THE McGRAW-HILL READER
Issues across the Disciplines

The McGraw-Hill Reader

SIXTH EDITION

Issues across the Disciplines

GILBERT H. MULLER

The City University of New York
LaGuardia

The McGraw-Hill Companies, Inc.

New York   St. Louis   San Francisco   Auckland   Bogotá   Caracas
Lisbon   London   Madrid   Mexico City   Milan   Montreal   New Delhi
San Juan   Singapore   Sydney   Tokyo   Toronto

McGraw-Hill

A Division of The **McGraw·Hill** Companies

THE McGRAW-HILL READER

Issues across the Disciplines

Acknowledgments appear on pages 695 to 704, and on this page by reference.

This book is printed on acid-free paper.

2 3 4 5 6 7 8 9 0   DOC   DOC   9 0 9 8 7

ISBN 0-07-044009-3

This book was set in Plantin Light by The Clarinda Company.
The editors were Tim Julet, Laura Lynch, and David A. Damstra;
  the designer was Joan Greenfield;
  the production supervisor was Elizabeth J. Strange;
  R. R. Donnelley & Sons Company was printer and binder.

Library of Congress Cataloging-in-Publication Data
    The McGraw-Hill reader: issues across the disciplines / [edited by]
    Gilbert H. Muller.
        p.   cm.
    Includes index.
    ISBN 0-07-044009-3
    1. College readers.   2. Interdisciplinary approach in education.
    3. English language—Rhetoric.   4. Academic writing.   I. Muller,
    Gilbert H., (date)
    PE1417.M44 1997
    808'.0427—dc20   96–14572

ABOUT THE AUTHOR

GILBERT H. MULLER, who received a Ph.D. in English and American Literature from Stanford University, is currently professor of English and Special Assistant to the President at the LaGuardia campus of the City University of New York. He has also taught at Stanford University, Vassar College, and several universities overseas. Dr. Muller is the author of the award-winning *Nightmares and Visions: Flannery O'Connor and the Catholic Grotesque, Chester Himes,* and other critical studies. His essays and reviews have appeared in *The New York Times, The New Republic, The Nation, The Sewanee Review, The Georgia Review,* and elsewhere. He is also a noted author and editor of textbooks in English and composition, including *The Short Prose Reader* with Harvey Wiener, and, with John A. Williams, *The McGraw-Hill Introduction to Literature, Bridges: Literature across Cultures,* and *Ways In: Reading and Writing about Literature.* Among Dr. Muller's awards are National Endowment for the Humanities Fellowships, a Fulbright Fellowship, and a Mellon Fellowship.

To Parisa and Darius
My favorite readers

CONTENTS

3: MANNERS AND CUSTOMS

4: SCHOOL AND COLLEGE

5: GENDER AND HUMAN DEVELOPMENT

6: SOCIAL PROCESSES AND INSTITUTIONS

7: WORK, BUSINESS, AND ECONOMICS

8: LANGUAGE AND COMMUNICATION

9: MEDIA AND THE ARTS

10: PHILOSOPHY, ETHICS AND RELIGION

11: NATURE AND THE ENVIRONMENT

12: SCIENCE, MEDICINE, AND MATHEMATICS

13: CIVILIZATION

❖

Contents

CONTENTS OF ESSAYS BY RHETORICAL MODE

NARRATION

DESCRIPTION

ILLUSTRATION

COMPARISON AND CONTRAST

ANALOGY

❖

*Contents of
Essays by
Rhetorical
Mode*

PROCESS ANALYSIS

CAUSAL ANALYSIS

ARGUMENT AND PERSUASION

LOGIC

HUMOR, IRONY, AND SATIRE

❖

*Contents of
Essays by
Rhetorical
Mode*

WRITERS IN DEPTH

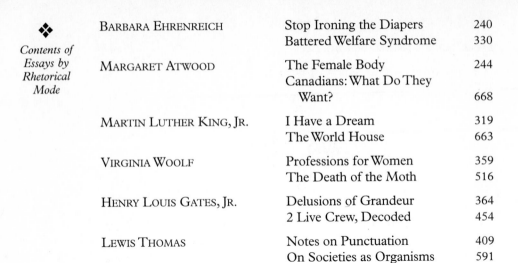

*Contents of
Essays by
Rhetorical
Mode*

PREFACE

*T*he sixth edition of *The McGraw-Hill Reader* preserves the form and spirit of earlier editions. It continues to present the finest classic and contemporary essays for today's college students. Addressing the continuing national interest in core liberal arts programs, interdisciplinary issues, and multicultural perspectives, this text offers students and teachers a full range of prose models important to writing courses, reading sequences, and key undergraduate disciplines. All the selections, consisting of complete essays, chapters, and self-contained sections of chapters, have been selected for their significance, vitality, and technical precision. With its high caliber of material, its consistent humanistic emphases, and its clear organization, *The McGraw-Hill Reader* is lively, sophisticated, and eminently usable for college composition and reading programs.

The organization of *The McGraw-Hill Reader* is one of its most significant features. Composed of thirteen chapters, the text embraces all major modes of writing and most disciplines that college students encounter as undergraduates. Chapters 1 to 3, dealing with childhood and family, the sense of place, and manners and customs, provide students with prose models largely of a personal, experiential, narrative, descriptive, or reflective nature—essays that enhance the acquisition of basic language skills while encouraging students to construct their own versions of social reality, a reality rooted in knowledge of cross-cultural perspectives. Following chapters cover core liberal arts disciplines, including education, the social sciences, business and economics, the humanities, and the sciences, and culminate in a final interdisciplinary chapter on civilization that is integral to the scope and method of *The McGraw-Hill Reader.* While reinforcing earlier modes of writing presented in the text, these disciplinary chapters offer prose models that provide practice in techniques of analysis, criticism, argumentation, and persuasion. As an integrated text, *The McGraw-Hill Reader* seeks to reconcile expressive and abstract varieties of thought in order to treat the total reading and writing process. An alternate table of contents, listing carefully selected essays in each of twelve rhetorical categories, adds to the flexibility of the text.

A second distinct advantage of *The McGraw-Hill Reader,* perhaps the primary one for teachers who prefer to create their own approaches to composition and reading courses, is the wide range of material and the varied constituencies represented in the text. The essays in this book have been selected carefully to embrace a rich international assortment of authors, to achieve balance among constituencies, to cover major historical periods, and to provide prose models and styles for class analysis, discussion, and imitation. The authors in this text—whether Plato or Maya Angelou, Swift or Joan Didion—have high visibility as writers and thinkers of value. Some of these authors are represented by two or three essays. All the authors—writing from such vantage points as literature, journalism, anthropology, sociology, art history, biology, and philosophy—presuppose that ideas exist in the world, that we should be alert to them, and that we should be able to deal with them in our own discourse. Because the selections extend from very simple essays to the most abstract and complex modes of prose, teachers and students will be able to use *The McGraw-Hill Reader* at virtually all levels of a program. Containing 131 complete essays, *The McGraw-Hill Reader* thus is a flexible companion for composition courses. It can be used from any of the major pedagogical perspectives common to the practice of composition today: as a writing-across-the-curricula text; as the basis for a rhetorically focused course; as a thematic reader; as a multicultural anthology; as an in-depth reader. Above all, teachers can develop their own sequence of essays that will contribute not only to their students' reading and writing proficiency but also to growing intellectual power.

The third major strength of *The McGraw-Hill Reader* is in the uniform apparatus that has been designed for every essay. Much can be learned from any well-written essay, especially if the apparatus is systematic in design. For each selection in this text there is a brief introduction. After each essay, there are questions organized in a common format created to reinforce essential reading, writing, and oral communication skills. Arranged in three categories—Comprehension, Rhetoric, and Writing—these questions reflect current compositional theory as they move students from audience analysis to various modes and processes of composition. All specialized terms used in the questions are defined for students in an extensive Glossary of Terms at the end of the text. The integrated design of these questions along with additional features that are new to the sixth edition makes each essay—simple or complex, short or long, old or new—accessible to college students who possess mixed reading and writing abilities.

Highlights of the Sixth Edition

Teachers planning a composition course around *The McGraw-Hill Reader* will discover that the sixth edition has several special features:

- approximately forty new selections—many on such topics as sex education, the death penalty, and affirmative action—that elicit provocative student writing

- the inclusion of even more women writers than in previous editions; 50 percent of all selections are by women

- the strengthening of the multicultural dimension through the incorporation of Judith Ortiz Cofer, Jamaica Kincaid, Pico Iyer, Michael Dorris, V. S. Naipaul, Richard Rodriguez, and others

- the presentation of an introductory chapter on the reading and writing process

- two recent chapters on gender and on the environment, along with several reconstituted chapters, such as "Childhood and Family" and "Media and the Arts," that make academic disciplines more comprehensible for students

- introductions to all chapters, with previewing sections that alert students to strategies for reading, discussion, and writing

- a "Classic and Contemporary" set of essays for each chapter, matching an older essayist with a more recent one so that students can gain fresh perspectives on influence and the essay tradition

- a "Connections" section at the end of each chapter that helps students to make comparative assessments of various groups of essays

- an alternate table of contents, "Writers in Depth," listing eighteen essayists who are represented by two or three selections each

All of these new features appear in response to suggestions made by composition teachers across the country whose reviews and advice have shaped the sixth edition of *The McGraw-Hill Reader*.

Supplementing *The McGraw-Hill Reader* is a comprehensive instructor's manual. Unlike many manuals, this one is a complete teacher's guide. *A Guide to the McGraw-Hill Reader* offers sample syllabi, well-considered strategies for teaching individual essays, sample rhetorical analyses, answers to questions, additional thought-provoking questions, comparative essay discussion formats, and tips for prewriting and guided writing activities. There is also a bibliography of criticism and research on the teaching of composition.

Eudora Welty, whose work appears in *The McGraw-Hill Reader,* speaks of reading as "a sweet devouring." This anthology alerts students to the vast and varied pleasures of reading and writing, while offering them opportunities to experience numerous perspectives on academic discourse. It is a reader that encourages students to make intelligent choices as they handle assignments for composition.

Acknowledgments

It is a pleasure to acknowledge the support, assistance, and guidance of numerous individuals who helped to create *The McGraw-Hill Reader*. Foremost among these people are the many McGraw-Hill sales representatives who obtained teacher responses to questionnaires when the text was in its formative stages. I also want to thank the excellent McGraw-Hill family of assistants, editors, and executives who participated enthusiastically in the project from the outset and who encouraged me at every step.

The final design and content of *The McGraw-Hill Reader*, Sixth Edition, reflects the expertise and advice offered by college teachers across the country who gave generously of their time when asked to respond to questionnaires submitted to them by McGraw-Hill sales representatives. These include: Jean Bauso, Peace College; Roberta Bienvenu, Johnson State College; Alvin W. Bowker, University of Maine at Machias; Alan Brown, Livingston University; Teresa Dalle, Memphis State University; Miriam Espinosa, Texas Wesleyan University; Florence Halle, Memphis State University; Vanessa Lynn Kerns, West Virginia University; Mary Kay Mahoney, Merrimack College; Frank Micklewright, San Joaquin Delta College; Meredith Morgan, Landmark College; Beth A. Rauer, West Virginia University; David Rogner, Concordia University; Edwina Romero, New Mexico Highlands University; Philip J. Skerry, Lakeland Community College; Lolly Smith, Everett Community College; Maria Solheim, Dawson Community College; Randall A. Wells, Coastal Carolina College; and Thomas Zolnay, Harold Washington College.

Warm appreciation is also extended to those college and university English professors who carefully read the manuscript in part or in its entirety and who made many constructive suggestions for improvement of the first three editions. I am most grateful to David Bartl, New Mexico Military Institute; Kathleen Bell, University of Miami; Robert L. Brown, University of Minnesota; Irene Clark, University of Southern California; David Fite, University of Santa Clara; Dennis R. Gabriel, Cuyahoga Community College; Alan Golding, University of California, Los Angeles; Lillian Gottesman, Bronx Community College; Eugene Hammond, University of Maryland; John Hanes, Duquesne University; Pamela Howell, Midland College; James Mauch, Foothill College; Mary McFarland, Fresno Community College; Susan Miller, University of Wisconsin; Albert Nicolai, Middlesex Community College; Patricia Owen, Nassau Community College; Robert J. Pelinski, University of Illinois; Linda H. Peterson, Yale University; Rosentine Purnell, California State University, Northridge; Carl Quesnell, Iowa State University; Grayce F. Salerno, Seton Hall University; Margaret A. Strom, George Washington University; Beverly Thorsen, Central State University; Randall Wells, University of South Carolina; Jack Wilson, Old Dominion University; Mary Ann Wilson, Georgia State University; and Carl Wooton, University of Southwestern Louisiana.

Special recognition must also be given to those specialists in various liberal arts fields who provided advice: Jane S. Zembaty, Department of Philosophy, University of Dayton; Linda Davidoff, Department of Psychology, Essex Community College; Curtis Williams, Department of Biology, The State University of New York; and Diane Papalia-Finlay, Department of Psychology, University of Wisconsin.

For the fourth edition, I thank the following reviewers for their supportive and most helpful evaluations: Susan Aylworth, California State University; Lynette Black, Memphis State University; Mary Edge Blevetty, Cardinal Stritch College; Nadia Creamer, Columbia-Greene

Community College; Paula Friedman, Cardinal Stritch College; James Fuller, Midland College; LaVerne Gonzalez, San Jose State University; Peter Hardon, Bradley University; Elyce Rae Helford, University of Iowa; Glenda Linsey Hicks, Midland College; Katherine Kernberger, Linfield College; Diane Koenig, Columbia-Greene Community College; Mary Kay Mahoney, Merrimack College; Ross Primm, Mount Senario College; Audrey Schmidt, Cardinal Stritch College; Patrick Shaw, Texas Tech University; Kathy Sheldon, Iowa University; Emma Johanne Thomas, Prairie View A&M University; Jeanne Wescott, Miami Dade Community College; Clifford Wood, University of Wisconsin; and Robert J. Wurster, Western Kentucky University.

For the fifth edition, I appreciate the assistance of the following scholars: Tuzyline Allan, Baruch College; Michael Cochran, Santa Fe Community College; Valerie Giroux, Miami Dade Community College; Lawrence Griffin, Midland College; Lee Hammer, Culver-Stockton College; Mary Katzif, University of South Carolina; Thomas Long, Thomas Nelson Community College; Alan Powers, Bristol Community College; Barbara Sloan, Santa Fe Community College; Theodore Tasis, Northeastern University; and Jeanne Wescott, Miami Dade Community College.

For the sixth edition, I have profited from the excellent advice offered by these reviewers: Carol Barrett, Austin Community College, Northridge Campus; David Lenoir, Western Kentucky University; Larry Beason, Eastern Washington University; James McBride, San Joaquin Delta College; Claudia Pineo, Fullerton College; Diane Koenig, Columbia-Greene Community College; Joseph Minton, Kingwood College; Claire Berger, Camden County College; Rita Wade Perkins, Camden County College; Andrew Fox, Camden County College.

Finally, I am pleased to acknowledge support from the Mellon Foundation, the Graduate Center of The City University of New York, and the United States Department of Education (Title III and Title VI) that enabled me to concentrate on the development of this text.

Gilbert H. Muller

THE McGRAW-HILL READER
Issues across the Disciplines

INTRODUCTION

Reading and Writing Essays

*F*or much of your college career, you will be reading and writing essays. An essay, as the eighteenth-century English wit Samuel Johnson observed, is "a loose sally of the mind; an irregular, undigested piece; not a regular and orderly performance." College essays that follow Dr. Johnson's prescription receive failing grades. However, if you reverse Johnson's advice, composing essays that are carefully and logically constructed, limited and clear in execution, and grammatically correct, you will produce passing—perhaps even commendable—papers.

You never know for certain what will happen when you sit down to read or write, for the nature of these reciprocal processes is complex. In both instances, words flow on paper (or on a computer screen). The eye and the brain—and the hand when writing, typing, or keyboarding—work in almost magical unison to move the reading and writing processes along. When reading critically, you absorb new ideas, develop perspectives on various bodies of knowledge, contend with competing viewpoints, learn something about yourself and your world. You also generate the raw stuff for writing, sifting information and also learning from significant authors the tricks of the trade that can help you become an effective essayist.

Critical reading *can* help produce sound critical writing, the sort of writing that college professors (and employers) like to see. The Renaissance philosopher Francis Bacon stresses the unity of reading and writing in his famous essay "Of Studies," where he asserts that "Reading maketh a full man, conference a ready man, and writing an exacting man." (In this era of gender-neutral usage, we would add "woman" to Bacon's remark in order to create a more truthful rendering of reality.) Through critical reading, discussion, and writing—the essential method used in this anthology—you can learn to communicate effectively in essay form.

1

Reading and Responding to Texts

When you read an essay or any type of text, you are creating meaning out of the material the author has presented. If the essay is relatively simple, clear, and concise, the experience that you construct from your reading may be very similar to what the author intended. Nevertheless, the way that you interact with even the most comprehensible texts will never be identical to the way another reader interacts.

Consider the first essay that you will encounter in this anthology, Langston Hughes's "Salvation." A chapter from his autobiography, *The Big Sea* (1940), this essay tells of a childhood incident in which the young Hughes's faith was tested. The narrative focuses on a church revival meeting that Hughes was taken to and the increasing pressure he sensed at the meeting to "testify" to the presence of Jesus in his life. At first the young Hughes holds out against the fervor of the congregation, but ultimately he pretends to be converted, or "saved." That night, however, he weeps and then testifies to something entirely unexpected: the loss of faith he experienced because Jesus did not "save" him in a time of need.

As your class reads this essay, individuals among you may be struck by the compressed energy of the narration and the description of the event; by the swift characterization and revealing dialogue; or by the conflict and mounting tension. Moreover, the heightened personal and spiritual conflict will force class members to consider the sad irony inherent in the title "Salvation."

Even if your class arrives at a broad consensus on the intentions of the author, individual reader responses to the text will vary. Readers who have ever attended a revival meeting will respond differently from those who have not. Evangelical Christians will see the text from a different perspective than will Catholics, Muslims, or Jews. African-American readers (Hughes himself was black) will respond differently than will white readers. Women may respond differently than men, and so on.

In this brief assessment of possible reader responses, we are trying to establish meaning from a shifting series of critical perspectives. Although we can establish a consensus of meaning over what Hughes probably intended, our own interpretation and evaluation of the text will be conditioned by our personal experiences, backgrounds, attitudes, biases, and beliefs. In other words, even as the class attempts to construct a common reading, each member of the class is also constructing a somewhat different meaning, one based on the individual's own interaction with the text.

Reading Essays Critically

As you read an essay, think critically about the meanings and perspectives the author is creating. When you think critically, you interact with the text to create your own meanings. Here are some key questions you should ask yourself about the text:

2

• Who is the author? What is the author's background—his or her age, education, ethnic and class affiliation, ideology? What credentials does the author bring to the subject? What authority does the author have to write about the subject? Does George Orwell, for example, possess a special authority to write about British imperialism because he experienced it firsthand?

• Who is the audience? Authors often address an essay to an intended group of readers. What information or knowledge does the author assume that the audience possesses? What other assumptions does the author make about the audience? What are the audience's expectations? Anna Quindlen, for instance, writes for women but also for all relatively literate readers of publications such as *The New York Times*.

• What is the writer's purpose? Why did the author write this essay? What is his or her thesis, or main idea? An author creates a text in order to inform, explain, entertain, educate, argue, evaluate, persuade, warn, justify, narrate, or describe. Often a combination of these purposes motivates a single text. What specifically does the writer hope to achieve? Is this purpose stated directly, as in Virginia Woolf's "Professions for Women," or must it be inferred, as in another essay by Woolf, "The Death of the Moth"?

• What strategies does the author use? Authors make basic stylistic and rhetorical choices as they compose essays. Often a particular form—narration, description, illustration, comparison and contrast, classification, definition, process analysis, causal analysis, or argumentation and persuasion—is selected. Which form predominates in any given essay, and why? Why does the subject lend itself to this form or forms? How does the author sustain the reader's attention? How does the essay develop? Why, for example, does J. B. Priestley employ classification in his essay "Wrong Ism"?

• What is your experience of the text? Ultimately, you have to clarify your relationship to the text. What personal experiences do you bring to the essay? How much do you know about the subject? What is your moral or ethical position on the subject? What biases or beliefs intervene as you read the text? How have your opinions been challenged or changed—as in Deborah Salazar's "My Abortion" or Martin Luther King Jr.'s "I Have a Dream"?

Preparing to Write

Thinking critically about the essays you read prepares you for writing. College writing is often a translation process in which you convert into your own words the knowledge, perceptions, and stylistic skills of established authors. If this translation process is effective, readers will be able to understand your own ways of thinking as well as appreciate your writing abilities.

The McGraw-Hill Reader has several distinctive features designed to facilitate this translation process. Every chapter contains a cluster of essays arranged around academic subject areas and key themes that you will encounter in the course of a standard college education. Thus the first chapter, "Childhood and Family," includes narratives by ten major authors dealing with the formative stages of human development from several multicultural perspectives. The sixth chapter, "Social Processes and Institutions," contains essays that encourage you to think about the significance of history and political science, while the last chapter, "Civilization," places a cluster of essays—and, indeed, the entire text—in a global, intercultural frame of reference.

Critical thinking about these readings is also facilitated by brief chapter introductions, followed by "Previewing the Chapter" questions that help you develop overviews of the essays. This attempt to establish critical overviews is reinforced by a comparative section of questions, entitled "Connections," at the end of each chapter. By utilizing these materials and your own critical powers, you develop an inquiring attitude about all of the essays in any given section. You discover fresh relationships among essays as well as an understanding of numerous forms of academic inquiry as they are defined by such disciplines as literature, psychology, anthropology, and science. A unique feature in each chapter is a paired set of readings entitled "Classic and Contemporary." This section pairs an established older author (typically deceased) with a present-day author for purposes of comparative assessment. For example, Virginia Woolf's "The Death of the Moth" is paired with Annie Dillard's "Death of a Moth" in the chapter on philosophy, ethics, and religion. Such comparative assessment will help you understand more clearly those influences that exist upon authors from age to age and generation to generation.

Every essay in this anthology is followed by a three-part set of exercises designed to take you from critical reading to directed writing. This set—"Comprehension," "Rhetoric," and "Writing"—stresses critical reflection and response. Critical reflection is typified by a willingness to test assertions and examine evidence, by a consistency in your viewpoints, by the detection and avoidance of faulty reasoning, by an understanding of relationships, by the creation of hypotheses (and theses), and by the prediction of outcomes. Through this active process of creating and forming ideas, you will be able to discover what you wish to say and write.

There is no one approach to reading and writing that will automatically solve your composing problems. Nevertheless, you *can* learn to model your writing after other authors, and many of the greatest essayists—from Swift to Orwell to Joan Didion—appear in this anthology. These authors engage you in a dialogue across centuries and numerous cultures. They encourage you to develop your own stylistic skills, rhetorical abilities, and intellectual positions. By following the course of readings in this text, you can identify and define a topic, develop methods to order your thoughts, and then translate these thoughts into print—an essay—for others to see.

CHAPTER ONE

Childhood and Family

*F*amilies and friendships are the two networks that nourish us during childhood. Essayists have always been aware of the rich subject of family life, and have created many superb narratives capturing the sweetness and innocence, as well as the terror and crazy logic, of children, families, and friends. Tolstoy wrote that "Happy families are all alike; every unhappy family is unhappy in its own way." In the opening chapter of this anthology, we will encounter both happy and unhappy families. We shall also discover that Tolstoy must have been wrong because our finest essayists can recreate or reimagine even happy families in decidedly unique ways.

The family, of course, is one of the few institutions that we find in virtually every society throughout the world. Anthropologists and sociologists tell us that family patterns are exceedingly diverse even in the same societies. The broad fact is that historically and today, children grow up in many ways: in "nuclear" and in nontraditional households; in single-parent and in dual-parent arrangements; in extended families and kinship networks; and in patriarchal and matriarchal, heterosexual and homosexual, monogamous and polygamous situations. And the dynamics of family life assume added dimensions as we move across cultures, studying European families, African-American families, Hispanic families, Asian families, and so forth.

Ultimately it is the emotional life of children as they relate to their families and friends that interest us the most when we read about them. It is easy to agree with the nineteenth-century English novelist Jane Austin, who, in *Emma*, wrote that "Nobody who has not been in the interior of a family can say what the difficulties of any individual of that family may be." This chapter contains vivid accounts of the interior lives—typically of narrators who as children confronted numerous difficulties as well as numerous possibilities for growth. We see the love that cuts across families, cultures, and generations in E. B. White's "Once More to the Lake," Judith Ortiz Cofer's "Silent Dancing," and Maya Angelou's "Momma, the Dentist, and Me." We witness family conflicts in essays such as Maxine Hong Kingston's "The Woman Warrior." We confront children trying to make sense of a complex and contradictory adult world in Langston Hughes's "Salvation" and Mark Twain's "A Boy's Life."

All of the writers in this chapter write from the vantage point of adults looking backward on their youth. They replay scenes from their childhoods involving family and friends. Some of them, like White and Angelou, seem haunted by the events that they narrate; others, like McCullers and Welty, are nostalgic in their memoirs; still others are amused by childhood events. These essayists objectify childhood memories sufficiently so that we, as readers, understand the importance of the tales they tell. They range over what Mark Twain in his essay terms the "comedy and tragedy" of life. In these narratives of childhood, we encounter young people coming to terms with their families and with the larger world unfolding for them.

Previewing the Chapter

As you read the essays in this chapter and respond to them in discussion and writing, consider the following questions:

• Where does the narrative take place? How important is the setting to the action?

• What are the strengths and weaknesses of the families and friendships described?

• Why is the culture of the family—its ethnic, racial, social, or economic background—important to your understanding of the narrative?

• How does the author present himself or herself to you? Is the author likable or not? Do you find the narrator to be honest and reliable? On what evidence do you base your response?

• Is the author subjective or objective in developing the narrative? How do you know?

• What stylistic devices does the author employ to recreate childhood memories as vividly as possible?

• What similarities and differences do you encounter in the family patterns the author presents? Are all families alike in certain ways and different in others?

• What does the author learn in the course of the narrative of childhood that has been presented?

• What have you learned or discovered about children, families, and friendships from reading these essays?

LANGSTON HUGHES James Langston Hughes (1902–1967), poet, playwright, fiction writer, biographer, and essayist, was for more than fifty years one of the most productive and significant modern American authors. In *The Weary Blues* (1926), *Simple Speaks His Mind* (1950), *The Ways of White Folks* (1940), *Selected Poems* (1959), and dozens of other books, he strove, in his own words, "to explain the Negro condition in America." This essay, from his 1940 autobiography, *The Big Sea,* reflects the sharp, humorous, often bittersweet insights contained in Hughes's examination of human behavior.

LANGSTON HUGHES

Salvation

I was saved from sin when I was going on thirteen. But not really saved. 1
It happened like this. There was a big revival at my Auntie Reed's church. Every night for weeks there had been much preaching, singing, praying, and shouting, and some very hardened sinners had been brought to Christ, and the membership of the church had grown by leaps and bounds. Then just before the revival ended, they held a special meeting for children, "to bring the young lambs to the fold." My aunt spoke of it for days ahead. That night I was escorted to the front row and placed on the mourners' bench with all the other young sinners, who had not yet been brought to Jesus.

My aunt told me that when you were saved you saw a light, and 2
something happened to you inside! And Jesus came into your life! And God was with you from then on! She said you could see and hear and feel Jesus in your soul. I believed her. I had heard a great many old people say the same thing and it seemed to me they ought to know. So I sat there calmly in the hot, crowded church, waiting for Jesus to come to me.

The preacher preached a wonderful rhythmical sermon, all moans 3
and shouts and lonely cries and dire pictures of hell, and then he sang a song about the ninety and nine safe in the fold, but one little lamb was left out in the cold. Then he said: "Won't you come? Won't you come to Jesus? Young lambs, won't you come?" And he held out his arms to all us young sinners there on the mourners' bench. And the little girls cried. And some of them jumped up and went to Jesus right away. But most of us just sat there.

A great many old people came and knelt around us and prayed, old 4
women with jet-black faces and braided hair, old men with work-gnarled hands. And the church sang a song about the lower lights are burning, some poor sinners to be saved. And the whole building rocked with prayer and song.

Still I kept waiting to *see* Jesus.   5

Finally all the young people had gone to the altar and were saved,   6
but one boy and me. He was a rounder's son named Westley. Westley
and I were surrounded by sisters and deacons praying. It was very hot
in the church, and getting late now. Finally Westley said to me in a
whisper: "God damn! I'm tired o' sitting here. Let's get up and be
saved." So he got up and was saved.

Then I was left all alone on the mourners' bench. My aunt came   7
and knelt at my knees and cried, while prayers and song swirled all
around me in the little church. The whole congregation prayed for me
alone, in a mighty wail of moans and voices. And I kept waiting
serenely for Jesus, waiting, waiting—but he didn't come. I wanted to see
him, but nothing happened to me. Nothing! I wanted something to
happen to me, but nothing happened.

I heard the songs and the minister saying: "Why don't you come? My   8
dear child, why don't you come to Jesus? Jesus is waiting for you. He
wants you. Why don't you come? Sister Reed, what is this child's name?"

"Langston," my aunt sobbed.   9

"Langston, why don't you come? Why don't you come and be   10
saved? Oh, Lamb of God! Why don't you come?"

Now it was really getting late. I began to be ashamed of myself, hold-   11
ing everything up so long. I began to wonder what God thought about
Westley, who certainly hadn't seen Jesus either, but who was now sitting
proudly on the platform, swinging his knickerbockered legs and grinning
down at me, surrounded by deacons and old women on their knees praying. God had not struck Westley dead for taking his name in vain or for
lying in the temple. So I decided that maybe to save further trouble, I'd
better lie, too, and say that Jesus had come, and get up and be saved.

So I got up.   12

Suddenly the whole room broke into a sea of shouting, as they saw   13
me rise. Waves of rejoicing swept the place. Women leaped in the air.
My aunt threw her arms around me. The minister took me by the hand
and led me to the platform.

When things quieted down, in a hushed silence, punctuated by a   14
few ecstatic "Amens," all the new young lambs were blessed in the
name of God. Then joyous singing filled the room.

That night, for the last time in my life but one—for I was a big boy   15
twelve years old—I cried. I cried, in bed alone, and couldn't stop. I
buried my head under the quilts, but my aunt heard me. She woke up
and told my uncle I was crying because the Holy Ghost had come into
my life, and because I had seen Jesus. But I was really crying because I
couldn't bear to tell her that I had lied, that I had deceived everybody
in the church, that I hadn't seen Jesus, and that now I didn't believe
there was a Jesus any more, since he didn't come to help me.

COMPREHENSION

1. What does the title tell you about the subject of this essay? How would you
state, in your own words, the thesis that emerges from the title and the essay?

2. How does Hughes recount the revival meeting he attended? What is the dominant impression?
3. Explain Hughes's shifting attitude toward salvation in this essay. Why is he disappointed in the religious answers provided by his church? What does he say about salvation in the last paragraph?

RHETORIC

1. Key words and phrases in this essay relate to the religious experience. Locate five of these words and expressions, and explain their connotations.
2. Identify the level of language in the essay. How does Hughes employ language effectively?
3. Where is the thesis statement in the essay? Consider the following: the use of dialogue; the use of phrases familiar to you *(idioms);* and the sentence structure. Cite examples of these elements.
4. How much time elapses, and why is this important to the effect? How does the author achieve narrative coherence?
5. Locate details and examples in the essay that are especially vivid and interesting. Compare your list with what others have listed. What are the similarities? The differences?
6. What is the tone of the essay? What is the relationship between tone and point of view?

WRITING

1. Describe a time in your life when you suppressed your feelings before adults because you thought they would misunderstand.
2. Recount an event in your life during which you surrendered to group pressures.
3. Write a narrative account of the most intense religious experience in your life.
4. Narrate an episode in which you played a trick on people simply to win their approval or satisfy their expectations.

EUDORA WELTY   Eudora Welty was born (in 1909) and raised in Mississippi. She attended the University of Wisconsin, from which she received a B.A. in 1929, and Columbia University, where she studied advertising. Rejecting a career in advertising, Welty turned to writing, publishing her first short story in 1936. After a decade of writing short fiction, she published her first novel, *Delta Wedding,* in 1946. Welty is considered one of our most important regional writers and one of the few contemporary masters of both the short story and the novel. Among her major works are *The Optimist's Daughter* (1972), which won a Pulitzer Prize, and *One Writer's Beginnings* (1984). She is a recipient of the National Medal for literature (1980) and the Presidential Medal of Freedom (1980). In this vivid reminiscence, Welty explores the relationship between reality and the imagination as she attempts to trace her origins as a writer.

EUDORA WELTY

One Writer's Beginnings

I had the window seat. Beside me, my father checked the progress of our train by moving his finger down the timetable and springing open his pocket watch. He explained to me what the position of the arms of the semaphore meant; before we were to pass through a switch we would watch the signal lights change. Along our track, the mileposts could be read; he read them. Right on time by Daddy's watch, the next town sprang into view, and just as quickly was gone.

Side by side and separately, we each lost ourselves in the experience of not missing anything, of seeing everything, of knowing each time what the blows of the whistle meant. But of course it was not the same experience: what was new to me, not older than ten, was a landmark to him. My father knew our way mile by mile; by day or by night, he knew where we were. Everything that changed under our eyes, in the flying countryside, was the known world to him, the imagination to me. Each in our own way, we hungered for all of this: my father and I were in no other respect or situation so congenial.

In Daddy's leather grip was his traveler's drinking cup, collapsible; a lid to fit over it had a ring to carry it by; it traveled in a round leather box. This treasure would be brought out at my request, for me to bear to the water cooler at the end of the Pullman car, fill to the brim, and bear back to my seat, to drink water over its smooth lip. The taste of silver could almost be relied on to shock your teeth.

After dinner in the sparkling dining car, my father and I walked back to the open-air observation platform at the end of the train and sat on the folding chairs placed at the railing. We watched the sparks we made fly behind us into the night. Fast as our speed was, it gave us time enough to see the rose-red cinders turn to ash, each one, and disappear from sight. Sometimes a house far back in the empty hills showed a light no bigger than a star. The sleeping countryside seemed itself to open a way through for our passage, then close again behind us.

The swaying porter would be making ready our berths for the night, pulling the shade down just so, drawing the green fishnet hammock across the window so the clothes you took off could ride along beside you, turning down the tight-made bed, standing up the two snowy pillows as high as they were wide, switching on the eye of the reading lamp, starting the tiny electric fan—you suddenly saw its blades turn into gauze and heard its insect murmur; and drawing across it all the pair of thick green theaterlike curtains—billowing, smelling of cigar smoke—between which you would crawl or dive headfirst to button them together with yourself inside, to be seen no more that night.

When you lay enclosed and enwrapped, your head on a pillow parallel to the track, the rhythm of the rail clicks pressed closer to your body as if it might be your heart beating, but the sound of the engine seemed to come from farther away than when it carried you in daylight. The whistle was almost too far away to be heard, its sound wavering back from the engine over the roofs of the cars. What you listened for was the different sound that ran under you when your own car crossed on a trestle, then another sound on an iron bridge; a low or a high bridge—each had its pitch, or drumbeat, for your car.

Riding in the sleeper rhythmically lulled me and waked me. From time to time, waked suddenly, I raised my window shade and looked out at my own strip of the night. Sometimes there was unexpected moonlight out there. Sometimes the perfect shadow of our train, with our car, with me invisibly included, ran deep below, crossing a river with us by the light of the moon. Sometimes the encroaching walls of mountains woke me by clapping at my ears. The tunnels made the train's passage resound like the "loud" pedal of a piano, a roar that seemed to last as long as a giant's temper tantrum.

But my father put it all into the frame of regularity, predictability, that was his fatherly gift in the course of our journey. I saw it going by, the outside world, in a flash. I dreamed over what I could see as it passed, as well as over what I couldn't. Part of the dream was what lay beyond, where the path wandered off through the pasture, the red clay road climbed and went over the hill or made a turn and was hidden in trees, or toward a river whose bridge I could see but whose name I'd never know. A house back at its distance at night showing a light from an open doorway, the morning faces of the children who stopped still in what they were doing, perhaps picking blackberries or wild plums, and watched us go by—I never saw with the thought of their continuing to be there just the same after we were out of sight. For now, and for a long while to come, I was proceeding in fantasy.

COMPREHENSION

1. At the end of the second paragraph, the narrator says, "Each in our own way, we hungered for all of this." Do father and child hunger for the same thing? Describe what each one is enjoying. In what way do they crave the same thing?
2. According to the author, what constitutes a writer's "beginnings"?
3. What does the narrator mean when she says that regularity and predictability were the gifts her father gave her "in the course of our journey"?

RHETORIC

1. The author makes vivid use of sensory language. Give instances where she employs her senses of touch, sound, taste, and smell.
2. Why is the "flying countryside" an important image? What other images of movement and acceleration can you find?

3. Is the time frame of this story one day or several? Why is the author compressing experience? What effect does this achieve?
4. Is the narrator writing this from the point of view of a child or an adult? Is there any place where the narrator judges something in retrospect? How is Welty's handling of point of view similar to that of Langston Hughes in "Salvation"?
5. What is the purpose of this narrative? Is the thesis overstated? Explain your answer.
6. In what sense is this trip a metaphor for the relationship between father and child?

WRITING

1. Discuss what qualities life had for you as a child. In what ways have your perceptions of the world changed over time?
2. In a narrative essay, describe an experience you had that served as a metaphor for your relationship to the world.
3. Select a particularly memorable childhood trip that you took with your family or a member of your family. As Welty does, try to recapture the event by using vivid sensory language.
4. Compare and contrast what we learn about Welty and Hughes from their respective essays about childhood events.

ANNIE DILLARD   Annie Dillard was born in Pittsburgh in 1945 and received her B.A. and M.A. degrees from Hollins College. Her first book, *Pilgrim at Tinker Creek* (1975), won the Pulitzer Prize for general nonfiction. Her other published works of nonfiction include *Teaching a Stone to Talk* (1982) and *An American Childhood* (1987). She has received awards from the National Endowment for the Arts and the Guggenheim Foundation as well as many other sources. As an essayist, poet, memoirist, and literary critic, her themes focus on the relationships among the self, nature, religion, and faith. Her writing is recognizable by its observations of the minutiae of life and its search for meaning in unlikely places, such as a stone or an insect. Dillard expanded her range of writing with the publication of her first novel, *The Living* (1992). In this passage from *An American Childhood,* the author gives us a portrait of her mother by focusing on her small idiosyncracies of speech, gesture, and attitude.

ANNIE DILLARD

An American Childhood

One Sunday afternoon Mother wandered through our kitchen, where   ₁
Father was making a sandwich and listening to the ball game. The
Pirates were playing the New York Giants at Forbes Field. In those

days, the Giants had a utility infielder named Wayne Terwilliger. Just as Mother passed through, the radio announcer cried—with undue drama—"Terwilliger bunts one!"

"Terwilliger bunts one?" Mother cried back, stopped short. She turned. "Is that English?"

"The player's name is Terwilliger," Father said. "He bunted." 3

"That's marvelous," Mother said. "'Terwilliger bunts one.' No won- 4
der you listen to baseball. 'Terwilliger bunts one.'"

For the next seven or eight years, Mother made this surprising 5
string of syllables her own. Testing a microphone, she repeated, "Terwilliger bunts one"; testing a pen or a typewriter, she wrote it. If, as happened surprisingly often in the course of various improvised gags, she pretended to whisper something else in my ear, she actually whispered, "Terwilliger bunts one." Whenever someone used a French phrase, or a Latin one, she answered solemnly, "Terwilliger bunts one." If Mother had had, like Andrew Carnegie, the opportunity to cook up a motto for a coat of arms, hers would have read simply and tellingly, "Terwilliger bunts one." (Carnegie's was "Death to Privilege.")

She served us with other words and phrases. On a Florida trip, she 6
repeated tremulously, "That . . . is a royal poinciana." I don't remember the tree; I remember the thrill in her voice. She pronounced it carefully, and spelled it. She also liked to say "portulaca."

The drama of the words "Tamiami Trail" stirred her, we learned on 7
the same Florida trip. People built Tampa on one coast, and they built Miami on another. Then—the height of visionary ambition and folly—they piled a slow, tremendous road through the terrible Everglades to connect them. To build the road, men stood sunk in muck to their armpits. They fought off cottonmouth moccasins and six-foot alligators. They slept in boats, wet. They blasted muck with dynamite, cut jungle with machetes; they laid logs, dragged drilling machines, hauled dredges, heaped limestone. The road took fourteen years to build up by the shovelful, a Panama Canal in reverse, and cost hundreds of lives from tropical, mosquito-carried diseases. Then, capping it all, some genius thought of the word Tamiami: they called the road from Tampa to Miami, this very road under our spinning wheels, the Tamiami Trail. Some called it Alligator Alley. Anyone could drive over this road without a thought.

Hearing this, moved, I thought all the suffering of road building was 8
worth it (it wasn't my suffering), now that we had this new thing to hang these new words on—Alligator Alley for those who liked things cute, and, for connoisseurs like Mother, for lovers of the human drama in all its boldness and terror, the Tamiami Trail.

Back home, Mother cut clips from reels of talk, as it were, and 9
played them back at leisure. She noticed that many Pittsburghers confuse "leave" and "let." One kind relative brightened our morning by mentioning why she'd brought her son to visit: "He wanted to come with me, so I left him." Mother filled in Amy and me on locutions we missed. "I can't do it on Friday," her pretty sister told a crowded dinner party, "because Friday's the day I lay in the stores."

(All unconsciously, though, we ourselves used some pure Pitts- 10
burghisms. We said "tele pole," pronounced "telly pole," for that splin-
tery sidewalk post I loved to climb. We said "slippy"—the sidewalks are
"slippy." We said, "That's all the farther I could go." And we said, as
Pittsburghers do say, "This glass needs washed," or "The dog needs
walked"—a usage our father eschewed; he knew it was not standard
English, nor even comprehensible English, but he never let on.)

"Spell 'poinsettia,'" Mother would throw out at me, smiling with 11
pleasure. "Spell 'sherbet.'" The idea was not to make us whizzes, but,
quite the contrary, to remind us—and I, especially, needed reminding—
that we didn't know it all just yet.

"There's a deer standing in the front hall," she told me one quiet 12
evening in the country.

"Really?" 13

"No. I just wanted to tell you something once without your saying, 14
'I know.'"

Supermarkets in the middle 1950s began luring, or bothering, cus- 15
tomers by giving out Top Value Stamps or Green Stamps. When, shopping with Mother, we got to the head of the checkout line, the checker,
always a young man, asked, "Save stamps?"

"No," Mother replied genially, week after week, "I build model air- 16
planes." I believe she originated this line. It took me years to determine
where the joke lay.

Anyone who met her verbal challenges she adored. She had surgery 17
on one of her eyes. On the operating table, just before she conked out,
she appealed feelingly to the surgeon, saying, as she had been planning
to say for weeks, "Will I be able to play the piano?" "Not on me," the
surgeon said. "You won't pull that old one on me."

It was, indeed, an old one. The surgeon was supposed to answer, 18
"Yes, my dear, brave woman, you will be able to play the piano after
this operation," to which Mother intended to reply, "Oh, good, I've
always wanted to play the piano." This pat scenario bored her; she
loved having it interrupted. It must have galled her that usually her
acquaintances were so predictably unalert; it must have galled her that,
for the length of her life, she could surprise everyone so continually, so
easily, when she had been the same all along. At any rate, she loved anyone who, as she put it, saw it coming, and called her on it.

She regarded the instructions on bureaucratic forms as straight 19
lines. "Do you advocate the overthrow of the United States government
by force or violence?" After some thought she wrote, "Force." She
regarded children, even babies, as straight men. When Molly learned to
crawl, Mother delighted in buying her gowns with drawstrings at the
bottom, like Swee'pea's, because, as she explained energetically, you
could easily step on the drawstring without the baby's noticing, so that
she crawled and crawled and crawled and never got anywhere except
into a small ball at the gown's top.

When we children were young, she mothered us tenderly and depend- 20
ably; as we got older, she resumed her career of anarchism. She collared

us into her gags. If she answered the phone on a wrong number, she told the caller, "Just a minute," and dragged the receiver to Amy or me, saying, "Here, take this, your name is Cecile," or, worse, just, "It's for you." You had to think on your feet. But did you want to perform well as Cecile, or did you want to take pity on the wretched caller?

During a family trip to the Highland Park Zoo, Mother and I were 21 alone for a minute. She approached a young couple holding hands on a bench by the seals, and addressed the young man in dripping tones: "Where have you been? Still got those baby-blue eyes; always did slay me. And this"—a swift nod at the dumbstruck young woman, who had removed her hand from the man's—"must be the one you were telling me about. She's not so bad, really, as you used to make out. But listen, you know how I miss you, you know where to reach me, same old place. And there's Ann over there—see how she's grown? See the blue eyes?"

And off she sashayed, taking me firmly by the hand, and leading us 22 around briskly past the monkey house and away. She cocked an ear back, and both of us heard the desperate man begin, in a high-pitched wail, "I swear, I never saw her before in my life . . ."

On a long, sloping beach by the ocean, she lay stretched out sunning 23 with Father and friends, until the conversation gradually grew tedious, when without forethought she gave a little push with her heel and rolled away. People were stunned. She rolled deadpan and apparently effortlessly, arms and legs extended and tidy, down the beach to the distant water's edge, where she lay at ease just as she had been, but half in the surf, and well out of earshot.

She dearly loved to fluster people by throwing out a game's rules at 24 whim—when she was getting bored, losing in a dull sort of way, and when everybody else was taking it too seriously. If you turned your back, she moved the checkers around on the board. When you got them all straightened out, she denied she'd touched them; the next time you turned your back, she lined them up on the rug or hid them under your chair. In a betting rummy game called Michigan, she routinely played out of turn, or called out a card she didn't hold, or counted backward, simply to amuse herself by causing an uproar and watching the rest of us do double takes and have fits. (Much later, when serious suitors came to call, Mother subjected them to this fast card game as a trial by ordeal; she used it as an intelligence test and a measure of spirit. If the poor man could stay a round without breaking down or running out, he got to marry one of us, if he still wanted to.)

She excelled at bridge, playing fast and boldly, but when the stakes 25 were low and the hands dull, she bid slams for the devilment of it, or raised her opponents' suit to bug them, or showed her hand, or tossed her cards in a handful behind her back in a characteristic swift motion accompanied by a vibrantly innocent look. It drove our stolid father crazy. The hand was over before it began, and the guests were appalled. How do you score it, who deals now, what do you do with a crazy person who is having so much fun? Or they were down seven, and the guests were appalled. "Pam!" "Dammit, Pam!" He groaned. What ails such people? What on earth possesses them? He rubbed his face.

She was an unstoppable force; she never let go. When we moved across town, she persuaded the U.S. Post Office to let her keep her old address—forever—because she'd had stationery printed. I don't know how she did it. Every new post office worker, over decades, needed to learn that although the Doaks' mail is addressed to here, it is delivered to there.

Mother's energy and intelligence suited her for a greater role in a larger arena—mayor of New York, say—than the one she had. She followed American politics closely; she had been known to vote for Democrats. She saw how things should be run, but she had nothing to run but our household. Even there, small minds bugged her; she was smarter than the people who designed the things she had to use all day for the length of her life.

"Look," she said. "Whoever designed this corkscrew never used one. Why would anyone sell it without trying it out?" So she invented a better one. She showed me a drawing of it. The spirit of American enterprise never faded in Mother. If capitalizing and tooling up had been as interesting as theorizing and thinking up, she would have fired up a new factory every week, and chaired several hundred corporations.

"It grieves me," she would say, "it grieves my heart," that the company that made one superior product packaged it poorly, or took the wrong tack in its advertising. She knew, as she held the thing mournfully in her two hands, that she'd never find another. She was right. We children wholly sympathized, and so did Father; what could she do, what could anyone do, about it? She was Samson in chains. She paced.

She didn't like the taste of stamps so she didn't lick stamps; she licked the corner of the envelope instead. She glued sandpaper to the sides of kitchen drawers, and under kitchen cabinets, so she always had a handy place to strike a match. She designed, and hounded workmen to build against all norms, doubly wide kitchen counters and elevated bathroom sinks. To splint a finger, she stuck it in a lightweight cigar tube. Conversely, to protect a pack of cigarettes, she carried it in a Band-Aid box. She drew plans for an over-the-finger toothbrush for babies, an oven rack that slid up and down, and—the family favorite—Lendalarm. Lendalarm was a beeper you attached to books (or tools) you loaned friends. After ten days, the beeper sounded. Only the rightful owner could silence it.

She repeatedly reminded us of P. T. Barnum's dictum: You could sell anything to anybody if you marketed it right. The adman who thought of making Americans believe they needed underarm deodorant was a visionary. So, too, was the hero who made a success of a new product, Ivory soap. The executives were horrified, Mother told me, that a cake of this stuff floated. Soap wasn't supposed to float. Anyone would be able to tell it was mostly whipped-up air. Then some inspired adman made a leap: Advertise that it floats. Flaunt it. The rest is history.

She respected the rare few who broke through to new ways. "Look," she'd say, "here's an intelligent apron." She called upon us to admire intelligent control knobs and intelligent pan handles, intelligent andirons and picture frames and knife sharpeners. She questioned everything, every pair of scissors, every knitting needle, gardening glove, tape dispenser. Hers was a restless mental vigor that just about ignited the dumb household objects with its force.

Torpid conformity was a kind of sin; it was stupidity itself, the mighty stream against which Mother would never cease to struggle. If you held no minority opinions, or if you failed to risk total ostracism for them daily, the world would be a better place without you.

Always I heard Mother's emotional voice asking Amy and me the same few questions: "Is that your own idea? Or somebody else's?" "*Giant* is a good movie," I pronounced to the family at dinner. "Oh, really?" Mother warmed to these occasions. She all but rolled up her sleeves. She knew I hadn't seen it. "Is that your considered opinion?"

She herself held many unpopular, even fantastic, positions. She was scathingly sarcastic about the McCarthy hearings while they took place, right on our living-room television; she frantically opposed Father's wait-and-see calm. "We don't know enough about it," he said. "I do," she said. "I know all I need to know."

She asserted, against all opposition, that people who lived in trailer parks were not bad but simply poor, and had as much right to settle on beautiful land, such as rural Ligonier, Pennsylvania, as did the oldest of families in the finest of hidden houses. Therefore, the people who owned trailer parks, and sought zoning changes to permit trailer parks, needed our help. Her profound belief that the country-club pool sweeper was a person, and that the department-store saleslady, the bus driver, telephone operator, and house-painter were people, and even in groups the steelworkers who carried pickets and the Christmas shoppers who clogged intersections were people—this was a conviction common enough in democratic Pittsburgh, but not altogether common among our friends' parents, or even, perhaps, among our parents' friends.

Opposition emboldened Mother, and she would take on anybody on any issue—the chairman of the board, at a cocktail party, on the current strike; she would fly at him in a flurry of passion, as a songbird selflessly attacks a big hawk.

"Eisenhower's going to win," I announced after school. She lowered her magazine and looked me in the eyes: "How do you know?" I was doomed. It was fatal to say, "Everyone says so." We all knew well what happened. "Do you consult this Everyone before you make your decisions? What if Everyone decided to round up all the Jews?" Mother knew there was no danger of cowing me. She simply tried to keep us all awake. And in fact it was always clear to Amy and me, and to Molly when she grew old enough to listen, that if our classmates came to cruelty, just as much as if the neighborhood or the nation came to madness, we were expected to take, and would be each separately capable of taking, a stand.

COMPREHENSION

1. The writer creates a picture of her mother's personality through a number of anecdotes and explanations. How would you sum up the mother's personality?
2. The mother appears to have a special appreciation for words and language. To what purpose does she apply this appreciation? What effect does it have on her family and acquaintances?
3. What values does the mother hold? What behaviors and attitudes does she abhor and discourage?

RHETORIC

1. In paragraph 7, the author explains that the highway from Tampa to Miami is referred to either as "Tamiami Trail" or "Alligator Alley." What is the connotation of each of these terms? Why does the mother prefer to call it "Tamiami Trail"?
2. The author herself seems to have inherited a special fascination for language. Study her use of dashes and semicolons in paragraphs 26 and 27. How do they help contribute to an energetic use of writing?
3. What are the functions of the space between paragraphs 19 and 20; 22 and 23; and 32 and 33? How do these divisions contribute to the structure of the essay as a whole?
4. How does the author use her writing talents to create paragraph 8 out of one long sentence? What other examples can you provide of long sentences in the essay? How do they contribute to the overall style of the writing?
5. What is the overall emotional "tone" of the writer toward her subject—admiring, loving, cautionary? What adjectives does the writer use in describing her mother that provides the reader with clues to the tone?
6. The author quotes her mother directly on several occasions. Can we assume that the author is quoting precisely, given that the essay was written years after the incidents described? Does it matter?
7. The final paragraph not only provides closure to the essay, but transmits a lesson the mother wants her family to learn. How does the style and structure of this paragraph contribute to the ultimate message of the essay? In other words, how does the form help to convey the meaning?

WRITING

1. Write a descriptive essay about someone you know, using at least five anecdotes from that person's life, so that by the end of the essay, we have a mental picture of your subject's personality, values, and attitudes.
2. Argue for or against the proposition that an effective parent should have—at least—a touch of unconventionality.

3. *Describe an incident in your life when the unexpected taught you an important lesson.*

JUDITH ORTIZ COFER   Judith Ortiz Cofer, who was born in 1952 in Puerto Rico, immigrated to the United States in 1956. Once a bilingual teacher in Florida public schools, Cofer has written collections of poetry, including *Native Dancer,* as well as plays, among them *Latin Women Pray* and *Reaching for the Mainland.* Her shorter work has appeared in anthologies, including *Hispanics in the United States.* One of the themes Cofer explores in her writing is the clash between Hispanic and American cultures. In the following autobiographical piece, she evokes the pain of assimilation.

JUDITH ORTIZ COFER

Silent Dancing

We have a home movie of this party. Several times my mother and I have 1 *watched it together, and I have asked questions about the silent revelers coming in and out of focus. It is grainy and of short duration, but it's a great visual aid to my memory of life at that time. And it is in color—the only complete scene in color I can recall from those years.*

We lived in Puerto Rico until my brother was born in 1954. Soon after, 2 because of economic pressures on our growing family, my father joined the United States Navy. He was assigned to duty on a ship in Brooklyn Yard—a place of cement and steel that was to be his home base in the States until his retirement more than twenty years later. He left the Island first, alone, going to New York City and tracking down his uncle who lived with his family across the Hudson River in Paterson, New Jersey. There my father found a tiny apartment in a huge tenement that had once housed Jewish families but was just being taken over and transformed by Puerto Ricans, overflowing from New York City. In 1955 he sent for us. My mother was only twenty years old, I was not quite three, and my brother was a toddler when we arrived at El Building, as the place had been christened by its newest residents.

My memories of life in Paterson during those first few years are all 3 in shades of gray. Maybe I was too young to absorb vivid colors and details, or to discriminate between the slate blue of the winter sky and the darker hues of the snow-bearing clouds, but that single color washes over the whole period. The building we lived in was gray, as were the streets, filled with slush the first few months of my life there.

The coat my father had bought for me was similar in color and too big; it sat heavily on my thin frame.

I do remember the way the heater pipes banged and rattled, star-   4
tling all of us out of sleep until we got so used to the sound that we automatically shut it out or raised our voices above the racket. The hiss from the valve punctuated my sleep (which has always been fitful) like a nonhuman presence in the room—a dragon sleeping at the entrance of my childhood. But the pipes were also a connection to all the other lives being lived around us. Having come from a house designed for a single family back in Puerto Rico—my mother's extended-family home—it was curious to know that strangers lived under our floor and above our heads, and that the heater pipe went through everyone's apartment. (My first spanking in Paterson came as a result of playing tunes on the pipes in my room to see if there would be an answer.) My mother was as new to this concept of beehive life as I was, but she had been given strict orders by my father to keep the doors locked, the noise down, ourselves to ourselves.

It seems that Father had learned some painful lessons about preju-   5
dice while searching for an apartment in Paterson. Not until years later did I hear how much resistance he had encountered with landlords who were panicking at the influx of Latinos into a neighborhood that had been Jewish for a couple of generations. It made no difference that it was the American phenomenon of ethnic turnover which was changing the urban core of Paterson, and that the human flood could not be held back with an accusing finger.

"You Cuban?" one man had asked my father, pointing at his name   6
tag on the navy uniform—even though my father had the fair skin and light brown hair of his northern Spanish background, and the name Ortiz is as common in Puerto Rico as Johnson is in the United States.

"No," my father had answered, looking past the finger into his   7
adversary's angry eyes. "I'm Puerto Rican."

"Same shit." And the door closed.   8

My father could have passed as European, but we couldn't. My   9
brother and I both have our mother's black hair and olive skin, and so we lived in El Building and visited our great-uncle and his fair children on the next block. It was their private joke that they were the German branch of the family. Not many years later that area too would be mainly Puerto Rican. It was as if the heart of the city map were being gradually colored brown—*café con leche* brown. Our color.

The movie opens with a sweep of the living room. It is "typical" immigrant   10
Puerto Rican decor for the time: the sofa and chairs are square and hard-looking, upholstered in bright colors (blue and yellow in this instance) and covered with the transparent plastic that furniture salesmen then were so adept at convincing women to buy. The linoleum on the floor is light blue; where it had been subjected to spike heels, as it was in most places, there were dime-size indentations all over it that cannot be seen in this movie. The room is full of people dressed up: dark suits for the men, red dresses for the women.

When I have asked my mother why most of the women are in red that night, she has shrugged and said, "I don't remember. Just a coincidence." She doesn't have my obsession for assigning symbolism to everything.

The three women in red sitting on the couch are my mother, my eighteen-year-old cousin, and her brother's girlfriend. The novia *is just up from the Island, which is apparent in her body language. She sits up formally, her dress pulled over her knees. She is a pretty girl, but her posture makes her look insecure, lost in her full-skirted dress, which she has carefully tucked around her to make room for my gorgeous cousin, her future sister-in-law. My cousin has grown up in Paterson and is in her last year of high school. She doesn't have a trace of what Puerto Ricans call* la mancha *(literally, the stain: the mark of the new immigrant—something about the posture, the voice, or the humble demeanor that makes it obvious to everyone the person has just arrived on the mainland). My cousin is wearing a tight, sequined, cocktail dress. Her brown hair has been lightened with peroxide around the bangs, and she is holding a cigarette expertly between her fingers, bringing it up to her mouth in a sensuous arc of her arm as she talks animatedly. My mother, who has come up to sit between the two women, both only a few years younger than herself, is somewhere between the poles they represent in our culture.*

It became my father's obsession to get out of the barrio, and thus we were never permitted to form bonds with the place or with the people who lived there. Yet El Building was a comfort to my mother, who never got over yearning for *la isla*. She felt surrounded by her language: the walls were thin, and voices speaking and arguing in Spanish could be heard all day. *Salsas* blasted out of radios, turned on early in the morning and left on for company. Women seemed to cook rice and beans perpetually—the strong aroma of boiling red kidney beans permeated the hallways.

Though Father preferred that we do our grocery shopping at the supermarket when he came home on weekend leaves, my mother insisted that she could cook only with products whose labels she could read. Consequently, during the week I accompanied her and my little brother to La Bodega—a hole-in-the-wall grocery store across the street from El Building. There we squeezed down three narrow aisles jammed with various products. Goya and Libby's—those were the trademarks that were trusted by her *mamá*, so my mother bought many cans of Goya beans, soups, and condiments, as well as little cans of Libby's fruit juices for us. And she also bought Colgate toothpaste and Palmolive soap. (The final *e* is pronounced in both these products in Spanish, so for many years I believed that they were manufactured on the Island. I remember my surprise at first hearing a commercial on television in which "Colgate" rhymed with "ate.") We always lingered at La Bodega, for it was there that Mother breathed best, taking in the familiar aromas of the foods she knew from Mamá's kitchen. It was also there that she got to speak to the other women of El Building without violating outright Father's dictates against fraternizing with our neighbors.

Yet Father did his best to make our "assimilation" painless. I can   14
still see him carrying a real Christmas tree up several flights of stairs to
our apartment, leaving a trail of aromatic pine. He carried it formally,
as if it were a flag in a parade. We were the only ones in El Building that
I knew of who got presents on both Christmas and *día de Reyes*, the day
when the Three Kings brought gifts to Christ and to Hispanic children.

Our supreme luxury in El Building was having our own television   15
set. It must have been a result of Father's guilt feelings over the isolation he had imposed on us, but we were among the first in the barrio
to have one. My brother quickly became an avid watcher of Captain
Kangaroo and Jungle Jim, while I loved all the series showing families.
By the time I started first grade, I could have drawn a map of Middle
America as exemplified by the lives of characters in *Father Knows Best,
The Donna Reed Show, Leave It to Beaver, My Three Sons,* and (my
favorite) *Bachelor Father,* where John Forsythe treated his adopted
teenage daughter like a princess because he was rich and had a Chinese
houseboy to do everything for him. In truth, compared to our neighbors in El Building, *we* were rich. My father's navy check provided us
with financial security and a standard of living that the factory workers
envied. The only thing his money could not buy us was a place to live
away from the barrio—his greatest wish, Mother's greatest fear.

In the home movie the men are shown next, sitting around a card table set   16
up in one corner of the living room, playing dominoes. The clack of the ivory
pieces was a familiar sound. I heard it in many houses on the Island and in
many apartments in Paterson. In Leave It to Beaver, *the Cleavers played*
bridge in every other episode; in my childhood, the men started every social
occasion with a hotly debated round of dominoes. The women would sit
around and watch, but they never participated in the games.

Here and there you can see a small child. Children were always brought   17
to parties and, whenever they got sleepy, were put to bed in the host's bed-
room. Babysitting was a concept unrecognized by the Puerto Rican women I
knew: a responsible mother did not leave her children with any stranger. And
in a culture where children are not considered intrusive, there was no need to
leave the children at home. We went where our mother went.

Of my preschool years I have only impressions: the sharp bite of the   18
wind in December as we walked with our parents toward the brightly
lit stores downtown; how I felt like a stuffed doll in my heavy coat,
boots, and mittens; how good it was to walk into the five-and-dime and
sit at the counter drinking hot chocolate. On Saturdays our whole family would walk downtown to shop at the big department stores on
Broadway. Mother bought all our clothes at Penney's and Sears, and
she liked to buy her dresses at the women's specialty shops like Lerner's
and Diana's. At some point we'd go into Woolworth's and sit at the soda
fountain to eat.

We never ran into other Latinos at these stores or when eating out,   19
and it became clear to me only years later that the women from El

Building shopped mainly in other places—stores owned by other Puerto Ricans or by Jewish merchants who had philosophically accepted our presence in the city and decided to make us their good customers, if not real neighbors and friends. These establishments were located not downtown but in the blocks around our street, and they were referred to generically as La Tienda, El Bazar, La Bodega, La Botánica. Everyone knew what was meant. These were the stores where your face did not turn a clerk to stone, where your money was as green as anyone else's.

One New Year's Eve we were dressed up like child models in the Sears catalogue: my brother in a miniature man's suit and bow tie, and I in black patent-leather shoes and a frilly dress with several layers of crinoline underneath. My mother wore a bright red dress that night, I remember, and spike heels; her long black hair hung to her waist. Father, who usually wore his navy uniform during his short visits home, had put on a dark civilian suit for the occasion: we had been invited to his uncle's house for a big celebration. Everyone was excited because my mother's brother Hernan—a bachelor who could indulge himself with luxuries—had bought a home movie camera, which he would be trying out that night.

Even the home movie cannot fill in the sensory details such a gathering left imprinted in a child's brain. The thick sweetness of women's perfumes mixing with the ever-present smells of food cooking in the kitchen: meat and plantain *pasteles,* as well as the ubiquitous rice dish made special with pigeon peas—*gandules*—and seasoned with precious *sofrito* sent up from the Island by somebody's mother or smuggled in by a recent traveler. *Sofrito* was one of the items that women hoarded, since it was hardly ever in stock at La Bodega. It was the flavor of Puerto Rico.

The men drank Palo Viejo rum, and some of the younger ones got weepy. The first time I saw a grown man cry was at a New Year's Eve party: he had been reminded of his mother by the smells in the kitchen. But what I remember most were the boiled *pasteles,* plantain or yucca rectangles stuffed with corned beef or other meats, olives, and many other savory ingredients, all wrapped in banana leaves. Everybody had to fish one out with a fork. There was always a "trick" *pastel*—one without stuffing—and whoever got that one was the "New Year's Fool."

There was also the music. Long-playing albums were treated like precious china in these homes. Mexican recordings were popular, but the songs that brought tears to my mother's eyes were sung by the melancholy Daniel Santos, whose life as a drug addict was the stuff of legend. Felipe Rodríguez was a particular favorite of couples, since he sang about faithless women and brokenhearted men. There is a snatch of one lyric that has stuck in my mind like a needle on a worn groove: *De piedra ha de ser mi cama, de piedra la cabezera . . . la mujer que a mi me quiera . . . ha de quererme de veras. Ay, Ay, Ay, corazón, porque no amas. . . .* I must have heard it a thousand times since the idea of a

20

21

22

23

bed made of stone, and its connection to love, first troubled me with its disturbing images.

The five-minute home movie ends with people dancing in a circle—the creative filmmaker must have set it up, so that all of them could file past him. It is both comical and sad to watch silent dancing. Since there is no justification for the absurd movements that music provides for some of us, people appear frantic, their faces embarrassingly intense. It's as if you were watching sex. Yet for years, I've had dreams in the form of this home movie. In a recurring scene, familiar faces push themselves forward into my mind's eye, plastering their features into distorted close-ups. And I'm asking them: "Who is *she?* Who is the old woman I don't recognize? Is she an aunt? Somebody's wife? Tell me who she is." 24

"See the beauty mark on her cheek as big as a hill on the lunar land- 25 scape of her face—well, that runs in the family. The women on your father's side of the family wrinkle early; it's the price they pay for that fair skin. The young girl with the green stain on her wedding dress is *la novia*—just up from the Island. See, she lowers her eyes when she approaches the camera, as she's supposed to. Decent girls never look at you directly in the face. *Humilde,* humble, a girl should express humility in all her actions. She will make a good wife for your cousin. He should consider himself lucky to have met her only weeks after she arrived here. If he marries her quickly, she will make him a good Puerto Rican-style wife; but if he waits too long, she will be corrupted by the city, just like your cousin there."

"She means me. I do what I want. This is not some primitive island 26 I live on. Do they expect me to wear a black mantilla on my head and go to mass every day? Not me. I'm an American woman, and I will do as I please. I can type faster than anyone in my senior class at Central High, and I'm going to be a secretary to a lawyer when I graduate. I can pass for an American girl anywhere—I've tried it. At least for Italian, anyway—I never speak Spanish in public. I hate these parties, but I wanted the dress. I look better than any of these *humildes* here. My life is going to be different. I have an American boyfriend. He is older and has a car. My parents don't know it, but I sneak out of the house late at night sometimes to be with him. If I marry him, even my name will be American. I hate rice and beans—that's what makes these women fat."

"Your *prima* is pregnant by that man she's been sneaking around 27 with. Would I lie to you? I'm your *tía política,* your great-uncle's com-mon-law wife—the one he abandoned on the Island to go marry your cousin's mother. I was not invited to this party, of course, but I came anyway. I came to tell you that story about your cousin that you've always wanted to hear. Do you remember the comment your mother made to a neighbor that has always haunted you? The only thing you heard was your cousin's name, and then you saw your mother pick up your doll from the couch and say: 'It was as big as this doll when they flushed it down the toilet.' This image has bothered you for years, hasn't it? You had nightmares about babies being flushed down the toilet, and you wondered why anyone would do such a horrible thing. You didn't dare ask your mother about it. She would only tell you that you had not heard her right, and yell at you for listening to adult conversations. But later, when you were old enough to know about abortions, you suspected.

"I am here to tell you that you were right. Your cousin was growing an *americanito* in her belly when this movie was made. Soon after, she put something long and pointy into her pretty self, thinking maybe she could get rid of the problem before breakfast and still make it to her first class at the high school. Well, *niña*, her screams could be heard downtown. Your aunt, her *mamá*, who had been a midwife on the Island, managed to pull the little thing out. Yes, they probably flushed it down the toilet. What else could they do with it—give it a Christian burial in a little white casket with blue bows and ribbons? Nobody wanted that baby—least of all the father, a teacher at her school with a house in West Paterson that he was filling with real children, and a wife who was a natural blonde.

"Girl, the scandal sent your uncle back to the bottle. And guess where your cousin ended up? Irony of ironies. She was sent to a village in Puerto Rico to live with a relative on her mother's side: a place so far away from civilization that you have to ride a mule to reach it. A real change in scenery. She found a man there—women like that cannot live without male company—but believe me, the men in Puerto Rico know how to put a saddle on a woman like her. La gringa, they call her. Ha, ha, ha. La gringa is what she always wanted to be. . . ."

The old woman's mouth becomes a cavernous black hole I fall into. And as I fall, I can feel the reverberations of her laughter. I hear the echoes of her last mocking words: *la gringa, la gringa!* And the conga line keeps moving silently past me. There is no music in my dream for the dancers.

When Odysseus visits Hades to see the spirit of his mother, he makes an offering of sacrificial blood, but since all the souls crave an audience with the living, he has to listen to many of them before he can ask questions. I, too, have to hear the dead and the forgotten speak in my dream. Those who are still part of my life remain silent, going around and around in their dance. The others keep pressing their faces forward to say things about the past.

My father's uncle is last in line. He is dying of alcoholism, shrunken and shriveled like a monkey, his face a mass of wrinkles and broken arteries. As he comes closer I realize that in his features I can see my whole family. If you were to stretch that rubbery flesh, you could find my father's face, and deep within *that* face—my own. I don't want to look into those eyes ringed in purple. In a few years he will retreat into silence, and take a long, long time to die. *Move back, Tío,* I tell him. *I don't want to hear what you have to say. Give the dancers room to move. Soon it will be midnight. Who is the New Year's Fool this time?*

COMPREHENSION

1. How did Cofer's parents differ in their views about life in the United States? Explain. Give concrete examples.
2. What is the attitude of those born or raised in the United States toward those Puerto Ricans still carrying *"la mancha"?* Cite evidence from the essay to support your opinion.
3. Cofer refers to learning "painful lessons about prejudice." What examples from the narrative illustrate these lessons?

RHETORIC

1. To what end does Cofer employ the italicized portions of the essay? How does this device contribute to the overall power of the narrative?
2. What is the mood of the essay? What phrases or passages reveal the narrator's point of view?
3. Cofer uses powerful images and sensory details in her narration. Which of these are especially evocative? Give examples, and explain how they enhance the emotional impact of her story.
4. What is the function of the Spanish idioms and phrases Cofer uses? Does she employ them successfully?
5. Toward the end of the essay, Cofer uses disembodied voices to recount the Latino experience in the United States. Is this an effective method? How do these voices affect the mood of the story?
6. Explain the overall pattern of essay development that emerges from this essay. In other words, how does Cofer unify the various scenes and episodes that constitute the narrative?

WRITING

1. There were many family gatherings in the Ortiz household. Write a narrative essay about a memorable family gathering you experienced as a child. Use sensory images to enrich your essay.
2. Write an essay recounting a time when you or someone you know experienced rejection or humiliation because of race, color, religion, or economic status. What happened, how did you feel, and what effect has it had on you?
3. As you read the next selection, consider Cofer's connotative labels of *"humilde"* and *"gringa"* and decide which category Maxine Hong Kingston, although Asian American, might fall under. Analyze this connection in the context of ethnic identity in the United States.

MAXINE HONG KINGSTON   Maxine Hong Kingston (b. 1940) has written three books on the Chinese-American experience that have established her as a major contemporary prose stylist. *The Woman Warrior* (1976) and *China Men* (1980) are brilliant explorations of personal and ethnic consciousness. Her newest work, a novel, is entitled *Tripmaster Monkey* (1989). This selection from her first book is filled with the mysteries, family tales, and legends that she uses to create the tapestry of her complex cultural identity.

*Chapter One
Childhood and
Family*

MAXINE HONG KINGSTON

The Woman Warrior

My American life has been such a disappointment. 1

"I got straight A's, Mama." 2

"Let me tell you a true story about a girl who saved her village." 3

I could not figure out what was my village. And it was important 4
that I do something big and fine, or else my parents would sell me when
we made our way back to China. In China there were solutions for
what to do with little girls who ate up food and threw tantrums. You
can't eat straight A's.

When one of my parents or the emigrant villagers said, "Feeding 5
girls is feeding cowbirds," I would thrash on the floor and scream so
hard I couldn't talk. I couldn't stop.

"What's the matter with her?" 6

"I don't know. Bad, I guess. You know how girls are. 'There's no 7
profit in raising girls. Better to raise geese than girls.'"

"I would hit her if she were mine. But then there's no use wasting 8
all that discipline on a girl. 'When you raise girls, you're raising children
for strangers.'"

"Stop that crying!" my mother would yell. "I'm going to hit you if 9
you don't stop. Bad girl! Stop!" I'm going to remember never to hit or
to scold my children for crying, I thought, because then they will only
cry more.

"I'm not a bad girl," I would scream. "I'm not a bad girl. I'm not a 10
bad girl." I might as well have said, "I'm not a girl."

"When you were little, all you had to say was 'I'm not a bad girl,' 11
and you could make yourself cry," my mother says, talking-story about
my childhood.

I minded that the emigrant villagers shook their heads at my sister 12
and me. "One girl—and another girl," they said, and made our parents ashamed to take us out together. The good part about my brothers being born was that people stopped saying, "All girls," but I
learned new grievances. "Did you roll an egg on *my* face like that
when *I* was born?" "Did you have a full-month party for *me*?" "Did
you turn on all the lights?" "Did you send *my* picture to Grandmother?" "Why not? Because I'm a girl? Is that why not?" "Why
didn't you teach me English?" "You like having me beaten up at
school, don't you?"

"She is very mean, isn't she?" the emigrant villagers would say. 13

"Come, children. Hurry. Hurry. Who wants to go out with Great-Uncle?" On Saturday mornings, my great-uncle, the ex-river pirate, did the shopping. "Get your coats, whoever's coming." 14

"I'm coming. I'm coming. Wait for me." 15

When he heard girls' voices, he turned on us and roared, "No girls!" and left my sisters and me hanging our coats back up, not looking at one another. The boys came back with candy and new toys. When they walked through Chinatown, the people must have said, "A boy—and another boy—and another boy!" At my great-uncle's funeral I secretly tested out feeling glad that he was dead—the six-foot bearish masculinity of him. 16

I went away to college—Berkeley in the sixties—and I studied, and I marched to change the world, but I did not turn into a boy. I would have liked to bring myself back as a boy for my parents to welcome with chickens and pigs. That was for my brother, who returned alive from Vietnam. 17

If I went to Vietnam, I would not come back; females desert families. It was said, "There is an outward tendency in females," which meant that I was getting straight A's for the good of my future husband's family, not my own. I did not plan ever to have a husband. I would show my mother and father and the nosey emigrant villagers that girls have no outward tendency. I stopped getting straight A's. 18

And all the time I was having to turn myself American-feminine, or no dates. 19

There is a Chinese word for the female *I*—which is "slave." Break the women with their own tongues! 20

I refused to cook. When I had to wash dishes, I would crack one or two. "Bad girl," my mother yelled, and sometimes that made me gloat rather than cry. Isn't a bad girl almost a boy? 21

"What do you want to be when you grow up, little girl?" 22

"A lumberjack in Oregon." 23

Even now, unless I'm happy, I burn the food when I cook. I do not feed people. I let the dirty dishes rot. I eat at other people's tables but won't invite them to mine, where the dishes are rotting. 24

If I could not-eat, perhaps I could make myself a warrior like the swordswoman who drives me. I will—I must—rise and plow the fields as soon as the baby comes out. 25

Once I get outside the house, what bird might call me; on what horse could I ride away? Marriage and childbirth strengthen the swordswoman, who is not a maid like Joan of Arc. Do the women's work; then do more work, which will become ours too. No husband of mine will say, "I could have been a drummer, but I had to think about the wife and kids. You know how it is." Nobody supports me at the expense of his own adventure. Then I get bitter: no one supports me; I am not loved enough to be supported. That I am not a burden has to compensate for the sad envy when I look at women loved enough to be supported. Even now China wraps double binds around my feet. 26

When urban renewal tore down my parents' laundry and paved over our slum for a parking lot, I only made up gun and knife fantasies and did nothing useful. 27

28

From the fairy tales, I've learned exactly who the enemy are. I easily recognize them—business-suited in their modern American executive guise, each boss two feet taller than I am and impossible to meet eye to eye.

I once worked at an art supply house that sold paints to artists. "Order more of that nigger yellow, willya?" the boss told me. "Bright, isn't it? Nigger yellow."

"I don't like that word," I had to say in my bad, smallperson's voice ₃₀ that makes no impact. The boss never deigned to answer.

I also worked at a land developer's association. The building indus- ₃₁ try was planning a banquet for contractors, real estate dealers, and real estate editors. "Did you know the restaurant you chose for the banquet is being picketed by CORE and the NAACP?" I squeaked.

"Of course I know." The boss laughed. "That's why I chose it." ₃₂

"I refuse to type these invitations," I whispered, voice unreliable. ₃₃

He leaned back in his leather chair, his bossy stomach opulent. He ₃₄ picked up his calendar and slowly circled a date. "You will be paid up to here," he said. "We'll mail you the check."

If I took the sword, which my hate must surely have forged out of ₃₅ the air, and gutted him, I would put color and wrinkles into his shirt.

It's not just the stupid racists that I have to do something about, but ₃₆ the tyrants who for whatever reason can deny my family food and work. My job is my own only land.

To avenge my family, I'd have to storm across China to take back ₃₇ our farm from the Communists; I'd have to rage across the United States to take back the laundry in New York and the one in California. Nobody in history has conquered and united both North America and Asia. A descendant of eighty pole fighters, I ought to be able to set out confidently, march straight down our street, get going right now. There's work to do, ground to cover. Surely, the eighty pole fighters, though unseen, would follow me and lead me and protect me, as is the wont of ancestors.

Or it may well be that they're resting happily in China, their spirits ₃₈ dispersed among the real Chinese, and not nudging me at all with their poles. I mustn't feel bad that I haven't done as well as the swordswoman did; after all, no bird called me, no wise old people tutored me. I have no magic beads, or water gourd sight, no rabbit that will jump in the fire when I'm hungry. I dislike armies.

I've looked for the bird. I've seen clouds make pointed angel wings ₃₉ that stream past the sunset, but they shred into clouds. Once at a beach after a long hike I saw a seagull, tiny as an insect. But when I jumped up to tell what miracle I saw, before I could get the words out I understood that the bird was insect-size because it was far away. My brain had momentarily lost its depth perception. I was that eager to find an unusual bird.

The news from China has been confusing. It also had something to ₄₀ do with birds. I was nine years old when the letters made my parents, who are rocks, cry. My father screamed in his sleep. My mother wept and crumpled up the letters. She set fire to them page by page in the ashtray, but new letters came almost every day. The only letters they opened without fear were the ones with red borders, the holiday letters that mustn't carry bad news. The other letters said that my uncles were made to kneel on broken glass during their trials and had confessed to being land-owners. They were all executed, and the aunt whose thumbs were twisted off drowned herself. Other aunts, mothers-in-law, and cousins disappeared; some suddenly began writing to us again from communes or from Hong Kong. They kept asking for money. The ones in communes got four ounces of fat and one cup of oil a week, they said, and had to work from 4 A.M. TO 9 P.M. They had to learn to do dances waving red kerchiefs; they had to sing nonsense syllables. The Communists gave axes to the old ladies and said, "Go and kill yourself. You're useless." If we overseas Chinese would just send money to the Communist bank, our relatives said, they might get a percentage of it for themselves. The aunts in Hong Kong said to send money quickly; their children were begging on the sidewalks and mean people put dirt in their bowls.

When I dream that I am wire without flesh, there is a letter on blue airmail paper that floats above the night ocean between here and China. It must arrive safely or else my grandmother and I will lose each other.

My parents felt bad whether or not they sent money. Sometimes they got angry at their brothers and sisters for asking. And they would not simply ask but have to talk-story too. The revolutionaries had taken Fourth Aunt and Uncle's store, house, and lands. They attacked the house and killed the grandfather and oldest daughter. The grandmother escaped with the loose cash and did not return to help. Fourth Aunt picked up her sons, one under each arm, and hid in the pig house, where they slept that night in cotton clothes. The next day she found her husband, who had also miraculously escaped. The two of them collected twigs and yams to sell while their children begged. Each morning they tied the faggots on each other's back. Nobody bought from them. They ate the yams and some of the children's rice. Finally Fourth Aunt saw what was wrong. "We have to shout 'Fuel for sale' and 'Yams for sale,'" she said, "We can't just walk unobtrusively up and down the street." "You're right," said my uncle, but he was shy and walked in back of her. "Shout," my aunt ordered, but he could not. "They think we're carrying these sticks home for our own fire," she said. "Shout." They walked about miserably, silently, until sundown, neither of them able to advertise themselves. Fourth Aunt, an orphan since the age of ten, mean as my mother, threw her bundle down at his feet and scolded Fourth Uncle, "Starving to death, his wife and children starving to death, and he's too damned shy to raise his voice." She left him standing by himself and afraid to return empty-handed to her. He sat under a tree to think, when he spotted a pair of nesting doves. Dumping his bag of yams, he climbed up and caught the birds. That was when the Communists trapped him, in the tree. They criticized him for selfishly taking food for his own family and killed him, leaving his body in the tree as an example. They took the birds to a commune kitchen to be shared.

It is confusing that my family was not the poor to be championed. They were executed like the barons in the stories, when they were not barons. It is confusing that birds tricked us.

What fighting and killing I have seen have not been glorious but slum grubby. I fought the most during junior high school and always cried. Fights are confusing as to who has won. The corpses I've seen had been rolled and dumped, sad little dirty bodies covered with a police khaki blanket. My mother locked her children in the house so we couldn't look at dead slum people. But at news of a body, I would find a way to get out; I had to learn about dying if I wanted to become a swordswoman. Once there was an Asian man stabbed next door, word on cloth pinned to his corpse. When the police came around asking questions, my father said, "No read Japanese. Japanese words. Me Chinese."

I've also looked for old people who could be my gurus. A medium with red hair told me that a girl who died in a far country follows me wherever I go. This spirit can help me if I acknowledge her, she said. Between the head line and heart line in my right palm, she said, I have the mystic cross. I could become a medium myself. I don't want to be a medium. I don't want to be a crank taking "offerings" in a wicker plate from the frightened audience, who, one after another, asked the spirits how to raise rent money, how to cure their coughs and skin diseases, how to find a job. And martial arts are for unsure little boys kicking away under fluorescent lights.

I live now where there are Chinese and Japanese, but no emigrants from my own village looking at me as if I had failed them. Living among one's own emigrant villagers can give a good Chinese far from China glory and a place. "That old busboy is really a swordsman," we whisper when he goes by, "He's a swordsman who's killed fifty. He has a tong ax in his closet." But I am useless, one more girl who couldn't be sold. When I visit the family now, I wrap my American successes around me like a private shawl; I *am* worthy of eating the food. From afar I can believe my family loves me fundamentally. They only say, "When fishing for treasures in the flood, be careful not to pull in girls," because that is what one says about daughters. But I watched such words come out of my own mother's and father's mouths; I looked at their ink drawing of poor people snagging their neighbor's flotage with long flood hooks and pushing the girl babies on down the river. And I had to get out of hating range. I read in an anthropology book that Chinese say, "Girls are necessary too"; I have never heard the Chinese I know make this concession. Perhaps it was a saying in another village. I refuse to shy my way anymore through our Chinatown, which tasks me with the old sayings and the stories.

The swordswoman and I are not so dissimilar. May my people understand the resemblance soon so that I can return to them. What we have in common are the words at our backs. The ideographs for *revenge* are "report at crime" and "report to five families." The reporting is the vengeance—not the beheading, not the gutting, but the words. And I have so many words—"chink" words and "gook" words too—that they do not fit on my skin.

COMPREHENSION

1. What is the historical context of this personal narrative? What assumptions does the author make about her audience?
2. Summarize the "autobiography" that Kingston presents of herself in this selection. What are her family and its individual members like?
3. Explain the author's American life. How does she relate to Chinese culture *and* to American culture? What is her major problem? How would she overcome it?

RHETORIC

1. What connotations does Kingston explore for the words *girls* and *females?* What connotations does she bring to the word *swordswoman?*
2. Locate five Chinese expressions or sayings in this selection. What is their effect on the tone of the essay?
3. The author's introductory paragraph consists of a single sentence. Is this strategy effective? Why?
4. Analyze the author's presentation of chronology. List the scenes into which the action is divided. Where are there stories within stories? Why does Kingston present such a complex tapestry of chronology and events? How, finally, does the author use narration to advance expository or explanatory ends?
5. Why is characterization important to the development of Kingston's thesis? How does the author *create* vivid characters? Cite specific examples and techniques.
6. Which paragraphs comprise the conclusion? How do these paragraphs reflect some of the major motifs of the essay?

WRITING

1. In *China Men,* Kingston speaks of "trying to unravel the mysteries" of her family. What mysteries does she explore here? Look up the word *mystery* in your dictionary. What "mysteries" concerning your family or your origins would you like to explore? Write an essay on this topic.
2. Write an autobiographical or narrative essay tracing a particular problem that you had to face while growing up in your family.
3. Narrate an event that happened to one of your relatives or ancestors in the "old country," the nation of your family's origin.

ZORA NEALE HURSTON   Zora Neale Hurston (1901–1960) was born in Eatonville, Florida. She studied anthropology at Barnard College and Columbia University with the eminent anthropologist Franz Boas. As a folklorist, she studied local customs and culture in places such as Jamaica, Haiti, Bermuda, and Honduras. She also worked as a college teacher and librarian. Her better-known works include the play *Mule Bone* (1931); a study of folklore, *Mules and Men* (1935); and a novel, *Their Eyes Were Watching God* (1937). Hurston was a complex figure. Ernest Hemingway described her as "flamboyant yet vulnerable, self-centered yet kind, a Republican conservative and an early black nationalist." In this excerpt from *Dust Tracks on the Road* (1942), Hurston provides an unsentimental yet lively account of the response of her community to her birth, allowing us to gain a glimpse of the culture into which she was born.

ZORA NEALE HURSTON

I Get Born

This is all hear-say. Maybe some of the details of my birth as told me might be a little inaccurate, but it is pretty well established that I really did get born.

The saying goes like this. My mother's time had come and my father was not there. Being a carpenter, successful enough to have other helpers on some jobs, he was away often on building business, as well as preaching. It seems that my father was away from home for months this time. I have never been told why. But I did hear that he threatened to cut his throat when he got the news. It seems that one daughter was all that he figured he could stand. My sister, Sarah, was his favorite child, but that one girl was enough. Plenty more sons, but no more girl babies to wear out shoes and bring in nothing. I don't think he ever got over the trick he felt that I played on him by getting born a girl, and while he was off from home at that. A little of my sugar used to sweeten his coffee right now. That is a Negro way of saying his patience was short with me. Let me change a few words with him—and I am of the word-changing kind—and he was ready to change ends. Still and all, I looked more like him than any child in the house. Of course, by the time I got born, it was too late to make any suggestions, so the old man had to put up with me. He was nice about it in a way. He didn't tie me in a sack and drop me in the lake, as he probably felt like doing.

People were digging sweet potatoes, and then it was hog-killing time. Not at our house, but it was going on in general over the country like, being January and a bit cool. Most people were either butchering for themselves, or off helping other folks do their butchering, which was almost just as good. It is a gay time. A big pot of hasslits cooking with plenty of seasoning, lean slabs of fresh-killed pork frying for the helpers to refresh themselves after the work is done. Over and above being neighborly and giving aid, there is the food, the drinks and the fun of getting together.

So there was no grown folks close around when Mama's water broke. She sent one of the smaller children to fetch Aunt Judy, the mid-wife, but she was gone to Woodbridge, a mile and a half away, to eat at a hog-killing. The child was told to go over there and tell Aunt Judy to come. But nature, being indifferent to human arrangements, was impatient. My mother had to make it alone. She was too weak after I rushed out to do anything for herself, so she just was lying there, sick in the body, and worried in mind, wondering what would become of her, as well as me. She was so weak, she couldn't even reach down to where I was. She had one consolation. She knew I wasn't dead, because I was crying strong.

Help came from where she never would have thought to look for it. 5
A white man of many acres and things, who knew the family well, had butchered the day before. Knowing that Papa was not at home, and that consequently there would be no fresh meat in our house, he decided to drive the five miles and bring a half of a shoat, sweet potatoes, and other garden stuff along. He was there a few minutes after I was born. Seeing the front door standing open, he came on in, and hollered, "Hello, there! Call your dogs!" That is the regular way to call in the country because nearly everybody who has anything to watch has biting dogs.

Nobody answered, but he claimed later that he heard me spreading 6
my lungs all over Orange County, so he shoved the door open and bolted on into the house.

He followed the noise and then he saw how things were, and, being 7
the kind of a man he was, he took out his Barlow Knife and cut the navel cord, then he did the best he could about other things. When the mid-wife, locally known as a granny, arrived about an hour later, there was a fire in the stove and plenty of hot water on. I had been sponged off in some sort of a way, and Mama was holding me in her arms.

As soon as the old woman got there, the white man unloaded what 8
he had brought, and drove off cussing about some blankety-blank people never being where you could put your hands on them when they were needed.

He got no thanks from Aunt Judy. She grumbled for years about it. 9
She complained that the cord had not been cut just right, and the belly-band had not been put on tight enough. She was mighty scared I was going to have a weak back, and that I would have trouble holding my water until I reached puberty. I did.

The next day or so a Mrs. Neale, a friend of Mama's, came in and 10
reminded her that she had promised to let her name the baby in case it was a girl. She had picked up a name somewhere which she thought was very pretty. Perhaps she had read it somewhere, or somebody back in those woods was smoking Turkish cigarettes. So I became Zora Neale Hurston.

There is nothing to make you like other human beings so much as 11
doing things for them. Therefore, the man who grannied me was back next day to see how I was coming along. Maybe it was pride in his own handiwork, and his resourcefulness in a pinch, that made him want to see it through. He remarked that I was a God-damned fine baby, fat and plenty of lung-power. As time went on, he came infrequently, but some-

how kept a pinch of interest in my welfare. It seemed that I was spying noble, growing like a gourd vine, and yelling bass like a gator. He was the kind of a man that had no use for puny things, so I was all to the good with him. He thought my mother was justified in keeping me.

But nine months rolled around, and I just would not get on with the walking business. I was strong, crawling well, but showed no inclination to use my feet. I might remark in passing, that I still don't like to walk. Then I was over a year old, but still I would not walk. They made allowances for my weight, but yet, that was no real reason for my not trying.

They tell me that an old sow-hog taught me how to walk. That is, she didn't instruct me in detail, but she convinced me that I really ought to try.

It was like this. My mother was going to have collard greens for dinner, so she took the dishpan and went down to the spring to wash the greens. She left me sitting on the floor, and gave me a hunk of cornbread to keep me quiet. Everything was going along all right, until the sow with her litter of pigs in convoy came abreast of the door. She must have smelled the cornbread I was messing with and scattering crumbs about the floor. So, she came right on in, and began to nuzzle around.

My mother heard my screams and came running. Her heart must have stood still when she saw the sow in there, because hogs have been known to eat human flesh.

But I was not taking this thing sitting down. I had been placed by a chair, and when my mother got inside the door, I had pulled myself up by that chair and was getting around it right smart.

As for the sow, poor misunderstood lady, she had no interest in me except my bread. I lost that in scrambling to my feet and she was eating it. She had much less intention of eating Mama's baby, than Mama had of eating hers.

With no more suggestions from the sow or anybody else, it seems that I just took to walking and kept the thing a-going. The strangest thing about it was that once I found the use of my feet, they took to wandering. I always wanted to go. I would wander off in the woods all alone, following some inside urge to go places. This alarmed my mother a great deal. She used to say that she believed a woman who was an enemy of hers had sprinkled "travel dust" around the doorstep the day I was born. That was the only explanation she could find. I don't know why it never occurred to her to connect my tendency with my father, who didn't have a thing on his mind but this town and the next one. That should have given her a sort of hint. Some children are just bound to take after their fathers in spite of women's prayers.

COMPREHENSION

1. To truly appreciate Hurston's story, one must have a keen sense of irony. How does irony act as a thread linking many of the events in this narrative together?

2. The author is describing life in a modest African-American community at the turn of the twentieth century; yet there is no hint of discrimination, oppression, or anger here. What is the tone of the author toward her environment and the individuals who populate it? Where do you find evidence of this tone?

3. The culture of a people can often be understood by the type of relationships, customs, and communication among them. Based upon the events in the story, how would you describe the cultural environment into which Hurston was born?

RHETORIC

1. How does the short, terse opening paragraph set the tone for the entire essay?

2. Regionalisms and ethnicity play a part in the author's choice of words and syntax—for example, "crying strong," "word-changing kind," "a white man of many acres and things," and "spying noble." Identify the meaning of these and other expressions in the essay that do not conform to standard American speech.

3. Note how Hurston makes use of transitional expressions when shifting from paragraph to paragraph—for example, "The saying goes like this" that begins paragraph 2. How does her use of such expressions establish an originality of voice that one is not liable to find in books on grammar instruction?

4. How is the final paragraph perhaps the most ironic of the essay? How does Hurston create a paradox between the way she describes her adult temperament and her beginnings?

5. Read the essay aloud. Does it help you to "hear" the way the writing resembles natural speech? Explain.

6. How we judge ourselves often results from the way others respond to us. When referring to her father, Hurston says, in paragraph 2, "He was nice about it in a way. He didn't tie me in a sack and drop me in the lake, as he probably felt like doing." Find other descriptions of the community's attitude toward the author's birth, and explain how these attitudes might shape the attitude of the writer.

7. Despite the conversational tone of the essay, there are several places where the author describes principles of human behavior. Identify these passages, and explain how they are incorporated into the narrative flow.

WRITING

1. Tape-record a senior member of your family or an elder from your community relating a story about their past. Transcribe the "story" and then convert it into a narrative, retaining the description, tone, dialogue, and any vernacular or "regionalisms" your subject uses.

2. Zora Neale Hurston had a varied, interesting, and tragic life. Using bibliographic research, write a paper demonstrating how Hurston's formative years contributed to aspects of her later life.

3. Write a first-person narrative essay about an incident in your life that was full of mishaps. Be sure that the tone of your writing conveys how you felt and how others involved in the incident felt.

CARSON McCULLERS Carson McCullers (1917–1967) is the author of a small but impressive body of fiction, including *The Heart Is a Lonely Hunter* (1940), *Reflections in a Golden Eye* (1941), *A Member of the Wedding* (1946), and *The Ballad of the Sad Cafe* (1951). Although she was preoccupied in her fiction with the theme of loneliness, this selection from her autobiography reveals instead the love, joy, and sense of community permeating one episode from her Georgia childhood.

CARSON McCULLERS

Home for Christmas

Sometimes in August, weary of the vacant, broiling afternoon, my ₁ younger brother and sister and I would gather in the dense shade under the oak tree in the back yard and talk of Christmas and sing carols. Once after such a conclave, when the tunes of the carols still lingered in the heat-shimmered air, I remember climbing up into the tree-house and sitting there alone for a long time.

Brother called up: "What are you doing?" ₂

"Thinking," I answered. ₃

"What are you thinking about?" ₄

"I don't know." ₅

"Well, how can you be thinking when you don't know what you are ₆ thinking about?"

I did not want to talk with my brother. I was experiencing the first ₇ wonder about the mystery of Time. Here I was, on this August afternoon, in the tree-house, in the burnt, jaded yard, sick and tired of all our summer ways. (I had read *Little Women* for the second time, *Hans Brinker and the Silver Skates, Little Men,* and *Twenty Thousand Leagues under the Sea.* I had read movie magazines and even tried to read love stories in the *Woman's Home Companion*—I was so sick of everything.) How could it be that I was I and now was now when in four months it would be Christmas, wintertime, cold weather, twilight and the glory of the Christmas tree? I puzzled about the *now* and *later* and rubbed the inside of my elbow until there was a little roll of dirt between my forefinger and thumb. Would the *now* I of the tree-house and the August afternoon be the same *I* of winter, firelight and the Christmas tree? I wondered.

My brother repeated: "You say you are thinking but you don't know ₈ what you are thinking about. What are you really doing up there? Have you got some secret candy?"

37

September came, and my mother opened the cedar chest and we ₉
tried on winter coats and last year's sweaters to see if they would do
again. She took the three of us downtown and bought us new shoes and
school clothes.

Christmas was nearer on the September Sunday that Daddy ₁₀
rounded us up in the car and drove us out on dusty country roads to
pick elderberry blooms. Daddy made wine from elderberry blossoms—
it was a yellow-white wine, the color of weak winter sun. The wine was
dry to the wry side—indeed, some years it turned to vinegar. The wine
was served at Christmastime with slices of fruitcake when company
came. On November Sundays we went to the woods with a big basket
of fried chicken dinner, thermos jug and coffee-pot. We hunted par-
tridge berries in the pine woods near our town. These scarlet berries
grew hidden underneath the glossy brown pine needles that lay in a
slick carpet beneath the tall wind-singing trees. The bright berries were
a Christmas decoration, lasting in water through the whole season.

In December the windows downtown were filled with toys, and my ₁₁
brother and sister and I were given two dollars apiece to buy our
Christmas presents. We patronized the ten-cent stores, choosing
between jackstones, pencil boxes, water colors and satin handkerchief
holders. We would each buy a nickel's worth of lump milk chocolate at
the candy counter to mouth as we trudged from counter to counter,
choice to choice. It was exacting and final—taking several afternoons—
for the dime stores would not take back or exchange.

Mother made fruitcakes, and for weeks ahead the family picked out ₁₂
the nut meats of pecans and walnuts, careful of the bitter layer of the
pecans that lined your mouth with nasty fur. At the last I was allowed
to blanch the almonds, pinching the scalded nuts so that they sometimes hit the ceiling or bounced across the room. Mother cut slices of
citron and crystallized pineapple, figs and dates, and candied cherries
were added whole. We cut rounds of brown paper to line the pans.
Usually the cakes were mixed and put into the oven when we were in
school. Late in the afternoon the cakes would be finished, wrapped in
white napkins on the breakfast-room table. Later they would be soaked
in brandy. These fruitcakes were famous in our town, and Mother gave
them often as Christmas gifts. When company came thin slices of fruitcake, wine and coffee were always served. When you held a slice of
fruitcake to the window or the firelight the slice was translucent, pale
citron green and yellow and red, with the glow and richness of our
church windows.

Daddy was a jeweler, and his store was kept open until midnight all ₁₃
Christmas week. I, as the eldest child, was allowed to stay up late with
Mother until Daddy came home. Mother was always nervous without
a "man in the house." (On those rare occasions when Daddy had to
stay overnight on business in Atlanta, the children were armed with a
hammer, saw and a monkey wrench. When pressed about her anxieties
Mother claimed she was afraid of "escaped convicts or crazy people." I
never saw an escaped convict, but once a "crazy" person did come to

see us. She was an old, old lady dressed in elegant black taffeta, my mother's second cousin once removed, and came on a tranquil Sunday morning and announced that she had always liked our house and she intended to stay with us until she died. Her sons and daughters and grandchildren gathered around to plead with her as she sat rocking in our front porch rocking chair and she left not unwillingly when they promised a car ride and ice cream.) Nothing ever happened on those evenings in Christmas week, but I felt grown, aged suddenly by trust and dignity. Mother confided in secrecy what the younger children were getting from Santa Claus. I knew where the Santa Claus things were hidden, and was appointed to see that my brother and sister did not go into the back-room closet or the wardrobe in our parents' room.

Christmas Eve was the longest day, but it was lined with the glory ₁₄ of tomorrow. The sitting-room smelled of floor wax and the clean, cold odor of the spruce tree. The Christmas tree stood in a corner of the front room, tall as the ceiling, majestic, undecorated. It was our family custom that the tree was not decorated until after we children were in bed on Christmas Eve night. We went to bed very early, as soon as it was winter dark. I lay in bed beside my sister and tried to keep her awake.

"You want to guess again about your Santa Claus?" ₁₅

"We've already done that so much," she said. ₁₆

My sister slept. And there again was another puzzle. How could it ₁₇ be that when she opened her eyes it would be Christmas while I lay awake in the dark for hours and hours? The time was the same for both of us, and yet not at all the same. What was it? How? I thought of Bethlehem and cherry candy, Jesus and skyrockets. It was dark when I awoke. We were allowed to get up on Christmas at five o'clock. Later I found out that Daddy juggled the clock Christmas Eve so that five o'clock was actually six. Anyway it was always still dark when we rushed in to dress by the kitchen stove. The rule was that we dress and eat breakfast before we could go in to the Christmas tree. On Christmas morning we always had fish roe, bacon and grits for breakfast. I grudged every mouthful—for who wanted to fill up on breakfast when there in the sitting-room was candy, at least three whole boxes? After breakfast we lined up, and carols were started. Our voices rose naked and mysterious as we filed through the door to the sitting-room. The carol, unfinished, ended in raw yells of joy.

The Christmas tree glittered in the glorious, candlelit room. There ₁₈ were bicycles and bundles wrapped in tissue paper. Our stockings hanging from the mantlepiece bulged with oranges, nuts and smaller presents. The next hours were paradise. The blue dawn at the window brightened, and the candles were blown out. By nine o'clock we had ridden the wheel presents and dressed in the clothes gifts. We visited the neighborhood children and were visited in turn. Our cousins came and grown relatives from distant neighborhoods. All through the morning we ate chocolates. At two or three o'clock the Christmas dinner was served. The dining-room table had been let out with extra leaves and the very best linen was laid—satin damask with a rose design. Daddy asked the blessing, then stood up to carve the turkey. Dressing, rice and giblet gravy were served. There were cut-glass dishes of sparkling jellies and stateliness of festal wine. For dessert there was always sillabub or charlotte and fruitcake. The afternoon was almost over when dinner was done.

At twilight I sat on the front steps, jaded by too much pleasure, sick at the stomach and worn out. The boy next door skated down the street in his new Indian suit. A girl spun around on a crackling son-of-a-gun. My brother waved sparklers. Christmas was over. I thought of the monotony of Time ahead, unsolaced by the distant glow of paler festivals, the year that stretched before another Christmas—eternity. 19

COMPREHENSION

1. What, according to the author, is the essence of Christmas?
2. Trace chronologically the preparations for Christmas by the McCullers family.
3. What is the author's attitude toward time? Paraphrase the last sentence of the essay.

RHETORIC

1. This essay is rich in sensory language. Cite five words or phrases that are especially vivid, and analyze their effect. To which senses does the writing appeal?
2. Define these words: *conclave* (paragraph 1); *patronized* (paragraph 11); *blanch* (paragraph 12); *tranquil* (paragraph 13); and *festal* (paragraph 18). Use them in sentences of your own.
3. McCullers writes in paragraph 7 that she "was experiencing the first wonder about the mystery of Time." How does this theme serve as the organizing principle for the essay? How does the author convey the mystery of time? What is her dual attitude toward time, and how does this serve as a structuring device in the essay? How does the author's treatment of time resemble that of Welty in "One Writer's Beginnings"?
4. What principles of emphasis do you find in McCullers's treatment of chronology?
5. How and why does the author connect the many and varied details in the essay? How effective are her details in conveying a sense of her childhood and evolving personality? How is this reflected in point of view?
6. How does the conclusion relate to the rest of the essay? Do you find the conclusion effective? Why, or why not?

WRITING

1. Do you still look forward to special holidays or celebrations, or does the type of anticipation of which McCullers speaks exist only for children? Why

do children have different perceptions of time than adults? Evaluate this matter in an essay.

2. Write a narrative account of a vivid holiday event in your childhood.

3. Analyze McCullers's use of sensory language to create a dominant impression in "Home for Christmas."

E. B. WHITE   Elwyn Brooks White (1899–1985), perhaps the finest contemporary American essayist, is at his most distinctive in his treatments of people and nature. A recipient of the National Medal for literature, and associated for years with *The New Yorker,* White is the author of *One Man's Meat* (1942), *Here Is New York* (1949), and *The Second Tree from the Corner* (1954), among numerous other works. He is also one of the most talented writers of literature for children, the author of *Stuart Little* (1945), *Charlotte's Web* (1952), and *The Trumpet of the Swan* (1970). In this essay, White combines narration and description to make a poignant and vivid statement about past and present, youth and age, life and death.

E. B. WHITE

Once More to the Lake

One summer, along about 1904, my father rented a camp on a lake in Maine and took us all there for the month of August. We all got ringworm from some kittens and had to rub Pond's Extract on our arms and legs night and morning, and my father rolled over in a canoe with all his clothes on; but outside of that the vacation was a success and from then on none of us ever thought there was any place in the world like that lake in Maine. We returned summer after summer—always on August 1st for one month. I have since become a salt-water man, but sometimes in summer there are days when the restlessness of the tides and the fearful cold of the sea water and the incessant wind which blows across the afternoon and into the evening make me wish for the placidity of a lake in the woods. A few weeks ago this feeling got so strong I bought myself a couple of bass hooks and a spinner and returned to the lake where we used to go, for a week's fishing and to revisit old haunts.

I took along my son, who had never had any fresh water up his nose and who had seen lily pads only from train windows. On the journey over to the lake I began to wonder what it would be like. I wondered how time would have marred this unique, this holy spot—the coves and streams, the hills that the sun set behind, the camps and the paths behind the camps. I was sure the tarred road would have found it out and I wondered in what other ways it would be desolated. It is strange how much you can remember about places like that once you allow your mind to return into the grooves which lead back. You remember one thing, and that suddenly reminds you of another thing. I guess I remembered clearest of all the early mornings, when the lake was cool and motionless, remembered how the bedroom smelled of the lumber it was made of and of the wet woods whose scent entered through the screen. The partitions in the camp were thin and did not extend clear to the top of the rooms, and as I was always the first up I would dress softly so as not to wake the others, and sneak out into the sweet out-doors and start out in the canoe, keeping close along the shore in the long shadows of the pines. I remembered being very careful never to rub my paddle against the gunwale for fear of disturbing the stillness of the cathedral.

The lake had never been what you would call a wild lake. There 3 were cottages sprinkled around the shores, and it was in farming coun-try although the shores of the lake were quite heavily wooded. Some of the cottages were owned by nearby farmers, and you would live at the shore and eat your meals at the farmhouse. That's what our family did. But although it wasn't wild, it was a fairly large and undisturbed lake and there were places in it which, to a child at least, seemed infinitely remote and primeval.

I was right about the tar: it led to within half a mile of the shore. But 4 when I got back there, with my boy, and we settled into a camp near a farmhouse and into the kind of summertime I had known, I could tell that it was going to be pretty much the same as it had been before—I knew it, lying in bed the first morning, smelling the bedroom, and hear-ing the boy sneak quietly out and go off along the shore in a boat. I began to sustain the illusion that he was I, and therefore, by simple transposition, that I was my father. This sensation persisted, kept crop-ping up all the time we were there. It was not an entirely new feeling, but in this setting it grew much stronger. I seemed to be living a dual existence. I would be in the middle of some simple act, I would be pick-ing up a bait box or laying down a table fork, or I would be saying something, and suddenly it would be not I but my father who was say-ing the words or making the gesture. It gave me a creepy sensation.

We went fishing the first morning. I felt the same damp moss cov- 5 ering the worms in the bait can, and saw the dragonfly alight on the tip of my rod as it hovered a few inches from the surface of the water. It was the arrival of this fly that convinced me beyond any doubt that everything was as it always had been, that the years were a mirage and there had been no years. The small waves were the same, chucking the rowboat under the chin as we fished at anchor, and the boat was the same boat, the same color green and the ribs broken in the same place, and under the floor-boards the same fresh-water leavings and débris—the dead hellgrammite, the wisps of moss, the rusty discarded fishhook, the dried blood from yesterday's catch. We stared silently at the tips of our rods, at the dragonflies that came and went. I lowered the tip of mine into the water, tentatively, pensively dislodging the fly, which darted two feet away, poised, darted two feet back, and came to rest again a little farther up the rod. There had been no years between the ducking of this dragonfly and the other one—the one that was part of memory. I looked at the boy, who was silently watching his fly, and it was my hands that held his rod, my eyes watching. I felt dizzy and didn't know which rod I was at the end of.

We caught two bass, hauling them in briskly as though they were mackerel, pulling them over the side of the boat in a businesslike manner without any landing net, and stunning them with a blow on the back of the head. When we got back for a swim before lunch, the lake was exactly where we had left it, the same number of inches from the dock, and there was only the merest suggestion of a breeze. This seemed an utterly enchanted sea, this lake you could leave to its own devices for a few hours and come back to, and find that it had not stirred, this constant and trustworthy body of water. In the shallows, the dark, water-soaked sticks and twigs, smooth and old, were undulating in clusters on the bottom against the clean ribbed sand, and the track of the mussel was plain. A school of minnows swam by, each minnow with its small individual shadow, doubling the attendance, so clear and sharp in the sunlight. Some of the other campers were in swimming, along the shore, one of them with a cake of soap, and the water felt thin and clear and unsubstantial. Over the years there had been this person with the cake of soap, this cultist, and here he was. There had been no years.

Up to the farmhouse to dinner through the teeming, dusty field, the road under our sneakers was only a two-track road. The middle track was missing, the one with the marks of the hooves and the splotches of dried, flaky manure. There had always been three tracks to choose from in choosing which track to walk in; now the choice was narrowed down to two. For a moment I missed terribly the middle alternative. But the way led past the tennis court, and something about the way it lay there in the sun reassured me; the tape had loosened along the backline, the alleys were green with plaintains and other weeds, and the net (installed in June and removed in September) sagged in the dry noon, and the whole place steamed with midday heat and hunger and emptiness. There was a choice of pie for dessert, and one was blueberry and one was apple, and the waitresses were the same country girls, there having been no passage of time, only the illusion of it as in a dropped curtain—the waitresses were still fifteen; their hair had been washed, that was the only difference—they had been to the movies and seen the pretty girls with the clean hair.

Summertime, oh summertime, pattern of life indelible, the fadeproof lake, the woods unshatterable, the pasture with the sweetfern and the juniper forever and ever, summer without end; this was the background, and the life along the shore was the design, the cottagers with their innocent and tranquil design, their tiny docks with the flagpole and the American flag floating against the white clouds in the blue sky, the little paths over the roots of the trees leading from camp to camp and the paths leading back to the outhouses and the can of lime for sprinkling, and at the souvenir counters at the store the miniature birch-bark canoes and the post cards that showed things looking a little better than they looked. This was the American family at play, escaping the city heat, wondering whether the newcomers in the camp at the head of the cove were "common" or "nice," wondering whether it was true that the people who drove up for Sunday dinner at the farmhouse were turned away because there wasn't enough chicken.

It seemed to me, as I kept remembering all this, that those times and those summers had been infinitely precious and worth saving. There had been jollity and peace and goodness. The arriving (at the beginning of August) had been so big a business in itself, at the railway station the farm wagon drawn up, the first smell of the pine-laden air, the first glimpse of the smiling farmer, and the great importance of the trunks and your father's enormous authority in such matters, and the feel of the wagon under you for the long ten-mile haul, and at the top of the last long hill catching the first view of the lake after eleven months of not seeing this cherished body of water. The shouts and cries of the other campers when they saw you, and the trunks to be unpacked, to give up their rich burden. (Arriving was less exciting nowadays, when you sneaked up in your car and parked it under a tree near the camp and took out the bags and in five minutes it was all over, no fuss, no loud wonderful fuss about trunks.)

Peace and goodness and jollity. The only thing that was wrong now, really, was the sound of the place, an unfamiliar nervous sound of the outboard motors. This was the note that jarred, the one thing that would sometimes break the illusion and set the years moving. In those other summertimes all motors were inboard; and when they were at a little distance, the noise they made was a sedative, an ingredient of summer sleep. They were one-cylinder and two-cylinder engines, and some were make-and-break and some were jump-spark, but they all made a sleepy sound across the lake. The one-lungers throbbed and fluttered, and the twin-cylinder ones purred and purred, and that was a quiet sound too. But now the campers all had outboards. In the day-time, in the hot mornings, these motors made a petulant, irritable sound; at night, in the still evening when the afterglow lit the water, they whined about one's ears like mosquitoes. My boy loved our rented out-board, and his great desire was to achieve singlehanded mastery over it, and authority, and he soon learned the trick of choking it a little (but not too much), and the adjustment of the needle valve. Watching him I would remember the things you could do with the old one-cylinder engine with the heavy flywheel, how you could have it eating out of your hand if you got really close to it spiritually. Motor boats in those days didn't have clutches, and you would make a landing by shutting off the motor at the proper time and coasting in with a dead rudder. But there was a way of reversing them, if you learned the trick, by cutting the switch and putting it on again exactly on the final dying revolution of the flywheel, so that it would kick back against compression

44

and begin reversing. Approaching a dock in a strong following breeze, it was difficult to slow up sufficiently by the ordinary coasting method, and if a boy felt he had complete mastery over his motor, he was tempted to keep it running beyond its time and then reverse it a few feet from the dock. It took a cool nerve, because if you threw the switch a twentieth of a second too soon you would catch the flywheel when it still had speed enough to go up past center, and the boat would leap ahead, charging bull-fashion at the dock.

We had a good week at the camp. The bass were biting well and the 11 sun shone endlessly, day after day. We would be tired at night and lie down in the accumulated heat of the little bedrooms after the long hot day and the breeze would stir almost imperceptibly outside and the smell of the swamp drift in through the rusty screens. Sleep would come easily and in the morning the red squirrel would be on the roof, tapping out his gay routine. I kept remembering everything, lying in bed in the mornings—the small steamboat that had a long rounded stern like the lip of a Ubangi, and how quietly she ran on the moonlight sails, when the older boys played their mandolins and the girls sang and we ate doughnuts dipped in sugar, and how sweet the music was on the water in the shining night, and what it had felt like to think about girls then. After breakfast we would go up to the store and the things were in the same place—the minnows in a bottle, the plugs and spinners disarranged and pawed over by the youngsters from the boys' camp, the fig newtons and the Beeman's gum. Outside, the road was tarred and cars stood in front of the store. Inside, all was just as it had always been, except there was more Coca-Cola and not so much Moxie and root beer and birch beer and sarsaparilla. We would walk out with a bottle of pop apiece and sometimes the pop would backfire up our noses and hurt. We explored the streams, quietly, where the turtles slid off the sunny logs and dug their way into the soft bottom; and we lay on the town wharf and fed worms to the tame bass. Everywhere we went I had trouble making out which was I, the one walking at my side, the one walking in my pants.

One afternoon while we were there at that lake a thunderstorm came 12 up. It was like the revival of an old melodrama that I had seen long ago with childish awe. The second-act climax of the drama of the electrical disturbance over a lake in America had not changed in any important respect. This was the big scene, still the big scene. The whole thing was so familiar, the first feeling of oppression and heat and a general air around camp of not wanting to go very far away. In midafternoon (it was all the same) a curious darkening of the sky, and a lull in everything that had made life tick; and then the way the boats suddenly swung the other way at their moorings with the coming of a breeze out of the new quarter, and the premonitory rumble. Then the kettle drum, then the snare, then the bass drum and cymbals, then crackling light against the dark, and the gods grinning and licking their chops in the hills. Afterward the calm, the rain steadily rustling in the calm lake, the return of light and hope and spirits, and the campers running out in joy and relief to go swimming in the rain, their bright cries perpetuating the deathless joke about how they were getting simply drenched, and the children screaming with delight at the new sensation of bathing in the rain, and the joke about getting drenched linking the generations in a strong indestructible chain. And the comedian who waded in carrying an umbrella.

When the others went swimming my son said he was going in too. 13 He pulled his dripping trunks from the line where they had hung all through the shower, and wrung them out. Languidly, and with no thought of going in, I watched him, his hard little body, skinny and bare, saw him wince slightly as he pulled up around his vitals the small, soggy, icy garment. As he buckled the swollen belt suddenly my groin felt the chill of death.

COMPREHENSION

1. At what point in the essay do you begin to sense White's main purpose? What is his purpose? What type of reader might his purpose appeal to?

2. What motivates White to return to the lake in Maine? Explain the "simple transposition" that he mentions in paragraph 4. List the illustrations that he gives of this phenomenon. What change does he detect in the lake?

3. Explain the significance of White's last sentence. Where are there foreshadowings of this statement?

RHETORIC

1. Describe the author's use of figurative language in paragraphs 2, 10, and 12.

2. Identify those words and phrases that White invokes to establish the sense of mystery about the lake. Why are these words and their connotations important to the nature of the illusion that he describes?

3. Explain the organization of the essay in terms of the following paragraph units: 1 to 4; 5 to 7; 8 to 10; and 11 to 13. Explain the function of paragraphs 8 and 12.

4. There are many vivid and unusual descriptive details in this essay—for example, the dragonfly in paragraph 5 and the two-track road in paragraph 7. How does White create symbolic overtones for these descriptive details and others? Why is the lake itself a complex symbol? Explain with reference to paragraph 6.

5. Describe the persona that White creates for himself in the essay. How does this persona function?

6. What is the relation between the introductory and concluding paragraphs, specifically in terms of irony of statement?

WRITING

1. Explore in an essay the theme of nostalgia in "Once More to the Lake." What are the beauties and the dangers of nostalgia? Can the past ever be recaptured or relived? Justify your answer.

2. Write a descriptive account of a return to a favorite location and of your reaction to the experience. Explore the interrelationship of past and present.

3. Explain, in a short essay, the appeal of this classic essay by White.

4. One of White's favorite authors was Thoreau. Read Thoreau's "Economy" (pp. 572–575) and, in a brief essay, identify the influence that you see at work in "Once More to the Lake."

CLASSIC AND CONTEMPORARY

MARK TWAIN Mark Twain (1835–1910) was the pseudonym of Samuel Langhorne Clemens. In *The Adventures of Tom Sawyer* (1876), *Life on the Mississippi* (1883), and *The Adventures of Huckleberry Finn* (1885), Twain celebrated the challenge of the frontier experience and the promise of a new world. Adventurous, democratic, individualistic, hardheaded, and sentimental, he projected the image of the essential American, a role that did not always correspond to the bitter and tragic aspects of his later life. In this selection from his autobiography, Twain successfully juggles tragedy and comedy in a bittersweet exploration of guilt and faith.

MARK TWAIN

A Boy's Life

In 1849, when I was fourteen years old, we were still living in Hanni- 1
bal, on the banks of the Mississippi, in the new "frame" house built by my father five years before. That is, some of us lived in the new part, the rest in the old part back of it and attached to it. In the autumn my sister gave a party and invited all the marriageable young people of the village. I was too young for this society and was too bashful to mingle with young ladies, anyway, therefore I was not invited—at least not for the whole evening. Ten minutes of it was to be my whole share. I was to do the part of a bear in a small fairy play. I was to be disguised all over in a close-fitting brown hairy stuff proper for a bear. About half past ten I was told to go to my room and put on this disguise and be ready in half an hour. I started but changed my mind, for I wanted to practice a little and that room was very small. I crossed over to the large unoccupied house on the corner of Main Street, unaware that a dozen of the young people were also going there to dress for their parts. I took the little black boy, Sandy, with me and we selected a roomy and empty chamber on the second floor. We entered it talking and this gave a couple of half-dressed young ladies an opportunity to take refuge behind a screen undiscovered. Their gowns and things were hanging on hooks

behind the door but I did not see them; it was Sandy that shut the door but all his heart was in the theatricals and he was as unlikely to notice them as I was myself.

That was a rickety screen with many holes in it but as I did not know there were girls behind it I was not disturbed by that detail. If I had known, I could not have undressed in the flood of cruel moonlight that was pouring in at the curtainless windows; I should have died of shame. Untroubled by apprehensions, I stripped to the skin and began my practice. I was full of ambition, I was determined to make a hit, I was burning to establish a reputation as a bear and get further engagements; so I threw myself into my work with an abandon that promised great things. I capered back and forth from one end of the room to the other on all fours, Sandy applauding with enthusiasm; I walked upright and growled and snapped and snarled, I stood on my head, I flung handsprings, I danced a lubberly dance with my paws bent and my imaginary snout sniffing from side to side, I did everything a bear could do and many things which no bear could ever do and no bear with any dignity would want to do, anyway; and of course I never suspected that I was making a spectacle of myself to anyone but Sandy. At last, standing on my head, I paused in that attitude to take a minute's rest. There was a moment's silence, then Sandy spoke up with excited interest and said:

"Mars Sam, has you ever seed a dried herring?"

"No. What is that?"

"It's a fish."

"Well, what of it? Anything peculiar about it?"

"Yes, suh, you bet you dey is. *Dey* eats 'em innards and all!"

There was a smothered burst of feminine snickers from behind the screen! All the strength went out of me and I toppled forward like an undermined tower and brought the screen down with my weight, burying the young ladies under it. In their fright they discharged a couple of piercing screams—and possibly others—but I did not wait to count. I snatched my clothes and fled to the dark hall below, Sandy following. I was dressed in half a minute and out the back way. I swore Sandy to eternal silence, then we went away and hid until the party was over. The ambition was all out of me. I could not have faced that giddy company after my adventure, for there would be two performers there who knew my secret and would be privately laughing at me all the time. I was searched for but not found, and the bear had to be played by a young gentleman in his civilized clothes. The house was still and everybody asleep when I finally ventured home. I was very heavy-hearted and full of a bitter sense of disgrace. Pinned to my pillow I found a slip of paper which bore a line which did not lighten my heart but only made my face burn. It was written in a laboriously disguised hand and these were its mocking terms:

> You probably couldn't have played bear but you played bare very well—oh, very *very* well!

We think boys are rude, unsensitive animals but it is not so in all cases. Each boy has one or two sensitive spots and if you can find out

48

where they are located you have only to touch them and you can scorch him as with fire. I suffered miserably over that episode. I expected that the facts would be all over the village in the morning but it was not so. The secret remained confined to the two girls and Sandy and me. That was some appeasement of my pain but it was far from sufficient—the main trouble remained: I was under four mocking eyes and it might as well have been a thousand, for I suspected all girls' eyes of being the ones I so dreaded. During several weeks I could not look any young lady in the face; I dropped my eyes in confusion when any one of them smiled upon me and gave me greeting; I said to myself, "That is one of them," and got quickly away. Of course I was meeting the right girls everywhere but if they ever let slip any betraying sign I was not bright enough to catch it. When I left Hannibal four years later the secret was still a secret; I had never guessed those girls out and was no longer hoping or expecting to do it.

One of the dearest and prettiest girls in the village at the time of my mishap was one whom I will call Mary Wilson, because that was not her name. She was twenty years old; she was dainty and sweet, peach-blooming and exquisite, gracious and lovely in character. I stood in awe of her, for she seemed to me to be made out of angel clay and rightfully unapproachable by just any unholy ordinary kind of boy like me. I probably never suspected *her*. But—

The scene changes to Calcutta—forty-seven years later. It was in 1896. I arrived there on a lecturing trip. As I entered the hotel a vision passed out of it, clothed in the glory of the Indian sunshine—the Mary Wilson of my long-vanished boyhood! It was a startling thing. Before I could recover from the pleasant shock and speak to her she was gone. I thought maybe I had seen an apparition but it was not so, she was flesh. She was the granddaughter of the other Mary. The other Mary, now a widow, was upstairs and presently sent for me. She was old and grayhaired but she looked young and was very handsome. We sat down and talked. We steeped our thirsty souls in the reviving wine of the past, the pathetic past, the beautiful past, the dear and lamented past; we uttered the names that had been silent upon our lips for fifty years and it was as if they were made of music; with reverent hands we unburied our dead, the mates of our youth, and caressed them with our speech; we searched the dusty chambers of our memories and dragged forth incident after incident, episode after episode, folly after folly, and laughed such good laughs over them, with the tears running down; and finally Mary said, suddenly, and without any leading up:

"Tell me! What is the special peculiarity of dried herrings?"

It seemed a strange question at such a hallowed time as this. And so inconsequential, too. I was a little shocked. And yet I was aware of a stir of some kind away back in the deeps of my memory somewhere. It set me to musing—thinking—searching. Dried herrings? Dried herrings? The peculiarity of dri . . . I glanced up. Her face was grave, but there was a dim and shadowy twinkle in her eye which— All of a sudden I knew and far away down in the hoary past I heard a remembered voice murmur, "Dey eats 'em innards and all!"

*Chapter One
Childhood and
Family*

"At—last! I've found one of you, anyway! Who was the other girl?" 15
But she drew the line there. She wouldn't tell me. 16

But a boy's life is not all comedy; much of the tragic enters into it. 17
The drunken tramp who was burned up in the village jail lay upon my
conscience a hundred nights afterward and filled them with hideous
dreams—dreams in which I saw his appealing face as I had seen it in
the pathetic reality, pressed against the window bars, with the red hell
glowing behind him—a face which seemed to say to me, "If you had
not given me the matches this would not have happened; you are
responsible for my death." I was *not* responsible for it, for I had meant
him no harm but only good, when I let him have the matches; but no
matter, mine was a trained Presbyterian conscience and knew but the
one duty—to hunt and harry its slave upon all pretexts and on all occasions, particularly when there was no sense nor reason in it. The
tramp—who was to blame—suffered ten minutes; I, who was not to
blame, suffered three months.

The shooting down of poor old Smarr in the main street at noon- 18
day supplied me with some more dreams; and in them I always saw
again the grotesque closing picture—the great family Bible spread open
on the profane old man's breast by some thoughtful idiot and rising
and sinking to the labored breathings and adding the torture of its
leaden weight to the dying struggles. We are curiously made. In all the
throng of gaping and sympathetic onlookers there was not one with
common sense enough to perceive that an anvil would have been in
better taste there than the Bible, less open to sarcastic criticism and
swifter in its atrocious work. In my nightmares I gasped and struggled
for breath under the crush of that vast book for many a night.

All within the space of a couple of years we had two or three other 19
tragedies and I had the ill luck to be too near by on each occasion.
There was the slave man who was struck down with a chunk of slag for
some small offense; I saw him die. And the young Californian emigrant
who was stabbed with a bowie knife by a drunken comrade; I saw the
red life gush from his breast. And the case of the rowdy young brothers and their harmless old uncle; one of them held the old man down
with his knees on his breast while the other one tried repeatedly to kill
him with an Allen revolver which wouldn't go off. I happened along
just then, of course.

Then there was the case of the young Californian emigrant who got 20
drunk and proposed to raid the "Welshman's house" all alone one dark
and threatening night. This house stood halfway up Holliday's Hill and
its sole occupants were a poor but quite respectable widow and her
blameless daughter. The invading ruffian woke the whole village with
his ribald yells and coarse challenges and obscenities. I went up there
with a comrade—John Briggs, I think—to look and listen. The figure of
the man was dimly visible; the women were on their porch, not visible
in the deep shadow of its roof, but we heard the elder woman's voice.
She had loaded an old musket with slugs and she warned the man that

if he stayed where he was while she counted ten it would cost him his life. She began to count, slowly; he began to laugh. He stopped laughing at "six"; then through the deep stillness, in a steady voice, followed the rest of the tale: "Seven . . . eight . . . nine"—a long pause, we holding our breaths—"ten!" A red spout of flame gushed out into the night and the man dropped with his breast riddled to rags. Then the rain and the thunder burst loose and the waiting town swarmed up the hill in the glare of the lightning like an invasion of ants. Those people saw the rest; I had had my share and was satisfied. I went home to dream and was not disappointed.

My teaching and training enabled me to see deeper into these tragedies than an ignorant person could have done. I knew what they were for. I tried to disguise it from myself but down in the secret deeps of my troubled heart I knew—and I *knew* I knew. They were inventions of Providence to beguile me to a better life. It sounds curiously innocent and conceited now, but to me there was nothing strange about it; it was quite in accordance with the thoughtful and judicious ways of Providence as I understood them. It would not have surprised me nor even over-flattered me if Providence had killed off that whole community in trying to save an asset like me. Educated as I had been, it would have seemed just the thing and well worth the expense. *Why* Providence should take such an anxious interest in such a property, that idea never entered my head, and there was no one in that simple hamlet who would have dreamed of putting it there. For one thing, no one was equipped with it.

It is quite true, I took all the tragedies to myself and tallied them off in turn as they happened, saying to myself in each case, with a sigh, "Another one gone—and on my account; this ought to bring me to repentance; the patience of God will not always endure." And yet privately I believed it would. That is, I believed it in the daytime; but not in the night. With the going down of the sun my faith failed and the clammy fears gathered about my heart. It was then that I repented. Those were awful nights, nights of despair, nights charged with the bitterness of death. After each tragedy I recognized the warning and repented; repented and begged; begged like a coward, begged like a dog; and not in the interest of those poor people who had been extinguished for my sake but only in my *own* interest. It seems selfish when I look back on it now.

My repentances were very real, very earnest; and after each tragedy they happened every night for a long time. But as a rule they could not stand the daylight. They faded out and shredded away and disappeared in the glad splendor of the sun. They were the creatures of fear and darkness and they could not live out of their own place. The day gave me cheer and peace and at night I repented again. In all my boyhood life I am not sure that I ever tried to lead a better life in the daytime—or wanted to. In my age I should never think of wishing to do such a thing. But in my age, as in my youth, night brings me many a deep remorse. I realize that from the cradle up I have been like the rest of the race—never quite sane in the night. When "Injun Joe" died. . . . But never mind. Somewhere I have already described what a raging hell of repentance I passed through then. I believe that for months I was as pure as the driven snow. After dark.

COMPREHENSION

1. Why does Twain the child feel responsible for the tragedies in his town? What role does religion play in his feelings of guilt?
2. What relation does the first episode have to the others recounted in the narrative?
3. How does the adult Twain feel about these childhood events and feelings?

RHETORIC

1. Does the essay contain a thesis? Where is it located?
2. How does Twain use dialogue and dialect in his essay? What does it add to his story?
3. Comment on the writer's use of language. Is it figurative or concrete? How does it contribute to the point the writer is making? Cite effective uses of language in the essay.
4. How does the author structure his narrative? Is there one narrative account or several? Explain why Twain's narrative approach is effective.
5. Discuss the author's use of symbolism in paragraph 18. Is this element used elsewhere in the story?
6. How does Twain's conclusion work? Does it provide a satisfactory closing to the essay? How does the writer use irony in the final phrase? Why is using a sentence fragment effective?

WRITING

1. Compose a narrative essay recounting an event in your life that was humorous, embarrassing, or tragic. Use details and dialogue to describe the situation and the people involved in it. Also consider how this event affected you later in life.
2. Write an essay exploring the effects of religion on the mind and behavior of a young person. How might young minds interpret and process religious learning? What effects might it have on them when they grow up? Use support from the essays of Twain and Hughes in your writing.

MAYA ANGELOU   Maya Angelou (b. 1928) is an American poet, playwright, television screenwriter, actress, and singer. Taken together, her autobiographical books—*I Know Why the Caged Bird Sings* (1970), *Gather Together in My*

Name (1974), *Singin' and Swingin' and Gettin' Merry Like Christmas* (1976), *The Heart of a Woman* (1981), and *I Shall Not Be Moved* (1990)—provide one of the fullest accounts of the black female experience in contemporary literature. Fluent in six languages and active in artistic, educational, and political affairs, Angelou often presents autobiographical material against the backdrop of larger cultural concerns. In the following selection from *I Know Why the Caged Bird Sings,* the physical pain of a toothache is overshadowed by the emotional pain of bigotry and humiliation.

MAYA ANGELOU

Momma, the Dentist, and Me

The angel of the candy counter had found me out at last, and was exacting excruciating penance for all the stolen Milky Ways, Mounds, Mr. Goodbars and Hersheys with Almonds. I had two cavities that were rotten to the gums. The pain was beyond the bailiwick of crushed aspirins or oil of cloves. Only one thing could help me, so I prayed earnestly that I'd be allowed to sit under the house and have the building collapse on my left jaw. Since there was no Negro dentist in Stamps, nor doctor either, for that matter, Momma had dealt with previous toothaches by pulling them out (a string tied to the tooth with the other end looped over her fist), pain killers and prayer. In this particular instance the medicine had proved ineffective; there wasn't enough enamel left to hook a string on, and the prayers were being ignored because the Balancing Angel was blocking their passage.

I lived a few days and nights in blinding pain, not so much toying with as seriously considering the idea of jumping in the well, and Momma decided I had to be taken to a dentist. The nearest Negro dentist was in Texarkana, twenty-five miles away, and I was certain that I'd be dead long before we reached half the distance. Momma said we'd go to Dr. Lincoln, right in Stamps, and he'd take care of me. She said he owed her a favor.

I knew there were a number of whitefolks in town that owed her favors. Bailey and I had seen the books which showed how she had lent money to Blacks and whites alike during the Depression, and most still owed her. But I couldn't aptly remember seeing Dr. Lincoln's name, nor had I ever heard of a Negro's going to him as a patient. However, Momma said we were going, and put water on the stove for our baths. I had never been to a doctor, so she told me that after the bath (which would make my mouth feel better) I had to put on freshly starched and ironed underclothes from inside out. The ache failed to respond to the bath, and I knew then that the pain was more serious than that which anyone had ever suffered.

Before we left the Store, she ordered me to brush my teeth and then wash my mouth with Listerine. The idea of even opening my clamped jaws increased the pain, but upon her explanation that when you go to a doctor you have to clean yourself all over, but most especially the part that's to be examined, I screwed up my courage and unlocked my teeth. The cool air in my mouth and the jarring of my molars dislodged what little remained of my reason. I had frozen to the pain, my family nearly had to tie me down to take the toothbrush away. It was no small effort to get me started on the road to the dentist. Momma spoke to all the passers-by, but didn't stop to chat. She explained over her shoulder that we were going to the doctor and she'd "pass the time of day" on our way home.

Until we reached the pond the pain was my world, an aura that 5 haloed me for three feet around. Crossing the bridge into whitefolks' county, pieces of sanity pushed themselves forward. I had to stop moaning and start walking straight. The white towel, which was drawn under my chin and tied over my head, had to be arranged. If one was dying, it had to be done in style if the dying took place in whitefolks' part of town.

On the other side of the bridge the ache seemed to lessen as if a 6 whitebreeze blew off the whitefolks and cushioned everything in their neighborhood—including my jaw. The gravel road was smoother, the stones smaller and the tree branches hung down around the path and nearly covered us. If the pain didn't diminish then, the familiar yet strange sights hypnotized me into believing that it had.

But my head continued to throb with the measured insistence of a 7 bass drum, and how could a toothache pass the calaboose, hear the songs of the prisoners, their blues and laughter, and not be changed? How could one or two or even a mouthful of angry tooth roots meet a wagonload of powhitetrash children, endure their idiotic snobbery and not feel less important?

Behind the building which housed the dentist's office ran a small 8 path used by servants and those tradespeople who catered to the butcher and Stamps' one restaurant. Momma and I followed that lane to the backstairs of Dentist Lincoln's office. The sun was bright and gave the day a hard reality as we climbed up the steps to the second floor.

Momma knocked on the back door and a young white girl opened 9 it to show surprise at seeing us there. Momma said she wanted to see Dentist Lincoln and to tell him Annie was there. The girl closed the door firmly. Now the humiliation of hearing Momma describe herself as if she had no last name to the young white girl was equal to the physical pain. It seemed terribly unfair to have a toothache and a headache and have to bear at the same time the heavy burden of Blackness.

It was always possible that the teeth would quiet down and maybe 10 drop out of their own accord. Momma said we would wait. We leaned in the harsh sunlight on the shaky railings of the dentist's back porch for over an hour.

He opened the door and looked at Momma. "Well, Annie, what can 11 I do for you?"

He didn't see the towel around my jaw or notice my swollen face. 12

54

Momma said, "Dentist Lincoln. It's my grandbaby here. She got two rotten teeth that's giving her a fit."

She waited for him to acknowledge the truth of her statement. He made no comment, orally or facially.

"She had this toothache purt' near four days now, and today I said, 'Young lady, you going to the Dentist.'" 15

"Annie?" 16

"Yes, sir, Dentist Lincoln." 17

He was choosing words the way people hunt for shells. "Annie, you know I don't treat nigra, colored people." 18

"I know, Dentist Lincoln. But this here is just my little grandbaby, and she ain't gone be no trouble to you. . . ." 19

"Annie, everybody has a policy. In this world you have to have a policy. Now, my policy is I don't treat colored people." 20

The sun had baked the oil out of Momma's skin and melted the Vaseline in her hair. She shone greasily as she leaned out of the dentist's shadow. 21

"Seem like to me, Dentist Lincoln, you might look after her, she ain't nothing but a little mite. And seems like maybe you owe me a favor or two." 22

He reddened slightly. "Favor or no favor. The money has all been repaid to you and that's the end of it. Sorry, Annie." He had his hand on the doorknob. "Sorry." His voice was a bit kinder on the second "Sorry," as if he really was. 23

Momma said, "I wouldn't press on you like this for myself but I can't take No. Not for my grandbaby. When you come to borrow my money you didn't have to beg. You asked me, and I lent it. Now, it wasn't my policy. I ain't no moneylender, but you stood to lose this building and I tried to help you out." 24

"It's been paid, and raising your voice won't make me change my mind. My policy. . . ." He let go of the door and stepped nearer Momma. The three of us were crowded on the small landing. "Annie, my policy is I'd rather stick my hand in a dog's mouth than in a nigger's." 25

He had never once looked at me. He turned his back and went through the door into the cool beyond. Momma backed up inside herself for a few minutes. I forgot everything except her face which was almost a new one to me. She leaned over and took the doorknob, and in her everyday soft voice she said, "Sister, go on downstairs. Wait for me. I'll be there directly." 26

Under the most common of circumstances I knew it did no good to argue with Momma. So I walked down the steep stairs, afraid to look back and afraid not to do so. I turned as the door slammed, and she was gone. 27

Momma walked in that room as if she owned it. She shoved that silly nurse aside with one hand and strode into the dentist's office. He was sitting in his chair, sharpening his mean instruments and putting extra sting into his medicines. Her eyes were blazing like live coals and her arms had doubled themselves in length. He looked up at her just before she caught him by the collar of his white jacket. 28

55

"Stand up when you see a lady, you contemptuous scoundrel." Her   29
tongue had thinned and the words rolled off well enunciated. Enunciated and
sharp like little claps of thunder.

The dentist had no choice but to stand at R.O.T.C. attention. His head   30
dropped after a minute and his voice was humble. "Yes, ma'am, Mrs. Henderson."

"You knave, do you think you acted like a gentleman, speaking to me like   31
that in front of my granddaughter?" She didn't shake him, although she had
the power. She simply held him upright.

"No, ma'am, Mrs. Henderson."   32

"No, ma'am, Mrs. Henderson, what?" Then she did give him the tiniest   33
of shakes, but because of her strength the action set his head and arms to
shaking loose on the ends of his body. He stuttered much worse than Uncle
Willie. "No, ma'am, Mrs. Henderson, I'm sorry."

With just an edge of her disgust showing, Momma slung him back in his   34
dentist's chair. "Sorry is as sorry does, and you're about the sorriest dentist
I ever laid my eyes on." (She could afford to slip into the vernacular because
she had such eloquent command of English.)

"I didn't ask you to apologize in front of Marguerite, because I don't   35
want her to know my power, but I order you, now and herewith. Leave
Stamps by sundown."

"Mrs. Henderson, I can't get my equipment. . . ." He was shaking ter-   36
ribly now.

"Now, that brings me to my second order. You will never again practice   37
dentistry. Never! When you get settled in your next place, you will be a vegetarian caring for dogs with the mange, cats with the cholera and cows with
the epizootic. Is that clear?"

The saliva ran down his chin and his eyes filled with tears. "Yes, ma'am.   38
Thank you for not killing me. Thank you, Mrs. Henderson."

Momma pulled herself back from being ten feet tall with eight-foot arms   39
and said, "You're welcome for nothing, you varlet, I wouldn't waste a killing
on the likes of you."

On her way out she waved her handkerchief at the nurse and turned her   40
into a crocus sack of chicken feed.

Momma looked tired when she came down the stairs, but who   41
wouldn't be tired if they had gone through what she had. She came close
to me and adjusted the towel under my jaw (I had forgotten the toothache;
I only knew that she made her hands gentle in order not to awaken the
pain). She took my hand. Her voice never changed. "Come on, Sister."

I reckoned we were going home where she would concoct a brew to   42
eliminate the pain and maybe give me new teeth too. New teeth that
would grow overnight out of my gums. She led me toward the drug-
store, which was in the opposite direction from the Store. "I'm taking
you to Dentist Baker in Texarkana."

I was glad after all that I had bathed and put on Mum and Cashmere   43
Bouquet talcum powder. It was a wonderful surprise. My toothache had
quieted to solemn pain, Momma had obliterated the evil white man, and
we were going on a trip to Texarkana, just the two of us.

On the Greyhound she took an inside seat in the back, and I sat beside her. I was so proud of being her granddaughter and sure that some of her magic must have come down to me. She asked if I was scared. I only shook my head and leaned over on her cool brown upper arm. There was no chance that a dentist, especially a Negro dentist, would dare hurt me then. Not with Momma there. The trip was uneventful, except that she put her arm around me, which was very unusual for Momma to do.

The dentist showed me the medicine and the needle before he 45 deadened my gums, but if he hadn't I wouldn't have worried. Momma stood right behind him. Her arms were folded and she checked on everything he did. The teeth were extracted and she bought me an ice cream cone from the side window of a drug counter. The trip back to Stamps was quiet, except that I had to spit into a very small empty snuff can which she had gotten for me and it was difficult with the bus humping and jerking on our country roads.

At home, I was given a warm salt solution, and when I washed out 46 my mouth I showed Bailey the empty holes, where the clotted blood sat like filling in a pie crust. He said I was quite brave, and that was my cue to reveal our confrontation with the peckerwood dentist and Momma's incredible powers.

I had to admit that I didn't hear the conversation, but what else 47 could she have said than what I said she said? What else done? He agreed with my analysis in a lukewarm way, and I happily (after all, I'd been sick) flounced into the Store. Momma was preparing our evening meal and Uncle Willie leaned on the door sill. She gave her version.

"Dentist Lincoln got right uppity. Said he'd rather put his hand in 48 a dog's mouth. And when I reminded him of the favor, he brushed it off like a piece of lint. Well, I sent Sister downstairs and went inside. I hadn't never been in his office before, but I found the door to where he takes out teeth, and him and the nurse was in there thick as thieves. I just stood there till he caught sight of me." Crash bang the pots on the stove. "He jumped just like he was sitting on a pin. He said, 'Annie, I done tole you, I ain't gonna mess around in no niggah's mouth.' I said, 'Somebody's got to do it then,' and he said, 'Take her to Texarkana to the colored dentist' and that's when I said, 'If you paid me my money I could afford to take her.' He said, 'It's all been paid.' I tole him every-thing but the interest been paid. He said "Twasn't no interest.' I said, "Tis now. I'll take ten dollars as payment in full.' You know, Willie, it wasn't no right thing to do, 'cause I lent that money without thinking about it.

"He tole that little snippety nurse of his'n to give me ten dollars and 49 make me sign a 'paid in full' receipt. She gave it to me and I signed the papers. Even though by rights he was paid up before, I figger, he gonna be that kind of nasty, he gonna have to pay for it."

Momma and her son laughed and laughed over the white man's 50 evilness and her retributive sin.

I preferred, much preferred, my version. 51

COMPREHENSION

1. Briefly describe the circumstances and social climate in which the narrator lived.
2. Why does the young Angelou need to imagine a different confrontation between Momma and the dentist than the one which actually took place? Why does she prefer the fantasy?
3. How would you describe the character of Angelou's grandmother?

RHETORIC

1. How does the writer structure her narrative? Why is this method effective?
2. What is the point of view of the writer? What response does it elicit from the reader?
3. Compare the diction and vocabulary Angelou's grandmother uses in the fantasy encounter to her language in the real event. How do they differ? Cite specific examples, and explain what the writer is trying to accomplish. How does the use of dialect affect the force of the narrative in general?
4. In paragraph 7, how does figurative language and the use of questions support the point of the paragraph?
5. What mood does Angelou create in her story? How does she achieve this? Use examples from the narrative.

WRITING

1. Compose a narrative essay describing an event that caused you embarrassment or humiliation. Describe what happened, who else was involved, and how you felt. Create a mood using figurative language and dialogue.
2. In an essay, explore the psychic damage caused by racism. How does it feel to be treated cruelly or thoughtlessly because of your racial or ethnic background? How might such treatment affect a child?
3. Compose an essay recounting an unpleasant event in your life that you wish had happened differently. Write what actually occurred as well as what you wish had occurred. Use Angelou's essay as a guide.

CLASSIC AND CONTEMPORARY: QUESTIONS FOR COMPARISON

1. Compare and contrast the childhood experiences of Twain and Angelou. How are they similar, and how are they different? In what ways did their childhood experiences influence their lives?
2. Explain the ways in which the authors structure their autobiographical accounts. Focus on their use of first-person narrators, the actual narrative order of events, the handling of time, the age of the narrator, and other relevant issues.
3. From one perspective, we can view these essays as reflections on the tragedy and comedy of life. How do Twain and Angelou approach this subject? What *is* their philosophy of life? Are they optimists or pessimists? Explain.

CONNECTIONS

1. Hurston, Cofer, and Angelou all address the issue of the minority experience in the United States. Do they also share a common voice or mood? What is distinctive about each essay? In your opinion, which essay is most effective? Why? Consider the style and emotional impact of the writing.

2. Kingston, Cofer, and Twain are haunted by ghosts, events, rumors in their narratives. Find examples in their writing, and examine the impact of these memories on the writers' lives and their perceptions as adults.

3. Analyze the roles of women as depicted in the narratives of Angelou, Kingston, Cofer, and Dillard.

4. Compare the essays of Twain and Hughes as regards childhood guilt and religion. What effect did the feeling of guilt have on the writers' religious beliefs, if any?

5. Examine the use of setting and evocative language in the works of Clemens and White. Cite examples in both essays in which language is especially effective in enriching the narrative.

6. In the essays of Angelou, Twain, and Hughes, examine the use of dialect and dialogue. How do these devices strengthen the stories being told? Use examples from the essays to support your views.

7. The issue of "family values" has provoked considerable political debate recently. Using examples from the essays in this section, write your own definition of family values.

8. Argue for or against the proposition that there is a "typical" family unit. Refer to at least three essays in this chapter to support your position.

9. Select your favorite writer from this chapter, and explain why you prefer his or her essay to others. Refer to the essays in your evaluation.

CHAPTER TWO

The Sense of Place

*I*n his award-winning book, *Arctic Dreams* (1986), Barry Lopez asks, "How do people imagine the landscape they find themselves in?" For Lopez, whose essay "The American Geographies" appears in this chapter, our sense of place should never be taken for granted. Instead, we must investigate and attempt to understand the ways in which landscape or place affects us physically, mentally, emotionally, and perhaps spiritually. Whether we love a place or hate it, feel an intimate relationship to it or feel alienated from it, we perceive that the places we inhabit mold our sense of identity.

Essayists who write about place sense that the subject is a perfect vehicle for self-discovery. Essays rooted in a sense of place also foster understanding of cultural diversity—of the complex interaction of human behavior, background, environment, and heritage. The essays in this chapter range over a broad and varied landscape: a colonial outpost in Burma; a college town in Florida; a postwar panorama of Vietnam; an island in the Caribbean; a house in Kiowa country; the cityscapes of New York and Miami. The authors of these essays invite us on voyages of discovery. The exterior landscapes that they depict so vividly tell us a great deal about the authors' own lives and values. Their essays arouse in us a desire to know more about the places that are so important to them.

"Only connect," wrote the English author E. M. Forster, whose famous essay "My Wood" appears in another chapter of this text. In many ways we spend our lives attempting to connect to a place or to a series of places. As a species, we are territorial, requiring "turf" or a "stamping ground." We know the importance of the place where we grew up; we recall the anxieties of emigration, or moving; we understand almost immediately the challenge of life on a new campus or in a new dormitory. We avoid or embrace certain places, mourn or celebrate others. Indeed, encountering and thinking about places inspires us, unlocks our creative impulses. And through language we attempt to capture the essence, or spirit, of a place—known or unknown, beautiful or ugly, urban or rural, settled or wild. Like the American novelist Harry Crews, we might want to celebrate the place we call home; or like George Orwell in "Shooting an Elephant," we might want to offer a cultural critique of a certain place. In short, the sense of place provokes many voices in us—sometimes in clear and sometimes in ambivalent tones.

Writing about a place may carry you from the personal to the objective. You may write about yourself, but extend the investigation outward to families, communities, regions, nations. Your memories of the past and present, understandings of your cultural legacies, may enrich your portrayal of diverse human relations nourished in one spot on Earth. In reading and writing about place, we acquire a better perception of human community and cultural cohesion. And we begin to unlock mysteries about our relationship to place for, as the American essayist, poet, and novelist Wendell Berry observes, if you don't know where you are, you don't know *who* you are.

Previewing the Chapter

As you read the essays in this chapter and respond to them in discussion and writing, consider the following questions:

• What is the writer's relationship to the place and his or her attitude toward it?

• What is the author's purpose in writing about a specific place?

• Is the place described friendly or hostile, known or unknown?

• Does the writer present an objective or a subjective picture of the place?

• What social, political, or ethical ideas does the author present?

• What are the main conflicts that the author presents?

• How well does the author know the place he or she is writing about? How do you know?

• What impact does the writer think a certain place has on culture?

• What does the author learn from his or her presentation of place?

• What have you learned from the author's presentation?

HARRY CREWS Harry Crews, born in Alma, Georgia, in 1935, was educated at the University of Florida in Gainesville, where he teaches English. He has written over ten novels, several collections of essays, and an autobiography. His work has been called tragic and comic, nostalgic and grotesque in the tradition of southern gothic writers. Crews grew up in an area where people had to struggle to survive and in a culture that took stock in faith healers and witchcraft. Many critics have hailed his work as being original and unique metaphors for American culture. In the following essay from *Esquire* magazine, the author unapologetically tells us of his values.

HARRY CREWS

Why I Live Where I Live

I can leave the place where I live a couple of hours before daylight and 1
be on a deserted little strip of sand called Crescent Beach in time to throw a piece of meat on a fire and then, in a few minutes, lie back sucking on a vodka bottle and chewing on a hunk of bloody beef while the sun lifts out of the Atlantic Ocean (somewhat unnerving but also mystically beautiful to a man who never saw a body of water bigger than a pond until he was grown) and while the sun rises lie on a blanket, brain singing from vodka and a bellyful of beef, while the beautiful bikinied children from the University of Florida drift down the beach, their smooth bodies sweating baby oil and the purest kind of innocent lust (which of course is the rankest sort) into the bright air. If all that starts to pall—and what *doesn't* start to pall?—I can leave the beach and be out on the end of a dock, sitting in the Captain's Table eating hearts-of-palm salad and hot boiled shrimp and sipping on a tall, icy glass of beer while the sun I saw lift out of the Atlantic that morning sinks into the warm, waveless Gulf of Mexico. It makes for a hell of a day. But that isn't really why I live in the north-central Florida town of Gainesville.

Nor do I live in Gainesville because seven blocks from my house 2
there are two enormous libraries filled with the most courteous, helpful people you can imagine, people who, after explaining some of the more intricate mysteries of how the place works, including the purposes of numerous indices, will go ahead and cheerfully find what I cannot: for example, the car capacity of drive-in theaters in Bakersfield, California, in 1950. A man never knows when he may need a bit of information like that, but it isn't enough to keep him living in a little town in Florida as opposed to, say, Ann Arbor, Michigan.

I love the size of Gainesville. I can walk anywhere I want to go, 3
and consequently I have very little to do with that abomination before the Lord, the car. It's a twenty-minute stroll to my two favorite bars, Lillian's Music Store and the Winnjammer; ten minutes to a lovely

square of grass and trees called the Plaza of the Americas; less than ten minutes to the house of a young lady who has been hypnotizing me for six years. Some people get analyzed; I get hypnotized. It leaves me with the most astonishing and pleasurable memories. But there must be ten thousand towns like Gainesville in this country, and surely several hundred of them would have good places to drink and talk and at least one house where a young lady lived who would consent to hypnotize me into astonishing and pleasurable memories. So I cannot lean too heavily on walking and memories to justify being where I am.

The reason I live where I do is more complicated than the sorts of ₄ things I've been talking about thus far—more complicated and, I expect, ultimately inexplicable. Or, said another way: anyone other than I may find that the explanation does not satisfy. To start, I live right in the middle of town on three acres of land, land thick with pines a hundred feet tall, oak, wild plum trees, and all manner of tangled, unidentifiable underbrush. The only cleared space is the very narrow road leading down to the house. No lawn. (There are many things I absolutely refuse to do in this world, but the three things leading the list are: wash my car, shine my shoes, and mow a lawn.) The back wall of the room I work in at the rear of the house is glass, and when I raise my eyes from the typewriter I look past an enormous bull bay tree through a thin stand of reeds into a tiny creek, the banks of which are thick with the greenest fern God ever made. In my imagination I can follow that little creek upstream to the place where, after a long, circuitous passage, it joins the Suwannee River, and then follow the dark waters of the Suwannee upriver to the place where it rises in the nearly impenetrable fastness of the Okefenokee Swamp. Okefenokee: Creek Indian word for Land of the Trembling Earth, because most of the islands in the swamp—some of them holding hundreds of huge trees growing so thick that their roots are matted and woven as closely as a blanket— actually float on the water, and when a black bear crashes across one of them, the whole thing trembles.

I saw the Okefenokee Swamp long before I saw the Suwannee ₅ River, and the Suwannee River long before I saw the little creek I'm looking at as I write this. When I was a boy, I was in the swamp a lot, on the edges of it practically all the time that I was not in the fields working. I went deep into the Okefenokee with T. J., the husband of one of my first cousins. His left leg was cut off at the knee and he wore a peg, but he got along fine with it because we were usually in a flat skiff casting nets for crawfish, which he sold for fish bait at a penny apiece. I did not know enough then and do not know enough now to go into the deep middle swamp, but T. J. did; he knew the twisting maze of sloughs like his back yard, could read every sign of every living thing in the swamp, and made a good living with the crawfish nets and his string of traps and his gun. He sold alligator, wore alligator, and ate alligator. This was long before the federal government made the place a national wildlife refuge.

T. J. made his living out of the swamp, and I make mine now out of how the swamp shaped me, how the rhythms and patterns of speech in that time and place are still alive in my mouth today and, more important, alive in my ear. I feed off now and hope always to feed off the stories I heard told in the early dark around fires where coffee boiled while our clothes, still wet from stringing traps all day, slowly dried to our bodies. Even when I write stories not set in Georgia and not at all about anything in the South, that writing is of necessity still informed by my notions of the world and of what it is to be caught in it. Those notions obviously come out of South Georgia and out of everything that happened to me there, or so I believe.

Living here in North Florida, I am a little more than a hundred 7 miles from where I was born and raised to manhood. I am just far enough away from the only place that was ever mine to still see it, close enough to the only people to whom I was ever kin in ways deeper than blood to still hear them. I know that what I have just written will sound precious and pretentious to many people. So be it. Let them do their work as they will, and I'll do mine.

I've tried to work—that is, to write—in Georgia, but I could not. 8 Even under the best of circumstances, at my mama's farm, for instance, it was all too much for me. I was too deep in it, too close to it to use it, to make anything out of it. My memory doesn't even seem to work when I'm writing in Georgia. I can't seem to hold a story in my head. I write a page, and five pages later what I wrote earlier has begun to slide out of focus. If this is all symptomatic of some more profound malaise, I don't want to know about it and I certainly don't want to understand it.

Living here in Gainesville seems to give me a kind of geographic 9 and emotional distance I need to write. I can't write if I get too far away. I tried to work on a novel in Tennessee once and after a ruined two months gave it up in despair. I once spent four months near Lake Placid in a beautiful house lent to me by a friend—perfect place to write—and I didn't do a damn thing but eat my guts and look out the window at the mountains.

And that, all of it, precious, pretentious, or whatever, is why I live 10 where I live. And unless something happens that I cannot control, I plan to die here.

COMPREHENSION

1. Summarize and categorize the reasons why the author lives where he lives.
2. The place in which the writer lives seems to mirror his life. What does it imply about his personality?
3. In paragraph 4, the author says his reason for living where he does is "ultimately inexplicable." Which aspects of his life does he convey articulately, and which are beyond his ability to relate to the reader?

1. Note the length of paragraph 1. How many different things does it describe? How many different senses does it invoke? In one word, how would you sum up the attitude of the author toward the scene he describes here?

2. Paragraph 5 describes the author's past. How does he use transition to connect this paragraph to his present life in paragraph 6?

3. The author, at various places in the essay, uses exposition, description, narrative, and argument. Locate and identify at least two examples of each of these rhetorical devices.

4. The author has what some people might consider eccentric opinions and habits. How does he integrate these into the text of his essay? What is his purpose in including them?

5. The idea of mystery is expressed throughout much of the essay; for example, in paragraph 7, the author claims that he lives "close enough to the only people to whom I was ever kin in ways deeper than blood to still hear them." Study the author's evocations of mystery. How does he incorporate them into his descriptions?

6. Why is the final paragraph so short? How does it differ from the other paragraphs in the essay?

7. Would you say that this essay emanates from a "man's" point of view? What about its style, voice, tone, and subject helped you to reach your conclusion?

WRITING

1. Write an essay entitled, "Why I Live Where I Live." Be sure to include elements of exposition, description, and narration.

2. Heraclitus, the Greek philosopher, stated, "You can't step into the same river twice." Write an essay comparing and contrasting two places you've lived, and explain why each was appropriate for the time you lived there.

3. Write an imaginary letter to Mr. Crews, explaining why you would or why you would not like to pay a visit to Gainesville. Be sure to base your letter on Mr. Crews's description.

BARRY LOPEZ   Barry Lopez (1945–   ) is a distinguished American writer on natural history, the environment, and our community obligations to the planet. He was born in Port Chester, New York; raised in rural California and New York City; and educated at the University of Notre Dame and the University of Oregon. His interests in nature, folklore, and the environment have led him on travels in the wilderness including the Arctic and remote regions of Australia, Africa, and Antarctica. Since the early 1970s, he has lived on the McKenzie River in western Oregon. His award-winning books include *Of Wolves and Men* (1978), *Winter Count* (1981), *Arctic Dreams* (1986), *Crow and Weasel* (1990, winner of the Parents Choice Foundation Award), and *The Rediscovery of North America* (1991). A frequent contributor to periodicals, Lopez has collected some of his best essays in *Crossing Open Ground* (1988). Lopez is a keen, poetic observer of landscape, by which he means "the complete lay of the land." In the following essay, Lopez warns of the dangers of viewing the American landscape as a symbol of patriotism or political agendas.

BARRY LOPEZ

The American Geographies

It has become commonplace to observe that Americans know little of the geography of their country, that they are innocent of it as a landscape of rivers, mountains, and towns. They do not know, supposedly, the location of the Delaware Water Gap, the Olympic Mountains, or the Piedmont Plateau; and, the indictment continues, they have little conception of the way the individual components of this landscape are imperiled, from a human perspective, by modern farming practices or industrial pollution.

I do not know how true this is, but it is easy to believe that it is truer than most of us would wish. A recent Gallup Organization and National Geographic Society survey found Americans woefully ignorant of world geography. Three out of four couldn't locate the Persian Gulf. The implication was that we knew no more about our own homeland, and that this ignorance undermined the integrity of our political processes and the efficiency of our business enterprises.

As Americans, we profess a sincere and fierce love for the American landscape, for our rolling prairies, free-flowing rivers, and "purple mountains' majesty"; but it is hard to imagine, actually, where this particular landscape is. It is not just that a nostalgic landscape has passed away—that Mark Twain's Mississippi is now dammed from Illinois to Louisiana and the prairies have all been sold and fenced. It is that it's *always* been a romantic's landscape. In the attenuated form in which it is presented on television today, in magazine articles, and in calendar photographs, the essential wildness of the American landscape is reduced to attractive scenery. We look out on a familiar, memorized landscape that portends adventure and promises enrichment. There are no distracting people in it and few artifacts of human life. The animals are all beautiful, diligent, one might even say well behaved. Nature's unruliness, the power of rivers and skies to intimidate, and any evidence of disastrous human land-management practices are all but invisible. It is, in short, a magnificent garden, a colonial vision of paradise imposed on real place that is, at best, only selectively known.

The real American landscape is a face of almost incomprehensible depth and complexity. If one were to sit for a few days, for example, among the ponderosa pine forest and black lava fields of the Cascade Mountains in western Oregon, inhaling the pines' sweet balm on an

evening breeze from some point on the barren rock, and then were to
step off onto the Olympic Peninsula in Washington, to those rain forests
with sphagnum moss floors soft as fleece underfoot and Douglas firs
too big around for five people to hug, and then head south to walk the
ephemeral creeks and sun-blistered playas of the Mojave Desert in
southern California, one would be reeling under the sensations. The
contrast is not only one of plants and soils, a different array, say, of brilliantly colored beetles. The shock to the senses comes from a different
shape to the silence, a difference in the very quality of light, in the
weight of the air. And this relatively short journey down the West Coast
would still leave the traveler with all that lay to the east to explore—the
anomalous sand hills of Nebraska, the heat and frog voices of Okefenokee Swamp, the fetch of Chesapeake Bay, and the hardwood
corpses and black bears of the Ozark Mountains.

No one of these places, of course, can be entirely fathomed, biologically or aesthetically. They are mysteries upon which we impose
names. Enchantments. We tick the names off glibly but lovingly. We
mean no disrespect. Our genuine desire, though we may be skeptical
about the time it would take and uncertain of its practical value to
us, is to actually know these places. As deeply ingrained in the American psyche as the desire to conquer and control the land is the
desire to sojourn in it, to sail up and down Pamlico Sound, to paddle a canoe through Minnesota's boundary waters, to walk on the
desert of the Great Salt Lake, to camp in the stony hardwood valleys
of Vermont.

To do this well, to really come to an understanding of the specific
American geography, requires not only time but a kind of local expertise, an intimacy with place few of us ever develop. There is no way
around the former requirement: If you want to know, you must take the
time. It is not in books. A specific geographical understanding, however, can be sought out and borrowed. It resides with men and women
more or less sworn to a place, who abide there, who have a feel for the
soil and history, for the turn of leaves and night sounds. Often they are
glad to take the outlander in tow.

These local geniuses of American landscape, in my experience, are
people in whom geography thrives. They are the antithesis of geographical ignorance. Rarely known outside their own communities,
they often seem, at the first encounter, unremarkable and anonymous.
They may not be able to recall the name of a particular wildflower—or
they may have given it a name known only to them. They might have
forgotten the precise circumstances of a local historical event. Or they
can't say for certain when the last of the Canada geese passed through
in the fall, or can't differentiate between two kinds of trout in the same
creek. Like all of us, they have fallen prey to the fallacies of memory
and are burdened with ignorance; but they are nearly flawless in the
respect they bear these places they love. Their knowledge is intimate
rather than encyclopedic, human but not necessarily scholarly. It rings
with the concrete details of experience.

America, I believe, teems with such people. The paradox here, between a faulty grasp of geographical knowledge for which Americans are indicted and the intimate, apparently contradictory familiarity of a group of largely anonymous people, is not solely a matter of confused scale. (The local landscape is easier to know than a national landscape—and many local geographers, of course, are relatively ignorant of a national geography.) And it is not simply ironic. The paradox is dark. To be succinct: The politics and advertising that seek a national audience must project a national geography; to be broadly useful that geography must, inevitably, be generalized, and it is often romantic. It is therefore frequently misleading and imprecise. Yet the same films, magazines, and television features that tout this imaginary American landscape also honor the anonymous men and women who interpret it. Their affinity for the land is lauded, their local allegiance admired. But the rigor of their local geographies, taken together, contradicts the patriotic, national vision of unspoiled, untroubled land. These men and women are ultimately forgotten, along with the details of the landscapes they speak for, in the face of more pressing national matters. It is the chilling nature of modern society to find an ignorance of geography, local or national, as excusable as an ignorance of hand tools; and to find the commitment of people to their home places only momentarily entertaining. And finally naive.

If one were to pass time among Basawara people in the Kalahari Desert, or with Kreen-Akrora in the Amazon Basin, or with Pitjantjatjara Aborigines in Australia, the most salient impression they might leave is of an absolutely stunning knowledge of their local geography— geology, hydrology, biology, and weather. In short, the extensive particulars of their intercourse with it.

In 40,000 years of human history, it has been only in the last few hundred years or so that a people could afford to ignore their local geographies as completely as we do and still survive. Technological innovations, from refrigerated trucks to artificial fertilizers, from sophisticated cost accounting to mass air transportation, have utterly changed concepts of season, distance, soil productivity, and the real cost of drawing sustenance from the land. It is now possible for a resident of Boston to bite into a fresh strawberry in the dead of winter; for someone in San Francisco to travel to Atlanta in a few hours with no worry about how formidable might be crossings of the Great Basin Desert or the Mississippi River; for an absentee farmer to gain a tax advantage from a farm that leaches poisons into its water table and on which crops are left to rot. The Pitjantjatjara might shake their heads in bewilderment and bemusement, not because they are primitive or ignorant people, not because they have no sense of irony or are incapable of marveling, but because they have not (many would say not yet) realized a world in which such manipulation of the land—surmounting the imperatives of distance it imposes, for example, or turning the large-scale destruction of forests and arable land into wealth— is desirable or plausible.

Chapter Two
The Sense of
Place

In the years I have traveled through America, in cars and on horseback, on foot and by raft, I have repeatedly been brought to a sudden state of awe by some gracile or savage movement of animal, some odd wrapping of a tree's foliage by the wind, and unimpeded run of dew-laden prairie stretching to a horizon flat as a coin where a pin-dot sun pales the dawn sky pink. I know these things are beyond intellection, that they are the vivid edges of the world that includes but also transcends the human world. In memory, when I dwell on these things, I know that in a truly national literature there should be odes to the Triassic reds of the Colorado Plateau, to the sharp and ghostly light of the Florida Keys, to the aeolian soils of southern Minnesota and the Palouse in Washington, though the modern mind abjures the literary potential of such subjects. (If the sand and floodwater farmers of Arizona and New Mexico were to take the black loams of Louisiana in their hands they would be flabbergasted, and that is the beginning of literature.) I know there should be eloquent evocations of the cobbled beaches of Maine, the plutonic walls of the Sierra Nevada, the orange canyons of the Kaibab Plateau. I have no doubt, in fact, that there are. They are as numerous and diverse as the eyes and fingers that ponder the country—it is that only a handful of them are known. The great majority are to be found in the drawers and boxes, in the letters and private journals of millions of workaday people who have regarded their encounters with the land as an engagement bordering on the spiritual, as being fundamentally linked to their state of health.

One cannot acknowledge the extent and the history of this kind of testimony without being forced to the realization that something strange, if not dangerous, is afoot. Year by year, the number of people with firsthand experience in the land dwindles. Rural populations continue to shift to the cities. The family farm is in a state of demise, and government and industry continue to apply pressure on the native peoples of North America to sever their ties with the land. In the wake of this loss the personal and local knowledge, the knowledge from which a real geography is derived, the knowledge upon which a country must ultimately stand, has come something hard to define but, I think, sinister and unsettling—the packaging and marketing of land as a form of entertainment. An incipient industry, capitalizing on the nostalgia Americans feel for the imagined virgin landscapes of their fathers, and on a desire for adventure, now offers people a convenient though sometimes incomplete or even spurious geography as an inducement to purchase a unique experience. But the line between authentic experience and a superficial exposure to the elements of experience is blurred. And the real landscape, in all its complexity, is distorted even further in the public imagination. No longer innately mysterious and dignified, a ground from which experience grows, it becomes a curiously generic backdrop on which experience is imposed.

In theme parks the profound, subtle, and protracted experience of running a river is reduced to a loud, quick, safe equivalence, a pleasant distraction. People only able to venture into the countryside on annual vacations are, increasingly, schooled in the belief that wild land will, and should, provide thrills and exceptional scenery on a timely basis. If it does not, something is wrong, either the land itself or possibly with the company outfitting the trip.

People in America, then, face a convoluted and ultimately destruc- 14 tive situation. The land itself, vast and differentiated, defies the notion of a national geography. Yet Americans are daily presented with, and have become accustomed to talking about, a homogenized national geography, one that seems to operate independently of the land, a collection of objects appearing in advertisements, as a background in movies, and in patriotic calendars. The suggestion is that there *can* be a national geography because the constituent parts are interchangeable and can be treated as commodities. On reflection, this is an appalling condescension and a terrible imprecision, the very antithesis of knowledge. The idea that either the Green River in Utah or the Salmon River in Idaho will do, or that the valleys of Kentucky and West Virginia are virtually interchangeable, is not just misleading. For people still dependent on the soil for their sustenance, or for people whose memories tie them to those places, it betrays a numbing casualness, a utilitarian, expedient, and commercial frame of mind. It heralds a society in which it is no longer necessary for human beings to know where they live, except as those places are described and fixed by numbers. The truly difficult and lifelong task of discovering where one lives is finally disdained.

If a society forgets or no longer cares where it lives, then anyone 15 with the political power and the will to do so can manipulate the landscape to conform to certain social ideas or nostalgic visions. People may hardly notice that anything has happened, or assume that whatever happens—a mountain stripped of timber and eroding into its creeks— is for the common good. The more superficial—or artificial—becomes a society's knowledge of the real dimensions of the land it occupies, the more vulnerable the land is to exploitation, to manipulation for short-term gain. The land, virtually powerless before political and commercial entities, finds itself finally with no defenders. It finds itself bereft of intimates with indispensable, concrete knowledge. (Oddly, or perhaps not oddly, while American society continues to value local knowledge as a quaint part of its heritage, it continues to cut such people off from any real political power. This is as true for small farmers and illiterate cowboys as it is for American Indians, native Hawaiians, and Eskimos.)

The intense pressure of imagery in America, and the manipulation 16 of images necessary to a society with specific goals, means the land will inevitably be treated like a commodity; and voices that tend to contradict the proffered image will, one way or another, be silenced or discredited by those in power. This is not new to America; the promulgation in America of a false or imposed geography has been the case from the beginning. All local geographies, as they were defined by hundreds of separate, independent native traditions, were denied in favor of an imported and unifying vision of America's natural history. The country,

71

the landscape itself, was eventually defined according to dictates of progress like Manifest Destiny and laws like the Homestead Act, which reflected a poor understanding of the physical lay of the land.

When I was growing up in southern California, I formed the rudiments of a local geography—eucalyptus trees, February rains, Santa Ana winds. I lost much of it when my family moved to New York City, a move typical of the modern, peripatetic style of American life, responding to the exigencies of divorce and employment. As a boy I felt a hunger to know the American landscape that was extreme; when I was finally able to travel on my own, I did so. Eventually I visited most of the United States, living for brief periods of time in Arizona, Indiana, Alabama, Georgia, Wyoming, New Jersey, and Montana before settling twenty years ago in western Oregon. 17

The astonishing level of my ignorance confronted me everywhere I went. I knew early on that the country could not be held together in a few phrases, that its geography was magnificent and incomprehensible, that a man or woman could devote a lifetime to its elucidation and still feel in the end that he had but sailed many thousands of miles over the surface of the ocean. So I came into the habit of traversing landscapes I wanted to know with local tutors and reading what had previously been written about, and in, those places. I came to value exceedingly novels and essays and works of nonfiction that connected human enterprise to real and specific places, and I grew to be mildly distrustful of work that occurred in no particular place, work so cerebral and detached as to be refutable only in an argument of ideas. 18

These sojourns in various corners of the country infused me, somewhat to my surprise on thinking about it, with a great sense of hope. Whatever despair I had come to feel at a waning sense of the real land and the emergence of false geographies—elements of the land being manipulated, for example, to create erroneous but useful patterns in advertising—was dispelled by the depth of a single person's local knowledge, by the serenity that seemed to come with that intelligence. Any harm that might be done by people who cared nothing for the land, to whom it was not innately worthy but only something ultimately for sale, I thought, would one day have to meet this kind of integrity, people with the same dignity and transcendence as the land they occupied. So when I traveled, when I rolled my sleeping bag out on the shores of the Beaufort Sea or in the high pastures of the Absaroka Range in Wyoming, or at the bottom of the Grand Canyon, I absorbed those particular testaments of life, the indigenous color and songbird song, the smell of sunbleached rock, damp earth, and wild honey, with some crude appreciation of the singular magnificence of each of those places. And the reassurance I felt expanded in the knowledge that there were, and would likely always be, people speaking out whenever they felt the dignity of the Earth imperiled in these places. 19

This promulgation of false geographies, which threaten the fundamental notion of what it means to live somewhere, is a current with a stable and perhaps growing countercurrent. There are people living in New York City who are familiar with the stone basements, the cratonic 20

72

geology, of that island and have a feeling for birds migrating through in the fall, their sequence and number. They do not find the city alien but human, its attenuated natural history merely different from that of rural Georgia or Kansas. I find the countermeasure, too, among Eskimos who cannot read but who might engage you for days on the subtleties of sea-ice topography. And among men and women who, though they have followed in the footsteps of their parents, have come to the conclusion that they can no longer farm or fish or log in the way their ancestors did; they recognize that finite boundaries to this sort of wealth have appeared in their lifetime. Or among young men and women who have taken several decades of book-learned agronomy, zoology, silviculture and horticulture, ecology, ethnobotany, and fluvial geomorphology and turned it into a new kind of local knowledge, who have taken up residence in a place and sought, both because of and in spite of their education, to develop a deep intimacy with it. Or they have gone to work, idealistically, for the National Park Service or the fish and wildlife services or for a private institution like The Nature Conservancy. These are people to whom the land is more than politics or economics. These are people for whom the land is alive. It feeds them, directly, and that is how and why they learn its geography.

In the end, then, if one begins among the blue crabs of Chesapeake 21 Bay and wanders for several years, down through the Smoky Mountains and back to the bluegrass hills, along the drainages of the Ohio and into the hill country of Missouri, where in summer a chorus of cicadas might drown out human conversation, then up the Missouri itself, reading on the way the entries of Meriwether Lewis and William Clark and musing on the demise of the plains grizzly and the sturgeon, crosses west into the drainage of the Platte and spends the evenings with Gene Weltfish's *The Lost Universe,* her book about the Pawnee who once thrived there, then drops south to Palo Duro Canyon and the irrigated farms of the Llano Estacado in Texas, turns west across the Sangre de Christo, southernmost of the Rocky Mountain ranges, and moves north and west up onto the slickrock mesas of Utah, those browns and oranges, the ocherous hues reverberating in the deep canyons, then goes north, swinging west to the insular ranges that sit like battleships in the pelagic space of Nevada, camps at the steaming edge of sulphur springs in the Black Rock Desert, where alkaline pans are glazed with a ferocious light, a heat to melt iron, then crosses the northern Sierra Nevada, waist-deep in summer snow in the passes, to descend to the valley of the Sacramento, and rises through groves of elephantine redwoods in the Coast Range, to arrive at Cape Mendocino, before Balboa's Pacific, cormorants and gulls, gray whales headed north for Unimak Pass in the Aleutians, the winds crashing down on you, facing the ocean over the blue ocean that gives the scene its true vastness, making this crossing, having been so often astonished at the line and the color of the land, the ingenious lives of its plants and animals, the varieties of its darknesses, the intensity of the stars overhead, you would be ashamed to discover, then, in yourself, any capacity to focus on ravages in the land that left you unsettled. You would have seen so much, breathtaking, startling, and outsize, that you might not be able for a long time to break the spell, the sense, especially finishing your journey in the West, that the land had not been as rearranged or quite as compromised as you had first imagined.

After you had slept some nights on the beach, however, with that finite line of the ocean before you and the land stretching out behind you, the wind first battering then cradling you, you would be compelled by memory, obligated by your own involvement, to speak of what left you troubled. To find the rivers dammed and shrunken, the soil washed away, the land fenced, a tracery of pipes and wires and roads laid down everywhere, blocking and channeling the movement of water and animals, cutting the eye off repeatedly and confining it—you had expected this. It troubles you no more than your despair over the ruthlessness, the insensitivity, the impetuousness of modern life. What underlies this obvious change, however, is a less noticeable pattern of disruption: acidic lakes, skies empty of birds, fouled beaches, the poisonous slags of industry, the sun burning like a molten coin in ruined air.

It is a tenet of certain ideologies that man is responsible for all that is ugly, that everything nature creates is beautiful. Nature's darkness goes partly unreported, of course, and human brilliance is often perversely ignored. What is true is that man has a power, literally beyond his comprehension, to destroy. The lethality of some of what he manufactures, the incompetence with which he stores it or seeks to dispose of it, the cavalier way in which he employs in his daily living substances that threaten his health, the leniency of the courts in these matters (as though products as well as people enjoyed the protection of the Fifth Amendment), and the treatment of open land, rivers, and the atmosphere as if, in some medieval way, they could still be regarded as disposal sinks of infinite capacity, would make you wonder, standing face to in the wind at Cape Mendocino, if we weren't bent on an errand of madness.

The geographies of North America, the myriad small landscapes that make up the national fabric, are threatened—by ignorance of what makes them unique, by utilitarian attitudes, by failure to include them in the moral universe, and by brutal disregard. A testament of minor voices can clear away an ignorance of any place, can inform us of its special qualities; but no voice, by merely telling a story, can cause the poisonous wastes that saturate some parts of the land to decompose, to evaporate. This responsibility falls ultimately to the national community, a vague and fragile entity to be sure, but one that, in America, can be ferocious in exerting its will.

Geography, the formal way in which we grapple with this areal mystery, is finally knowledge that calls up something in the land we recognize and respond to. It gives us a sense of place and a sense of community. Both are indispensable to a state of well-being, an individual's and a country's.

One afternoon on the Sīuslaw River in the Coast Range of Oregon, in January, I hooked a steelhead, as sea-run trout, that told me, through the muscles of my hands and arms and shoulders, something of the nature of the thing I was calling "the Sīuslaw River." Years ago I had stood under a pecan tree in Upson County, Georgia, idly eating the nuts, when slowly it occurred to me that these nuts would taste different from pecans growing somewhere up in South Carolina. I didn't need a sharp sense of taste to know this, only to pay attention at a level no one had ever told me was necessary. One November dawn, long before the sun rose, I began a vigil at the Dumont Dunes in the Mojave Desert in California, which I kept until a few minutes after the sun broke the horizon. During that time I named to myself the colors by which the sky changed and by which the sand itself flowed like a rising tide through grays and silvers and blues into yellows, pinks, washed duns, and fallow beiges.

It is through the power of observation, the gifts of eye and ear, of 27 tongue and nose and finger, that a place first rises up in our mind; afterward it is memory that carries the place, that allows it to grow in depth and complexity. For as long as our records go back, we have held these two things dear: landscape and memory. Each infuses us with a different kind of life. The one feeds us, figuratively and literally. The other protects us from lies and tyranny. To keep landscapes intact—and the memory of them, our history in them, alive—seems as imperative a task in modern time as finding the extent to which individual expression can be accommodated, before it threatens to destroy the fabric of society.

If I were now to visit another country, I would ask my local com- 28 panion, before I saw any museum or library, any factory or fabled town, to walk me in the country of his or her youth, to tell me the names of things and how, traditionally, they have been fitted together in a community. I would ask for the stories, the voice of memory over the land. I would ask to taste the wild nuts and fruits, to see their fishing lures, their bouquets, their fences. I would ask about the history of storms there, the age of the trees, the winter color of the hills. Only then would I ask to see the museum. I would want first the sense of a real place, to know that I was not inhabiting an idea. I would want to know the lay of the land first, the real geography, and take some measure of the love of it in my companion before I stood before the paintings or read works of scholarship. I would want to have something real and remembered against which I might hope to measure their truth.

COMPREHENSION

1. According to Lopez, what is the difference between "real" geography and "imagined" geography?
2. What does Lopez mean by the phrase "the concrete details of experience"?
3. What connection does the author make between an intimate knowledge of geography and human survival?

RHETORIC

1. What is the thesis of the essay? Where is it expressed, and what support does Lopez provide for it?

2. What is the tone of Lopez's introductory paragraph? How does it establish the writer's point of view?

3. What is the origin of the phrase "purple mountains' majesty" in paragraph 3? What associations are triggered by its use, and how does it help the writer's argument?

4. In paragraph 4, how does Lopez support his statement about the diversity of America? Do his examples aid the reader's understanding? Would you have added or substituted other examples?

5. How does Lopez use a pattern of definitions to help structure his essay? Cite examples.

6. How do the examples in paragraph 10 contribute to the point being made? Examine the arrangement of examples. What is the significance of the final example?

WRITING

1. Is it possible for technological advances and environmental concerns to coexist, or must one always be sacrificed to the other? Write an essay in which you explore this question.

2. Lopez states, "If you want to know, you must take the time." Do you believe most Americans "take the time" to learn about their landscape? Write an essay examining this attitude and its possible consequences.

3. What role does politics play in a country's attitude toward its land? Use current news events, as well as quotes from Lopez's essay, to develop this theme in an essay.

4. Become a local geographer. Take an hour's walk through an area in your hometown. Then, using its various sights, smells, and sounds, write a descriptive essay in which you particularize this area for the reader.

GEORGE ORWELL   George Orwell (1903–1950) was the pseudonym of Eric Blair, an English novelist, essayist, and journalist. Orwell served with the Indian Imperial Police from 1922 to 1927 in Burma, fought in the Spanish Civil War, and acquired from his experiences a disdain of totalitarian and imperialistic systems. This attitude is reflected in his satiric fable, *Animal Farm* (1945), and in his bleak futuristic novel, *1984* (1949). In this essay, Orwell invokes personal experience to expose the contradictions inherent in British imperialism.

GEORGE ORWELL

Shooting an Elephant

In Moulmein, in Lower Burma, I was hated by large numbers of people—the only time in my life that I have been important enough for this   1 to happen to me. I was subdivisional police officer of the town, and in an aimless, petty kind of way anti-European feeling was very bitter. No one had the guts to raise a riot, but if a European woman went through the bazaars alone somebody would probably spit betel juice over her dress. As a police officer I was an obvious target and was baited whenever it seemed safe to do so. When a nimble Burman tripped me up on the football field and the referee (another Burman) looked the other way, the crowd yelled with hideous laughter. This happened more than once. In the end the sneering yellow faces of young men that met me everywhere, the insults hooted after me when I was at a safe distance, got badly on my nerves. The young Buddhist priests were the worst of all. There were several thousands of them in the town and none of them seemed to have anything to do except stand on street corners and jeer at Europeans.

All this was perplexing and upsetting. For at that time I had already 2 made up my mind that imperialism was an evil thing and the sooner I chucked up my job and got out of it the better. Theoretically—and secretly, of course—I was all for the Burmese and all against their oppressors, the British. As for the job I was doing, I hated it more bitterly than I can perhaps make clear. In a job like that you see the dirty work of Empire at close quarters. The wretched prisoners huddling in the stinking cages of the lock-ups, the grey, cowed faces of the long-term convicts, the scarred buttocks of the men who had been flogged with bamboos—all these oppressed me with an intolerable sense of guilt. But I could get nothing into perspective. I was young and ill-educated and I had had to think out my problems in the utter silence that is imposed on every Englishman in the East. I did not even know that the British Empire is dying, still less did I know that it is a great deal better than the younger empires that are going to supplant it. All I knew was that I was stuck between my hatred of the empire I served and my rage against the evil-spirited little beasts who tried to make my job impossible. With one part of my mind I thought of the British Raj as an unbreakable tyranny, as something clamped down, *in saecula saeculorum,* upon the will of prostrate peoples; with another part I thought that the greatest joy in the world would be to drive a bayonet into a Buddhist priest's guts. Feelings like these are the normal by-products of imperialism; ask any Anglo-Indian official, if you can catch him off duty.

One day something happened which in a roundabout way was 3 enlightening. It was a tiny incident in itself, but it gave me a better glimpse than I had had before of the real nature of imperialism—the real motives for which despotic governments act. Early one morning the sub-inspector at a police station the other end of the town rang me up on the phone and said that an elephant was ravaging the bazaar. Would I please come and do something about it? I did not know what I could do, but I wanted to see what was happening and I got on to a pony and started out. I took my rifle, an old .44 Winchester and much too small to kill an elephant, but I thought the noise might be useful *in terrorem*. Various Burmans stopped me on the way and told me about the elephant's doings. It was not, of course, a wild elephant, but a tame one which had gone "must." It had been chained up as tame elephants always are when their attack of "must" is due, but on the previous night it had broken its chain and escaped. Its mahout, the only person who could manage it when it was in that state, had set out in pursuit, but he had taken the wrong direction and was now twelve hours' journey away, and in the morning the elephant had suddenly reappeared in the town. The Burmese population had no weapons and were quite helpless against it. It had already destroyed somebody's bamboo hut, killed a cow and raided some fruit-stalls and devoured the stock; also it had met the municipal rubbish van, and, when the driver jumped out and took to his heels, had turned the van over and inflicted violence upon it.

The Burmese sub-inspector and some Indian constables were wait- 4 ing for me in the quarter where the elephant had been seen. It was a very poor quarter, a labyrinth of squalid bamboo huts, thatched with palm-leaf, winding all over a steep hillside. I remember that it was a cloudy stuffy morning at the beginning of the rains. We began questioning the people as to where the elephant had gone, and, as usual, failed to get any definite information. That is invariably the case in the East; a story always sounds clear enough at a distance, but the nearer you get to the scene of events the vaguer it becomes. Some of the people said that the elephant had gone in one direction, some said that he had gone in another, some professed not even to have heard of any elephant. I had almost made up my mind that the whole story was a pack of lies, when we heard yells a little distance away. There was a loud, scandalized cry of "Go away, child! Go away this instant!" and an old woman with a switch in her hand came round the corner of a hut, violently shooing away a crowd of naked children. Some more women followed, clicking their tongues and exclaiming; evidently there was something there that the children ought not to have seen. I rounded the hut and saw a man's dead body sprawling in the mud. He was an Indian, a black Dravidian coolie, almost naked, and he could not have been dead many minutes. The people said that the elephant had come suddenly upon him round the corner of the hut, caught him with its trunk, put its foot on his back and ground him into the earth. This was the rainy season and the ground was soft, and his face had scored a trench a foot deep and a couple of yards long. He was lying on his belly with arms crucified and head sharply twisted to one side. His face was coated with mud, the eyes wide open, the teeth bared and grinning with an expression of unendurable agony. (Never tell me, by the way, that the dead look peaceful. Most of the corpses I have seen looked devilish.) The friction of the great beast's foot had stripped the skin from his back as neatly as one skins a rabbit. As soon as I saw the dead man I sent an orderly to a friend's house nearby to borrow an elephant rifle. I had already sent back the pony, not wanting it to go mad with fright and throw me if it smelled the elephant.

The orderly came back in a few minutes with a rifle and five car- 5 tridges, and meanwhile some Burmans had arrived and told us that the elephant was in the paddy fields below, only a few hundred yards away. As I started forward practically the whole population of the quarter flocked out of their houses and followed me. They had seen the rifle and were all shouting excitedly that I was going to shoot the elephant. They had not shown much interest in the elephant when he was merely ravaging their homes, but it was different now that he was going to be shot. It was a bit of fun to them, as it would be to an English crowd; besides, they wanted the meat. It made me vaguely uneasy. I had no intention of shooting the elephant—I had merely sent for the rifle to defend myself if necessary—and it is always unnerving to have a crowd following you. I marched down the hill, looking, and feeling, a fool, with the rifle over my shoulder and an ever-growing army of people jostling at my heels. At the bottom, when you got away from the huts, there was a metalled road and beyond that a miry waste of paddy fields a thousand yards across, not yet ploughed but soggy from the first rains and dotted with coarse grass. The elephant was standing eighty yards from the road, his left side towards us. He took not the slightest notice of the crowd's approach. He was tearing up bunches of grass, beating them against his knees to clean them and stuffing them into his mouth.

I had halted on the road. As soon as I saw the elephant I knew with perfect certainty that I ought not to shoot him. It is a serious matter to shoot a working elephant—it is comparable to destroying a huge and costly piece of machinery—and obviously one ought not to do it if it can possibly be avoided. And at a distance, peacefully eating, the elephant looked no more dangerous than a cow. I thought then and I think now that his attack of "must" was already passing off; in which case he would merely wander harmlessly about until the mahout came back and caught him. Moreover, I did not in the least want to shoot him. I decided that I would watch him for a little while to make sure that he did not turn savage again, and then go home.

But at that moment I glanced round at the crowd that had followed me. It was an immense crowd, two thousand at the least and growing every minute. It blocked the road for a long distance on either side. I looked at the sea of yellow faces above the garish clothes—faces all happy and excited over this bit of fun, all certain that the elephant was going to be shot. They were watching me as they would watch a conjuror about to perform a trick. They did not like me, but with the magical rifle in my hands I was momentarily worth watching. And suddenly I realised that I should have to shoot the elephant after all. The people expected it of me and I had got to do it; I could feel their two thousand wills pressing me forward, irresistibly. And it was at this moment, as I stood there with the rifle in my hands, that I first grasped the hollowness, the futility of the white man's dominion in the East. Here was I, the white man with his gun, standing in front of the unarmed native crowd—seemingly the leading actor of the piece, but in reality I was only an absurd puppet pushed to and fro by the will of those yellow faces behind. I perceived in this moment that when the white man turns tyrant it is his own freedom that he destroys. He becomes a sort of hollow, posing dummy, the conventionalised figure of a sahib. For it is the condition of his rule that he shall spend his life in trying to impress the "natives" and so in every crisis he has got to do what the "natives" expect of him. He wears a mask, and his face grows to fit it. I had got to shoot the elephant. I had committed myself to doing it when I sent for the rifle. A sahib has got to act like a sahib; he has got to appear resolute, to know his own mind and do definite things. To come all that way, rifle in hand, with two thousand people marching at my heels, and then to trail feebly away, having done nothing—no, that was impossible. The crowd would laugh at me. And my whole life, every white man's life in the East, was one long struggle not to be laughed at.

But I did not want to shoot the elephant. I watched him beating his ⁸ bunch of grass against his knees, with that preoccupied grandmotherly air that elephants have. It seemed to me that it would be murder to shoot him. At that age I was not squeamish about killing animals, but I had never shot an elephant and never wanted to. (Somehow it always seems worse to kill a *large* animal.) Besides, there was the beast's owner to be considered. Alive, the elephant was worth at least a hundred pounds; dead, he would only be worth the value of his tusks—five pounds, possibly. But I had got to act quickly. I turned to some experi-enced-looking Burmans who had been there when we arrived, and asked them how the elephant had been behaving. They all said the same thing: he took no notice of you if you left him alone, but he might charge if you went too close to him.

It was perfectly clear to me what I ought to do. I ought to walk up ⁹ to within, say, twenty-five yards of the elephant and test his behaviour. If he charged I could shoot, if he took no notice of me it would be safe to leave him until the mahout came back. But also I knew that I was going to do no such thing. I was a poor shot with a rifle and the ground was soft mud into which one would sink at every step. If the elephant charged and I missed him, I should have about as much chance as a toad under a steam-roller. But even then I was not thinking particularly of my own skin, only the watchful yellow faces behind. For at that moment, with the crowd watching me, I was not afraid in the ordinary sense, as I would have been if I had been alone. A white man mustn't be frightened in front of "natives"; and so, in general, he isn't fright-ened. The sole thought in my mind was that if anything went wrong those two thousand Burmans would see me pursued, caught, trampled on and reduced to a grinning corpse like that Indian up the hill. And if that happened it was quite probable that some of them would laugh. That would never do. There was only one alternative. I shoved the car-tridges into the magazine and lay down on the road to get a better aim.

The crowd grew very still, and a deep, low, happy sigh, as of people ¹⁰ who see the theatre curtain go up at last, breathed from innumerable throats. They were going to have their bit of fun after all. The rifle was a beautiful German thing with cross-hair sights. I did not then know that in shooting an elephant one should shoot to cut an imaginary bar running from ear-hole to ear-hole. I ought therefore, as the elephant was sideways on, to have aimed straight at his ear-hole; actually I aimed several inches in front of this, thinking the brain would be further forward.

When I pulled the trigger I did not hear the bang or feel the kick— one never does when a shot goes home—but I heard the devilish roar of glee that went up from the crowd. In that instant, in too short a time, one would have thought, even for the bullet to get there, a mysterious, terrible change had come over the elephant. He neither stirred nor fell, but every line of his body had altered. He looked suddenly stricken, shrunken, immensely old, as though the frightful impact of the bullet had paralysed him without knocking him down. At last, after what seemed a long time—it might have been five seconds, I dare say—he sagged flabbily to his knees. His mouth slobbered. An enormous senility seemed to have settled upon him. One could have imagined him thousands of years old. I fired again into the same spot. At the second shot he did not collapse but climbed with desperate slowness to his feet and stood weakly upright, with legs sagging and head drooping. I fired a third time. That was the shot that did for him. You could see the agony of it jolt his whole body and knock the last remnant of strength from his legs. But in falling he seemed for a moment to rise, for as his hind legs collapsed beneath him he seemed to tower upwards like a huge rock toppling, his trunk reaching skyward like a tree. He trumpeted, for the first and only time. And then down he came, his belly towards me, with a crash that seemed to shake the ground even where I lay.

I got up. The Burmans were already racing past me across the mud. It was obvious that the elephant would never rise again, but he was not dead. He was breathing very rhythmically with long rattling gasps, his great mound of a side painfully rising and falling. His mouth was wide open—I could see far down into caverns of pale pink throat. I waited a long time for him to die, but his breathing did not weaken. Finally I fired my two remaining shots into the spot where I thought his heart must be. The thick blood welled out of him like red velvet, but still he did not die. His body did not even jerk when the shots hit him, the tortured breathing continued without a pause. He was dying, very slowly and in great agony, but in some world remote from me where not even a bullet could damage him further. I felt that I had got to put an end to that dreadful noise. It seemed dreadful to see the great beast lying there, powerless to move and yet powerless to die, and not even to be able to finish him. I sent back for my small rifle and poured shot after shot into his heart and down his throat. They seemed to make no impression. The tortured gasps continued as steadily as the ticking of a clock.

In the end I could not stand it any longer and went away. I heard later that it took him half an hour to die. Burmans were arriving with dahs and baskets even before I left, and I was told they had stripped his body almost to the bones by the afternoon.

Afterwards, of course, there were endless discussions about the 14 shooting of the elephant. The owner was furious, but he was only an Indian and could do nothing. Besides, legally I had done the right thing, for a mad elephant has to be killed, like a mad dog, if its owner fails to control it. Among the Europeans opinion was divided. The older men said I was right, the younger men said it was a damn shame to shoot an elephant for killing a coolie, because an elephant was worth more than any damn Coringhee coolie. And afterwards I was very glad that the coolie had been killed; it put me legally in the right and it gave me a sufficient pretext for shooting the elephant. I often wondered whether any of the others grasped that I had done it solely to avoid looking a fool.

COMPREHENSION

1. State in your own words the thesis of this essay.

2. How does the shooting of the elephant give Orwell a better understanding of "the real nature of imperialism—the real motives for which despotic governments act" (paragraph 3)? Why does Orwell kill the elephant? What is his attitude toward the Burmese people?

3. Why does Orwell concentrate on the prolonged death of the elephant? What effect does it have?

RHETORIC

1. How would you describe the level of language in the essay? Point to specific words, sentences, and phrases to support your answer.

2. Define *supplant* (paragraph 2); *labyrinth* (paragraph 4); *jostling* (paragraph 5); *conjuror* (paragraph 7); *and senility* (paragraph 11).

3. What is the function of the first two paragraphs? Where is the thesis stated in the essay?

4. Analyze Orwell's use of dramatic techniques to develop the narrative. Examine consecutive paragraphs in the essay to determine the author's presentation of action from different perspectives. What other essays in this chapter strike you as dramatic, and why?

5. Select and analyze some of the details in the essay that are designed to impress the reader's senses and emotions. Why does Orwell rely so heavily on the presentation and accumulation of detail in the essay?

6. How is the entire essay structured by irony of situation and paradox? How do these devices relate to the ethical issues raised by Orwell?

WRITING

1. In this essay, written in 1936, Orwell declares: "I did not even know that the British Empire is dying, still less did I know that it is a great deal better than the younger empires that are going to supplant it" (paragraph 2). In what ways is Orwell's statement prophetic?

2. Write a narrative essay about an episode in your life that brought you into conflict with social or political forces.
3. For a research project, consult library sources, and then write a report, employing proper documentation, on the importance of Orwell as an essayist.

ELIZABETH HARDWICK   Elizabeth Hardwick, who was born in Lexington, Kentucky, in 1916, received her bachelor's and master's degrees from the University of Kentucky. Drawn to the intellectual and literary life of New York City, she soon made a name for herself there as a novelist; essayist; and literary, theatrical, and cultural critic. She writes regularly for the *Partisan Review, The New Republic,* and *The New York Review of Books* as well as for a number of newspapers. Her essays have been published in various collections over three decades. One critic called her "the voice of toughminded gentility." Evidence of this voice is apparent in the following essay, first published in *Harper's Magazine* in 1959.

ELIZABETH HARDWICK

Boston: The Lost Ideal

With Boston and its mysteriously enduring reputation, "the reverbera-   1
tion is longer than the thunderclap," as Emerson observed about the tenacious fame of certain artists. Boston—wrinkled, spindlylegged, depleted of nearly all her spiritual and cutaneous oils, provincial, self-esteeming—has gone on spending and spending her inflated bills of pure reputation decade after decade. Now, one supposes it is all over at last. The old jokes embarrass, the anecdotes are so many thrice-squeezed lemons, and no new fruit hangs on the boughs.

All the American regions are breaking up, ground down to a stan-   2
dard American corn meal. And why not Boston, which would have been the most difficult to maintain? There has never been anything quite like Boston as a creation of the American imagination, or perhaps one should say as a creation of the American scene. Some of the legend was once real, surely. Our utilitarian, fluid landscape has produced a handful of regional conceptions, popular images, brief and naked; the conservative Vermonter, the boastful Texan, the honeyed Southerner. "Graciousness is ours," brays a coarsened South; and the sheiks of Texas cruise around in their desert.

The Boston image is more complex. The city is felt to have, in the   3
end, a pure and special nature, absurd no doubt but somehow valuable. An author can hardly fail to turn a penny or two on this magical sub-

ject. Everyone will consent to be informed on it, to be slyly entertained by it. The image lends itself to exaggerations, to dreams of social and ethnic purity, to notions of grand old families still existing as grand old families are supposed to exist. *Actual* Boston, the living city, is governed largely by people of Irish descent and more and more, recently, by men of Italian descent. Not long ago, the old Yankee, Senator Saltonstall, remarked wistfully that there were still a good many Anglo-Saxons in Massachusetts, his own family among them. Extinction is foreshadowed in the defense.

Plainness and pretension restlessly feuding and combining; wealth 4
and respectability and firmness of character ending in the production of a number of diverting individual tics or, at the best, instances of high culture. Something of that sort is the legendary Boston soul or so one supposes without full confidence because the old citizens of Boston vehemently hold to the notion that the city and their character are ineffable, unknowable. When asked for an opinion on the admirable novel, *Boston Adventure,* or even the light social history, *The Proper Bostonians,* the answer invariably comes, "Not Boston." The descriptive intelligence, the speculative mind, the fresh or even the merely open eye are felt to discover nothing but errors here, be they errors of praise or censure. Still, wrong-headedness flourishes, the subject fascinates, and the Athenaeum's list of written productions on this topic is nearly endless.

The best book on Boston is Henry James's novel, *The Bostonians.* By 5
the bald and bold use of the place name, the unity of situation and person is dramatized. But poor James, of course, was roundly and importantly informed by everyone, including his brother William, that this too was "not Boston," and, stricken, he pushed aside a superb creation, and left the impregnable, unfathomable Boston to its mysteries. James's attitude toward the city's intellectual consequence and social charm is one of absolute impiety. A view of the Charles River reveals ". . . an horizon indented at empty intervals with wooden spires, the masts of lonely boats, the chimneys of dirty 'works,' over a brackish expanse of anomalous character, which is too big for a river and too small for a bay." A certain house has "a peculiar look of being both new and faded—a kind of modern fatigue—like certain articles of commerce which are sold at a reduction as shopworn." However, there is little natural landscape in James's novel. The picture is, rather, of the psychological Boston of the 1870s, a confused scene, slightly mad with neurotic repressions, provincialism, and earnestness without intellectual seriousness.

James's view of Boston is not the usual one, although his irony and 6
dissatisfaction are shared by Henry Adams, who says that "a simpler manner of life and thought could hardly exist, short of cave-dwelling," and by Santayana who spoke of Boston as a "moral and intellectual nursery, always busy applying first principles to trifles." The great majority of the writings on Boston are in another spirit altogether—frankly unctuous, for the town has always attracted men of quiet and timid and tasteful opinion, men interested in old families and things, in the charms of times recently past, collectors of anecdotes about those

Boston worthies hardly anyone can still clearly identify, men who spoke and preached and whose style and fame deteriorated quickly. Rufus Choate, Dr. Channing, Edward Everett Hale, Phillips Brooks, and Theodore Parker: names that remain in one's mind, without producing an image or a fact, as the marks are left on the wall after the picture has been removed. William Dean Howells held a more usual view than Henry James or Adams or Santayana. Indeed Howells' original enthusiasm for garden and edifice, person and setting, is more than a little *exalté*. The first sight of the Chapel at Mount Auburn Cemetery moved him more than the "Acropolis, Westminster Abbey, and Santa Croce in one." The massive, gray stones of "the Public Library and the Athenaeum are hardly eclipsed by the Vatican and the Pitti." And so on.

The importance of Boston was intellectual and as its intellectual [7] donations to the country have diminished, so it has declined from its lofty symbolic meaning, to become a more lowly image, a sort of farce of conservative exclusiveness and snobbish humor. Marquand's George Apley is a figure of the decline—fussy, sentimental, farcically mannered, archaic. He cannot be imagined as an Abolitionist, an author, a speaker; he is merely a "character," a very idiosyncratic and simpleminded one. The old Boston had something of the spirit of Bloomsbury: clannish, worldly, and intellectually serious. About the historian, Prescott, Van Wyck Brooks could say, ". . . for at least ten years, Prescott had been hard at work, harder, perhaps, than any Boston merchant."

History, indeed, with its long, leisurely, gentlemanly labors, the [8] books arriving by post, the cards to be kept and filed, the sections to be copied, the documents to be checked, is the ideal pursuit for the New England mind. All the Adamses spent a good deal of their lives on one kind of history or another. The eccentricity, studiousness, and study-window slow pace of life of the historical gentleman lay everywhere about the Boston scene. For money, society, fashion, extravagance, one went to New York. But now, the descendants of the old, intellectual aristocracy live in the respectable suburbs and lead the healthy, restless, outdoor life that atrophies the sedentary nerves of culture. The bluestocking, the eccentric, the intransigent bring a blush of uncertainty and embarrassment to the healthy young couple's cheek.

Boston today can still provide a fairly stimulating atmosphere for the [1] banker, the broker, for doctors and lawyers. "Open end" investments prosper, the fish come in at the dock, the wool market continues, and workers are employed in the shoe factories in the nearby towns. For the engineer, the physicist, the industrial designer, for all the highly trained specialists of the electronic age, Boston and its area are of seemingly unlimited promise. Sleek, well-designed factories and research centers pop up everywhere; the companies plead, in the Sunday papers, for more chemists, more engineers, and humbly relate the executive benefits of salary and pension and advancement they are prepared to offer.

But otherwise, for the artist, the architect, the composer, the writer, ₂
the philosopher, the historian, for those humane pursuits for which the
town was once noted and even for the delights of entertainment, for
dancing, acting, cooking, Boston is a bewildering place. There is, first
of all, the question of Boston or New York. (The question is not new;
indeed it was answered in the last decades of the last century in favor
of New York as the cultural center of America.) It is, in our day, only a
private and personal question: where or which of the two Eastern cities
should one try to live and work in? It is a one-sided problem. For the
New Yorker, San Francisco or Florida, perhaps—Boston, never. In
Boston, New York tantalizes; one of the advantages of Boston is said,
wistfully, to be its nearness to New York. It is a bad sign when a man
who has come to Boston or Cambridge, Massachusetts, from another
place begins to show an undivided acceptance of his new town. Smug-
ness is the great vice of the two places. Between puffy self-satisfaction
and the fatiguing wonder if one wouldn't be happier, more productive,
more appreciated in New York a thoughtful man makes his choice.

Boston is not a small New York, as they say a child is not a small ₃
adult but is, rather, a specially organized small creature with its small-
creature's temperature, balance, and distribution of fat. In Boston there
is an utter absence of that wild electric beauty of New York, of the marvelous, excited rush of people in taxicabs at twilight, of the great
Avenues and Streets, the restaurants, theatres, bars, hotels, deli-
catessens, shops. In Boston the night comes down with an incredibly
heavy, small-town finality. The cows come home; the chickens go to
roost; the meadow is dark. Nearly every Bostonian is in his own house
or in someone else's house, dining at the home board, enjoying domestic and social privacy. The "nice little dinner party"—for this the
Bostonian would sell his soul. In the evenings, the old "accommoda-
tors" dart about the city, carrying their black uniforms and white
aprons in a paper bag. They are on call to go, anywhere, to cook and
serve dinners. Many of these women are former cooks and maids, now
living on Social Security retirement pensions, supplemented by the fees
for these evening "accommodations" to the community. Their style and
the bland respectability of their cuisine keep up the social tone of the
town. They are like those old slaves who stuck to their places and, even
in the greatest deprivation, graciously went on toting things to the
Massa.

There is a curious flimsiness and indifference in the commercial life ₄
of Boston. The restaurants are, charitably, to be called mediocre, the
famous sea food is only palatable when raw. Otherwise it usually has to
endure the deep-fry method that makes everything taste like those
breaded pork chops of the Middle West, which in turn taste like the
fried sole of Boston. Here, French restaurants quickly become tea-
roomy, as if some sort of rapid naturalization had taken place. There is
not a single attractive eating place on the water front. An old downtown
restaurant of considerable celebrity, LockeOber's, has been expanded,
let out, and "costumed" by one of the American restaurant decorators

whose productions have a ready-made look, as if the designs had been chosen from a catalogue. But for the purest eccentricity, there is the "famous" restaurant, DurginPark, which is run like a boarding house in a mining town. And so it goes.

Downtown Boston at night is a dreary jungle of honky-tonks for sailors, dreary department-store windows, Loew's movie houses, hill-billy bands, strippers, parking lots, undistinguished new buildings. Mid-town Boston—small, expensive shops, the inevitable Elizabeth Arden and Helena Rubinstein "salons," Brooks Brothers—is deserted at night, except for people going in and out of the Ritz Carlton Hotel, the only public place in Boston that could be called "smart." The merchandise in the Newbury Street shops is designed in a high fashion, elaborate, furred and sequined, but it is never seen anywhere. Perhaps it is for out-of-town use, like a traveling man's mistress.

Just as there is no smart life, so there is no Soho, no Greenwich Vil-lage. Recently a man was murdered in a parking lot in the Chinatown area. His address was given as the South End, a lowerclass section, and he was said to be a free-spender, making enough money as a summer bartender on Cape Cod to lead a free-wheeling life the rest of the year. One paper referred to the unfortunate man as a "member of the Bea-con Hill Bohemia set." This designation is of considerable interest because there is no "Bohemia" in Boston, neither upper nor lower; the detergent of bourgeois Boston cleans everything, effortlessly, com-pletely. If there *were* a Bohemia, its members would indeed live on Bea-con Hill, the most beautiful part of Boston and, like the older parts of most cities, fundamentally classless, providing space for the rich in the noble mansions and for the people with little money in the run-down alleys. For both of these groups the walled gardens of Beacon Hill, the mews, the coach houses, the river views, the cobblestone streets are a necessity and the yellow-brick, sensible structures of the Fenway—a plausible but unpoetical residential section near the Art Museum—are poison. Espresso bars have sprung up, or rather dug down in base-ments, but no summer of wild Bohemia is ushered into town. This reluctance is due to the Boston legend and its endurance as a lost ideal, a romantic quest.

Something transcendental is always expected in Boston. There is, one imagines, behind the drapery on Mount Vernon Street a person of democratic curiosity and originality of expression, someone alas—and this is the tiresome Boston note—*well-born*. It is likely to be, even in imagination, a she, since women now and not the men provide the links with the old traditions. Of her, then, one expects a certain unprofes-sionalism, but it is not expected that she will be superficial; she is pro-foundly conventional in manner of life but capable of radical insights. To live in Boston means to seek some connection with this famous local excellence, the regional type and special creation of the city. An angry disappointment attends the romantic soul bent upon this quest. When the archaeological diggings do turn up an authentic specimen it will be someone old, nearly gone, "whom you should have known when she was young"—and still could hear.

The younger Bostonians seem in revolt against the old excellence, with its indulgent, unfettered development of the self. Revolt, however, is too active a word for a passive failure to perpetuate the ideal high-mindedness and intellectual effort. With the fashionable young women of Boston, one might just as well be on Long Island. Only in the nervous, shy, earnest women is there a lingering hint of the peculiar local development. Terrible *faux pas* are constantly being made by this reasonable, honorable person, followed by blushes and more false steps and explanations and the final blinking, retreating blush.

Among the men, the equivalent of the blushing, blurting, sensitive, and often "fine" woman, is a person who exists everywhere perhaps but nowhere else with such elaboration of type, such purity of example. This is the well-born failure, the amateur not by choice but from some fatal reticence of temperament. They are often descendants of intellectual Boston, odd-ball grandsons, charming and sensitive, puzzlingly complicated, living on a "small income." These unhappy men carry on their conscience the weight of unpublished novels, half-finished paintings, impossible historical projects, old-fashioned poems, unproduced plays. Their inevitable "small income" is a sort of dynastic flaw, like hemophilia. Much money seems often to impose obligations of energetic management; from great fortunes the living cells receive the hints of the possibilities of genuine power, enough to make some enormously rich Americans endure the humiliations and fatigues of political office. Only the most decadent and spoiled think of living in idleness on millions; but this notion does occur to the man afflicted with ten thousand a year. He will commit himself with a dreamy courage to whatever traces of talent he may have and live to see himself punished by the New England conscience which demands accomplishments, duties performed, responsibilities noted, and energies sensibly used. The dying will accuses and the result is a queer kind of Boston incoherence. It is literally impossible much of the time to tell what some of the most attractive men in Boston are talking about. Half-uttered witticisms, grave and fascinating obfuscations, points incredibly qualified, hesitations infinitely refined—one staggers about, charmed and confused, by the twilight.

But this person, with his longings, connects with the old possibilities and, in spite of his practical failure, keeps alive the memory of the best days. He may have a brother who has retained the mercantile robustness of nature and easy capacity for action and yet has lost all belief in anything except money and class, who may practice private charities, but entertain profoundly trivial national and world views. A Roosevelt, Harriman, or Stevenson is impossible to imagine as a member of the Boston aristocracy; in Boston the vein of self-satisfaction and conservatism cuts too deeply.

Harvard (across the river in Cambridge) and Boston are two ends of one mustache. Harvard is now so large and international it has altogether avoided the whimsical stagnation of Boston. But the two places need each other, as we knowingly say of a mismatched couple. Without the faculty, the visitors, the events that Harvard brings to the life here, Boston would be intolerable to anyone except genealogists, antique dealers, and those who find repletion in a closed local society. Unfortunately, Harvard, like Boston, has "tradition" and in America this always carries with it the risk of a special staleness of attitude, and of pride, incredibly and comically swollen like the traits of hypocrisy, selfishness, or lust in the old dramas. At Harvard some of the vices of "society" exist, of Boston society that is—arrogance and the blinding dazzle of being, *being at Harvard.*

The moral and social temptations of Harvard's unique position in American academic life are great and the pathos is seen in those young faculty members who are presently at Harvard but whose appointments are not permanent and so they may be thrown down, banished from the beatific condition. The young teacher in this position lives in a dazed state of love and hatred, pride and fear; their faces have a look of desperate yearning, for they would rather serve in heaven than reign in hell. For those who are not banished, for the American at least, since the many distinguished foreigners at Harvard need not endure these piercing and fascinating complications, something of Boston seems to seep into their characters. They may come from anywhere in America and yet to be at Harvard unites them with the transcendental, legendary Boston, with New England in flower. They begin to revere the old worthies, the houses, the paths trod by so many before, and they feel a throb of romantic sympathy for the directly-gazing portraits on the walls, for the old graves and old names in the Mount Auburn Cemetery. All of this has charm and may even have a degree of social and intellectual value—and then again it may not. Devious parochialisms, irrelevant snobberies, a bemused exaggeration of one's own productions, pimple the soul of a man upholding tradition in a forest of relaxation, such as most of America is thought to be. Henry James's observation in his book on Hawthorne bears on this:

> It is only in a country where newness and change and brevity of tenure are the common substance of life, that the fact of one's ancestors having lived for a hundred and seventy years in a single spot would become an element of one's morality. It is only an imaginative American that would feel urged to keep reverting to this circumstance, to keep analyzing and cunningly considering it.

If the old things of Boston are too heavy and plushy, the new either hasn't been born or is appallingly shabby and poor. As early as Thanksgiving, Christmas decorations unequaled for cheap ugliness go up in the Public Garden and on the Boston Common. Year after year,

89

the city fathers bring out crèches and camels and Mother and Child so badly made and of such tasteless colors they verge on blasphemy, or would seem to do so if it were not for the equally dismal, although secular, little men blowing horns and the canes of peppermint hanging on the lamps. The shock of the first sight is the most interesting; later the critical senses are stilled as year after year the same bits are brought forth and gradually one realizes that the whole thing is a permanent exhibition.

Recently the dying downtown shopping section of Boston was to be graced with flowers, an idea perhaps in imitation of the charming potted geraniums and tulips along Fifth Avenue in New York. Commercial Boston produced a really amazing display: old, gray square bins, in which were stuck a few bits of yellowing, drying evergreen. It had the look of exhausted greenery thrown out in the garbage and soon the dust-bins were full of other bits of junk and discard—people had not realized or recognized the decorative hope and saw only the rubbishy result.

The municipal, civic backwardness of Boston does not seem to bother its more fortunate residents. For them and for the observer, Boston's beauty is serene and private, an enclosed, intense personal life, rich with domestic variation, interesting stuffs and things, showing the hearthside vitality of a Dutch genre painting. Of an evening the spirits quicken, not to public entertainment, but instead to the sights behind the draperies, the glimpses of drawing-rooms on Louisburg Square, paneled walls, and French chandeliers on Commonwealth Avenue, bookshelves and flower-filled bays on Beacon Street. Boston is a winter city. Every apartment has a fireplace. In the town houses, old persons climb steps without complaint, four or five floors of them, cope with the maintenance of roof and gutter, and survive the impractical kitchen and resign themselves to the useless parlors. This is life: the house, the dinner party, the charming gardens, one's high ceilings, fine windows, lacy grillings, magnolia trees, inside shutters, glassed-in studios on the top of what were once stables, outlook on the "river side." Setting is serious.

When it is not serious, when a splendid old private house passes into less dedicated hands, an almost exuberant swiftness of deterioration can be noticed. A rooming house, although privately owned, is no longer in the purest sense a private house and soon it partakes of some of the reckless, ugly municipal neglect. The contrasts are startling. One of two houses of almost identical exterior design will have shining windows, a bright brass door-knocker, and its twin will show a "Rooms" sign peering out of dingy glass, curtained by those lengths of flowered plastic used in the shower bath. Garbage lies about in the alleys behind the rooming houses, discarded furniture blocks old garden gateways. The vulnerability of Boston's way of life, the meanness of most things that fall outside the needs of the upper classes are shown with a bleak and terrible fullness in the rooming houses on Beacon Street. And even some of the best houses show a spirit of mere "maintenance," which, while useful for the individual with money, leads to civic dullness, architectural torpor, and stagnation. In the Back Bay area, a voluntary, casual association of property owners exists for the purpose of trying to keep the alleys clean, the streets lighted beyond their present medieval darkness, and to pursue other worthy items of neighborhood value. And yet this same group will "protest" against the attractive Café Florian on Newbury Street (smell of coffee too strong!) and against the brilliantly exciting Boston Arts Festival held in the beautiful Public Garden for two weeks in June. The idea that Boston might be a vivacious, convenient place to live in is not uppermost in most residents' thoughts. Trying to buy groceries in the best sections of the Back Bay region is an interesting study in commercial apathy.

A great many of the young Bostonians leave town, often taking off with a sullen demand for a freer, more energetic air. And yet many of them return later, if not to the city itself, to the beautiful sea towns and old villages around it. For the city itself, who will live in it after the present human landmarks are gone? No doubt, some of the young people there at the moment will persevere, and as a reward for their fidelity and endurance will themselves later become monuments, old types interesting to students of what our colleges call American Civilization. Boston is defective, out-of-date, vain, and lazy, but if you're not in a hurry it has a deep, secret appeal. Or, more accurately, those who like it may make of its appeal a secret. The weight of the Boston legend, the tedium of its largely fraudulent posture of traditionalism, the disillusionment of the Boston present as a cultural force, make quick minds hesitate to embrace a region so deeply compromised. They are on their guard against falling for it, but meanwhile they can enjoy its very defects, its backwardness, its slowness, its position as one of the large, possible cities on the Eastern seacoast, its private, residential charm. They speak of going to New York and yet another season finds them holding back, positively enjoying the Boston life. . . .

. . . Outside it is winter, dark. The curtains are drawn, the wood is on the fire, the table has been checked, and in the stillness one waits for the guests who come stamping in out of the snow. There are lectures in Cambridge, excellent concerts in Symphony Hall, bad plays being tried out for the hungry sheep of Boston before going to the hungry sheep of New York. Arnold Toynbee or T. S. Eliot or Robert Frost or Robert Oppenheimer or Barbara Ward is in town again. The cars are double-parked so thickly along the narrow streets that a moving vehicle can scarcely maneuver; the pedestrians stumble over the cobbles; in the back alleys a cat cries and the rats, enormously fat, run in front of the car lights creeping into the parking spots. Inside it is cozy, Victorian, and gossipy. Someone else has *not* been kept on at Harvard. The old Irish "accommodator" puffs up stairs she had never seen before a few hours previously and announces that dinner is ready. A Swedish journalist is just getting off the train at the Back Bay Station. He has been exhausted by cocktails, reality, life, taxis, telephones, bad connections in New York and Chicago, pulverized by "a good time." Sighing, he alights, seeking old Boston, a culture that hasn't been alive for a long time . . . and rest.

COMPREHENSION

1. What are the major differences between the "idealized" Boston and the contemporary city it has become?
2. Who is the intended audience of this essay—for example, Bostonians, the general public, the educated reader, the informed traveler? How does the level of diction in the essay help determine the audience?
3. What is the attitude of the writer toward her subject? Does she feel angry, betrayed, superior, disappointed? Or is her role that of the objective reporter? What elements of the writing led you to your conclusion?

RHETORIC

1. There is a plethora of places and names in the essay; for example, in paragraph 6, the author refers to nine personages and two locales. What assumptions is the author making about her intended audience by making the essay replete with these references?
2. The essay is divided into five parts, separated by space. How does this structure relate to the essay as a whole? Pay particular attention to the final and first lines of each segment for clues regarding this structural device.
3. Hardwick has a penchant for using the rhetorical device of the *series* (a sentence that describes three or more things or actions) in her essay. For example, in paragraph 1, she states, "The old jokes embarrass, the anecdotes are so many thrice-squeezed lemons, and no new fruit hangs on the boughs." Explore this device throughout the essay. How does it contribute to the author's style?
4. Another device favored by the author is the image. For example, in paragraph 5 of section 2, she says, "Downtown Boston at night is a dreary jungle of honky-tonks" and in paragraph 6 she states "the detergent of bourgeois Boston cleans everything." Locate five other uses of imagery in the essay. How do they contribute to the overall style?
5. The author focuses one section of her essay on Harvard University. How does she distinguish life at Harvard from the general tenor of Bostonian life? Is she positive or negative toward the Harvard students' and professors' attitudes? Where and how does she express this distinction?
6. The author uses several direct quotations from other observers of Boston. What is her purpose in including these quotations? Study the writing of the quotations. How similar are their styles to the author's style?
7. The level of the author's diction is not that of everyday speech. Take, for example, the following sentence from paragraph 2 in section IV: "Devious parochialisms, irrelevant snobberies, a bemused exaggeration of one's own productions, pimple the soul of a man upholding tradition in a forest of

relaxation." What does this sentence mean within the context of the paragraph? What makes the language "literary"?

WRITING

1. A *glossary* is a type of specialized dictionary to explain terms in a piece of writing that are uncommon or generally unfamiliar. Underline all the words, people, and sites in this essay with which you are not familiar. Look them up in reference books, and write a glossary for the essay.
2. Argue for or against the proposition that "Boston: The Lost Ideal" is an essay for a particular type of audience and not suitable for the general public. Be sure to use standard argumentation, with a thesis, supporting points, and examples.
3. Think of a time in your life when you had a high expectation of a person, place, event, or thing and were betrayed or "let down" by your anticipation. Title your essay "Betrayed by ———," with the blank filled in by the circumstance or locale of the betrayal.

PICO IYER   Pico Iyer was born in Oxford, England, and educated at Eton, Oxford, and Harvard. He now lives in Santa Barbara, California. A correspondent for *Time* magazine, Iyer also contributes articles and reviews to *Partisan Review,* the *Village Voice,* and numerous other publications. His book *Video Night in Kathmandu* (1988) places Iyer in the forefront of contemporary travel writers. In the following essay, Iyer trains his camera-sharp eye on one Asian nation in order to offer a comparative assessment of culture.

PICO IYER

Vietnam: A Delicate Innocence

In Hue, the gracious, reticent capital of old Vietnam, I drifted one morning, by sampan, down to the Linh Mu pagoda, its gardens scented with orchids, frangipani, and jackfruit and scattered with a flutter of white and crimson butterflies. Monks with girlish faces ushered me into the kitchen, where eleven-year-old novices, tassel-haired, were slicing vegetables and stoking fires. Then, over tea and green bean cake, the head abbot, smiling-eyed, told me about how Buddhism had long been suppressed in his country and pointed out to me the grayish Austin, sitting neatly in the temple garden, in which a monk from the pagoda had driven to Saigon to immolate himself in 1963. Later that day, I walked around the lakeside pavilion where the emperor Tu Duc had once composed poems, sipped lotus tea, and dallied with his 104 courtesans; I wandered into the shaded, pink-walled French colonial school where Ho Chi Minh, General Vo Nguyen Giap, and former prime minister Ngo Dinh Diem had all been educated (and, as ever in Hue, felt as if I were walking through an avenue of smiles); and that night I returned to the kind of lyric pleasures that I had come to expect in Vietnam—the couples gathered in cafés along the waterside, sitting on wicker chairs, their glasses balanced on stones, watching the lights on the river while a syrupy female singer softened the night.

In Hue, watching the famous local beauties, flowerlike in their traditional *ao dais*, bicycling with queenly serenity the bridge across the Perfume River, long hair falling to their waists and pink parasols held up against the sun, I felt that here was a scene that could move even a journalist to poetry. Just one week later, to my astonishment, I read in Morley Safer's *Flashbacks* that even this most hard-headed of investigative journalists had, he confessed, written a poem in Hue (which "mercifully [he had] both lost and forgotten"). 2

A few days later, I found myself inside the busiest and brashest circus I had ever seen. Saigon could be called Scooter City, the home of the Motorcycle Revolution, a 350 cc Beijing. For, every weekend night, all the bright young things of town dress up in their Sunday best, get onto their bikes, and start racing and roaring around the central streets, swerving in and out of packs, speeding along in swarms; girls in cocktail dresses, boys in white shirts and ties, whole families on a single scooter, teenagers in denim skirts, even demure old gray-haired couples, all of them roaring around and around and around, past high-rise murals that say "To Keep Money in the Bank Is Patriotic," past packs of others lined up along the sidewalks, the whole group of them enacting a kind of crazy, revved-up *thé dansant* on wheels. 3

The feverish carnival atmosphere was like nothing I had ever known before: In Italian towns, teenagers famously promenade around the main plaza in the evenings, exchanging glances and flirtations, but here the whole ritual was speeded up, intensified, and played out at top volume, half of Saigon caught up in this surging mass, trading smiles as they went, catching the eyes of strangers, or simply exulting in a literal version of their brand-new motto of *song voi*, or "living fast." It seemed an almost perfect metaphor for the sudden explosion of energy and excitement in Saigon, as sharp as if a rubber band, stretched out for fifteen years, had suddenly snapped back, and with a vengeance. 4

As the night wore on, the feverish sense of abandon grew ever more surreal. Somehow, in Saigon it is always 9:30 at night in some flashy, shady dive, and a chanteuse in a sequined microskirt is belting out "I'm on the top of the world, looking down on creation . . ." to the accompaniment of violins and cellos played by girls in shocking pink miniskirts. 5

Vietnam, to me, seemed two distinct, almost contradictory, countries: Saigon (Ho Chi Minh City) and the rest. And almost anything I might say about the one would be contradicted by the other. In part, of course, this reflects nothing more than the universal disjunction 6 between big city and unspoiled countryside, equally apparent around New York, Paris, Buenos Aires, and Bangkok. In part, it reflects merely the geography of a country that was divided into two—twenty years ago and two hundred years ago. Hanoi is as far north of Ho Chi Minh City as Boston is of Charleston, and the character, the pace, and even the climate of the quiet, unshowy northern capital bear little relation to the helter-skelter, anything-goes vitality of the south (in ten days in the north, I never saw the sun; in ten days in the south, I almost got charbroiled). Even now, North and South Vietnam are as different as past and future, silence and frenzy, maiden aunt and bar girl; as different, ultimately, as Beijing and Hong Kong. Ask someone in Saigon if she's ever been to Hanoi, and she'll say, "No, I've never been outside Vietnam." Her cousin in the north will say, with equal conviction, "In Saigon, you can do anything. But in Vietnam. . . ." Saigon and Vietnam are as different, almost literally, as night and day.

Yet both places are distinctly new to foreign eyes, and both places— that of an aging bicycle and of a juiced-up Honda—have their own exhilarations. Vietnam is a smiling Southeast Asian country set amid the systems and institutions of old China, yet it is more unspoiled than Thailand and more gentle than the Middle Kingdom. Indeed, it is hard not to grow woozily romantic when enumerating the holiday seductions of the place. There are the mist-wreathed rain forests of the west and north, where you can find fifty-three distinct minority tribes—each with its own colorful costumes, customs, and tongue—hunting, still with bows and arrows, and, if asked how old they are, answering, "Ten or fifteen water buffaloes' lives."

COMPREHENSION

1. According to the essay, what sets Saigon apart from the rest of the country? What evidence does Iyer provide?
2. How does the writer feel about his subject?
3. Is Iyer promoting or condemning tourism in Vietnam?

RHETORIC

1. Iyer employs exotic words and images to help convey an impression of Vietnam. Give some examples of his use of language. How does it help you understand the subject?
2. Why has Iyer written this essay? What message is he conveying? Specifically where in the essay does his intention become clear?
3. Who is Iyer's audience? What support can you find in the essay?
4. What kind of mood does Iyer set up in his introductory paragraph? What details elicit a sense of history and culture? How do these help the reader understand the land and its people?
5. How does Iyer use a pattern of comparison and contrast to develop his essay?

6. What transition does Iyer make in paragraph 7? What purpose do the colorful details serve?

WRITING

1. If you were planning a vacation in Asia, would you consider visiting Vietnam? Write an essay in which you develop the reasons for your answer. How would Iyer's descriptions and opinions influence your choice? Be specific.
2. Compare Lopez's view of landscape as entertainment to Iyer's views on tourism. Do they share a common view of place? In what ways do they differ? Use support from both writers.
3. Write an essay examining America's historic link to Vietnam and its impact on the people and geography. Some research may be necessary. In addition, evidence from Iyer's essay should be considered.
4. Consider in an essay the effects of tourism on a country's people, land, economy. What are the advantages of marketing a culture? How can it be detrimental to a country's resources and identity?

JAMAICA KINCAID   Jamaica Kincaid remains a citizen of Antigua, the small island in the Caribbean where she was born in 1949, though she resides in Vermont with her husband and two children. Kincaid graduated from Bennington College and has been a staff writer for the *New Yorker* since 1976. She has written a collection of short stories, *At the Bottom of the River* (1985), *Annie John* (1985), *A Small Place* (1988) and, most recently, *Lucy* (1991). Using language as sensuous and evocative as the place she's describing, Kincaid takes us to her birthplace, with its lush beauty and harsh historical realities, in the following selection.

JAMAICA KINCAID

An Excerpt from *A Small Place*

Antigua is beautiful. Antigua is too beautiful. Sometimes the beauty of   1
it seems unreal. Sometimes the beauty of it seems as if it were stage sets
for a play, for no real sunset could look like that; no real seawater could
strike that many shades of blue at once; no real sky could be that shade
of blue—another shade of blue, completely different from the shades of
blue seen in the sea—and no real cloud could be that white and float
just that way in that blue sky; no real day could be that sort of sunny
and bright, making everything seem transparent and shallow; and no
real night could be that sort of black, making everything seem thick and

deep and bottomless. No real day and no real night could be that evenly divided—twelve hours of one and twelve hours of the other; no real day would begin that dramatically or end that dramatically (there is no dawn in Antigua: one minute, you are in the complete darkness of night; the next minute, the sun is overhead and it stays there until it sets with an explosion of reds on the horizon, and then the darkness of night comes again, and it is as if the open lid of a box you are inside suddenly snaps into place). No real sand on any real shore is that fine or that white (in some places) or that pink (in other places); no real flowers could be these shades of red, purple, yellow, orange, blue, white; no real lily would bloom only at night and perfume the air with a sweetness so thick it makes you slightly sick; no real earth is that colour brown; no real grass is that particular shade of dilapidated, run-down green (not enough rain); no real cows look that poorly as they feed on the unreal-looking grass in the unreal-looking pasture, and no real cows look quite that miserable as some unreal-looking white egrets sit on their backs eating insects; no real rain would fall with that much force, so that it tears up the parched earth. No real village in any real countryside would be named Table Hill Gordon, and no real village with such a name would be so beautiful in its pauperedness, its simple-ness, its one-room houses painted in unreal shades of pink and yellow and green, a dog asleep in the shade, some flies asleep in the corner of the dog's mouth. Or the market on a Saturday morning, where the colours of the fruits and vegetables and the colours of the clothes peo-ple are wearing and the colour of the day itself, and the colour of the nearby sea, and the colour of the sky, which is just overhead and seems so close you might reach up and touch it, and the way the people there speak English (they break it up) and the way they might be angry with each other and the sound they make when they laugh, all of this is so beautiful, all of this is not real like any other real thing that there is. It is as if, then, the beauty—the beauty of the sea, the land, the air, the trees, the market, the people, the sounds they make—were a prison, and as if everything and everybody inside it were locked in and everything and everybody that is not inside it were locked out. And what might it do to ordinary people to live in this way every day? What might it do to them to live in such heightened, intense surroundings day after day? They have nothing to compare this incredible constant with, no big his-torical moment to compare the way they are now to the way they used to be. No Industrial Revolution, no revolution of any kind, no Age of Anything, no world wars, no decades of turbulence balanced by decades of calm. Nothing, then, natural or unnatural, to leave a mark on their character. It is just a little island. The unreal way in which it is beautiful now is the unreal way in which it was always beautiful. The unreal way in which it is beautiful now that they are a free people is the unreal way in which it was beautiful when they were slaves.

Again, Antigua is a small place, a small island. It is nine miles wide by twelve miles long. It was discovered by Christopher Columbus in 1493. Not too long after, it was settled by human rubbish from Europe, who used enslaved but noble and exalted human beings from Africa (all masters of every stripe are rubbish, and all slaves of every stripe are noble and exalted; there can be no question about this) to satisfy their desire for wealth and power, to feel better about their own miserable existence, so that they could be less lonely and empty—a European disease. Eventually, the masters left, in a kind of way; eventually, the slaves were freed, in a kind of way. The people in Antigua now, the people who really think of themselves as Antiguans (and the people who would immediately come to your mind when you think about what Antiguans might be like; I mean, supposing you were to think about it), are the descendants of those noble and exalted people, the slaves. Of course, the whole thing is, once you cease to be a master, once you throw off your master's yoke, you are no longer human rubbish, you are just a human being, and all the things that adds up to. So, too, with the slaves. Once they are no longer slaves, once they are free, they are no longer noble and exalted; they are just human beings.

COMPREHENSION

1. What actual facts about Antigua and its people does the reader extract from the writer's lyrical descriptions?
2. What is the significance of the title?
3. How does Kincaid define *master and slave?*

RHETORIC

1. What situation does the writer set up with the first two sentences of the essay? What effect does the use of "too" have on the reader? How does it help set a tone for the following images?
2. How does repetition and rhythm help to set up a mood in the first paragraph? What response is called for? Identify specific words that resonate through the passage, and explain why they're powerful.
3. Why does Kincaid break the mood of her descriptions in several places with parenthetical information? How do these interruptions serve to alert the reader?
4. Find the line in the first paragraph where the images in Kincaid's piece begin to change. What does the writer wish to convey with this change? Locate a couple of images that show the writer's shift.
5. How does the "prison" metaphor work? What is Kincaid saying about Antigua's place in the world? How does the rest of the paragraph help define "little island" in a historical context?
6. How does the juxtaposition of "real" and "unreal" elements aid in the development of Kincaid's thesis?
7. What tone and style does Kincaid adopt in the last paragraph? Contrast them to the language and mood originally set up.

1. Write an essay in which you attempt to answer Kincaid's question: "And what might it do to ordinary people to live in this way every day?" referring to Antigua's beauty as a prison. How does such isolation help or hinder the inhabitants?

2. Using support from Kincaid's essay as well as Orwell's "Shooting an Elephant," consider the effects of slavery on the native population of a country as well as on the landscape itself.

3. Write a research paper that combines Kincaid's personal view of Antigua with factual, historical information about its geography and inhabitants. How does one approach enrich the other?

WILLIAM ZINSSER   William Zinsser was born in New York City in 1922 and educated at Princeton University, where he received his A.B. degree in 1944. Zinsser is a writer who sees his job primarily as a craft rather than an art. His best-selling book, *On Writing Well: An Informal Guide to Writing,* has been popular for two decades as a manual for developing a straightforward writing style. He has been a journalist since 1946, when he started with the *New York Herald Tribune* as a feature writer. He has also worked as a drama and film critic and has taught writing at a number of colleges and universities. He has authored or edited over twenty books, including eight books on various aspects of the writer's craft. His most recent book, *Willie and Dwike,* is a biography of a jazz duo, an appropriate topic for the author, who is himself an amateur jazz pianist. The following portrait of Disneyland demonstrates his measured, focused style. It is taken from *American Places,* published in 1992.

WILLIAM ZINSSER

Disneyland

When I first called Disneyland and was put on hold, the canned music I got was "When You Wish Upon a Star." It made my day, or at least that two minutes of it. Of all the affable songs that ran through the Walt Disney movies I grew up on, none conveyed with such assurance—not even "Some Day My Prince Will Come," from *Snow White and the Seven Dwarfs*—the Disney message of infinite possibility. When you wished upon a star, the song said, it didn't matter who you were; anything your heart desired would come true. Jiminy Cricket sang it in the opening scene of *Pinocchio,* 50 years ago, and in 1991 it was still on the job, epitomizing not only Disneyland but its surrounding homeland of southern California, world capital of make-believe.

It was to that far-off Eldorado that a young man named Cecil B. 2
DeMille came from New York in 1913 on an exploring trip, dispatched
by his partners—Jesse L. Lasky and Samuel Goldfish, who later
changed his name to Goldwyn—in a newly formed film-producing
company. Their first picture was *The Squaw Man,* and they needed a
rural site that they could populate with cowboys and Indians. DeMille
found an old barn with some fruit trees and chicken coops in a drowsy
section of Los Angeles called Hollywood, and he proposed to Lasky
that they rent the barn and an acre of land as their production center.

"O.K.," Lasky wired back, "but be careful." 3

That may have been the last time that restraint was urged on any of 4
the moguls who founded "Hollywood," one of the most famous civilizations that man has built, a synonym in every corner of the world for
glamour and wish fulfillment. Goldwyn would become the "G" of M-
G-M, the mightiest dream factory of them all, and the second "M,"
Louis B. Mayer, would impose on the colony an almost religious belief
in the happy ending and the punished sin. I was reared on the movies
that were spun out of that factory, and when I grew up and toured the
studios as a writer in the twilight of their golden age, in the 1950s, I saw
the sets that had once transported me to distant lands and dynasties. I
saw the Middle Kingdom pylons from *The Egyptian* and the medieval
castle from *Prince Valiant* and the Siamese court from *The King and I.* I
saw Caligula's Rome and Napoleon's Paris and Disraeli's London and
Diamond Jim Brady's New York and Wyatt Earp's Dodge City. I saw
the columns of Tara and the train that finished off Greta Garbo in *Anna
Karenina.* I saw the Chinese village from *The Good Earth* and the
picket-fenced street where Andy Hardy lived. Huddled on the back lot,
the ghostly sets waited to be reanimated by the rustle of costumed
extras and the director's cry of "Action!"

Instead the sounds that were heard were the sounds of demolition. 5
The founding moguls died, the back lots were sold off to developers,
and a new breed of independent producers began to forge a new Hollywood, where agents would be quoted more often than stars, where
studios would be bought and sold like junk bonds, and where the
movies that did get produced were not made according to the gospel of
Louis B. Mayer. Hollywood as the purveyor of happy dreams was shutting down. But 27 miles to the south, in Anaheim, on a rural acreage
not unlike the one that DeMille and Lasky and Goldfish bought in
1913 to start it all, another dream merchant was about to take over the
franchise.

Walt Disney first talked in the early 1940s about building a "magical 1
little park" next to his movie studio in Burbank. It would cover eight
acres and would feature pony rides, train rides, "singing waterfalls" and
statues of Mickey Mouse, Donald Duck and other Disney cartoon figures with whom tourists could pose for pictures. He wanted to create
something different in entertainment parks, having found as a father

trying to entertain his young daughters that existing parks were "dirty, phony places, run by tough-looking people." His plans were halted by World War II, and when they were revived a decade later they had outgrown the small tract in Burbank, reaching a level of aspiration that was unheard of in America and unwelcomed by its banks. Bankers were not persuaded that a family park called Disneyland was what American families were waiting for.

"Dreams offer too little collateral," Walt later said, explaining the banks' aversion, and to raise the money he and his brother Roy did the traditional borrowing against their life insurance and selling of treasured assets that are the stuff of American capitalist legend. They bought 180 acres of orange groves in Anaheim, began "imagineering" the new kind of theme park they had in mind, cleared the land, built their Sleeping Beauty Castle and their Rocket to the Moon and their fantasy villages and rivers and rides, and opened on July 17, 1955. More than 300 million people have since paid their way in.

Thus Disney dreams were proved to be prime collateral after all, and in the 1970s they financed the orgy of land acquisition and construction in Florida that created Walt Disney World and Epcot Center. But Anaheim was where the brothers first tried out their idea on the American people and found that they had struck a deep psychic need. Disneyland, not Walt Disney World, was the true icon—carved, like Mount Rushmore, out of virgin America—and that's where I went next, flying to an airport so aptly named for Orange County, John Wayne Airport, that just landing there made me feel better. Walt and the Duke would watch over me and see that all my endings were happy.

The psychic need that Disneyland fills is the need to be whisked away to any time and place except present-day America. Being transported—on mechanical rides or on the wings of imagination—is the essence of the park. Its central metaphor, anchoring all the other contraptions of escape, is the old-fashioned Main Street that constitutes its entrance. It looks the way we like to think America looked in its late-Victorian age of innocence, or at least the way Disney chose to reimagine his boyhood town of Marceline, Missouri, and as soon as I saw its genial facades and storefronts—mansard roofs with red-white-and-blue bunting, ice cream parlors and candy palaces and penny arcades—I gladly let myself sink into the warm bath of that turn-of-the-century world. Given a choice of turning centuries, there was no choice; Disney's late 1890s were a far nicer place than my 1990s, which I had left just outside the main gate—a vast tundra of asphalt, parked cars, tourist buses and sightseer hotels. Greater Anaheim was greater nowhere.

I began my visit by taking a ride on the old-fashioned steam train that leaves from an old-fashioned brick station at the head of Main Street. Hanging on the wall of the station was a French barometer in an ornate Victorian frame, and I wasn't surprised to see that its needle was at *très sec*, safely beyond *variable* and well past *grande pluie* and *tempête*. There is no *pluie* in Disneyland. Nor is there a speck of dirt, as I noticed when I got back to Main Street. The pavement is hospital clean, and even the horses that draw the horse-drawn trolleys leave no evidence behind. I stopped to look in the window of the clockmaker and the Blue Ribbon Bakery and the Silhouette Studio and the Market House ("Jellies and Jams") and then went up onto a turn-of-the-century front porch and sat on one of its turn-of-the-century chairs and watched the day's arriving crowds as they hurried by.

Actually they *strolled* by, their gait subliminally set by the music, all 6 of which was in three-quarter time. One after another the gently lilting waltzes came and went—"East Side, West Side," "On a Bicycle Built for Two," "I'm in Love with the Man in the Moon"—and I realized that no other time signature in music is so suggestive of good old summer pleasures, of picnics in a grove and rowboats on a lake. Three-quarter time is an intravenous drip of yesteryear. Sometimes I heard competing music from the coin-operated nickelodeon in the Penny Arcade across the street, but it never violated the emotional codes—it was ragtime piano or steam calliope, ingenuous and jaunty, with no harsh edges, just as the colors of the buildings had no hard tones. They were pastel yellows and greens and gray-blues, or, at the loudest, the pink of a strawberry ice cream soda. The saleswomen in the shops wore peppermint-striped shirtwaists, high at the neck, and tied their hair up in ribbons—definitely not "tough-looking people." The men wore vests and suspenders and boaters, and occasionally four of them came gliding by on a bicycle built for four. It was an old Alice Faye Technicolor musical brought to life, and what it said as an architectural statement was that Main Street circa 1900 was America's lost paradise, recoverable only in facsimile.

I thought about that architecture, that Disney haute nostalgia. 7 Hadn't I seen it somewhere else? I had. I had seen it replicated in upscale shopping malls in upscale towns across America—towns like Aspen, Colorado, and Naples, Florida. I remembered from a visit to Naples that the twin ideas of "postmodern" (reinventing the past) and "retro" (re-creating the past) have merged there to form the collective taste. Though taste is seldom easy to define, Naples, it's safe to say, is united in the belief that yesterday was wonderful. Proof of that homage was a six-block complex of 110 stores, restaurants and art galleries that were as aggressively charming as the set of *Meet Me in St. Louis*. I also remembered a visit to the Georgetown section of Washington, D.C. Walking along its main street, admiring its authentic Federal facades, I turned through an archway and found myself in a vast turn-of-the-century world. It was a three-story mall called Georgetown Park, with every *faux* gaslight and lamppost and storefront in place—a pure appropriation, I realized, of Disneyland. I wondered whether this influence is taught in architecture schools. Just as America's postwar architects inflicted on our landscape the glass boxes of their revered Bauhaus modernism, their successors have taken their inspiration from Anaheim Victorian, building mini-Disneylands across the country to soothe our worries away. Thus Main Street America comes full circle. Though we have eagerly abandoned our actual Main Streets for the new mall out on the strip, we don't have to give up the *idea* of Main Street. Thanks to Disney, we can still make believe that the good old days never went away.

At the far end of Main Street, Disneyland fans out into other "lands," including Fantasyland, Frontierland, Adventureland, Tomorrowland and New Orleans Square—each of them, like Main Street, a perfect amalgam of preformed ideas and memories. Fantasyland, which I reached by crossing a moat perpetually washed by a dulcet rendition of "When You Wish Upon a Star," was "a timeless land of enchantment," as Walt Disney once called it, invoking two of the park's operative words. Many of its attractions have "enchanted" in their name, and what makes Fantasyland "timeless" is that it is a tapestry of images that go back to the fairy tales of our early childhood, which in turn go back to folk myth. Fantasyland could have been built by Bavarian elves, not Anaheim carpenters. The turreted Sleeping Beauty Castle was every castle from every illustrated storybook about princes, princesses, wicked stepsisters and enchanted toads, and the town that lies at its feet, with its half-timbered stucco houses and weathered beams, was every medieval European village from the tales of Grimm to the opera *Hansel and Gretel*.

No less familiar to me were the neighboring principalities of Adventureland and Frontierland, where I went next. Adventureland was all-purpose exotic: the South Seas of Maugham and Gauguin and Jack London, with an Amazon cruise and appropriate jungle drums thrown in. Every Pacific culture from Melanesia to Maui had been rifled for an identifying artifact—tribal masks and tiki statues, tapa cloth and thatched roofs, Hawaiian music and bamboo porch railings—and the resulting town was the generic "away" of every dreamer who dreams of getting away from it all, just as Frontierland was the generic Old West that Hollywood has planted in our minds as the real Old West, instantly recognizable for its trading posts and cowboy outfitters and wooden sidewalks. The genius of Disneyland is that it has no shocks of nonrecognition; we are safely cushioned against change. Walt Disney wasn't Wilbur Wright, or Gutzon Borglum, or Thoreau; he was at the other end of the American rainbow from those peppery individualists. He was Mr. Mainstream, a boy who never entirely grew up and who intuitively knew that the rest of us haven't entirely grown up either.

I spent my two days at Disneyland taking rides. I took a bobsled through the Matterhorn and a submarine under the Polar Ice Cap and a rocket jet to the Cosmic Vapor Curtain. I took Peter Pan's Flight, Mr. Toad's Wild Ride, Alice's Scary Adventures and Pinocchio's Daring Journey. I took a steamboat and a jungle boat. I took the Big Thunder Mountain railroad to coyote country and the Splash Mountain roller coaster to Critter Country. I took a "Pirates of the Caribbean" ride (black cats and buried treasure) and a "Haunted Mansion" ride (creaking hinges and ghostly laughter). I took monorails and Skyways and Autopias and PeopleMovers. More precisely, those rides took *me:* up and down and around sudden corners and through dark tunnels and over rooftops, and all I had to do was sit back and let whatever conveyance I was sitting in do the driving. I had no desire to be at the wheel myself. In Disneyland that primal American urge—the urge to drive—gets suspended, replaced by the still more primal urge to be eternally transported to timeless lands of enchantment.

I didn't even mind waiting for the rides. The lines had been 4 shrewdly configured in bends and loops to look shorter than they were, and the crowds moved along without impatience, the children cheerful and well behaved. Parents with very small children had dutifully left their strollers in one of the areas designated for "Stroller Parking": ultimate tidiness. The crowds were also very white. Although I noticed a number of Mexican-American and Asian tourists, I saw only one black family in two days. American blacks, I suspect, know that it will take more than wishing upon a star to make their hearts' desires come true.

How the Disney people view their park—what dreams and needs they 1 think their millions of visitors bring to Disneyland to be fulfilled—I never found out; they weren't allowed to talk to me. When I first called to introduce myself, I was told that if I were writing an article there would be no problem—I could interview anybody. But books were another matter: anything connected with a book had to be cleared by the Disney legal department.

On one level that was good news. At a time when writing and read- 2 ing are increasingly devalued, books were still important enough for lawyers to worry about. Books got into libraries. Magazines and newspapers were mere visitors in our midst, leaving no imprint on the culture; as a young reporter I was often told that the morning newspaper is what fish get wrapped in at night. But now, because I was working on a book, I would have to write Disneyland a formal letter of request. I did, and word came back that the legal department would process my letter soon. That "soon" never arrived. When I got to Disneyland the publicity staff refused to see me, or give me any publicity material, or even let me cross their doorstep. "Our hands are tied," they told me on the phone— the closest I came to meeting them—and no untying was ever done.

I couldn't help thinking about the American values I had seen cer- 3 tified and glorified on Disneyland's turn-of-the-century Main Street— such things as neighborliness and trust. At all my previous stops I had been replenished by hearing men and women talk about the place where they work and what it means to them. Their sense of work as useful and satisfying was an old-fashioned value that I found alive and well, especially in the National Park Service. In towns like Abilene, I was reminded that the people who traditionally lubricated small-town America in Disney's beloved yesteryear, helping people to get on with their lives, were the bankers and the doctors and the lawyers. None of them could have imagined that with the turn of another century Americans would be so protective of their image that they would cede to lawyers much of their freedom to act. Half the country, it often seemed, was waiting for legal clearance.

Because Disneyland is a collage of many cherished American myths, I found myself encountering in its synthetic "lands" many of the folk heroes I had met earlier on their authentic turf. The Mississippi steamboat I took in Frontierland was the *Mark Twain,* and the island it circumnavigated was Tom Sawyer Island. Davy Crockett, late of the Alamo, appeared to me three times. In Critter Country I rode in a Davy Crockett Explorer Canoe; in Frontierland I shopped in a store called Davy Crockett's Pioneer Mercantile; and at a nearby log stockade I saw a sign informing me that a string of such forts, like Fort Pitt and Fort Duquesne, once linked the American frontier. "Davy Crockett and other famous scouts," it said, "spent much time in and around such wilderness outposts acting as 'eyes and ears' of the woods."

Therefore I should have known that I hadn't seen the last of Abraham Lincoln. Earlier I had seen him in granite at Mount Rushmore and had felt his healing presence at Appomattox. Now, as I was about to leave, I noticed a building called the Disneyland Opera House. GREAT MOMENTS WITH MR. LINCOLN, its marquee said. That was for me—I'm always up for great moments with Mr. Lincoln. Inside, I watched a brief film in which Walt Disney explains his process of Audio-Animatronics, the technology that has become a trademark of his parks, enabling all manner of seemingly real people, animals, birds, fish and other critters to hail us as we come riding by. "Ever since I was a small boy I've had a great personal admiration for Abraham Lincoln," Disney says, recalling that he first Audio-Animated Mr. Lincoln for the New York World's Fair of 1964, using a life mask of the 16th President that was taken in 1860, before he grew a beard. "The final result is so lifelike you may find it hard to believe," the narrator of the film said, and we were duly ushered into a theater to try to believe it.

After a brief slide show recapitulating the Civil War, the curtain went up and I saw on the stage a tall man in a black suit who somewhat resembled Abraham Lincoln. He was sitting in a chair, with a diorama of the Capitol behind him, and something in me kept hoping he wouldn't try to get up. But he did, struggling arthritically to his feet and moving a few steps forward. He wanted to talk to us about liberty, he said, and he began to expatiate on respect for duty, the law, faith in divine Providence, and dangers facing the nation. They sounded like disconnected homilies, and as I later learned, they were: snippets plucked from five speeches delivered during the mainly beardless years of 1838 to 1864. This was not my writer's Lincoln. In fact, was it anybody's Lincoln? As the tall man rambled on, emphasizing his points with hand and arm gestures that were angular and spasmodic, his long legs just a little unsteady—would he *fall?*—I was reminded of another tall figure from the dim recesses of Hollywood make-believe who moved with the same mechanical vulnerability, the same endearing wish to be human. It was Boris Karloff in *Frankenstein*.

With mingled joy and regret, as they said in the old Hollywood travelogues, I bade farewell to Disneyland and stole out into the parking lot. There I caught a shuttle bus that took me to my modern hotel across a landscape that was not spotless and not beautiful; I didn't see a single orange tree. But it was real, and I was glad to get back to my America. Two days in Disneyland had been a welcome release from the stressful present into an America as long gone and as deeply longed for as the boyhood of Tom Sawyer. I could only tell myself that Walt Disney's turn-of-the-century Main Street and Mark Twain's mid-19th-century Hannibal—the handiwork of two masters of make-believe—were also not as ideal as they made themselves believe.

4

COMPREHENSION

1. What is the thesis of this essay? Is it directly asserted in the writing, or must one infer it?

2. The author seems to have a mixed view of nostalgia, both a positive and a negative one. Which passages in the essay provide evidence of each view?

3. What are the major ironies Zinsser encounters in his exploration of Disneyland?

RHETORIC

1. Study the five parts of the essay. What is the focus of each of the parts? How does the author create a "bridge" from one part to the next?

2. What is the purpose of the transition that occurs between paragraphs 4 and 5? How does it foreshadow the transition between the old Hollywood and the new one?

3. Disneyland borrows from many styles of architecture, styles, and artifacts of different eras; and Zinsser refers to them to provide us with an image of what he is describing. For example, he mentions a "French barometer in an ornate Victorian frame," "coin-operated nickelodeon in the Penny Arcade," and "half-timbered stucco houses." Must one be acquainted with these objects to appreciate Zinsser's description? Is Zinsser making any assumptions about his intended audience?

4. The author mixes both traditional and original terms to convey the sights of Disneyland. What is the purpose of using such expressions as *"faux gaslight,"* "Anaheim Victorian," "Bauhaus modernism" (section II, paragraph 7)? What other terms, proper names of people and places must one know in order to acquire a complete picture of what the author describes?

5. In paragraph 1 of section 4, dashes, a colon, and a semicolon are used to create a tone of officiousness. How does the punctuation assist the tone of the paragraph? How does the paragraph add variety to the tone of the essay?

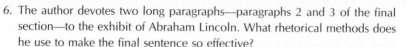

6. The author devotes two long paragraphs—paragraphs 2 and 3 of the final section—to the exhibit of Abraham Lincoln. What rhetorical methods does he use to make the final sentence so effective?

7. Summarize the overall tone of the essay. Is it one of sadness, irony, joy, disappointment, contempt, something else, or a combination of tones? What evidence do you have to support your view? Do you believe the tone of the essay reflects the true response of the writer? If he were writing the essay for a close friend, say, rather than for a book intended for public consumption, would he give a different account of his experience?

WRITING

1. Visit a local museum, zoo, park, or other public place. Write an essay describing the relationship between its structure and its purpose, paying particular attention to its intended effect on its audience.

2. Argue for or against the proposition that caricatures of real life, whether they be theme parks, movies, cartoons, or virtual reality, are inherently dangerous because they provide a distorted picture of the way things really are. Be sure to use supporting points and illustrations to support your thesis.

3. For a research paper, study the latest trends in technology, and write a descriptive essay entitled "The Future of Fantasy."

N. SCOTT MOMADAY   Navarre Scott Momaday (b. 1934), Pulitzer Prize–winning poet, critic, and academician, is the author of *House Made of Dawn* (1968), *The Way to Rainy Mountain* (1969), *The Names* (1976), and other works. "I am an American Indian (Kiowa), and am vitally interested in American Indian art, history and culture," Momaday has written. In this essay, he elevates personal experience to the realm of poetry and tribal myth.

N. SCOTT MOMADAY

The Way to Rainy Mountain

A single knoll rises out of the plain in Oklahoma, north and west of the Wichita Range. For my people, the Kiowas, it is an old landmark, and they gave it the name Rainy Mountain. The hardest weather in the world is there. Winter brings blizzards, hot tornadic winds arise in the spring, and in summer the prairie is an anvil's edge. The grass turns brittle and brown, and it cracks beneath your feet. There are green belts along the rivers and creeks, linear groves of hickory and pecan, willow and witch hazel. At a distance in July or August the steaming foliage seems almost to writhe in fire. Great green and yellow grasshoppers are everywhere in the tall grass, popping up like corn to sting the flesh, and tortoises crawl about on the red earth, going nowhere in the plenty of time. Loneliness is an aspect of the land. All things in the plain are isolate; there is no confusion of objects in the eye, but *one* hill or *one* tree or *one* man. To look upon that landscape in the early morning, with the sun at your back, is to lose the sense of proportion. Your imagination comes to life, and this, you think, is where Creation was begun.

I returned to Rainy Mountain in July. My grandmother had died in the spring, and I wanted to be at her grave. She had lived to be very old and at last infirm. Her only living daughter was with her when she died, and I was told that in death her face was that of a child.

I like to think of her as a child. When she was born, the Kiowas were living the last great moment of their history. For more than a hundred years they had controlled the open range from the Smoky Hill River to the Red, from the headwaters of the Canadian to the fork of the Arkansas and Cimarron. In alliance with the Comanches, they had ruled the whole of the southern Plains. War was their sacred business, and they were among the finest horsemen the world has ever known. But warfare for the Kiowas was preeminently a matter of disposition rather than of survival, and they never understood the grim, unrelenting advance of the U.S. Cavalry. When at last, divided and ill-provisioned, they were driven onto the Staked Plains in the cold rains of autumn, they fell into panic. In Palo Duro Canyon they abandoned their crucial stores to pillage and had nothing then but their lives. In order to save themselves, they surrendered to the soldiers at Fort Sill and were imprisoned in the old stone corral that now stands as a military museum. My grandmother was spared the humiliation of those high gray walls by eight or ten years, but she must have known from birth the affliction of defeat, the dark brooding of old warriors.

Her name was Aho, and she belonged to the last culture to evolve in North America. Her forebears came down from the high country in western Montana nearly three centuries ago. They were a mountain people, a mysterious tribe of hunters whose language has never been positively classified in any major group. In the late seventeenth century they began a long migration to the south and east. It was a journey toward the dawn, and it led to a golden age. Along the way the Kiowas were befriended by the Crows, who gave them the culture and religion of the Plains. They acquired horses, and their ancient nomadic spirit was suddenly free of the ground. They acquired Tai-me, the sacred Sun Dance doll, from that moment the object and symbol of their worship, and so shared in the divinity of the sun. Not least, they acquired the sense of destiny, therefore courage and pride. When they entered upon the southern Plains they had been transformed. No longer were they slaves to the simple necessity of survival; they were a lordly and dangerous society of fighters and thieves, hunters and priests of the sun. According to their origin myth, they entered the world through a hollow log. From one point of view, their migration was the fruit of an old prophecy, for indeed they emerged from a sunless world.

Although my grandmother lived out her long life in the shadow of Rainy Mountain, the immense landscape of the continental interior lay like memory in her blood. She could tell of the Crows, whom she had never seen, and of the Black Hills, where she had never been. I wanted to see in reality what she had seen more perfectly in the mind's eye, and traveled fifteen hundred miles to begin my pilgrimage.

Yellowstone, it seemed to me, was the top of the world, a region of deep lakes and dark timber, canyons and waterfalls. But, beautiful as it is, one might have the sense of confinement there. The skyline in all directions is close at hand, the high wall of the woods and deep cleavages of shade. There is a perfect freedom in the mountains, but it belongs to the eagle and the elk, the badger and the bear. The Kiowas reckoned their stature by the distance they could see, and they were bent and blind in the wilderness.

Descending eastward, the highland meadows are a stairway to the plain. In July the inland slope of the Rockies is luxuriant with flax and buckwheat, stonecrop and larkspur. The earth unfolds and the limit of the land recedes. Clusters of trees, and animals grazing far in the distance, cause the vision to reach away and wonder to build upon the mind. The sun follows a longer course in the day, and the sky is immense beyond all comparison. The great billowing clouds that sail upon it are shadows that move upon the grain like water, dividing light. Farther down, in the land of the Crows and Blackfeet, the plain is yellow. Sweet clover takes hold of the hills and bends upon itself to cover and seal the soil. There the Kiowas paused on their way; they had come to the place where they must change their lives. The sun is at home on the plains. Precisely there does it have the certain character of a god. When the Kiowas came to the land of the Crows, they could see the dark lees of the hills at dawn across the Bighorn River, the profusion of light on the grain shelves, the oldest deity ranging after the solstices. Not yet would they veer southward to the caldron of the land that lay below; they must wean their blood from the northern winter and hold the mountains a while longer in their view. They bore Tai-me in procession to the east.

A dark mist lay over the Black Hills, and the land was like iron. At the top of a ridge I caught sight of Devil's Tower upthrust against the gray sky as if in the birth of time the core of the earth had broken through its crust and the motion of the world was begun. There are things in nature that engender an awful quiet in the heart of man; Devil's Tower is one of them. Two centuries ago, because they could not do otherwise, the Kiowas made a legend at the base of the rock. My grandmother said:

> Eight children were there at play, seven sisters and their brother. Suddenly the boy was struck dumb; he trembled and began to run upon his hands and feet. His fingers became claws, and his body was covered with fur. Directly there was a bear where the boy had been. The sisters were terrified; they ran, and the bear after them. They came to the

109

stump of a great tree, and the tree spoke to them. It bade them climb upon it, and as they did so it began to rise into the air. The bear came to kill them, but they were just beyond its reach. It reared against the tree and scored the bark all around with its claws. The seven sisters were borne into the sky, and they became the stars of the Big Dipper.

From that moment, and so long as the legend lives, the Kiowas have kinsmen in the night sky. Whatever they were in the mountains, they could be no more. However tenuous their well-being, however much they had suffered and would suffer again, they had found a way out of the wilderness.

My grandmother had a reverence for the sun, a holy regard that now is all but gone out of mankind. There was a wariness in her, and an ancient awe. She was a Christian in her later years, but she had come a long way about, and she never forgot her birthright. As a child she had been to the Sun Dances; she had taken part in those annual rites, and by them she had learned the restoration of her people in the presence of Tai-me. She was about seven when the last Kiowa Sun Dance was held in 1887 on the Washita River above Rainy Mountain Creek. The buffalo were gone. In order to consummate the ancient sacrifice—to impale the head of a buffalo bull upon the medicine tree—a delegation of old men journeyed into Texas, there to beg and barter for an animal from the Goodnight herd. She was ten when the Kiowas came together for the last time as a living Sun Dance culture. They could find no buffalo; they had to hang an old hide from the sacred tree. Before the dance could begin, a company of soldiers rode out from Fort Sill under orders to disperse the tribe. Forbidden without cause the essential act of their faith, having seen the wild herds slaughtered and left to rot upon the ground, the Kiowas backed away forever from the medicine tree. That was July 20, 1890, at the great bend of the Washita. My grandmother was there. Without bitterness, and for as long as she lived, she bore a vision of deicide.

Now that I can have her only in memory, I see my grandmother in the several postures that were peculiar to her: standing at the wood stove on a winter morning and turning meat in a great iron skillet; sitting at the south window, bent above her beadwork, and afterwards, when her vision failed, looking down for a long time into the fold of her hands; going out upon a cane, very slowly as she did when the weight of age came upon her; praying. I remember her most often at prayer. She made long, rambling prayers out of suffering and hope, having seen many things. I was never sure that I had the right to hear, so exclusive were they of all mere custom and company. The last time I saw her she prayed standing by the side of her bed at night, naked to the waist, the light of a kerosene lamp moving upon her dark skin. Her long, black hair, always drawn and braided in the day, lay upon her shoulders and against her breasts like a shawl. I do not speak Kiowa, and I never understood her prayers, but there was something inherently sad in the sound, some merest hesitation upon the syllables of sorrow. She began in a high and descending pitch, exhausting her breath to silence; then again and again—and always the same intensity of effort, of something that is, and is not, like urgency in the human voice. Transported so in the dancing light among the shadows of her room, she seemed beyond the reach of time. But that was illusion; I think I knew then that I should not see her again.

Houses are like sentinels in the plain, old keepers of the weather watch. There, in a very little while, wood takes on the appearance of great age. All colors wear soon away in the wind and rain, and then the wood is burned gray and the grain appears and the nails turn red with rust. The windowpanes are black and opaque; you imagine there is nothing within, and indeed there are many ghosts, bones given up to the land. They stand here and there against the sky, and you approach them for a longer time than you expect. They belong in the distance; it is their domain.

Once there was a lot of sound in my grandmother's house, a lot of coming and going, feasting and talk. The summers there were full of excitement and reunion. The Kiowas are a summer people; they abide the cold and keep to themselves, but when the season turns and the land becomes warm and vital they cannot hold still; an old love of going returns upon them. The aged visitors who came to my grandmother's house when I was a child were made of lean and leather, and they bore themselves upright. They wore great black hats and bright ample shirts that shook in the wind. They rubbed fat upon their hair and wound their braids with strips of colored cloth. Some of them painted their faces and carried the scars of old and cherished enmities. They were an old council of warlords, come to remind and be reminded of who they were. Their wives and daughters served them well. The women might indulge themselves; gossip was at once the mark and compensation of their servitude. They made loud and elaborate talk among themselves, full of jest and gesture, fright and false alarm. They went abroad in fringed and flowered shawls, bright beadwork and German silver. They were at home in the kitchen, and they prepared meals that were banquets.

There were frequent prayer meetings, and great nocturnal feasts. When I was a child I played with my cousins outside, where the lamplight fell upon the ground and the singing of the old people rose up around us and carried away into the darkness. There were a lot of good things to eat, a lot of laughter and surprise. And afterwards, when the quiet returned, I lay down with my grandmother and could hear the frogs away by the river and feel the motion of the air.

Now there is funeral silence in the rooms, the endless wake of some final word. The walls have closed in upon my grandmother's house. When I returned to it in mourning, I saw for the first time in my life how small it was. It was late at night, and there was a white moon, nearly full. I sat for a long time on the stone steps by the kitchen door. From there I could see out across the land; I could see the long row of trees by the creek, the low light upon the rolling plains, and the stars of the Big Dipper. Once I looked at the moon and caught sight of a strange thing. A cricket had perched upon the handrail, only a few inches away from me. My line of vision was such that the creature filled the moon like a fossil. It had gone there, I thought, to live and die, for there, of all places, was its small definition made whole and eternal. A warm wind rose up and purled like the longing within me.

The next morning I awoke at dawn and went out on the dirt road to Rainy Mountain. It was already hot, and the grasshoppers began to fill the air. Still, it was early in the morning, and the birds sang out of the shadows. The long yellow grass on the mountain shone in the bright light, and a scissortail hied above the land. There, where it ought to be, at the end of a long and legendary way, was my grandmother's grave. Here and there on the dark stones were ancestral names. Looking back once, I saw the mountain and came away.

COMPREHENSION

1. What is the significance of Momaday's title? How does the title help to explain the author's purpose?
2. Why does Momaday return to his grandmother's house and journey to her grave?
3. List the various myths and legends the author mentions in the essay. What subjects do they treat? How are these subjects interrelated?

RHETORIC

1. Locate and explain instances of sensory, metaphorical, and symbolic language in the essay. Why are these modes of language consistent with the subject and theme elaborated by Momaday?
2. How does Momaday's use of abstract language affect the concrete vocabulary in the essay?
3. What is the method of development in the first paragraph? How does the introduction serve as a vehicle for the central meanings in the essay?
4. Consider the relationship of narration to description in the organization of the essay. What forms of narrative serve to unify the selection? Are the narrative patterns strictly linear, or do they shift for other purposes? Explain. In what sense is Momaday's descriptive technique cinematic?
5. How do the land, the Kiowas, and Momaday's grandmother serve as reinforcing frames of the essay?
6. Describe in detail the creation of mood in this essay. Explain specifically the mood at the conclusion.

WRITING

1. Momaday implies that myth is central to his life and the life of the Kiowas. What *is* myth? Do you think that myth is as strong in general American culture as it is in Kiowa culture? In what ways does it operate? How can myth sustain the individual, community, and nation? Write an analytical essay on this subject.
2. Write about a person and place that, taken together, inspire a special reverence in you.

3. In an essay, explore the ways in which environment molds personality in "The Way to Rainy Mountain" and in "Wyoming: The Solace of Open Spaces" by Gretel Ehrlich (see pp. 543–549).

CLASSIC AND CONTEMPORARY

E. B. WHITE   Elwyn Brooks White (1899–1985), one of the finest American essayists, is at his most distinctive when treating people and nature. A recipient of the National Medal for literature and associated for years with *The New Yorker,* White is the author of *One Man's Meat* (1942), *Here Is New York* (1949), and *The Second Tree from the Corner* (1954), among numerous other works. A selection of his essays appeared in 1977. In the following essay, White brings to life the excitingly complex rhythms of one of the world's great cities.

E. B. WHITE

Here Is New York

There are roughly three New Yorks. There is, first, the New York of the man or woman who was born here, who takes the city for granted and accepts its size and its turbulence as natural and inevitable. Second, there is the New York of the commuter—the city that is devoured by locusts each day and spat out each night. Third, there is the New York of the person who was born somewhere else and came to New York in quest of something. Of these three trembling cities the greatest is the last—the city of final destination, the city that is a goal. It is this third city that accounts for New York's high-strung disposition, its poetical deportment, its dedication to the arts, and its incomparable achievements. Commuters give the city its tidal restlessness; natives give it solidity and continuity; but the settlers give it passion. And whether it is a farmer arriving from Italy to set up a small grocery store in a slum, or a young girl arriving from a small town in Mississippi to escape the indignity of being observed by her neighbors, or a boy arriving from the Corn Belt with a manuscript in his suitcase and a pain in his heart, it makes no difference: each embraces New York with the intense excitement of first love, each absorbs New York with the fresh eyes of an adventurer, each generates heat and light to dwarf the Consolidated Edison Company.

   The commuter is the queerest bird of all. The suburb he inhabits has no essential vitality of its own and is a mere roost where he comes at day's end to go to sleep. Except in rare cases, the man who lives in

113

Mamaroneck or Little Neck or Teaneck, and works in New York, discovers nothing much about the city except the time of arrival and departure of trains and buses, and the path to a quick lunch. He is desk-bound, and has never, idly roaming in the gloaming, stumbled suddenly on Belvedere Tower in the Park, seen the ramparts rise sheer from the water of the pond, and the boys along the shore fishing for minnows, girls stretched out negligently on the shelves of the rocks; he has never come suddenly on anything at all in New York as a loiterer, because he has had no time between trains. He has fished in Manhattan's wallet and dug out coins, but has never listened to Manhattan's breathing, never awakened to its morning, never dropped off to sleep in its night. About 400,000 men and women come charging onto the Island each week-day morning, out of the mouths of tubes and tunnels. Not many among them have ever spent a drowsy afternoon in the great rustling oaken silence of the reading room of the Public Library, with the book elevator (like an old water wheel) spewing out books onto the trays. They tend their furnaces in Westchester and in Jersey, but have never seen the furnaces of the Bowery, the fires that burn in oil drums on zero winter nights. They may work in the financial district downtown and never see the extravagant plantings of Rockefeller Center—the daffodils and grape hyacinths and birches and the flags trimmed to the wind on a fine morning in spring. Or they may work in a midtown office and may let a whole year swing round without sighting Governors Island from the sea wall. The commuter dies with tremendous mileage to his credit, but he is no rover. His entrances and exits are more devious than those in a prairie-dog village; and he calmly plays bridge while buried in the mud at the bottom of the East River. The Long Island Rail Road alone carried forty million commuters last year; but many of them were the same fellow retracing his steps.

The terrain of New York is such that a resident sometimes travels ₃ farther, in the end, than a commuter. Irving Berlin's journey from Cherry Street in the lower East Side to an apartment uptown was through an alley and was only three or four miles in length; but it was like going three times around the world.

COMPREHENSION

1. What are the three New Yorks in White's essay?
2. When do you think this essay was written? What is your evidence from the text?
3. Which New York is White's favorite, and why?

RHETORIC

1. What is the writer's thesis? Is it stated explicitly? Explain.
2. How does the author support his claim that New York's "settlers give it passion"?

114

3. What concrete examples aid in establishing the city's reality? Which images conjure an "imagined" place?
4. Explain White's scheme of classification. Do all New Yorks get an equal share of attention?
5. Examine White's writing style, explaining how it is compatible with his subject matter.

WRITING

1. Compare and contrast New York (or any large city) with the suburbs. Do you agree with White's unflattering portrait of suburbia? Use figurative as well as concrete language to support your views.
2. If you live in or near a big city, which of White's categories do you fit into? Describe your relation to the city and its people. How do you experience the city?
3. Write your own classification essay, entitled "The Three." Focus on a specific place as the subject of this classification essay.

JOAN DIDION   Joan Didion (b. 1934) grew up in California and graduated from the University of California at Berkeley in 1956. She began writing for national magazines such as *Mademoiselle, The Saturday Evening Post,* and *Life.* She published her first novel, *Run River,* in 1963. Although she has continued to write novels and has written several screenplays, her most acclaimed work is nonfiction. This includes *Slouching Towards Bethlehem* (1968), *The White Album* (1979), *Salvador* (1983), *Democracy* (1984), *Miami* (1987), and her latest collection, *After Henry* (1992). In the following selection from *Miami,* Didion describes a city rich in ethnic diversity yet torn along lines of mistrust and fear.

JOAN DIDION

Miami: The Cuban Presence

On the 150th anniversary of the founding of Dade County, in February of 1986, the *Miami Herald* asked four prominent amateurs of local history to name "the ten people and the ten events that had the most impact on the county's history." Each of the four submitted his or her own list of "The Most Influential People in Dade's History," and among the names mentioned were Julia Tuttle ("pioneer businesswoman"), Henry Flagler ("brought the Florida East Coast Railway to Miami"), Alexander Orr, Jr. ("started the research that saved Miami's drinking water from salt"), Everest George Sewell ("publicized the city and fostered its deepwater seaport"). . . . There was Dr. James M. Jackson, an early Miami physician. There was Napoleon Bonaparte Broward, the governor of Florida who initiated the draining of the

115

Everglades. There appeared on three of the four lists the name of the developer of Coral Gables, George Merrick. There appeared on one of the four lists the name of the coach of the Miami Dolphins, Don Shula.

On none of these lists of "The Most Influential People in Dade's ₂ History" did the name Fidel Castro appear, nor for that matter did the name of any Cuban, although the presence of Cubans in Dade County did not go entirely unnoted by the *Herald* panel. When it came to naming the Ten Most Important "Events," as opposed to "People," all four panelists mentioned the arrival of the Cubans, but at slightly off angles ("Mariel Boatlift of 1980" was the way one panelist saw it), and as if the arrival had been just another of those isolated disasters or innovations which deflect the course of any growing community, on an approximate par with the other events mentioned, for example the Freeze of 1895, the Hurricane of 1926, the opening of the Dixie Highway, the establishment of Miami International Airport, and the adoption, in 1957, of the metropolitan form of government, "enabling the Dade County Commission to provide urban services to the increasingly populous unincorporated area."

This set of mind, in which the local Cuban community was seen as ₃ a civic challenge determinedly met, was not uncommon among Anglos to whom I talked in Miami, many of whom persisted in the related illusions that the city was small, manageable, prosperous in a predictable broad-based way, Southern in a progressive Sunbelt way, American, and belonged to them. In fact 43 percent of the population of Dade County was by that time "Hispanic," which meant mostly Cuban. Fifty-six percent of the population of Miami itself was Hispanic. The most visible new buildings on the Miami skyline, the Arquitectonica buildings along Brickell Avenue, were by a firm with a Cuban founder. There were Cubans in the board rooms of the major banks, Cubans in clubs that did not admit Jews or blacks, and four Cubans in the most recent mayoralty campaign, two of whom, Raul Masvidal and Xavier Suarez, had beaten out the incumbent and all other candidates to meet in a runoff, and one of whom, Xavier Suarez, a thirty-six-year-old lawyer who had been brought from Cuba to the United States as a child, was by then mayor of Miami.

The entire tone of the city, the way people looked and talked and ₄ met one another, was Cuban. The very image the city had begun presenting of itself, what was then its newfound glamour, its "hotness" (hot colors, hot vice, shady dealings under the palm trees), was that of prerevolutionary Havana, as perceived by Americans. There was even in the way women dressed in Miami a definable Havana look, a more distinct emphasis on the hips and décolletage, more black, more veiling, a generalized flirtatiousness of style not then current in American cities. In the shoe departments at Burdine's and Jordan Marsh there were more platform soles than there might have been in another American city, and fewer displays of the running shoe ethic. I recall being struck, during an afternoon spent at La Liga Contra el Cancer, a prominent exile charity which raises money to help cancer patients, by the appearance of the volunteers who had met that day to stuff envelopes for a benefit. Their hair was sleek, of a slightly other period, immaculate pageboys and French twists. They wore Bruno Magli pumps, and silk and linen dresses of considerable expense. There seemed to be a preference for strictest gray or black, but the effect remained lush, tropical, like a room full of perfectly groomed mangoes.

This was not, in other words, an invisible 56 percent of the population. Even the social notes in *Diario Las Americas* and in *El Herald,* the daily Spanish edition of the *Herald* written and edited for *el exilio,* suggested a dominant culture, one with money to spend and a notable willingness to spend it in public. La Liga Contra el Cancer alone sponsored, in a single year, two benefit dinner dances, one benefit ball, a benefit children's fashion show, a benefit telethon, a benefit exhibition of jewelry, a benefit presentation of Miss Universe contestants, and a benefit showing, with Saks Fifth Avenue and chicken *vol-au-vent,* of the Adolfo (as it happened, a Cuban) fall collection.

One morning *El Herald* would bring news of the gala at the Pavillon of the Amigos Latinamericanos del Museo de Ciencia y Planetarium; another morning, of an upcoming event at the Big Five Club, a Miami club founded by former members of five fashionable clubs in prerevolutionary Havana: a *coctel,* or cocktail party, at which tables would be assigned for yet another gala, the annual "Baile Imperial de las Rosas" of the American Cancer Society, Hispanic Ladies Auxiliary. Some members of the community were honoring Miss America Latina with dinner dancing at the Doral. Some were being honored themselves, at the Spirit of Excellence Awards Dinner at the Omni. Some were said to be enjoying the skiing at Vail; others to prefer Bariloche, in Argentina. Some were reported unable to attend (but sending checks for) the gala at the Pavillon of the Amigos Latinamericanos del Museo de Ciencia y Planetarium because of a scheduling conflict, with *el coctel de* Paula Hawkins.

Fete followed fete, all high visibility. Almost any day it was possible to drive past the limestone arches and fountains which marked the boundaries of Coral Gables and see little girls being photographed in the tiaras and ruffled hoop skirts and maribou-trimmed illusion capes they would wear at their *quinces,* the elaborate fifteenth-birthday parties at which the community's female children come of official age. The favored facial expression for a *quince* photograph was a classic smolder. The favored backdrop was one suggesting Castilian grandeur, which was how the Coral Gables arches happened to figure. Since the idealization of the virgin implicit in the *quince* could exist only in the presence of its natural foil, *machismo,* there was often a brother around, or a boyfriend. There was also a mother, in dark glasses, not only to protect the symbolic virgin but to point out the better angle, the more aristocratic location. The *quinceanera* would pick up her hoop skirts and move as directed, often revealing the scuffed Jellies she had worn that day to school. A few weeks later there she would be, transformed in *Diario Las Americas,* one of the morning battalion of smoldering fifteen-year-olds, each with her arch, her fountain, her borrowed scenery, the gift if not exactly the intention of the late George Merrick, who built the arches when he developed Coral Gables.

Neither the photographs of the Cuban *quinceaneras* nor the notes 8 about the *coctel* at the Big Five were apt to appear in the newspapers read by Miami Anglos, nor, for that matter, was much information at all about the daily life of the Cuban majority. When, in the fall of 1986, Florida International University offered an evening course called "Cuban Miami: A Guide for Non-Cubans," the *Herald* sent a staff writer, who covered the classes as if from a distant beat. "Already I have begun to make some sense out of a culture, that, while it totally surrounds us, has remained inaccessible and alien to me," the *Herald* writer was reporting by the end of the first meeting, and, by the end of the fourth:

> What I see day to day in Miami, moving through mostly Anglo corridors of the community, are just small bits and pieces of that other world, the tip of something much larger than I'd imagined. . . . We may frequent the restaurants here, or wander into the occasional festival. But mostly we try to ignore Cuban Miami, even as we rub up against this teeming, incomprehensible presence.

Only thirteen people, including the *Herald* writer, turned up for the 9 first meeting of "Cuban Miami: A Guide for Non-Cubans" (two more appeared at the second meeting, along with a security guard, because of telephone threats prompted by what the *Herald* writer called "somebody's twisted sense of national pride"), an enrollment which suggested a certain willingness among non-Cubans to let Cuban Miami remain just that, Cuban, the "incomprehensible presence." In fact there had come to exist in South Florida two parallel cultures, separate but not exactly equal, a key distinction being that only one of the two, the Cuban, exhibited even a remote interest in the activities of the other. "The American community is not really aware of what is happening in the Cuban community," an exiled banker named Luis Botifoll said in a 1983 *Herald* Sunday magazine piece about ten prominent local Cubans. "We are clannish, but at least we know who is whom in the American establishment. They do not." About another of the ten Cubans featured in this piece, Jorge Mas Canosa, the *Herald* had this to say:

> He is an advisor to U.S. senators, a confidant of federal bureaucrats, a lobbyist for anti-Castro U.S. policies, a near unknown in Miami. When his political group sponsored a luncheon speech in Miami by Secretary of Defense Caspar Weinberger, almost none of the American business leaders attending had ever heard of their Cuban host.

The general direction of this piece, which appeared under the cover 10 line "THE CUBANS: *They're ten of the most powerful men in Miami. Half the population doesn't know it,*" was, as the *Herald* put it,

> to challenge the widespread presumption that Miami's Cubans are not really Americans, that they are a foreign presence here, an exile com-

munity that is trying to turn South Florida into North Cuba. . . . The top ten are not separatists; they have achieved success in the most traditional ways. They are the solid, bedrock citizens, hard-working humanitarians who are role models for a community that seems determined to assimilate itself into American society.

This was interesting. It was written by one of the few Cubans then on the *Herald* staff, and yet it described, however unwittingly, the precise angle at which Miami Anglos and Miami Cubans were failing to connect: Miami Anglos were in fact interested in Cubans only to the extent that they could cast them as aspiring immigrants, "determined to assimilate," a "hard-working" minority not different in kind from other groups of resident aliens. (But had I met any Haitians, a number of Anglos asked when I said that I had been talking to Cubans.) Anglos (who were, significantly, referred to within the Cuban community as "Americans") spoke of cross-culturalization, and of what they believed to be a meaningful second-generation preference for hamburgers, and rock-and-roll. They spoke of "diversity," and of Miami's "Hispanic flavor," an approach in which 56 percent of the population was seen as decorative, like the Coral Gables arches.

Fixed as they were on this image of the melting pot, of immigrants fleeing a disruptive revolution to find a place in the American sun, Anglos did not on the whole understand that assimilation would be considered by most Cubans a doubtful goal at best. Nor did many Anglos understand that living in Florida was still at the deepest level construed by Cubans as a temporary condition, an accepted political option shaped by the continuing dream, if no longer the immediate expectation, of a vindicatory return. *El exilio* was for Cubans a ritual, a respected tradition. *La revolución* was also a ritual, a trope fixed in Cuban political rhetoric at least since José Martí, a concept broadly interpreted to mean reform, or progress, or even just change. Ramón Grau San Martín, the president of Cuba during the autumn of 1933 and from 1944 until 1948, had presented himself as a revolutionary, as had his 1948 successor, Carlos Prío. Even Fulgencio Batista had entered Havana life calling for *la revolución,* and had later been accused of betraying it, even as Fidel Castro was now.

This was a process Cuban Miami understood, but Anglo Miami did not, remaining as it did arrestingly innocent of even the most general information about Cuba and Cubans. Miami Anglos for example still had trouble with Cuban names, and Cuban food. When the Cuban novelist Guillermo Cabrera Infante came from London to lecture at Miami-Dade Community College, he was referred to by several Anglo faculty members to whom I spoke as "Infante." Cuban food was widely seen not as a minute variation on that eaten throughout both the Caribbean and the Mediterranean but as "exotic," and full of garlic. A typical Thursday food section of the *Herald* included recipes for Broiled Lemon-Curry Cornish Game Hens, Chicken Tetrazzini, King Cake, Pimiento Cheese,

Raisin Sauce for Ham, Sauteed Spiced Peaches, Shrimp Scampi, Easy Beefy Stir-Fry, and four ways to use dried beans ("Those cheap, humble beans that have long sustained the world's poor have become the trendy set's new pet"), none of them Cuban.

This was all consistent, and proceeded from the original construction, that of the exile as an immigration. There was no reason to be curious about Cuban food, because Cuban teenagers preferred hamburgers. There was no reason to get Cuban names right, because they were complicated, and would be simplified by the second generation, or even by the first. "Jorge L. Mas" was the way Jorge Mas Canosa's business card read. "Raul Masvidal" was the way Raul Masvidal y Jury ran for mayor of Miami. There was no reason to know about Cuban history, because history was what immigrants were fleeing.

Even the revolution, the reason for the immigration, could be covered in a few broad strokes: "Batista," "Castro," "26 Julio," this last being the particular broad stroke that inspired the Miami Springs Holiday Inn, on July 26, 1985, the thirty-second anniversary of the day Fidel Castro attacked the Moncada Barracks and so launched his six-year struggle for power in Cuba, to run a bar special on Cuba Libres, thinking to attract local Cubans by commemorating their holiday. "It was a mistake," the manager said, besieged by outraged exiles. "The gentleman who did it is from Minnesota."

There was in fact no reason, in Miami as well as in Minnesota, to know anything at all about Cubans, since Miami Cubans were now, if not Americans, at least aspiring Americans, and worthy of Anglo attention to the exact extent that they were proving themselves, in the *Herald's* words, "role models for a community that seems determined to assimilate itself into American society"; or, as George Bush put it in a 1986 Miami address to the Cuban American National Foundation, "the most eloquent testimony I know to the basic strength and success of America, as well as to the basic weakness and failure of Communism and Fidel Castro."

The use of this special lens, through which the exiles were seen as a tribute to the American system, a point scored in the battle of the ideologies, tended to be encouraged by those outside observers who dropped down from the Northeast corridor for a look and a column or two. George Will, in *Newsweek,* saw Miami as "a new installment in the saga of America's absorptive capacity," and Southwest Eighth Street as the place where "these exemplary Americans," the seven Cubans who had been gotten together to brief him, "initiated a columnist to fried bananas and black-bean soup and other Cuban contributions to the tanginess of American life." George Gilder, in *The Wilson Quarterly,* drew pretty much the same lesson from Southwest Eighth Street, finding it "more effervescently thriving than its crushed prototype," by which he seemed to mean Havana. In fact Eighth Street was for George Gilder a street that seemed to "percolate with the forbidden commerce of the dying island to the south . . . the Refrescos Cawy, the Competidora and El Cuño cigarettes, the *guayaberas*,[1] the Latin music pulsing from the storefronts, the pyramids of mangoes and tubers, gourds and plantains, the iced coconuts served with a straw, the new theaters showing the latest anti-Castro comedies."

There was nothing on this list, with the possible exception of the "anti-Castro comedies," that could not most days be found on Southwest Eighth Street, but the list was also a fantasy, and a particularly *gringo* fantasy, one in which Miami Cubans, who came from a culture which had represented western civilization in this hemisphere since before there was a United States of America, appeared exclusively as vendors of plantains, their native music "pulsing" behind them. There was in any such view of Miami Cubans an extraordinary element of condescension, and it was the very condescension shared by Miami Anglos, who were inclined to reduce the particular liveliness and sophistication of local Cuban life to a matter of shrines on the lawn and love potions in the *botanicas,* the primitive exotica of the tourist's Caribbean.

Cubans were perceived as most satisfactory when they appeared most fully to share the aspirations and manners of middle-class Americans, at the same time adding "color" to the city on appropriate occasions, for example at their *quinces* (the *quinces* were one aspect of Cuban life almost invariably mentioned by Anglos, who tended to present them as evidence of Cuban extravagance, i.e., Cuban irresponsibility, or childishness), or on the day of the annual Calle Ocho Festival, when they could, according to the *Herald,* "samba" in the streets and stir up a paella for two thousand (ten cooks, two thousand mussels, two hundred and twenty pounds of lobster, and four hundred and forty pounds of rice), using rowboat oars as spoons. Cubans were perceived as least satisfactory when they "acted clannish," "kept to themselves," "had their own ways," and, two frequent flash points, "spoke Spanish when they didn't need to" and "got political"; complaints, each of them, which suggested an Anglo view of what Cubans should be at significant odds with what Cubans were.

This question of language was curious. The sound of spoken Spanish was common in Miami, but it was also common in Los Angeles, and Houston, and even in the cities of the Northeast. What was unusual about Spanish in Miami was not that it was so often spoken, but that it was so often heard: In, say, Los Angeles, Spanish remained a language only barely registered by the Anglo population, part of the ambient noise, the language spoken by the people who worked in the car wash and came to trim the trees and cleared the tables in restaurants. In Miami Spanish was spoken by the people who ate in the restaurants, the people who owned the cars and the trees, which made, on the

[1]*guayaberas:* summer shirts. (Ed.)

121

socio-auditory scale, a considerable difference. Exiles who felt isolated or declassed by language in New York or Los Angeles thrived in Miami. An entrepreneur who spoke no English could still, in Miami, buy, sell, negotiate, leverage assets, float bonds, and, if he were so inclined, attend galas twice a week, in black tie. "I have been after the *Herald* ten times to do a story about millionaires in Miami who do not speak more than two words in English," one prominent exile told me. "'Yes' and 'no.' Those are the two words. They come here with five dollars in their pockets and without speaking another word of English they are millionaires."

The truculence a millionaire who spoke only two words of English might provoke among the less resourceful native citizens of a nominally American city was predictable, and manifested itself rather directly. In 1980, the year of Mariel, Dade County voters had approved a referendum requiring that county business be conducted exclusively in English. Notwithstanding the fact that this legislation was necessarily amended to exclude emergency medical and certain other services, and notwithstanding even the fact that many local meetings continued to be conducted in that unbroken alternation of Spanish and English which had become the local patois ("I will be in Boston on Sunday and *desafortunadamente yo tengo un compromiso en* Boston *qu no puedo romper y yo no podre estar con Vds.,*" read the minutes of a 1984 Miami City Commission meeting I had occasion to look up. "*En espiritu, estaré, pero* the other members of the commission I am sure are invited . . ."),[2] the very existence of this referendum was seen by many as ground regained, a point made. By 1985 a St. Petersburg optometrist named Robert Melby was launching his third attempt in four years to have English declared the official language of the state of Florida, as it would be in 1986 of California. "I don't know why your legislators here are so, how should I put it?—spineless," Robert Melby complained about those South Florida politicians who knew how to count. "No one down here seems to want to run with the issue."

Even among those Anglos who distanced themselves from such efforts, Anglos who did not perceive themselves as economically or socially threatened by Cubans, there remained considerable uneasiness on the matter of language, perhaps because the inability or the disinclination to speak English tended to undermine their conviction that assimilation was an ideal universally shared by those who were to be assimilated. This uneasiness had for example shown up repeatedly during the 1985 mayoralty campaign, surfacing at odd but apparently irrepressible angles. The winner of that contest, Xavier Suarez, who was born in Cuba but educated in the United States, a graduate of Harvard Law, was reported in a wire service story to speak, an apparently unexpected accomplishment, "flawless English."

[2] "I will be in Boston on Sunday and unfortunately I have an appointment in Boston that I can't break and I won't be able to be with you. In spirit, I will be, but the other members of the commission I am sure are invited. . . ."

A less prominent Cuban candidate for mayor that year had unsettled reporters at a televised "meet the candidates" forum by answering in Spanish the questions they asked in English. "For all I or my dumbstruck colleagues knew," the *Herald* political editor complained in print after the event, "he was reciting his high school's alma mater or the ten Commandments over and over again. The only thing I understood was the occasional *Cubanos vota Cubano* he tossed in." It was noted by another *Herald* columnist that of the leading candidates, only one, Raul Masvidal, had a listed telephone number, but: ". . . if you call Masvidal's 661-0259 number on Kiaora Street in Coconut Grove—during the day, anyway—you'd better speak Spanish. I spoke to two women there, and neither spoke enough English to answer the question of whether it was the candidate's number."

On the morning this last item came to my attention in the *Herald* I studied it for some time. Raul Masvidal was at that time the chairman of the board of the Miami Savings Bank and the Miami Savings Corporation. He was a former chairman of the Biscayne Bank, and a minority stockholder in the M Bank, of which he had been a founder. He was a member of the Board of Regents for the state university system of Florida. He had paid $600,000 for the house on Kiaora Street in Coconut Grove, buying it specifically because he needed to be a Miami resident (Coconut Grove is part of the city of Miami) in order to run for mayor, and he had sold his previous house, in the incorporated city of Coral Gables, for $1,100,000.

The Spanish words required to find out whether the number listed for the house on Kiaora Street was in fact the candidate's number would have been roughly these: *"¿Es la casa de Raul Masvidal?"* The answer might have been *"Si,"* or the answer might have been *"No."* It seemed to me that there must be very few people working on daily newspapers along the southern borders of the United States who would consider this exchange entirely out of reach, and fewer still who would not accept it as a commonplace of American domestic-life that daytime telephone calls to middle-class urban households will frequently be answered by women who speak Spanish.

Something else was at work in this item, a real resistance, a balkiness, a coded version of the same message Dade County voters had sent when they decreed that their business be done only in English: WILL THE LAST AMERICAN TO LEAVE MIAMI PLEASE BRING THE FLAG, the famous bumper stickers had read the year of Mariel. "It was the last American stronghold in Dade County," the owner of the Gator Kicks Longneck Saloon, out where Southwest Eighth Street runs into the Everglades, had said after he closed the place for good the night of Super Bowl Sunday, 1986. "Fortunately or unfortunately, I'm not alone in my inability," a *Herald* columnist named Charles Whited had written a week or so later, in a column about not speaking Spanish. "A good many Americans have left Miami because they want to live someplace where everybody speaks one language: theirs." In this context the call to the house on Kiaora Street in Coconut Grove which did or did not belong to Raul Masvidal appeared not as a statement of literal fact but as shorthand, a glove thrown down, a stand, a cry from the heart of a beleaguered raj.

COMPREHENSION

1. What are the two Miamis depicted in Didion's essay?
2. How do Cubans view the issue of assimilation?
3. What stereotypical perceptions do Anglos in Miami have about their Cuban neighbors? What differences do the Anglos find most threatening?
4. In your opinion, where do the writer's sympathies lie? Justify your answer.

RHETORIC

1. Examine Didion's opening paragraph. Why did she choose to begin this way? Does it prepare the reader for her views? Why does she also mention the accomplishments of the people in the introduction?
2. What is Didion's thesis? Where is it stated or implied? What support does she give?
3. How does the writer use language to bring the Cuban community to life in her essay? Cite specific images, words, phrases; and show how they contribute to her exposition.
4. Is Didion stating her case objectively? What indications are there in the piece that demonstrate this?
5. How does Didion's use of quotes from various sources strengthen her credibility? Give examples.
6. In paragraph 6, Didion lists Cuban social and charity events, using specific names and places. What point is she making?
7. Consider Didion's use of the term "beleaguered raj" in her final paragraph. What connection is she making between the social climate in the two Miamis and a more global perspective? Does the image hold?

WRITING

1. Conduct an interview with an older member of your community, and discuss the changing face of the community in terms of racial or cultural differences. What impact has immigration had on your state, town, or city? How are this person's views representative of others in the community?
2. In an argumentation essay, give your views on assimilation. Consider its benefits to immigrants and natives as well as its drawbacks.
3. Write a personal essay in which you describe the ethnic and racial diversity of your community. How comfortable do you feel with the differences? Have you made any attempts to interact with members of other nationalities? Why, or why not? Do you sense any conflicts within yourself similar to the ones in Didion's essay? Use your personal experience to support your views.

1. White and Didion both discuss life in big cities. How do their visions differ? Examine the strategies they use. What moods do they establish in their essays, and how? Do they have similar goals? Discuss in an essay.

2. When were these essays written? What details provide a sense of time? What impact did the prevailing political and social realities of the time have on the writers? Write an essay addressing these questions.

3. Consider the level of language in both essays. How does the presence or absence of abstract or concrete images help to advance the writers' views? How appropriate or effective are they?

4. Write an essay in which you either "update" White's portrait of New York or describe Didion's Miami of two or three decades ago. Research your subject, choose an effective strategy, and use quotes from either or both writers in your own piece.

CONNECTIONS

Chapter Two
The Sense of
Place

1. Using the essays of Iyer, Lopez, and Kincaid as support, consider the ramifications of imposing a foreign consciousness on a country's people and geography.

2. Momaday and Crews write about their homes. How do they establish mood in their works? Do they share similar feelings about their homes? How are their aims similar, and how do they differ? Use examples from the essays to support your views.

3. Both Orwell and Kincaid deal with the influences of foreign domination on a country's landscape. How do the writers approach this theme? How do they establish a mood? Are they equally effective? Is there a historical link between the two? Compare and contrast.

4. Titles play an important part in establishing an essay's theme and setting a mood. Pick three of the writers in this section, and discuss why these writers chose the particular titles for their pieces and how appropriate their choices were.

5. The link between human beings and the land is crucial. Using the essays of Crews, Lopez, Iyer, and White, discuss the writers' attitudes. How do these writers see humanity's impact on the landscape?

6. Discuss the contribution made by figurative language and details in an essay. Consider the level of language in the works of Momaday, Kincaid, and Zinsser in your discussion.

7. Some essays in this section are expository while others are of a more personal nature. Choose two writers using dissimilar strategies, and consider why the strategy used works for that writer.

8. Select one of the specific places or landmarks mentioned in any of the essays and research it. How did the writer spark your interest in the place? How did the place in the essay compare to the information you found?

9. Compare and contrast Didion's and White's vision of city life.

10. Select the essay in this section that most satisfied you as a reader. What feelings and ideas did it evoke? How did it accomplish this? What personal connections did it make? Compare it to an essay in this section that you feel was less effective.

CHAPTER THREE

Manners and Customs

*E*very society lives by certain rituals and rules, and observes certain tastes and fashions. These manners and customs help us to understand our culture and the traditions that mold it. In fact, manners and customs—such as handing down your great-grandmother's wedding ring from bride to bride, following a favorite family recipe faithfully, and celebrating a holiday in a specific way—are our inheritance.

The way in which we behave in a culture is determined by manners and customs. Sometimes these customs cut across cultures; at other times they conflict. Moreover, in modern times, it is increasingly difficult to find manners and customs that are unchanging, for social life today is characterized by innovation and transformation. Take as an example the culture of food. On or near any typical college campus, you can find Chinese, Italian, Mexican, Greek, and Japanese restaurants and more, including the ubiquitous American diner. As Imamu Amiri Baraka tells us in his essay "Soul Food," the habits we bring to the simple act of eating define our values, lifestyles, and cultural identity. And when we experience the cuisines of other cultures, we learn something about the social patterns of those cultures.

Our ability to understand the manners and customs of other people is one of the best antidotes to cultural ignorance. As Jade Snow Wong observes in her essay in this chapter, immigrants to this nation are under special challenges to comprehend new manners and customs while preserving their own traditions. Conversely, when we encounter other customs at home or abroad, we often have our own notions of "heritage" challenged. We might have set notions about marriage customs, but as Ann Grace Mojtabai reminds us in "Polygamy," other patterns of marriage exist around the world. Similarly, Alice Walker reminds us that notions of beauty are often gender- and culture-specific, adhering to unspoken but understood rules of the cultural game.

People who parade their manners and customs are often blind to other perspectives. What, for example, is your favorite holiday? How do you celebrate it? Would everyone else necessarily find this holiday as appealing as you do? What if you were a Native American, like Michael Dorris, and you were asked to celebrate Thanksgiving? You might discover, as Dorris does in "For the Indians No Thanksgiving," that a holiday that you celebrate actually might offend the traditions or heritage of others.

Some customs and cultural habits might seem strange to us and even defy logic—read the essay on superstition by Pogrebin—but if we are fair-minded, we make an effort to comprehend them and perhaps even to honor them. Thomas Carlyle wrote, "Good breeding differs, if at all, from high breeding only as it gracefully remembers the rights of others, rather than insisting on its own rights." In learning to understand others' manners and customs, we gain wisdom about other cultures and learn to structure our social relations in new and more useful ways.

Previewing the Chapter

As you read the essays in this chapter and respond to them in discussion and writing, consider the following questions:

• What is the author's purpose? Does the author have a personal motive in addressing the topic in the way he or she does?

• Does the writer present a negative or a positive picture of the manners and customs under consideration? How do you know?

• What cultural problems and conflicts are raised by the author in his or her treatment of the subject?

• What is the writer's tone? Is it serious, humorous, critical, biased, unbiased, or what?

• Which writers focus simply on the need to understand certain customs and manners, and which authors advocate changing rather than preserving them?

• What strengths and weaknesses does the author find in the customs under discussion?

• Does the author have a broad or narrow focus on the relationship of manners to the larger society?

• What is your position or perspective on the subjects and themes raised by each author?

• Which authors altered your position on a topic, and why?

LETTY COTTIN POGREBIN   Letty Cottin Pogrebin (b. 1939) is deeply committed to women's issues, family politics, and the nonsexist rearing and education of children. A native of New York, she graduated from Brandeis University and, from 1971–1987, was the editor of *Ms.* magazine, for which she remains a contributing editor. She has also contributed to such publications as *The New York Times* and *The Nation* and has written a number of books, among them *Among Friends* (1986); *Debra, Golda and Me: Being Female and Jewish in America* (1991); and *Family Politics* (1983). Pogrebin lectures frequently and is a founder of the Women's Political Caucus. In the following essay, she reminisces about her fearful, superstitious mother, whom she understands much better since becoming a mother herself.

LETTY COTTIN POGREBIN

Superstitious Minds

I am a very rational person. I tend to trust reason more than feeling.   1
But I also happen to be superstitious—in my fashion. Black cats and rabbits' feet hold no power for me. My superstitions are my mother's superstitions, the amulets and incantations she learned from her mother and taught me.

I don't mean to suggest that I grew up in an occult atmosphere. On   2
the contrary, my mother desperately wanted me to rise above her immigrant ways and become an educated American. She tried to hide her superstitions, but I came to know them all: Slap a girl's cheeks when she first gets her period. Never take a picture of a pregnant woman. Knock wood when speaking about your good fortune. Eat the ends of bread if you want to have a boy. Don't leave a bride alone on her wedding day.

When I was growing up, my mother often would tiptoe in after I   3
seemed to be asleep and kiss my forehead three times, making odd noises that sounded like a cross between sucking and spitting. One night I opened my eyes and demanded an explanation. Embarrassed, she told me she was excising the "Evil Eye"—in case I had attracted its attention that day by being especially wonderful. She believed her kisses could suck out any envy or ill will that those less fortunate may have directed at her child.

By the time I was in my teens, I was almost on speaking terms with   4
the Evil Eye, a jealous spirit that kept track of those who had "too much" happiness and zapped them with sickness and misery to even the score. To guard against this mischief, my mother practiced rituals of interference, evasion, deference, and above all, avoidance of situations where the Evil Eye might feel at home.

This is why I wasn't allowed to attend funerals. This is also why my ₅ mother hated to mend my clothes while I was wearing them. The only garment one should properly get sewn *into* is a shroud. To ensure that the Evil Eye did not confuse my pinafore with a burial outfit, my mother insisted that I chew a thread while she sewed, thus proving myself very much alive. Outwitting the Evil Eye also accounted for her closing the window shades above my bed whenever there was a full moon. The moon should only shine on cemeteries, you see; the living need protection from the spirits.

Because we were dealing with a deadly force, I also wasn't supposed ₆ to say any words associated with mortality. This was hard for a 12-year-old who punctuated every anecdote with the verb "to die," as in "You'll die when you hear this!" or "If I don't get home by ten, I'm dead." I managed to avoid using such expressions in the presence of my mother until the day my parents brought home a painting I hated and we were arguing about whether it should be displayed on our walls. Unthinking, I pressed my point with a melodramatic idiom: "That picture will hang over my dead body!" Without a word, my mother grabbed a knife and slashed the canvas to shreds.

I understand all this now. My mother emigrated in 1907 from a ₇ small Hungarian village. The oldest of seven children, she had to go out to work before she finished the eighth grade. Experience taught her that life was unpredictable and often incomprehensible. Just as an athlete keeps wearing the same T-shirt in every game to prolong a winning streak, my mother's superstitions gave her a means of imposing order on a chaotic system. Her desire to control the fates sprung from the same helplessness that makes the San Francisco 49ers' defensive more superstitious than its offensive team. Psychologists speculate this is because the defense has less control; they don't have the ball.

Women like my mother never had the ball. She died when I was 15, ₈ leaving me with deep regrets for what she might have been—and a growing understanding of who she was. *Superstitious* is one of the things she was. I wish I had a million sharp recollections of her, but when you don't expect someone to die, you don't store up enough memories. Ironically, her mystical practices are among the clearest impressions she left behind. In honor of this matrilineal heritage—and to symbolize my mother's effort to control her life as I in my way try to find order in mine—I knock on wood and I do not let the moon shine on those I love. My children laugh at me, but they understand that these tiny rituals have helped keep my mother alive in my mind.

A year ago, I awoke in the night and realized that my son's window ₉ blinds had been removed for repair. Smiling at my own compulsion, I got a bed sheet to tack up against the moonlight and I opened his bedroom door. What I saw brought tears to my eyes. There, hopelessly askew, was a blanket my son, then 18, had taped to his window like a curtain.

My mother never lived to know David, but he knew she would not ₁₀ want the moon to shine upon him as he slept.

COMPREHENSION

1. What is the function of superstition in the writer's life? What purpose did it serve in her mother's life?
2. What was Pogrebin's reaction to her mother's behavior while she was growing up? How does the adult feel?
3. How does the writer use superstitions now as an adult? Has she passed on these beliefs to her children? Explain.

RHETORIC

1. Examine Pogrebin's first sentence. How does it prepare the reader for the content of the essay? How does its simplicity add to its force?
2. How do the accumulated examples in paragraph 2 illustrate the point of the paragraph?
3. What is the writer's tone? Justify your answer.
4. What is the point of paragraph 7? How does the metaphor work to support Pogrebin's point?
5. What is the purpose of the essay? Where does it become apparent? How do the other paragraphs reinforce it?
6. Comment on the author's final sentence. What effect does it have on the reader? How does it help to hold the essay together?

WRITING

1. Children are often annoyed or embarrassed by their parents' behavior or beliefs. Write an essay describing something your parents repeatedly said or did that caused you discomfort or confusion. Include how you now feel about their actions and any insight you may have since gained about their motives or feelings.
2. Write an essay about superstition. Consider the meaning of the word. What connection, if any, does it have with religion? How do superstitions affect the people who believe in them? Why do they believe? What is the role of superstition in your family? Provide examples of superstitions.
3. Write an essay in which you consider how your parents raised you—the values, opinions, beliefs they instilled in you. Would you want to pass these on to your children? Why, or why not?

JADE SNOW WONG   Jade Snow Wong, the daughter of a manufacturer father, was born in San Francisco in 1922. Wong has been a secretary, co-owner of a travel agency, and owner of a ceramics gallery. She has won prizes for her work in pottery and enamel. As a writer, she is known best for her auto-biography, *Fifth Chinese Daughter,* and has contributed to periodicals such as *Holiday* magazine. Through her life and work, Wong hopes to bridge the gap between Chinese and Americans. In the following narrative, she develops the theme of mainstreaming and its effects on her family.

JADE SNOW WONG

Pilgrims from the Orient

From infancy to my sixteenth year, I was reared according to nine- 1
teenth-century ideals of Chinese womanhood. I was never left alone,
though it was not unusual for me to feel lonely, while surrounded by a
family of seven others, and often by ten (including bachelor cousins) at
meals.

My father (who enjoyed our calling him Daddy in English) was the 2
unquestioned head of our household. He was not talkative, being preoccupied with his business affairs and with reading constantly otherwise. My mother was mistress of domestic affairs. Seldom did these
two converse before their children, but we knew them to be a united
front, and suspected that privately she both informed and influenced
him about each child.

In order to support the family in America, Daddy tried various 3
occupations—candy making, the ministry to which he was later
ordained—but finally settled on manufacturing men's and children's
denim garments. He leased sewing equipment, installed machines in a
basement where rent was cheapest, and there he and his family lived
and worked. There was no thought that dim, airless quarters were terrible conditions for living and working, or that child labor was
unhealthful. The only goal was for all in the family to work, to save, and
to become educated. It was possible, so it would be done.

My father, a meticulous bookkeeper, used only an abacus, a brush, 4
ink, and Chinese ledgers. Because of his newly learned ideals, he pio-
neered for the right of women to work. Concerned that they have economic independence, but not with the long hours of industrial home
work, he went to shy housewives' apartments and taught them sewing.

My earliest memories of companionship with my father were as his 5
passenger in his red wheelbarrow, sharing space with the piles of blue-
jean materials he was delivering to a worker's home. He must have been
forty. He was lean, tall, inevitably wearing blue overalls, rolled shirt
sleeves, and high black kid shoes. In his pockets were numerous keys,
tools, and pens. On such deliveries, I noticed that he always managed
time to show a mother how to sew a difficult seam, or to help her repair
a machine, or just to chat.

I observed from birth that living and working were inseparable. My 6
mother was short, sturdy, young looking, and took pride in her appearance. She was at her machine the minute housework was done, and she
was the hardest-working seamstress, seldom pausing, working after I
went to bed. The hum of sewing machines continued day and night,
seven days a week. She knew that to have more than the four necessi-

ties, she must work and save. We knew that to overcome poverty, there were only two methods: working and education.

Having provided the setup for family industry, my father turned his attention to our education. Ninety-five percent of the population in his native China had been illiterate. He knew that American public schools would take care of our English, but he had to nurture our Chinese knowledge. Only the Cantonese tongue was ever spoken by him or my mother. When the two oldest girls arrived from China, the schools of Chinatown received only boys. My father tutored his daughters each morning before breakfast. In the midst of a foreign environment, he clung to a combination of the familiar old standards and what was permissible in the newly learned Christian ideals.

My eldest brother was born in America, the only boy for fourteen 8 years, and after him three daughters—another older sister, myself, and my younger sister. Then my younger brother, Paul, was born. That older brother, Lincoln, was cherished in the best Chinese tradition. He had his own room; he kept a German shepherd as his pet; he was tutored by a Chinese scholar; he was sent to private school for American classes. As a male Wong, he would be responsible some day for the preservation of and pilgrimages to ancestral graves—his privileges were his birthright. We girls were content with the unusual opportunities of working and attending two schools. By day, I attended American public school near our home. From 5:00 P.M. to 8:00 P.M. on five weekdays and from 9:00 A.M. to 12 noon on Saturdays, I attended the Chinese school. Classes numbered twenty to thirty students, and were taught by educated Chinese from China. We studied poetry, calligraphy, philosophy, literature, history, correspondence, religion, all by exacting memorization.

Daddy emphasized memory development; he could still recite flu- 9 ently many lengthy lessons of his youth. Every evening after both schools, I'd sit by my father, often as he worked at his sewing machine sing-songing my lessons above its hum. Sometimes I would stop to hold a light for him as he threaded the difficult holes of a specialty machine, such as one for bias bindings. After my Chinese lessons passed his approval, I was allowed to attend to American homework. I was made to feel luckier than other Chinese girls who didn't study Chinese, and also luckier than Western girls without a dual heritage.

There was little time for play, and toys were unknown to me. In any 10 spare time, I was supplied with embroidery and sewing for my mother. The Chinese New Year, which by the old lunar calendar would fall sometime in late January or early February of the Western Christian calendar, was the most special time of the year, for then the machine stopped for three days. Mother would clean our living quarters very thoroughly, decorate the sitting room with flowering branches and fresh oranges, and arrange candied fruits or salty melon seeds for callers. All of us would be dressed in bright new clothes, and relatives or close friends, who came to call, would give each of us a red paper packet containing a good luck coin—usually a quarter. I remember how my classmates would gleefully talk of *their* receipts. But my mother made us give our money to her, for she said that she needed it to reciprocate to others.

Yet there was little reason for unhappiness. I was never hungry. Though we had no milk, there was all the rice we wanted. We had hot and cold running water—a rarity in Chinatown—as well as our own bathtub. Our sheets were pieced from dishtowels, but we had sheets. I was never neglected, for my mother and father were always at home. During school vacation periods, I was taught to operate many types of machines—tacking (for pockets), overlocking (for the raw edges of seams), buttonhole, double seaming; and I learned all the stages in producing a pair of jeans to its final inspection, folding, and tying in bundles of a dozen pairs by size, ready for pickup. Denim jeans are heavy—my shoulders ached often. My father set up a modest nickel-and-dime piecework reward for me, which he recorded in my own notebook, and paid me regularly.

My mother dutifully followed my father's leadership. She was extremely thrifty, but the thrifty need pennies to manage, and the old world had denied her those. Upon arrival in the new world of San Francisco, she accepted the elements her mate had selected to shape her new life: domestic duties, seamstress work in the factory-home, mothering each child in turn, church once a week, and occasional movies. Daddy frowned upon the community Chinese operas because of their very late hours (they did not finish till past midnight) and their mixed audiences.

Very early in my life, the manners of a traditional Chinese lady were taught to me: how to hold a pair of chopsticks (palm up, not down); how to hold a bowl of rice (one thumb on top, not resting in an open palm); how to pass something to elders (with both hands, never one); how to pour tea into the tiny, handleless porcelain cups (seven-eighths full so that the top edge would be cool enough to hold); how to eat from a center serving dish (only the piece in front of your place, never pick around); not to talk at table, not to show up outside of one's room without being fully dressed; not to be late, ever; not to be too playful. In a hundred and one ways, we were molded to be trouble-free, unobtrusive, cooperative.

We were disciplined by first being told, and then by punishment if we didn't remember. Punishment was instant and unceremonious. At the table, it came as a sudden whack from Daddy's chopsticks. Away from the table, punishment could be the elimination of a privilege or the blow on our legs from a bundle of cane switches.

Only Daddy and Oldest Brother were allowed individual idiosyncrasies. Daughters were all expected to be of one standard. To allow each one of many daughters to be different would have posed enormous problems of cost, energy, and attention. No one was shown physical affection. Such familiarity would have weakened my parents and endangered the one-answer authoritative system. One standard from past to present, whether in China or in San Francisco, was simpler to enforce. My parents never said "please" and "thank you" for any service or gift. In Chinese, both "please" and "thank you" can be literally translated as "I am not worthy" and naturally, no parent is going to say that about a service which should be their just due.

Traditional Chinese parents pit their children against a standard of perfection without regard to personality, individual ambitions, tolerance for human error, or exposure to the changing social scene. It never occurred to that kind of parent to be friends with their children on common ground.

During the Depression, my mother and father needed even more hours to work. Daddy had been shopping daily for groceries (we had no icebox) and my mother cooked. Now I was told to assume both those duties. My mother would give me fifty cents to buy enough fresh food for dinner and breakfast. In those years, twenty-five cents could buy a small chicken or three sanddabs, ten cents bought three bunches of green vegetables, and fifteen cents bought some meat to cook with these. After American school I rushed to the stores only a block or so away, returned and cleaned the foods, and cooked in a hurry in order to eat an early dinner and get to Chinese school on time. When I came home at 8:00 P.M., I took care of the dinner dishes before starting to do my homework. Saturdays and Sundays were for housecleaning and the family laundry, which I scrubbed on a board, using big galvanized buckets in our bathtub.

I had no sympathetic guidance as an eleven-year-old in my own reign in the kitchen, which lasted for four years. I finished junior high school, started high school, and continued studying Chinese. With the small earnings from summer work in my father's basement factory (we moved back to the basement during the Depression), I bought materials to sew my own clothes. But the routine of keeping house only to be dutiful, to avoid tongue or physical lashings, became exasperating. The tiny space which was the room for three sisters was confining. After I graduated from Chinese evening school, I began to look for part-time paying jobs as a mother's helper. Those jobs varied from cleaning house to baking a cake, amusing a naughty child to ironing shirts, but wearying, exhausting as they were, they meant money earned for myself.

As I advanced in American high school and worked at those jobs, I was gradually introduced to customs not of the Chinese world. American teachers were mostly kind. I remember my third-grade teacher's skipping me half a year. I remember my fourth-grade teacher—with whom I am still friendly. She was the first person to hold me to her physically and affectionately—because a baseball bat had been accidentally flung against my hand. I also remember that I was confused by being held, since physical comfort had not been offered by my parents. I remember my junior high school principal, who skipped me half a grade and commended me before the school assembly, to my great embarrassment.

In contrast, Chinese schoolteachers acted as extensions of Chinese parental discipline. There was a formal "disciplinarian dean" to apply the cane to wayward boys, and girls were not exempt either. A whisper during chapel was sufficient provocation to be called to the dean's office. No humor was exchanged; no praise or affection expressed by the teachers. They presented the lessons, and we had to learn to memorize all the words, orally, before the class. Then followed the written test, word for word. Without an alphabet, the Chinese language requires exact memorization. No originality or deviation was permitted and grading was severe. One word wrong during an examination could reduce a grade by 10 percent. It was the principle of learning by punishment.

Interest and praise, physical or oral, were rewards peculiar to the American world. Even employers who were paying me thanked me for a service or complimented me on a meal well cooked, and sometimes helped me with extra dishes. Chinese often said that "foreigners" talked too much about too many personal things. My father used to tell me to think three times before saying anything, and if I said nothing, no one would say I was stupid. I perceived a difference between two worlds. 21

By the time I was graduating from high school, my parents had done their best to produce an intelligent, obedient daughter, who would know more than the average Chinatown girl and should do better than average at a conventional job, her earnings brought home to them in repayment for their years of child support. Then, they hoped, she would marry a nice Chinese boy and make him a good wife, as well as an above-average mother for his children. Chinese custom used to decree that families should "introduce" chosen partners to each other's children. The groom's family should pay handsomely to the bride's family for rearing a well-bred daughter. They should also pay all bills for a glorious wedding banquet for several hundred guests. Then the bride's family could consider their job done. Their daughter belonged to the groom's family and must henceforth seek permission from all persons in his home before returning to her parents for a visit. 22

But having been set upon a new path, I did not oblige my parents with the expected conventional ending. At fifteen, I had moved away from home to work for room and board and a salary of twenty dollars per month. Having found that I could subsist independently, I thought it regrettable to terminate my education. Upon graduating from high school at the age of sixteen, I asked my parents to assist me in college expenses. I pleaded with my father, for his years of encouraging me to be above mediocrity in both Chinese and American studies had made me wish for some undefined but brighter future. 23

My father was briefly adamant. He must conserve his resources for my oldest brother's medical training. Though I desired to continue on an above-average course, his material means were insufficient to support that ambition. He added that if I had the talent, I could provide for my own college education. When he had spoken, no discussion was expected. After his edict, no daughter questioned. 24

But this matter involved my whole future—it was not simply asking for permission to go to a night church meeting (forbidden also). 25

Though for years I had accepted the authority of the one I honored most, his decision that night embittered me as nothing ever had. My oldest brother had so many privileges, had incurred unusual expenses for luxuries which were taken for granted as his birthright, yet these were part of a system I had accepted. Now I suddenly wondered at my father's interpretation of the Christian code: was it intended to discriminate against a girl after all, or was it simply convenient for my father's economics and cultural prejudice? Did a daughter have any right to expect more than a fate of obedience, according to the old Chinese standard? As long as I could remember, I had been told that a female followed three men during her lifetime: as a girl, her father; as a wife, her husband; as an old woman, her son.

My indignation mounted against that tradition and I decided then that my past could not determine my future. I knew that more education would prepare me for a different expectation than my other female schoolmates, few of whom were to complete a college degree. I, too, had my father's unshakable faith in the justice of God, and I shared his unconcern with popular opinion.

So I decided to enter junior college, now San Francisco's City College, because the fees were lowest. I lived at home and supported myself with an after-school job which required long hours of housework and cooking but paid me twenty dollars per month, of which I saved as much as possible. The thrills derived from reading and learning, in ways ranging from chemistry experiments to English compositions, from considering new ideas of sociology to the logic of Latin, convinced me that I had made a correct choice. I was kept in a state of perpetual mental excitement by new Western subjects and concepts and did not mind long hours of work and study. I also made new friends, which led to another painful incident with my parents, who had heretofore discouraged even girlhood friendships.

The college subject which had most jolted me was sociology. The instructor fired my mind with his interpretation of family relationships. As he explained to our class, it used to be an economic asset for American farming families to be large, since children were useful to perform agricultural chores. But this situation no longer applied and children should be regarded as individuals with their own rights. Unquestioning obedience should be replaced with parental understanding. So at sixteen, discontented as I was with my parents' apparent indifference to me, those words of my sociology professor gave voice to my sentiments. How old-fashioned was the dead-end attitude of my parents! How ignorant they were of modern thought and progress! The family unit had been China's strength for centuries, but it had also been her weakness, for corruption, nepotism, and greed were all justified in the name of the family's welfare. My new ideas festered; I longed to release them.

One afternoon on a Saturday, which was normally occupied with my housework job, I was unexpectedly released by my employer, who was departing for a country weekend. It was a rare joy to have free time

137

and I wanted to enjoy myself for a change. There had been a Chinese-American boy who shared some classes with me. Sometimes we had found each other walking to the same 8:00 A.M. class. He was not a special boyfriend, but I had enjoyed talking to him and had confided in him some of my problems. Impulsively, I telephoned him. I knew I must be breaking rules, and I felt shy and scared. At the same time, I was excited at this newly found forwardness, with nothing more purposeful than to suggest another walk together.

He understood my awkwardness and shared my anticipation. He asked me to "dress up" for my first movie date. My clothes were limited but I changed to look more graceful in silk stockings and found a bright ribbon for my long black hair. Daddy watched, catching my mood, observing the dashing preparations. He asked me where I was going without his permission and with whom. 30

I refused to answer him. I thought of my rights! I thought he surely would not try to understand. Thereupon Daddy thundered his displeasure and forbade my departure. 31

I found a new courage as I heard my voice announce calmly that I was no longer a child, and if I could work my way through college, I would choose my own friends. It was my right as a person. 32

My mother heard the commotion and joined my father to face me; both appeared shocked and incredulous. Daddy at once demanded the source of this unfilial, non-Chinese theory. And when I quoted my college professor, reminding him that he had always felt teachers should be revered, my father denounced that professor as a foreigner who was disregarding the superiority of our Chinese culture, with its sound family strength. My father did not spare me; I was condemned as an ingrate for echoing dishonorable opinions which should only be temporary whims, yet nonetheless inexcusable. 33

The scene was not yet over. I completed my proclamation to my father, who had never allowed me to learn how to dance, by adding that I was attending a movie, unchaperoned, with a boy I met at college. 34

My startled father was sure that my reputation would be subject to whispered innuendos. I must be bent on disgracing the family name; I was ruining my future, for surely I would yield to temptation. My mother underscored him by saying that I hadn't any notion of the problems endured by parents of a young girl. 35

I would not give in. I reminded them that they and I were not in China, that I wasn't going out with just anybody but someone I trusted! Daddy gave a roar that no man could be trusted, but I devastated them in declaring that I wished the freedom to find my own answers. 36

Both parents were thoroughly angered, scolded me for being shameless, and predicted that I would some day tell them I was wrong. But I dimly perceived that they were conceding defeat and were perplexed at this breakdown of their training. I was too old to beat and too bold to intimidate. 37

1. How were boys and girls treated in the Wong family? What was expected of each?
2. What kind of child was Jade? What precipitated her change?
3. What values were instilled in the Wong children?

RHETORIC

1. Who are the "pilgrims" in Wong's title? Does the title effectively convey the thematic content of the essay? What is Wong's thesis? Where is it stated?
2. What is Wong emphasizing by the capitalization of "Daddy"? Is there any evidence of irony in the word? Explain.
3. What comparative strategy does Wong employ in her essay?
4. What specific examples does the writer use to illustrate the clash between Chinese and American values and customs?
5. How does the writer present the confrontation with Daddy at the end of the essay? Does this approach work to intensify or dilute the drama of the scene?
6. What is the significance of the essay's final line: "I was too old to beat and too bold to intimidate"? What resolution does the writer seem to have come to?

WRITING

1. Write an essay in which you argue for or against the necessity of rejecting your parents' values and traditions in order to develop independence and selfhood. Use examples from Wong's essay as well as personal experience in your development.
2. Wong's essay explores some of the ways in which Chinese traditions defined her role as a girl and, later, as a woman. What restrictions does American society place on sexual identity? What were the messages (subtle or overt) sent by your family as you were growing up?
3. Wong spends some time in her essay comparing the educational system in China to the American system. Using the information she provides, which method seems more effective to you? Write an essay in which you explore what one could learn from the other.

ELIZABETH WHELAN   Elizabeth Whelan was born in New York City in 1945 and educated at Connecticut College, Yale University, and Harvard University. She has served on the staff of several government health departments and has been a moderator of the nationally syndicated radio program *Healthline*. She has authored or coauthored a dozen books on a range of health issues as well as contributing to numerous periodicals, including *Glamour, Cosmopolitan,* and the *National Review.* She is a member of several national health associations and serves as president of the American Council on Science and Health.

"Perils of Prohibition," a logical argument for the lowering of the drinking age, was first published in *Newsweek* in 1995.

ELIZABETH M. WHELAN

Perils of Prohibition

My colleagues at the Harvard School of Public Health, where I studied   1
preventive medicine, deserve high praise for their recent study on
teenage drinking. What they found in their survey of college students
was that they drink "early and . . . often," frequently to the point of
getting ill.

As a public-health scientist with a daughter, Christine, heading to   2
college this fall, I have professional and personal concerns about teen
binge drinking. It is imperative that we explore *why* so many young
people abuse alcohol. From my own study of the effects of alcohol
restrictions and my observations of Christine and her friends' predicament about drinking, I believe that today's laws are unrealistic. Prohibiting the sale of liquor to responsible young adults creates an atmosphere where binge drinking and alcohol abuse have become a problem.
American teens, unlike their European peers, don't learn how to drink
gradually, safely and in moderation.

Alcohol is widely accepted and enjoyed in our culture. Studies show   3
that moderate drinking can be good for you. But we legally proscribe
alcohol until the age of 21 (why not 30 or 45?). Christine and her classmates can drive cars, fly planes, marry, vote, pay taxes, take out loans
and risk their lives as members of the U.S. armed forces. But laws in all
50 states say that no alcoholic beverages may be sold to anyone until
that magic 21st birthday. We didn't always have a national "21" rule.
When I was in college, in the mid-'60s, the drinking age varied from
state to state. This posed its own risks, with underage students crossing
state lines to get a legal drink.

In parts of the Western world, moderate drinking by teenagers and   4
even children under their parents' supervision is a given. Though the
per capita consumption of alcohol in France, Spain and Portugal is
higher than in the United States, the rate of alcoholism and alcohol
abuse is lower. A glass of wine at dinner is normal practice. Kids learn
to regard moderate drinking as an enjoyable family activity rather than
as something they have to sneak away to do. Banning drinking by
young people makes it a badge of adulthood—a tantalizing forbidden
fruit.

Christine and her teenage friends like to go out with a group to a   5
club, comedy show or sports bar to watch the game. But teens today
have to go on the sly with fake IDs and the fear of getting caught. Oth-

erwise, they're denied admittance to most places and left to hang out on the street. That's hardly a safer alternative. Christine and her classmates now find themselves in a legal no man's land. At 18, they're considered adults. Yet when they want to enjoy a drink like other adults, they are, as they put it, "disenfranchised."

Comparing my daughter's dilemma with my own as an "underage" college student, I see a difference—and one that I think has exacerbated the current dilemma. Today's teens are far more sophisticated than we were. They're treated less like children and have more responsibilities than we did. This makes the 21 restriction seem anachronistic.

For the past few years, my husband and I have been preparing Christine for college life and the inevitable partying—read keg of beer—that goes with it. Last year, a young friend with no drinking experience was violently ill for days after he was introduced to "clear liquids in small glasses" during freshman orientation. We want our daughter to learn how to drink sensibly and avoid this pitfall. Starting at the age of 14, we invited her to join us for a glass of champagne with dinner. She'd tried it once before, thought it was "yucky" and declined. A year later, she enjoyed sampling wine at family meals.

When, at 16, she asked for a Mudslide (a bottled chocolate-milk-and-rum concoction), we used the opportunity to discuss it with her. We explained the alcohol content, told her the alcohol level is lower when the drink is blended with ice and compared it with a glass of wine. Since the drink of choice on campus is beer, we contrasted its potency with wine and hard liquor and stressed the importance of not drinking on an empty stomach.

Our purpose was to encourage her to know the alcohol content of what she is served. We want her to experience the effects of liquor in her own home, not on the highway and not for the first time during a college orientation week with free-flowing suds. Although Christine doesn't drive yet, we regularly reinforce the concept of choosing a designated driver. Happily, that already seems a widely accepted practice among our daughter's friends who drink.

We recently visited the Ivy League school Christine will attend in the fall. While we were there, we read a story in the college paper about a student who was nearly electrocuted when, in a drunken state, he climbed on top of a moving train at a railroad station near the campus. The student survived, but three of his limbs were later amputated. This incident reminded me of a tragic death on another campus. An intoxicated student maneuvered himself into a chimney. He was found three days later when frat brothers tried to light a fire in the fireplace. By then he was dead.

These tragedies are just two examples of our failure to teach young people how to use alcohol prudently. If 18-year-olds don't have legal access to even a beer at a public place, they have no experience handling liquor on their own. They feel "liberated" when they arrive on campus. With no parents to stop them, they have a "let's make up for lost time" attitude. The result: binge drinking.

We should make access to alcohol legal at 18. At the same time, we 12 should come down much harder on alcohol abusers and drunk drivers of all ages. We should intensify our efforts at alcohol education for adolescents. We want them to understand that it is perfectly OK not to drink. But if they do, alcohol should be consumed in moderation.

After all, we choose to teach our children about safe sex, including 13 the benefits of teen abstinence. Why, then, can't we—schools and parents alike—teach them about safe drinking?

COMPREHENSION

1. In which paragraph of this essay is its thesis most clearly articulated?
2. Why does the author call the current minimum drinking age the "magic 21st birthday"?
3. What major forms of inquiry does the author use to back up her thesis? What role does her profession as a public-health scientist play in defending her argument?

RHETORIC

1. How does the phrasing in paragraph 1 contribute to introducing a major irony in the theme of teenage drinking?
2. In paragraph 2, the author states that she has based her argument on two methods. What are these methods? Are the use of these methods sufficient to back up her arguments, or should she have used others? If so, what others?
3. In the final paragraph, the author asks a pertinent question about teaching teenagers about "safe drinking." What rhetorical purpose did she have for waiting until the conclusion to raise the question?
4. Does the author effectively use description in creating an emotional and attitudinal portrait of her daughter? If so, what elements of the essay help evoke this portrait?
5. The author combines general observations of teenage psychology with specific examples to buttress these observations. Enumerate both the generalities and the examples.
6. Based upon your review of the essay's tone, structure, and vocabulary, is it geared toward parents alone or to their teenage children as well? Explain your view.
7. Does the author have an implicit portrait of the average teenager? How do her examples either support or refute a particular portrait?

WRITING

1. Argue for or against the proposition that the author's argument is faulty because her essay uses a privileged group of teenagers to represent *all* teenagers.
2. Argue for or against the proposition that the author is unfair because she cites the drinking practices of some countries and omits to mention those where teenage alcoholism *is* a problem.

3. For a research paper, write a concise history of teenage drinking in America.

4. For a research paper, compare and contrast the laws and customs of two countries regarding teenage drinking.

IMAMU AMIRI BARAKA   Imamu Amiri Baraka (b. 1934) is a playwright, novelist, editor, poet, essayist, and community leader. Baraka's most famous work, the play *Dutchman* (1964), is about the often destructive relations between black and white Americans. During his career, Baraka has, through the powerful use of the black idiom, introduced the public to the richness of African-American culture.

IMAMU AMIRI BARAKA

Soul Food

Recently, a young Negro novelist writing in *Esquire* about the beauties of America mentioned that one of the things wrong with Negroes was that, unlike the Chinese, boots have neither a language of their own nor a characteristic cuisine. And this to me is the deepest stroke, the unkindest cut, of oppression, especially as it has distorted Black Americans. America, where the suppliant, far from rebelling or even disagreeing with the forces that have caused him to suffer, readily backs them up and finally tries to become an honorary oppressor himself.

No language? No characteristic food? Oh, man, come on.

Maws are things ofays seldom get to peck, nor are you likely ever to hear about Charlie eating a chitterling. Sweet potatoe pies, a good friend of mine asked recently, "Do they taste anything like pumpkin?" Negative. They taste more like memory, if you're not uptown.

All those different kinds of greens (now quick frozen for anyone) once were all Sam got to eat. (Plus the potlikker, into which one slipped some throwed away meat.) Collards and turnips and kale and mustards were not fit for anybody but the woogies. So they found a way to make them taste like something somebody would want to freeze and sell to a Negro going to Harvard as exotic European spinach.

The watermelon, friend, was imported from Africa (by whom?) where it had been growing many centuries before it was necessary for some people to deny that they had ever tasted one.

Did you ever hear of a black-eyed pea? (Whitey used it for forage, but some folks couldn't.) And all those weird parts of the hog? (After the pig was stripped of its choicest parts, the feet, snout, tail, intestines, stomach, etc., were all left for the "members," who treated them mercilessly.) Is it mere myth that shades are death on chickens? (Deep fat frying, the Dutch found out in 17th century New Amsterdam, was an

African speciality: and if you can get hold of a fried chicken leg, or a fried porgie, you can find out what happened to that tradition.)

I had to go to Rutgers before I found people who thought grits were 7 meant to be eaten with milk and sugar, instead of gravy and pork sausage . . . and that's one of the reasons I left.

Away from home, you must make the trip uptown to get really 8 straight as far as a good grease is concerned. People kill chickens all over the world, but chasing them through the dark on somebody else's property would probably insure, once they went in the big bag, that you'd find some really beautiful way to eat them. I mean, after all the risk involved. The fruit of that tradition unfolds everywhere above 100th Street. There are probably more restaurants in Harlem whose staple is fried chicken, or chicken in the basket, than any other place in the world. Ditto, barbecued ribs—also straight out of the South with the West Indians, *i.e.*, Africans from farther south in the West, having developed the best sauce for roasting whole oxen and hogs, spicy and extremely hot.

Hoppin' John (black-eyed peas and rice), hushpuppies (crusty 9 cornmeal bread cooked in fish grease and best with fried fish, especially fried salt fish, which ought to soak overnight unless you're over fifty and can take all that salt), hoecake (pan bread), buttermilk biscuits and pancakes, fatback (i.e., streak'alean-streak'afat), dumplings, neck bones, knuckles (*both* good for seasoning limas or string beans), okra (another African importation, other name gumbo), pork chops—some more staples of the Harlem cuisine. Most of the food came North when the people did.

There are hundreds of tiny restaurants, food shops, rib joints, 10 shrimp shacks, chicken shacks, "rotisseries" throughout Harlem that serve "soul food"—say, a breakfast of grits, eggs and sausage, pancakes and Alaga syrup—and even tiny booths where it's at least possible to get a good piece of barbecue, hot enough to make you whistle, or a chicken wing on a piece of greasy bread. You can *always* find a fish sandwich: a fish sandwich is something you walk with, or "Two of those small sweet potato pies to go." The Muslim temple serves bean pies which are really separate. It is never necessary to go to some big expensive place to get a good filling grease. You *can* go to the Red Rooster, or Wells, or Joch's, and get a good meal, but Jennylin's, a little place on 135th near Lenox, is more filling, or some place like the A&A food shop in a basement up in the 140's, and you can really get away. I guess a square is somebody who's in Harlem and eats at Nedicks.

COMPREHENSION

1. Who is Baraka's primary audience for this essay? What is the author's attitude toward this audience? Cite evidence to support your answer.

2. According to Baraka, what foods and cooking styles originated in African or African-American culture?

3. The theme of white oppression and the black response to it recurs frequently in the essay. Identify some of the different ways in which the theme is put forth. Why does the author state and restate the theme?

RHETORIC

1. List the various words that come from the black language, and define them. There are also several references to "uptown" in the essay, references which can be considered examples of metonymy. Explain.
2. Why is slang so effective in this essay?
3. What are the two opinions Baraka sets out to disprove? He uses two different methods of refuting these opinions. What are they?
4. How does the essay use inductive reasoning?
5. Why does Baraka present historical information in parentheses?
6. Analyze the way that Baraka develops his concluding paragraph.

WRITING

1. Write an essay that develops your own definition of *soul food, ethnic food, or junk food.*
2. Write an argumentative essay on the value of the "separate" language used by a particular ethnic, social, or professional group.
3. Develop an appreciative essay on your favorite national cuisine.

ANN GRACE MOJTABAI   Ann Grace Mojtabai (b. 1938) spent several years living in Iran. She has written several novels, including *Mundome* (1974), *The Four Hundred Eels of Sigmund Freud* (1976), and *A Stopping Place* (1979). In the following essay, Mojtabai tries to look clearly at a particularly disturbing—from our perspective—aspect of Iranian culture.

ANN GRACE MOJTABAI

Polygamy

Teheran, 1960. A warm evening. The courtyard in which we were sitting was not very beautiful. There was a narrow strip of ground that ran along the edge of the wall, spotted with shrubbery and some insignificant roses; the rest was flagstone surrounding the customary small pool for ablutions, set like a turquoise in the center.

I had come to Iran expecting nightingales and roses, but had not yet heard a nightingale above the sounds of streets hawkers and traffic, and the famed rose gardens of Persia were nowhere in evidence; they remained out of sight, if they ever existed, sealed off by high proprietary walls.

But my interest of the moment was not in the garden; my eyes were fixed on my father-in-law. He was a large, imposing man in his mid-90's, with high color, still-black eyebrows and the scrub of a heavy beard. He might have passed for a much younger man and, in fact, claimed to be in his young, vigorous 70's.

"What do you think of this?" he asked, pointing to his wives, one large, one small, on either side of him. His wives smiled in my direction, then at each other. My father-in-law continued to stare at me and to wait; he really wanted to know what I thought.

For the few separate moments it took to translate his question and my reply (with what distortion I shall never know), we gazed coolly at each other, each an anthropologist confronting opacity—the mind of a stranger. I thought I could hear him taking notes. I, for my part, was certainly jotting things down—but only impressions. I would see; I wasn't going to judge prematurely. My judgment, when it came, wouldn't be narrow, biased or culture-bound. "Customs differ," I said.

Long before meeting my father-in-law, I had been prepared for this—or, rather, I had been briefed, and imagined that I was prepared. It had been a briefing full of history (polygamy as a practical solution to the decimation of the male population in warfare and the resulting disproportionate preponderance of females over males); it had been a briefing on principle as well (the Koranic requirement that the husband distribute his affection equally among the co-wives).

But, of course, I was not ready to confront the live instance—three individuals who would bear an intimate family relation to me. Mother, father and what—aunt? mother-surrogate? I decided that the other party would simply be my Other Mother-in-Law. At that moment, the language barrier turned out to be an opportune cover for, really, I did not know what I thought.

The happy threesome sat cross-legged on a takhte, a low wooden platform, covered with a rug. My particular mother-in-law, the tiny one, was the junior wife, chosen, I later learned, by the older woman as someone agreeable to herself, someone she thought the old man would like, too. The senior wife's passion was for talking, and her husband's silence had long been wearing her down. She wanted someone in the house willing to hear her out and, she hoped, to respond from time to time.

I was left to imagine the precise formalities, but it seemed to me to be a marriage welcome to all the parties concerned. It was an arrangement not without its share of bickerings and quarrels, for however well-disposed the women were to each other, their respective children were rivals, and the wives were partisan for their children.

Still, as marriages go, theirs seemed to be a reasonably happy one.

When it grew chilly, we moved indoors. The sitting room was also my father-in-law's bedroom. He sat on a fine, ancient rug, with bolsters at his back, a bay of windows on his left and, in front of him, an array of small vials: vitamins, elixirs, purges. He didn't believe in modern medicine, but was taking no chances.

Stiff, wooden chairs of mismatching shapes were lined against the walls of the room. I eyed them, but, noticing that they were mantled in dust, furred with a thin, unbroken velvet, decided they were not really for use, and sat on the floor instead. In fact, the chairs were chiefly ceremonial, a reluctant concession to the times, to the imposition of Westernization around the world. Not like the television set, which was an ecstatic testimony to the march of *universal* human progress, and which held, along with the samovar, pride of place among the old man's possessions.

The wives stepped out to bring refreshments. With a sinking sense, 13 I noticed my husband getting up to speak to his mother in private. I was utterly adrift, alone with my father-in-law, a total stranger. The old man turned to me and said what I later learned was: "When hearts speak, no language is necessary." I recognized none of the words, but I guessed from his face and tone that whatever it was he had said was meant to be comforting and, trusting in a language of gesture and sign, I ventured a smile by way of reply.

Even today, I do not know what I think about polygamy. Or, per- 14 haps, I know what I think—it's only that my feelings are mixed. Abstractly, I oppose the custom. These bonds ought to be reciprocal, one-to-one. Sexual favors *may* be distributed equally as required (a night with A, a night with B), but I doubt whether affection can be distributed so neatly. And, of course, the custom speaks of the poverty of opportunities for women.

On the other hand, the custom of mut'a, or temporary marriage, 15 practiced by Shiites, though not by Sunnites, seems to me to be possessed of some merits and, on the whole, somewhat more enlightened than prostitution, or the vaguely polygamous custom of balancing wife (with legal rights) with mistress (having no rights), which is so widely prevalent in the West.

In the mut'a marriage, a term is stipulated—a night, a year, a decade, 16 an hour, whatever. A set term, a mehr—a wedding endowment for the woman—mutual consent and a contract specifying all this are required. The children of such unions are legitimate and entitled to a share of the father's inheritance, although the sigheh, the temporary wife, has no claim to maintenance beyond the initial marriage endowment.

But polygamy is meant to be more than a mere alternative to such 17 clearly deficient institutions as prostitution. And my feelings for polygamy as a true and viable form of marriage remain contrary, held in suspension. My opposition in theory is muffled by my observation of one palpable contrary fact. I saw a polygamous marriage work, and work well. That my mothers-in-law were deeply attached to each other, I have no doubt. I tend to question rather more their devotion to the husband who brought them together.

As for two mothers-in-law in one household, an old proverb would 18 seem to apply: "Better two tigers in one cage than two mistresses in one household." But, in point of fact, the laws of addition don't always apply. After all, one shark and one codfish equal one shark; one raindrop and one raindrop equal one raindrop. The two women worked off their intensities on each other, with less energy left for me. So, actually, I had one mother-in-law, which, as all the proverbs of all nations attest, was quite sufficient.

COMPREHENSION

1. How do paragraphs 1 to 5 serve the author's purpose?
2. What effects of Westernization appear in the essay? Of which ones do the Iranians approve? Of which ones do they disapprove?
3. What academic-sounding reasons for polygamy has Mojtabai been given? Do they help her to confront the reality of it? Why, or why not? What is her final attitude toward polygamy?

RHETORIC

1. Identify Iranian words in the essay, and explain what they mean.
2. What does Mojtabai mean when she describes her first meeting with her father-in-law as "each an anthropologist confronting opacity" (paragraph 5)? What level of language does that suggest Mojtabai uses in the essay? Can these words be used by Westerners to describe aspects of Western culture?
3. What is the function of the opening narrative? Why is it effective?
4. In this essay, the narrator is both actor and observer. How does this affect the tone of the essay? Where else in the anthology have we seen this strategy?
5. Why does Mojtabai spend considerable time describing *mut'a? What elements of contrast does she utilize here? For what purpose?*
6. One paragraph is considerably shorter than the others. How does this contribute to the structure and meaning of the essay?

WRITING

1. Discuss a custom you have confronted that was alien to your own values. Compare your response to Mojtabai's response.
2. Write your own evaluation of polygamy.
3. Does the United States have a more enlightened perspective on women and marriage than does the Iran depicted by Mojtabai? Discuss this question in an essay.

MICHAEL DORRIS   Michael Dorris (b. 1945), a member of the Modoc tribe and a native of Washington, is a professor of anthropology and Native-American studies at Dartmouth College. He has written, among other works, *The Broken Cord: A Family's Ongoing Struggles with Fetal Alcohol Syndrome* (1987). He has also written about the Native-American experience in books such as *Native Americans: Five Hundred Years After Cromwell* (1975). He and his wife, Louise Erdrich, coauthored a novel, *The Crown of Columbus* (1991). In this essay, Dorris wonders how the first Thanksgiving might have been seen through the eyes of non-Pilgrims.

MICHAEL DORRIS

For the Indians No Thanksgiving

Maybe those Pilgrims and Wampanoags actually got together for a November picnic, maybe not. It matters only as a facile, ironical footnote.

For the former group, it would have been a celebration of a precarious hurdle successfully crossed on the path to the political domination first of a continent and eventually of a planet. For the latter, it would have been, at best, a naïve extravaganza—the last meeting as equals with invaders who, within a few years, would win King Philip's War and decorate the city limits of their towns with rows of stakes, each topped with an Indian head.

The few aboriginal survivors of the ensuing violence were either sold into Caribbean slavery by their better armed, erstwhile hosts, or were ruthlessly driven from their Cape Cod homes. Despite the symbolic idealism of the first potluck, New England—from the emerging European point of view—simply wasn't big enough for two sets of societies.

An enduring benefit of success, when one culture clashes with another, is that the victorious group controls the record. It owns not only the immediate spoils but also the power to edit, embellish and concoct the facts of the original encounter for the generations to come. Events, once past, reside at the small end of the telescope, the vague and hazy antecedents to accepted reality.

Our collective modern fantasy of Thanksgiving is a case in point. It has evolved into a ritual pageant in which almost everyone of us, as children, either acted or were forced to watch a 17th century vision that we can conjure whole in the blink of an eye.

The cast of stock characters is as recognizable as those in any Macy's parade: long-faced Pilgrim men, pre-N.R.A. muskets at their sides, sitting around a rude outdoor table while their wives, dressed in long dresses, aprons and linen caps, bustle about lifting the lids off steaming kettles—pater and materfamilias of New World hospitality.

They dish out the turkey to a scattering of shirtless Indian invitees. But there is no ambiguity as to who is in charge of the occasion, who could be asked to leave, whose protocol prevails.

Only good Indians are admitted into this tableau, of course: those who accept the manifest destiny of a European presence and are prepared to adopt English dining customs and, by inference, English everything else.

These compliant Hollywood extras are, naturally enough, among ⁹ the blessings the Pilgrims are thankful for—and why not? They're colorful, bring the food and vanish after dessert. They are something exotic to write home about, like a visit to Frontierland. In the sound bite of national folklore, they have metamorphosed into icons, totems of America as evocative, and ultimately as vapid, as a flag factory.

And these particular Indians did not all repair to the happy hunting ¹⁰ grounds during the first Christmas rush. They lived on, smoking peace pipes and popping up at appropriate crowd-pleasing moments.

They lost mock battles from coast to coast in Wild West shows. In ¹¹ 19th century art, they sat bareback on their horses and watched a lot of sunsets. Whole professional teams of them take the home field every Sunday afternoon in Cleveland or Washington.

They are the sources of merit badges for Boy Scouts and the emblem ¹² of purity for imitation butter. They are, and have been from the beginning, predictable, manageable, domesticated cartoons, inventions without depth or reality apart from that bestowed by their creators.

These appreciative Indians, as opposed to the pesky flesh and blood ¹³ native peoples on whom they are loosely modeled, did not question the enforced exchange of their territories for a piece of pie. They did not protest when they died by the millions of European diseases.

They did not resist—except for the "bad" ones, the renegades— ¹⁴ when solemn pacts made with them were broken or when their religions and customs were declared illegal. They did not make a fuss in courts in defense of their sovereignty. They never expected all the fixings anyway.

As for Thanksgiving 1988, the descendants of those first partygoers ¹⁵ sit at increasingly distant tables, the pretense of equity all but abandoned. Against great odds, native Americans have maintained political identity—hundreds of tribes have Federal recognition as "domestic, dependent nations."

But, in a country so insecure about heterogeneity that it votes its ¹⁶ dominant language as "official," this refusal to melt into the pot has been an expensive choice.

A majority of reservation Indians reside in among the most impov- ¹⁷ erished counties in the nation. They constitute the ethnic group at the wrong peak of every scale: most undernourished, most short-lived, least educated, least healthy.

For them, that long ago Thanksgiving was not a milestone, not a ¹⁸ promise. It was the last full meal.

COMPREHENSION

1. Where in the essay does Dorris state his main idea? Would you say that he is arguing his point or simply presenting it? How do you know?

2. In your own words, state what Dorris explains about the myth and reality of the Native American.
3. How does Dorris explain the "collective modern fantasy" of Thanksgiving?

RHETORIC

1. Which paragraphs constitute the author's introduction? How does the author unify these paragraphs?
2. At what point does the body of the essay actually begin? What is the position of the thesis in relation to the body?
3. Explain Dorris's style, tone, and approach to paragraph development. What do these elements tell us about his intended audience?
4. How does Dorris develop an extended example of the "collective modern fantasy of Thanksgiving"? Which paragraphs constitute this extended example?
5. How does Dorris employ definition and comparison and contrast to advance his point?
6. Where does the conclusion of this essay begin? How do you know? Does the conclusion satisfy the reader's earlier expectations? Explain your response.

WRITING

1. Write a letter to Michael Dorris defending Thanksgiving. In the course of your argumentative essay, rebut the issues raised by the author.
2. Write an essay about your favorite holiday. Provide examples and details, narration and description.
3. In an explanatory essay, examine why it is desirable to be able to approach holidays from various perspectives and at least to understand why some people might not want to celebrate certain holidays the way you do.

VLADIMIR NABOKOV   Vladimir Nabokov (1899–1977) was born into an aristocratic family in czarist Russia. Following the Russian Revolution, he went into exile in England in 1919. In 1922, he graduated with honors from Cambridge University. Subsequently he lived in Germany and France, writing in Russian, giving tennis lessons, and collecting butterflies—all recounted in his poignant autobiography, *Speak Memory* (1966). He came to the United States in 1940. Nabokov taught at Wellesley College from 1944 to 1948 and at Cornell University from 1948 to 1958. Nabokov, who once termed himself the greatest Russian novelist writing in English, gained enormous success with *Lolita* (1956). His later novels include *Pale Fire* (1962) and *Ada* (1969). He died in Montreux, Switzerland. With stylistic grace and satiric precision, Nabokov in the following essay defines both a state of mind and a social condition of our times.

VLADIMIR NABOKOV

Philistines and Philistinism

A philistine is a full-grown person whose interests are of a material and
commonplace nature, and whose mentality is formed of the stock ideas
and conventional ideals of his or her group and time. I have said "full-
grown person" because the child or the adolescent who may look like a
small philistine is only a small parrot mimicking the ways of confirmed
vulgarians, and it is easier to be a parrot than to be a white heron. "Vulgarian" is more or less synonymous with "philistine": the stress in a
vulgarian is not so much on the conventionalism of a philistine as on
the vulgarity of some of his conventional notions. I may also use the
terms *genteel* and *bourgeois*. *Genteel* implies the lace-curtain refined vulgarity which is worse than simple coarseness. To burp in company may
be rude, but to say "excuse me" after a burp is genteel and thus worse
than vulgar. The term *bourgeois* I use following Flaubert, not Marx.
Bourgeois in Flaubert's sense is a state of mind, not a state of pocket. A
bourgeois is a smug philistine, a dignified vulgarian.

A philistine is not likely to exist in a very primitive society although
no doubt rudiments of philistinism may be found even there. We may
imagine, for instance, a cannibal who would prefer the human head he
eats to be artistically colored, just as the American philistine prefers his
oranges to be painted orange, his salmon pink, and his whisky yellow.
But generally speaking philistinism presupposes a certain advanced
state of civilization where throughout the ages certain traditions have
accumulated in a heap and have started to stink.

Philistinism is international. It is found in all nations and in all
classes. An English duke can be as much of a philistine as an American
Shriner or a French bureaucrat or a Soviet citizen. The mentality of a
Lenin or a Stalin or a Hitler in regard to the arts and the sciences was
utterly bourgeois. A laborer or a coal miner can be just as bourgeois as
a banker or a housewife or a Hollywood star.

Philistinism implies not only a collection of stock ideas but also the
use of set phrases, clichés, banalities expressed in faded words. A true
philistine has nothing but these trivial ideas of which he entirely consists. But it should be admitted that all of us have our cliché side; all of
us in everyday life often use words not as words but as signs, as coins,
as formulas. This does not mean that we are all philistines, but it does
mean that we should be careful not to indulge too much in the automatic process of exchanging platitudes. On a hot day every other person will ask you, "Is it warm enough for you?" but that does not necessarily mean that the speaker is a philistine. He may be merely a parrot
or a bright foreigner. When a person asks you "Hullo, how *are* you?" it

is perhaps a sorry cliché to reply, "Fine"; but if you made to him a detailed report of your condition you might pass for a pedant and a bore. It also happens that platitudes are used by people as a kind of disguise or as the shortest cut for avoiding conversation with fools. I have known great scholars and poets and scientists who in the cafeteria sank to the level of the most commonplace give and take.

The character I have in view when I say "smug vulgarian" is, thus, not the part-time philistine, but the total type, the genteel bourgeois, the complete universal product of triteness and mediocrity. He is the conformist, the man who conforms to his group, and he also is typified by something else: he is a pseudo-idealist, he is pseudo-compassionate, he is pseudo-wise. The fraud is the closest ally of the true philistine. All such great words as "Beauty," "Love," "Nature," "Truth," and so on become masks and dupes when the smug vulgarian employs them. In *Dead Souls* you have heard Chichikov. In *Bleak House* you have heard Skimpole. You have heard Homais in *Madame Bovary.* The philistine likes to impress and he likes to be impressed, in consequence of which a world of deception, of mutual cheating, is formed by him and around him.

The philistine in his passionate urge to conform, to belong, to join, is torn between two longings: to act as everybody does, to admire, to use this or that thing because millions of people do; or else he craves to belong to an exclusive set, to an organization, to a club, to a hotel patronage or an ocean liner community (with the captain in white and wonderful food), and to delight in the knowledge that there is the head of a corporation or a European count sitting next to him. The philistine is often a snob. He is thrilled by riches and rank—"Darling, I've actually talked to a duchess!"

A philistine neither knows nor cares anything about art, including literature—his essential nature is anti-artistic—but he wants information and he is trained to read magazines. He is a faithful reader of the *Saturday Evening Post,* and when he reads he identifies himself with the characters. If he is a male philistine he will identify himself with the fascinating executive or any other big shot—aloof, single, but a boy and a golfer at heart; or if the reader is a female philistine—a philistinette—she will identify herself with the fascinating strawberry-blond secretary, a slip of a girl but a mother at heart, who eventually marries the boyish boss. The philistine does not distinguish one writer from another; indeed, he reads little and only what may be useful to him, but he may belong to a book club and choose beautiful, *beautiful* books, a jumble of Simone de Beauvoir, Dostoevski, Marquand, Somerset Maugham, *Dr. Zhivago,* and Masters of the Renaissance. He does not much care for pictures, but for the sake of prestige he may hang in his parlor reproductions of Van Gogh's or Whistler's respective mothers, although secretly preferring Norman Rockwell.

In his love for the useful, for the material goods of life, he becomes an easy victim of the advertisement business. Ads may be very good ads—some of them are very artistic—that is not the point. The point is that they tend to appeal to the philistine's pride in possessing things whether silverware or underwear. I mean the following kind of ad: just come to the family is a radio set or a television set (or a car, or a refrigerator, or table silver—anything will do). It has just come to the family: mother clasps her hands in dazed delight, the children crowd around all agog: junior and the dog strain up to the edge of the table where the Idol is enthroned; even Grandma of the beaming wrinkles peeps out somewhere in the background; and somewhat apart, his thumbs gleefully inserted in the armpits of his waistcoat, stands triumphant Dad or Pop, the Proud Donor. Small boys and girls in ads are invariably freckled, and the smaller fry have front teeth missing. I have nothing against freckles (in fact I find them very becoming in live creatures) and quite possibly a special survey might reveal that the majority of small American-born Americans *are* freckled, or else perhaps another survey might reveal that all successful executives and handsome housewives had been freckled in their childhood. I repeat, I have really nothing against freckles as such. But I do think there is considerable philistinism involved in the use made of them by advertisers and other agencies. I am told that when an unfreckled, or only slightly freckled, little boy actor has to appear on the screen in television, an artificial set of freckles is applied to the middle of his face. Twenty-two freckles is the minimum: eight over each cheekbone and six on the saddle of the pert nose. In the comics, freckles look like a case of bad rash. In one series of comics they appear as tiny circles. But although the good cute little boys of the ads are blond or redhaired, with freckles, the handsome young men of the ads are generally dark haired and always have thick dark eyebrows. The evolution is from Scotch to Celtic.

The rich philistinism emanating from advertisements is due not to ⁹ their exaggerating (or inventing) the glory of this or that serviceable article but to suggesting that the acme of human happiness is purchasable and that its purchase somehow ennobles the purchaser. Of course, the world they create is pretty harmless in itself because everybody knows that it is made up by the seller with the understanding that the buyer will join in the make-believe. The amusing part is not that it is a world where nothing spiritual remains except the ecstatic smiles of people serving or eating celestial cereals, or a world where the game of the senses is played according to bourgeois rules, but that it is a kind of satellite shadow world in the actual existence of which neither sellers nor buyers really believe in their heart of hearts—especially in this wise quiet country.

Russians have, or had, a special name for smug philistinism— ¹⁰ *posh-lust. Poshlism* is not only the obviously trashy but mainly the falsely important, the falsely beautiful, the falsely clever, the falsely attractive. To apply the deadly label of *poshlism* to something is not only an esthetic judgment but also a moral indictment. The genuine, the guileless, the good is never *poshlust*. It is possible to maintain that a simple, uncivilized man is seldom if ever a *poshlust* since *poshlism* presupposes the veneer of civilization. A peasant has to become a townsman

154

in order to become vulgar. A painted necktie has to hide the honest Adam's apple in order to produce *poshlism*.

It is possible that the term itself has been so nicely devised by Russians because of the cult of simplicity and good taste in old Russia. The Russia of today, a country of moral imbeciles, of smiling slaves and poker-faced bullies, has stopped noticing *poshlism* because Soviet Russia is so full of its special brand, a blend of despotism and pseudo-culture; but in the old days a Gogol, a Tolstoy, a Chekhov in quest of the simplicity of truth easily distinguished the vulgar side of things as well as the trashy systems of pseudo-thought. But *poshlists* are found everywhere, in every country, in this country as well as in Europe—in fact *poshlism* is more common in Europe than here, despite our American ads.

COMPREHENSION

1. What does Nabokov reveal of his own background, beliefs, and behavior in this essay?
2. What, according to the author, is a philistine? Explain the representative characteristics of a philistine.
3. What does philistinism tell us about the state of society? Why is philistinism international? What does Nabokov say about the degrees of philistinism in Europe and in America?

RHETORIC

1. Nabokov employs several synonyms for *philistine* and *philistinism*. List them, and explain their shades of meaning.
2. Identify and explain the effectiveness of the various literary allusions in the essay.
3. Identify the topic sentence in each paragraph. Why are they so consistently placed? Relate their placement to the movement from general or abstract to specific and concrete in three representative paragraphs.
4. Does the author use actual examples or hypothetical examples in the essay? Explain.
5. How does Nabokov use definition? For what purpose does he employ it? What instances of comparison and contrast and causal analysis do you find?
6. What is the tone of the essay? What effect does that tone have on the way that Nabokov describes the philistine?

WRITING

1. What is your opinion of Nabokov's assertion that philistinism is rampant in the modern world? Respond to this question in an argumentative essay.
2. Write an extended definition of *philistinism,* using examples drawn from personal experience, reading, and the media.

3. Write an essay that uses definition to make a comic or satiric point about manners or social behavior.

ALICE WALKER   Alice Walker was born in Eatonton, Georgia, in 1944 and now lives in San Francisco and Mendocino County, California. A celebrated poet, short-story writer, and novelist, she is the author of *Revolutionary Petunias and Other Poems, In Love and Trouble: Stories of Black Women,* and *Meridian,* among other works. Her 1983 novel, *The Color Purple,* won the American Book Award and the Pulitzer Prize in fiction. Her latest book, *Possessing the Secret of Joy,* was published in 1992 and continues the story of the characters introduced in *The Color Purple.* In the following narrative, Walker writes of a childhood accident that almost destroyed her self-esteem.

ALICE WALKER

Beauty: When the Other Dancer Is the Self

It is a bright summer day in 1947. My father, a fat, funny man with beautiful eyes and a subversive wit, is trying to decide which of his eight children he will take with him to the county fair. My mother, of course, will not go. She is knocked out from getting most of us ready: I hold my neck stiff against the pressure of her knuckles as she hastily completes the braiding and then beribboning of my hair.

My father is the driver for the rich old white lady up the road. Her name is Miss Mey. She owns all the land for miles around, as well as the house in which we live. All I remember about her is that she once offered to pay my mother thirty-five cents for cleaning her house, raking up piles of her magnolia leaves, and washing her family's clothes, and that my mother—she of no money, eight children, and a chronic earache—refused it. But I do not think of this in 1947. I am two and a half years old. I want to go everywhere my daddy goes. I am excited at the prospect of riding in a car. Someone has told me fairs are fun. That there is room in the car for only three of us doesn't faze me at all. Whirling happily in my starchy frock, showing off my biscuit-polished patent-leather shoes and lavender socks, tossing my head in a way that makes my ribbons bounce, I stand, hands on hips, before my father. "Take me, Daddy," I say with assurance: "I'm the prettiest!"

Later, it does not surprise me to find myself in Miss Mey's shiny black car, sharing the back seat with the other lucky ones. Does not surprise me that I thoroughly enjoy the fair. At home that night I tell the unlucky ones all I can remember about the merry-go-round, the man who eats live chickens, and the teddy bears, until they say: that's enough, baby Alice. Shut up now, and go to sleep.

It is Easter Sunday, 1950. I am dressed in a green, flocked, scalloped-hem dress (handmade by my adoring sister, Ruth) that has its own smooth satin petticoat and tiny hot-pink roses tucked into each scallop. My shoes, new T-strap patent leather, again highly biscuit-polished. I am six years old and have learned one of the longest Easter speeches to be heard that day, totally unlike the speech I said when I was two: "Easter lilies/pure and white/blossom in/the morning light." When I rise to give my speech I do so on a great wave of love and pride and expectation. People in the church stop rustling their new crinolines. They seem to hold their breath. I can tell they admire my dress, but it is my spirit, bordering on sassiness (womanishness), they secretly applaud.

"That girl's a little *mess*," they whisper to each other, pleased. 5

Naturally I say my speech without stammer or pause, unlike 6 those who stutter, stammer, or, worst of all, forget. This is before the word "beautiful" exists in people's vocabulary, but "Oh, isn't she the *cutest* thing!" frequently floats my way. "And got so much sense!" they gratefully add . . . for which thoughtful addition I thank them to this day.

It was great fun being cute. But then, one day, it ended. 7

I am eight years old and a tomboy. I have a cowboy hat, cowboy 8 boots, checkered shirt and pants, all red. My playmates are my brothers, two and four years older than I. Their colors are black and green, the only difference in the way we are dressed. On Saturday nights we all go to the picture show, even my mother; Westerns are her favorite kind of movie. Back home, "on the ranch," we pretend we are Tom Mix, Hopalong Cassidy, Lash LaRue (we've even named one of our dogs Lash LaRue); we chase each other for hours rustling cattle, being outlaws, delivering damsels from distress. Then my parents decide to buy my brothers guns. These are not "real" guns. They shoot "BBs," copper pellets my brothers say will kill birds. Because I am a girl, I do not get a gun. Instantly I am relegated to the position of Indian. Now there appears a great distance between us. They shoot and shoot at everything with their new guns. I try to keep up with my bow and arrows.

One day while I am standing on top of our makeshift "garage"— 9 pieces of tin nailed across some poles—holding my bow and arrow and looking out toward the fields, I feel an incredible blow in my right eye. I look down just in time to see my brother lower his gun.

Both brothers rush to my side. My eye stings, and I cover it with my 10 hand. "If you tell," they say, "we will get a whipping. You don't want that to happen, do you?" I do not. "Here is a piece of wire," says the older brother, picking it up from the roof; "say you stepped on one end of it and the other flew up and hit you." The pain is beginning to start. "Yes," I say, "Yes, I will say that is what happened." If I do not say this is what happened, I know my brothers will find ways to make me wish I had. But now I will say anything that gets me to my mother.

Confronted by our parents we stick to the lie agreed upon. They 11 place me on a bench on the porch and I close my left eye while they examine the right. There is a tree growing from underneath the porch that climbs past the railing to the roof. It is the last thing my right eye sees. I watch as its trunk, its branches, and then its leaves are blotted out by the rising blood.

I am in shock. First there is intense fever, which my father tries to 12 break using lily leaves bound around my head. Then there are chills: my mother tries to get me to eat soup. Eventually, I do not know how, my parents learn what has happened. A week after the "accident" they take me to see a doctor. "Why did you wait so long to come?" he asks, looking into my eye and shaking his head. "Eyes are sympathetic," he says. "If one is blind, the other will likely become blind too."

This comment of the doctor's terrifies me. But it is really how I look 13 that bothers me most. Where the BB pellet struck there is a glob of whitish scar tissue, a hideous cataract, on my eye. Now when I stare at people—a favorite pastime, up to now—they will stare back. Not at the "cute" little girl, but at her scar. For six years I do not stare at anyone, because I do not raise my head.

Years later, in the throes of a mid-life crisis, I ask my mother and sister 14 whether I changed after the "accident." "No," they say, puzzled. "What do you mean?"

What do I mean? 15

I am eight, and, for the first time, doing poorly in school, where I 16 have been something of a whiz since I was four. We have just moved to the place where the "accident" occurred. We do not know any of the people around us because this is a different county. The only time I see the friends I knew is when we go back to our old church. The new school is the former state penitentiary. It is a large stone building, cold and drafty, crammed to overflowing with boisterous, ill-disciplined children. On the third floor there is a huge circular imprint of some partition that has been torn out.

"What used to be here?" I ask a sullen girl next to me on our way 17 past it to lunch.

"The electric chair," says she. 18

At night I have nightmares about the electric chair, and about all the 19 people reputedly "fried" in it. I am afraid of the school, where all the students seem to be budding criminals.

"What's the matter with your eye?" they ask, critically. 20

When I don't answer (I cannot decide whether it was an "accident" 21 or not), they shove me, insist on a fight.

158

My brother, the one who created the story about the wire, comes to my rescue. But then brags so much about "protecting" me, I become sick.

After months of torture at the school, my parents decide to send me back to our old community, to my old school. I live with my grandparents and the teacher they board. But there is no room for Phoebe, my cat. By the time my grandparents decide there *is* room, and I ask for my cat, she cannot be found. Miss Yarborough, the boarding teacher, takes me under her wing, and begins to teach me to play the piano. But soon she marries an African—a "prince," she says—and is whisked away to his continent.

At my old school there is at least one teacher who loves me. She is the 24 teacher who "knew me before I was born" and bought my first baby clothes. It is she who makes life bearable. It is her presence that finally helps me turn on the one child at the school who continually calls me "one-eyed bitch." One day I simply grab him by his coat and beat him until I am satisfied. It is my teacher who tells me my mother is ill.

My mother is lying in bed in the middle of the day, something I have 25 never seen. She is in too much pain to speak. She has an abscess in her ear. I stand looking down on her, knowing that if she dies, I cannot live. She is being treated with warm oils and hot bricks held against her cheek. Finally a doctor comes. But I must go back to my grandparents' house. The weeks pass but I am hardly aware of it. All I know is that my mother might die, my father is not so jolly, my brothers still have their guns, and I am the one sent away from home.

"You did not change," they say. 26

Did I imagine the anguish of never looking up? 27

I am twelve. When relatives come to visit I hide in my room. My 28 cousin Brenda, just my age, whose father works in the post office and whose mother is a nurse, comes to find me. "Hello," she says. And then she asks, looking at my recent school picture, which I did not want taken, and on which the "glob," as I think of it, is clearly visible, "You still can't see out of that eye?"

"No," I say, and flop back on the bed over my book. 29

That night, as I do almost every night, I abuse my eye. I rant and 30 rave at it, in front of the mirror. I plead with it to clear up before morning. I tell it I hate and despise it. I do not pray for sight. I pray for beauty.

"You did not change," they say. 31

I am fourteen and baby-sitting for my brother Bill, who lives in Boston. 32 He is my favorite brother and there is a strong bond between us. Understanding my feelings of shame and ugliness he and his wife take me to a local hospital, where the "glob" is removed by a doctor named O. Henry. There is still a small bluish crater where the scar tissue was, but the ugly white stuff is gone. Almost immediately I become a differ-ent person from the girl who does not raise her head. Or so I think. Now that I've raised my head I win the boyfriend of my dreams. Now that I've raised my head I have plenty of friends. Now that I've raised my head classwork comes from my lips as faultlessly as Easter speeches did, and I leave high school as valedictorian, most popular student, and *queen,* hardly believing my luck. Ironically, the girl who was voted most beautiful in our class (and was) was later shot twice through the chest by a male companion, using a "real" gun, while she was pregnant. But that's another story in itself. Or is it?

"You did not change," they say. ₃₃

It is now thirty years since the "accident." A beautiful journalist comes ₃₄ to visit and to interview me. She is going to write a cover story for her magazine that focuses on my latest book. "Decide how you want to look on the cover," she says. "Glamorous, or whatever."

Never mind "glamorous," it is the "whatever" that I hear. Suddenly ₃₅ all I can think of is whether I will get enough sleep the night before the photography session: if I don't, my eye will be tired and wander, as blind eyes will.

At night in bed with my lover I think up reasons why I should not ₃₆ appear on the cover of a magazine. "My meanest critics will say I've sold out," I say. "My family will now realize I write scandalous books."

"But what's the real reason you don't want to do this?" he asks. ₃₇

"Because in all probability," I say in a rush, "my eye won't be ₃₈ straight."

"It will be straight enough," he says. Then, "Besides, I thought ₃₉ you'd made your peace with that."

And I suddenly remember that I have. ₄₀

I remember:

I am talking to my brother Jimmy, asking if he remembers anything ₄₁ unusual about the day I was shot. He does not know I consider that day the last time my father, with his sweet home remedy of cool lily leaves, chose me, and that I suffered and raged inside because of this. "Well," he says, "all I remember is standing by the side of the highway with Daddy, trying to flag down a car. A white man stopped, but when Daddy said he needed somebody to take his little girl to the doctor, he drove off."

I remember:

I am in the desert for the first time. I fall totally in love with it. I am ₄₂ so overwhelmed by its beauty, I confront for the first time, consciously, the meaning of the doctor's words years ago: "Eyes are sympathetic. If one is blind, the other will likely become blind too." I realize I have dashed about the world madly, looking at this, looking at that, storing up images against the fading of the light. *But I might have missed seeing the desert!* The shock of that possibility—and gratitude for over twenty-five years of sight—sends me literally to my knees. Poem after poem comes—which is perhaps how poets pray.

On Sight

I am so thankful I have seen
The Desert
And the creatures in the desert
And the desert Itself.

The desert has its own moon
Which I have seen
With my own eye.
There is no flag on it.

Trees of the desert have arms
All of which are always up
That is because the moon is up
The sun is up
Also the sky
The stars
Clouds
None with flags.
If there were flags, I doubt
the trees would point.
Would you?

But mostly, I remember this:

I am twenty-seven, and my baby daughter is almost three. Since her birth I have worried about her discovery that her mother's eyes are different from other people's. Will she be embarrassed? I think. What will she say? Every day she watches a television program called "Big Blue Marble." It begins with a picture of the earth as it appears from the moon. It is bluish, a little battered-looking, but full of light, with whitish clouds swirling around it. Every time I see it I weep with love, as if it is a picture of Grandma's house. One day when I am putting Rebecca down for her nap, she suddenly focuses on my eye. Something inside me cringes, gets ready to try to protect myself. All children are cruel about physical differences, I know from experience, and that they don't always mean to be is another matter. I assume Rebecca will be the same.

But no-o-o-o. She studies my face intently as we stand, her inside and me outside her crib. She even holds my face maternally between her dimpled little hands. Then, looking every bit as serious and lawyerlike as her father, she says, as if it may just possibly have slipped my attention: "Mommy, there's a *world* in your eye." (As in, "Don't be alarmed, or do anything crazy.") And then, gently, but with great interest: "Mommy, where did you get that world in your eye?"

161

For the most part, the pain left then. (So what, if my brothers ₄₅ grew up to buy even more powerful pellet guns for their sons and to carry real guns themselves. So what, if a young "Morehouse man" once nearly fell off the steps of Trevor Arnett Library because he thought my eyes were blue.) Crying and laughing I ran to the bathroom, while Rebecca mumbled and sang herself off to sleep. Yes indeed, I realized, looking into the mirror. There was a world in my eye. And I saw that it was possible to love it: that in fact, for all it had taught me of shame and anger and inner vision, I *did* love it. Even to see it drifting out of orbit in boredom, or rolling up out of fatigue, not to mention floating back at attention in excitement (bearing witness, a friend has called it), deeply suitable to my personality, and even characteristic of me.

That night I dream I am dancing to Stevie Wonder's song "Always" ₄₆ (the name of the song is really "As," but I hear it as "Always"). As I dance, whirling and joyous, happier than I've ever been in my life, another bright-faced dancer joins me. We dance and kiss each other and hold each other through the night. The other dancer has obviously come through all right, as I have done. She is beautiful, whole and free. And she is also me.

COMPREHENSION

1. Describe Walker's self-image before and after the accident.
2. How do the adults' perceptions differ from Walker's when she confronts them years later?
3. How does Walker's daughter react to her mother's deformity? What effect does this have on the writer?

RHETORIC

1. Why does Walker go into detail when describing clothing and appearance in paragraphs 2, 4, and 8? How do these descriptions underscore the thesis of her essay?
2. Examine the use of the word *mess* (paragraph 5); look it up in the dictionary, and compare its meaning to the way it is used in the paragraph.
3. What device does Walker utilize to take us through the key points in the narrative? How does this device help to "ground" the story for the reader?
4. Why is paragraph 7 italicized and set apart from surrounding paragraphs? What is Walker trying to emphasize here? What effect does this paragraph have on the reader?
5. Identify the devices and strategies that Walker uses to divide her essay into sections.
6. What point is Walker making toward the end of paragraph 32, where she recounts the tragic end of the girl voted "most beautiful"? What is its value to the narrative?

1. Write an essay in which you analyze the emphasis placed on physical beauty in American society. Is the pressure placed equally on males and females? Would a man write an essay similar to Walker's? Why, or why not?

2. Write an essay defining *beauty*. Consider both the denotative and connotative meanings. Where does human physical beauty fit in your definition?

3. Write a personal narrative describing your own body image. What positive or negative messages did you receive from your family and environment as a child? How did other people's opinions help shape your current body image?

CLASSIC AND CONTEMPORARY

ALEXIS DE TOCQUEVILLE Alexis Charles Henri Clerél de Tocqueville (1805–1859), descended from an aristocratic Norman family, was a French lawyer, politician, statesman, and historian. Sent to the United States in 1831 to study the American penal system, he wrote instead one of the most penetrating inquiries into the nature of the American system, *Democracy in America* (1835). In this chapter from his study, Tocqueville compares and contrasts manners as manifested in the political and social contexts of democracy and aristocracy.

ALEXIS DE TOCQUEVILLE

Some Reflections on American Manners

Nothing, at first sight, seems less important than the external formalities of human behavior, yet there is nothing to which men attach more importance. They can get used to anything except living in a society which does not share their manners. The influence of the social and political system on manners is therefore worth serious examination.

Manners, speaking generally, have their roots in mores; they are also sometimes the result of an arbitrary convention agreed between certain men. They are both natural and acquired.

When some see that, without dispute or effort of their own, they stand first in society; when they daily have great aims in view which keep them occupied, leaving details to others; and when they live surrounded by wealth they have not acquired and do not fear to lose, one can see that they will feel a proud disdain for all the petty interests and material cares of life and that there will be a natural grandeur in their thoughts that will show in their words and manners.

In democracies there is generally little dignity of manner, as private ₄ life is very petty. Manners are often vulgar, as thoughts have small occasion to rise above preoccupation with domestic interests.

True dignity in manners consists in always taking one's proper ₅ place, not too high and not too low; that is as much within the reach of a peasant as of a prince. In democracies everybody's status seems doubtful; as a result, there is often pride but seldom dignity of manners. Moreover, manners are never well regulated or well thought out.

There is too much mobility in the population of a democracy for ₆ any definite group to be able to establish a code of behavior and see that it is observed. So everyone behaves more or less after his own fashion, and a certain incoherence of manners always prevails, because they conform to the feelings and ideas of each individual rather than to an ideal example provided for everyone to imitate.

In any case, this is much more noticeable when an aristocracy has ₇ just fallen than when it has long been destroyed.

New political institutions and new mores then bring together in the ₈ same places men still vastly different in education and habits and compel them to a life in common; this constantly leads to the most ill-assorted juxtapositions. There is still some memory of the former strict code of politeness, but no one knows quite what it said or where to find it. Men have lost the common standard of manners but have not yet resolved to do without it, so each individual tries to shape, out of the ruins of former customs, some rule, however arbitrary and variable. Hence manners have neither the regularity and dignity frequent in aristocracies nor the qualities of simplicity and freedom which one sometimes finds in democracies; they are both constrained and casual.

But this is not a normal state of things. ₉

When equality is complete and old-established, all men, having ₁₀ roughly the same ideas and doing roughly the same things, do not need to come to an understanding or to copy each other in order to behave and talk in the same way; one sees a lot of petty variations in their manners but no great differences. They are never exactly alike, since they do not copy one pattern; they are never very unlike, because they have the same social condition. At first sight one might be inclined to say that the manners of all Americans are exactly alike, and it is only on close inspection that one sees all the variations among them.

The English make game of American manners, but it is odd that ₁₁ most of those responsible for those comic descriptions belong themselves to the English middle classes, and the cap fits them very well too. So these ruthless critics generally themselves illustrate just what they criticize in America; they do not notice that they are abusing themselves, to the great delight of their own aristocracy.

Nothing does democracy more harm than its outward forms of ₁₂ behavior; many who could tolerate its vices cannot put up with its manners.

But I will not admit that there is nothing to praise in democratic ₁₃ manners.

In aristocracies, all within reach of the ruling class are at pains to imitate it, and very absurd and insipid imitations result. Democracies, with no models of high breeding before them, at least escape the necessity of daily looking at bad copies thereof.

In democracies manners are never so refined as among aristocracies, but they are also never so coarse. One misses both the crude words of the mob and the elegant and choice phrases of the high nobility. There is much triviality of manner, but nothing brutal or degraded.

I have already said that a precise code of behavior cannot take shape in democracies. That has its inconveniences and its advantages. In aristocracies rules of propriety impose the same demeanor on all, making every member of the same class seem alike in spite of personal characteristics; they bedizen and conceal nature. Democratic manners are neither so well thought out nor so regular, but they often are more sincere. They form, as it were, a thin, transparent veil through which the real feelings and personal thoughts of each man can be easily seen. Hence there is frequently an intimate connection between the form and the substance of behavior; we see a less decorative picture, but one truer to life. One may put the point this way: democracy imposes no particular manners, but in a sense prevents them from having manners at all.

Sometimes the feelings, passions, virtues, and vices of an aristocracy may reappear in a democracy, but its manners never. They are lost and vanish past return when the democratic revolution is completed. It would seem that nothing is more lasting than the manners of an aristocratic class, for it preserves them for some time after losing property and power, nor more fragile, for as soon as they have gone, no trace of them is left, and it is even difficult to discover what they once were when they have ceased to exist. A change in the state of society works this marvel, and a few generations are enough to bring it about.

The principal characteristics of the aristocracy remain engraved in history after its destruction, but the slight and delicate forms of its manners are lost to memory almost immediately after its fall. No one can imagine them when they are no longer seen. Their disappearance is unnoted and unfelt. For the heart needs an apprenticeship of custom and education to appreciate the refined pleasure derived from distinguished and fastidious manners; once the habit is lost, the taste for them easily goes too.

Thus, not only are democratic peoples unable to have aristocratic manners, but they cannot even conceive or desire them. As they cannot imagine them, from their point of view it is as if they had never existed.

One should not attach too much importance to this loss, but it is permissible to regret it.

I know it has happened that the same men have had very distinguished manners and very vulgar feelings; the inner life of courts has shown well enough what grand appearances may conceal the meanest hearts. But though the manners of an aristocracy by no means create virtue, they may add grace to virtue itself. It was no ordinary sight to see a numerous and powerful class whose every gesture seemed to

16

17

18

19

20

21

165

show a constant and natural dignity of feeling and thought, an ordered refinement of taste and urbanity of manners.

The manners of the aristocracy created a fine illusion about human nature; though the picture was often deceptive, it was yet a noble satisfaction to look on it. 22

COMPREHENSION

1. Summarize Tocqueville's observations about American manners, and explain why he believes they got that way.

2. Explain the positive and negative aspects that Tocqueville finds in both aristocratic manners and democratic ones.

3. Why are manners the one element in the transition from an aristocracy to a democracy that cannot be transmitted?

RHETORIC

1. The author makes a number of points concerning the nature of manners. What method, if any, does he use to reach his conclusions?

2. The author seems quite concerned about the concepts of "formal" and "informal." Would you rate his writing as formal or informal? What educational level does the author assume his intended audience has attained? Explain your answer.

3. Paragraph 3 is one long sentence. What punctuation devices does the author use to achieve this? How does his use of the word *when* help to give the paragraph a logical structure?

4. We ordinarily think of rhythm as a component of music, yet, by mixing long and short sentences, the author is able to establish a rhythm to his prose. How do the short sentences help to keep the prose "moving"? How do they function as transitional devices?

5. One commonly learns in school not to begin a sentence with the word *but.* Tocqueville breaks this convention three times in his essay—in paragraphs 9, 13, and 21. Explain why or why not this is effective.

6. The author uses comparison and contrast in many of his sentences. For example, in paragraph 15, he lists three distinctions between democratic manners and aristocratic ones. How often does he use this device in the essay? What is the total effect of using it so consistently?

7. Paragraph 13 offers the reader a rare example of the "double negative" in English. How does this reflect upon the style of the writing? How would the tone be different if the sentence were, "But I will admit there is something to praise in democratic manners"?

WRITING

1. Select an aspect of American behavior or perspective—such as language, attire, or taste—and write a three-paragraph essay explaining your subject, using Tocqueville's writing style.

2. For a research project, use anthropological, cultural, and historical source material in your library to write an essay about daily life in one American city during the early nineteenth century.

3. All cultures have rituals concerning things such as conversation, comfort zones, greeting and leave-taking signals. Browse through a book featuring photographs of a range of people from another era or culture, and write a brief descriptive essay describing their gestures or expressions.

P. J. O'ROURKE   Patrick Jake O'Rourke was born in Toledo, Ohio, in 1947. He received a B.A. from Miami University and an M.A. from The Johns Hopkins University. From his early days, as writer and editor of a left-wing underground newspaper titled *Baltimore Harry,* to today, as head of the international affairs desk of *Rolling Stone* magazine, O'Rourke has been an iconoclast. He is best known for his satirical articles and books on government. A libertarian, O'Rourke perceives the state as an intrusive and incompetent institution and has railed against it in such books as *Parliament of Whores: A Lone Humorist Attempts to Explain the Entire U.S. Government* (1991) and *Give War a Chance: Eyewitness Accounts of Mankind's Struggle against Tyranny, Injustice and Alcohol-Free Beer* (1992). He writes regularly for such magazines as *Harper's, Playboy, Vanity Fair, American Spectator,* and *Esquire.* The following, from his book *Modern Manners: An Etiquette Book for Rude People* (1989), demonstrates his whimsical yet biting style.

P. J. O'ROURKE

The Fundamentals of Contemporary Courtesy

*Good breeding consists in concealing how much we think of ourselves and
how little we think of the other person.*   —Samuel Clemens

The purpose of old-fashioned manners was to avoid attracting attention. The reason for this was that old-fashioned manners were possessed by only a few hundred rich people. These few hundred rich people didn't want all the hundreds of millions of poor people to notice who had the money. If the rich, polite few started attracting attention, the poor, rude many might get together and commit mayhem the way they did in Russia. The heck with that, said rich people.

But nowadays there are hundreds of millions of rich people, and poor people have been pretty much rendered harmless by drugs and sleeping on sidewalks. Plus it's getting so you can't tell rich from poor anyway, what with Nigerian illegal immigrants selling Rolexes on street corners and Gloria Vanderbilt putting her name on blue jean behinds. The problem modern people have is trying to be special. Therefore, the purpose of modern manners is to attract as much attention as possible.

Greetings

The importance of conspicuousness in modern life has led to the ³ phenomenon of "greeting inflation." Once, even the closest friends greeted each other with a polite bow. Today such reticence is almost extinct. A loud "Sweetheart," a slap on the back, chuck on the arm, tousling of hair, and a cheerful "Have a nice day!" will do if you don't know a person at all. But if you have even the slightest acquaintance with someone, it is usual to embrace him physically no matter what the circumstances. If you're carrying a briefcase or package, just throw it into the gutter. This makes a dramatic gesture of good fellowship.

If you actually know someone's name, twin kisses on both cheeks ⁴ are expected and should be accompanied by some highly original term of endearment. "I love you" or "You're my best friend" isn't nearly strong enough. In California, where manners are more modern than anywhere else, people say, "I'd murder my parents to have lunch with you" or even "I'm so glad to see you that I'm going to give you gross points in my new movie." (The latter statement is a lie, by the way.)

Rebuffs

At one time there was not only an etiquette of greeting people but ⁵ also an etiquette of not greeting them. This ranged in degree from the coldly formal bow to the "cut direct." The cut direct was delivered by looking right at a person and not acknowledging his acquaintance or even his existence. This is no longer done. It has been replaced by the lawsuit. Opposing parties in a lawsuit (and other enemies) are expected to greet each other like lovers—especially now when it's so fashionable for hostesses to invite people who hate each other to the same dinners. If the enmity is minor or philosophical in nature, argument—or, better, tableware throwing—may resume after a drink or two. But if the hatred is deep and well occasioned, the mutual detestors are expected to chat amicably throughout the evening.

Hat, Cane, and Gloves

What to do with your hat and cane is a perennial awkwardness ⁶ when greeting people. If the cane is necessary, it should be replaced with a crutch, which will gain you much more sympathy.

A hat should be taken off when you greet a lady and left off for the ⁷ rest of your life. Nothing looks more stupid than a hat. When you put on a hat you are surrendering to the same urge that makes children

wear mouse ears at Disney World or drunks wear lampshades at parties. Wearing a hat implies that you are bald if you are a man and that
your hair is dirty if you are a woman. Every style of hat is identified
with some form of undesirable (derby = corrupt ward heeler; fedora =
male model; top hat = rich bum; pillbox = Kennedy wife, et cetera).
Furthermore, the head is symbolically identified with the sexual organs,
so that when you walk down the street wearing a hat, anyone who has
the least knowledge of psychology will see you as having . . . a problem. A hat should only be worn if you are employed as a baseball player
or are hunting ducks in the rain.

Gloves present another problem, especially when shaking hands. 8
Men must always remove their gloves before a handshake. There is a
good reason for this. A man can be very accurately judged by his hand.
A soft hand indicates a lazy, unemployed person. A hard, calloused
hand shows that a person is an ignorant and dull manual laborer. A
cold, clammy hand means that a person is guilty and nervous. And a
warm, dry hand means a person is incapable of feeling guilt and has the
nerve to pull anything on you. A woman never removes her gloves.
There's a good reason for this, too. A woman can also be very accurately judged by her hand, and why would she want to be?

The Handshake

Despite the popularity of more effusive forms of greeting, the hand- 9
shake is omnipresent. It is now extended to everyone—men, women,
old people, young children, and, especially, pet dogs.

It's important to develop a limp and affected handshake. A firm, 10
hearty handshake gives a good first impression, and you'll never be forgiven if you don't live up to it. Also, a firm, hearty handshake inspires
confidence in others. People who go around inspiring confidence in
others are probably looking to sell them something. You don't want to
appear to be that sort.

Farewells

Much more important than greeting people is saying good-bye to 11
them or getting them to say good-bye to you or getting rid of them
somehow anyway. The one thing that can be safely said about the great
majority of people is that we don't want them around. Be sincere and
forthright about the problem. Take the person you want to get rid of
aside and tell him he has to leave because the people you're with hate
him. Say, "I'm sorry, Fred, but you can't sit down with us. Molly and
Bill Dinnersworth hate you because you're so much smarter and more
successful than they are."

This is nasty and flattering at the same time. And it makes life more 12
interesting, which, if you're too sophisticated to just want attention, is
the point of existence.

In Public

If you don't manage to get rid of everyone and end up having to go 13
somewhere with a group of people, make sure the couples are separated and that each partner is escorted by somebody new. This will give
everyone something different to fight about later.

Generally speaking, a man is supposed to walk to the left of a 14
woman and also keep himself between her and the curb. Of course, it
is frequently impossible to do both. But the great thinkers of all ages
have been unanimous in their admiration of paradoxes.

Unless he is helping her into an ambulance or a paddy wagon, a 15
man is never supposed to touch a woman in public. That is, he
shouldn't if he's married to the woman. Nothing is more deleterious to
the spirit of romance than watching a married couple hold hands.

If a man is walking down the street with two women, he should 16
keep them both on his right and not appear between them like an
acrobat taking a bow. Every authority on etiquette mentions this precept. But what no authority on etiquette mentions is how a man can
manage to get two women in the first place. The best idea is for him
to convince his wife or girlfriend to talk a friend of hers into a threesome. Most likely the result will be physically and emotionally disastrous. But everyone will get something juicy to tell the psychiatrist and
something to romanticize in diary or memoirs. Again, life is made
more interesting.

It's no longer *de rigueur* for a man to burden himself with anything 17
heavy that a woman is carrying, especially not a mortgage or someone
else's baby. Nor should a man necessarily hold a door for a woman,
unless it is a revolving door. It's not good manners to hold a revolving
door, but it is lots of fun when other people are trapped inside.

Restaurants, Taxicabs, and the Theater

When entering a restaurant, a man should allow the woman to pre- 18
cede him to their seats. This lets her find a friend whose table she can
stand at and chat for half an hour while the man gets a chance to
glimpse the prices on the menu and has a clear shot to bolt for the door
when he sees those prices.

A wise woman allows a man to enter a taxicab ahead of her so she 19
can slam his hand in the door if he's been acting like an ass.

At the theater, concert, or ballet, a man allows a woman to take her 20
seat first. He then holds her coat on his lap, along with his own coat,
her purse, her umbrella, both programs, and any other personal effects.
Safely hidden behind this mound of belongings, he can go to sleep.

The Importance of Being on Time

Whatever type of event you're attending, it's important to be on 21
time. Being on time should not be confused with being prompt. Being

prompt means arriving at the beginning. Being on time means arriving at the most interesting moment. Excepting love affairs, that moment is rarely the beginning.

"On time" is between midnight and four A.M. in New York, even for an eight o'clock play. Between midnight and four A.M. the actors will be getting drunk in a bar, and they'll be much more fun to talk to than when they're up on the stage.

In most other urban areas, "on time" is between twenty minutes 23 and an hour late. This gives everyone else time to be late, too, and they'll appreciate it.

In the country being on time more nearly approximates being 24 prompt. But don't overdo it. Being early is an unpardonable sin. If you are early, you'll witness the last-minute confusion and panic that always attend making anything seem effortlessly gracious.

In California, "on time" doesn't mean anything at all. An appoint- 25 ment for a meeting at three o'clock on Tuesday indicates there won't be a meeting and there might not be a Tuesday. Few words and no numbers have any meaning west of the Nevada border.

At Home

One popular way to avoid the problem of being on time is to stay at 26 home and conduct your life over the telephone. This is very chic in New York. Even New Yorkers who occasionally go outdoors have taken to telephoning every person they know once a day and twice if any of them has anything awful to say about the others.

Living over the telephone has a number of advantages. It saves on 27 cab fare and clothing budgets, and love affairs can be conducted without the bother of contraception or hairdressers. In fact, with judicious use of answering machines, a love affair can be conducted without the bother of ever talking to the loved one.

Making Up in Public

It's bad manners to apply cosmetics in public. It reminds people 28 that you need them.

Smoking in Public

Smoking was once subject to all sorts of polite restrictions, but 29 now it's just illegal. Therefore, there's only one remaining rule of etiquette about smoking in public: make sure you don't smoke anywhere else. Smoking is an inexpensive and convenient means of showing fashionable contempt for middle-class rules and regulations. Smoking also looks good. People who don't smoke have a terrible time finding something polite to do with their lips. But, when no one's around to see you, it doesn't matter what you do so there's no point in smoking then.

If someone asks you not to smoke, tell him you have no intentions ³⁰ of living to be an embittered old person. But thank him for his concern.

Nonchalance

Nonchalance about health and well-being is what gives smoking its ³¹ charm. That same nonchalance is at the heart of all really good manners. The most fundamental lesson of etiquette is "be unconcerned." Proper behavior means always giving the appearance of unperturbed grace. This appearance is much easier to achieve if you really don't care about anything. And this is why people always seem to be on their best behavior right before they commit suicide.

COMPREHENSION

1. What is the relationship between the essay and the epigram by Samuel Clemens that precedes it?

2. Humor is an important element in this essay. How would you characterize the audience for whom this humor is intended? Are there segments of society that wouldn't "get it"? If so, which ones?

3. State the thesis of the essay. Is it implied or directly expressed?

RHETORIC

1. The author has divided the essay into sections with titles. Is there any rationale for ordering the sections as they are, or does it appear arbitrary? Explain your view.

2. The author uses both understatement and hyperbole for comic purposes. For example, in paragraph 1 he refers to the Russian revolution as "the poor, rude many . . . get[ting] together and commit[ting] mayhem." In paragraph 1 of the "Greetings" section, he states, "If you're carrying a briefcase or package, just throw it into the gutter." Find at least three other examples of each device (understatement and hyperbole) and explain why they are effective as comedy.

3. The author uses definition and equivalences as rhetorical devices to create comic effect. Find examples of each. Are the definitions accurate, or used solely for rhetorical purposes, or both? Explain.

4. A good example of irony can be found in the section entitled "Smoking In Public," where the author states, "Smoking was once subject to all sorts of polite restrictions, but not it's just illegal." Explain how this statement is ironic, and find two other ironic statements in the essay.

5. In paragraph 2 of the "At Home" section, the author escalates the values of "living over the telephone," going from the nearly sensible to the downright absurd. How does this device achieve a comic effect?

6. How does the final sentence give a sense of closure to the essay?

1. Create your own comic guidebook for the newly initiated. Examples include "How to Get Along Well in College," "How to Deal Successfully with Your Boss," and "How to Make a Good Impression on a First Date." Compare your comic methods with those of O'Rourke.

2. A popular expression states that comics are disappointed idealists. Argue for against the proposition that O'Rourke's purpose in this essay is to write a critical commentary on our society.

3. Interview one of your grandparents or someone from your grandparents' generation concerning his or her view of the various types of behaviors depicted in this essay. Write an essay comparing and contrasting the differences between their attitudes toward manners and those expressed in the essay.

CLASSIC AND CONTEMPORARY: QUESTIONS FOR COMPARISON

1. Although both Tocqueville and O'Rourke write about manners in the United States, their purposes seem to differ. What are the purposes of each writer in reporting his observations?

2. Compare and contrast Tocqueville's statement that "Nothing, at first sight, seems less important than the external formalities of human behavior" with O'Rourke's claim that "The purpose of old-fashioned manners was to avoid attracting attention."

3. Using your own observations of everyday life, argue for or against the accuracy of either author's view on manners.

4. Tocqueville considers the style of American manners to be based directly on the effects of democracy. How appropriate or inappropriate is this view in the light of the role that manners play in contemporary America? Pay particular attention to O'Rourke's comment that "the purpose of modern manners is to attract as much attention as possible."

CONNECTIONS

1. Baraka writes about food and Whelan about alcohol in their essays. What connections do they make between their subjects and cultural alienation? How do they present their ideas? How does Baraka's tone differ from Whelan's?

2. Write an essay exploring the role of the father in the essays of Walker and Wong. Compare the impact these men had on the writers' lives. How strong is the maternal presence in these essays?

3. How do Whelan, Walker, and Pogrebin use experiences with their children to support or illustrate their respective points of view? Give examples from these writers.

4. Consider the current position of women in the world. What determines beauty or desirability in a woman? Do women own their own bodies? Explore these issues, using support for your views from Mojtabai, Wong, and Walker.

5. What role have manner and custom played in shaping contemporary American culture? Mention specific customs you're familiar with, and describe the lessons they teach about life in America today. Make a connection between your views and those of Michael Dorris.

6. Consider the use of dialogue, slang, and syntax in the essays of Walker and Baraka. How does language help to promote the writers' points of view? Are they using language in a similar manner? Who are they writing for?

7. How does one's experience of being an *outsider,* or stranger to a culture, affect one's understanding of that culture? Use the essays by Pogrebin, Wong, and Mojtabai as a basis for your discussion.

CHAPTER FOUR

School and College

*I*n "Learning to Read and Write," a chapter from his autobiography, Frederick Douglass offers a spirited affirmation of the rights we all should have to pursue an education. For Douglass, who began his life in slavery, knowledge began with experience but also with the need to articulate that experience through literacy. The ability to read and write should be the possession of all human beings, and Douglass was willing to risk punishment—even death—to gain that ability.

Perhaps the struggle for an education always involves a certain amount of effort and risk, but the struggle also conveys excitement and the deep, abiding satisfaction that derives from achieving knowledge of oneself and of the world. Time and again in the essays comprising this chapter, we discover that there is always a price to be paid for acquiring knowledge, developing intellectual skills, and attaining wisdom. However, numerous task forces and national commissions tell us that students today are not willing to pay this price and that, as a consequence, we have become academically mediocre. Is it true that we no longer delight in educating ourselves through reading, as Richard Rodriguez recounts in "The Lonely Good Company of Books"? Is it true that we take libraries for granted but never visit them, a thought that would have been anathema to Richard Wright, who educated himself through them? A democratic society requires an educated citizenry, people who refuse to commit intellectual suicide. The writers in this chapter, who take many pathways to understanding, remind us that we cannot afford to be passive or compliant when our right to an education is challenged.

Today we are in an era of dynamic change in attitudes toward education. Such issues as sex education, multiculturalism, and affirmative action—subjects treated by three of the essayists in this chapter—suggest the liveliness of the educational debate. Any debate over contemporary education touches on the themes of politics, economics, religion, or the social agenda, forcing us to recognize that configurations of power are at the heart of virtually all educational issues in society today.

Mark Twain, whom you encountered in an earlier chapter, called "petrified opinion" the opposite of true knowledge and the enemy of democratic processes. Indeed, if we judge the tenor of the essayists in this section, we discover that many of them are subversives, waging war against both ignorance *and* received dogma. These writers treat education as the key vehicle to upset the status quo and effect change. Operating from diverse backgrounds and cultural traditions, they reveal many pathways to knowledge and wisdom, inviting us to think critically about the purpose of education.

Previewing the Chapter

As you read the essays in this chapter and respond to them in discussion and writing, consider the following questions:

- What is the main educational issue that the author deals with?
- What tone does the author establish in treating the subject? Does the author take a positive or a negative approach to the topic?
- How does the author define *education?* How closely is the definition tied to the author's own experience?
- Which problems and conflicts influence the writer's attitude toward education? How did the writer overcome these problems?
- What is the impact of race, ethnicity, class, and gender on the educational issues discussed?
- How does education change the writer's view of himself or herself?
- According to the author, what is the purpose or end of education?
- Do you share the writer's viewpoint on education, or do you oppose it?
- How closely does the author's educational experience or attitude parallel your own?
- What have you learned about the value of education from reading these selections?

E. B. WHITE   Elwyn Brooks White (1899–1985), perhaps the finest contemporary American essayist, is at his most distinctive in his treatments of people, nature, and social conventions. Associated for years with *The New Yorker,* White is the author of *One Man's Meat* (1942), and *Here Is New York* (1949). Most writers and lovers of language have enjoyed his witty, explanation of English grammar in his revision of William Strunk Jr.'s *The Elements of Style* (1959). In the following essay, White reveals his love for the country experience as he muses on the comparative values of urban and rural, private and public education.

E. B. WHITE

Education

I have an increasing admiration for the teacher in the country school where we have a third-grade scholar in attendance. She not only undertakes to instruct her charges in all the subjects of the first three grades, but she manages to function quietly and effectively as a guardian of their health, their clothes, their habits, their mothers, and their snowball engagements. She has been doing this sort of Augean task for twenty years, and is both kind and wise. She cooks for the children on the stove that heats the room, and she can cool their passions or warm their soup with equal competence. She conceives their costumes, cleans up their messes, and shares their confidences. My boy already regards his teacher as his great friend, and I think tells her a great deal more than he tells us.

The shift from city school to country school was something we worried about quietly all last summer. I have always rather favored public school over private school, if only because in public school you meet a greater variety of children. This bias of mine, I suspect, is partly an attempt to justify my own past (I never knew anything but public schools) and partly an involuntary defense against getting kicked in the shins by a young ceramist on his way to the kiln. My wife was unacquainted with public schools, never having been exposed (in her early life) to anything more public than the washroom of Miss Winsor's. Regardless of our backgrounds, we both knew that change in schools was something that concerned not us but the scholar himself. We hoped it would work out all right. In New York our son went to a medium-priced private institution with semi-progressive ideas of education, and modern plumbing. He learned fast, kept well, and we were satisfied. It was an electric, colorful, regimented existence with moments of pleasurable pause and giddy incident. The day the Christmas angel fainted and had to be carried out by one of the Wise Men was educational in the highest sense of the term. Our scholar gave imitations of it around the house for weeks afterward, and I doubt if it ever goes completely out of his mind.

His days were rich in formal experience. Wearing overalls and an ₃ old sweater (the accepted uniform of the private seminary), he sallied forth at morn accompanied by a nurse or a parent and walked (or was pulled) two blocks to a corner where the school bus made a flag stop. This flashy vehicle was as punctual as death: seeing us waiting at the cold curb, it would sweep to a halt, open its mouth, suck the boy in, and spring away with an angry growl. It was a good deal like a train picking up a bag of mail. At school the scholar was worked on for six or seven hours by half a dozen teachers and a nurse, and was revived on orange juice in mid-morning. In a cinder court he played games supervised by an athletic instructor, and in a cafeteria he ate lunch worked out by a dietitian. He soon learned to read with gratifying facility and discernment and to make Indian weapons of a semi-deadly nature. Whenever one of his classmates fell low of a fever the news was put on the wires and there were breathless phone calls to physicians, discussing periods of incubation and allied magic.

In the country all one can say is that the situation is different, and ₄ somehow more casual. Dressed in corduroys, sweatshirt, and short rubber boots, and carrying a tin dinner-pail, our scholar departs at crack of dawn for the village school, two and a half miles down the road, next to the cemetery. When the road is open and the car will start, he makes the journey by motor, courtesy of his old man. When the snow is deep or the motor is dead or both, he makes it on the hoof. In the afternoons he walks or hitches all or part of the way home in fair weather, gets transported in foul. The schoolhouse is a two-room frame building, bungalow type, shingles stained a burnt brown with weather-resistant stain. It has a chemical toilet in the basement and two teachers above stairs. One takes the first three grades, the other the fourth, fifth, and sixth. They have little or no time for individual instruction, and no time at all for the esoteric. They teach what they know themselves, just as fast and as hard as they can manage. The pupils sit still at their desks in class, and do their milling around outdoors during recess.

There is no supervised play. They play cops and robbers (only they ₅ call it "Jail") and throw things at one another—snowballs in winter, rose hips in fall. It seems to satisfy them. They also construct darts, pinwheels, and "pick-up sticks" (jackstraws), and the school itself does a brisk trade in penny candy, which is for sale right in the classroom and which contains "surprises." The most highly prized surprise is a fake cigarette, made of cardboard, fiendishly lifelike.

The memory of how apprehensive we were at the beginning is still ₆ strong. The boy was nervous about the change too. The tension, on that first fair morning in September when we drove him to school, almost blew the windows out of the sedan. And when later we picked him up on the road, wandering along with his little blue lunch-pail, and got his laconic report "All right" in answer to our inquiry about how the day had gone, our relief was vast. Now, after almost a year of it, the only difference we can discover in the two school experiences is that in the country he sleeps better at night—and *that* probably is more the air than the education. When grilled on the subject of school-in-country vs. school-in-city, he replied that the chief difference is that the day seems to go so much quicker in the country. "Just like lightning," he reported.

COMPREHENSION

1. How does White define his subject in this essay? Does he present a limited or comprehensive view of his subject? Justify your answer.
2. Why were the Whites "quietly" worried about the shift from private to public school? What were the two schools like? Which school does the author prefer? How do you know?
3. Explain the connections between the city and private schools and the country and public schools.

RHETORIC

1. White refers to his son as the "scholar" several times in this essay. What are the purpose and effect of this strategy?
2. What is the significance of the word "Education" as used in the title? Is this significance a matter of connotation or denotation? Explain.
3. What is White's thesis? Is it ever explicitly stated? Why, or why not?
4. What standard means of exposition does the author employ in the introduction? Why is the introductory paragraph especially effective?
5. How does the author develop his pattern of comparison and contrast in this essay? What major and minor points in the contrast does he develop?
6. How are the rhetorical strategies of narration, description, and argumentation reflected in this essay?

WRITING

1. Debate this proposition: Rural schools cannot provide the educational advantages of urban private schools.
2. Write a comparative essay on the type of school that you prefer—public or private.
3. Compare and contrast the relative advantages and disadvantages of urban and rural (or, if you wish, suburban) education.
4. In a comparative essay, examine the father-son relationship in this essay and in White's "Once More to the Lake."

MAYA ANGELOU   Maya Angelou (b. 1928) is an American poet, playwright, television writer, actress, and singer. Her autobiographical books, notably *I Know Why the Caged Bird Sings* (1970), from which the following selection is taken, provide rich accounts of the black female experience. Fluent in six languages and active in artistic, educational, and political affairs, Angelou often presents autobiographical material against the backdrop of larger cultural concerns. In this vivid reminiscence of her 1940 graduation from grade school in Stamps, Arkansas, she provides insights into a community of young scholars who gain inspiration and wisdom from their experience during commencement ceremonies.

MAYA ANGELOU

Graduation

The children in Stamps trembled visibly with anticipation. Some   1
adults were excited too, but to be certain the whole young population
had come down with graduation epidemic. Large classes were graduating from both the grammar school and the high school. Even those who
were years removed from their own day of glorious release were anxious to help with preparations as a kind of dry run. The junior students
who were moving into the vacating classes' chairs were tradition-bound
to show their talents for leadership and management. They strutted
through the school and around the campus exerting pressure on the
lower grades. Their authority was so new that occasionally if they
pressed a little too hard it had to be overlooked. After all, next term was
coming, and it never hurt a sixth grader to have a play sister in the
eighth grade, or a tenth-year student to be able to call a twelfth grader
Bubba. So all was endured in a spirit of shared understanding. But the
graduating classes themselves were the nobility. Like travelers with
exotic destinations on their minds, the graduates were remarkably for-
getful. They came to school without their books, or tablets or even pencils. Volunteers fell over themselves to secure replacements for the missing equipment. When accepted, the willing workers might or might not
be thanked, and it was of no importance to the pregraduation rites.
Even teachers were respectful of the now quiet and aging seniors, and
tended to speak to them, if not as equals, as beings only slightly lower
than themselves. After tests were returned and grades given, the student
body, which acted like an extended family, knew who did well, who
excelled, and what piteous ones had failed.

Unlike the white high school, Lafayette County Training School dis-   2
tinguished itself by having neither lawn, nor hedges, nor tennis court,
nor climbing ivy. Its two buildings (main classrooms, the grade school
and home economics) were set on a dirt hill with no fence to limit
either its boundaries or those of bordering farms. There was a large
expanse to the left of the school which was used alternately as a baseball diamond or a basketball court. Rusty hoops on the swaying poles
represented the permanent recreational equipment, although bats and
balls could be borrowed from the P.E. teacher if the borrower was qualified and if the diamond wasn't occupied.

Over this rocky area relieved by a few shady tall persimmon trees   3
the graduating class walked. The girls often held hands and no longer
bothered to speak to the lower students. There was a sadness about
them, as if this old world was not their home and they were bound for
higher ground. The boys, on the other hand, had become more

friendly, more outgoing. A decided change from the closed attitude they projected while studying for finals. Now they seemed not ready to give up the old school, the familiar paths and classrooms. Only a small percentage would be continuing on to college—one of the South's A & M (agricultural and mechanical) schools, which trained Negro youths to be carpenters, farmers, handymen, masons, maids, cooks and baby nurses. Their future rode heavily on their shoulders, and blinded them to the collective joy that had pervaded the lives of the boys and girls in the grammar school graduating class.

Parents who could afford it had ordered new shoes and ready-made clothes for themselves from Sears and Roebuck or Montgomery Ward. They also engaged the best seamstresses to make the floating graduating dresses and to cut down secondhand pants which would be pressed to a military slickness for the important event.

Oh, it was important, all right. Whitefolks would attend the ceremony, and two or three would speak of God and home, and the Southern way of life, and Mrs. Parsons, the principal's wife, would play the graduation march while the lower-grade graduates paraded down the aisles and took their seats below the platform. The high school seniors would wait in empty classrooms to make their dramatic entrance.

In the Store I was the person of the moment. The birthday girl. The center. Bailey had graduated the year before, although to do so he had had to forfeit all pleasures to make up for his time lost in Baton Rouge.

My class was wearing butter-yellow piqué dresses, and Momma launched out on mine. She smocked the yoke into tiny crisscrossing puckers, then shirred the rest of the bodice. Her dark fingers ducked in and out of the lemony cloth as she embroidered raised daisies around the hem. Before she considered herself finished she had added a crocheted cuff on the puff sleeves, and a pointy crocheted collar.

I was going to be lovely. A walking model of all the various styles of fine hand sewing and it didn't worry me that I was only twelve years old and merely graduating from the eighth grade. Besides, many teachers in Arkansas Negro schools had only that diploma and were licensed to impart wisdom.

The days had become longer and more noticeable. The faded beige of former times had been replaced with strong and sure colors. I began to see my classmates' clothes, their skin tones, and the dust that waved off pussy willows. Clouds that lazed across the sky were objects of great concern to me. Their shiftier shapes might have held a message that in my new happiness and with a little bit of time I'd soon decipher. During that period I looked at the arch of heaven so religiously my neck kept a steady ache. I had taken to smiling more often, and my jaws hurt from the unaccustomed activity. Between the two physical sore spots, I suppose I could have been uncomfortable, but that was not the case. As a member of the winning team (the graduating class of 1940) I had outdistanced unpleasant sensations by miles. I was headed for the freedom of open fields.

181

Youth and social approval allied themselves with me and we tram-   10
meled memories of slights and insults. The wind of our swift passage
remodeled my features. Lost tears were pounded to mud and then to
dust. Years of withdrawal were brushed aside and left behind, as hanging ropes of parasitic moss.

My work alone had awarded me a top place and I was going to be   11
one of the first called in the graduating ceremonies. On the classroom
blackboard, as well as on the bulletin board in the auditorium, there
were blue stars and white stars and red stars. No absences, no tardi-
ness, and my academic work was among the best of the year. I could
say the preamble to the Constitution even faster than Bailey. We timed
ourselves often: "WethepeopleoftheUnitedStatesinordertoformamore-
perfectunion. . . ." I had memorized the Presidents of the United
States from Washington to Roosevelt in chronological as well as alpha-
betical order.

My hair pleased me too. Gradually the black mass had lengthened   12
and thickened, so that it kept at last to its braided pattern, and I didn't
have to yank my scalp off when I tried to comb it.

Louise and I had rehearsed the exercises until we tired out our-   13
selves. Henry Reed was class valedictorian. He was a small, very black
boy with hooded eyes, a long, broad nose and an oddly shaped head.
I had admired him for years because each term he and I vied for the
best grades in our class. Most often he bested me, but instead of being
disappointed, I was pleased that we shared top places between us.
Like many Southern black children, he lived with his grandmother,
who was as strict as Momma and as kind as she knew how to be. He
was courteous, respectful and softspoken to elders, but on the play-
ground he chose to play the roughest games. I admired him. Anyone,
I reckoned, sufficiently afraid or sufficiently dull could be polite. But
to be able to operate at a top level with both adults and children was
admirable.

His valedictory speech was entitled "To Be or Not to Be." The rigid   14
tenth-grade teacher had helped him write it. He'd been working on the
dramatic stresses for months.

The weeks until graduation were filled with heady activities. A   15
group of small children were to be presented in a play about buttercups
and daisies and bunny rabbits. They could be heard throughout the
building practicing their hops and their little songs that sounded like silver bells. The older girls (non-graduates, of course) were assigned the
task of making refreshments for the night's festivities. A tangy scent of
ginger, cinnamon, nutmeg and chocolate wafted around the home economics building as the budding cooks made samples for themselves
and their teachers.

In every corner of the workshop, axes and saws split fresh timber as   17
the woodshop boys made sets and stage scenery. Only the graduates
were left out of the general bustle. We were free to sit in the library at
the back of the building or look in quite detachedly, naturally, on the
measures being taken for our event.

Even the minister preached on graduation the Sunday before. His subject was, "Let your light so shine that men will see your good works and praise your Father, Who is in Heaven." Although the sermon was purported to be addressed to us, he used the occasion to speak to backsliders, gamblers and general ne'er-do-wells. But since he had called our names at the beginning of the service we were mollified.

Among Negroes the tradition was to give presents to children going only from one grade to another. How much more important this was when the person was graduating at the top of the class. Uncle Willie and Momma had sent away for a Mickey Mouse watch like Bailey's. Louise gave me four embroidered handkerchiefs. (I gave her three crocheted doilies.) Mrs. Sneed, the minister's wife, made me an underskirt to wear for graduation, and nearly every customer gave me a nickel or maybe even a dime with the instruction "Keep on moving to higher ground," or some such encouragement.

Amazingly the great day finally dawned and I was out of bed before I knew it. I threw open the back door to see it more clearly, but Momma said, "Sister, come away from that door and put your robe on."

I hoped the memory of that morning would never leave me. Sunlight was itself still young, and the day had none of the insistence maturity would bring it in a few hours. In my robe and barefoot in the backyard, under cover of going to see about my new beans, I gave myself up to the gentle warmth and thanked God that no matter what evil I had done in my life He had allowed me to live to see this day. Somewhere in my fatalism I had expected to die, accidentally, and never have the chance to walk up the stairs in the auditorium and gracefully receive my hard-earned diploma. Out of God's merciful bosom I had won reprieve.

Bailey came out in his robe and gave me a box wrapped in Christmas paper. He said he had saved his money for months to pay for it. It felt like a box of chocolates, but I knew Bailey wouldn't save money to buy candy when we had all we could want under our noses.

He was as proud of the gift as I. It was a soft-leather-bound copy of a collection of poems by Edgar Allan Poe, or, as Bailey and I called him, "Eap." I turned to "Annabel Lee" and we walked up and down the garden rows, the cool dirt between our toes, reciting the beautifully sad lines.

Momma made a Sunday breakfast although it was only Friday. After we finished the blessing, I opened my eyes to find the watch on my plate. It was a dream of a day. Everything went smoothly and to my credit. I didn't have to be reminded or scolded for anything. Near evening I was too jittery to attend to chores, so Bailey volunteered to do all before his bath.

Days before, we had made a sign for the Store, and as we turned out the lights Momma hung the cardboard over the doorknob. It read clearly: CLOSED. GRADUATION.

My dress fitted perfectly and everyone said that I looked like a sunbeam in it. On the hill, going toward the school, Bailey walked behind

183

with Uncle Willie, who muttered, "Go on, Ju." He wanted him to walk ahead with us because it embarrassed him to have to walk so slowly. Bailey said he'd let the ladies walk together, and the men would bring up the rear. We all laughed, nicely.

Little children dashed by out of the dark like fireflies. Their ²⁶ crepe-paper dresses and butterfly wings were not made for running and we heard more than one rip, dryly, and the regretful "uh uh" that followed.

The school blazed without gaiety. The windows seemed cold and ²⁷ unfriendly from the lower hill. A sense of ill-fated timing crept over me, and if Momma hadn't reached for my hand I would have drifted back to Bailey and Uncle Willie, and possibly beyond. She made a few slow jokes about my feet getting cold, and tugged me along to the now-strange building.

Around the front steps, assurance came back. There were my fellow ²⁸ "greats," the graduating class. Hair brushed back, legs oiled, new dresses and pressed pleats, fresh pocket handkerchiefs and little hand-bags, all homesewn. Oh, we were up to snuff, all right. I joined my comrades and didn't even see my family go in to find seats in the crowded auditorium.

The school band struck up a march and all classes filed in as had ²⁹ been rehearsed. We stood in front of our seats, as assigned, and on a signal from the choir director, we sat. No sooner had this been accomplished than the band started to play the national anthem. We rose again and sang the song, after which we recited the pledge of allegiance. We remained standing for a brief minute before the choir director and the principal signaled to us, rather desperately I thought, to take our seats. The command was so unusual that our carefully rehearsed and smooth-running machine was thrown off. For a full minute we fumbled for our chairs and bumped into each other awkwardly. Habits change or solidify under pressure, so in our state of nervous tension we had been ready to follow our usual assembly pattern: the American national anthem, then the pledge of allegiance, then the song every Black person I knew called the Negro National Anthem. All done in the same key, with the same passion and most often standing on the same foot.

Finding my seat at last, I was overcome with a presentiment of ³⁰ worse things to come. Something unrehearsed, unplanned, was going to happen, and we were going to be made to look bad. I distinctly remember being explicit in the choice of pronoun. It was "we," the graduating class, the unit, that concerned me then.

The principal welcomed "parents and friends" and asked the Bap- ³¹ tist minister to lead us in prayer. His invocation was brief and punchy, and for a second I thought we were getting back on the high road to right action. When the principal came back to the dais, however, his voice had changed. Sounds always affected me profoundly and the principal's voice was one of my favorites. During assembly it melted and lowered weakly into the audience. It had not been in my plan to listen to him, but my curiosity was piqued and I straightened up to give him my attention.

He was talking about Booker T. Washington, our "late great leader," who said we can be as close as the fingers on the hand, etc. . . . . Then he said a few vague things about friendship and the friendship of kindly people to those less fortunate than themselves. With that his voice nearly faded, thin, away. Like a river diminishing to a stream and then to a trickle. But he cleared his throat and said, "Our speaker tonight, who is also our friend, came from Texarkana to deliver the commencement address, but due to the irregularity of the train schedule, he's going to, as they say, 'speak and run.'" He said that we understood and wanted the man to know that we were most grateful for the time he was able to give us and then something about how we were willing always to adjust to another's program, and without more ado—"I give you Mr. Edward Donleavy."

Not one but two white men came through the door offstage. The 33 shorter one walked to the speaker's platform, and the tall one moved over to the center seat and sat down. But that was our principal's seat, and already occupied. The dislodged gentleman bounced around for a long breath or two before the Baptist minister gave him his chair, then with more dignity than the situation deserved, the minister walked off the stage.

Donleavy looked at the audience once (on reflection, I'm sure that 34 he wanted only to reassure himself that we were really there), adjusted his glasses and began to read from a sheaf of papers.

He was glad "to be here and to see the work going on just as it was 35 in the other schools."

At the first "Amen" from the audience I willed the offender to 36 immediate death by choking on the word. But Amens and Yes, sir's began to fall around the room like rain through a ragged umbrella.

He told us of the wonderful changes we children in Stamps had in 37 store. The Central School (naturally, the white school was Central) had already been granted improvements that would be in use in the fall. A well-known artist was coming from Little Rock to teach art to them. They were going to have the newest microscopes and chemistry equipment for their laboratory. Mr. Donleavy didn't leave us long in the dark over who made these improvements available to Central High. Nor were we to be ignored in the general betterment scheme he had in mind.

He said that he had pointed out to people at a very high level that 38 one of the first-line football tacklers at Arkansas Agricultural and Mechanical College had graduated from good old Lafayette County Training School. Here fewer Amens were heard. Those few that did break through lay dully in the air with the heaviness of habit.

He went on to praise us. He went on to say how he had bragged 39 that "one of the best basketball players at Fisk sank his first ball right here at Lafayette County Training School."

The white kids were going to have a chance to become Galileos 40 and Madame Curies and Edisons and Gauguins, and our boys (the girls weren't even in on it) would try to be Jesse Owenses and Joe Louises.

Owens and the Brown Bomber were great heroes in our world, but 41 what school official in the white-goddom of Little Rock had the right to decide that those two men must be our only heroes? Who decided that for Henry Reed to become a scientist he had to work like George Washington Carver, as a bootblack, to buy a lousy microscope? Bailey was obviously always going to be too small to be an athlete, so which concrete angel glued to what country seat had decided that if my brother wanted to become a lawyer he had to first pay penance for his skin by picking cotton and hoeing corn and studying correspondence books at night for twenty years?

The man's dead words fell like bricks around the auditorium and 42 too many settled in my belly. Constrained by hard-learned manners I couldn't look behind me, but to my left and right the proud graduating class of 1940 had dropped their heads. Every girl in my row had found something new to do with her handkerchief. Some folded the tiny squares into love knots, some into triangles, but most were wadding them, then pressing them flat on their yellow laps.

On the dais, the ancient tragedy was being replayed. Professor Parsons sat, a sculptor's reject, rigid. His large, heavy body seemed devoid of will or willingness, and his eyes said he was no longer with us. The other teachers examined the flag (which was draped stage right) or their notes, or the windows which opened on our now-famous playing diamond.

Graduation, the hush-hush magic time of frills and gifts and congratulations and diplomas, was finished for me before my name was called. The accomplishment was nothing. The meticulous maps, drawn in three colors of ink, learning, and spelling decasyllabic words, memorizing the whole of *The Rape of Lucrece*—it was for nothing. Donleavy had exposed us.

We were maids and farmers, handymen and washerwomen, and 45 anything higher that we aspired to was farcical and presumptuous.

Then I wished that Gabriel Prosser and Nat Turner had killed all 46 whitefolks in their beds and that Abraham Lincoln had been assassinated before the signing of the Emancipation Proclamation, and that Harriet Tubman had been killed by that blow on her head and Christopher Columbus had drowned in the *Santa Maria*.

It was awful to be Negro and have no control over my life. It was 47 brutal to be young and already trained to sit quietly and listen to charges brought against my color with no chance of defense. We should all be dead. I thought I should like to see us all dead, one on top of the other. A pyramid of flesh with the whitefolks on the bottom, as the broad base, then the Indians with their silly tomahawks and tepees and wigwams and treaties, the Negroes with their mops and recipes and cotton sacks and spirituals sticking out of their mouths. The Dutch children should all stumble in their wooden shoes and break their necks. The French should choke to death on the Louisiana Purchase

(1803) while silkworms ate all the Chinese with their stupid pigtails. As a species, we were an abomination. All of us.

Donleavy was running for election, and assured our parents that if he won we could count on having the only colored paved playing field in that part of Arkansas. Also—he never looked up to acknowledge the grunts of acceptance—also, we were bound to get some new equipment for the home economics building and the workshop.

He finished, and since there was no need to give any more than the most perfunctory thank-you's, he nodded to the men on the stage, and the tall white man who was never introduced joined him at the door. They left with the attitude that now they were off to something really important. (The graduation ceremonies at Lafayette County Training School had been a mere preliminary.)

The ugliness they left was palpable. An uninvited guest who wouldn't leave. The choir was summoned and sang a modern arrangement of "Onward, Christian Soldiers," with new words pertaining to graduates seeking their place in the world. But it didn't work. Elouise, the daughter of the Baptist minister, recited "Invictus," and I could have cried at the impertinence of "I am the master of my fate, I am the captain of my soul."

My name had lost its ring of familiarity and I had to be nudged to go and receive my diploma. All my preparations had fled. I neither marched up to the stage like a conquering Amazon, nor did I look in the audience for Bailey's nod of approval. Marguerite Johnson, I heard the name again, my honors were read, there were noises in the audience of appreciation, and I took my place on the stage as rehearsed.

I thought about colors I hated: ecru, puce, lavender, beige and black.

There was shuffling and rustling around me, then Henry Reed was giving his valedictory address, "To Be or Not to Be." Hadn't he heard the whitefolks? We couldn't *be* so the question was a waste of time. Henry's voice came clear and strong. I feared to look at him. Hadn't he got the message? There was no "nobler in the mind" for Negroes because the world didn't think we had minds, and they let us know it. "Outrageous fortune"? Now, that was a joke. When the ceremony was over I had to tell Henry Reed some things. That is, if I still cared. Not "rub," Henry, "erase." "Ah, there's the erase." Us.

Henry had been a good student in elocution. His voice rose on tides of promise and fell on waves of warnings. The English teacher had helped him to create a sermon winging through Hamlet's soliloquy. To be a man, a doer, a builder, a leader, or to be a tool, an unfunny joke, a crusher of funky toadstools, I marveled that Henry could go through the speech as if we had a choice.

I had been listening and silently rebutting each sentence with my eyes closed; then there was a hush, which in an audience warns that something unplanned is happening. I looked up and saw Henry Reed, the conservative, the proper, the A student, turn his back to the audience and turn to us (the proud graduating class of 1940) and sing, nearly speaking,

Lift ev'ry voice and sing
Till earth and heaven ring
Ring with the harmonies of Liberty. . . .

It was the poem written by James Weldon Johnson. It was the music composed by J. Rosamond Johnson. It was the Negro national anthem. Out of habit we were singing it.

Our mothers and fathers stood in the dark hall and joined the hymn 56 of encouragement. A kindergarten teacher led the small children onto the stage and the buttercups and daisies and bunny rabbits marked time and tried to follow:

Stony the road we trod
Bitter the chastening rod
Felt in the days when hope, unborn, had died.
Yet with a steady beat
Have not our weary feet
Come to the place for which our father sighed?

Every child I knew had learned that song with his ABC's and along 57 with "Jesus Loves Me This I Know." But I personally had never heard it before. Never heard the words, despite the thousands of times I had sung them. Never thought they had anything to do with me.

On the other hand, the words of Patrick Henry had made such an 58 impression on me that I had been able to stretch myself tall and trembling and say, "I know not what course others may take, but as for me, give me liberty or give me death."

And now I heard, really for the first time: 59

We have come over a way that with tears has been watered,
We have come, treading our path through the blood of the slaughtered.

While echoes of the song shivered in the air, Henry Reed bowed his 60 head, said "Thank you," and returned to his place in the line. The tears that slipped down many faces were not wiped away in shame.

We were on top again. As always, again. We survived. The depths 61 had been icy and dark, but now a bright sun spoke to our souls. I was no longer simply a member of the proud graduating class of 1940; I was a proud member of the wonderful beautiful Negro race.

COMPREHENSION

1. Is Angelou a neutral observer or subjective participant in the events of this narrative? How can you tell?

2. How is the author's "presentiment of worse things to come" actually borne out? What is the "ancient tragedy" alluded to? How, specifically, does education relate to this allusion?

3. What do you learn about Marguerite—the young Maya Angelou—from this essay? What are her moods, emotions, thoughts, and attitudes? In what way is she "bound for higher ground"?

1. Angelou is a highly impressionistic stylist in this essay. Provide examples of details that create vivid descriptive impressions. How do these details control the shifting moods of the selection?
2. Explain Angelou's allusions to *The Rape of Lucrece,* Gabriel Prosser and Nat Turner, Harriet Tubman, and "Invictus." How are these allusions and others related to the thesis? State that thesis in your own words.
3. What is the purpose of the relatively long five-paragraph introduction? What contrasts and latent ironies do you detect?
4. Cite examples of the author's ability to blend description, narration, and exposition. At what points is the expository mode the strongest? What is Angelou's purpose?
5. Why are the descriptions of Henry Reed and Donleavy juxtaposed?
6. Which paragraphs constitute the conclusion? How does Angelou achieve the transition from the body to the end?

WRITING

1. To what extent does American education still try to "track" students? What are the implications of such tracking? Discuss this issue in an essay; be certain to provide appropriate evidence.
2. Reconstruct your own graduation from grade school or high school.
3. Analyze and evaluate the many strategies that Angelou employs to honor and celebrate black culture and black wisdom in this essay.

SANTHA RAMA RAU   Santha Rama Rau (b. 1923) is an Indian novelist and essayist who, throughout her career, has interpreted the Eastern experience for Western audiences. She is a gifted travel writer and memoirist. Her principal works include *Home to India* (1944), *Remember the House* (1955), and *Gifts of Passage* (1961). This narrative essay sensitively portrays the conflict in cultures perceived by the author in her early childhood.

SANTHA RAMA RAU

By Any Other Name

At the Anglo-Indian day school in Zorinabad to which my sister and I were sent when she was eight and I was five and a half, they changed our names. On the first day of school, a hot, windless morning of a north Indian September, we stood in the head-mistress's study and she said, "Now you're the *new* girls. What are your names?"

My sister answered for us. "I am Premila, and she"—nodding in my direction—"is Santha."

The headmistress had been in India, I suppose, fifteen years or so, but she still smiled her helpless inability to cope with Indian names. Her rimless half-glasses glittered, and the precarious bun on top of her head trembled as she shook her head. "Oh, my dears, those are much too hard for me. Suppose we give you pretty English names. Wouldn't that be more jolly? Let's see, now—Pamela for you, I think." She shrugged in a baffled way at my sister. "That's as close as I can get. And for *you*," she said to me, "how about Cynthia? Isn't that nice?"

My sister was always less easily intimidated than I was, and while she kept a stubborn silence, I said, "Thank you," in a very tiny voice.

We had been sent to that school because my father, among his responsibilities as an officer of the civil service, had a tour of duty to perform in the villages around that steamy little provincial town, where he had his headquarters at that time. He used to make his shorter inspection tours on horseback, and a week before, in the stale heat of a typically postmonsoon day, we had waved good-by to him and a little procession—an assistant, a secretary, two bearers, and the man to look after the bedding rolls and luggage. They rode away through our large garden, still bright green from the rains, and we turned back into the twilight of the house and the sound of fans whispering in every room.

Up to then, my mother had refused to send Premila to school in the British-run establishments of that time, because, she used to say, "you can bury a dog's tail for seven years and it still comes out curly, and you can take a Britisher away from his home for a lifetime, and he still remains insular." The examinations and degrees from entirely Indian schools were not, in those days, considered valid. In my case, the question had never come up, and probably never would have come up if Mother's extraordinary good health had not broken down. For the first time in my life, she was not able to continue the lessons she had been giving us every morning. So our Hindi books were put away, the stories of the Lord Krishna as a little boy were left in midair, and we were sent to the Anglo-Indian school.

That first day at school is still, when I think of it, a remarkable one. At that age, if one's name is changed, one develops a curious form of dual personality. I remember having a certain detached and disbelieving concern in the actions of "Cynthia," but certainly no responsibility. Accordingly, I followed the thin, erect back of the headmistress down the veranda to my classroom feeling, at most, a passing interest in what was going to happen to me in this strange, new atmosphere of School.

The building was Indian in design, with wide verandas opening onto a central courtyard, but Indian verandas are usually whitewashed, with stone floors. These, in the tradition of British schools, were painted dark brown and had matting on the floors. It gave a feeling of extra intensity to the heat.

I suppose there were about a dozen Indian children in the school— which contained perhaps forty children in all—and four of them were in my class. They were all sitting at the back of the room, and I went to join them. I sat next to a small, solemn girl who didn't smile at me. She had long, glossy-black braids and wore a cotton dress, but she still kept on her Indian jewelry—a gold chain around her neck, thin gold bracelets, and tiny ruby studs in her ears. Like most Indian children, she had a rim of black kohl around her eyes. The cotton dress should have looked strange, but all I could think of was that I should ask my mother if I couldn't wear a dress to school, too, instead of my Indian clothes.

I can't remember too much about the proceedings in class that day,   10
except for the beginning. The teacher pointed to me and asked me to stand up. "Now, dear, tell the class your name."

I said nothing.   11

"Come along," she said, frowning slightly. "What's your name,   12
dear?"

"I don't know," I said, finally.   13

The English children in the front of the class—there were about   14
eight or ten of them—giggled and twisted around in their chairs to look at me. I sat down quickly and opened my eyes very wide, hoping in that way to dry them off. The little girl with the braids put out her hand and very lightly touched my arm. She still didn't smile.

Most of that morning I was rather bored. I looked briefly at the chil-   15
dren's drawings pinned to the wall, and then concentrated on a lizard clinging to the ledge of the high, barred window behind the teacher's head. Occasionally it would shoot out its long yellow tongue for a fly, and then it would rest, with its eyes closed and its belly palpitating, as though it were swallowing several times quickly. The lessons were mostly concerned with reading and writing and simple numbers— things that my mother had already taught me—and I paid very little attention. The teacher wrote on the easel blackboard words like "bat" and "cat," which seemed babyish to me; only "apple" was new and incomprehensible.

When it was time for the lunch recess, I followed the girl with braids   16
out onto the veranda. There the children from the other classes were assembled. I saw Premila at once and ran over to her, as she had charge of our lunchbox. The children were all opening packages and sitting down to eat sandwiches. Premila and I were the only ones who had Indian food—thin wheat chapatties, some vegetable curry, and a bottle of buttermilk. Premila thrust half of it into my hand and whispered fiercely that I should go and sit with my class, because that was what the others seemed to be doing.

The enormous black eyes of the little Indian girl from my class   17
looked at my food longingly, so I offered her some. But she only shook her head and plowed her way solemnly through her sand- wiches.

I was very sleepy after lunch, because at home we always took a   18
siesta. It was usually a pleasant time of day, with the bedroom darkened against the harsh afternoon sun, the drifting off into sleep with the

sound of Mother's voice reading a story in one's mind, and, finally, the shrill, fussy voice of the ayah waking one for tea.

At school, we rested for a short time on low, folding cots on the veranda, and then we were expected to play games. During the hot part of the afternoon we played indoors, and after the shadows had begun to lengthen and the slight breeze of the evening had come up we moved outside to the wide courtyard.

I had never really grasped the system of competitive games. At home, whenever we played tag or guessing games, I was always allowed to "win"—"because," Mother used to tell Premila, "she is the youngest, and we have to allow for that." I had often heard her say it, and it seemed quite reasonable to me, but the result was that I had no clear idea of what "winning" meant.

When we played twos-and-threes that afternoon at school, in accordance with my training, I let one of the small English boys catch me, but was naturally rather puzzled when the other children did not return the courtesy. I ran about for what seemed like hours without ever catching anyone, until it was time for school to close. Much later I learned that my attitude was called "not being a good sport," and I stopped allowing myself to be caught, but it was not for years that I really learned the spirit of the thing.

When I saw our car come up to the school gate, I broke away from my classmates and rushed toward it yelling, "Ayah! Ayah!" It seemed like an eternity since I had seen her that morning—a wizened, affectionate figure in her white cotton sari, giving me dozens of urgent and useless instructions on how to be a good girl at school. Premila followed more sedately, and she told me on the way home never to do that again in front of the other children.

When we got home we went straight to Mother's high, white room to have tea with her, and I immediately climbed onto the bed and bounced gently up and down on the springs. Mother asked how we had liked our first day in school. I was so pleased to be home and to have left that peculiar Cynthia behind that I had nothing whatever to say about school, except to ask what "apple" meant. But Premila told Mother about the classes, and added that in her class they had weekly tests to see if they learned their lessons well.

I asked, "What's a test?"

Premila said, "You're too small to have them. You won't have them in your class for donkey's years." She had learned the expression that day and was using it for the first time. We all laughed enormously at her wit. She also told Mother, in an aside, that we should take sandwiches to school the next day. Not, she said, that *she* minded. But they would be simpler for me to handle.

That whole lovely evening I didn't think about school at all. I sprinted barefoot across the lawns with my favorite playmate, the cook's son, to the stream at the end of the garden. We quarreled in our usual way, waded in the tepid water under the lime trees, and waited for the night to bring out the smell of the jasmine. I listened with fascination to his stories of ghosts and demons, until I was too frightened to cross the garden alone in the semidarkness. The ayah found me, shouted at the cook's son, scolded me, hurried me into supper—it was an entirely usual, wonderful evening.

It was a week later, the day of Premila's first test, that our lives changed rather abruptly. I was sitting at the back of my class, in my usual inattentive way, only half listening to the teacher. I had started a rather guarded friendship with the girl with the braids, whose name turned out to be Nalini (Nancy, in school). The three other Indian children were already fast friends. Even at that age it was apparent to all of us that friendship with the English or Anglo-Indian children was out of the question. Occasionally, during the class, my new friend and I would draw pictures and show them to each other secretly.

The door opened sharply and Premila marched in. At first, the teacher smiled at her in a kindly and encouraging way and said, "Now, you're little Cynthia's sister?" 28

Premila didn't even look at her. She stood with her feet planted firmly apart and her shoulders rigid, and addressed herself directly to me. "Get up," she said. "We're going home." 29

I didn't know what had happened, but I was aware that it was a crisis of some sort. I rose obediently and started to walk toward my sister. 30

"Bring your pencils and your notebook," she said. 31

I went back for them, and together we left the room. The teacher started to say something just as Premila closed the door, but we didn't wait to hear what it was. 32

In complete silence we left the school grounds and started to walk home. Then I asked Premila what the matter was. All she would say was "We're going home for good." 33

It was a very tiring walk for a child of five and a half, and I dragged along behind Premila with my pencils growing sticky in my hand. I can still remember looking at the dusty hedges, and the tangles of thorns in the ditches by the side of the road, smelling the faint fragrance from the eucalyptus trees and wondering whether we would ever reach home. Occasionally a horse-drawn tonga passed us, and the women, in their pink or green silks, stared at Premila and me trudging along on the side of the road. A few coolies and a line of women carrying baskets of vegetables on their heads smiled at us. But it was nearing the hottest time of day, and the road was almost deserted. I walked more and more slowly, and shouted to Premila, from time to time, "Wait for me!" with increasing peevishness. She spoke to me only once, and that was to tell me to carry my notebook on my head, because of the sun. 34

When we got to our house the ayah was just taking a tray of lunch into Mother's room. She immediately started a long, worried questioning about what are you children doing back here at this hour of the day. 35

Mother looked very startled and very concerned, and asked Premila what had happened. 36

Premila said, "We had our test today, and she made me and the other Indians sit at the back of the room, with a desk between each one." 37

Mother said, "Why was that, darling?" 38

"She said it was because Indians cheat," Premila added. "So I don't 39 think we should go back to that school."

Mother looked very distant, and was silent a long time. At last she 40 said, "Of course not, darling." She sounded displeased.

We all shared the curry she was having for lunch, and afterward I 41 was sent off to the beautifully familiar bedroom for my siesta. I could hear Mother and Premila talking through the open door.

Mother said, "Do you suppose she understood all that?" 42

Premila said, "I shouldn't think so. She's a baby." 43

Mother said, "Well, I hope it won't bother her." 44

Of course, they were both wrong. I understood it perfectly, and I 45 remember it all very clearly. But I put it happily away, because it had all happened to a girl called Cynthia, and I never was really particularly interested in her.

COMPREHENSION

1. What does the title of this essay mean? State the thesis that emerges from it.

2. Cite five examples the author gives to demonstrate that her attendance at the Anglo-Indian day school was an alien experience for her. How is the author's experience similar to Angelou's in "Graduation"?

3. According to the author's inferences, what was the effect of British rule on Indian society? How does the headmistress embody this impact? Compare and contrast Rau's perception of colonialism and that of Orwell in "Shooting an Elephant."

RHETORIC

1. Define these Indian words, preferably from the contexts in which they are used: *kohl* (paragraph 9); *chapatties* (paragraph 16); *ayah* (paragraph 18); *sari* (paragraph 22); and *tonga* (paragraph 34).

2. Explain the author's use of sensory language in paragraphs 1, 3, 5, 8, 9, 15, 26, and 34.

3. What is the theme of this narrative essay? How does the author state it?

4. Identify the tone and mood of the essay.

5. What is the utility and value of the author's use of dialogue in the essay?

6. How do various causal patterns inform the narrative?

WRITING

1. Although dealing specifically with a colonial situation, the author also illuminates the universal experience of being made to feel different, strange, or alien. Why is this ironic for the author? Why does it remain so vivid in her memory? Do we become more or less conscious of this phenomenon at a later age? Write a narrative essay centering on a time when you were made to feel strange or foreign in an educational situation.

2. Tell of a time when you felt that someone or some group was trying to change your identity or sense of self.

3. Write a comparative essay on this selection and Angelou's "Graduation."

DAVID GELERNTER   David Gelernter is a professor of computer science at Yale University. He is a leading figure in the field of human cognition and a seminal thinker in the field known as *parallel computing*. Gelernter, who was injured by a package sent by the Unabomber in 1993, is the author of *Mirror Worlds* (1991), *The Muse in the Machine* (1994), and *1939: The Lost World of the Fair* (1995). In the following essay, published in *The New Republic* in 1994, Gelernter offers a cogent analysis of the limits of technology in the classroom.

DAVID GELERNTER

Unplugged: The Myth of Computers in the Classroom

Over the last decade an estimated $2 billion has been spent on more than 2 million computers for America's classrooms. That's not surprising. We constantly hear from Washington that the schools are in trouble and that computers are a godsend. Within the education establishment, in poor as well as rich schools, the machines are awaited with nearly religious awe. An inner-city principal bragged to a teacher friend of mine recently that his school "has a computer in every classroom . . . despite being in a bad neighborhood!"

Computers should be in the schools. They have the potential to accomplish great things. With the right software, they could help make science tangible or teach neglected topics like art and music. They could help students form a concrete idea of society by displaying on-screen a version of the city in which they live—a picture that tracks real life moment by moment.

In practice, however, computers make our worst educational nightmares come true. While we bemoan the decline of literacy, computers discount words in favor of pictures and pictures in favor of video. While we fret about the decreasing cogency of public debate, computers dismiss linear argument and promote fast, shallow romps across the information landscape. While we worry about basic skills, we allow into the classroom software that will do a student's arithmetic or correct his spelling.

Take multimedia. The idea of multimedia is to combine text, sound and pictures in a single package that you browse on screen. You don't just *read* Shakespeare; you watch actors performing, listen to songs, view Elizabethan buildings. What's wrong with that? By offering children candy-coated books, multimedia is guaranteed to sour them on unsweetened reading. It makes the printed page look even more boring than it used to look. Sure, books will be available in the classroom, too—but they'll have all the appeal of a dusty piano to a teen who has a Walkman handy.

So what if the little nippers don't read? If they're watching Olivier 5 instead, what do they lose? The text, the written word along with all of its attendant pleasures. Besides, a book is more portable than a computer, has a higher-resolution display, can be written on and dog-eared and is comparatively dirt cheap.

Hypermedia, multimedia's comrade in the struggle for a brave new 6 classroom, is just as troubling. It's a way of presenting documents on screen without imposing a linear start-to-finish order. Disembodied paragraphs are linked by theme; after reading one about the First World War, for example, you might be able to choose another about the technology of battleships, or the life of Woodrow Wilson, or hemlines in the '20s. This is another cute idea that is good in minor ways and terrible in major ones. Teaching children to understand the orderly unfolding of a plot or a logical argument is a crucial part of education. Authors don't merely agglomerate paragraphs; they work hard to make the narrative read a certain way, prove a particular point. To turn a book or a document into hypertext is to invite readers to ignore exactly what counts—the story.

The real problem, again, is the accentuation of already bad habits. 7 Dynamiting documents into disjointed paragraphs is one more expression of the sorry fact that sustained argument is not our style. If you're a newspaper or magazine editor and your readership is dwindling, what's the solution? Shorter pieces. If you're a politician and you want to get elected, what do you need? Tasty sound bites. Logical presentation be damned.

Another software species, "allow me" programs, is not much better. 8 These programs correct spelling and, by applying canned grammatical and stylistic rules, fix prose. In terms of promoting basic skills, though, they have all the virtues of a pocket calculator.

In Kentucky, as *The Wall Street Journal* recently reported, students 9 in grades K-3 are mixed together regardless of age in a relaxed environment. It works great, the *Journal* says. Yes, scores on computation tests have dropped 10 percent at one school, but not to worry: "Drilling addition and subtraction in an age of calculators is a waste of time," the principal reassures us. Meanwhile, a Japanese educator informs University of Wisconsin mathematician Richard Akey that in his country, "calculators are not used in elementary or junior high school because the primary emphasis is on helping students develop their mental abilities." No wonder Japanese kids blow the pants off American kids in math. Do we really think "drilling addition and subtraction in an age of calculators is a waste of time"? If we do, then "drilling reading in an age of multimedia is a waste of time" can't be far behind.

Prose-correcting programs are also a little ghoulish, like asking a computer for tips on improving your personality. On the other hand, I ran this article through a spell-checker, so how can I ban the use of such programs in schools? Because to misspell is human; to have no idea of correct spelling is to be semiliterate.

There's no denying that computers have the potential to perform 11 inspiring feats in the classroom. If we are ever to see that potential realized, however, we ought to agree on three conditions. First, there should be a completely new crop of children's software. Most of today's offerings show no imagination. There are hundreds of similar reading and geography and arithmetic programs, but almost nothing on electricity or physics or architecture. Also, they abuse the technical capacities of new media to glitz up old forms instead of creating new ones. Why not build a time-travel program that gives kids a feel for how history is structured by zooming you backward? A spectrum program that lets users twirl a frequency knob to see what happens?

Second, computers should be used only during recess or relaxation 12 periods. Treat them as fillips, not as surrogate teachers. When I was in school in the '60s, we all loved educational films. When we saw a movie in class, everybody won: teachers didn't have to teach, and pupils didn't have to learn. I suspect that classroom computers are popular today for the same reasons.

Most important, educators should learn what parents and most 13 teachers already know: you cannot teach a child anything unless you look him in the face. We should not forget what computers are. Like books—better in some ways, worse in others—they are devices that help children mobilize their own resources and learn for themselves. The computer's potential to do good is modestly greater than a book's in some areas. Its potential to do harm is vastly greater, across the board.

COMPREHENSION

1. State the author's main thesis in one sentence.
2. In the final paragraph, Gelernter defines what he believes to be the most important shortcoming of the computer as a teaching tool. Explain the reason why this weakness is so significant.
3. In your own words, explain the author's dislike of hypermedia as a pedagogic tool (as expressed in paragraph 6) and why the orderly arrangement of paragraphs in a book is superior to this newer technological capability.

RHETORIC

1. The introductory paragraph goes from a general fact to a specific quotation. What is the effect of this method of paragraph patterning?

2. Much of the author's argument hinges on showing preference for the form of one medium over another. Explain terms such as "linear argument" (paragraph 3), "agglomerate paragraphs," (paragraph 6), and "'allow me' programs" (paragraph 8).

3. The essay has a three-part structure, each section divided by space. How would you characterize the purpose of each section? How does the author use transitions to move from one section to the next?

4. The author states that the overuse of computers in the classroom can hinder the development of clear thinking and reasoned argument. How clearly written is *his* essay? How reasoned is his argument? Base your answer by reviewing whether each sentence seems to flow logically from the next and how each paragraph seems to move reasonably to the next.

5. The author uses devices such as metaphors, similes, and other rhetorical modes of speech. Explain the effectiveness of terms such as "have all the appeal of a dusty piano to a teen who has a Walkman handy" (paragraph 4), "dynamiting documents" (paragraph 7), and "software species" (paragraph 8). Locate other unconventional descriptions.

6. Who is the intended audience for this essay? Educators, parents, students, politicians? What evidence can you show to back up your view?

7. What rhetorical device is the author using in his title? What is the implicit meaning of the title?

WRITING

1. Select one of the teaching capabilities of modern computers—multimedia, hypertext, or spell- and grammar-check programs. Argue *for* the benefits of one of these features.

2. Visit the writing or reading computer lab in your school. As an objective observer, study the interaction of student and computer. Write a descriptive essay focusing on the demeanor and behavior of the student and the atmosphere of the classroom. If you wish, compare it to a traditional classroom.

3. Copy a paragraph from the essay, and enter it into a word-processing program that has a grammar-check function. Record any comments that the program makes in response to its evaluation of the writing. Does the computer's responses to the sentence structure make sense?

ANNA QUINDLEN   Anna Quindlen (b. 1953), a journalist and editor, began her writing career as a reporter for the *New York Post* and later moved on to *The New York Times,* where she was a syndicated columnist. A graduate of Barnard College, Quindlen has written a number of books, including *Living out Loud* (1986) and *Object Lessons* (1991). Quindlen received the Pulitzer Prize for Commentary in 1992. In this essay, she focuses on the problem of teenage pregnancy and suggests children be given more than textbook information to help them cope with their sexuality.

ANNA QUINDLEN

Sex Ed

Several years ago I spent the day at a family planning clinic in one ₁ of New York City's poorest neighborhoods. I sat around a Formica table with a half-dozen sixteen-year-old girls and listened with some amazement as they showed off their knowledge of human sexuality.

They knew how long sperm lived inside the body, how many ₂ women out of a hundred using a diaphragm were statistically likely to get pregnant and the medical term for the mouth of the cervix. One girl pointed out all the parts of the female reproductive system on a placard; another recited the stages of the ovulation cycle from day one to twenty-eight. There was just one problem with this performance: although the results of their laboratory tests would not be available for fifteen more minutes, every last one of them was pregnant.

I always think of that day when someone suggests that sex education ₃ at school is a big part of the answer to the problem of teenage pregnancy. I happen to be a proponent of such programs; I think human sexuality is a subject for dispassionate study, like civics and ethics and dozens of other topics that have a moral component. I'd like my sons to know as much as possible about how someone gets pregnant, how pregnancy can be avoided, and what it means when avoidance techniques have failed.

I remember adolescence about as vividly as I remember anything, ₄ however, and I am not in the least convinced that that information alone will significantly alter the rate of teenage pregnancy. It seemed to me that day in the clinic, and on days I spent at schools and on street corners, that teenage pregnancy has a lot more to do with what it means to be a teenager than with how someone gets pregnant. When I was in high school, at the tail end of the sixties, there was a straightforward line on sex among my friends. Boys could have it; girls couldn't. A girl who was not a virgin pretended she was. A girl who was sleeping with her boyfriend, no matter how long-playing the relationship, pretended she was not.

It is the nature of adolescence that there is no past and no future, only ₅ the present, burning as fierce, bright, and merciless as a bare light bulb. Girls had sex with boys because nothing seemed to matter except right now, not pregnancy, not parental disapprobation, nothing but those minutes, this dance, that face, those words. Most of them knew that pregnancy could result, but they assured themselves that they would be the lucky ones who would not get caught. Naturally, some of them were wrong, and in my experience they did one of three things: they went to Puerto Rico for a mysterious weekend trip; visited an aunt in some faraway state for three months and came back with empty eyes and a vague reputation, or got married, quickly, in Empire-waist dresses.

What seems to have changed most since then is that there is little   6
philosophical counterpoint, hypocritical or not, to the raging hormones
of adolescence, and that so many of the once-hidden pregnancies are
hidden no more.

Not long after the day at the family planning clinic, I went to a pub-   7
lic high school in the suburbs. In the girl's room was this graffito: Jen-
nifer Is a Virgin. I asked the kids about it and they said it was shorthand
for geek, nerd, weirdo, somebody who was so incredibly out of it that
they were in high school and still hadn't had sex. If you were a virgin,
they told me, you just lied about it so that no one would think you were
that immature. The girls in the family planning clinic told me much the
same thing—that everyone did it, that the boys wanted it, that not
doing it made them seem out of it. The only difference, really, was that
the girls in the clinic were poor and would have their babies, and the
girls in the high school were well-to-do and would have abortions. Pleasure didn't seem to have very much to do with sex for either group.
After she learned she was pregnant, one of the girls at the clinic said,
without a trace of irony, that she hoped childbirth didn't hurt as much
as sex had. Birth control was easily disposed of in both cases. The pill,
the youngsters said, could give you a stroke; the IUD could make you
sterile. A diaphragm was disgusting.

One girl told me the funniest thing her boyfriend—a real original   8
thinker—had told her: they couldn't use condoms because it was like
taking a shower with a raincoat on. She was a smart girl, and pretty,
and I wanted to tell her that it sounded as if she was sleeping with a jerk
who didn't deserve her. But that is the kind of basic fact of life that
must be taught not in the classroom, not by a stranger, but at home by
the family. It is this that, finally, I will try to teach my sons about sex,
after I've explained fertile periods and birth control and all the other
mechanics that are important to understand but never really go to the
heart of the matter: I believe I will say that when you sleep with someone you take off a lot more than your clothes.

COMPREHENSION

1. Does Quindlen approve of sex education? Explain.
2. How does the writer characterize the attitude of adolescents regarding sex
   and pregnancy?
3. What advice or information about sex will the writer give her sons? Why?

RHETORIC

1. Why did Quindlen choose "Sex Ed" as a title? What is its significance in
   relation to the thesis?
2. What is Quindlen's thesis? Where is it contained in the essay? Is it directly
   stated or implied?
3. Is Quindlen's writing an argumentative essay? Support your position with
   citations from the text.

4. What point is the writer making through use of accumulated details in paragraph 2?
5. What does Quindlen mean by the term "moral component" in paragraph 3? Where else in the essay does she allude to it? How does the author employ definition in this essay?
6. What does Quindlen mean by her final statement that "when you sleep with someone you take off a lot more than your clothes"? How does this ending serve to underscore the thesis of the essay?

WRITING

1. Write a letter to a teenage son or daughter in which you discuss sexuality and pregnancy.
2. Write a research paper describing the most common forms of birth control available and listing the advantages and disadvantages of each.
3. In an essay, consider possible solutions to the problem of teenage pregnancy. What role do you think sex education has in ameliorating the problem? Use support from the Quindlen essay if applicable.

ANDREW ROONEY   Andrew Rooney was born in Albany, New York, in 1919 and attended the Albany Academy and Colgate University. Rooney is perhaps the most recognized writer in America, being seen by 40 million viewers each week on one of television's top-rated shows, *60 Minutes.* Rooney began his writing career during World War II as a reporter for the *Stars and Stripes.* Since then, he has worked primarily in television, beginning in the 1940s and continuing to the present. Besides his work on *60 Minutes,* Rooney has written many documentaries and specials for television. His syndicated columns run in over 250 newspapers, and his television essays and newspaper columns have been collected in seven books. His work for television has garnered four Emmy awards. Always the humorist, when Rooney was asked what he would most like to do that he has not yet done, he replied, "live to be a hundred." Nonetheless, Rooney does tackle important issues in his television essays and writings. The following is an example of his serious concerns for American society. It is taken from a collection of essays entitled *Sweet and Sour* (1992).

ANDREW ROONEY

The Need for National Testing

Never has the nation been safer from foreign menaces, and never   ₁ before has the nation been graduating students less well educated than those of the immediately preceding generation. These facts warrant this conclusion: Today the principal threat to America is America's public-education establishment.

It tenaciously opposes national testing of primary and secondary school students. As Chester Finn of Vanderbilt says in his indispensable new book, *We Must Take Charge,* the education establishment knows that testing would shatter the public's complacency and bring demands for accountability.

Sixty-three percent of those ages 18 to 24 cannot find France on an unlabeled map (fewer than half find New York); 60 percent of 11th-graders do not know why *The Federalist* papers were written; 94 percent of 11th-graders cannot compute simple interest; in tests comparing their math and science skills with those of five foreign countries and four Canadian provinces, American 13-year-olds finish last; New York Telephone finds that 115,000 of 117,000 applicants flunk its employment exam; 80 percent of applicants flunk Motorola's exam seeking levels of seventh-grade English and fifth-grade math. Every American employer knows it is possible—indeed, common—for high school graduates to be functionally illiterate.

National testing would be a lever for moving the entire world of education. Measurable standards for cognitive learning would shape curricula and teacher education, and would provide criteria for pay differentials among teachers, and for declaring the educational bankruptcy of some schools.

Some conservatives are afraid national tests would further institutionalize the political ideology of the education establishment. Testing might be an occasion for indoctrination through politicized questioning. Furthermore, say conservatives, any movement toward a more national curriculum would make possible continent-wide mistakes.

Momentum toward national testing, and all that it entails, was imparted by the 1989 "education summit" with the president and all 50 governors at the University of Virginia—Mr. Jefferson's university. Any permeation of education by national standards does involve another departure from Jeffersonian impulses, toward those of his rival, Hamilton, that apostle of centralization and national, rather than local, consciousness.

However, many conservatives, like most Americans, are alarmed enough to put aside their traditional preference for educational localism. National testing is necessary for acquiring information about educational results that can galvanize and guide reform. Anyway, localism makes less and less sense in a nation of increasing mobility among regions, a nation flunking—as a nation—the international test of competitiveness.

The parlous condition of public education was the foremost domestic concern voiced by voters in 1990 Election Day exit polls. More than 70 percent of Americans (the figure is higher among parents) support standardized national testing, including a national high school graduation exam, keyed to a national curriculum.

Conservatives' qualms about national tests should be assuaged by the ferocity of the education establishment's opposition to such tests.

That establishment wants to preserve America's unwarranted sense of well-being that is based on lax or tendentious assessments of cognitive learning. Most Americans like the illusion of living in Lake Wobegon, where "all the children are above average."

It is no coincidence that the philosophy and interests of the education establishment coincide exactly. Testing is "judgmental" and hence jars the educators' warm, "caring," empathetic, "child-centered" therapeutic ethic that nurtures "self-esteem." This produces today's toxic mixture of low expectations and grade inflation.

Testing would make possible a result-oriented assessment of educa- 11 tion, would end today's practice of gauging the quality of education by the amount of money spent on it. Testing is necessary for a system of accountability—clearly stated goals, accurate information about progress toward them and positive and negative consequences of the information. Thus, Finn says, national testing is a first step toward transforming America from a culture of lassitude back into a culture of achievement:

> When it comes to consumer information about outcomes, the Ameri- 12
> can education system has been engaged in a massive cover-up. If the
> Securities and Exchange Commission allowed publicly traded corpora-
> tions to conceal this much data about their profits and losses, we'd have
> a crisis of investor confidence—and a lot of ruinous investments.

Finn notes that few people think doctors should autonomously set 13 health policy. Everyone knows war is too important to be left to soldiers. It is time for "civilian" control of education, the largest item in every state's budget—a $230 million enterprise at the primary and secondary levels.

Education is second only, and not by much, to defense as the 14 nation's most expensive common provision. National testing is a step toward facing this fact: The safer the world becomes militarily, the less prepared America is to prosper in it, because knowledge matters more as military prowess matters less.

COMPREHENSION

1. What is the significance of calling the University of Virginia "Mr. Jefferson's university"?
2. Rooney claims that both conservatives and the "education establishment" have something to lose by introducing national testing. What is each group afraid of?
3. Without outside assistance, perform the three cognitive tasks Rooney specifically refers to in paragraph 3.

RHETORIC

1. The author cites the same authority at the beginning and toward the end of his essay. Does this method bolster his argument? Why, or why not?

2. In paragraph 10, Rooney uses five consecutive adjectives to describe the education ethic. What function does this rhetorical device serve in shading the tone of his argument?

3. Rooney refers to the education establishment several times without actually naming any organization or department. What effect does this use of unspecified generalization in describing a group have on the author's argument? Explain your view.

4. As a college student, your school assumes that you have a certain level of reading competency. Without the aid of a dictionary, test your own vocabulary by defining words such as *tenaciously, galvanize, ideology, apostle, qualms,* and *parlous.* How many of these were you able to identify? How does the use of these words contribute to the authority of the writer?

5. Rooney has gained fame as a humorist on national television. Is the tone of this essay humorous? Explain your view.

6. In paragraph 1, Rooney uses the phrase "been graduating students." What is the difference in connotation between a school graduating students and students graduating from a school? How does this reflect upon the attitude of the author toward the relationship between schools and students?

7. Rate this essay as though it were an argumentative essay submitted to an English professor. What alphabetic grade would you give it in the areas of structure, coherence, vocabulary, and punctuation? Explain your evaluation.

WRITING

1. Argue for or against the proposition that it is social forces outside the school that have lowered educational standards, not the schools themselves.

2. Argue for or against the proposition that one cannot compare one generation of students to another because technology changes what should or should not be taught in school.

3. Write a process analysis essay wherein you offer a "recipe" on how to improve your school. You may include teacher and student preparation, class size, testing requirements, physical environment, policies, or anything else you feel is appropriate.

DINESH D'SOUZA   Dinesh D'Souza was born in Bombay, India, in 1961. He graduated from Dartmouth College in 1983 and rapidly established himself as a neoconservative spokesperson on education and other public policy issues. He has written a biography of the television evangelist Jerry Falwell (1985) and the controversial *Illiberal Education* (1991), in which he charges that liberals control the nation's universities. In this essay, D'Souza takes issue with the multicultural curriculum.

DINESH D'SOUZA

"Bogus" Multiculturalism

At Stanford University a couple of years ago, Jesse Jackson led ₁
protesting students who chanted, "Hey, hey, ho, ho, Western culture has
got to go." Ultimately, the university administration acquiesced to the
call for the abolition of Stanford's so-called "Great Books" course,
which had focused on the classics of Western civilization, and installed
a new requirement called "Cultures, Ideas, and Values," which emphasized non-Western and minority cultures. Stanford's example has been
inspirational and has been emulated by many other schools and colleges across the country as well.

I have spent some time over the last couple of years auditing Stan- ₂
ford's new non-Western curriculum to see what it was that Stanford
professors were teaching about the Third World, which is my place of
origin and of birth. I realized that Stanford professors were presenting
a picture of the Third World that bore no resemblance to what I, as a
native of the Third World, knew. Something very funny seemed to be
going on. What could this be? What was the shape that multicultural
education was taking in practice?

I would like to illustrate this problem briefly by talking about one ₃
book that I see as a kind of emblem for the new multicultural curriculum at Stanford. The book is called *I, Rigoberta Menchu,* and is
subtitled "The Story of a Young Woman in Guatemala." In the introduction, Rigoberta, who is a young woman, says, "I am speaking not
for myself, I am speaking for the people, the oppressed people of
Latin America."

Rigoberta does not claim any individual distinction, but she is ₄
speaking on behalf of minority oppression. This is the significance of
her book. One might expect that it is a valuable perspective.

Rigoberta further says that because she is "in the oral tradition," she ₅
has narrated this book to a French feminist writer, Elisabeth Burgos
Debray.

One interesting question that occurred to me at the outset was ₆
where did young Rigoberta meet Elisabeth Burgos Debray, the
French feminist writer? In reading the book's acknowledgments, you
realize that they met in Paris, where Rigoberta was apparently
attending a socialist conference. Paris, I need not remind you, is not
a venue to which many of the Third World's poor routinely travel.
Therefore, one might suspect that Rigoberta is not typical of the
Latin American or Third World peasantry. As you read the book, this
impression is reinforced. You run across a chapter, for example, that
is titled "Rigoberta Renounces Marriage and Motherhood." The

book describes in some detail Rigoberta's sequential embrace of socialism, of Marxism, of feminism, of gay rights, and so on. This is her story. It dawns on the critical reader that Rigoberta does not, by any stretch of the imagination, represent the poor people or the peasants of Guatemala or of the Third World. This raises the interesting question: Why read this book? Whom does Rigoberta represent? Whom does she speak for?

Perhaps she speaks for the political prejudices of some Stanford professors and Stanford students, who are very interested in her embrace of Marxism, of socialism, of feminism, and so on. The Third World is not like that, but that is the way that some people at Stanford would like to see it. Rigoberta represents, in short, a projection of Western ideological predilections and prejudices onto the Third World.

Multicultural education, in general, is inspired by political activists who are alienated from what they see to be the racism, the sexism, and homophobia of the West. They would like to find in other cultures a better alternative to this terrible Western way of life. But, anybody who looks carefully and critically at non-Western cultures, at Third World cultures, realizes that the Third World cultures are generally quite inhospitable to the basic passions of these multicultural activists. There is not a strong tradition of racial equality in many parts of the Third World. In India, for example, there is the terrible legacy of the caste system. Women are treated very badly in many non-Western cultures. Homosexuality is often a crime, if not a medical ailment, in many Third World countries.

The classics of non-Western cultures have produced important works. But, for example, the *Koran* evinces a notion of male superiority. The great Japanese classic *The Tale of Genji* is a celebration of courtship and of hierarchy. The Indian classics, the *Bhagavad-Gita* and so on, are a rejection of Western materialism and atheism.

The multicultural activists, when they look abroad, don't like what they see and so they engage very routinely in what one may call the *Rigoberta* model: They put aside the reality and great works of non-Western cultures; then they ransack these cultures to find utterly non-representative figures like Rigoberta, figures who reflect not the temper or the accomplishment of their own cultures, but who reflect the political prejudices of Western culture. This is what I call a bogus multiculturalism.

There is no reason that we can't have a curriculum that emphasizes what Matthew Arnold once called "the best that has been thought and said." Arnold had in mind Western culture, but there is no reason we can't apply his criterion to non-Western cultures, as well. If we take a critical and honest look at both Western and non-Western cultures, we can then arrive at a sensible basis for the norms according to which we would like to live our lives and shape this multiracial society. Multicultural education is too important, in short, to leave to multicultural ideologues and activists.

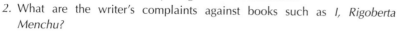

COMPREHENSION

1. What does D'Souza mean by "bogus" multiculturalism?
2. What are the writer's complaints against books such as *I, Rigoberta Menchu?*
3. What changes would D'Souza like to see at Stanford?

RHETORIC

1. State the thesis of the essay in your own words.
2. What is D'Souza's tone? Cite specific evidence in the essay.
3. Does D'Souza's major example strongly support his thesis? Explain.
4. How does the author structure his argument? Can you find examples of logical fallacies? Explain.
5. Where does D'Souza employ definition in this essay? What is his purpose in using this strategy?
6. What is the purpose of paragraph 9? How does it serve to support the writer's point?

WRITING

1. Write an essay agreeing or disagreeing with D'Souza's statement that multiculturalism "is inspired by political activists who are alienated from what they see to be the racism, the sexism, and homophobia of the West."
2. Pretend you are a college professor teaching an "introduction to civilization" class or any liberal arts course of your choice. What five books would you use in your class, and why? Discuss your choices in the context of a multicultural curriculum.
3. Write a personal essay in which you describe the reading material used in your elementary or high school years. What was the first book in which a different culture was depicted? How was this culture portrayed, and what impressions did you form of it?

SHELBY STEELE   Shelby Steele was born in Chicago, Illinois, in 1946 and raised, along with his twin brother, the psychologist Claude Steele, in an interracial family. He graduated from Coe College in 1968 and received a Ph.D. in English from the University of Utah in 1974. Now a professor of English at San Jose State University, Steele won the National Magazine Award in 1989 for his essays on race. His work has appeared in *Harper's, The American Scholar, The New Republic,* and elsewhere. A leading intellectual, who is uncomfortable with the labels "conservative" and "liberal," Steele, in the following chapter from *The Content of Our Character* (1990), offers a revisionist look at one of America's enduring social dilemmas.

SHELBY STEELE

Affirmative Action:
The Price of Preference

In a few short years, when my two children will be applying to col- 1
lege, the affirmative action policies by which most universities offer
black students some form of preferential treatment will present me with
a dilemma. I am a middle-class black, a college professor, far from
wealthy, but also well-removed from the kind of deprivation that would
qualify my children for the label "disadvantaged." Both of them have
endured racial insensitivity from whites. They have been called names,
have suffered slights, and have experienced firsthand the peculiar
malevolence that racism brings out in people. Yet, they have never experienced racial discrimination, have never been stopped by their race on
any path they have chosen to follow. Still, their society now tells them
that if they will only designate themselves as black on their college
applications, they will likely do better in the college lottery than if they
conceal this fact. I think there is something of a Faustian bargain in
this.

Of course, many blacks and a considerable number of whites would 2
say that I was sanctimoniously making affirmative action into a test of
character. They would say that this small preference is the meagerest
recompense for centuries of unrelieved oppression. And to these arguments other very obvious facts must be added. In America, many mar-
ginally competent or flatly incompetent whites are hired everyday—
some because their white skin suits the conscious or unconscious racial
preference of their employer. The white children of alumni are often
grandfathered into elite universities in what can only be seen as a resid-
ual benefit of historic white privilege. Worse, white incompetence is
always an individual matter, while for blacks it is often confirmation of
ugly stereotypes. The Peter Principle was not conceived with only
blacks in mind. Given that unfairness cuts both ways, doesn't it only
balance the scales of history that my children now receive a slight preference over whites? Doesn't this repay, in a small way, the systematic
denial under which their grandfather lived out his days?

So, in theory, affirmative action certainly has all the moral symme- 3
try that fairness requires—the injustice of historical and even contemporary white advantage is offset with black advantage; preference
replaces prejudice, inclusion answers exclusion. It is reformist and corrective, even repentent and redemptive. And I would never sneer at
these good intentions. Born in the late forties in Chicago, I started my
education (a charitable term in this case) in a segregated school and

suffered all the indignities that come to blacks in a segregated society. My father, born in the South, only made it to the third grade before the white man's fields took permanent priority over his formal education. And though he educated himself into an advanced reader with an almost professorial authority, he could only drive a truck for a living and never earned more than ninety dollars a week in his entire life. So yes, it is crucial to my sense of citizenship, to my ability to identify with the spirit and the interests of America, to know that this country, however imperfectly, recognizes its past sins and wishes to correct them.

Yet good intentions, because of the opportunity for innocence they offer us, are very seductive and can blind us to the effects they generate when implemented. In our society, affirmative action is, among other things, a testament to white goodwill and to black power, and in the midst of these heavy investments, its effects can be hard to see. But after twenty years of implementation, I think affirmative action has shown itself to be more bad than good and that blacks—whom I will focus on in this essay—now stand to lose more from it than they gain.

In talking with affirmative action administrators and with blacks and whites in general, it is clear that supporters of affirmative action focus on its good intentions while detractors emphasize its negative effects. Proponents talk about "diversity" and "pluralism"; opponents speak of "reverse discrimination," the unfairness of quotas and set-asides. It was virtually impossible to find people outside either camp. The closest I came was a white male manager at a large computer company who said, "I think it amounts to reverse discrimination, but I'll put up with a little of that for a little more diversity." I'll live with a little of the effect to gain a little of the intention, he seemed to be saying. But this only makes him a halfhearted supporter of affirmative action. I think many people who don't really like affirmative action support it to one degree or another anyway.

I believe they do this because of what happened to white and black Americans in the crucible of the sixties when whites were confronted with their racial guilt and blacks tasted their first real power. In this stormy time white absolution and black power coalesced into virtual mandates for society. Affirmative action became a meeting ground for these mandates in the law, and in the late sixties and early seventies it underwent a remarkable escalation of its mission from simple anti-discrimination enforcement to social engineering by means of quotas, goals, timetables, set-asides and other forms of preferential treatment.

Legally, this was achieved through a series of executive orders and EEOC guidelines that allowed racial imbalances in the workplace to stand as proof of racial discrimination. Once it could be assumed that discrimination explained racial imbalances, it became easy to justify group remedies to presumed discrimination, rather than the normal case-by-case redress for proven discrimination. Preferential treatment through quotas, goals, and so on is designed to correct imbalances based on the assumption that they always indicate discrimination. This expansion of what constitutes discrimination allowed affirmative action

209

to escalate into the business of social engineering in the name of anti-discrimination, to push society toward statistically proportionate racial representation, without any obligation of proving actual discrimination.

What accounted for this shift, I believe, was the white mandate to achieve a new racial innocence and the black mandate to gain power. Even though blacks had made great advances during the sixties without quotas, these mandates, which came to a head in the very late sixties, could no longer be satisfied by anything less than racial preferences. I don't think these mandates in themselves were wrong, since whites clearly needed to do better by blacks and blacks needed more real power in society. But, as they came together in affirmative action, their effect was to distort our understanding of racial discrimination in a way that allowed us to offer the remediation of preference on the basis of mere color rather than actual injury. By making black the color of preference, these mandates have reburdened society with the very marriage of color and preference (in reverse) that we set out to eradicate. The old sin is reaffirmed in a new guise.

But the essential problem with this form of affirmative action is the way it leaps over the hard business of developing a formerly oppressed people to the point where they can achieve proportionate representation on their own (given equal opportunity) and goes straight for the proportionate representation. This may satisfy some whites of their innocence and some blacks of their power, but it does very little to truly uplift blacks.

A white female affirmative action officer at an Ivy League university told me what many supporters of affirmative action now say: "We're after diversity. We ideally want a student body where racial and ethnic groups are represented according to their proportion in society." When affirmative action escalated into social engineering, diversity became a golden word. It grants whites an egalitarian fairness (innocence) and blacks an entitlement to proportionate representation (power). *Diversity* is a term that applies democratic principles to races and cultures rather than to citizens, despite the fact that there is nothing to indicate that real diversity is the same thing as proportionate representation. Too often the result of this on campuses (for example) has been a democracy of colors rather than of people, an artificial diversity that gives the appearance of an educational parity between black and white students that has not yet been achieved in reality. Here again, racial preferences allow society to leapfrog over the difficult problem of developing blacks to parity with whites and into a cosmetic diversity that covers the blemish of disparity—a full six years after admission, only about 26 percent of black students graduate from college.

Racial representation is not the same thing as racial development, yet affirmative action fosters a confusion of these very different needs. Representation can be manufactured; development is always hard-earned. However, it is the music of innocence and power that we hear in affirmative action that causes us to cling to it and to its distracting emphasis on representation. The fact is that after twenty years of racial

8

9

10

11

preferences, the gap between white and black median income is greater than it was in the seventies. None of this is to say that blacks don't need policies that ensure our right to equal opportunity, but what we need more is the development that will let us take advantage of society's efforts to include us.

I think that one of the most troubling effects of racial preferences for blacks is a kind of demoralization, or put another way, an enlargement of self-doubt. Under affirmative action the quality that earns us preferential treatment is an implied inferiority. However this inferiority is explained—and it is easily enough explained by the myriad deprivations that grew out of our oppression—it is still inferiority. There are explanations, and then there is the fact. And the fact must be borne by the individual as a condition apart from the explanation, apart even from the fact that others like himself also bear this condition. In integrated situations where blacks must compete with whites who may be better prepared, these explanations may quickly wear thin and expose the individual to racial as well as personal self-doubt.

All of this is compounded by the cultural myth of black inferiority that blacks have always lived with. What this means in practical terms is that when blacks deliver themselves into integrated situations, they encounter a nasty little reflex in whites, a mindless, atavistic reflex that responds to the color black with alarm. Attributions may follow this alarm if the white cares to indulge them, and if they do, they will most likely be negative—one such attribution is intellectual ineptness. I think this reflex and the attributions that may follow it embarrass most whites today, therefore, it is usually quickly repressed. Nevertheless, on an equally atavistic level, the black will be aware of the reflex his color triggers and will feel a stab of horror at seeing himself reflected in this way. He, too, will do a quick repression, but a lifetime of such stabbings is what constitutes his inner realm of racial doubt.

The effects of this may be a subject for another essay. The point here is that the implication of inferiority that racial preferences engender in both the white and black mind expands rather than contracts this doubt. Even when the black sees no implication of inferiority in racial preferences, he knows that whites do, so that—consciously or unconsciously—the result is virtually the same. The effect of preferential treatment—the lowering of normal standards to increase black representation—puts blacks at war with an expanded realm of debilitating doubt, so that the doubt itself becomes an unrecognized preoccupation that undermines their ability to perform, especially in integrated situations. On largely white campuses, blacks are five times more likely to drop out than whites. Preferential treatment, no matter how it is justified in the light of day, subjects blacks to a midnight of self-doubt, and so often transforms their advantage into a revolving door.

Another liability of affirmative action comes from the fact that it indirectly encourages blacks to exploit their own past victimization as a source of power and privilege. Victimization, like implied inferiority, is what justifies preference, so that to receive the benefits of preferential treatment one must, to some extent, become invested in the view of one's self as a victim. In this way, affirmative action nurtures a victim-focused identity in blacks. The obvious irony here is that we become inadvertently invested in the very condition we are trying to overcome. Racial preferences send us the message that there is more power in our past suffering than our present achievements—none of which could bring us a *preference* over others.

When power itself grows out of suffering, then blacks are encouraged to expand the boundaries of what qualifies as racial oppression, a situation that can lead us to paint our victimization in vivid colors, even as we receive the benefits of preference. The same corporations and institutions that give us preference are also seen as our oppressors. At Stanford University minority students—some of whom enjoy as much as $15,000 a year in financial aid—recently took over the president's office demanding, among other things, more financial aid. The power to be found in victimization, like any power, is intoxicating and can lend itself to the creation of a new class of super-victims who can feel the pea of victimization under twenty mattresses. Preferential treatment rewards us for being underdogs rather than for moving beyond that status—a misplacement of incentives that, along with its deepening of our doubt, is more a yoke than a spur. 16

But, I think, one of the worst prices that blacks pay for preference has to do with an illusion. I saw this illusion at work recently in the mother of a middle-class black student who was going off to his first semester of college. "They owe us this, so don't think for a minute that you don't belong there." This is the logic by which many blacks, and some whites, justify affirmative action—it is something "owed," a form of reparation. But this logic overlooks a much harder and less digestible reality, that it is impossible to repay blacks living today for the historic suffering of the race. If all blacks were given a million dollars tomorrow morning it would not amount to a dime on the dollar of three centuries of oppression, nor would it obviate the residues of that oppression that we still carry today. The concept of historic reparation grows out of man's need to impose a degree of justice on the world that simply does not exist. Suffering can be endured and overcome, it cannot be repaid. Blacks cannot be repaid for the injustice done to the race, but we can be corrupted by society's guilty gestures of repayment. 17

Affirmative action is such a gesture. It tells us that racial preferences can do for us what we cannot do for ourselves. The corruption here is in the hidden incentive *not* to do what we believe preferences will do. This is an incentive to be reliant on others just as we are struggling for self-reliance. And it keeps alive the illusion that we can find some deliverance in repayment. The hardest thing for any sufferer to accept is that his suffering excuses him from very little and never has enough currency to restore him. To think otherwise is to prolong the suffering. 18

Several blacks I spoke with said they were still in favor of affirmative action because of the "subtle" discrimination blacks were subject to 19 once on the job. One photojournalist said, "They have ways of ignoring you." A black female television producer said, "You can't file a lawsuit when your boss doesn't invite you to the insider meetings without ruining your career. So we still need affirmative action." Others mentioned the infamous "glass ceiling" through which blacks can see the top positions of authority but never reach them. But I don't think racial preferences are a protection against this subtle discrimination; I think they contribute to it.

In any workplace, racial preferences will always create two-tiered [20] populations composed of preferreds and unpreferreds. This division makes automatic a perception of enhanced competence for the unpreferreds and of questionable competence for the preferreds—the former earned his way, even though others were given preference, while the latter made it by color as much as by competence. Racial preferences implicitly mark whites with an exaggerated superiority just as they mark blacks with an exaggerated inferiority. They not only reinforce America's oldest racial myth but, for blacks, they have the effect of stigmatizing the already stigmatized.

I think that much of the "subtle" discrimination that blacks talk [21] about is often (not always) discrimination against the stigma of questionable competence that affirmative action delivers to blacks. In this sense, preferences scapegoat the very people they seek to help. And it may be that at a certain level employers impose a glass ceiling, but this may not be against the race so much as against the race's reputation for having advanced by color as much as by competence. Affirmative action makes a glass ceiling virtually necessary as a protection against the corruptions of preferential treatment. This ceiling is the point at which corporations shift the emphasis from color to competency and stop playing the affirmative action game. Here preference backfires for blacks and becomes a taint that holds them back. Of course, one could argue that this taint, which is, after all, in the minds of whites, becomes nothing more than an excuse to discriminate against blacks. And certainly the result is the same in either case—blacks don't get past the glass ceiling. But this argument does not get around the fact that racial preferences now taint this color with a new theme of suspicion that makes it even more vulnerable to the impulse in others to discriminate. In this crucial yet gray area of perceived competence, preferences make whites look better than they are and blacks worse, while doing nothing whatever to stop the very real discrimination that blacks may encounter. I don't wish to justify the glass ceiling here, but only to suggest the very subtle ways that affirmative action revives rather than extinguishes the old rationalizations for racial discrimination.

In education, a revolving door; in employment, a glass ceiling. [22]

I believe affirmative action is problematic in our society because it [23] tries to function like a social program. Rather than ask it to ensure equal opportunity we have demanded that it create parity between the races. But preferential treatment does not teach skills, or educate, or instill motivation. It only passes out entitlement by color, a situation

213

that in my profession has created an unrealistically high demand for black professors. The social engineer's assumption is that this high demand will inspire more blacks to earn Ph.D.'s and join the profession. In fact, the number of blacks earning Ph.D.'s has declined in recent years. A Ph.D. must be developed from preschool on. He requires family and community support. He must acquire an entire system of values that enables him to work hard while delaying gratification. There are social programs, I believe, that can (and should) help blacks *develop* in all these areas, but entitlement by color is not a social program; it is a dubious reward for being black.

It now seems clear that the Supreme Court, in a series of recent 24 decisions, is moving away from racial preferences. It has disallowed preferences except in instances of "identified discrimination," eroded the precedent that statistical racial imbalances are *prima facie* evidence of discrimination, and in effect granted white males the right to challenge consent degrees that use preference to achieve racial balances in the workplace. One civil rights leader said, "Night has fallen on civil rights." But I am not so sure. The effect of these decisions is to protect the constitutional rights of everyone rather than take rights away from blacks. What they do take away from blacks is the special entitlement to more rights than others that preferences always grant. Night has fallen on racial preferences, not on the fundamental rights of black Americans. The reason for this shift, I believe, is that the white mandate for absolution from past racial sins has weakened considerably during the eighties. Whites are now less willing to endure unfairness to themselves in order to grant special entitlements to blacks, even when these entitlements are justified in the name of past suffering. Yet the black mandate for more power in society has remained unchanged. And I think part of the anxiety that many blacks feel over these decisions has to do with the loss of black power they may signal. We had won a certain specialness and now we are losing it.

But the power we've lost by these decisions is really only the power 25 that grows out of our victimization—the power to claim special entitlements under the law because of past oppression. This is not a very substantial or reliable power, and it is important that we know this so we can focus more exclusively on the kind of development that will bring enduring power. There is talk now that Congress will pass new legislation to compensate for these new limits on affirmative action. If this happens, I hope that their focus will be on development and anti-discrimination rather than entitlement, on achieving racial parity rather than jerry-building racial diversity.

I would also like to see affirmative action go back to its original pur- 26 pose of enforcing equal opportunity—a purpose that in itself disallows racial preferences. We cannot be sure that the discriminatory impulse in America has yet been shamed into extinction, and I believe affirmative action can make its greatest contribution by providing a rigorous vigilance in this area. It can guard constitutional rather than racial rights, and help institutions evolve standards of merit and selection that are appropriate to the institution's needs yet as free of racial bias as possible (again, with the understanding that racial imbalances are not always an indication of racial bias). One of the most important things affirmative action can do is to define exactly what racial discrimination is and how it might manifest itself within a specific institution. The impulse to discriminate *is* subtle and cannot be ferreted out unless its many guises are made clear to people. Along with this there should be monitoring of institutions and heavy sanctions brought to bear when actual discrimination is found. This is the sort of affirmative action that America owes to blacks and to itself. It goes after the evil of discrimination itself, while preferences only sidestep the evil and grant entitlement to its *presumed* victims.

But if not preferences, then what? I think we need social policies   27 that are committed to two goals: the educational and economic development of disadvantaged people, regardless of race, and the eradication from our society—through close monitoring and severe sanctions—of racial, ethnic, or gender discrimination. Preferences will not deliver us to either of these goals, since they tend to benefit those who are not disadvantaged—middle-class white women and middle-class blacks—and attack one form of discrimination with another. Preferences are inexpensive and carry the glamour of good intentions—change the numbers and the good deed is done. To be against them is to be unkind. But I think the unkindest cut is to bestow on children like my own an undeserved advantage while neglecting the development of those disadvantaged children on the East Side of my city who will likely never be in a position to benefit from a preference. Give my children fairness; give disadvantaged children a better shot at development—better elementary and secondary schools, job training, safer neighborhoods, better financial assistance for college, and so on. Fewer blacks go to college today than ten years ago; more black males of college age are in prison or under the control of the criminal justice system than in college. This despite racial preferences.

The mandates of black power and white absolution out of which   28 preferences emerged were not wrong in themselves. What was wrong was that both races focused more on the goals of these mandates than on the means to the goals. Blacks can have no real power without taking responsibility for their own educational and economic development. Whites can have no racial innocence without earning it by eradicating discrimination and helping the disadvantaged to develop. Because we ignored the means, the goals have not been reached, and the real work remains to be done.

COMPREHENSION

1. In your own words, explain just what is meant by *affirmative action.*
2. In your own words, summarize the major arguments Steele offers against the current affirmative-action program.

3. In paragraph 1, Steele claims that the affirmative-action program is a "Faustian bargain." What are the historical and literary roots of this term? What does it mean?

4. The author makes a distinction between "racial representation" and "racial development." What is the difference?

RHETORIC

1. What forms of argument (for example, appeals to authority, direct quotes, statistics, and so on) does the author call upon to support his thesis? Cite specific examples in the text that demonstrate these forms.

2. The author uses the terms "I believe" and "I think" several times in the essay. How do these terms help indicate the overall rhetorical category of the essay?

3. The author peppers his argument with descriptions such as "a cosmetic diversity that covers the blemish of disparity," "the black will be aware of the reflex his color triggers and will feel a stab of horror," and "preferential treatment . . . subjects blacks to a midnight of self-doubt." Does this incorporation of imagistic language make the essay more interesting to read?

4. Often those who criticize our society fail to provide alternatives to the shortcomings they uncover. Does Steele offer any solutions to the problems posed by affirmative action? If so, what are they? How does he weave them into the body of his argument?

5. Most of Steele's paragraphs follow a specific structure that lends them coherence. What is the general line of reasoning the author follows in his paragraphs to focus his points concerning the failure of affirmative action?

6. Examine the six paragraphs in the essay that begin with the coordinating conjunctions *yet, but,* and *so.* Why has the author selected these words as transitions from one paragraph to the next?

7. It seems that everyone has an opinion concerning affirmative action. What is the implied audience for whom Steele is offering his opinion? How does the way he offers his opinion differ from other opinions you have heard?

WRITING

1. Through a step-by-step process, argue for or against each supporting point Steele raises in his essay on the failure of affirmative action.

2. Convert each of Steele's arguments into interview questions. Interview at least four professionals (two white, two black), and record their responses to the points the author raises. Write an essay summarizing your findings.

3. Using your library as a source of research, write a research paper entitled, "The History of Affirmative Action in the United States."

4. Suspending your judgment on whether you agree with Steele, write an essay entitled "The Art of Argument," using the author's essay as a case study.

CLASSIC AND CONTEMPORARY

FREDERICK DOUGLASS   Frederick Douglass (1817–1895) was an American abolitionist, orator, and journalist. Born of the union between a slave and a white man, Douglass later escaped to Massachusetts. An impassioned anti-slavery speech brought him recognition as a powerful orator; thereafter he was much in demand for speaking engagements. He described his experience as a black man in America in *Narrative of the Life of Frederick Douglass* (1845). After managing to buy his freedom, Douglass founded the *North Star,* a newspaper he published for the next seventeen years. In the following exerpt from his stirring autobiography, Douglass recounts the tremendous obstacles he overcame in his efforts to become literate.

FREDERICK DOUGLASS

Learning to Read and Write

I lived in Master Hugh's family about seven years. During this time, ₁
I succeeded in learning to read and write. In accomplishing this, I was compelled to resort to various stratagems. I had no regular teacher. My mistress, who had kindly commenced to instruct me, had, in compliance with the advice and direction of her husband, not only ceased to instruct, but had set her face against my being instructed by any one else. It is due, however, to my mistress to say of her, that she did not adopt this course of treatment immediately. She at first lacked the depravity indispensable to shutting me up in mental darkness. It was at least necessary for her to have some training in the exercise of irresponsible power, to make her equal to the task of treating me as though I were a brute.

My mistress was, as I have said, a kind and tender-hearted woman; ₂
and in the simplicity of her soul she commenced, when I first went to live with her, to treat me as she supposed one human being ought to treat another. In entering upon the duties of a slaveholder, she did not seem to perceive that I sustained to her the relation of a mere chattel, and that for her to treat me as a human being was not only wrong, but dangerously so. Slavery proved as injurious to her as it did to me. When I went there, she was a pious, warm, and tender-hearted woman. There was no sorrow or suffering for which she had not a tear. She had bread for the hungry, clothes for the naked, and comfort for every mourner that came within her reach. Slavery soon proved its ability to divest her of these heavenly qualities. Under its influence, the tender heart became stone, and the lamb-like disposition gave way to one of tiger-

like fierceness. The first step in her downward course was in her ceasing to instruct me. She now commenced to practise her husband's precepts. She finally became even more violent in her opposition than her husband himself. She was not satisfied with simply doing as well as he had commanded; she seemed anxious to do better. Nothing seemed to make her more angry than to see me with a newspaper. She seemed to think that here lay the danger. I have had her rush at me with a face made all up of fury, and snatch from me a newspaper, in a manner that fully revealed her apprehension. She was an apt woman; and a little experience soon demonstrated, to her satisfaction, that education and slavery were incompatible with each other.

From this time I was most narrowly watched. If I was in a separate   3
room any considerable length of time, I was sure to be suspected of having a book, and was at once called to give an account of myself. All this, however, was too late. The first step had been taken. Mistress, in teaching me the alphabet, had given me the *inch,* and no precaution could prevent me from taking the *ell.*

The plan which I adopted, and the one by which I was most suc-   4
cessful, was that of making friends of all the little white boys whom I met in the street. As many of these as I could, I converted into teachers. With their kindly aid, obtained at different times and in different places, I finally succeeded in learning to read. When I was sent on errands, I always took my book with me, and by doing one part of my errand quickly, I found time to get a lesson before my return. I used also to carry bread with me, enough of which was always in the house, and to which I was always welcome; for I was much better off in this regard than many of the poor white children in our neighborhood. This bread I used to bestow upon the hungry little urchins, who, in return, would give me that more valuable bread of knowledge. I am strongly tempted to give the names of two or three of those little boys, as a testimonial of the gratitude and affection I bear them; but prudence forbids;—not that it would injure me, but it might embarrass them; for it is almost an unpardonable offence to teach slaves to read in this Christian country. It is enough to say of the dear little fellows, that they lived on Philpot Street, very near Durgin and Bailey's ship-yard. I used to talk this matter of slavery over with them. I would sometimes say to them, I wished I could be as free as they would be when they got to be men. "You will be free as soon as you are twenty-one, *but I am a slave for life!* Have not I as good a right to be free as you have?" These words used to trouble them; they would express for me the liveliest sympathy, and console me with the hope that something would occur by which I might be free.

I was now about twelve years old, and the thought of being *a slave*   5
for life began to bear heavily upon my heart. Just about this time, I got hold of a book entitled "The Columbian Orator." Every opportunity I got, I used to read this book. Among much of other interesting matter, I found in it a dialogue between a master and his slave. The slave was represented as having run away from his master three times. The dia-

logue represented the conversation which took place between them, when the slave was retaken the third time. In this dialogue, the whole argument in behalf of slavery was brought forward by the master, all of which was disposed of by the slave. The slave was made to say some very smart as well as impressive things in reply to his master—things which had the desired though unexpected effect; for the conversation resulted in the voluntary emancipation of the slave on the part of the master.

In the same book, I met with one of Sheridan's mighty speeches on and in behalf of Catholic emancipation. These were choice documents to me. I read them over and over again with unabated interest. They gave tongue to interesting thoughts of my own soul, which had frequently flashed through my mind, and died away for want of utterance. The moral which I gained from the dialogue was the power of truth over the conscience of even a slaveholder. What I got from Sheridan was a bold denunciation of slavery, and a powerful vindication of human rights. The reading of these documents enabled me to utter my thoughts, and to meet the arguments brought forward to sustain slavery; but while they relieved me of one difficulty, they brought on another even more painful than the one of which I was relieved. The more I read, the more I was led to abhor and detest my enslavers. I could regard them in no other light than a band of successful robbers, who had left their homes, and gone to Africa, and stolen us from our homes, and in a strange land reduced us to slavery. I loathed them as being the meanest as well as the most wicked of men. As I read and contemplated the subject, behold! that very discontentment which Master Hugh had predicted would follow my learning to read had already come, to torment and sting my soul to unutterable anguish. As I writhed under it, I would at times feel that learning to read had been a curse rather than a blessing. It had given me a view of my wretched condition, without the remedy. It opened my eyes to the horrible pit, but to no ladder upon which to get out. In moments of agony, I envied my fellow-slaves for their stupidity. I have often wished myself a beast. I preferred the condition of the meanest reptile to my own. Any thing, no matter what, to get rid of thinking! It was this everlasting thinking of my condition that tormented me. There was no getting rid of it. It was pressed upon me by every object within sight or hearing, animate or inanimate. The silver trump of freedom had roused my soul to eternal wakefulness. Freedom now appeared, to disappear no more forever. It was heard in every sound, and seen in every thing. It was ever present to torment me with a sense of my wretched condition. I saw nothing without seeing it, I heard nothing without hearing it, and felt nothing without feeling it. It looked from every star, it smiled in every calm, breathed in every wind, and moved in every storm.

I often found myself regretting my own existence, and wishing myself dead; and but for the hope of being free, I have no doubt but that I should have killed myself, or done something for which I should have been killed. While in this state of mind, I was eager to hear anyone

219

speak of slavery. I was a ready listener. Every little while, I could hear something about the abolitionists. It was some time before I found what the word meant. It was always used in such connections as to make it an interesting word to me. If a slave ran away and succeeded in getting clear, or if a slave killed his master, set fire to a barn, or did any thing very wrong in the mind of a slaveholder, it was spoken of as the fruit of *abolition.* Hearing the word in this connection very often, I set about learning what it meant. The dictionary afforded me little or no help. I found it was "the act of abolishing;" but then I did not know what was to be abolished. Here I was perplexed. I did not dare to ask any one about its meaning, for I was satisfied that it was something they wanted me to know very little about. After a patient waiting, I got one of our city papers, containing an account of the number of petitions from the north, praying for the abolition of slavery in the District of Columbia, and of the slave trade between the States. From this time I understood the words *abolition* and *abolitionist,* and always drew near when that word was spoken, expecting to hear something of importance to myself and fellow-slaves. The light broke in upon me by degrees. I went one day down on the wharf of Mr. Waters; and seeing two Irishmen unloading a scow of stone, I went, unasked, and helped them. When we had finished, one of them came to me and asked me if I were a slave. I told him I was. He asked, "Are ye a slave for life?" I told him that I was. The good Irishman seemed to be deeply affected by the statement. He said to the other that it was a pity so fine a little fellow as myself should be a slave for life. He said it was a shame to hold me. They both advised me to run away to the north; that I should find friends there, and that I should be free. I pretended not to be interested in what they said, and treated them as if I did not understand them; for I feared they might be treacherous. White men have been known to encourage slaves to escape, and then, to get the reward, catch them and return them to their masters. I was afraid that these seemingly good men might use me so; but I nevertheless remembered their advice, and from that time I resolved to run away. I looked forward to a time at which it would be safe for me to escape. I was too young to think of doing so immediately; besides, I wished to learn how to write, as I might have occasion to write my own pass. I consoled myself with the hope that I should one day find a good chance. Meanwhile, I would learn to write.

The idea as to how I might learn to write was suggested to me by being in Durgin and Bailey's ship-yard, and frequently seeing the ship carpenters, after hewing, and getting a piece of timber ready for use, write on the timber the name of that part of the ship for which it was intended. When a piece of timber was intended for the larboard side, it would be marked thus—"L." When a piece was for the starboard side, it would be marked thus—"S." A piece for the larboard side forward, would be marked thus—"L. F." When a piece was for starboard side forward, it would be marked thus—"S. F." For larboard aft, it would be marked thus—"L. A." For starboard aft, it would be marked thus—"S. A." I soon learned the names of these letters, and for what they were intended when placed upon a piece of timber in the ship-yard. I immediately commenced copying them, and in a short time was able to make the four letters named. After that, when I met with any boy who I knew could write, I would tell him I could write as well as he. The next word would be, "I don't believe you. Let me see you try it." I would then make the letters which I had been so fortunate as to learn, and ask him to beat that. In this way I got a good many lessons in writing, which it is quite possible I should never have gotten in any other way. During this time, my copy-book was the board fence, brick wall, and pavement; my pen and ink was a lump of chalk. With these, I learned mainly how to write. I then commenced and continued copying the Italics in Webster's Spelling Book, until I could make them all without looking on the book. By this time, my little Master Thomas had gone to school, and learned how to write, and had written over a number of copy-books. These had been brought home, and shown to some of our near neighbors, and then laid aside. My mistress used to go to class meeting at the Wilk Street meeting-house every Monday afternoon, and leave me to take care of the house. When left thus, I used to spend the time in writing in the spaces left in Master Thomas's copy-book, copying what he had written. I continued to do this until I could write a hand very similar to that of Master Thomas. Thus, after a long, tedious effort for years, I finally succeeded in learning how to write.

COMPREHENSION

1. What strategies does Douglass use to continue his education after his mistress's abandonment?
2. Why did the author's mistress find his reading newspapers particularly threatening?
3. Why does Douglass call learning to read "a curse rather than a blessing"?

RHETORIC

1. What is the thesis of Douglass's narration? How well is it supported and developed by the body paragraphs? Explain.
2. The first couple of sentences in the story, though simple, are very powerful. How do they serve to set up the mood of the piece and the reader's expectations?
3. Cite examples of Douglass's use of metaphors, and discuss why they work in those paragraphs.
4. How would you describe Douglass's writing style and level of language? Does it reveal anything about the writer's character? Justify your response.
5. Explain the way in which the author uses comparison and contrast.
6. What is Douglass's definition of *abolition,* and how does Douglass help the reader define it? How does this method contribute to the reader's understanding of the learning process?

1. What does Douglass mean when he writes that "education and slavery were incompatible with each other"? Write an essay in which you consider the relationship between the two.
2. Both Douglass and his mistress were in inferior positions to Master Hugh. Write an essay in which you compare and contrast their positions in society at the time.
3. Literacy is still a major problem in the United States. Write an account of what your day-to-day life would be like if you couldn't write or read. What impact would this deficiency have on your life? Use concrete examples to illustrate your narrative.

RICHARD RODRIGUEZ   Richard Rodriguez was born in 1944 in San Francisco and received degrees from Stanford University and Columbia University. He also did graduate study at the University of California, Berkeley, and at the Warburg Institute, London. Rodriguez became a nationally known writer with the publication of his autobiography, *Hunger of Memory: The Education of Richard Rodriguez* (1982). In it, he describes the struggles of growing up biculturally—feeling alienated from his Spanish-speaking parents yet not wholly comfortable in the dominant culture of the United States. He opposes bilingualism and affirmative action as they are now practiced in the United States, and his stance has caused much controversy in educational and intellectual circles. Rodriguez continues to write about social issues such as acculturation, education, and language. In the following essay, Rodriguez records his childhood passion for reading.

RICHARD RODRIGUEZ

The Lonely, Good Company of Books

From an early age I knew that my mother and father could read and write both Spanish and English. I had observed my father making his way through what, I now suppose, must have been income tax forms. On other occasions I waited apprehensively while my mother read onion-paper letters air-mailed from Mexico with news of a relative's illness or death. For both my parents, however, reading was something done out of necessity and as quickly as possible. Never did I see either of them read an entire book. Nor did I see them read for pleasure. Their reading consisted of work manuals, prayer books, newspapers, recipes. . . .

In our house each school year would begin with my mother's careful instruction: "Don't write in your books so we can sell them at the end of the year." The remark was echoed in public by my teachers, but only in part: "Boys and girls, don't write in your books. You must learn to treat them with great care and respect."

OPEN THE DOORS OF YOUR MIND WITH BOOKS, read the red and white poster over the nun's desk in early September. It soon was apparent to me that reading was the classroom's central activity. Each course had its own book. And the information gathered from a book was unquestioned. READ TO LEARN, the sign on the wall advised in December. I privately wondered: What was the connection between reading and learning? Did one learn something only by reading it? Was an idea only an idea if it could be written down? In June, CONSIDER BOOKS YOUR BEST FRIENDS. Friends? Reading was, at best, only a chore. I needed to look up whole paragraphs of words in a dictionary. Lines of type were dizzying, the eye having to move slowly across the page, then down, and across. . . . The sentences of the first books I read were coolly impersonal. Toned hard. What most bothered me, however, was the isolation reading required. To console myself for the loneliness I'd feel when I read, I tried reading in a very soft voice. Until: "Who is doing all that talking to his neighbor?" Shortly after, remedial reading classes were arranged for me with a very old nun.

At the end of each school day, for nearly six months, I would meet ⁴ with her in the tiny room that served as the school's library but was actually only a storeroom for used textbooks and a vast collection of *National Geographics.* Everything about our sessions pleased me: the smallness of the room; the noise of the janitor's broom hitting the edge of the long hallway outside the door; the green of the sun, lighting the wall; and the old woman's face blurred white with a beard. Most of the time we took turns. I began with my elementary text. Sentences of astonishing simplicity seemed to me lifeless and drab: "The boys ran from the rain. . . . She wanted to sing. . . . The kite rose in the blue." Then the old nun would read from her favorite books, usually biographies of early American presidents. Playfully she ran through complex sentences, calling the words alive with her voice, making it seem that the author somehow was speaking directly to me. I smiled just to listen to her. I sat there and sensed for the very first time some possibility of fellowship between a reader and a writer, a communication, never *intimate* like that I heard spoken words at home convey, but one nonetheless *personal.*

One day the nun concluded a session by asking me why I was so ⁵ reluctant to read by myself. I tried to explain; said something about the way written words made me feel all alone—almost, I wanted to add but didn't, as when I spoke to myself in a room just emptied of furniture. She studied my face as I spoke; she seemed to be watching more than listening. In an uneventful voice she replied that I had nothing to fear. Didn't I realize that reading would open up whole new worlds? A book could open doors for me. It could introduce me to people and show me places I never imagined existed. She gestured toward the bookshelves. (Bare-breasted African women danced, and the shiny hubcaps of automobiles on the back covers of the *Geographic* gleamed in my mind.) I listened with respect. But her words were not very influential. I was thinking then of another consequence of literacy, one I was too shy to

223

admit but nonetheless trusted. Books were going to make me "educated." *That* confidence enabled me, several months later, to overcome my fear of the silence.

In fourth grade I embarked upon a grandiose reading program. 6 "Give me the names of important books," I would say to startled teachers. They soon found out that I had in mind "adult books." I ignored their suggestion of anything I suspected was written for children. (Not until I was in college, as a result, did I read *Huckleberry Finn* or *Alice's Adventures in Wonderland.*) Instead, I read *The Scarlet Letter* and Franklin's *Autobiography.* And whatever I read I read for extra credit. Each time I finished a book, I reported the achievement to a teacher and basked in the praise my effort earned. Despite my best efforts, however, there seemed to be more and more books I needed to read. At the library I would literally tremble as I came upon whole shelves of books I hadn't read. So I read and I read and I read: *Great Expectations;* all the short stories of Kipling; *The Babe Ruth Story;* the entire first volume of the *Encyclopaedia Britannica* (A-ANSTEY); the *Iliad; Moby Dick; Gone with the Wind; The Good Earth; Ramona; Forever Amber; The Lives of the Saints; Crime and Punishment; The Pearl.* . . . Librarians who initially frowned when I checked out the maximum ten books at a time started saving books they thought I might like. Teachers would say to the rest of the class, "I only wish the rest of you took reading as seriously as Richard obviously does."

But at home I would hear my mother wondering, "What do you see 7 in your books?" (Was reading a hobby like her knitting? Was so much reading even healthy for a boy? Was it the sign of "brains"? Or was it just a convenient excuse for not helping around the house on Saturday mornings?) Always, "What do you see . . . ?"

What *did* I see in my books? I had the idea that they were crucial 8 for my academic success, though I couldn't have said exactly how or why. In the sixth grade I simply concluded that what gave a book its value was some major idea or theme it contained. If that core essence could be mined and memorized, I would become learned like my teachers. I decided to record in a notebook the themes of the books that I read. After reading *Robinson Crusoe,* I wrote that its theme was "the value of learning to live by oneself." When I completed *Wuthering Heights,* I noted the danger of "letting emotions get out of control." Rereading these brief moralistic appraisals usually left me disheartened. I couldn't believe that they were really the source of reading's value. But for many years, they constituted the only means I had of describing to myself the educational value of books.

In spite of my earnestness, I found reading a pleasurable activity. I 9 came to enjoy the lonely good company of books. Early on weekday mornings, I'd read in my bed. I'd feel a mysterious comfort then, reading in the dawn quiet—the blue-gray silence interrupted by the occasional churning of the refrigerator motor a few rooms away or the more distant sounds of a city bus beginning its run. On weekends I'd go to the public library to read, surrounded by old men and women. Or, if the weather was fine, I would take my books to the park and read in the shade of a tree. Neighbors would leave for vacation and I would water their lawns. I would sit through the twilight on the front porches or in backyards, reading to the cool, whirling sounds of the sprinklers.

I also had favorite writers. But often those writers I enjoyed most I was least able to value. When I read William Saroyan's *The Human Comedy,* I was immediately pleased by the narrator's warmth and the charm of his story. But as quickly I became suspicious. A book so enjoyable to read couldn't be very "important." Another summer I determined to read all the novels of Dickens. Reading his fat novels, I loved the feeling I got—after the first hundred pages—of being at home in a fictional world where I knew the names of the characters and cared about was going to happen to them. And it bothered me that I was forced away at the conclusion, when the fiction closed tight, like a fortune-teller's fist—the futures of all the major characters neatly resolved. I never knew how to take such feelings seriously, however. Nor did I suspect that these experiences could be part of a novel's meaning. Still, there were pleasures to sustain me after I'd finish my books. Carrying a volume back to the library, I would be pleased by its weight. I'd run my fingers along the edge of the pages and marvel at the breadth of my achievement. Around my room, growing stacks of paperback books reinforced my assurance.

I entered high school having read hundreds of books. My habit of reading made me a confident speaker and writer of English. Reading also enabled me to sense something of the shape, the major concerns, of Western thought. (I was able to say something about Dante and Descartes and Engels and James Baldwin in my high school term papers.) In these various ways, books brought me academic success as I hoped that they would. But I was not a good reader. Merely bookish, I lacked a point of view when I read. Rather, I read in order to acquire a point of view. I vacuumed books for epigrams, scraps of information, ideas, themes—anything to fill the hollow within me and make me feel educated. When one of my teachers suggested to his drowsy tenth-grade English class that a person could not have a "complicated idea" until he had read at least two thousand books, I heard the remark without detecting either its irony or its very complicated truth. I merely determined to compile a list of all the books I had ever read. Harsh with myself, I included only once a title I might have read several times. (How, after all, could one read a book more than once?) And I included only those books over a hundred pages in length. (Could anything shorter be a book?)

There was yet another high school list I compiled. One day I came across a newspaper article about the retirement of an English professor at a nearby state college. The article was accompanied by a list of the "hundred most important books of Western Civilization." "More than anything else in my life," the professor told the reporter with finality, "these books have made me all that I am." That was the kind of remark I couldn't ignore. I clipped out the list and kept it for the several months it took me to read all of the titles. Most books, of course, I barely understood. While reading Plato's *Republic*, for instance, I needed to keep looking at the book jacket comments to remind myself what the text was about. Nevertheless, with the special patience and superstition of a scholarship boy, I looked at every word of the text. And by the time I reached the last word, relieved, I convinced myself that I had read *The Republic*. In a ceremony of great pride, I solemnly crossed Plato off my list.

COMPREHENSION

1. What was Rodriguez's parents' attitude toward reading? Did it influence his attitude? Cite examples from the essay that support your opinion.
2. What does Rodriguez mean by "the fellowship between a reader and a writer"? Why does he differentiate between "intimate" and "personal" forms of communication?
3. Rodriguez hoped that reading would fill "the hollow" inside him. What was the cause of his emptiness? Did he succeed in filling the void? Why did he find reading a lonely experience? Did reading fulfill any of his expectations?

RHETORIC

1. What is the thesis of Rodriguez's essay? Is it stated or implied? Explain.
2. How does the author's use of narrative advance his views on reading and education?
3. What is the writer's tone? How effective is it in conveying his point of view?
4. Rodriguez uses uppercase letters when referring to signs advocating reading. Why does he use this device? How does it support his point of view?
5. The essay ends with an ironic anecdote. Why did Rodriguez choose to conclude this way? Does it satisfactorily illustrate the writer's attitude?
6. What words or phrases imply that there is an ethnic component in Rodriguez's conflict? Is the subtlety effective? Justify your response.

WRITING

1. Rodriguez's parents had a pragmatic attitude toward reading. What was the attitude in your home as you were growing up? Did your parents encourage your interest in reading? Did they read themselves? What is the first book you remember reading by yourself? Write an essay in which you describe your reading history.
2. Rodriguez believed reading would make him "educated." Do you agree or disagree? Is reading vitally important to a person's education? How do you define *education*? Can it only be acquired through reading, or are there other contributing factors? Write an argumentative essay on this topic.

3. Is reading still a significant source of information and entertainment, or has it been usurped by television? Is it important (or necessary) to be a reader today?

CLASSIC AND CONTEMPORARY: QUESTIONS FOR COMPARISON

1. Both Rodriguez and Douglass were motivated to educate themselves in a society inimical to this achievement. Compare and contrast their struggles and attitudes in their quest for knowledge.
2. Pretend you are Richard Rodriguez, and write a letter to Douglass addressing the issues of minorities and education in present-day America. What would Rodriguez say about the progress of minorities in our society?
3. Although Rodriguez and Douglass treat a similar theme, they communicate their messages differently. Which narration do you consider more powerful, and why?
4. Rodriguez explores the theme of isolation in his story. Is there any evidence that this feeling was shared by Douglass in his efforts to learn how to read? Use proof from both narratives to support your view.
5. Slavery was an obvious obstacle to Douglass's attempt to educate himself. What impeded Rodriguez's progress? Were there similar forces at work? Cite examples from Rodriguez's narrative to prove your point.

CONNECTIONS

1. Using the essays of D'Souza and Steele, write an essay examining the positive and negative consequences of multiculturalism in American schools.

2. Write an essay about the special significance of education for African Americans and other minorities in the United States and elsewhere. Refer to at least three essays in this section to support your evaluation.

3. Write a personal narrative recreating an important event connected to your education. Describe the event itself and its impact on your personality. Was it a bittersweet experience like Angelou's, a galvanizing one like Rau's, or a dawning shift in perspective like Rodriguez's? Refer to the writers in this section where relevant.

4. Which writers in this section would you classify as progressive on the subject of education, and which ones are conservative? Refer to specific authors and their essays to support your contentions.

5. Gelernter's essay raises the issue of computers in education. Research the issue, and then present your insights into the subject.

6. Write an essay in which you favor or oppose affirmative action at work and in school. Use the essays of D'Souza and Steele to make your case.

7. Write an essay arguing that sex and morality should be taught at home by parents and not left up to the schools.

8. Using the essays of Rooney, Gelernter, and others, write an essay that speculates on the shape of American education in the twenty-first century.

CHAPTER FIVE

Gender and Human Development

*T*here is an essay in this chapter by the anthropologist Mary Leakey. In it, she offers readers one of the most memorable images in this anthology. The image is of two sets of footprints moving toward us out of "the ashes of time." The smaller set of footprints might have been those of a female. These footprints, Leakey speculates, signify our original human prototypes—the first woman and man. These two sets of footprints suggest to Leakey that human development is rooted in gender or "sexual dimorphism."

In many cultures, we still find the smaller set of footprints moving behind the larger because issues of gender stereotyping still dominate many discussions of human development. Today, more than seventy years after they won the right to vote, women in the United States still earn less than men, still hold far fewer high corporate and political positions, and are still expected to be traditional "homemakers." They may be freer than are women in other cultures to determine their own destinies—to walk beside or ahead of men or to dispense with men altogether—but their footprints inevitably cross paths with their male counterparts as American society continues to map out destiny on the basis of gender.

Admittedly, every culture has its own idea of what it means to be a man or a woman; and these ideas affect our major institutions, from the family to school to numerous other social relationships. And although it is difficult to reconcile these various cross-cultural ideas, the writers in this chapter attempt to make sense of sex roles and to liberate themselves from the tyranny of sexual stereotyping. Freud, of course, in his essay "Libidinal Types," asserts that human behavior is rooted in sexuality, that sex is destiny. Whether you agree or disagree with his premise, it is clear that notions of what it means to be a woman or a man have a definite impact on the way we conduct our lives. For example, when Margaret Atwood provides an innovative, multipart catalogue on "the female body," she investigates and critiques lines of sexual power while offering a satire on attitudes that reduce women to sexual objects. Gloria Steinem extends this critique to the realm of literature and art in her evaluation of erotica and pornography and their relationship to human sexual response.

All of the writers in this chapter tend to challenge attitudes that reflect various forms of sexual discrimination and gender stereotyping. They each suggest, in their own ways, that men and women can be better in their relationships than they have been historically. Paul Theroux and Michael Dorris extend this theme in their essays, both of which offer revisionist definitions of what it means to be a man in American culture. The gender issues discussed by writers in this chapter might prove to be controversial. They will force you to confront your own sense of sexual identity. These essays are like a mirror in which you can see and evaluate the ways in which you behave as a man or a woman.

Previewing the Chapter

As you read the essays in this chapter and respond to them in discussion and writing, consider the following questions:

• How does the author define what it means to be a woman or a man?

• What specific gender issues does the author raise?

• Is the author concerned with male behavior, female behavior, or both?

• What perspective does the writer take on the subject of gender stereotyping? Is the writer optimistic, pessimistic, or neutral?

• How does the writer present power relationships between the sexes?

• What social, political, and economic issues are raised by the author?

• Does the author demonstrate a bias for or against men or women? How do you know?

• What changes in human behavior, if any, does the author propose for men and women?

• According to the author, how do women perceive the world? How do men perceive it? How do they judge each other's behavior?

• Do you agree or disagree with the presentation of gender and human development presented by the author?

• Based on your reading of these essays, what overall attitude do you have on gender and human behavior? Have any of the essayists encouraged you to examine your own behavior and beliefs?

GAIL SHEEHY   Gail Sheehy was born in Mamaroneck, New York in 1937 and received a B.S. degree from the University of Vermont in 1958. Although her first published book was a novel, *Lovesounds* (1970), Sheehy is primarily known for magazine articles and nonfiction books that deal with contemporary issues of daily life. Her most famous book, *Passages,* was published in 1976; its sequel, *New Passages* (1995), has raised some eyebrows in American society that is currently at grips with dealing with the nature of the family, aging, and work. Sheehy claims to be a popularizer, borrowing research done by scholars and scientists and transforming it into material that will appeal to the general population. Some critics claim her work does not accurately present scholarly information, while others say her work nonetheless makes a tremendous contribution to a society trying to understand itself. The following is an excerpt from *New Passages* that was published in *U.S. News & World Report.*

GAIL SHEEHY

New Passages

In the space of one short generation, the whole shape of the life   1
cycle has been fundamentally altered. Since the publication of my book
Passages in 1976, age norms have shifted and are no longer normative.

Consider: Nine-year-old girls are developing breasts and pubic hair;   2
9-year-old boys carry guns to school; 16-year-olds can "divorce" a parent; 30-year-old men still live at home with Mom; 40-year-old women
are just getting around to pregnancy; 50-year-old men are forced into
early retirement; 55-year-old women can have egg donor babies; 60-
year-old women start first professional degrees; 70-year-old men
reverse aging by 20 years with human growth hormone; 80-year-olds
run marathons; 85-year-olds remarry and still enjoy sex; and every day,
the "Today" show's Willard Scott says "Happy Birthday!" to more 100-
year-old women.

What's going on? There is a revolution in the adult life cycle. Peo-   3
ple today are leaving childhood sooner, but they are taking longer to
grow up and much longer to die. That is shifting all the stages of adulthood ahead—by 10 years. Adolescence is now prolonged for the middle class until the end of the 20s. Today, our First Adulthood only
begins at 30. Most baby boomers don't feel fully "grown up" until they
are into their 40s. When our parents turned 50, we thought they were
old! But today, women and men I've interviewed routinely feel they are
five to 10 years younger than the age on their birth certificates. Fifty is
what 40 used to be; 60 is what 50 used to be. Middle age has already

been pushed far into the 50s—in fact, if you listen to boomers, there is no more middle age. So what's next?

Welcome to Middlescence. It's adolescence the second time around. 4

The territory of the 50s, 60s and beyond is changing so radically 5 that it now opens up whole new passages leading to stages of life that are nothing like what our parents experienced. An American woman who today reaches age 50 free of cancer and heart disease can expect to see her 92nd birthday. The average man who is 65 today—an age now reached by more than 70 percent of the U.S. population—can expect to live until 81. That amounts to a second adult lifetime.

Stop and recalculate. Imagine the day you turn 45 as the old age 6 of your First Adulthood. Fifty then becomes the youth of your Second Adulthood. First Adulthood just happens to you. Second Adulthood, you can custom-design. It's a potential rebirth that offers exhilarating new possibilities. But only for those who are aware and who prepare.

For those who are approaching 50, the question increasingly 7 becomes, "How shall we live the rest of our lives?" And the tantalizing dynamic that has emerged in our era is that the second half of adult life is not the stagnant, depressing downward slide we have always assumed it to be.

In the hundreds of interviews I have done with men and women in 8 middle life, especially pacesetters in the educated middle class, I have discovered that people are beginning to see there is the exciting potential of a new life to live: one in which they can concentrate on becoming better, stronger, deeper, wiser, funnier, freer, sexier and more attentive to living the privileged moments—even as they are getting older, lumpier, bumpier, slower and closer to the end. Instead of being a dreary tale of decline, our middle life is a progress story, a series of little victories over little deaths.

We now have not one but three adult lives to anticipate: Provisional 9 Adulthood from age 18 to 30, First Adulthood from 30 to 45 and Second Adulthood from 45 to 85 and beyond. The most exciting development is that Second Adulthood contains two new territories—an Age of Mastery from 45 to 65 and an Age of Integrity from 65 to 85 and beyond. The startling life changes awaiting all of us are now being charted by path breakers from the World War II generation and the "silent" generation of those who came of age in the 1950s, who are writing new maps for everyone else to follow.

The Flourishing Forties

The two generations of baby boomers—the Vietnam generation of 10 the 1960s and the "me" generation of the 1970s—are set to become the longest-living humans in American history. The first of them will officially turn 50 in 1996. A million of them, the Census Bureau predicts, will live past 100. Having indulged themselves in the longest adolescence in history, they betray a collective terror and disgust of aging.

Early in life, baby boomers got used to having two things: choice and control. That means that when life's storm clouds threaten, people in their 40s today are likely to feel more out of control than ever. Wally Scott, a participant in one of many "Midlife Passages" group discussions I've attended in recent years, put it this way: "All of a sudden, you have to start listening to the little voices inside: What do I really want to invest my life in? How can I construct a life that fits the me of today as opposed to the me of 15 years ago?"

The Flourishing Forties can be complicated for women by the 12
storms of perimenopause and menopause. Men may face their own version of biological meltdown. Although it is not strictly a male menopause, many men in middle or later life do experience a lapse in virility and vitality and a decline in well-being. About half of American men over 40 have experienced middle-life impotence to varying degrees. This decline can definitely be delayed. It can even be corrected. In the near future, it may even become preventable. But first a man must understand it.

The social arena contains its own challenges as women in their 40s 13
continue to explore new roles, struggle with late child rearing or mourn their lack of children. As couples are forced to renegotiate traditional relationships and medical crises intrude on well-laid plans, men and women in this age group begin to feel their mortality.

Today, smart men and women will use their early 40s as prepara- 14
tion for a custom-designed Second Adulthood. What do you need to learn to maximize your ability to respond quickly to a fluid marketplace? A single, fixed identity is a liability today. Recent research also suggests that developing multiple identities is one of the best buffers against mental and physical illness. When a marriage blows up or the company shuts down or the whole nature of a profession is changed by technology, people with more than one identity can draw upon other sources of self-esteem while they regroup. Such resilience is essential.

Second Adulthood

John Guare has been doing exactly what he most loves since he was 15
9 years old—writing plays. But even the brilliant creator of *Six Degrees of Separation* and *House of Blue Leaves* knows he cannot rest on his laurels. He was 56 when I mentioned to him that I was exploring our Second Adulthood. "I was just saying to my wife, 'I've got to reinvent my life, right now!'" he exploded. "Or we'll be dead. Worse than dead—the walking dead."

That is the challenge of making the passage to Second Adulthood. 16
This new life must be precipitated by a moment of change—the "Aha!" moment. It forces us to look upon our lives differently and to make a transition from survival to mastery. In young adulthood we survive by figuring out how best to please or perform for the powerful ones who will protect and reward us—parents, teachers, lovers, mates, bosses, mentors. It is all about proving ourselves. The transformation of middle

life is to move into a more stable psychological state of mastery, where we control much of what happens in our life and can often act on the world rather than react to whatever the world throws at us. Reaching this state of mastery is also one of the best predictors of good mental and psychological functioning in old age.

Second Adulthood takes us beyond the preoccupation with self. We are compelled to search for a greater significance in our engagement in the world. "We are all hungry for connection," said James Sniechowski, a 51-year-old men's group leader in Santa Monica, Calif. *Connection* was a word that came up again and again in my discussions with groups of middle-aged men. 17

Increasingly, women who have mastered the silent passage through menopause feel a power surge—postmenopausal zest. As family obligations fade away, many become motivated to stretch their independence, learn new skills, return to school, plunge into new careers, rediscover the creativity and adventurousness of their youth and, at last, find their own voices. 18

The Flaming Fifties

By the time they reach their Flaming Fifties, most educated women have acquired the skills and self-knowledge to master complex environments and change the conditions around them. Over and over, women who have crossed into their 50s tell me with conviction, "I would not go back to being young again." They remember vividly what it was like to wake up not knowing exactly who they were, to be torn between demands of family and commands of career, to be constantly changing hats (and hairstyles) in the attempt to fit many roles and often losing focus in the blur of it all. 19

In three major national opinion surveys I have done in the past seven years, I have learned that by Second Adulthood, the dominant influence on a woman's well-being is not income level or social class or marital status. The most decisive factor is age. Older is happier. 20

"Fifty for me was a time when I really, for the first time, owned my body," said Ginny Ford, a Rochester, N.Y., businesswoman, whose blond hair and dimpled smile evoke Doris Day movies. "I had been very ashamed of my body, and now I love it. Now, there's all this inner stuff going on. I'm probably 10 pounds heavier, my thighs are a little rumply, my arms have flab. Fifteen years ago I would have starved myself. But now I'm enjoying my husband's pasta. I exercise every day, I enjoy myself sexually and I'm proud of this body. It really works!" 21

For men entering their 50s today, there is no script. It has traditionally been assumed that aging is kinder to men, but a different truth comes out in personal interviews. I found far more uncertainty among men in middle life than among women; indeed, they often appear to be going in opposite directions. Overall, the over-50 men in my surveys don't experience the great transformation from First to Second Adulthood that women do. Most appear to be more resigned to accepting life 22 as it is: Two thirds are not anticipating any major change, and one third feel more concerned about just getting by. Half of these men feel tired and like they're "running out of gas." Their greatest worry is that they can no longer take their health for granted.

But among those men I have studied who are well educated, particularly those with an entrepreneurial temperament, a good many are enjoying a sense of mastery. They say the best things about being over 45 are being able to rely on their experience and being clearer about what is truly important in life. Still others find new richness in forging closer, more intimate attachments with their wives or in becoming start-over dads.

How can we make this passage more positively? Find your passion, 24 and pursue it. How do you know where to look? You can start by seeing if it passes the time-flies test. What activity do you do in which time goes by without your even knowing it? What did you most love to do when you were 12 years old? Somewhere in that activity there is a hook to be found that might pull up your dormant self.

Men and women who emerge psychologically healthiest at 50 are 25 those who, as their expectations and goals change with age, "shape a 'new self' that calls upon qualities that were dormant earlier." This was the principal finding of longitudinal studies at the University of California at Berkeley. Men have always been able to start over, and not once but more than once. What is really new is that women now have the option of starting second lives in their mid-40s or 50s, and increasingly they are doing so.

For some that will lead to intellectual pursuits. A remarkable surge 26 is already occurring in higher education among older women. Only 3.2 percent of the women in the World War II generation went back to post-high-school education between the ages of 40 and 54. But fully 11 percent of the "silent" generation of the 1950s went back for some college education in those middle years. In 1991, nearly 1 million women over 40 were enrolled in college nationwide.

This stage brings with it much greater emotional and social license, 27 and a majority of these women have claimed it, becoming more outspoken and less self-conscious. After interviewing 14 women from my national survey who emerged in their 50s with optimum well-being, I learned that they see themselves as survivors. That is not the same as seeing themselves as former victims of terrible physical or emotional abuse, although some do describe overcoming such situations in their lives. What they have "survived" are the economic biases and stereotypical sex roles that threatened to inhibit their development as fully independent adults. They are so strong that they do not expect to feel "old" until they are about 70.

One striking finding among researchers is that men over 50 are 28 becoming somewhat more dependent on their wives, emotionally and financially, and less certain about their future goals. The special stresses of an economy in transition, with its punishing wage declines for non-college-educated workers and corporate downsizing that now robs many college-educated men of identity and meaning, have been added to classic biological stresses, especially the decline of men's physical prowess and, for many, the sagging of their sexual performance. Given this new set of conditions, men at middle life probably face the roughest patch of all in mapping the new adult life across time.

"Men over 45 are becoming the new at-risk population for significant problems with anxiety and depression," says Ellen McGrath, a psychologist and author of *When Feeling Bad Is Good*. "And for the first time ever, some of them are acknowledging it and reaching out for help. This is a brand-new trend." 29

Making a passage to the Age of Mastery often means men are giving up being the master. Alan Alhadeff, a Seattle lawyer of 45, described his "Aha!" moment on a basketball court: "This 20-year-old kid was checking me real hard in the back court. I'm then about 20 pounds heavier than people my height should be. So I pushed him away, somewhat aggressively. I said, 'C'mon. I'm old enough to be your dad.'" The young man looked the older man straight in the eye: "Then get off the court." 30

"After that day on the basketball court, I mellowed. I realized I don't have to prove myself in physical contests anymore. I don't see that as a negative at all." Indeed, this freed Alhadeff to try other forms of expression he had never entertained before: art, music, gardening, gourmet cooking. "And they're all a lot easier on the knees!" 31

The real winners among men in middle life do make this shift. Nearly all have developed passions or hobbies that happily occupy and challenge them outside their workaday routines. Such occupations are crucial in offsetting the disenchantment with their profession that polls show is now felt by large numbers of doctors, or the boredom of the accountant defending yet another tax audit of a rich client, or the weariness of the dentist who cannot expect to be wildly stimulated by drilling his billionth bicuspid. 32

The Serene Sixties

The 60s have changed just as dramatically as the earlier stages of middle life. What with beta blockers and hip replacements, you're as likely to run into a man of 65 roller-blading in the park as to see him biking with his youngest child, enjoying the adolescent boy in himself as well as the recycled father. Only 10 percent of Americans 65 and over have a chronic health problem that restricts them from carrying on a major physical activity. 33

Clearly the vast majority of American women and men now in their 60s have reached the stage where maximum freedom coexists with a minimum of physical limitations. And another passage looms: the one from mastery to integrity. Experts in gerontology make a clear distinction between passive aging and successful aging. To engage in successful aging is actually a career choice—a conscious commitment 34 to continuing self-education and the development of a whole set of strategies.

Resilience is probably the most important protection one can have entering the Age of Integrity. An impressive study of the sources of well-being in men at 65 found that the harbinger of emotional health was not a stable childhood or a highflying career. Rather, it was much more important to have developed an ability to handle life's accidents and conflicts without passivity, blaming or bitterness. "It's having the capacity to hold a conflict or impulse in consciousness without acting on it," concludes George Vaillent, a psychiatrist now at Harvard Medical School, who has been scrutinizing—in the Grant Study—the same 173 Harvard men at five-year intervals since they graduated in the early 1940s.

A related finding in the Grant Study: Time does heal. The research 36 shows that even the most traumatic events in childhood had virtually no effect on the well-being of these men by their mid-60s, although severe depression earlier in life did predispose them to continuing problems. Traits that turned out to contribute to happiness in the golden years were not the same ones that had influenced people back in their college days: spontaneity, creative flair and easy sociability. Instead, the traits important to smooth functioning as we get older are being dependable, well organized and pragmatic.

The major predictable passage in this period for most people is 37 retirement, though many consider part-time work to help pay for their longer lives and perhaps to handle other family cares like aged parents or the needs of grandchildren. Forty-one percent of retirees surveyed in New York City in 1993 said the adjustment to retirement was difficult. The younger the retiree, the harder the transition. And the higher the status one's work conferred, the steeper the slide to anonymity.

The comfort of mature love is the single most important determi- 38 nant of older men's outlook on life. Continued excitement about life is the other factor in high well-being for men at this stage. My research with members of the Harvard Business School class of 1949 shows that those who enjoy the highest well-being had reached out for new adventures in half a dozen new directions *before* retiring. They see semi- or full retirement as an enticing opportunity to add richness to their lives.

Grandparenthood can jump-start the transition to the Age of 38 Integrity. For women or men who had to learn, painfully, in First Adulthood how to compartmentalize their nurturing selves and achieving selves, grandparenthood is a particularly welcome second chance to bring all the parts of their lives into harmony.

The Sage Seventies

Those who thrive into their 70s and beyond "live very much in the 40 present, but they always have plans for the future," argues Cecelia Hur-

237

wich in her doctoral thesis at the Center for Psychological Studies in Albany, Calif. The seventysomethings Hurwich studied had mastered the art of "letting go" of their egos gracefully, so they could focus their attention on a few fine-tuned priorities. These zestful women were not in unusually good physical shape, but believing they still had living to do, they concentrated on what they could do rather than on what they had lost. Every one acknowledged the need for some form of physical intimacy. They found love through sharing a variety of pleasures: music, gardening, hiking, traveling. Several spoke enthusiastically of active and satisfying sex lives.

After that life stage, the most successful octogenarians I have come   41 across seem to share a quality of directness. Robust and unaffected, often hilariously uninhibited in expressing what they really think, they are liable to live with a partner rather than get married or to pick up an old sweetheart and marry despite their kids' disapproval. They have nothing left to lose.

The Age of Integrity is primarily a stage of spiritual growth. Instead   42 of focusing on time running out, we should make it a daily exercise to mark the moment. The present never ages. And instead of trying to maximize our control over our environment, a goal that was perfectly appropriate to the earlier Age of Mastery, now we must cultivate greater appreciation and acceptance of that which we cannot control. Some of the losses of Second Adulthood are inconsolable losses. To accept them without bitterness usually requires making a greater effort to discern the highest spiritual truths that shape the changes and losses of the last passage of life.

COMPREHENSION

1. Define such neologisms as "Middlescence," "Provisional Adulthood," "First Adulthood," "Second Adulthood," and the "Age of Integrity."
2. According to the author, is the major cause of the "New Passages" phenomenon biological, social, psychological, or a combination of all three? Explain.
3. Which group of individuals does Sheehy claim have become the new "at-risk" population for psychological problems? Why?

RHETORIC

1. What is the author's purpose in providing her essay with a "newly-coined term"? What is its intended effect on the reader?
2. The author cites many studies in arguing her point. What evidence does she present that these studies are valid and reliable? How does the presence or absence of an explanation of their methods help to advance or detract from her argument?

3. Is there any particular social group to which the author is referring as she traces the "new passages"? If so, is this social group implied or made explicit?

4. The original essay was divided into sections with bold headlines. What does this suggest about the media format in which the essay was presented? What would be the function of presenting the headlines in bold?

5. Consider the following two sentences in paragraph 3: "There is a revolution in the adult life cycle. People today are leaving childhood sooner, but they are taking longer to grow up and much longer to die." Is this fact, opinion, or a combination of each? Explain.

6. Consider the following evaluative phrases: "smart men and women," "brilliant creator of *Six Degrees of Separation*," "feel a power surge—postmenopausal zest," and "optimum well-being." Do any of these descriptors indicate the bias of the writer? If so, which ones? Do they advance or detract from the main argument?

7. What rhetorical devices in this piece demonstrate that it was written for a general audience rather than for a group of professionals, such as gerontologists, social workers, or nurses?

WRITING

1. Gail Sheehy wrote *Passages* in 1976 and its sequel, *New Passages*, in 1995. Write a 500-word imaginative essay entitled *"Newer Passages"* as it would appear in the year 2015.

2. Write an essay comparing and contrasting two individuals who are approximately the same age but have outlooks on the future vastly different in terms of objectives, goals, and ambitions.

3. Write an autobiography describing yourself as you will be during the stages of life defined in the essay.

BARBARA EHRENREICH   Barbara Ehrenreich was born in Butte, Montana, in 1941. She received a B.A. degree from Reed College and a Ph.D. from Rockefeller University. Ehrenreich, an outspoken feminist and socialist, has challenged many of the theories concerning the changing roles of the sexes in contemporary America. A firm believer that male domination of the health care system, the world of work, and politics has contributed to a growing gap between the "haves" and "have-nots" in America, Ehrenreich's books and essays have brought major attention to issues which many Americans shy away from. Ehrenreich's ideas are articulately discussed in *The Hearts of Men: American Dreams and the Flight from Commitment* (1983), *Fear of Failing: The Inner Life of the Middle Class* (1989), and *The Worst Years of Our Lives: Irreverent Notes from a Decade of Greed* (1990). Ehrenreich is a serious social critic, yet the following essay reveals the lighter side of the author.

BARBARA EHRENREICH

Stop Ironing the Diapers

I was saddened to read, a few weeks ago, that a group of young   1
women is planning a conference on that ancient question: is it possible to raise children and have a career at the same time? A group of
young *men*—now that would be interesting. But I had thought that
among women the issue had been put to rest long ago with the simple retort, Is it possible to raise children *without* having some dependable source of income with which to buy them food, clothing, and
Nintendo?

Of course, what the young women are worried about is whether it's   2
possible to raise children *well* while at the same time maintaining one's
membership in the labor force. They have heard of "quality time." They
are anxious about "missing a stage." They are afraid they won't have
the time to nudge their offsprings' tiny intellects in the direction of the
inevitable SATs.

And no wonder they are worried: while everything else in our lives   3
has gotten simpler, speedier, more microwavable and user-friendly,
child-raising seems to have expanded to fill the time no longer available
for it. At least this is true in the trendsetting, postyuppie class, where it
is not uncommon to find busy young lawyers breast-feeding until the
arrival of molars, reserving entire weekdays for the company of five-
year-olds, and feeling guilty about not ironing the diapers.

This is not only silly but dangerous. Except under the most   4
adverse circumstances—such as homelessness, unsafe living conditions, or lack of spouse and child care—child-raising was not *meant* to
be a full-time activity. No culture on earth outside of mid-century
suburban America has ever deployed one woman per child without
simultaneously assigning her such major productive activities as weav-
ing, farming, gathering, temple maintenance, and tent building. The
reason is that full-time, one-on-one child-raising is not good for
women *or* children. And it is on the strength of that anthropological
generalization, as well as my own two decades of motherhood, that I
offer you my collected tips on *how to raise your children at home in
your spare time.*

1. *Forget the "stages."* The women who are afraid to leave home   5
because they might "miss a stage" do not realize that all "stages" last
more than ten minutes. Sadly, some of them last fifteen years or more.
Even the most cursory parent, who drops in only to change clothes and
get the messages off the answering machine, is unlikely to miss a
"stage." Once a "stage" is over—and let us assume it is a particularly

charming one, involving high-pitched squeals of glee and a rich flow of spittle down the chin—the best thing you can do is *forget it* at once. The reason for this is that no self-respecting six-year-old wants to be reminded that she was once a fat little fool in a high chair; just as no thirteen-year-old wants to be reminded that she was ever, even for a moment, a six-year-old.

I cannot emphasize this point strongly enough: the parent who insists on remembering the "stages"—and worse still, bringing them up—risks turning that drool-faced little darling into a *lifelong enemy*. I mean, try to see it from the child's point of view: suppose you were condemned to being two and a half feet tall, unemployed, and incontinent for an indefinite period of time. Would you want people reminding you of this unfortunate phase for the rest of your life?

2. Forget "quality time." I tried it once on May 15, 1978. I know because it is still penciled into my 1978 appointment book. "Kids," I announced, "I have forty-five minutes. Let's have some quality time!" They looked at me dully in the manner of rural retirees confronting a visitor from the Census Bureau. Finally, one of them said, in a soothing tone, "Sure, Mom, but could it be after *Gilligan's Island?*"

The same thing applies to "talks," as in "Let's sit down and have a little talk." In response to that—or the equally lame "How's school?"— any self-respecting child will assume the demeanor of a prisoner of war facing interrogation. The only thing that works is *low-quality* time: time in which you—and they—are ostensibly doing something else, like housework. Even a two-year-old can dust or tidy and thereby gain an exaggerated sense of self-importance. In fact, this is the only sensible function of housework, the other being to create the erroneous impression that you do not live with children at all.

Also, do not underestimate the telephone as a means of parent-child communication. Teenagers especially recognize it as an instrument demanding full disclosure, in infinite detail, of their thoughts, ambitions, and philosophical outlook. If you want to know what's on their minds, call them from work. When you get home, they'll be calling someone else.

3. Do not overload their intellects. Many parents, mindful of approaching nursery-school entrance exams, PSATs, GREs, and so forth, stay up late into the night reading back issues of *Scientific American* and the *Cliff's Notes* for the *Encyclopaedia Britannica*. This is in case the child should ask a question, such as "Why do horses walk on their hands?" The *overprepared* parent answers with a twenty-minute disquisition on evolution, animal husbandry, and DNA, during which the child slinks away in despair, determined never to ask a question again, except possibly the indispensable "Are we there yet?"

The part-time parent knows better, and responds only in vague and elusive ways, letting her voice trail off and her eyes wander to some mythical landscape, as in: "Well, they don't when they fight. . . . No, then they rear up. . . . Or when they fly . . . like Pegasus . . .

mmmm." This system invariably elicits a stream of eager questions, which can then be referred to a more reliable source.

4. Do not attempt to mold them. First, because it takes too much ₁₂ time. Second, because a child is not a salmon mousse. A child is a temporarily disabled and stunted version of a larger person, whom you will someday know. Your job is to help them overcome the disabilities associated with their size and inexperience so that they get on with being that larger person, and in a form that you might *like* to know.

Hence the part-time parent encourages self-reliance in all things. ₁₃ For example, from the moment my children mastered Pidgin English, they were taught one simple rule: Never wake a sleeping adult. I was mysterious about the consequences, but they became adept, at age two, at getting their own cereal and hanging out until a reasonable hour. Also, contrary to widespread American myth, no self-respecting toddler enjoys having wet and clammy buns. Nor is the potty concept alien to the one-year-old mind. So do not make the common mistake of withholding the toilet facilities until the crisis of nursery-school matriculation forces the issue.

5. Do not be afraid they will turn on you, someday, for being a lousy ₁₄ *parent.* They *will* turn on you. They will also turn on the full-time parents, the cookie-making parents, the Little League parents, and the all-sacrificing parents. If you are at work every day when they get home from school, they will turn on you, eventually, for being a selfish, neglectful careerist. If you are at home every day, eagerly awaiting their return, they will turn on you for being a useless, unproductive layabout. This is all part of the normal process of "individuation," in which one adult ego must be trampled into the dust in order for one fully formed teenage ego to emerge. Accept it.

Besides, a part-time parent is unlikely to ever harbor that most poi- ₁₅ sonous of all parental thoughts: "What I gave up for you. . . !" No child should have to take the rap for wrecking a grown woman's brilliant career. The good part-time parent convinces her children that they are positive assets, without whose wit and insights she would never have gotten the last two promotions.

6. Whether you work outside the home or not, never tell them that being ₁₆ *a mommy is your "job."* Being a mommy is a relationship, not a profession. Nothing could be worse for a child's self-esteem than to think that you think that being with her is *work.* She may come to think that you are involved in some obscure manufacturing process in which she is only the raw material. She may even come to think that her real mom was switched at birth, and that you are the baby-sitter. Which leads to my final tip:

7. Even if you are not a part-time parent, even if you haven't the ₁₇ slightest intention of entering the wide world of wage earning, *pretend that you are one.*

COMPREHENSION

1. What can we infer about Ehrenreich's view of the appropriate role of a mother *outside* the family? Explain.
2. Based upon the content of the essay, would you consider the author to be a "feminist writer"? Why, or why not?
3. What does Ehrenreich mean when she says, "what the young women are worried about is whether it's possible to raise children *well*"?

RHETORIC

1. What is the effect of listing tips on parenthood in a mock instruction-manual format? How would a more conventional essay structure change the tone of the essay?
2. Why does the author place quotation marks around terms such as "stages," "quality time," and "talks"?
3. Ehrenreich provides much irony in challenging contemporary beliefs and rituals among working mothers. How does the accrual of these ironies help to support her thesis?
4. Much of contemporary psychology focuses on the need to nurture children to assure their proper development. How does the author use examples to demonstrate the need for more responsibility among children toward their parents?
5. Why does the author italicize the last five words of her essay?
6. In paragraph 4, the author mentions activities engaged in by previous generations of mothers. Why might she have chosen these particular tasks over more culturally familiar ones?

WRITING

1. Argue for or against the proposition that Ehrenreich has a cold, insensitive view of raising children.
2. Write an essay counseling one group on how to relate to another; for example, children vis-à-vis parents, employees vis-à-vis bosses, and students vis-à-vis teachers.
3. Videotape and watch a two-family comedy television show. Write a descriptive essay exploring the behaviors mothers show toward their children; and compare and contrast these behaviors to the admonitions voiced in Ehrenriech's essay.

MARGARET ATWOOD   Margaret Atwood (b. 1939) is a Canadian poet, novelist, short-story writer, and critic whose work explores the role of personal consciousness in a troubled world. Her second collection of poems, *The Circle Game* (1966), brought her recognition; she is also well known for her novels, including *Surfacing* (1973), *Life before Man* (1979), *The Handmaid's Tale*

(1986), and *Cat's Eye* 1988). Atwood is interested in the complexities of language, and her subjects are wide-ranging, from the personal to the global. In the following essay, Atwood uses a lively, unconventional style to address a serious theme.

MARGARET ATWOOD

The Female Body

. . . entirely devoted to the subject of "The Female Body." Knowing how well
you have written on this topic . . . this capacious topic . . .
—Letter from the *Michigan Quarterly Review*

1. I agree, it's a hot topic. But only one? Look around, there's a wide range. Take my own, for instance.

I get up in the morning. My topic feels like hell. I sprinkle it with water, brush parts of it, rub it with towels, powder it, add lubricant. I dump in the fuel and away goes my topic, my topical topic, my controversial topic, my capacious topic, my limping topic, my nearsighted topic, my topic with back problems, my badly behaved topic, my vulgar topic, my outrageous topic, my aging topic, my topic that is out of the question and anyway still can't spell, in its oversized coat and worn winter boots, scuttling along the sidewalk as if it were flesh and blood, hunting for what's out there, an avocado, an alderman, an adjective, hungry as ever.

2. The basic Female Body comes with the following accessories: garter belt, panti-girdle, crinoline, camisole, bustle, brassiere, stomacher, chemise, virgin zone, spike heels, nose ring, veil, kid gloves, fishnet stockings, fichu, bandeau, Merry Widow, weepers, chokers, barrettes, bangles, beads, lorgnette, feather boa, basic black, compact, Lycra stretch one-piece with modesty panel, designer peignoir, flannel nightie, lace teddy, bed, head.

3. The Female Body is made of transparent plastic and lights up when you plug it in. You press a button to illuminate the different systems. The circulatory system is red, for the heart and arteries, purple for the veins; the respiratory system is blue; the lymphatic system is yellow; the digestive system is green, with liver and kidneys in aqua. The nerves are done in orange and the brain is pink. The skeleton, as you might expect, is white.

The reproductive system is optional, and can be removed. It comes with or without a miniature embryo. Parental judgment can thereby be exercised. We do not wish to frighten or offend.

4. He said, I won't have one of those things in the house. It gives a young girl a false notion of beauty, not to mention anatomy. If a real woman was built like that she'd fall on her face.

She said, If we don't let her have one like all the other girls she'll feel singled out. It'll become an issue. She'll long for one and she'll long to turn into one. Repression breeds sublimation. You know that.

He said, It's not just the pointy plastic tits, it's the wardrobes. The 8 wardrobes and that stupid male doll, what's his name, the one with the underwear glued on.

She said, Better to get it over with when she's young. He said, All 9 right, but don't let me see it.

She came whizzing down the stairs, thrown like a dart. She was 10 stark naked. Her hair had been chopped off, her head was turned back to front, she was missing some toes and she'd been tattooed all over her body with purple ink in a scrollwork design. She hit the potted azalea, trembled there for a moment like a botched angel, and fell.

He said, I guess we're safe. 11

5. The Female Body has many uses. It's been used as a door 12 knocker, a bottle opener, as a clock with a ticking belly, as something to hold up lampshades, as a nutcracker, just squeeze the brass legs together and out comes your nut. It bears torches, lifts victorious wreaths, grows copper wings and raises aloft a ring of neon stars; whole buildings rest on its marble heads.

It sells cars, beer, shaving lotion, cigarettes, hard liquor; it sells diet 13 plans and diamonds, and desire in tiny crystal bottles. Is this the face that launched a thousand products? You bet it is, but don't get any funny big ideas, honey, that smile is a dime a dozen.

It does not merely sell, it is sold. Money flows into this country 14 or that country, flies in, practically crawls in, suitful after suitful, lured by all those hairless pre-teen legs. Listen, you want to reduce the national debt, don't you? Aren't you patriotic? That's the spirit. That's my girl.

She's a natural resource, a renewable one luckily, because those 15 things wear out so quickly. They don't make 'em like they used to. Shoddy goods.

6. One and one equals another one. Pleasure in the female is not a 16 requirement. Pair-bonding is stronger in geese. We're not talking about love, we're talking about biology. That's how we all got here, daughter.

Snails do it differently. They're hermaphrodites, and work in threes. 17

7. Each Female Body contains a female brain. Handy. Makes things 18 work. Stick pins in it and you get amazing results. Old popular songs. Short circuits. Bad dreams.

Anyway: each of these brains has two halves. They're joined 19 together by a thick cord; neural pathways flow from one to the other, sparkles of electric information washing to and fro. Like light on waves. Like a conversation. How does a woman know? She listens. She listens in.

The male brain, now, that's a different matter. Only a thin connec- 20 tion. Space over here, time over there, music and arithmetic in their own sealed compartments. The right brain doesn't know what the left brain is doing. Good for aiming though, for hitting the target when you pull the trigger. What's the target? Who's the target? Who cares? What matters is hitting it. That's the male brain for you. Objective.

This is why men are so sad, why they feel so cut off, why they think 21 of themselves as orphans cast adrift, footloose and stringless in the deep void. What void? she asks. What are you talking about? The void of the universe, he says, and she says Oh and looks out the window and tries to get a handle on it, but it's no use, there's too much going on, too many rustlings in the leaves, too many voices, so she says, Would you like a cheese sandwich, a piece of cake, a cup of tea? And he grinds his teeth because she doesn't understand, and wanders off, not just alone but Alone, lost in the dark, lost in the skull, searching for the other half, the twin who could complete him.

Then it comes to him: he's lost the Female Body! Look, it shines in 22 the gloom, far ahead, a vision of wholeness, ripeness, like a giant melon, like an apple, like a metaphor for "breast" in a bad sex novel; it shines like a balloon, like a foggy noon, a watery moon, shimmering in its egg of light.

Catch it. Put it in a pumpkin, in a high tower, in a compound, in a 23 chamber, in a house, in a room. Quick, stick a leash on it, a lock, a chain, some pain, settle it down, so it can never get away from you again.

COMPREHENSION

1. Why do you think this essay was written? Justify your response.
2. List the different ways in which Atwood views the female body.
3. What distinction does Atwood make between the male and female brains?

RHETORIC

1. What is the tone of Atwood's essay? Supply concrete evidence from her writing.
2. Does the essay contain a thesis? Is it stated or implied?
3. Define the following words in section 2: *fichu, bandeau, Merry Widow, weepers.* Why do the words *bed* and *head* also appear in this list?
4. How does Atwood's use of details and metaphors strengthen her points in the essay? Cite specific examples.
5. What is the object being described in section 4? How does its inclusion help underscore Atwood's point?
6. Why did Atwood choose this particular way to organize her essay? What does it tell the reader about her attitude toward the subject?

7. Is the tone of the final paragraph similar to that of the rest of the essay? Provide evidence from the writing and explain.

WRITING

1. Using a style similar to Atwood's, write a brief essay in which you describe "the female brain," "the male brain," or "the male body".
2. In an argumentative essay, consider the role played by sex-specific toys in reinforcing sexual stereotyping in children. Use Atwood's essay as well as your personal experience as support.
3. Analyze the ways in which sex and the female body have been used in sales and advertising.

MARY LEAKEY   Mary Douglas Leakey (b. 1913) is the director of the Olduvai Gorge Excavations, one of the most important paleontological sites in the world. Among her publications are *Olduvai Gorge* (1971); *Africa's Vanishing Art* (1983); and *Disclosing the Past* (1984), an autobiography. In addition, Mrs. Leakey has contributed numerous papers to *Nature* and other scientific journals. In this essay, a preliminary report on a remarkable find, Leakey provides insight into the challenging field of paleontology.

MARY LEAKEY

Footprints in the Ashes of Time

It happened some 3,600,000 years ago, at the onset of a rainy season. The East African landscape stretched then, much as it does now, in a series of savannas punctuated by wind-sculptured acacia trees. To the east the volcano now called Sadiman heaved restlessly, spewing ash over the flat expanse known as Laetoli.

The creatures that inhabited the region, and they were plentiful, showed no panic. They continued to drift on their random errands. Several times Sadiman blanketed the plain with a thin layer of ash. Tentative showers, precursors of the heavy seasonal rains, moistened the ash. Each layer hardened, preserving in remarkable detail the footprints left by the ancient fauna. The Laetolil Beds, as geologists designate the oldest deposits at Laetoli, captured a frozen moment of time from the remote past—a pageant unique in prehistory.

Our serious survey of the beds, which lie in northern Tanzania 30 miles by road south of Olduvai Gorge, began in 1975 and gained intensity last summer after the discovery of some startling footprints. This article must stand as a preliminary report; further findings will almost certainly modify early interpretations.

Still, what we have discovered to date at Laetoli will cause yet 4
another upheaval in the study of human origins. For in the gray, petrified ash of the beds—among the spoor of the extinct predecessors of
today's elephants, hyenas, hares—we have found hominid footprints
that are remarkably similar to those of modern man. Prints that, in my
opinion, could only have been left by an ancestor of man. Prints that
were laid down an incredible 3,600,000 years ago . . . !

In 1976 Peter Jones, my assistant and a specialist in stone tools, and 5
my youngest son, Philip, noticed what they believed to be a trail of
hominid footprints. After considerable analysis I agreed and announced
the discovery the following year. Of the five prints, three were obscured
by overlying sediment impossible to remove. The two clear examples,
broad and rather curiously shaped, offered few clues to the primate
that had trudged across the plain so long ago.

Nonetheless, the implications of this find were enormous. Dr. Gar- 6
niss Curtis of the University of California at Berkeley undertook to date
the footprint strata. These deposits possess relatively large crystals of
biotite, or black mica. Biotite from ash overlying the prints, when subjected to potassium-argon testing, showed an age of about 3.6 million
years; that from below tested at about 3.8 million years. The footprints
had been preserved sometime within this span. Dr. Richard L. Hay,
also of Berkeley, showed that the ash forming the layers fell within a
month's time.

The hominid footprints attested, in my considered opinion, to the 7
existence of a direct ancestor of man half a million years before the earliest previous evidence—fossils unearthed by Dr. Donald C. Johanson
and his party in the Afar triangle of Ethiopia beginning in 1973.

Faced with this, we largely abandoned our hunt for fossils and 8
focused our three-month campaign of 1978 on the footprints—plotting
and photographing them, making plaster and latex casts, and even
removing certain specimens. While Dr. Paul Abell of the University of
Rhode Island was attempting—delicately and successfully—to quarry
out a block of rhinoceros tracks, he noticed a barely exposed, hominid-
like heel print.

When we removed the surrounding overburden, we found a trail 9
some 23 meters long; only the end of the excavation season in September prevented our following it still farther. Two individuals, one larger,
one smaller, had passed this way 3,600,000 years ago.

The footsteps come from the south, progress northward in a fairly 10
straight line, and end abruptly where seasonal streams have eroded a
small, chaotic canyon through the beds. The nature of the terrain leads
us to believe that the footprints, though now covered, remain largely
intact to the south. And that is where we will continue our effort.

The closeness of the two sets of prints indicates that their owners 11
were not walking abreast. Other clues suggest that the hominids may
have passed at different times. For example, the imprints of the smaller
individual stand out clearly. The crispness of definition and sharp out-

lines convince me that they were left on a damp surface that retained the form of the foot.

On the other hand, the prints of the larger are blurred, as if he had shuffled or dragged his feet. In fact, I think that the surface when he passed was loose and dusty, hence the collapsed appearance of his prints. Nonetheless, luck favored us again; the bigger hominid left one absolutely clear print, probably on a patch of once damp ash.

What do these footprints tell us? First, they demonstrate once and for all that at least 3,600,000 years ago, in Pliocene times, what I believe to be man's direct ancestor walked fully upright with a bipedal, free-striding gait. Second, that the form of his foot was exactly the same as ours.

One cannot overemphasize the role of bipedalism in hominid development. It stands as perhaps the salient point that differentiated the forebears of man from other primates. This unique ability freed the hands for myriad possibilities—carrying, tool-making, intricate manipulation. From this single development, in fact, stems all modern technology.

Somewhat oversimplified, the formula holds that this new freedom of forelimbs posed a challenge. The brain expanded to meet it. And mankind was formed.

Even today, millions of years beyond that unchronicled Rubicon, *Homo sapiens* is the only primate to walk upright as a matter of course. And, for better or for worse, *Homo sapiens* dominates the world.

But what of those two hominids who crossed the Laetolil Beds so long ago? We have measured their footprints and the length of their stride. Was the larger one a male, the smaller a female? Or was one mature, the other young? It is unlikely that we will ever know with certainty. For convenience, let us postulate a case of sexual dimorphism and consider the smaller one a female.

Incidentally, following her path produces, at least for me, a kind of poignant time wrench. At one point, and you need not be an expert tracker to discern this, she stops, pauses, turns to the left to glance at some possible threat or irregularity, and then continues to the north. This motion, so intensely human, transcends time. Three million six hundred thousand years ago, a remote ancestor—just as you or I—experienced a moment of doubt.

The French have a proverb: *Plus ça change, plus c'est la même chose*— "The more it changes, the more it is the same." In short, nothing really alters. Least of all, the human condition.

Measurements show the length of the smaller prints to be 18.5 centimeters (slightly more than 7 inches) and 21.5 centimeters for the larger. Stride length averages 38.7 centimeters for the smaller hominid, 47.2 centimeters for the larger. Clearly we are dealing with two small creatures.

An anthropological rule of thumb holds that the length of the foot represents about 15 percent of an individual's height. On this basis—

and it is far from exact—we can estimate the height of the male as perhaps four feet eight inches (1.4 meters); the female would have stood about four feet.

Leg structure must have been very similar to our own. It seems clear to me that the Laetoli hominid, although much older, relates very closely to the remains found by Dr. Johanson in Ethiopia. Dr. Owen Lovejoy of Kent State University in Ohio studied a knee joint from Ethiopia—the bottom of the femur and the top of the tibia—and concluded that the Afar hominid had walked upright, with a free, bipedal gait. 22

Our footprints confirm this. Furthermore, Dr. Louise Robbins of the University of North Carolina, Greensboro, an anthropologist who specializes in the analysis of footprints, visited Laetoli and concluded: "The movement pattern of the individual is a bipedal walking gait, actually a stride—and quite long relative to the creature's small size. Weight-bearing pressure patterns in the prints resemble human ones." 23

I can only assume that the prints were left by the hominids whose fossils we also found in the beds. In addition to part of a child's skeleton, we uncovered adult remains—two lower jaws, a section of upper jaw, and a number of teeth. 24

Where can we place the Laetoli hominids and their Afar cousins in the incomplete mosaic of the rise of man? This question, quite honestly, is a subject of some contention among paleontologists. One school, including Dr. Johanson, classifies them as australopithecines. 25

But the two forms of *Australopithecus*, gracile and robust, represent, in my opinion, evolutionary dead ends. These man apes flourished for their season, and perished—unsuccessful twigs on the branch that produced mankind. Of course, the Laetoli hominid resembles the gracile *Australopithecus*, but I believe that, so far back in time, all the hominids shared certain characteristics. However, the simple evidence of the footprints, so very much like our own, indicates to me that the Laetoli hominid stands in the direct line of man's ancestry. 26

We have encountered one anomaly. Despite three years of painstaking search by Peter Jones, no stone tools have been found in the Laetolil Beds. With their hands free, one would have expected this species to have developed tools or weapons of some kind. But, except for the ejecta of erupting volcanoes, we haven't found a single stone introduced into the beds. So we can only conclude, at least for the moment, that the hominids we discovered had not yet attained the toolmaking stage. 27

But in the end one cannot escape the supreme importance of the presence of hominids at Laetoli. Sometimes, during the excavating season, I go out and watch the dusk settle over the gray tuff with its eerie record of time long past. The slanting light of evening throws the hominid prints into sharp relief, so sharp that they could have been left this morning. 28

I cannot help but think about the distant creatures who made them. Where did they come from? Where were they going? We simply do not 29 know. It has been suggested that they were merely crossing this scorched plain toward the greener ridges to the north. Perhaps so.

In any case, those footprints out of the deep past, left by the oldest known hominids, haunt the imagination. Across the gulf of time I can only wish them well on that prehistoric trek. It was, I believe, part of a greater and more perilous journey, one that—through millions of years of evolutionary trial and error, fortune and misfortune—culminated in the emergence of modern man.

COMPREHENSION

1. What is the author's main purpose in this essay? Cite evidence to support your answer.
2. In which paragraph do you discover that Leakey is describing human footprints? What effect is she trying to achieve by delaying this revelation? Does Leakey do an effective job of proving that the footprints "could only have been left by an ancestor of man"? What other interpretation is there? What facts support another interpretation?
3. What is the author's relationship to Donald C. Johanson? How often and where do his theories appear?

RHETORIC

1. Define the following words: *hominid* (paragraph 4); *Pliocene* (paragraph 13); and *dimorphism* (paragraph 17). Is the language in this section specialized? Explain.
2. Use a dictionary or encyclopedia to define *Rubicon* (paragraph 16). In what sense is "that unchronicled Rubicon" a turning point? How does the allusion strengthen the idea?
3. How does the author create her introduction in this essay?
4. What sort of reasoning process does Leakey apply to the development of her essay? Trace this process as carefully as you can.
5. Many of Leakey's paragraphs are relatively short. Cite representative examples, and explain why the overall strategy is successful.
6. Is this report meant to be read by scientists or by lay people? What clues tell you this?

WRITING

1. If Leakey is right, what implications are there to the discovery that humankind is far older than we once believed? In what ways are we like our hominid ancestors? Write an essay explaining the connection between humans and hominids.
2. There is a school of thought that entirely rejects the findings of Leakey and others on the subject of evolution and fossil remains. This school, called "creationism," argues that the biblical account in the Book of Genesis is

incompatible with scientific evidence and that where the two disagree, the revealed word of God is a better indicator than is a fossil record. Write an essay explaining which side of this debate you find more compelling. Offer reasons and evidence to support your position.

3. Leakey asserts that "nothing really alters. Least of all the human condition." From your reading of this essay and your perspective, is she right or wrong? Answer this question in an argumentative essay.

PAUL THEROUX Paul Theroux (b. 1941) has explored the effects of colonialism on Americans and Europeans—effects which he experienced firsthand as a teacher in Malawi, Uganda, and Singapore—in books such as *Saint Jack* (1973) and *The Consul's File* (1977). Theroux's other fictional works include *The Mosquito Coast* (1982), *O-Zone* (1986), and *Chicago Loop* (1990). In addition, he has written a number of travel books, among them *The Great Railway Bazaar* (1975) and *The Old Patagonian Express* (1979). In the following essay, Theroux explores the meaning of masculinity and its relation to writing.

PAUL THEROUX

Being a Man

There is a pathetic sentence in the chapter "Fetishism" in Dr. Norman Cameron's book *Personality Development and Psychopathology.* It goes, "Fetishists are nearly always men; and their commonest fetish is a woman's shoe." I cannot read that sentence without thinking that it is just one more awful thing about being a man—and perhaps it is an important thing to know about us.

I have always disliked being a man. The whole idea of manhood in America is pitiful, in my opinion. This version of masculinity is a little like having to wear an ill-fitting coat for one's entire life (by contrast, I imagine femininity to be an oppressive sense of nakedness). Even the expression "Be a man!" strikes me as insulting and abusive. It means: Be stupid, be unfeeling, obedient, soldierly, and stop thinking. Man means "manly"—how can one think about men without considering the terrible ambition of manliness? And yet it is part of every man's life. It is a hideous and crippling lie; it not only insists on difference and connives at superiority, it is also by its very nature destructive—emotionally damaging and socially harmful.

The youth who is subverted, as most are, into believing in the masculine ideal is effectively separated from women and he spends the rest of his life finding women a riddle and a nuisance. Of course, there is a female version of this male affliction. It begins with mothers encouraging little girls to say (to other adults) "Do you like my new dress?" In a sense, little girls are traditionally urged to please adults with a kind of coquettishness, while boys are enjoined to behave like monkeys towards each other. The nine-year-old coquette proceeds to become womanish in a subtle power game in which she learns to be sexually indispensable, socially decorative, and always alert to a man's sense of inadequacy.

Femininity—being ladylike—implies needing a man as witness and seducer; but masculinity celebrates the exclusive company of men. That is why it is so grotesque; and that is also why there is no manliness without inadequacy—because it denies men the natural friendship of women.

It is very hard to imagine any concept of manliness that does not belittle women, and it begins very early. At an age when I wanted to meet girls—let's say the treacherous years of thirteen to sixteen—I was told to take up a sport, get more fresh air, join the Boy Scouts, and I was urged not to read so much. It was the 1950s and if you asked too many questions about sex you were sent to camp—boy's camp, of course: the nightmare. Nothing is more unnatural or prisonlike than a boy's camp, but if it were not for them we would have no Elks' Lodges, no pool rooms, no boxing matches, no Marines.

And perhaps no sports as we know them. Everyone is aware of how few in number are the athletes who behave like gentlemen. Just as high school basketball teaches you how to be a poor loser, the manly attitude towards sports seems to be little more than a recipe for creating bad marriages, social misfits, moral degenerates, sadists, latent rapists, and just plain louts. I regard high school sports as a drug far worse than marijuana, and it is the reason that the average tennis champion, say, is a pathetic oaf.

Any objective study would find the quest for manliness essentially right-wing, puritanical, cowardly, neurotic, and fueled largely by a fear of women. It is also certainly philistine. There is no book-hater like a Little League coach. But indeed all the creative arts are obnoxious to the manly ideal, because at their best the arts are pursued by uncompetitive and essentially solitary people. It makes it very hard for a creative youngster, for any boy who expresses the desire to be alone seems to be saying that there is something wrong with him.

It ought to be clear by now that I have something of an objection to the way we turn boys into men. It does not surprise me that when the President of the United States has his customary weekend off he dresses like a cowboy—it is both a measure of his insecurity and his willingness to please. In many ways, American culture does little more for a man than prepare him for modeling clothes in the L. L. Bean catalogue. I take this as a personal insult because for many years I found it impossible to admit to myself that I wanted to be a writer. It was my guilty secret, because being a writer was incompatible with being a man.

There are people who might deny this, but that is because the American writer, typically, has been so at pains to prove his manliness that we have come to see literariness and manliness as mingled qualities. But first there was a fear that writing was not a manly profession—indeed, not a profession at all. (The paradox in American letters is that it has always been easier for a woman to write and for a man to be published.) Growing up, I had thought of sports as wasteful and humiliating, and the idea of manliness was a bore. My wanting to become a writer was not a flight from that oppressive role-playing, but I quickly saw that it was at odds with it. Everything in stereotyped manliness goes against the life of the mind. The Hemingway personality is too tedious to go into here, and in any case his exertions are well known, but certainly it was not until this aberrant behavior was examined by feminists in the 1960s that any male writer dared question the pugnacity in Hemingway's fiction. All the bullfighting and arm wrestling and elephant shooting diminished Hemingway as a writer, but it is consistent with a prevailing attitude in American writing: one cannot be a male writer without first proving that one is a man.

It is normal in America for a man to be dismissive or even somewhat apologetic about being a writer. Various factors make it easier. There is a heartiness about journalism that makes it acceptable—journalism is the manliest form of American writing and, therefore, the profession the most independent-minded women seek (yes, it is an illusion, but that is my point). Fiction-writing is equated with a kind of dispirited failure and is only manly when it produces wealth—money is masculinity. So is drinking. Being a drunkard is another assertion, if misplaced, of manliness. The American male writer is traditionally proud of his heavy drinking. But we are also a very literal-minded people. A man proves his manhood in America in old-fashioned ways. He kills lions, like Hemingway; or he hunts ducks, like Nathanael West, or he makes pronouncements like, "A man should carry enough knife to defend himself with," as James Jones once said to a *Life* interviewer. Or he says he can drink you under the table. But even tiny drunken William Faulkner loved to mount a horse and go fox hunting, and Jack Kerouac roistered up and down Manhattan in a lumberjack shirt (and spent every night of *The Subterraneans* with his mother in Queens). And we are familiar with the lengths to which Norman Mailer is prepared, in his endearing way, to prove that he is just as much a monster as the next man.

When the novelist John Irving was revealed as a wrestler, people took him to be a very serious writer, and even a bubble reputation like Eric *(Love Story)* Segal's was enhanced by the news that he ran the marathon in a respectable time. How surprised we would be if Joyce Carol Oates were revealed as a sumo wrestler or Joan Didion active in pumping iron. "Lives in New York City with her three children" is the typical woman writer's biographical note, for just as the male writer must prove he has achieved a sort of muscular manhood, the woman writer—or rather her publicists—must prove her motherhood.

There would be no point in saying any of this if it were not generally accepted that to be a man is somehow—even now in feminist-influenced America—a privilege. It is on the contrary an unmerciful and punishing burden. Being a man is bad enough; being manly is appalling (in this sense, women's lib has done much more for men than for women). It is the sinister silliness of men's fashions and a clubby attitude in the arts. It is the subversion of good students. It is the so-called Dress Code of the Ritz-Carlton Hotel in Boston, and it is the institutionalized cheating in college sports. It is the most primitive insecurity.

And this is also why men often object to feminism, but are afraid to explain why: of course women have a justified grievance, but most men believe—and with reason—that their lives are just as bad.   13

COMPREHENSION

1. What does Theroux hate about being a man?

2. What does the writer mean by "the terrible ambition of manliness"?

3. According to Theroux, why are writing and manliness at odds?

RHETORIC

1. What is Theroux's thesis? Where is it stated?

2. Explain Theroux's choice for an introductory paragraph. How does it help to set up the reader for what follows? What was the writer's intention?

3. Does the writer's example in paragraph 5 help validate the paragraph's topic sentence? Why, or why not?

4. Explain the reference to the L. L. Bean catalogue in paragraph 8. What connection is Theroux making between it and the American concept of masculinity?

5. Trace the sequence of ideas through the paragraphs in the essay. Do they follow a coherent pattern? How does the conclusion help to unify the ideas presented?

6. What argumentative strategies does Theroux employ in this essay?

WRITING

1. Write a definition essay on *manliness,* considering both the denotative and the connotative meanings of the word. Use support from Theroux's work.

2. Theroux states that being a man is "an unmerciful and punishing burden." Write an argumentative essay in which you agree or disagree with this assessment.

3. Write an essay in which you pretend to be a member of the opposite sex for a day. Describe how your conditions, behaviors, and perceptions might be different. Consider how others would respond to you.

GLORIA STEINEM   Gloria Steinem was born in 1934 and raised in Toledo, Ohio; she attended Smith College, receiving a B.A. in government in 1956. A noted feminist and political activist, Steinem in 1968 helped to found *New York* magazine; in 1971 she cofounded *Ms.* magazine and has served as its

*Chapter Five
Gender and
Human
Development*

editor since then. Whether campaigning for Robert Kennedy and George McGovern or helping to defend and raise money for Angela Davis and the United Farmworkers, Steinem has been on the cutting edge of American politics for more than two decades. Her books include a collection of essays, *Outrageous Acts and Everyday Rebellions* (1983) and *Revolution from Within: A Book of Self-Esteem* (1992). The essay that follows reflects Steinem's keen ability to relate ideas and issues to the lives of women today.

GLORIA STEINEM

Erotica and Pornography

Human beings are the only animals that experience the same sex 1 drive at times when we can—and cannot—conceive.

Just as we developed uniquely human capacities for language, plan- 2 ning, memory, and invention along our evolutionary path, we also developed sexuality as a form of expression; a way of communicating that is separable from our need for sex as a way of perpetuating ourselves. For humans alone, sexuality can be and often is primarily a way of bonding, of giving and receiving pleasure, bridging differentness, discovering sameness, and communicating emotion.

We developed this and other human gifts through our ability to 3 change our environment, adapt physically, and in the long run, to affect our own evolution. But as an emotional result of this spiraling path away from other animals, we seem to alternate between periods of exploring our unique abilities to change new boundaries, and feelings of loneliness in the unknown that we ourselves have created; a fear that sometimes sends us back to the comfort of the animal world by encouraging us to exaggerate our sameness.

The separation of "play" from "work," for instance, is a problem 4 only in the human world. So is the difference between art and nature, or an intellectual accomplishment and a physical one. As a result, we celebrate play, art, and invention as leaps into the unknown; but any imbalance can send us back to nostalgia for our primate past and the conviction that the basics of work, nature, and physical labor are somehow more worthwhile or even moral.

In the same way, we have explored our sexuality as separable from 5 conception: a pleasurable, empathetic bridge to strangers of the same species. We have even invented contraception—a skill that has probably existed in some form since our ancestors figured out the process of birth—in order to extend this uniquely human difference. Yet we also have times of atavistic suspicion that sex is not complete—or even legal or intended-by-god—if it cannot end in conception.

256

No wonder the concepts of "erotica" and "pornography" can be so crucially different, and yet so confused. Both assume that sexuality can be separated from conception, and therefore can be used to carry a personal message. That's a major reason why, even in our current culture, both may be called equally "shocking" or legally "obscene," a word whose Latin derivative means "dirty, containing filth." This gross condemnation of all sexuality that isn't harnessed to childbirth and marriage has been increased by the current backlash against women's progress. Out of fear that the whole patriarchal structure might be upset if women really had the autonomous power to decide our reproductive futures (that is, if we controlled the most basic means of production), right-wing groups are not only denouncing prochoice abortion literature as "pornographic," but are trying to stop the sending of all contraceptive information through the mails by invoking obscenity laws. In fact, Phyllis Schlafly recently denounced the entire Women's Movement as "obscene."

Not surprisingly, this religious, visceral backlash has a secular, intellectual counterpart that relies heavily on applying the "natural" behavior of the animal world to humans. That is questionable in itself, but these Lionel Tiger-ish studies make their political purpose even more clear in the particular animals they select and the habits they choose to emphasize. The message is that females should accept their "destiny" of being sexually dependent and devote themselves to bearing and rearing their young.

Defending against such reaction in turn leads to another temptation: to merely reverse the terms, and declare that *all* nonprocreative sex is good. In fact, however, this human activity can be as constructive or destructive, moral or immoral, as any other. Sex as communication can send messages as different as life and death; even the origins of "erotica" and "pornography" reflect that fact. After all, "erotica" is rooted in *eros* or passionate love, and thus in the idea of positive choice, free will, the yearning for a particular person. (Interestingly, the definition of erotica leaves open the question of gender.) "Pornography" begins with a root meaning "prostitution" or "female captives," thus letting us know that the subject is not mutual love, or love at all, but domination and violence against women. (Though, of course, homosexual pornography may imitate this violence by putting a man in the "feminine" role of victim.) It ends with a root meaning "writing about" or "description of" which puts still more distance between subject and object, and replaces a spontaneous yearning for closeness with objectification and a voyeur.

The difference is clear in the words. It becomes even more so by example.

Look at any photo or film of people making love; really making love. The images may be diverse, but there is usually a sensuality and touch and warmth, an acceptance of bodies and nerve endings. There is always a spontaneous sense of people who are there because they *want* to be, out of shared pleasure.

Now look at any depiction of sex in which there is clear force, or an unequal power that spells coercion. It may be very blatant, with weapons or torture or bondage, wounds and bruises, some clear humiliation, or an adult's sexual power being used over a child. It may be much more subtle: a physical attitude of conqueror and victim, the use of race or class difference to imply the same thing, perhaps a very unequal nudity, with one person exposed and vulnerable while the other is clothed. In either case, there is no sense of equal choice or equal power.

The first is erotic: a mutually pleasurable, sexual expression between people who have enough power to be there by positive choice. It may or may not strike a sense-memory in the viewer, or be creative enough to make the unknown seem real; but it doesn't require us to identify with a conquerer or a victim. It is truly sensuous, and may give us a contagion of pleasure.

The second is pornographic: its message is violence, dominance, and conquest. It is sex being used to reinforce some inequality, or to create one, or to tell us the lie that pain and humiliation (ours or someone else's) are really the same as pleasure. If we are to feel anything, we must identify with conqueror or victim. That means we can only experience pleasure through the adoption of some degree of sadism or masochism. It also means that we may feel diminished by the role of conqueror, or enraged, humiliated, and vengeful by sharing identity with the victim.

Perhaps one could simply say that erotica is about sexuality, but pornography is about power and sex-as-weapon—in the same way we have come to understand that rape is about violence, and not really about sexuality at all.

Yes, it's true that there are women who have been forced by violent families and dominating men to confuse love with pain; so much so that they have become masochists. (A fact that in no way excuses those who administer such pain.) But the truth is that, for most women—and for men with enough humanity to imagine themselves into the predicament of women—true pornography could serve as aversion therapy for sex.

Of course, there will always be personal differences about what is and is not erotic, and there may be cultural differences for a long time to come. Many women feel that sex makes them vulnerable and therefore may continue to need more sense of personal connection and safety before allowing any erotic feelings. We now find competence and expertise erotic in men, but that may pass as we develop those qualities in ourselves. Men, on the other hand, may continue to feel less vulnerable, and therefore more open to such potential danger as sex with strangers. As some men replace the need for submission from childlike women with the pleasure of cooperation from equals, they may find a partner's competence to be erotic, too.

Such group changes plus individual differences will continue to be reflected in sexual love between people of the same gender, as well as between women and men. The point is not to dictate sameness, but to discover ourselves and each other through sexuality that is an exploring, pleasurable, empathetic part of our lives; a human sexuality that is unchained both from unwanted pregnancies and from violence.

But that is a hope, not a reality. At the moment, fear of change is increasing both the indiscriminate repression of all nonprocreative sex in the religious and "conservative" male world, and the pornographic vengeance against women's sexuality in the secular world of "liberal" and "radical" men. It's almost futuristic to debate what is and is not truly erotic, when many women are again being forced into compulsory motherhood, and the number of pornographic murders, tortures, and woman-hating images are on the increase in both popular culture and real life.

It's a familiar division: wife or whore, "good" woman who is constantly vulnerable to pregnancy or "bad" woman who is unprotected from violence. *Both* roles would be upset if we were to control our own sexuality. And that's exactly what we must do. 19

In spite of all our atavistic suspicions and training for the "natural" role of motherhood, we took up the complicated battle for reproductive freedom. Our bodies had borne the health burden of endless births and poor abortions, and we had a greater motive for separating sexuality and conception. 20

Now we have to take up the equally complex burden of explaining that all nonprocreative sex is *not* alike. We have a motive: our right to a uniquely human sexuality, and sometimes even to survival. As it is, our bodies have too rarely been enough our own to develop erotica in our own lives, much less in art and literature. And our bodies have too often been the objects of pornography and the woman-hating, violent practice that it preaches. Consider also our spirits that break a little each time we see ourselves in chains or full labial display for the conquering male viewer, bruised or on our knees, screaming a real or pretended pain to delight the sadist, pretending to enjoy what we don't enjoy, to be blind to the images of our sisters that really haunt us—humiliated often enough ourselves by the truly obscene idea that sex and the domination of women must be combined. 21

Sexuality *is* human, free, separate—and so are we. 22

But until we untangle the lethal confusion of sex with violence, there will be more pornography and less erotica. There will be little murders in our beds—and very little love. 23

COMPREHENSION

1. What thesis does the author develop in this essay?

2. How does Steinem define the terms *erotica* and *pornography?* What is the essential distinction that the author draws between these two words?

3. In what ways do the concepts of erotica and pornography affect women's lives?

1. Look up the words *erotica* and *pornography* in the *Oxford English Dictionary (OED)* or any large dictionary. Trace the etymology of these two words and any shifts in meaning.

2. Use the dictionary as necessary to understand the following biological, psychological, and sociological terms: *evolutionary* (paragraph 2); *environment* (paragraph 3); *primate* (paragraph 4); *atavistic* (paragraph 5); *patriarchal* (paragraph 6); *voyeur* (paragraph 8); *sadism* and *masochism* (paragraph 13); and *aversion therapy* (paragraph 15).

3. Why does the author delay the introduction of her key topic until paragraph 6? What is the relevance of the first five paragraphs? How are these paragraphs developed?

4. What is the relevance of definition to the essay's development?

5. Explain Steinem's use of comparison and contrast to structure parts of this essay.

6. Examine the author's use of illustration in the essay.

WRITING

1. Do you accept the author's distinction between erotica and pornography? Answer this question in an argumentative essay.

2. Describe and evaluate an erotic scene that you have viewed in a film or read in a book.

3. Should pornography be banned? Answer this question in an essay.

MICHAEL DORRIS   Michael Dorris (b. 1945), a member of the Modoc tribe and a native of Washington, is a professor of anthropology and Native-American studies at Dartmouth College. He has written, among other works, *The Broken Cord: A Family's Ongoing Struggles with Fetal Alcohol Syndrome* (1987). He has also written about the Native-American experience in books such as *Native Americans: Five Hundred Years After Cromwell* (1975). He and his wife, Louise Erdrich, coauthored a novel, *The Crown of Columbus* (1991). In the article below, Dorris shares his feelings about parenting.

MICHAEL DORRIS

What Men Are Missing

I've been changing diapers now for twenty years, half of that time
as the single adoptive parent of three young children, and half—with
three more daughters, the oldest of whom is now seven—as a partner
in a two-career marriage. I started with cloth in 1971, graduated to

plastic in 1976, and am ending up, in 1991, with biodegradable. That's progress. By necessity, I've learned to become sanguine about certain inevitable tribulations (chicken pox, science fairs, the escalating price of sneakers) and fairly proficient at handling others (laundry, birthday parties, interviewing baby-sitters). I can tell a snappy version of "Cinderella," make peanut-butter-and-jelly sandwiches in the dark, and qualify for membership in the chauffeur's union.

When I was growing up as an only child, I used to envy my friends with younger siblings. I'd listen to their complaints about tagalong brothers and sisters, about the combustion around the breakfast table or the chaos of bedtime, and long for the excitement of a crowded house. My mother, widowed after only four years of marriage, had moved back to Louisville to live with my grandmother and my aunt, and throughout my youth I was doted upon, listened to, encouraged in every project by three smart and independent women. They led me to believe that I could accomplish anything I set my mind to, that nothing was impossible.

Perhaps as an adult I was especially impatient to be a father because I missed having one of my own as I grew up, though probably the impulse is not so obscure. Due to the unusual circumstances of my upbringing, I was spared much of the gender typecasting that discourages a good number of men from taking an active role in the primary care of their offspring—because of embarrassment or ignorance of the rewards, or through a basic lack of self-confidence.

Women, it should be noted, can be as susceptible to the mythos of the bumbling, inept man-about-the-house as men, though they suffer a different, less abstract consequence when the prophecy is fulfilled. During the tenure of my bachelor fatherhood, the immediate reaction to my situation on the part of certain female acquaintances was to express condolence for my mommy-deprived children and to wonder who, for instance, bathed and dressed the babies—as if the only way our family could function was via Mary Poppins. There's no explaining to people weaned on *The Donna Reed Show* and *Father Knows Best* that the nuclear family is but one style among several or that children tend to accept as "normal" any arrangement that is loving, consistent, and secure.

I never theorized about such matters all that much—there was too much else to do in the space of each day—but then again I never quite anticipated that fatherhood would turn out to be my most demanding profession (though teaching at Dartmouth College and writing books paid the bills) and constant occupation: a never-ending round of shopping, cleaning, cajoling, and being late for appointments. I didn't expect to be stigmatized with stereotypes, whether of the patronizing, sexist *3 Men and a Baby* variety or of the unctuous, flat-footed, loser-tinged "house husband" stripe.

In my family, the choice to be a single parent was regarded as a viable, normal option, as potentially available (except for the hurdle of biology) to a male who wanted children as it was to a female. After all, gender does not, on a day-to-day basis, make the balancing act of work and responsibility for children easier to manage. When a school or a day-care center closes for "spring vacation" right when a deadline or important meeting is scheduled, you get no extra points for having a Y chromosome.

That's not to say you don't receive a few strange, perhaps even initially sympathetic, glances—the body-language equivalent of "Huh?" or "Ah!"—when you decline an opportunity because you have a prior engagement to read *The Little Engine That Could.* When "real" work is on the table, career men *and* women are expected to be 100 percent on the job.

Last week, for instance, when my wife had to go to Seattle for an important conference, I was unexpectedly summoned to be interviewed the next morning on a national TV news program as a result of my 1989 book on fetal alcohol syndrome, *The Broken Cord.* The good news was that I didn't have time to be nervous, because—the bad news—it meant I had to have our three little girls dressed for school, fed, and in the studio waiting room by 6:30 A.M. I did have the forethought to ask the producer to make sure that the small Vermont affiliate station would provide child care while I was on the air, but somehow that request got lost in the scramble, and no one was free when I arrived. My face and voice may have been beamed to a million viewers by satellite for five minutes, but all the while my mind was on the pointy-edged glass table in the room where my daughters watched cartoons. Don't ask me what I said.

The truth is, though, I wouldn't trade my decades of crayons ground into the carpet and playpens set up in the living room. To experience intimately the freshness of life with a child is to be dazzled all over again by the surprise of snow, the gratification of a wish come true. Fathers who for whatever reason miss these moments are forever cut off from the quintessentially human acts repeated by a new generation. To nurture is, on some basic level, to *be* nurtured—and no matter how old, how successful, we become, we never cease to yearn for that consolation. To divide the labor of parenthood too rigidly along conventional lines—the men on one side, women and children on the other—may satisfy the accepted practice of patriarchal tradition, but it's not a mode of existence carved in stone. Other societies have always organized family life differently. The goal should be to find an equitable pattern that satisfies all parties rather than one that simply conforms to a generic sitcom plot.

When in 1981 I fell in love with Louise Erdrich (and she, miraculously, fell in love back) and we got married, at least one thing soon became clear: parenthood is a new ball game when done in concert. Raising children with a spouse or a partner as opposed to solo is, at best, like the difference between pedaling a bicycle and traveling in a car with alternating drivers: there's a greater chance to occasionally look at a map, to notice where you're headed, and to view the scenery along the way.

As the oldest of seven siblings, Louise was practiced, relatively confident, and calmly undaunted as the new mother of my three older children. That doesn't mean that the transition from living in a household headed by a single man to one operated by a husband and a wife was automatic or free of stress. Much of my identity had become anchored in "doing it alone," and at first it wasn't easy to share decision making, responsibility—or credit.

Moreover, Louise and I both aspire to careers as writers as well as to warm, rewarding relationships with our children. In delineating our jointly inhabited territory we were determined not to respect artificial or hypothetical boundaries. She no more wanted to completely take over the province of the home than I wanted to totally give it up, but how to carve up the individual precincts? Who cooked, and on what days? Who did the laundry and the shopping? Who went to PTA while who put the children to bed? Who put the kid into the car seat and who took her out? And of course: diapers.

With the births—in 1984, 1985, and 1989—of three more daughters, our lives became even more hectic. (The resolution of at least one issue was incontrovertible: Louise gave birth.) From our collective gene pool (Chippewa-Modoc-Irish-German-French) emerged a trio of personalities so disparate as to define the limits of diversity within the species.

Persia, now seven, is pure heart. Even as a baby she was empathic, looking up at us in condolence when she needed a midnight change or a feeding. She's an actress, a ballerina, a would-be equestrienne. She weeps freely for either joy or sorrow, and always with great gusto. Her dolls are dressed in the latest styles, told stories, and bathed daily. Persia has the look in her eye that as a child the French Lieutenant's Woman must have sported: romantic, enigmatic, mesmerizing.

Pallas, just turned six, is all mind. As a toddler she insisted upon sleeping each night not with a teddy bear but with a red block of wood. Her passion is spiders, and her joy is that one tiny brown arachnid has spun a delicate web in an eave above her bed. When we asked what she wanted for her birthday this year, she said wistfully and despondently, "I have a dream, but I know it can't come true."

"Try us," her mother implored.

"Well," she said, "I've decided I want to be a carpenter. Do you think I could have a tool chest?"

Compared with her older sisters, Aza already, at two, is iron will, Gertrude Stein's soul transmigrated. Before the age of one she had taught herself how to instantly dismantle, from within, any crib or other restraint devised by modern science. Her first words were, emphatically, "good girl," and she has seemed ever afterward to be immune to self-doubt. The other day, as I was zipping her jacket, I said, "You're a sweetie pie."

"No," she corrected me. "I'm a woman."

It's no accident that whatever Louise and I write, whether fiction or nonfiction, there always seems to be a baby getting born and being

263

cared for. When you're typing with one hand while aiming a bottle of juice at an open mouth with the other, you take your inspiration where you find it. And not just for fiction.

I doubt that we'll ever get all the duties parceled out, or that once distributed they'll stay constant. For now, Louise sorts the laundry. I wash and fold it. We each function periodically as a single parent while the other is immersed in a project or away from home. It's an ongoing trek, with no posted directions, no Michelin guide, no paved surfaces. But we all seem headed in the same direction. 21

COMPREHENSION

1. Why did Dorris want to become a father?
2. What is the "mythos" Dorris refers to in paragraph 4?
3. Does Dorris see a difference between parenting and "real" work?

RHETORIC

1. What is the purpose of the accumulation of details and examples in the introductory paragraph? What do they help to establish about the essay's thesis or writer?
2. What is the point of Dorris's essay? Where does his main idea become apparent?
3. Who is Dorris's audience? What evidence can you find for this?
4. What tone does Dorris use in his essay? Cite examples to support your response.
5. Define these terms used in the essay: *gender typecasting* (paragraph 3); *nuclear family* (paragraph 4); *stereotypes* (paragraph 5).
6. What is the reason for the extended example used in paragraph 8, and how does it serve the overall thrust of the essay?
7. What forms of comparison appear in this essay? How is the comparative method reflected in the essay's conclusion?

WRITING

1. Dorris's essay argues that children can grow up reasonably well in any loving household regardless of how it deviates from the nuclear-family norm. Do you agree or disagree?
2. Debate this proposition in an essay: If given the choice, most American men would choose *not* to be full-time fathers.
3. Write a definition essay entitled "What Is a Father?"

SIGMUND FREUD Sigmund Freud (1856–1939), founder of psychoanalysis, was an excellent writer. His theories concerning the pleasure principle, repression, and infantile sexuality are still controversial; nevertheless, they have had a profound impact upon culture, education, and art. Some of Freud's psychological works include *The Interpretation of Dreams* (1900), *The Psychopathology of Everyday Life* (1904), and *The Ego and the Id* (1923). He also analyzed the relation of culture and psychology in *Totem and Taboo* (1913) and *Moses and Monotheism* (1939). In the following essay, Freud discusses several character types derived from his theory of the libido.

SIGMUND FREUD

Libidinal Types

Observation teaches us that in individual human beings the general features of humanity are embodied in almost infinite variety. If we follow the promptings of a legitimate desire to distinguish particular types in this multiplicity, we must begin by selecting the characteristics to look for and the points of view to bear in mind in making our differentiation. For this purpose physical qualities will be no less useful than mental; it will be most valuable of all if we can make our classification on the basis of a regularly occurring combination of physical and mental characteristics.

It is doubtful whether we are as yet able to discover types of this order, although we shall certainly be able to do so sometime on a basis of which we are still ignorant. If we confine our efforts to defining certain purely psychological types, the libidinal situation will have the first claim to serve as the basis of our classification. It may fairly be demanded that this classification should not merely be deduced from our knowledge or our conjectures about the libido, but that it should be easily verified in actual experience and should help to clarify the mass of our observations and enable us to grasp their meaning. Let it be admitted at once that there is no need to suppose that, even in the psychical sphere, these libidinal types are the only possible ones; if we take other characteristics as our basis of classification we might be able to distinguish a whole series of other psychological types. But there is one rule which must apply to all such types: they must not coincide with specific clinical pictures. On the contrary, they should embrace all the variations which according to our practical standards fall within the category of the normal. In their extreme developments, however, they may well approximate to clinical pictures and so help to bridge the gulf which is assumed to exist between the normal and the pathological.

Now we can distinguish three main libidinal types, according as the subject's libido is mainly allocated to one or another region of the mental apparatus. To name these types is not very easy; following the lines of our depth-psychology, I should be inclined to call them the *erotic,* the *narcissistic* and the *obsessional* type.

The *erotic* type is easily characterized. Erotics are persons whose ⁴ main interest—the relatively largest amount of their libido—is focused on love. Loving, but above all being loved, is for them the most important thing in life. They are governed by the dread of loss of love, and this makes them peculiarly dependent on those who may withhold their love from them. Even in its pure form this type is a very common one. Variations occur according as it is blended with another type and as the element of aggression in it is strong or weak. From the social and cultural standpoint this type represents the elementary instinctual claims of the id, to which the other psychical agencies have become docile.

The second type is that which I have termed the *obsessional*—a ⁵ name which may at first seem rather strange; its distinctive characteristic is the supremacy exercised by the super-ego, which is segregated from the ego with great accompanying tension. Persons of this type are governed by anxiety of conscience instead of by the dread of losing love; they exhibit, we might say, an inner instead of an outer dependence; they develop a high degree of self-reliance, from the social standpoint they are the true upholders of civilization, for the most part in a conservative spirit.

The characteristics of the third type, justly called the *narcissistic,* are ⁶ in the main negatively described. There is no tension between ego and super-ego—indeed, starting from this type one would hardly have arrived at the notion of a super-ego; there is no preponderance of erotic needs; the main interest is focused on self-preservation; the type is independent and not easily overawed. The ego has a considerable amount of aggression available, one manifestation of this being a proneness to activity; where love is in question, loving is preferred to being loved. People of this type impress others as being "personalities"; it is on them that their follow-men are specially likely to lean; they readily assume the role of leader, give a fresh stimulus to cultural development or break down existing conditions.

These pure types will hardly escape the suspicion of being ⁷ deduced from the theory of the libido. But we feel that we are on the firm ground of experience when we turn to the mixed types which are to be found so much more frequently than the unmixed. These new types: the *erotic-obsessional,* the *erotic-narcissistic* and the *narcissistic-obsessional* do really seem to provide a good grouping of the individual psychical structures revealed in analysis. If we study these mixed types we find in them pictures of characters with which we have long been familiar. In the *erotic-obsessional* type the preponderance of the instincts is restricted by the influence of the super-ego: dependence on persons who are *contemporary* objects and, at the same time, on the residues of *former* objects—parents, educators and ideal figures—

is carried by this type to the furthest point. The *erotic-narcissistic* type is perhaps the most common of all. It combines contrasting characteristics which are thus able to moderate one another; studying this type in comparison with the other two erotic types, we can see how aggressiveness and activity go with a predominance of narcissism. Finally, the *narcissistic-obsessional* type represents the variation most valuable from the cultural standpoint, for it combines independence of external factors and regard for the requirements of conscience with the capacity for energetic action, and it reinforces the ego against the super-ego.

It might be asked in jest why no mention has been made of another mixed type which is theoretically possible: the *erotic-obsessional-narcissistic*. But the answer to this jest is serious: such a type would no longer be a type at all, but the absolute norm, the ideal harmony. We thereupon realize that the phenomenon of different *types* arises just in so far as one or two of the three main modes of expending the libido in the mental economy have been favoured at the cost of the others.

Another question that may be asked is what is the relation of these libidinal types to pathology, whether some of them have a special disposition to pass over into neurosis and, if so, which types lead to which forms of neurosis. The answer is that the hypothesis of these libidinal types throws no fresh light on the genesis of the neuroses. Experience testifies that persons of all these types can live free from neurosis. The pure types marked by the undisputed predominance of a single psychical agency seem to have a better prospect of manifesting themselves as pure character-formations, while we might expect that the mixed types would provide a more fruitful soil for the conditioning factors of neurosis. But I do not think that we should make up our mind on these points until they have been carefully submitted to appropriate tests.

It seems easy to infer that when persons of the erotic type fall ill they will develop hysteria, just as those of the obsessional type will develop obsessional neurosis; but even this conclusion partakes of the uncertainty to which I have just alluded. People of the narcissistic type, who, being otherwise independent, are exposed to frustration from the external world, are peculiarly disposed to psychosis; and their mental composition also contains some of the essential conditioning factors which make for criminality.

We know that we have not as yet exact certainty about the aetiological conditions of neurosis. The precipitating occasions are frustrations and inner conflicts: conflicts between the three great psychical agencies, conflicts arising in the libidinal economy by reason of our bisexual disposition, conflicts between the erotic and the aggressive instinctual components. It is the endeavor of the psychology of the neurosis to discover what imparts a pathogenic character to these processes, which are a part of the normal course of mental life.

COMPREHENSION

1. State, in your own words, Freud's thesis in this selection.
2. According to Freud, what types of individuals uphold society? What are their psychological characteristics?
3. What relationship does Freud see between mental illness and these character types?

RHETORIC

1. Freud assumes that the reader is familiar with several psychological terms. Make sure you understand the following: *depth-psychology* (paragraph 3); *id* (paragraph 4); *ego* (paragraph 5); *neuroses* (paragraph 9); *psychosis* (paragraph 10); and *aetiological* (paragraph 11).
2. Does Freud use general or specific language in this essay? How does his choice of language relate to the conclusions he draws in paragraphs 9 to 11?
3. Freud's primary rhetorical technique is classification. Identify his categories, and list the distinguishing characteristics of each class.
4. Explain the relations of paragraphs 1 and 2 to the body of the essay.
5. Freud uses definition frequently in this essay. What kinds of definitions does he use? How do they contribute to the structuring of the essay?
6. Explain the importance of paragraph 7 to the essay's structure. What effect does it have on the classification the author has established?

WRITING

1. Judging from your own observations, how valid is Freud's classification of libidinal types? Write an essay defending or attacking Freud's system.
2. There are innumerable ways to classify people. In a classification essay, devise your own method for analyzing a particular group of people.
3. Take one of Freud's terms—for example, *neurosis*—and write an extended definition of it.

CLASSIC AND CONTEMPORARY

D. H. LAWRENCE David Herbert Lawrence (1885–1930), novelist, essayist, and poet, wrote in the great tradition of English romanticism. He chafed under the conventions of his age and zealously extended the content and style of the English novel. His novels, such as *Sons and Lovers* (1913), *The Rainbow* (1915), *Women in Love* (1921), *The Plumed Serpent* (1926), and *Lady Chatterley's Lover* (1928) are famous for their often disquieting depictions of love and ambition in the modern world. Lawrence also wrote criticism: His *Studies in*

Classic American Literature (1923) is still a revealing, if idiosyncratic, look at American literature. In the following provocative piece, Lawrence equates beauty with sex appeal.

D. H. LAWRENCE

Sex versus Loveliness

It is a pity that *sex* is such an ugly little word. An ugly little word, and really almost incomprehensible. What *is* sex, after all? The more we think about it the less we know.

Science says it is an instinct; but what is an instinct? Apparently an instinct is an old, old habit that has become ingrained. But a habit, however old, has to have a beginning. And there is really no beginning to sex. Where life is, there it is. So sex is no "habit" that has been formed.

Again, they talk of sex as an appetite, like hunger. An appetite; but for what? An appetite for propagation? It is rather absurd. They say a peacock puts on all his fine feathers to dazzle the peahen into letting him satisfy his appetite for propagation. But why should the peahen not put on fine feathers, to dazzle the peacock, and satisfy *her* desire for propagation? She has surely quite as great a desire for eggs and chickens as he has. We cannot believe that her sex-urge is so weak that she needs all that blue splendour of feathers to rouse her. Not at all.

As for me, I never even saw a peahen so much as look at her lord's bronze and blue glory. I don't believe she ever sees it. I don't believe for a moment that she knows the difference between bronze, blue, brown or green.

If I had ever seen a peahen gazing with rapt attention on her lord's flamboyancy, I might believe that he had put on all those feathers just to "attract" her. But she never looks at him. Only she seems to get a little perky when he shudders all his quills at her, like a storm in the trees. Then she does seem to notice, just casually, his presence.

These theories of sex are amazing. A peacock puts on his glory for the sake of a wall-eyed peahen who never looks at him. Imagine a scientist being so naïve as to credit the peahen with a profound, dynamic appreciation of a peacock's colour and pattern. Oh, highly aesthetic peahen!

And a nightingale sings to attract his female. Which is mighty curious, seeing he sings his best when courtship and honeymoon are over and the female is no longer concerned with him at all, but with the young. Well, then, if he doesn't sing to attract her, he must sing to distract her and amuse her while she's sitting.

How delightful, how naïve theories are! But there is a hidden will behind them all. There is a hidden will behind all theories of sex, implacable. And that is the will to deny, to wipe out the mystery of beauty.

269

Because beauty is a mystery. You can neither eat it nor make flannel 9 out of it. Well, then, says science, it is just a trick to catch the female and induce her to propagate. How naïve! As if the female needed inducing. She will propagate in the dark, even—so where, then, is the beauty trick?

Science has a mysterious hatred of beauty, because it doesn't fit in 10 the cause-and-effect chain. And society has a mysterious hatred of sex, because it perpetually interferes with the nice money-making schemes of social man. So the two hatreds made a combine, and sex and beauty are mere propagation appetite.

Now sex and beauty are one thing, like flame and fire. If you hate 11 sex you hate beauty. If you love *living* beauty, you have a reverence for sex. Of course you can love old, dead beauty and hate sex. But to love living beauty you must have a reverence for sex.

Sex and beauty are inseparable, like life and consciousness. And the 12 intelligence which goes with sex and beauty, and arises out of sex and beauty, is intuition. The great disaster of our civilization is the morbid hatred of sex. What, for example, could show a more poisoned hatred of sex than Freudian psycho-analysis?—which carries with it a morbid fear of beauty, "alive" beauty, and which causes the atrophy of our intuitive faculty and our intuitive self.

The deep psychic disease of modern men and women is the dis- 13 eased, atrophied condition of the intuitive faculties. There is a whole world of life that we might know and enjoy by intuition, and by intuition alone. This is denied us, because we deny sex and beauty, the source of the intuitive life and of the insouciance which is so lovely in free animals and in plants.

Sex is the root of which intuition is the foliage and beauty the 14 flower. Why is a woman lovely, if ever, in her twenties? It is the time when sex rises softly to her face, as a rose to the top of a rose bush.

And the appeal is the appeal of beauty. We deny it wherever we can. 15 We try to make the beauty as shallow and trashy as possible. But, first and foremost, sex appeal is the appeal of beauty.

Now beauty is a thing about which we are so uneducated we can 16 hardly speak of it. We try to pretend it is a fixed arrangement: straight nose, large eyes, etc. We think a lovely woman must look like Lillian Gish, a handsome man must look like Rudolph Valentino. So we *think*.

In actual life we behave quite differently. We say: "She's quite beau- 17 tiful, but I don't care for her." Which shows we are using the word *beautiful* all wrong. We should say: "She has the stereotyped attributes of beauty, but she is not beautiful to me."

Beauty is an *experience*, nothing else. It is not a fixed pattern or an 18 arrangement of features. It is something *felt*, a glow or a communicated sense of fineness. What ails us is that our sense of beauty is so bruised and blunted, we miss all the best.

But to stick to the films—there is a greater essential beauty in 19 Charlie Chaplin's odd face than ever there was in Valentino's. There is a bit of true beauty in Chaplin's brows and eyes, a gleam of something pure.

But our sense of beauty is so bruised and clumsy, we don't see it, and don't know it when we do see it. We can only see the blatantly obvious, like the so-called beauty of Rudolph Valentino, which only pleases because it satisfies some ready-made notion of handsomeness.

But the plainest person can look beautiful, can *be* beautiful. It only 21 needs the fire of sex to rise delicately to change an ugly face to a lovely one. That is really sex appeal: the communicating of a sense of beauty.

And in the reverse way, no one can be quite so repellent as a 22 really pretty woman. That is, since beauty is a question of experience, not of concrete form, no one can be as acutely ugly as a really pretty woman. When the sex-glow is missing, and she moves in ugly coldness, how hideous she seems, and all the worse for her externals of prettiness.

What sex is, we don't know, but it must be some sort of fire. For it 23 always communicates a sense of warmth, of glow. And when the glow becomes a pure shine, then we feel the sense of beauty.

But the communicating of the warmth, the glow of sex, is true sex 24 appeal. We all have the fire of sex slumbering or burning inside us. If we live to be ninety, it is still there. Or, if it dies, we become one of those ghastly living corpses which are unfortunately becoming more numerous in the world.

Nothing is more ugly than a human being in whom the fire of sex 25 has gone out. You get a nasty clayey creature whom everybody wants to avoid.

But while we are fully alive, the fire of sex smoulders or burns in us. 26 In youth it flickers and shines; in age it glows softer and stiller, but there it is. We have some control over it; but only partial control. That is why society hates it.

While ever it lives, the fire of sex, which is the source of beauty and 27 anger, burns in us beyond our understanding. Like actual fire, while it lives it will burn our fingers if we touch it carelessly. And so social man, who only wants to be "safe," hates the fire of sex.

Luckily, not many men succeed in being merely social men. The fire 28 of the old Adam smoulders. And one of the qualities of fire is that it calls to fire. Sex-fire here kindles sex-fire there. It may only rouse the smoulder into a soft glow. It may call up a sharp flicker. Or rouse a flame; and then flame leans to flame, and starts a blaze.

Whenever the sex-fire glows through, it will kindle an answer some- 29 where or other. It may only kindle a sense of warmth and optimism. Then you say: "I like that girl; she's a real good sort." It may kindle a glow that makes the world look kindlier, and life feel better. Then you say: "She's an attractive woman. I like her."

Or she may rouse a flame that lights up her own face first, before it 30 lights up the universe. Then you say: "She's a lovely woman. She looks lovely to me."

It takes a rare woman to rouse a real sense of loveliness. It is not that 31 a woman is born beautiful. We say that to escape our own poor, bruised, clumsy understanding of beauty. There have been thousands and thousands of women quite as good-looking as Diane de Poitiers, or Mrs. Langtry, or any of the famous ones. There are today thousands and thousands of superbly good-looking women. But oh, how few lovely women!

And why? Because of the failure of their sex appeal. A good-looking 32 woman becomes lovely when the fire of sex rouses pure and fine in her and flickers through her face and touches the fire in me.

Then she becomes a lovely woman to me, then she is in the living 33 flesh a lovely woman: not a mere photograph of one. And how lovely a lovely woman! But, alas! how rare! How bitterly rare in a world full of unusually handsome girls and women!

Handsome, good-looking, but not lovely, not beautiful. Handsome 34 and good-looking women are the women with good features and the right hair. But a lovely woman is an experience. It is a question of communicated fire. It is a question of sex appeal in our poor, dilapidated modern phraseology. Sex appeal applied to Diane de Poitiers, or even, in the lovely hours, to one's wife—why, it is a libel and a slander in itself. Nowadays, however, instead of the fire of loveliness, it is sex appeal. The two are the same thing, I suppose, but on vastly different levels.

The business man's pretty and devoted secretary is still chiefly valu- 35 able because of her sex appeal. Which does not imply "immoral relations" in the slightest.

Even today a girl with a bit of generosity likes to feel she is helping 36 a man if the man will take her help. And this desire that he shall take her help is her sex appeal. It is the genuine fire, if of a very mediocre heat.

Still, it serves to keep the world of "business" alive. Probably, but 37 for the introduction of the lady secretary into the business man's office, the business man would have collapsed entirely by now. She calls up the sacred fire in her and she communicates it to her boss. He feels an added flow of energy and optimism, and—business flourishes.

There is, of course, the other side of sex appeal. It can be the 38 destruction of the one appealed to. When a woman starts using her sex appeal to her own advantage it is usually a bad moment for some poor devil. But this side of sex appeal has been overworked lately, so it is not nearly as dangerous as it was.

The sex-appealing courtesans who ruined so many men in Balzac 39 no longer find it smooth running. Men have grown canny. They fight shy even of the emotional vamp. In fact, men are inclined to think they smell a rat the moment they feel the touch of feminine sex appeal today.

Which is a pity, for sex appeal is only a dirty name for a bit of life- 40 flame. No man works so well and so successfully as when some woman has kindled a little fire in his veins. No woman does her housework with real joy unless she is in love—and a woman may go on being quietly in love for fifty years almost without knowing it.

If only our civilization had taught us how to let sex appeal flow properly and subtly, how to keep the fire of sex clear and alive, flickering or glowing or blazing in all its varying degrees of strength and communication, we might, all of us, have lived all our lives in love, which means we should be kindled and full of zest in all kinds of ways and for all kinds of things. . . .

Whereas, what a lot of dead ash there is in life now. 42

COMPREHENSION

1. How does Lawrence define *beauty* in his essay?

2. Which scientific definitions of *sex* does the writer oppose? Why?

3. What does Lawrence mean by "Beauty is an *experience*" (paragraph 18)?

RHETORIC

1. In your own words, what is Lawrence's thesis? Where is it in the essay?

2. How does the writer employ humor in his writing? Does it reflect his attitude? Why, or why not? Provide examples of his use of humor.

3. How does Lawrence use comparison in his essay? Does he use any other rhetorical strategies? Justify your response.

4. Where does Lawrence use repetition and parallel structure in his essay? Why does he use these techniques? How do they contribute to his argument?

5. Examine his use of metaphor and similes in paragraph 14. How do they clarify his point? Where else in the essay does Lawrence use figurative language? Cite especially effective uses in the essay.

6. What is the purpose of paragraphs 35, 36, and 37? How do they serve to expand or support Lawrence's views? Do they add coherence to the essay's structure? Why, or why not?

WRITING

1. In an essay entitled "What Is Beauty?" write a definition of the term *beauty,* using both its denotative and connotative meanings. Use examples from Lawrence's essay if applicable.

2. Write an essay that examines how the media (television, movies, magazines, books) influence our notions of beauty and sex appeal. How do their definitions compare or contrast with your own personal view of these issues? Give concrete examples and details.

SUSAN SONTAG Susan Sontag (b. 1933) is an intelligent, witty observer of new trends in literature, art, film, photography, and culture. An American essayist, novelist, short-story writer, and filmmaker, Sontag has written *Against*

Interpretation (1966), advocating the use of the senses when critiquing art, as well as *On Photography* (1976). While battling cancer, she wrote *Illness as Metaphor* (1978), and in 1989 she wrote *AIDS and Its Metaphors.* Sontag's fictional works include *Death Kit* (1967) and *The Volcano Lover* (1992). In the following essay, written in 1975, she reexamines ancient and modern notions of beauty, especially as they apply to women.

SUSAN SONTAG

Beauty

For the Greeks, beauty was a virtue: a kind of excellence. Persons then were assumed to be what we now have to call—lamely, enviously—*whole* persons. If it did occur to the Greeks to distinguish between a person's "inside" and "outside," they still expected that inner beauty would be matched by beauty of the other kind. The well-born young Athenians who gathered around Socrates found it quite paradoxical that their hero was so intelligent, so brave, so honorable, so seductive—and so ugly. One of Socrates' main pedagogical acts was to be ugly—and teach those innocent, no doubt splendid-looking disciples of his how full of paradoxes life really was.

They may have resisted Socrates' lesson. We do not. Several thousand years later, we are more wary of the enchantments of beauty. We not only split off—with the greatest facility—the "inside" (character, intellect) from the "outside" (looks); but we are actually surprised when someone who is beautiful is also intelligent, talented, good.

It was principally the influence of Christianity that deprived beauty of the central place it had in classical ideals of human excellence. By limiting excellence (*virtus* in latin) to *moral* virtue only, Christianity set beauty adrift—as an alienated, arbitrary, superficial enchantment. And beauty has continued to lose prestige. For close to two centuries it has become a convention to attribute beauty to only one of the two sexes: the sex which, however Fair, is always Second. Associating beauty with women has put beauty even further on the defensive, morally.

A beautiful woman, we say in English. But a handsome man. "Handsome" is the masculine equivalent of—and refusal of—a compliment which has accumulated certain demeaning overtones, by being reserved for women only. That one can call a man "beautiful" in French and in Italian suggests that Catholic countries—unlike those countries shaped by the Protestant version of Christianity—still retain some vestiges of the pagan admiration for beauty. But the difference, if one exists, is of degree only. In every modern country that is Christian or post-Christian, women *are* the beautiful sex—to the detriment of the notion of beauty as well as of women.

To be called beautiful is thought to name something essential to women's character and concerns. (In contrast to men—whose essence is to be strong, or effective, or competent.) It does not take someone in the throes of advanced feminist awareness to perceive that the way women are taught to be involved with beauty encourages narcissism, reinforces dependence and immaturity. Everybody (women and men) knows that. For it is "everybody," a whole society, that has identified being feminine with caring about how one *looks*. (In contrast to being masculine—which is identified with caring about what one *is* and *does* and only secondarily, if at all, about how one looks.) Given these stereotypes, it is no wonder that beauty enjoys, at best, a rather mixed reputation.

It is not, of course, the desire to be beautiful that is wrong but the obligation to be—or to try. What is accepted by most women as a flattering idealization of their sex is a way of making women feel inferior to what they actually are—or normally grow to be. For the ideal of beauty is administered as a form of self-oppression. Women are taught to see their bodies in *parts,* and to evaluate each part separately. Breasts, feet, hips, waistline, neck, eyes, nose, complexion, hair, and so on—each in turn is submitted to an anxious, fretful, often despairing scrutiny. Even if some pass muster, some will always be found wanting. Nothing less than perfection will do.

In men, good looks is a whole, something taken in at a glance. It does not need to be confirmed by giving measurements of different regions of the body, nobody encourages a man to dissect his appearance, feature by feature. As for perfection, that is considered trivial— almost unmanly. Indeed, in the ideally good-looking man a small imperfection or blemish is considered positively desirable. According to one movie critic (a woman) who is a declared Robert Redford fan, it is having that cluster of skin-colored moles on one cheek that saves Redford from being merely a "pretty face." Think of the depreciation of women—as well as of beauty—that is implied in that judgment.

"The privileges of beauty are immense," said Cocteau. To be sure, beauty is a form of power. And deservedly so. What is lamentable is that it is the only form of power that most women are encouraged to seek. This power is always conceived in relation to men; it is not the power to do but the power to attract. It is a power that negates itself. For this power is not one that can be chosen freely—at least, not by women— or renounced without social censure.

To preen, for a woman, can never be just a pleasure. It is also a duty. It is her work. If a woman does real work—and even if she has clambered up to a leading position in politics, law, medicine, business, or whatever—she is always under pressure to confess that she still works at being attractive. But in so far as she is keeping up as one of the Fair Sex, she brings under suspicion her very capacity to be objective, professional, authoritative, thoughtful. Damned if they do— women are. And damned if they don't.

One could hardly ask for more important evidence of the dangers of considering persons as split between what is "inside" and what is "outside" than that interminable half-comic half-tragic tale, the oppres-

275

sion of women. How easy it is to start off by defining women as care-takers of their surfaces, and then to disparage them (or find them adorable) for being "superficial." It is a crude trap, and it has worked for too long. But to get out of the trap requires that women get some critical distance from that excellence and privilege which is beauty, enough distance to see how much beauty itself has been abridged in order to prop up the mythology of the "feminine." There should be a way of saving beauty *from* women—and *for* them.

COMPREHENSION

1. How did the Greeks define *beauty?*
2. To what does Sontag attribute the lowered prestige of beauty in our society?
3. According to the author, what are the consequences of associating beauty exclusively with women?

RHETORIC

1. State Sontag's thesis in your own words. What are her supporting ideas? What transitions does she employ?
2. Describe the level of language used by Sontag. Cite specific examples from the essay. What does the level of language tell us about Sontag's intended audience?
3. Discuss the writer's use of punctuation marks in paragraph 7. Consider the purpose they serve in the paragraph and their effectiveness. Why does Sontag begin with a quotation in paragraph 8? How well is it supported by the subsequent sentences?
4. How does Sontag develop an extended definition in this essay?
5. Where does the comparative method appear in this essay?
6. Examine the essay's conclusion. How well does it help to round out Sontag's ideas? How does it compare to the essay's introduction?

WRITING

1. Write an argumentative essay entitled "Beauty Is Power."
2. Write an essay analyzing the importance of physical appearance in your family. Consider issues such as the amount of time, energy, and money individual family members spend on makeup, hair products, and clothes. Do you feel obligated to look attractive at all times?
3. Compare and contrast Sontag's thoughts on beauty to Atwood's essay on the female body. What ideas do these two writers hold in common? In what areas do they differ? Use quotes from both writers to support your claims.

CLASSIC AND CONTEMPORARY:
QUESTIONS FOR COMPARISON

❖

*Chapter Five
Gender and
Human
Development*

1. Compare Lawrence's and Sontag's definitions of *beauty.* What, if anything, do they have in common, and where do they differ? Use particular examples from the essays to support your opinion.

2. Examine the language, style, and content of both essays. Is there anything in either that is indicative of the time it was written? What use do the writers make of figurative language? How do the essays compare and contrast in tone and organization?

3. Consider the social climates in which these essays were written. Are the writers' views consistent with the beliefs of the society in which they exist? Are Sontag's views acceptable today? How were Lawrence's ideas on beauty and sexuality viewed during his lifetime?

CONNECTIONS

1. Evaluate the way that Atwood, Leakey, and Steinem view the human body and the way it functions. Where do they differ in their views? What might Leakey tell Atwood and Steinem about the human female body? Do you think Leakey might share their feminist sensibilities? Consider these questions in essay form.

2. Pretend you are Michael Dorris writing a letter to Barbara Ehrenreich. What advice would he give about parenting? What insights do you think he might share?

3. Using the writings of Freud and Lawrence, explore the issues of sex, love, and personality types. What connections can you make between the views of these two men? Use evidence from their work as well as evidence from the work of any other relevant writer in this section.

4. Write a classification essay entitled "Gender Typecasting," using support from any writer in this section.

5. Compare the level of language and writing styles in the scientific essays of Freud and Leakey. What do they have in common, and how do they differ? Use examples from both works.

6. Using the essay of Theroux (as well as any others in this section), write an essay in which you discuss the role of sports in masculine development.

7. Establish your own definition of what it means to be a man or woman. Refer to at least three of the essays in this section to support your definition.

CHAPTER SIX

Social Processes
and Institutions

Recent studies indicate that American students have a decidedly weak understanding of history and politics. In fact, one-third of all high school juniors cannot identify the main purpose of the Declaration of Independence or say in which fifty-year period it was signed. The Declaration of Independence is one of the selections in this chapter. It appears with other notable essays on history and politics that help us understand our cultural legacies.

Major writers can bring history and politics to life, enabling us to develop a sense of the past and of the various social processes that have influenced the development of cultures over time. By studying the course of history, we develop causal notions of how events are interrelated and how traditions have evolved. Essays, speeches, documents, biographies, narratives, and many other literary forms capture events and illuminate the past while holding up a mirror to the present. History can be brought to life out of the plain but painfully eloquent artifacts of oral culture. On the other hand, Thomas Jefferson employs classical rhetorical structures—notably argumentation—in outlining democratic vistas in the Declaration of Independence. By studying history, we learn to appreciate the texture of past events and their impact on our lives today. This is what the historian Barbara Tuchman terms wisdom, "a decent appreciation of probability."

Even the briefest reflection will remind us of how important social processes and institutions are. But simply, a knowledge of history validates our memory, a remembrance of how important the past is to our current existence. When, for example, Mary Gordon investigates her "roots" in a decidedly subjective essay, she taps into a collective memory of the immigrant experience that most Americans share. Or when Doris Lessing and Martin Luther King, Jr., approach the subject of oppression from diverse perspectives, we are reminded of how important the freedom to know our past is to the creation and preservation of democratic societies.

Only through a knowledge of history and politics can we make informed choices. Through a study of history and politics, we learn about challenges and opportunities, conflicts and their resolutions, and the use and abuse of power across time in numerous cultures and civilizations. It is through the study of historical processes and political institutions that we seek to define ourselves and to learn how we have evolved.

Previewing the Chapter

As you read the selections in this chapter and respond to them in discussion and writing, consider the following questions:

• What specific events does the author concentrate on? What is the time frame?

• What larger historical and political issues concern the author?

• From what perspective does the author treat the subject, from that of participant, observer, commentator, or what?

• What is the author's purpose in treating historical events and personalities: to explain, to instruct, to amuse, to criticize, or to celebrate?

• What does the author learn about history and politics from his or her inquiry into events?

• What sorts of conflicts—historical, political, economic, social, religious—emerge in the essay?

• Are there any correspondences among the essays? What analogies do the authors themselves draw?

• What is the relationship of people and personalities to the events under consideration?

• Which biases and ideological positions do you detect in the authors' works?

• How has your understanding of history and politics been challenged by the essays in this section?

GEORGE WILL George Will (b. 1941) was educated at Trinity College and then at Princeton University, where he received his Ph.D. degree in 1967 in the field of philosophy. Recognized as a leading conservative writer and thinker, he was awarded the Pulitzer Prize for distinguished commentary in 1977. A champion of the idea that only through reason, reflection, and responsibility can humans move toward a more equitable society, his ideas are expressed clearly in many books and in his syndicated columns. Will believes strongly that American society and culture are in a state of crisis; this excerpt from his book *The Leveling Word* addresses one aspect of this crisis.

GEORGE WILL

Straight Line to Calamity

The Senator glanced at the numbers and saw in his mind's eye 1
something frightening: a straight line, ascending. Pat Moynihan had in hand the 1991 natal statistics which, together with those from 1970–1990, produce a graph line pointing straight to calamity.

Fifty years ago 5 percent of American births were to unmarried 2
women. That began to change in the 1960s. By 1970 it was 10 percent. Since then the increasing rate has produced a virtually straight line— almost one percentage point a year for 21 years.

We bandy the word "crisis" so casually it is drained of power. How- 3
ever, America's real crisis can be presented numerically in the percentages of births to unmarried women:

	All Races	Whites	Blacks
1970	10.7	5.6	37.5
1975	14.3	7.3	46.8
1980	17.8	10.2	55.5
1985	22.0	14.5	60.1
1990	28.0	20.1	65.2
1991	29.5	21.8	67.9

What makes the natal statistics alarming is the ascending straight 4
line for the whole society. What makes the statistics terrifying is that the graph line of births to unmarried black women remains straight. That is, the rate of increase is not slowing even at extraordinarily high levels.

Minority births are primarily responsible for the fact that the per- 5
centage of births to unmarried women is over 70 percent in Detroit, over 60 percent in Atlanta, Baltimore, Cleveland, Newark, St. Louis and Washington, D.C., over 50 percent in Chicago, Miami, Philadelphia and Pittsburgh. But Moynihan surmises that San Francisco's lower ratio—31.5—is the result of a minority: Asian-Americans.

Lee Rainwater, a Harvard sociologist emeritus, testifying to the 6

Finance Committee that Moynihan chairs, foresees 40 percent of all American births, and 80 percent of minority births, occurring out of wedlock by the turn of the century. In 1976 there was an ominous portent during the Bicentennial: The percentage of black births to unmarried women passed 50 percent. Forty years after that, in 2016, if the ascending line on the graph stays straight, 50 percent of births to all races will be out of wedlock.

Now, trends are not inevitabilities. However, rising illegitimacy is a 7 self-reinforcing trend because of the many mechanisms of the intergenerational transmission of poverty. The principal one is: People tend to parent as they were parented.

What has all this to do with the subject of the hearings—"Social 8 Behavior and Health Care Costs"—at which Moynihan examined the natal statistics? Lots.

America is undergoing a demographic transformation the cost of 9 which will be crushing. Why? Because poverty is, strictly speaking, sickening. The children of unmarried women are particularly apt to be poor. And poverty, with its attendant evils—ignorance, dropping out of school, domestic and other violence, drug abuse, joblessness—is unhealthy.

In the inaugural issue of *MediaCritic,* a new quarterly devoted to 10 analysis of contemporary journalism, Fred Barnes, a senior editor of *The New Republic,* examines various myths purveyed by some journalism concerning the "health care crisis," including the myth that there is such a crisis. Two supposed signs of the "crisis" are America's high rate of infant mortality and low rate of immunization of preschool children.

Barnes notes that America's high rate of teenage pregnancy means 11 a large number of low-birth-weight babies and a high mortality rate. "Doctors," says Barnes, "make heroic efforts to save these babies, many of whom would be declared 'born dead' in other countries and thus not counted toward the infant mortality rate."

Regarding immunization rates, Barnes reports that about 98 per- 12 cent of children are fully vaccinated by the time they are of school age because vaccination is required for admission to school. Says Barnes, "Faced with a mandate, parents comply." Negligent or otherwise incompetent parents behave responsibly only when required. Such parents are particularly apt to be young and unmarried.

High infant mortality rates and low immunization rates are less health 13 care problems—less problems of the distribution of medicine—than problems of social behavior, although the political class, other than Moynihan, is reluctant to say so. Moynihan quotes Dr. Reynolds Farley of the University of Michigan: "Shifts in attitudes imply that our norms may no longer abjure childbearing by unmarried women." What can be done?

One clue may be in William Buckley's words that Moynihan cites: 14 "It is increasingly recognized that the most readily identifiable tragedy in modern life is the illegitimate child."

To many people today there is something anachronistic about the 15 word "illegitimate." They find it jarring because it is "judgmental." But reviving the value judgments behind that locution may be the only way to bend down the line on Moynihan's graph.

COMPREHENSION

1. What is the major thesis of this essay?
2. Explain the double meaning of the title "Straight Line to Calamity."
3. What is the main point of the final paragraph?

RHETORIC

1. Will calls the escalating percentage of births to unmarried women "America's real crisis." What supporting evidence does he provide to back this up?
2. Will appeals to several authorities during the course of his argument. Do these appeals strengthen his view? If so, how?
3. In the final paragraph, Will makes the statement, "To many people today there is something anachronistic about the word "'illegitimate.'" To what group of people is he referring? Does he offer any evidence that such a group exists? How does this strengthen or weaken his argument?
4. Define the following words used in the essay: *natal, ominous, portent, abjure, anachronistic,* and *locution.* What do these words suggest about the level of discourse of the essay?
5. In paragraph 8, the author states, "trends are not inevitabilities." Where does he demonstrate that the rising tide of illegitimate births is not inevitable?
6. In paragraph 13, Will asks the question, "What can be done?" Where does he answer the question? How effective is his answer?
7. Examine the first sentence of paragraph 130. Does the author exercise faulty logic in this sentence? If so, what is it? If not, explain the accuracy of the rationale behind it.

WRITING

1. Respond to "Straight Line to Calamity" with your own argument entitled, "Easy to Criticize, Hard to Solve."
2. Respond to "Straight Line to Calamity" with your own argument entitled, "'Straight Line to Calamity': Only the Tip of the Iceberg."
3. Prepare an interview with a mother or father who is a caretaker for his or her out-of-wedlock child. Be sure that your questions cover all the salient details mentioned in the Will essay and any others you think are important. Transform your answers into a descriptive portrait of your subject.

MARY GORDON   Mary Gordon was born in 1949 on Long Island, New York. The daughter of a writer and a legal secretary, she was educated at Barnard College and Syracuse University. Gordon has taught English and is known for both her novels and short stories, which often contain the Catholic themes of devotion, goodness, and redemption. Her major novels are *Final Payments* (1978), *The Company of Women* (1981), and *The Other Side* (1989). Gordon has been a contributor to *Mademoiselle, Harper's,* and *Ms.* In this piece she describes a trip to Ellis Island in which she reestablished bonds with her heritage.

MARY GORDON

More Than Just a Shrine: Paying Homage to the Ghosts of Ellis Island

I once sat in a hotel in Bloomsbury trying to have breakfast alone. 1 A Russian with a habit of compulsively licking his lips asked if he could join me. I was afraid to say no; I thought it might be bad for détente. He explained to me that he was a linguist and that he always liked to talk to Americans to see if he could make any connection between their speech and their ethnic background. When I told him about my mixed ancestry—my mother is Irish and Italian, my father was a Lithuanian Jew—he began jumping up and down in his seat, rubbing his hands together and licking his lips even more frantically.

"Ah," he said, "so you are really somebody who comes from what 2 is called the boiling pot of America." Yes, I told him; yes, I was; but I quickly rose to leave. I thought it would be too hard to explain to him the relation of the boiling potters to the main course, and I wanted to get to the British Museum. I told him that the only thing I could think of that united people whose backgrounds, histories, and points of view were utterly diverse was that their people had landed at a place called Ellis Island.

I didn't tell him that Ellis Island was the only American landmark I'd 3 ever visited. How could I describe to him the estrangement I'd always felt from the kind of traveler who visits shrines to America's past greatness, those rebuilt forts with muskets behind glass, sabers mounted on the walls and gift shops selling maple syrup candy in the shape of Indian headdresses, those reconstructed villages with tables set for fifty and the Paul Revere silver gleaming. All that Americana—Plymouth Rock, Gettysburg, Mount Vernon, Valley Forge—it all inhabits for me a zone of blurred abstraction with far less hold on my imagination than the Bastille or Hampton Court. I suppose I've always known that my uninterest in it contains a large component of the willed: I am American, and those places purport to be my history. But they are not mine.

Ellis Island is, though; it's the one place I can be sure my people are 4 connected to. And so I made a journey there to find my history like any Rotarian traveling in his Winnebago to Antietam to find his. I had become part of that humbling democracy of people looking in some site for a past that has grown unreal. The monument I traveled to was not, however, a tribute to some old glory. The minute I set foot upon the island I could feel all that it stood for: insecurity, obedience, anxiety, dehumanization, the terrible and careful deference of the displaced. I hadn't traveled to the Battery and boarded a ferry across from the

Statue of Liberty to raise flags or breathe a richer, more triumphant air. I wanted to do homage to the ghosts.

I felt them everywhere, from the moment I disembarked I saw the building with its high-minded brick, its hopeful little land, its ornamental cornices. The place was derelict when I arrived; it had not functioned for more than thirty years—almost as long as the time it had operated at full capacity as a major immigration center. I was surprised to learn what a small part of history Ellis Island had occupied. The main building was constructed in 1892, then rebuilt between 1898 and 1900 after a fire. Most of the immigrants who arrived during the latter half of the nineteenth century, mainly northern and western Europeans, landed not at Ellis Island but on the western tip of the Battery, at Castle Garden which had opened as a receiving center for immigrants in 1855.

By the 1880s, the facilities at Castle Garden had grown scandalously inadequate. Officials looked for an island on which to build a new immigration center, because they thought that on an island immigrants could be more easily protected from swindlers and quickly transported to railroad terminals in New Jersey. Bedloe's Island was considered, but New Yorkers were aghast at the idea of a "Babel" ruining their beautiful new treasure, "Liberty Enlightening the World." The statue's sculptor, Frédéric-Auguste Bartholdi, reacted to the prospect of immigrants landing near his masterpiece in horror; he called it a "monstrous plan." So much for Emma Lazarus.

Ellis Island was finally chosen because the citizens of New Jersey petitioned the federal government to remove from the island an old naval powder magazine that they thought dangerously close to the Jersey shore. The explosives were removed; no one wanted the island for anything. It was the perfect place to build an immigration center.

I thought about the island's history as I walked into the building and made my way to the room that was the center in my imagination of the Ellis Island experience: the Great Hall. It had been made real for me in the stark, accusing photographs of Louis Hine and others, who took those pictures to make a point. It was in the Great Hall that everyone had waited—waiting, always, the great vocation of the dispossessed. The room was empty, except for me and a handful of other visitors and the park ranger who showed us around. I felt myself grow insignificant in that room, with its huge semicircular windows, its air, even in dereliction, of solid and official probity.

I walked in the deathlike expansiveness of the room's disuse and tried to think of what it might have been like, filled and swarming. More than sixteen million immigrants came through that room; approximately 250,000 were rejected. Not really a large proportion, but the implications for the rejected were dreadful. For some, there was nothing to go back to, or there was certain death; for others, who left as adventurers, to return would be to adopt in local memory the fool's role, and the failure's. No wonder that the island's history includes reports of three thousand suicides.

Sometimes immigrants could pass through Ellis Island in mere 10 hours, though for some the process took days. The particulars of the experience in the Great Hall were often influenced by the political events and attitudes on the mainland. In the 1890s and the first years of the new century, when cheap labor was needed, the newly built receiving center took in its immigrants with comparatively little question. But as the century progressed, the economy worsened, eugenics became both scientifically respectable and popular, and World War I made American xenophobia seem rooted in fact.

Immigration acts were passed; newcomers had to prove, besides 11 moral correctness and financial solvency, their ability to read. Quota laws came into effect, limiting the number of immigrants from southern and eastern Europe to less than 14 percent of the total quota. Intelligence tests were biased against all non-English-speaking persons, and medical examinations became increasingly strict, until the machinery of immigration nearly collapsed under its own weight. The Second Quota Law of 1924 provided that all immigrants be inspected and issued visas at American consular offices in Europe, rendering the center almost obsolete.

On the day of my visit, my mind fastened upon the medical inspec- 12 tions, which had always seemed to me most emblematic of the ignominy and terror the immigrants endured. The medical inspectors, sometimes dressed in uniforms like soldiers, were particularly obsessed with a disease of the eyes called trachoma, which they checked for by flipping back the immigrants' top eyelids with a hook used for buttoning gloves—a method that sometimes resulted in the transmission of the disease to healthy people. Mothers feared that if their children cried too much, their red eyes would be mistaken for a symptom of the disease and the whole family would be sent home. Those immigrants suspected of some physical disability had initials chalked on their coats. I remembered the photographs I'd seen of people standing, dumbstruck and innocent as cattle, with their manifest numbers hung around their necks and initials marked in chalk upon their coats: "E" for eye trouble, "K" for hernia, "L" for lameness, "X" for mental defects, "H" for heart disease.

I thought of my grandparents as I stood in the room: my seventeen- 13 year-old grandmother, coming alone from Ireland in 1896, vouched for by a stranger who had found her a place as a domestic servant to some Irish who had done well. I tried to imagine the assault it all must have been for her; I've been to her hometown, a collection of farms with a main street—smaller than the athletic field of my local public school. She must have watched the New York skyline as the first- and second-class passengers were whisked off the gangplank with the most cursory of inspections while she was made to board a ferry to the new immigration center.

What could she have made of it—this buff-painted wooden struc- 14 ture with its towers and its blue slate roof, a place *Harper's Weekly* described as "a latter-day watering place hotel"? It would have been the first time she had heard people speaking something other than English. She would have mingled with people carrying baskets on their heads and eating foods unlike any she had ever seen—dark-eyed people, like the Sicilian she would marry ten years later, who came over with his family at thirteen, the man of the family, responsible even then for his mother and sister. I don't know what they thought, my grandparents, for they were not expansive people, nor romantic; they didn't like to think of what they called "the hard times," and their trip across the ocean was the single adventurous act of lives devoted after landing to security, respectability, and fitting in.

What is the potency of Ellis Island for someone like me—an 15 American, obviously, but one who has always felt that the country really belonged to the early settlers, that, as J. F. Powers wrote in *Morte D'Urban,* it had been "handed down to them by the Pilgrims, George Washington and others, and that they were taking a risk in letting you live in it." I have never been the victim of overt discrimination; nothing I have wanted has been denied me because of the accidents of blood. But I suppose it is part of being an American to be engaged in a somewhat tiresome but always self-absorbing process of national definition. And in this process, I have found in traveling to Ellis Island an important piece of evidence that could remind me I was right to feel my differentness. Something had happened to my people on that island, a result of the eternal wrongheadedness of American protectionism and the predictabilities of simple greed. I came to the island, too, so I could tell the ghosts that I was one of them, and that I honored them—their stoicism, and their innocence, the fear that turned them inward, and their pride. I wanted to tell them that I liked them better than I did the Americans who made them pass through the Great Hall and stole their names and chalked their weaknesses in public on their clothing. And to tell the ghosts what I have always thought: that American history was a very classy party that was not much fun until they arrived, brought the good food, turned up the music, and taught everyone to dance.

COMPREHENSION

1. Why does the writer visit Ellis Island?
2. How were the new arrivals treated on the island?
3. What effect does the visit have on the writer? Does she accomplish her goal?

RHETORIC

1. What purpose is served by the first two paragraphs in the essay? Could the essay have begun with the third paragraph without losing any power? Justify your response.
2. What is Gordon's thesis? Where is it contained?

3. Give a brief sketch of Ellis Island in your own words. Why is this information important to the essay?
4. What is Gordon's tone in paragraph 6? How does it fit in with the rest of
   the essay?
5. Explain Gordon's choice of title. How appropriate is it?
6. Examine Gordon's use of language in her essay. Are there any particularly
   strong images or details? Cite them, and explain why they are evocative.

WRITING

1. Write a research paper on the history of Ellis Island. If possible, conduct an
   interview with an elderly relative or neighbor who came through the island
   as a child, and relate his or her experiences.
2. Write a narrative essay in which you pretend to be an immigrant newly
   arrived on Ellis Island. What are your impressions of America and its people? How would you respond to the procedures Gordon depicts in her
   essay? Use sensory details to evoke a sense of place.
3. Gordon writes: "But I suppose it is part of being an American to be engaged
   in a somewhat tiresome but always self-absorbing process of national definition." Write an essay in which you analyze the meaning and validity of
   this statement.

NICCOLO MACHIAVELLI Niccolo Machiavelli (1469–1527), Italian patriot,
statesman, and writer, is one of the seminal figures in the history of Western
political thought. His inquiries into the nature of the state, the amoral quality
of political life, and the primacy of power are distinctly modernist in outlook.
He began his studies of political and historical issues after being forced to
retire from Florentine politics in 1512. Exiled outside the city, Machiavelli
wrote *The Prince* (1513), *The Discourses* (1519), *The Art of War* (1519–1520),
and *The Florentine History* (1525). The following selection from *The Discourses* (conceived by the author as commentaries on the first ten books of
Livy's *History of Rome*) analyzes the varieties of government and their political implications in history.

NICCOLO MACHIAVELLI

The Circle of Governments

Having proposed to myself to treat of the kind of government estab-   1
lished at Rome, and of the events that led to its perfection, I must at the
beginning observe that some of the writers on politics distinguished
three kinds of government, vis. the monarchical, the aristocratic, and

the democratic; and maintain that the legislators of a people must choose from these three the one that seems to them most suitable. Other authors, wiser according to the opinion of many, count six kinds of governments, three of which are very bad, and three good in themselves, but so liable to be corrupted that they become absolutely bad. The three good ones are those which we have just named; the three bad ones result from the degradation of the other three, and each of them resembles its corresponding original, so that the transition from the one to the other is very easy. Thus monarchy becomes tyranny; aristocracy degenerates into oligarchy; and the popular government lapses readily into licentiousness. So that a legislator who gives to a state which he founds either of these three forms of government, constitutes it but for a brief time; for no precautions can prevent either one of the three that are reputed good from degenerating into its opposite kind; so great are in these the attractions and resemblances between the good and the evil.

Chance has given birth to these different kinds of governments 2 amongst men; for at the beginning of the world the inhabitants were few in number and lived for a time dispersed, like beasts. As the human race increased, the necessity for uniting themselves for defence made itself felt; the better to attain this object they chose the strongest and most courageous from amongst themselves and placed him at their head promising to obey him. Thence they began to know the good and the honest, and to distinguish them from the bad and vicious; for seeing a man injure his benefactor aroused at once two sentiments in every heart, hatred against the ingrate and love for the benefactor. They blamed the first, and on the contrary honoured those the more who showed themselves grateful, for each felt that he in turn might be subject to a like wrong; and to prevent similar evils, they set to work to make laws, and to institute punishments for those who contravened them. Such was the origin of justice. This caused them, when they had afterwards to choose a prince, neither to look to the strongest nor bravest, but to the wisest and most just. But when they began to make sovereignty hereditary and non-elective, the children quickly degenerated from their fathers; and, so far from trying to equal their virtues, they considered that a prince had nothing else to do than to excel all the rest in luxury, indulgence, and every other variety of pleasure. The prince consequently soon drew upon himself the general hatred. An object of hatred, he naturally felt fear; fear in turn dictated to him precautions and wrongs, and thus tyranny quickly developed itself. Such were the beginning and causes of disorders, conspiracies, and plots against the sovereigns, set on foot, not by the feeble and timid, but by those citizens who, surpassing the others in grandeur of soul, in wealth, and in courage, could not submit to the outrages and excesses of their princes.

Under such powerful leaders the masses armed themselves against 3 the tyrant, and after having rid themselves of him, submitted to these chiefs as their liberators. These, abhorring the very name of prince, constituted themselves a new government; and at first bearing in mind the past tyranny, they governed in strict accordance with the laws which they had established themselves; preferring public interests to their own, and to administer and protect with greatest care both public and private affairs. The children succeeded their fathers, and ignorant of the changes of fortune, having never experienced its reverses, and indisposed to remain content with this civil equality, they in turn gave themselves up to cupidity, ambition, libertinage, and violence, and soon caused the aristocratic government to degenerate into an oligarchic tyranny, regardless of all civil rights. They soon, however, experienced the same fate as the first tyrant; the people, disgusted with their government, placed themselves at the command of whoever was willing to attack them, and this disposition soon produced an avenger, who was sufficiently well seconded to destroy them. The memory of the prince and the wrongs committed by him being still fresh in their minds, and having overthrown the oligarchy, the people were not willing to return to the government of a prince. A popular government was therefore resolved upon, and it was so organized that the authority would not again fall into the hands of a prince or a small number of nobles. And as all governments are at first looked up to with some degree of reverence, the popular state also maintained itself for a time, but which was never of long duration, and lasted generally only about as long as the generation that had established it; for it soon ran into that kind of licence which inflicts injury upon public as well as private interests. Each individual only consulted his own passions, and a thousand acts of injustice were daily committed, so that, constrained by necessity, or directed by the counsels of some good man, or for the purpose of escaping from this anarchy, they returned anew to the government of a prince, and from this they generally lapsed again into anarchy, step-by-step, in the same manner and from the same causes as we have indicated.

Such is the circle which all republics are destined to run through. ◄ Seldom, however, do they come back to the original form of government, which results from the fact that their duration is not sufficiently long to be able to undergo these repeated changes and preserve their existence. But it may well happen that a republic lacking strength and good counsel in its difficulties becomes subject after a while to some neighbouring state, that is better organized than itself; and if such is not the case, then they will be apt to revolve indefinitely in the circle of revolutions. I say, then, that all kinds of government are defective; those three which we have qualified as good because they are too short-lived, and the three bad ones because of their inherent viciousness. Thus sagacious legislators, knowing the vices of each of these systems of government by themselves, have chosen one that should partake of all of them, judging that to be the most stable and solid. In fact, when there is combined under the same constitution a prince, a nobility, and the power of the people, then these three powers will watch and keep each other reciprocally in check.

COMPREHENSION

1. Where in the essay does Machiavelli state his thesis? What is his thesis?
2. Explain in your own words the three types of government Machiavelli describes, their origins, and their pitfalls.
3. Ultimately, who determines what system of government a country will have—the governed or the legislators? Explain your view.

RHETORIC

1. In paragraph 1, Machiavelli states the motivation for writing his essay. How does he create a transition from explaining this motivation to addressing his subject directly?
2. Machiavelli explains the three forms of government in a particular order. What is the unifying rhetoric behind the order in which he describes them? How does it relate to the theme of the essay?
3. Both paragraphs 2 and 3 describe the process by which governments are formed. What methods does the author use to create coherent paragraphs in providing a step-by-step description of these formations?
4. Would you consider this essay descriptive, narrative, expository, or a combination of two or more of these methods? Explain your answer.
5. Define *oligarchy, benefactor, licentiousness, cupidity, libertinage,* and *sagacious*. What does the use of these words in the essay suggest about the author and his intended audience?
6. From what vantage point does the author appear to view his subject matter: participant, reporter, critic, or teacher? Explain your view.

WRITING

1. Argue for or against the proposition that the United States has an ideal form of government, according to Machiavelli's view of what a government should be.
2. Argue for or against *one* of the forms of government that Machiavelli describes in his essay.
3. Using the terms *monarchy, oligarchy,* and *democracy,* describe the various governing bodies of your school, their functions, and where they fit into Machiavelli's taxonomy.

DORIS LESSING   Doris Lessing, a major British novelist, was born in 1919 in Kermanshah, Iran, of English parents. She moved at an early age with her parents to a large farm in Southern Rhodesia. At the age of 18, she went to Salisbury, entering quickly into the artistic and political life there. Lessing left Africa for London in 1949, and in 1950 she published her first novel, *The Grass Is Singing.* Her later novels include *The Golden Notebook* (1962), *Briefing for a Descent into Hell* (1971), and the four-volume *Canopus in Argos: Archives* (1981). Lessing's short stories, many of the best drawn from her African experience, have been collected in five volumes. In "Being Prohibited," taken from her essay collection *A Small Personal Voice* (1975), Lessing plots over a period of time her several confrontations with apartheid.

DORIS LESSING

Being Prohibited

The border is Mafeking, a little dorp with nothing interesting about it but its name. The train waits (or used to wait) interminably on the empty tracks, while immigration and customs officials made their leisurely way through the coaches, and pale gritty dust settled over everything. Looking out, one saw the long stretch of windows, with the two, three, or four white faces at each; then at the extreme end, the single coach for "natives" packed tight with black humans; and, in between, two or three Indians or Coloured people on sufferance in the European coaches.

Outside, on the scintillating dust by the tracks, a crowd of ragged black children begged for *bonsellas*. One threw sandwich crusts or bits of spoiled fruit and watched them dive and fight to retrieve them from the dirt.

I was sixteen. I was not, as one says, politically conscious; nor did I know the score. I knew no more, in fact, than on which side my bread was buttered. But I already felt uneasy about being a member of the Herrenvolk. When the immigration official reached me, I had written on the form; *Nationality,* British, *Race,* European; and it was the first time in my life I had had to claim myself as a member of one race and disown the others. I remember distinctly that I had to suppress an impulse opposite *Race:* Human. Of course I *was* very young.

The immigration man had the sarcastic surliness which characterises the Afrikaans official, and he looked suspiciously at my form for a long time before saying that I was in the wrong part of the train. I did not understand him. (I forgot to mention that where the form asked, Where were you born?, I had written, Persia.)

"Asiatics," said he, "have to go to the back of the train; and anyway you are prohibited from entry unless you have documents proving you conform to the immigration quota for Asians."

"But," I said, "I am not an Asiatic."

The compartment had five other females in it; skirts were visibly being drawn aside. To prove my bona fides I should, of course, have exclaimed with outraged indignation at any such idea.

"You were born in Persia?"

"Yes."

"Then you are an Asiatic. You know the penalties for filling in the form wrongly?"

This particular little imbroglio involved my being taken off the train, escorted to an office, and kept under watch while they telephoned Pretoria for a ruling.

When next I entered the Union it was 1939. Sophistication had set in in the interval, and it took me no more than five minutes to persuade the official that one could be born in a country without being its citizen. The next two times there was no trouble at all, although my political views had in the meantime become nothing less than inflammatory: in a word, I had learned to disapprove of the colour bar.

This time, two weeks ago, what happened was as follows: one gets off the plane and sits for about fifteen minutes in a waiting room while they check the plane list with a list, or lists, of their own. They called my name first, and took me to an office which had two tables in it. At one sat a young man being pleasant to the genuine South African citizens. At the one where they made me sit was a man I could have sworn I had seen before. He proceeded to go through my form item by item, as follows: "You *say*, Mrs. Lessing, that, etc. . . ." From time to time he let out a disbelieving laugh and exchanged ironical looks with a fellow official who was standing by. Sure enough, when he reached that point on my form when he had to say: "You *claim* that you are British; you *say* you were born in Persia," I merely said *"Yes,"* and sat still while he gave me a long, exasperated stare. Then he let out an angry exclamation in Afrikaans and went next door to telephone Pretoria. Ten minutes later I was informed I must leave at once. A plane was waiting and I must enter it immediately.

I did so with dignity. Since then I have been unable to make up my mind whether I should have made a scene or not. I never have believed in the efficacy of dignity.

On the plane I wanted to sit near the window but was made to sit by myself and away from the window. I regretted infinitely that I had no accomplices hidden in the long grass by the airstrip, but, alas, I had not thought of it beforehand.

It was some time before it came home to me what an honour had been paid me. But now I am uneasy about the whole thing: suppose that I owe these attentions, not to my political views, but to the accident of my birthplace?

COMPREHENSION

1. Trace the sequence of conflicts that the author has with South African apartheid. How does her attitude shift with each confrontation? In what way does the conflict come full circle?

2. What do you learn about the author's personality and her beliefs? Cite evidence from the narrative to support your response.

1. What would you say is the thesis of Lessing's essay? Is it apparent in the narrative?
2. Analyze the imagery in the first paragraph of the essay. What mood or impression is created?
3. Trace Lessing's development of conflict in this narrative. How many episodes are there? How does the author handle the matter of time? Why does she shift tenses from present, to past, to present?
4. Lessing is especially effective in using dialogue to reveal character. Cite examples of this method, and analyze the results.
5. Lessing uses several words drawn from South African dialect: *dorp* (paragraph 1); *Herrenvolk* (paragraph 3); and *Afrikaans* (paragraph 4). Define each word. What do such terms contribute to the tone of the essay?
6. Lessing concludes her narrative with a question. How effective is that device?

WRITING

1. Write a research paper examining the current state of apartheid in South Africa. Use quotes from the Lessing essay for purposes of comparison. What changes, if any, have occurred since the time of her essay?
2. In an analytical essay, compare South Africa's apartheid policies with similar policies in recent U.S. history. Some research may be necessary.
3. Write a personal narrative describing an experience similar to Lessing's where you were "prohibited" because of your nationality, color, sex, or economic situation.

SCOTT RUSSELL SANDERS Scott Russell Sanders was born in Memphis, Tennessee, in 1945. He received his B.A. degree from Brown University in 1967 and a Ph.D. degree from Cambridge University in 1971. Since then, Sanders has divided his time between science and the arts. He is comfortable writing about theoretical physics as he is giving typical accounts of everyday life. Particularly concerned with community and nature, his ecological writings combine a humanistic look at the relationship between humans and their environment with technical knowledge that helps him explain complex subject matter to the lay reader. He believes that writing should value, not experimentation in form or style, but rather clarity of language and vision. His nonfiction includes *The Engineer of Beats* (1988), *The Invisible Company* (1989), and *Aurora Means Dawn* (1989). He has also contributed essays to such well-known publications as *Omni, Harper's, New York Times Book Review,* and *Sewanee Review.* Sanders believes the role of the writer should be to teach humans how to live in greater harmony with their neighbors and communities. He is also a writer of fiction—science fiction, folktales, children's literature, and historical novels among other forms. The range of his writing demonstrates the breadth of his knowledge. The following shows his concern about the interrelationship of the self and society based upon general study and personal experience. It is excerpted from *The Georgia Review* (spring 1994).

SCOTT RUSSELL SANDERS

Community: The Web of Life

A woman who recently moved from Los Angeles to Bloomington, 1
Indiana, told me that she would not be able to stay here long, because
she was already beginning to recognize people in the grocery stores, on
the sidewalks, in the library. Being surrounded by familiar faces made
her nervous, after years in a city where she could range about anony-
mously. Every traveler knows the sense of liberation that comes from
journeying to a place where nobody expects anything of you. Everyone
who has gone to college knows the exhilaration of slipping away from
the watchful eyes of Mom and Dad. We all need seasons of withdrawal
from responsibility. But if we make a career of being unaccountable, we
have lost something essential to our humanity, and we may well become
a burden or a threat to those around us.

Ever since the eclipse of our native cultures, the dominant Ameri- 2
can view has been that we should cultivate the self rather than the community; that we should look to the individual as the source of hope and
the center of value, while expecting hindrance and harm from society.
We have understood freedom for the most part negatively rather than
positively, as release from constraints rather than as a condition for
making a decent life in common. Hands off, we say; give me elbow
room; good fences make good neighbors; my home is my castle; don't
tread on me. I'm looking out for number one, we say; I'm doing my
own thing. We have a Bill of Rights, which protects each of us from a
bullying society, but no Bill of Responsibilities, which would oblige us
to answer the needs of others.

What other view could have emerged from our history? The first 3
Europeans to reach America were daredevils and treasure seekers, as
were most of those who mapped the interior. Many colonists were
renegades of one stripe or another, some of them religious noncon-
formists, some political rebels, more than a few of them fugitives from
the law. The trappers, hunters, traders, and freebooters who pushed the
frontier westward seldom recognized any authority beyond the reach of
their own hands. Coast to coast, our land has been settled and our cities
have been filled by generations of immigrants more intent on leaving
behind old tyrannies than on seeking new social bonds.

The cult of the individual shows up everywhere in American lore, 4
which celebrates drifters, rebels, and loners while pitying or reviling the
pillars of the community. The backwoods explorer like Daniel Boone,
the riverboat rowdy like Mike Fink, the lumberjack, the prospector, the

rambler and gambler, the daring crook like Jesse James or the resource-ful killer like Billy the Kid, along with countless lonesome cowboys, all wander, unattached, through the great spaces of our imagination.

Fortunately, while our tradition is heavily tilted in favor of private life, we also inherit a tradition of caring for the community. Writing about what he had seen in the 1830s, Alexis de Tocqueville judged Americans to be avaricious, self-serving, and aggressive: but he was also amazed by our eagerness to form clubs, to raise barns or town halls, to join together in one cause or another: "In no country in the world," he wrote, "do the citizens make such exertions for the common weal. I know of no people who have established schools so numerous and efficacious, places of public worship better suited to the wants of the inhabitants, or roads kept in better repair."

Today we might revise Tocqueville's estimate of our schools or roads, but we can still see all around us the fruits of that concern for the common weal—the libraries, museums, courthouses, hospitals, orphanages, universities, parks, on and on. No matter where we live, our home places have also benefited from the Granges and unions, the volunteer fire brigades, the art guilds and garden clubs, the chari-ties, food kitchens, homeless shelters, soccer and baseball teams, the Scouts and 4-H, the Girls and Boys Clubs, the Lions and Elks and Rotarians, the countless gatherings of people who saw a need and responded to it.

This history of local care hardly ever makes it into our literature, for it is less glamorous than rebellion, yet it is a crucial part of our heritage. Any of us could cite examples of people who dug in and joined with others to make our home places better places. Women and men who invest themselves in their communities, fighting for good schools or green spaces, paying attention to where they are, seem to me as worthy of celebration as those adventurous loners who keep drifting on, prospecting for pleasure.

The words *community, communion,* and *communicate* all derive from *common,* and the two syllables of *common* grow from separate roots, the first meaning "together" or "next to," the second having to do with barter or exchange. Embodied in that word is a sense of our shared life as one of giving and receiving—music, touch, ideas, recipes, stories, medicine, tools, the whole range of artifacts and talents. After 25 years with my wife, Ruth, that is how I have come to understand marriage, as a constant exchange of labor and love. We do not calculate who gives how much; if we had to, the marriage would be in trouble. Looking outward from this community of two, I see my life embedded in ever larger exchanges—those of family and friendship, neighborhood and city, countryside and country—and on every scale there is giving and receiving, calling and answering.

Many people shy away from community out of a fear that it may become suffocating, confining, even vicious; and of course it may, if it grows rigid or exclusive. A healthy community is dynamic, stirred up by the energies of those who already belong, open to new members and fresh influences, kept in motion by the constant bartering of gifts. It is fashionable just now to speak of this open quality as "tolerance," but that word sounds too grudging to me—as though, to avoid strife, we must grit our teeth and ignore whatever is strange to us. The community I desire is not grudging; it is exuberant, joyful, grounded in affection, pleasure, and mutual aid. Such a community arises not from duty or money but from the free interchange of people who share a place, share work and food, sorrows and hope. Taking part in the common life means dwelling in a web of relationships, the many threads tugging at you while also holding you upright.

I have told elsewhere the story of a man who lived in the Ohio township where I grew up, a builder who refused to join the volunteer fire department. Why should he join, when his house was brick, properly wired, fitted out with new appliances? Well, one day that house caught fire. His wife dialed the emergency number, the siren wailed, and pretty soon the volunteer firemen, my father among them, showed up with the pumper truck. But they held back on the hoses, asking the builder if he still saw no reason to join, and the builder said he could see a pretty good reason to join right there and then, and the volunteers let the water loose.

I have also told before the story of a family from that township whose house burned down. The local people sheltered the family, then built them a new house. This was a poor township. But nobody thought to call in the government or apply to a foundation. These were neighbors in a fix, and so you helped them, just as you would harvest corn for an ailing farmer or pull a flailing child from the creek or put your arm around a weeping friend.

My daughter Eva and I recently went to a concert in Bloomington's newly opened arts center. The old limestone building had once been the town hall, then a fire station and jail, then for several years an abandoned shell. Volunteers bought the building from the city for a dollar and renovated it with materials, labor, and money donated by local people. Now we have a handsome facility that is in constant use for pottery classes, theater productions, puppet shows, art exhibits, poetry readings, and every manner of musical event.

The music Eva and I heard was *Hymnody of Earth*, for hammer dulcimer, percussion, and children's choir. Composed by our next-door neighbor Malcolm Dalglish and featuring lyrics by our Ohio Valley neighbor Wendell Berry, it was performed that night by Malcolm, percussionist Glen Velez, and the Bloomington Youth Chorus. As I sat there with Eva in a sellout crowd—about a third of whom I knew by name, another third by face—I listened to music that had been elaborated within earshot of my house, and I heard my friend play his instrument, and I watched those children's faces shining with the colors of the human spectrum, and I felt the restored building clasping us like the cupped hands of our community. I knew once more that I was in the right place, a place created and filled and inspired by our lives together.

I am not harking back to some idyllic past, like the one embalmed   14
in the *Saturday Evening Post* covers by Norman Rockwell or the prints of Currier and Ives. The past was never golden. As a people, we still need to unlearn some of the bad habits we formed during the long period of settlement. One good habit we might reclaim, however, is looking after those who live nearby. For much of our history, neighbors have kept one another going, kept one another sane. Still today, in town and country, in apartment buildings and barrios, even in suburban estates, you are certain to lead a narrower life without the steady presence of neighbors. It is neither quaint nor sentimental to advocate neighborliness; it is far more sentimental to suggest that we can do without such mutual aid.

Even Emerson, preaching self-reliance, knew the necessity of neigh-   15
bors. He lived in a village, gave and received help, and delivered his essays as lectures for fellow citizens whom he hoped to sway. He could have left his ideas in his journals, where they first took shape, but he knew those ideas would only have effect when they were shared. I like to think he would have agreed with the Lakota shaman Black Elk, who said, "A man who has a vision is not able to use the power of it until after he has performed the vision on earth for the people to see." If you visit Emerson's house in Concord, you will find leather buckets hanging near the door, for he belonged to the village fire brigade, and even in the seclusion of his study, in the depths of thought, he kept his ears open for the alarm bell.

We should not have to wait until our houses are burning before we   16
see the wisdom of facing our local needs by joining in common work. We should not have to wait until gunfire breaks out in our schools, rashes break out on our skin, dead fish float in our streams, or beggars sleep on our streets before we act on behalf of the community. On a crowded planet, we had better learn how to live well together, or we will live miserably apart.

COMPREHENSION

1. Explain the thesis of this essay.
2. According to the author, what ingredients must exist in order to have a healthy community?
3. What central paradox does the author allude to that has existed since the formation of the United States?

RHETORIC

1. In paragraph 2, the author makes effective use of the series as a rhetorical device. What is his purpose?
2. Locate at least one of the following rhetorical devices in the essay: direct quotation, example, definition, and anecdote.

3. How would you describe the tone of the essay? Where in the essay is the author's tone most pronounced?

4. In paragraph 14, the author claims that a sense of community is essential in all areas and regions, yet his only examples seem to focus on the midwest. Does this selectivity hinder Sanders' argument? Explain.

5. What is the effect of juxtaposing references to Emerson and Black Elk in paragraph 15?

6. Although written in an argumentative form, the essay does not offer any specific proscriptions or recommendations for social change. Does this weaken his argument? Explain your view.

7. The author goes into rather precise detail in describing attendance at a concert at Bloomington's arts center. What is the purpose of this detailing?

WRITING

1. Demonstrate the presence or absence of a "community spirit" in the town, region, or city in which you live.

2. Write a compendium of instructions entitled, "Ten things you can do to create a community spirit in your neighborhood."

3. Describe an event in your life that demonstrated or failed to demonstrate a sense of community concern.

BRUCE CATTON   Bruce Catton (1899–1978) was born in Petosky, Michigan. After serving in the Navy during World War I, he attended Oberlin College but left in his junior year to pursue a career in journalism. From 1942 to 1952, Catton served in the government, first on the War Production Board and later in the departments of Commerce and the Interior. He left government to devote himself to literary work as a columnist for the *Nation* and a historian of the Civil War. His many works include *A Stillness at Appomattox* (1953), which won the 1954 Pulitzer Prize; *Mr. Lincoln's Army* (1951); *The Centennial History of the Civil War* (1961–1965); and *Prefaces to History*. In this selection, Catton presents vivid portraits of two well-known but little-understood figures from American history.

BRUCE CATTON

Grant and Lee: A Study in Contrasts

When Ulysses S. Grant and Robert E. Lee met in the parlor of a modest house at Appomattox Court House, Virginia, on April 9, 1865, to work out the terms for the surrender of Lee's Army of Northern Virginia, a great chapter in American life came to a close, and a great new chapter began.

These men were bringing the Civil War to its virtual finish. To be sure, other armies had yet to surrender, and for a few days the fugitive Confederate government would struggle desperately and vainly, trying to find some way to go on living now that its chief support was gone. But in effect it was all over when Grant and Lee signed the papers. And the little room where they wrote out the terms was the scene of one of the poignant, dramatic contrasts in American history.

They were two strong men, these oddly different generals, and they represented the strengths of two conflicting currents that, through them, had come into final collision.

Back of Robert E. Lee was the notion that the old aristocratic concept might somehow survive and be dominant in American life.

Lee was tidewater Virginia, and in his background were family, culture, and tradition . . . the age of chivalry transplanted to a New World which was making its own legends and its own myths. He embodied a way of life that had come down through the age of knighthood and the English country squire. America was a land that was beginning all over again, dedicated to nothing much more complicated than the rather hazy belief that all men had equal rights and should have an equal chance in the world. In such a land Lee stood for the feeling that it was somehow of advantage to human society to have a pronounced inequality in the social structure. There should be a leisure class, backed by ownership of land; in turn, society itself should be keyed to the land as the chief source of wealth and influence. It would bring forth (according to this ideal) a class of men with a strong sense of obligation to the community; men who lived not to gain advantage for themselves, but to meet the solemn obligations which had been laid on them by the very fact that they were privileged. From them the country would get its leadership; to them it could look for the higher values—of thought, of conduct, of personal deportment—to give it strength and virtue.

Lee embodied the noblest elements of this aristocratic ideal. Through him, the landed nobility justified itself. For four years, the Southern states had fought a desperate war to uphold the ideals for which Lee stood. In the end, it almost seemed as if the Confederacy fought for Lee; as if he himself was the Confederacy . . . the best thing that the way of life for which the Confederacy stood could ever have to offer. He had passed into legend before Appomattox. Thousands of tired, underfed, poorly clothed Confederate soldiers, long since past the simple enthusiasm of the early days of the struggle, somehow considered Lee the symbol of everything for which they had been willing to die. But they could not quite put this feeling into words. If the Lost Cause, sanctified by so much heroism and so many deaths, had a living justification, its justification was General Lee.

Grant, the son of a tanner on the Western frontier, was everything Lee was not. He had come up the hard way and embodied nothing in particular except the eternal toughness and sinewy fiber of the men who grew up beyond the mountains. He was one of a body of men who owed reverence and obeisance to no one, who were self-reliant to a fault, who cared hardly anything for the past but who had a sharp eye for the future.

These frontier men were the precise opposites of the tidewater aristocrats. Back of them, in the great surge that had taken people over the Alleghenies and into the opening Western country, there was a deep, implicit dissatisfaction with a past that had settled into grooves. They stood for democracy, not from any reasoned conclusion about the proper ordering of human society, but simply because they had grown up in the middle of democracy and knew how it worked. Their society might have privileges, but they would be privileges each man had won for himself. Forms and patterns meant nothing. No man was born to anything, except perhaps to a chance to show how far he could rise. Life was competition. 8

Yet along with this feeling had come a deep sense of belonging to a national community. The Westerner who developed a farm, opened a shop, or set up in business as a trader, could hope to prosper only as his own community prospered—and his community ran from the Atlantic to the Pacific and from Canada down to Mexico. If the land was settled, with towns and highways and accessible markets, he could better himself. He saw his fate in terms of the nation's own destiny. As its horizons expanded, so did his. He had, in other words, an acute dollars-and-cents stake in the continued growth and development of his country. 9

And that, perhaps, is where the contrast between Grant and Lee becomes most striking. The Virginia aristocrat, inevitably, saw himself in relation to his own region. He lived in a static society which could endure almost anything except change. Instinctively, his first loyalty would go to the locality in which that society existed. He would fight to the limit of endurance to defend it, because in defending it he was defending everything that gave his own life its deepest meaning. 10

The Westerner, on the other hand, would fight with an equal tenacity for the broader concept of society. He fought so because everything he lived by was tied to growth, expansion, and a constantly widening horizon. What he lived by would survive or fall with the nation itself. He could not possibly stand by unmoved in the face of an attempt to destroy the Union. He would combat it with everything he had, because he could only see it as an effort to cut the ground out from under his feet. 11

So Grant and Lee were in complete contrast, representing two diametrically opposed elements in American life. Grant was the modern man emerging; beyond him, ready to come on the stage, was the great age of steel and machinery, of crowded cities and a restless burgeoning vitality. Lee might have ridden down from the old age of chivalry, lance in hand, silken banner fluttering over his head. Each man was the perfect champion of his cause, drawing both his strengths and his weaknesses from the people he led. 12

301

Yet it was not all contrast, after all. Different as they were—in back- 13
ground, in personality, in underlying aspiration—these two great soldiers had much in common. Under everything else, they were marvelous fighters. Furthermore, their fighting qualities were really very
much alike.

Each man had, to begin with, the great virtue of utter tenacity and 14
fidelity. Grant fought his way down the Mississippi Valley in spite of
acute personal discouragement and profound military handicaps. Lee
hung on in the trenches at Petersburg after hope itself had died. In each
man there was an indomitable quality . . . the born fighter's refusal to
give up as long as he can still remain on his feet and lift his two fists.

Daring and resourcefulness they had, too; the ability to think faster 15
and move faster than the enemy. These were the qualities which gave
Lee the dazzling campaigns of Second Manassas and Chancellorsville
and won Vicksburg for Grant.

Lastly, and perhaps greatest of all, there was the ability, at the end, to 16
turn quickly from war to peace once the fighting was over. Out of the way
these two men behaved at Appomattox came the possibility of a peace of
reconciliation. It was a possibility not wholly realized, in the years to
come, but which did, in the end, help the two sections to become one
nation again . . . after a war whose bitterness might have seemed to make
such a reunion wholly impossible. No part of either man's life became him
more than the part he played in their brief meeting in the McLean house
at Appomattox. Their behavior there put all succeeding generations of
Americans in their debt. Two great Americans, Grant and Lee—very different, yet under everything very much alike. Their encounter at Appomattox was one of the great moments of American history.

COMPREHENSION

1. What is the central purpose of Catton's study? Cite evidence to support your
view. Who is his audience?

2. What is the primary appeal to readers of describing history through the
study of individuals rather than through the recording of events? How does
Catton's essay reflect this appeal?

3. According to Catton, what special qualities did Grant and Lee share, and
what qualities set them apart?

RHETORIC

1. What role does the opening paragraph have in setting the tone for the
essay? Is the tone typical of what you would expect of an essay describing
military generals? Explain your view. How does the conclusion echo the
introductory paragraph?

2. Note that the sentence, "Two great Americans, Grant and Lee—very different,
yet under everything very much alike" (paragraph 16), has no verb. What does
this indicate about Catton's style? What other sentences contain atypical syntax? What is *their* contribution to the unique quality of the writing?

Chapter Six
Social Processes
and Institutions

3. While this essay is about a historical era, there is a notable lack of specific facts—dates, statistics, and events. What has Catton focused on instead?
4. What is the function of the one-sentence paragraph 3?
5. Paragraphs 9, 10, 12, and 13 begin with coordinating conjunctions. How do these transitional words give the paragraphs their special coherence? How would more typical introductory expressions, such as *in addition, furthermore,* or *moreover,* have altered this coherence?
6. What strategy does Catton use in comparing and contrasting the two generals? Study paragraphs 5 through 16. Which are devoted to describing each man separately, and which include aspects of each man? What is the overall development of the comparisons?

WRITING

1. Does Lee's vision of society exist in the United States today? If not, why not? If so, where do you find this vision? Write a brief essay on this topic.
2. Select two well-known individuals in the same profession—for example, politics, entertainment, or sports. Make a list for each, enumerating the different aspects of their character, behavior, beliefs, and background. Using this as an outline, devise an essay comparing and contrasting the two.
3. Apply, in a comparative essay, Catton's observation about "two diametrically opposed elements in American life" to the current national scene.

WILLIAM BENNETT   William J. Bennett was born in 1943 and grew up in Brooklyn, New York. He received a doctorate in political philosophy from the University of Texas and a law degree from Harvard University. He served as secretary of education and director of the National Endowment for the Humanities under President Reagan and as director of the Office of National Drug Control Policy under President Bush. He is a senior editor at the magazine *National Review* and a fellow at the Heritage Foundation. In 1993, he published *The Book of Virtues: A Treasury of Great Moral Stories,* which became a best-seller. He often criticizes what he perceives to be a growing amorality in our society.

WILLIAM J. BENNETT

What Really Ails America

A few months ago I lunched with a friend who now lives in Asia. During our conversation the topic turned to America as seen through the eyes of foreigners. My friend had observed that while the world still regards the United States as the leading economic and military power on earth, this same world no longer beholds us with the moral respect it once did, as a "shining city on a hill." Instead, it sees a society in decline.

Recently, a Washington, D.C., cabdriver—a graduate student from Africa—told me that when he receives his degree, he is returning to his homeland. His reason? He doesn't want his children to grow up in a country where his daughter will be an "easy target" for young men and where his son might also be a target for violence at the hands of other young males. "It is more civilized where I come from," he said.

Last year an article in the Washington *Post* described how exchange students adopt the life-style of American teens. Paulina, a Polish high-school student studying in the United States, said that when she first came here she was amazed at the way teenagers spent their time. "In Warsaw, we would come home after school, eat with our parents and then do four or five hours of homework. Now, I go to Pizza Hut and watch TV and do less work in school. I can tell it is not a good thing to get used to."

I have an instinctive aversion to foreigners harshly judging my nation; yet, I must concede that much of what they say is true. Something has gone wrong with us.

Yes, there are families, schools, churches and neighborhoods that work. But there is a lot less virtue than there ought to be.

Last year I compiled *The Index of Leading Cultural Indicators,* a statistical portrait of American behavioral trends of the past three decades. Among the findings: Since 1960, while the gross domestic product has nearly tripled, violent crime has increased at least 560 percent. Divorces have more than doubled. The percentage of children in single-parent homes has tripled. And by the end of the decade 40 percent of all American births and 80 percent of minority births will occur out of wedlock.

These are not good things to get used to.

The United States leads the industrialized world in murder, rape and violent crime. At the same time, our elementary-school students rank at or near the bottom in tests of math and science skills. Since 1960, average SAT scores in our high schools have dropped 75 points.

In 1940, teachers identified the top problems in America's schools as: talking out of turn, chewing gum, making noise and running in the hall. In 1990, teachers listed drugs, alcohol, pregnancy, suicide, rape and assault.

These are not good things to get used to, either.

There is a coarseness, a callousness and a cynicism to our era. The worst of it has to do with our children. Our culture seems almost dedicated to the corruption of the young.

Last year, Snoop Doggy Dogg, indicted for murder, saw his rap album "Doggystyle," which celebrates marijuana use and the degradation of women, debut at No. 1 on the pop chart. What will happen when young boys who grow up on mean streets, without fathers in their lives, are constantly exposed to such music?

On television, indecent exposure is celebrated by all ages as a virtue. There was a time when personal failures, subliminal desires and perverse tastes were accompanied by guilt, or at least silence. Today they are tickets to appear as guests on talk shows. In one recent two-week period, these shows featured cross-dressing couples, a three-way love affair, a man who fools women into thinking he is using a condom during sex, and prostitutes who love their jobs. These shows present a two-edged problem: people want to expose themselves, and other people want to watch.

We have become inured to the cultural rot that is setting in. People [14] are losing their capacity for shock, disgust and outrage. During the 1992 Los Angeles riots, Damian Williams was filmed crushing an innocent man's skull with a brick, while Henry Watson held the victim down. When Williams was finished, he did a victory dance. Watson and Williams's lawyers then built a legal defense on the premise that people cannot be held accountable for getting caught up in mob violence. ("I guess maybe they were in the wrong place at the wrong time," one juror told the New York *Times.*) When these men were acquitted on most counts, the sound you heard throughout the land was not outrage, but relief.

This is not a good thing to get used to. [15]

What's to blame for this change? The hard fact is that it was not [16] something done to us; it is something we have done to ourselves. Thoughtful people have pointed to materialism, an overly permissive society, or the legacy of the 1960s. There is truth in almost all these accounts. But in my view our real crisis is spiritual, a corruption of the heart.

The ancients called our problem acedia, an aversion to spiritual [17] things and an undue concern for the external and the worldly. Acedia also is the seventh capital sin—sloth—but it does not mean mere laziness. The slothful heart is steeped in the worldly and carnal, hates the spiritual and wants to be free of its demands.

When the novelist Walker Percy was asked what concerned him [18] most about America's future, he answered, "Probably the fear of seeing America, with all its great strength and beauty and freedom . . . gradually subside into decay through default and be defeated, not by the communist movement, but from within, from weariness, boredom, cynicism, greed and in the end helplessness before its great problems."

I realize this is a tough indictment. If my diagnosis is wrong, then [19] why, amid our economic prosperity and military security, do almost 70 percent of the public say we are off track? I submit that only when we turn to the right things—enduring, noble, spiritual things—will life get better.

During the last decade of the 20th century, there is a disturbing [20] reluctance to talk seriously about matters spiritual and religious. We have become used to not talking about the things that matter most. One will often hear that religious faith is a private matter. But whatever your faith—or even if you have none at all—it is a fact that when millions of people stop believing in God, enormous public consequences follow. Dostoyevsky reminded us in *The Brothers Karamazov* that "if God does not exist, everything is permissible." We are now seeing "everything."

What can be done? For one, we must once again connect public policies to our deepest beliefs. Right now we say one thing and do another.

• We *say* we want law and order, but we allow violent criminals to return to the streets.

• We *say* we want to stop illegitimacy, but we subsidize behavior that leads to it.

• We *say* we want to discourage teen-age sex, but educators across America treat teen-agers as if they were young animals in heat, and are more eager to dispense condoms than moral guidance.

• We *say* we want more families to stay together, but we make divorce easier to attain.

• We *say* we want a colorblind society, but we continue to count people by race and skin pigment.

Furthermore, America desperately needs to recover the purpose of education, which is to provide for the intellectual *and* moral education of the young. Plato made the point that good education makes good men, and good men act nobly.

Until a quarter-century or so ago, this time-honored belief virtually went unchallenged. But having departed from it, we are now reaping the whirlwind. We say we desire more civility and responsibility from our children, but many schools refuse to teach right and wrong. And so we talk about "skills facilitation," "self-esteem" and being "comfortable with ourselves."

Most important, we must return religion to its proper place. Religion provides us with moral bearings, and the solution to our chief problem of spiritual impoverishment depends on spiritual renewal. The surrendering of strong beliefs, in our private and public lives, has demoralized society.

Today, much of society ridicules and mocks those who are serious about their faith. America's only respectable form of bigotry is bigotry against religious people. And the only reason for hatred of religion is that it forces us to confront matters many would prefer to ignore.

Nobel Prize-winning author William Faulkner once declared, "I decline to accept the end of man." Man will prevail because, as Faulkner said, he alone among creatures "has a soul, a spirit capable of compassion and sacrifice and endurance."

In our time, we have seen America make enormous gains—a standard of living unimagined 50 years ago, with extraordinary advances in medicine, science and technology. Life expectancy has increased by more than 20 years in the past seven decades. Opportunity has been extended to those who were once denied it. And, of course, America prevailed in our "long, twilight struggle" against communism.

Today we must carry on a new struggle for the country we love. We must push hard against an age that is pushing hard against us. If we have full employment and greater economic growth—if we have cities of gold and alabaster—but our children have not learned how to walk in goodness, justice and mercy, then the American experiment, no matter how gilded, will have failed.

Do not surrender. Get mad. Get in the fight.

COMPREHENSION

1. In one sentence, summarize what Bennett believes to be the major factor that "ails America." Where in the essay does Bennett most clearly express his general thesis?
2. In paragraph 11, the author states, "Our culture seems almost dedicated to the corruption of the young." What does he mean by the word *culture,* and what does he mean by the term *the young*?
3. What is the significance of using the word *really* in the title? How would the connotation of the title have changed if the word had not been included?
4. The author states, "The ancients called our problem acedia." To whom does the term *ancients* refer?

RHETORIC

1. The first three paragraphs include anecdotes. How does the juxtaposition of these anecdotes serve to benefit Bennett's argument that "what ails America" is pervasive?
2. What information does the author provide to directly or indirectly suggest that he is an authority on the essay's subject matter?
3. Bennett uses a one-sentence paragraph three times in the essay nearly verbatim. Locate the three sentences. What is their rhetorical effect, and how do they contribute toward asserting the author's polemical style?
4. The author uses the generic "we" in describing America's troubles; for example, "We have become inured to the cultural rot," "It is something we have done to ourselves," "We *say* we want law and order," and so on. How does the repetition of this word emphasize his argument? Why would this method of repetition be particularly effective in a speech (from which this essay is condensed)?
5. What is the effect of the final paragraph? Does it provide closure to the essay? Does it provoke further thought on the subject? Does it seem abrupt and unsatisfying? Explain your view.
6. Where, if at all, does the author use *proof* to buttress his thesis? How does its presence or absence strengthen or weaken his argument?
7. The author makes direct or indirect references to historical figures and famous authors. Does he assume his audience is familiar with these references? What can you infer about the intended audience for this essay?

1. Argue for or against the proposition that public policy can legislate morality. Use examples that directly affect *you,* such as rules and laws governing drinking, smoking, driving, sex, work, and school.

2. Bennett claims that America "hates the spiritual." For a research paper, investigate studies on church attendance, published studies on America's beliefs and values, the rise of religious programming in the media, the Christian Coalition, and so on. Then write an informed, opinionated essay based upon your own research.

3. Many social critics blame unemployment and slow economic growth for many of our social ills, while the author implies in paragraph 33 that these are not such significant issues. Argue for or against Bennett's dismissal of them.

J. B. PRIESTLEY   John Boynton Priestley (1894–1984), best-selling English novelist and popular dramatist, was also a prolific writer of essays, many of them involving social and political criticism. His work includes *The English Novel* (1927), *The Good Companions* (1929), *Time and the Conways* (1937), *An Inspector Calls* (1946), and *The English* (1973). This selection from *Essays of Five Decades* (1968) offers an astute analysis of contemporary political habits.

J. B. PRIESTLEY

Wrong Ism

There are three isms that we ought to consider very carefully— regionalism, nationalism, internationalism. Of these three the one there is most fuss about, the one that starts men shouting and marching and shooting, the one that seems to have all the depth and thrust and fire, is of course nationalism. Nine people out of ten, I fancy, would say that of this trio it is the one that really counts, the big boss. Regionalism and internationalism, they would add, are comparatively small, shadowy, rather cranky. And I believe all this to be quite wrong. Like many another big boss, nationalism is largely bogus. It is like a bunch of flowers made of plastics.

The real flowers belong to regionalism. The mass of people everywhere may never have used the term. They are probably regionalists without knowing it. Because they have been brought up in a certain part of the world, they have formed perhaps quite unconsciously a deep attachment to its landscape and speech, its traditional customs, its food and drink, its songs and jokes. (There are of course always the rebels, often intellectuals and writers, but they are not the mass of people.) They are rooted in their region. Indeed, without this attachment a man can have no roots.

So much of people's lives, from earliest childhood onwards, is deeply intertwined with the common life of the region, they cannot help feeling strongly about it. A threat to it is a knife pointing at the heart. How can life ever be the same if bullying strangers come to change everything? The form and colour, the very taste and smell of dear familiar things will be different, alien, life-destroying. It would be better to die fighting. And it is precisely this, the nourishing life of the region, for which common men have so often fought and died.

This attachment to the region exists on a level far deeper than that of any political hocus-pocus. When a man says "my country" with real feeling, he is thinking about his region, all that has made up his life, and not about that political entity, the nation. There can be some confusion here simply because some countries are so small—and ours is one of them—and so old, again like ours, that much of what is national is also regional. Down the centuries, the nation, itself, so comparatively small, has been able to attach to itself the feeling really created by the region. (Even so there is something left over, as most people in Yorkshire or Devon, for example, would tell you.) This probably explains the fervent patriotism developed early in small countries. The English were announcing that they were English in the Middle Ages, before nationalism had arrived elsewhere.

If we deduct from nationalism all that it has borrowed or stolen from regionalism, what remains is mostly rubbish. The nation, as distinct from the region, is largely the creation of power-men and political manipulators. Almost all nationalist movements are led by ambitious frustrated men determined to hold office. I am not blaming them. I would do the same if I were in their place and wanted power so badly. But nearly always they make use of the rich warm regional feeling, the emotional dynamo of the movement, while being almost untouched by it themselves. This is because they are not as a rule deeply loyal to any region themselves. Ambition and a love of power can eat like acid into the tissues of regional loyalty. It is hard, if not impossible, to retain a natural piety and yet be for ever playing both ends against the middle.

Being itself a power structure, devised by men of power, the nation tends to think and act in terms of power. What would benefit the real life of the region, where men, women and children actually live, is soon sacrificed for the power and prestige of the nation. (And the personal vanity of presidents and ministers themselves, which historians too often disregard.) Among the new nations of our time innumerable peasants and labourers must have found themselves being cut down from five square meals a week to three in order to provide unnecessary airlines, military forces that can only be used against them and nobody else, great conference halls and official yachts and the rest. The last traces of imperialism and colonialism may have to be removed from Asia and Africa, where men can no longer endure being condemned to a permanent inferiority by the colour of their skins; but even so, the modern world, the real world of our time, does not want and would be far better without more and more nations, busy creating for themselves the very paraphernalia that western Europe is now trying to abolish. You are compelled to answer more questions when trying to spend half a day in Cambodia than you are now travelling from the Hook of Holland to Syracuse.

This brings me to internationalism. I dislike this term, which I used only to complete the isms. It suggests financiers and dubious promoters living nowhere but in luxury hotels; a shallow world of entrepreneurs and impresarios. (Was it Sacha Guitry who said that impresarios were men who spoke many languages but all with a foreign accent?) The internationalism I have in mind here is best described as world civilisation. It is life considered on a global scale. Most of our communications and transport already exist on this high wide level. So do many other things from medicine to meteorology. Our astronomers and physicists (except where they have allowed themselves to be hush-hushed) work here. The UN special agencies, about which we hear far too little, have contributed more and more to this world civilisation. All the arts, when they are arts and not chunks of nationalist propaganda, naturally take their place in it. And it grows, widens, deepens, in spite of the fact that for every dollar, ruble, pound or franc spent in explaining and praising it, a thousand are spent by the nations explaining and praising themselves.

This world civilisation and regionalism can get along together, especially if we keep ourselves sharply aware of their quite different but equally important values and rewards. A man can make his contribution to world civilisation and yet remain strongly regional in feeling: I know several men of this sort. There is of course the danger—it is with us now—of the global style flattening out the regional, taking local form, colour, flavour, away for ever, disinheriting future generations, threatening them with sensuous poverty and a huge boredom. But to understand and appreciate regionalism is to be on guard against this danger. And we must therefore make a clear distinction between regionalism and nationalism.

It is nationalism that tries to check the growth of world civilisation. And nationalism, when taken on a global scale, is more aggressive and demanding now than it has ever been before. This in the giant powers is largely disguised by the endless fuss in public about rival ideologies, now a largely unreal quarrel. What is intensely real is the glaring nationalism. Even the desire to police the world is nationalistic in origin. (Only the world can police the world.) Moreover, the nation-states of today are for the most part far narrower in their outlook, far more inclined to allow prejudice against the foreigner to impoverish their own style of living, than the old imperial states were. It should be part of world civilisation that men with particular skills, perhaps the product of the very regionalism they are rebelling against, should be able to move easily from country to country, to exercise those skills, in anything from teaching the violin to running a new type of factory to managing an old hotel. But nationalism, especially of the newer sort, would rather see everything done badly than allow a few non-nationals to get to work. And people face a barrage of passports, visas, immigration controls, labour permits; and in this respect are worse off than they were in 1900. But even so, in spite of all that nationalism can do—so long as it keeps its nuclear bombs to itself—the internationalism I have in mind, slowly creating a world civilisation, cannot be checked.

Nevertheless, we are still backing the wrong ism. Almost all our   10
money goes on the middle one, nationalism, the rotten meat between the two healthy slices of bread. We need regionalism to give us roots and that very depth of feeling which nationalism unjustly and greedily claims for itself. We need internationalism to save the world and to broaden and heighten our civilisation. While regional man enriches the lives that international man is already working to keep secure and healthy, national man, drunk with power, demands our loyalty, money and applause, and poisons the very air with his dangerous nonsense.

COMPREHENSION

1. What thesis does Priestley present? State the thesis in your own words.

2. Define *regionalism, nationalism,* and *internationalism* as Priestley presents these terms.

3. Explain Priestley's objections to nationalism. Where does he state these objections in the essay? What alternative does he propose?

RHETORIC

1. What striking metaphor does the author develop to capture the essence of nationalism? What is its sensory impact? Analyze another example of metaphorical language in the essay.

2. How does the suffix *-ism* function stylistically in the essay?

3. What is Priestley's principle of classification in this essay? How does he maintain proportion in the presentation of categories?

4. Analyze the relationship between definition and classification in the essay.

5. Examine Priestley's use of comparison and contrast.

6. Explain the connection between the introductory and concluding paragraphs.

WRITING

1. Priestley makes many assumptions about regionalism, nationalism, and internationalism. Which assumptions do you accept? Which assumptions do you reject? Explain in an essay.

2. Write a classification essay on at least three related "isms": capitalism, socialism, and communism; Protestantism, Catholicism, and Judaism; or regionalism, nationalism, and internationalism.

BARBARA TUCHMAN   Barbara Wertheim Tuchman (1912–1989) was born in New York City and received her B.A. degree from Radcliffe College in 1933. She is one of the most famous historians of the twentieth century, perhaps because of her strong literary style and popularity with the average reader. She was awarded two Pulitzer Prizes for general nonfiction, one in 1963 for *The Guns of August* and one in 1972 for *Stilwell and the American Experience in China, 1911–1945.* The former was a description and an interpretation of the opening days of World War I; the latter, about Joseph Warren Stilwell, an American who saw China's transformation from a feudal society to a communist state. Another work of major importance is *A Distant Mirror: The Calamitous Fourteenth Century* (1978), a book that attempted to demonstrate the similarities between the fourteenth century and our own. Her narrative style has helped to make her books best-sellers. She partly attributed her success to maintaining a spot outside the academic environment, which she felt would have cramped her style as a writer and thinker. Her book *The March of Folly: From Troy to Vietnam* (1984) sought to link different historical periods to demonstrate that nations and humans do not learn from their past mistakes but repeat them because of the same ambitions. Besides her ten books on history, she was a regular contributor to magazines such as *Harper's, Atlantic, American Scholar,* and *Foreign Affairs,* among others. The following essay demonstrates her accessible yet informative style. It is taken from *Practicing History* (1981).

BARBARA TUCHMAN

On Our Birthday—America as Idea

The United States is a nation consciously conceived, not one that ₁
evolved slowly out of an ancient past. It was a planned idea of democracy, of liberty of conscience and pursuit of happiness. It was the promise of equality of opportunity and individual freedom within a just social order, as opposed to the restrictions and repressions of the Old World. In contrast to the militarism of Europe, it would renounce standing armies and "sheathe the desolating sword of war." It was an experiment in Utopia to test the thesis that, given freedom, independence, and local self-government, people, in Kossuth's words, "will in due time ripen into all the excellence and all the dignity of humanity." It was a new life for the oppressed, it was enlightenment, it was optimism.

Regardless of hypocrisy and corruption, of greed, chicanery, brutal ₂
ity, and all the other bad habits man carries with him whether in the New World or Old, the founding idea of the United States remained, on the whole, dominant through the first hundred years. With reservations,

it was believed in by Americans, by visitors who came to aid our Revolution or later to observe our progress, by immigrants who came by the hundreds of thousands to escape an intolerable situation in their native lands.

The idea shaped our politics, our institutions, and to some extent our national character, but it was never the only influence at work. Material circumstances exerted an opposing force. The open frontier, the hardships of homesteading from scratch, the wealth of natural resources, the whole vast challenge of a continent waiting to be exploited, combined to produce a prevailing materialism and an American drive bent as much, if not more, on money, property, and power than was true of the Old World from which we had fled. The human resources we drew upon were significant: Every wave of immigration brought here those people who had the extra energy, gumption, or restlessness to uproot themselves and cross an unknown ocean to seek a better life. Two other factors entered the shaping process—the shadow of slavery and the destruction of the native Indian.

At its Centennial the United States was a material success. Through its second century the idea and the success have struggled in continuing conflict. The Statue of Liberty, erected in 1886, still symbolized the promise to those "yearning to breathe free." Hope, to them, as seen by a foreign visitor, was "domiciled in America as the Pope is in Rome." But slowly in the struggle the idea lost ground, and at a turning point around 1900, with American acceptance of a rather half-hearted imperialism, it lost dominance. Increasingly invaded since then by self-doubt and disillusion, it survives in the disenchantment of today, battered and crippled but not vanquished.

What has happened to the United States in the twentieth century is not a peculiarly American phenomenon but a part of the experience of the West. In the Middle Ages plague, wars, and social violence were seen as God's punishment upon man for his sins. If the concept of God can be taken as man's conscience, the same explanation may be applicable today. Our sins in the twentieth century—greed, violence, inhumanity—have been profound, with the result that the pride and self-confidence of the nineteenth century have turned to dismay and self-disgust.

In the United States we have a society pervaded from top to bottom by contempt for the law. Government—including the agencies of law enforcement—business, labor, students, the military, the poor no less than the rich, outdo each other in breaking the rules and violating the ethics that society has established for its protection. The average citizen, trying to hold a footing in standards of morality and conduct he once believed in, is daily knocked over by incoming waves of venality, vulgarity, irresponsibility, ignorance, ugliness, and trash in all senses of the word. Our government collaborates abroad with the worst enemies of humanity and liberty. It wastes our substance on useless proliferation of military hardware that can never buy security no matter how high the pile. It learns no lessons, employs no wisdom, and corrupts all who succumb to Potomac fever.

Yet the idea does not die. Americans are not passive under their 7 faults. We expose them and combat them. Somewhere every day some group is fighting a public abuse—openly and, on the whole, notwithstanding the FBI, with confidence in the First Amendment. The U.S. has slid a long way from the original idea. Nevertheless, somewhere between Gulag Archipelago and the featherbed of cradle-to-the-grave welfare, it still offers a greater opportunity for social happiness—that is to say, for well-being combined with individual freedom and initiative—than is likely elsewhere. The ideal society for which mankind has been striving through the ages will remain forever beyond our grasp. But if the great question, whether it is still possible to reconcile democracy with social order and individual liberty, is to find a positive answer, it will be here.

COMPREHENSION

1. What is the thesis of Tuchman's essay? How does it relate to her views concerning the founding of America?
2. Identify the four major forces that shaped the social development of America.
3. In paragraph 5, Tuchman states, "What has happened to the United States in the twentieth century is not a peculiarly American phenomenon but a part of the experience of the West." What does she mean by "the West" in terms of geography, culture, ideas, religion, and technology?

RHETORIC

1. What does Tuchman imply by citing the bicentennial of America with the phrase "Our Birthday"? How does the title set the tone for the rest of the essay?
2. Nouns can be considered concrete or abstract. How many abstract nouns are there in paragraph 1? Are the meanings of these words the same to all people? How does the use and frequency of these words in paragraph 1 and throughout the essay contribute to its tone?
3. Identify three *facts* in the essay. Identify three *opinions*. How did you distinguish between these two rhetorical forms. Does the essay seem "overloaded" with one at the expense of the other? Explain your view.
4. In the final sentence, Tuchman refers to "the great question." How does the substance of the final sentence provide closure to the entire essay? How does it reconcile the contradictions that Tuchman notes about American society throughout the essay? How does deleting the final sentence change the tenor of the entire essay?
5. Does this essay have a purpose? If so, is the purpose primarily to inform, to argue, to entertain, to celebrate, or to do a combination of these things? Explain your view.

6. A well-written essay consists of well-structured, coherent prose with no extraneous words or needlessly repetitive ideas. Does this essay fulfill these criteria? Explain your view.
7. Study the topic sentences of each paragraph. Do they fulfill the standard purpose of topic sentences; that is, do they summarize and preview the information contained in the paragraph that follows?

WRITING

1. Argue for or against the proposition that "we have a society pervaded from top to bottom by contempt for the law." Use recent examples from the news media to support your argument.
2. Many "histories" have been written: histories of nations, of sports, of war, of cultures, and so on. For a research paper, trace the origins of the concept of the "history of ideas." How is it defined? Who have been some of its major proponents? What have been some of its significant milestones?
3. For a creative writing project, write an essay from the perspective of someone in the year 2076 reviewing the success or failure of "America as Idea" for the country's tricentennial.

CLASSIC AND CONTEMPORARY

THOMAS JEFFERSON   Thomas Jefferson (1743–1826) was governor of Virginia during the American Revolution, America's first secretary of state, and the third President of the United States. He had a varied and monumental career as politician, public servant, scientist, architect, educator (he founded the University of Virginia), and man of letters. Jefferson attended the Continental Congress in 1775, where he wrote the rough draft of the Declaration of Independence and revised it; other hands made contributions to the document that was signed on July 4, 1776; but the wording, style, structure, and spirit of the final version are distinctly Jefferson's. Like Thomas Paine, Benjamin Franklin, James Madison, and other major figures of the Revolutionary era, Jefferson was notable for his use of prose as an instrument for social and political change. In the Declaration of Independence, we see the direct, precise, logical, and persuasive statement of revolutionary principles that makes the document one of the best known and best written texts in world history. Jefferson died in his home at Monticello on July 4, fifty years to the day from the signing of the Declaration of Independence.

THOMAS JEFFERSON

The Declaration of Independence

In Congress, July 4, 1776

The Unanimous Declaration of the thirteen united States of America

When in the Course of human events it becomes necessary for one [1] people to dissolve the political bands which have connected them with another, and to assume among the powers of the earth, the separate and equal station to which the Laws of Nature and of Nature's God entitle them, a decent respect to the opinions of mankind requires that they should declare the causes which impel them to the separation.

We hold these truths to be self-evident, that all men are created [2] equal, that they are endowed by their Creator with certain unalienable Rights, that among these are Life, Liberty and the pursuit of Happiness.—That to secure these rights, Governments are instituted among Men, deriving their just powers from the consent of the governed.— That whenever any Form of Government becomes destructive of these ends, it is the Right of the People to alter or to abolish it, and to institute new Government, laying its foundation on such principles and organizing its powers in such form, as to them shall seem most likely to effect their Safety and Happiness. Prudence, indeed, will dictate that Governments long established should not be changed for light and transient causes; and accordingly all experience hath shewn that mankind are more disposed to suffer, while evils are sufferable, than to right themselves by abolishing the forms to which they are accustomed. But when a long train of abuses and usurpations, pursuing invariably the same Object evinces a design to reduce them under absolute Despotism, it is their right, it is their duty, to throw off such Government, and to provide new Guards for their future security.—Such has been the patient sufferance of these Colonies; and such is now the necessity which constrains them to alter their former Systems of Government. The history of the present King of Great Britain is a history of repeated injuries and usurpations, all having in direct object the establishment of an absolute Tyranny over these States. To prove this, let Facts be submitted to a candid world.

He has refused his Assent to Laws, the most wholesome and neces- [3] sary for the public good.

He has forbidden his Governors to pass Laws of immediate and [4] pressing importance, unless suspended in their operation till his Assent should be obtained; and when so suspended, he has utterly neglected to attend to them.

He has refused to pass other Laws for the accommodation of large [5] districts of people, unless those people would relinquish the right of Representation in the Legislature, a right inestimable to them and formidable to tyrants only.

He has called together legislative bodies at places unusual, uncomfortable, and distant from the depository of their public Records, for the sole purpose of fatiguing them into compliance with his measures.

He has called together legislative bodies at places unusual, uncomfortable, and distant from the depository of their public Records, for the sole purpose of fatiguing them into compliance with his measures.

He has dissolved Representative Houses repeatedly, for opposing with manly firmness his invasions on the rights of the people.

8 He has refused for a long time, after such dissolutions, to cause others to be elected; whereby the Legislative powers, incapable of Annihilation, have returned to the People at large for their exercise; the State remaining in the mean time exposed to all the dangers of invasion from without, and convulsions within.

9 He has endeavoured to prevent the population of these States; for that purpose obstructing the Laws for Naturalization of Foreigners; refusing to pass others to encourage their migrations hither, and raising the conditions of new Appropriations of Lands.

10 He has obstructed the Administration of Justice, by refusing his Assent to Laws for establishing Judiciary powers.

11 He was made Judges dependent on his Will alone, for the tenure of their offices, and the amount and payment of their salaries.

12 He has erected a multitude of New Offices, and sent hither swarms of Officers to harass our people, and eat out their substance.

13 He has kept among us, in times of peace, Standing Armies without the Consent of our legislatures.

14 He has affected to render the Military independent of and superior to the Civil power.

15 He has combined with others to subject us to a jurisdiction foreign to our constitution, and unacknowledged by our laws; giving his Assent to their Acts of pretended Legislation:

For quartering large bodies of armed troops among us:

For protecting them, by a mock Trial, from punishment for any Murders which they should commit on the Inhabitants of these States:

For cutting off our Trade with all parts of the world:

For imposing Taxes on us without our Consent:

For depriving us in many cases, of the benefits of Trial by Jury:

For transporting us beyond Seas to be tried for pretended offences:

For abolishing the free System of English Laws in a neighboring Province, establishing therein an Arbitrary government, and enlarging its Boundaries so as to render it at once an example and fit instrument for introducing the same absolute rule into these Colonies:

For taking away our Charters, abolishing our most valuable Laws and altering fundamentally the Forms of our Governments:

For suspending our own Legislatures, and declaring themselves invested with power to legislate for us in all cases whatsoever.

16 He has abdicated Government here, by declaring us out of his Protection and waging War against us.

17 He has plundered our seas, ravaged our Coasts, burnt our towns, and destroyed the lives of our people.

18 He is at this time transporting large Armies of foreign Mercenaries to complete the works of death, desolation and tyranny, already begun

with circumstances of Cruelty & Perfidy scarcely paralleled in the most barbarous ages, and totally unworthy the Head of a civilized nation.

He has constrained our fellow Citizens taken Captive on the high 19 Seas to bear Arms against their Country, to become the executioners of their friends and Brethren, or to fall themselves by their Hands.

He has excited domestic insurrections amongst us, and has endeav- 20 oured to bring on the inhabitants of our frontiers, the merciless Indian Savages, whose known rule of warfare, is an undistinguished destruction of all ages, sexes and conditions.

In every stage of these Oppressions We have Petitioned for Redress 21 in the most humble terms: Our repeated Petitions have been answered only by repeated injury. A Prince, whose character is thus marked by every act which may define a Tyrant, is unfit to be the ruler of a free people.

Nor have We been wanting in attentions to our British brethren. We 22 have warned them from time to time of attempts by their legislature to extend an unwarrantable jurisdiction over us. We have reminded them of the circumstances of our emigration and settlement here. We have appealed to their native justice and magnanimity, and we have conjured them by the ties of our common kindred to disavow these usurpations, which would inevitably interrupt our connections and correspondence. They too have been deaf to the voice of justice and of consanguinity. We must, therefore, acquiesce in the necessity, which denounces our Separation, and hold them, as we hold the rest of mankind, Enemies in War, in Peace Friends.

We, therefore, the Representatives of the United States of America, 23 in General Congress, Assembled, appealing to the Supreme Judge of the world for the rectitude of our intentions, do, in the Name, and by Authority of the good People of these Colonies, solemnly publish and declare, That these United Colonies are, and of Right ought to be Free and Independent States; that they are Absolved from all Allegiance to the British Crown, and that all political connection between them and the State of Great Britain, is and ought to be totally dissolved; and that as Free and Independent States, they have full Power to levy War, conclude Peace, contract Alliances, establish Commerce, and to do all other Acts and Things which Independent States may of right do. And for the support of this Declaration, with a firm reliance on the protection of divine Providence, we mutually pledge to each other our Lives, our Fortunes and our sacred Honor.

COMPREHENSION

1. Explain Jefferson's main and subordinate purposes in this document.
2. What is Jefferson's key assertion, or argument? Mention several reasons that he gives to support his argument.
3. Summarize Jefferson's definition of human nature and of government. Read Forster's "My Wood" in Chapter 7 and consider how Forster might respond to Jefferson's definition.

1. There are many striking words and phrases in the Declaration of Independence, notably in the beginning. Locate three such examples, and explain their connotative power and effectiveness.
2. Jefferson and his colleagues had to draft a document designed for several audiences. What audiences did they have in mind? How do their language and style reflect their awareness of multiple audiences?
3. The Declaration of Independence is a classic model of syllogistic reasoning and deductive argument (see the Glossary). What is its major premise, and where is this premise stated? The minor premise? The conclusion?
4. What sort of inductive evidence does Jefferson offer?
5. Why is the middle portion, or body, of the Declaration of Independence considerably longer than the introduction or conclusion? What holds the body together?
6. Explain the function and effect of parallel structure in this document.

WRITING

1. Do you believe that "all men are created equal"? Justify your answer.
2. Discuss the relevance of the Declaration of Independence to politics today.
3. Explain why the Declaration of Independence is a model of effective prose.
4. Write your own declaration of independence—from family, employer, required courses, or the like. Develop this declaration as an Op-Ed piece for a newspaper.

MARTIN LUTHER KING, JR.   Martin Luther King, Jr. (1929–1968) was born in Atlanta, Georgia, and earned degrees from Morehouse College, Crozer Theological Seminary, Boston University, and Chicago Theological Seminary. As Baptist clergyman, civil rights leader, founder and president of the Southern Christian Leadership Conference, and, in 1964, Nobel Peace Prize winner, King was a celebrated advocate of nonviolent resistance to achieve equality and racial integration in the world. King was a gifted orator and a highly persuasive writer. His books include *Stride toward Freedom* (1958); *Letter from Birmingham City Jail* (1963); *Strength to Love* (1963); *Why We Can't Wait* (1964); and *Where Do We Go from Here: Chaos or Community?* (1967), a book published shortly before Reverend King was assassinated on April 4, 1968, in Memphis, Tennessee. This selection, a milestone of American oratory, was the keynote address at the March on Washington, August 28, 1963.

MARTIN LUTHER KING, JR.

I Have a Dream

I am happy to join with you today in what will go down in history as the greatest demonstration for freedom in the history of our nation.

Fivescore years ago, a great American, in whose symbolic shadow we stand today, signed the Emancipation Proclamation. This momentous decree came as a great beacon light of hope to millions of Negro slaves who had been seared in the flames of withering injustice. It came as a joyous daybreak to end the long night of their captivity.

But one hundred years later, the Negro still is not free; one hundred years later, the life of the Negro is still sadly crippled by the manacles of segregation and the chains of discrimination; one hundred years later, the Negro lives on a lonely island of poverty in the midst of a vast ocean of material prosperity; one hundred years later, the Negro is still languishing in the corners of American society and finds himself in exile in his own land.

So we've come here today to dramatize a shameful condition. In a sense we've come to our nation's capital to cash a check. When the architects of our republic wrote the magnificent words of the Constitution and the Declaration of Independence, they were signing a promissory note to which every American was to fall heir. This note was the promise that all men, yes, black men as well as white men, would be guaranteed the unalienable rights of life, liberty, and the pursuit of happiness.

It is obvious today that America has defaulted on this promissory note in so far as her citizens of color are concerned. Instead of honoring this sacred obligation, America has given the Negro people a bad check; a check which has come back marked "insufficient funds." We refuse to believe that there are insufficient funds in the great vaults of opportunity of this nation. And so we've come to cash this check, a check that will give us upon demand the riches of freedom and the security of justice.

We have also come to this hallowed spot to remind America of the fierce urgency of now. This is no time to engage in the luxury of cooling off or to take the tranquilizing drug of gradualism. Now is the time to make real the promises of democracy; now is the time to rise from the dark and desolate valley of segregation to the sunlit path of racial justice; now is the time to lift our nation from the quicksands of racial injustice to the solid rock of brotherhood; now is the time to make justice a reality for all God's children. It would be fatal for the nation to overlook the urgency of the moment. This sweltering summer of the Negro's legitimate discontent will not pass until there is an invigorating autumn of freedom and equality.

Nineteen sixty-three is not an end, but a beginning. And those who hope that the Negro needed to blow off steam and will now be content, will have a rude awakening if the nation returns to business as usual.

There will be neither rest nor tranquility in America until the Negro is granted his citizenship rights. The whirlwinds of revolt will continue to shake the foundations of our nation until the bright day of justice emerges.

But there is something that I must say to my people who stand on the warm threshold which leads into the palace of justice. In the process of gaining our rightful place we must not be guilty of wrongful deeds.

Let us not seek to satisfy our thirst for freedom by drinking from the cup of bitterness and hatred. We must forever conduct our struggle on the high plane of dignity and discipline. We must not allow our creative protest to degenerate into physical violence. Again and again we must rise to the majestic heights of meeting physical force with soul force.

The marvelous new militancy which has engulfed the Negro community must not lead us to a distrust of all white people, for many of our white brothers, as evidenced by their presence here today, have come to realize that their destiny is tied up with our destiny and they have come to realize that their freedom is inextricably bound to our freedom. This offense we share mounted to storm the battlements of injustice must be carried forth by a biracial army. We cannot walk alone.

And as we walk, we must make the pledge that we shall always march ahead. We cannot turn back. There are those who are asking the devotees of civil rights, "When will you be satisfied?" We can never be satisfied as long as the Negro is the victim of the unspeakable horrors of police brutality.

We can never be satisfied as long as our bodies, heavy with fatigue of travel, cannot gain lodging in the motels of the highways and the hotels of the cities. We cannot be satisfied as long as the Negro's basic mobility is from a smaller ghetto to a larger one.

We can never be satisfied as long as our children are stripped of their selfhood and robbed of their dignity by signs stating "for whites only." We cannot be satisfied as long as a Negro in Mississippi cannot vote and a Negro in New York believes he has nothing for which to vote. No, we are not satisfied, and we will not be satisfied until justice rolls down like waters and righteousness like a mighty stream.

I am not unmindful that some of you have come here out of excessive trials and tribulation. Some of you have come fresh from narrow jail cells. Some of you have come from areas where your quest for freedom left you battered by the storms of persecution and staggered by the winds of police brutality. You have been the veterans of creative suffering. Continue to work with the faith that unearned suffering is redemptive.

Go back to Mississippi; go back to Alabama; go back to South Carolina; go back to Georgia; go back to Louisiana; go back to the slums and ghettos of the northern cities, knowing that somehow this situation can, and will be changed. Let us not wallow in the valley of despair.

So I say to you, my friends, that even though we must face the difficulties of today and tomorrow, I still have a dream. It is a dream deeply rooted in the American dream that one day this nation will rise up and live out the true meaning of its creed—we hold these truths to be self-evident, that all men are created equal.

I have a dream that one day on the red hills of Georgia, sons of for- 18
mer slaves and sons of former slave-owners will be able to sit down
together at the table of brotherhood.

I have a dream that one day, even the state of Mississippi, a state 19
sweltering with the heat of injustice, sweltering with the heat of oppression, will be transformed into an oasis of freedom and justice.

I have a dream my four little children will one day live in a nation 20
where they will not be judged by the color of their skin but by content
of their character. I have a dream today!

I have a dream that one day, down in Alabama, with its vicious 21
racists, with its governor having his lips dripping with the words of
interposition and nullification, that one day, right there in Alabama, little black boys and black girls will be able to join hands with little white
boys and white girls as sisters and brothers. I have a dream today!

I have a dream that one day every valley shall be exalted, every hill 22
and mountain shall be made low, the rough places shall be made plain,
and the crooked places shall be made straight and the glory of the Lord
will be revealed and all flesh shall see it together.

This is our hope. This is the faith that I go back to the South with. 23

With this faith we will be able to hear out of the mountain of 24
despair a stone of hope. With this faith we will be able to transform the
jangling discords of our nation into a beautiful symphony of brotherhood.

With this faith we will be able to work together, to pray together, to 25
struggle together, to go to jail together, to stand up for freedom
together, knowing that we will be free one day. This will be the day
when all of God's children will be able to sing with new meaning—"my
country 'tis of thee; sweet land of liberty; of thee I sing; land where my
fathers died, land of the pilgrim's pride; from every mountain side, let
freedom ring"—and if America is to be a great nation, this must
become true.

So let freedom ring from the prodigious hilltops of New Hamp- 26
shire.

Let freedom ring from the mighty mountains of New York. 27

Let freedom ring from the heightening Alleghenies of Pennsylvania. 28

Let freedom ring from the snow-capped Rockies of Colorado. 29

Let freedom ring from the curvaceous slopes of California. 30

But not only that. 31

Let freedom ring from Stone Mountain of Georgia. 32

Let freedom ring from Lookout Mountain of Tennessee. 33

Let freedom ring from every hill and molehill of Mississippi, from 34
every mountainside, let freedom ring.

And when we allow freedom to ring, when we let it ring from every 35
village and hamlet, from every state and city, we will be able to speed
up that day when all of God's children—black men and white men,
Jews and Gentiles, Catholics and Protestants—will be able to join hands
and to sing in the words of the old Negro spiritual, "Free at last, free at
last; thank God Almighty, we are free at last."

1. What is the main purpose behind this speech? Where does King state this purpose most clearly?
2. Why does King make use of "fivescore years ago" (paragraph 2)? How is this more appropriate than simply saying, "a hundred years ago"?
3. Who is King's audience? Where does he acknowledge the special historic circumstances influencing his speech?

RHETORIC

1. From what sources else does King adapt phrases to give his work allusive richness?
2. What do the terms *interposition* and *nullification* (paragraph 21) mean? What is their historical significance?
3. Why does King make use of repetition? Does this technique work well in print? Explain.
4. What is the purpose of the extended metaphor in paragraphs 4 and 5? Which point in paragraph 3 does it refer to?
5. In which paragraphs does King address the problems of African Americans?
6. Why is this selection entitled "I Have a Dream"? How do dreams serve as a motif for this speech?

WRITING

1. "I Have a Dream" is considered by many people to be among the greatest speeches delivered by an American. Do you think that it deserves to be? Explain in an essay.
2. Write a comparative essay analyzing King's assessment of black Americans' condition in 1963 and their condition today. What do you think King would say if he knew of contemporary conditions?
3. Write your own "I Have a Dream" essay, basing it on your vision of America or of a special people.
4. Prepare a newspaper editorial advocating a solution to one aspect of racial, ethnic, or sexual injustice.

CLASSIC AND CONTEMPORARY: QUESTIONS FOR COMPARISON

1. Compare the Declaration of Independence with King's speech in terms of the level of language, style, and content. Are they equally powerful and resonant? Cite specific passages from the essays to illustrate your responses.
2. Rewrite the Declaration of Independence in modern English as you believe Dr. King might, reflecting his concerns about the African American and other minorities in this country. Include a list of grievances similar to the one concerning British rule.
3. Write a research paper about the lives and times of King and Jefferson. Compare and contrast any significant events or pertinent biographical data in their backgrounds.

1. Using the essays of Gordon, Tuchman, and others in this chapter, write an essay in which you develop the topic "What Is an American?"

2. Write an essay that links the Declaration of Independence and Tuchman's essay.

3. Examine one of the issues developed in this section (for example, immigration or apartheid), and argue how wisely or unwisely governments have dealt with this issue.

4. Compare and contrast the opinions expressed by Machiavelli and Priestley about government in their essays.

5. King speaks of the Declaration of Independence as a promissory note to the people of the United States. Using the essays of Gordon and Sanders, write an essay which considers what the United States may still owe its citizens.

6. Using the essays of Will and Bennett as support, write a causal-analysis essay on the wisdom or folly of U.S. public policy.

7. Both Thomas Jefferson and Martin Luther King, Jr., made powerful appeals to the U.S. government on behalf of their people. Write a comparison/contrast essay that examines the language, style, and content of both essays.

CHAPTER SEVEN

Work, Business, and Economics

W ork is central to the human experience; in fact, it is work in its economic and social outcomes that provides us with the keys to an understanding of culture and civilization. It tells us much about scarcity and abundance, poverty and affluence, the "haves" and "have-nots" in any society, as well as a nation's economic imperatives. Whether it is the rise and fall of cities, the conduct of businesses and corporations, or the economic policies of government, we see in the culture of work an attempt to impose order on nature. Work is our handprint—much like the handprints discovered in underwater caves in southern France—upon the world.

The work we perform and the careers we pursue also define us in very personal ways. "I'm a professor at Harvard" or "I work for IBM" serve as identity badges, for what we do explains, at least in part, what and who we are. The very act of "looking for work" illuminates one's status in society, one's background, one's aspirations. And as several writers in this chapter argue, notably Jonathan Swift in his classic "A Modest Proposal," labor reveals those configurations of power—both economic and political—that exist in any society or nation.

According to Freud, whom you encountered in a previous chapter, work is the basis of one's social reality. We speak, for example, of "the work ethic" that is ingrained in the American character as if the very reality of labor uniquely defines our culture. You might like your work, or you might loathe it; be employed or unemployed; enjoy the reputa-tion of a workaholic or a person who lives for leisure time; view work as a curse or as a duty. In each instance, it is work that occupies a cen-tral position in your relationship to society. Indeed, the complex nature and economy of work, as Jessica Mitford demonstrates in her savagely satiric essay on American funeral practices, pursues us to the grave.

Regardless of your perspective on the issue, it is important to understand the multiple dimensions of work. In both traditional and modern societies, work prepares us for economic and social roles. It affects families, school curricula, public policy. Ultimately, as many authors here suggest, it determines our self-esteem. Through work we come to terms with ourselves and our environment. The nature and purpose of the work we do provide us with a powerful measure of our worth.

Previewing the Chapter

As you read the essays in this chapter and respond to them in discussion and writing, consider the following questions:

• Does the author have a subjective or an objective view of work? How do you know?

• What assumptions does the author make about the value of work?

• Does the author discuss work in general or focus on one particular aspect of work?

• How does the writer define *work?* In what ways, if any, does the author expand on the simple definition of *work* as "paid employment"?

• What issues of race, class, and gender does the author raise?

• What is the relationship of work to the economic system depicted in the author's essay?

• What tone does the writer take in his or her presentation of the work experience?

• What psychological insights does the author offer into the culture of work?

• What does the writer's style reveal about his or her attitude toward work?

• Considering these essays, identify the needs that people must have met if their labor is to assume significance for them.

ANNA QUINDLEN   Anna Quindlen was born in 1953 in Philadelphia. She has worked as a reporter and columnist for the *New York Post* and *The New York Times*. She published a novel entitled *Object Lessons* in 1991. In 1992, she received the Pulitzer Prize for commentary. An outspoken feminist, she stated in an interview in *Commonweal* that "I write for me. . . . I tend to write about what we have come, unfortunately, to call women's issues. Those are issues that directly affect my life and those are issues that are historically underreported." The following is an essay about the contemporary father, published in a collection of her work entitled *Thinking Out Loud* (1993).

ANNA QUINDLEN

Men at Work

Overheard in a Manhattan restaurant, one woman to another: "He's a terrific father, but he's never home."

The five o'clock dads can be seen on cable television these days, just after that time in the evening the stay-at-home moms call the arsenic hours. They are sixties sitcom reruns, Ward and Steve and Alex, and fifties guys. They eat dinner with their television families and provide counsel afterward in the den. Someday soon, if things keep going the way they are, their likenesses will be enshrined in a diorama in the Museum of Natural History, frozen in their recliner chairs. The sign will say, "Here sit lifelike representations of family men who worked only eight hours a day." 1

The five o'clock dad has become an endangered species. A corporate culture that believes presence is productivity, in which people of ambition are afraid to be seen leaving the office, has lengthened his workday and shortened his homelife. So has an economy that makes it difficult for families to break even at the end of the month. For the man who is paid by the hour, that means never saying no to overtime. For the man whose loyalty to the organization is measured in time at his desk, it means goodbye to nine to five. 2

To lots of small children it means a visiting father. The standard joke in one large corporate office is that the dads always say their children look like angels when they're sleeping because that's the only way they ever see them. A Gallup survey taken several years ago showed that roughly 12 percent of the men surveyed with children under the age of six worked more than sixty hours a week, and an additional 25 percent worked between fifty and sixty hours. (Less than 8 percent of the working women surveyed who had children of that age worked those hours.) 3

No matter how you divide it up, those are twelve-hour days. When ₄ the talk-show host Jane Wallace adopted a baby recently, she said one reason she was not troubled by becoming a mother without becoming a wife was that many of her married female friends were "functionally single," given the hours their husbands worked. The evening commuter rush is getting longer. The 7:45 to West Backofbeyond is more crowded than ever before. The eight o'clock dad. The nine o'clock dad.

There's a horribly sad irony to this, and it is that the quality of ₅ fathering is better than it was when the dads left work at five o'clock and came home to café curtains and tuna casserole. The five o'clock dad was remote, a "Wait till your father gets home" kind of dad with a newspaper for a face. The roles he and his wife had were clear: she did nurture and home, he did discipline and money.

The role fathers have carved out for themselves today is a vast ₆ improvement, a muddling of those old boundaries. Those of us obliged to convert behavior into trends have probably been a little heavy-handed on the shared childbirth and egalitarian diaper-changing. But fathers today do seem to be more emotional with their children, more nurturing, more open. Many say, "My father never told me he loved me," and so they tell their own children all the time that they love them.

When they're home. ₇

There are people who think that this is changing even as we speak, ₈ that there is a kind of perestroika of home and work that we will look back on as beginning at the beginning of the 1990s. A nonprofit organization called the Families and Work Institute advises corporations on how to balance personal and professional obligations and concerns, and Ellen Galinsky, its cofounder, says she has noticed a change in the last year.

"When we first started doing this the groups of men and of women ₉ sounded very different," she said. "If the men complained at all about long hours, they complained about their wives' complaints. Now if the timbre of the voice was disguised I couldn't tell which is which. The men are saying: 'I don't want to live this way anymore. I want to be with my kids.' I think the corporate culture will have to begin to respond to that."

This change can only be to the good, not only for women but espe- ₁₀ cially for men, and for kids, too. The stereotypical five o'clock dad belongs in a diorama, with his "Ask your mother" and his "Don't be a crybaby." The father who believes hugs and kisses are sex-blind and a dirty diaper requires a change, not a woman, is infinitely preferable. What a joy it would be if he were around more.

"This is the man's half of having it all," said Don Conway-Long, ₁₁ who teaches a course at Washington University in St. Louis about men's relationships that drew 135 students this year for thirty-five places. "We're trying to do what women want of us, what children want of us, but we're not willing to transform the workplace." In other words, the hearts and minds of today's fathers are definitely in the right place. If only their bodies could be there, too.

COMPREHENSION

1. According to the author, contemporary fathers and "traditional" fathers both have faults. Describe the specific problems in each group.
2. What is the thesis of this essay? Where in the essay is this thesis most succinctly articulated?
3. Is this a "regional" essay? Does it address a particular class or geographic area of America? Would the examples need to be expanded if the author were to include *all* types of American fathers? Explain.

RHETORIC

1. The author uses some unique phrasing and vocabulary in her essay. What is the effect on the tone of the essay of expressions such as "arsenic hours," "visiting father," "'functionally single,'" "West Backofbeyond," and "perestroika"?
2. The opening paragraph of an essay often sets the tone for the rest. How does the tone of paragraph 1 help direct the tone of the essay's argument?
3. In paragraph 5, the author states that there is a "horribly sad irony" in the fact that fathers are better nurturers now but have less time to nurture. What other ironies does the author use to advance her argument?
4. What is the purpose of the rhetorical strategy of using the three-word paragraph "When they're home"? Does it add or detract from the coherence of the essay?
5. Paragraph 5 contains the rather oddly structured sentence. "The roles he and his wife had were clear: she did nurture and home, he did discipline and money." Conduct a grammatical analysis of the sentence. Does it make sense? Does it transgress any rules of grammar? Explain.
6. In paragraph 6, the author states, "fathers today do seem to be more emotional with their children, more nurturing, more open." Where in the essay does she provide documentation of this? Is this assertion argued sufficiently, or is it merely presented as an assumption without evidence?
7. Does the author provide a solution or a recommendation on how to solve the problems she raises? Does its presence or absence strengthen or weaken the argument? Explain.

WRITING

1. Argue for or against the proposition that the author's description of the modern father is a narrow one, based on biases of class and culture.
2. The author cites television portraits of fifties fathers as her evidence for the family behavior of the traditional father. For a research project, explore whether her comparison between the contemporary father and the traditional one is accurate by comparing two books on family roles: one written during the 1950s, the other during the 1990s.
3. For a creative writing project, write an imaginary letter to a supervisor, stating your view that your work hours should be reduced so that you can spend more time with your family. Be sure to include appropriate supporting material.

BARBARA EHRENREICH Barbara Ehrenreich was born in 1941 in Butte, Montana. She received a B.A. degree from Reed College and a Ph.D. from Rockefeller University. Ehrenreich is an outspoken feminist and socialist who has challenged many of our theories about the changing roles of the sexes in contemporary America. A firm believer that male domination of the health care system, the world of work, and politics has contributed to a growing gap between the "haves" and "have-nots" in America, Ehrenreich's books and essays have brought major attention to issues that many Americans shy away from. Ehrenreich's ideas are articulately discussed in *The Fears of Men: American Dreams and the Flight from Commitment* (1983), *Fear of Falling: The Inner Life of the Middle Class* (1989), and *The Worst Years of Our Lives: Irreverent Notes from a Decade of Greed* (1990). Ehrenreich is a serious social critic, as the following essay suggests.

BARBARA EHRENREICH

Battered Welfare Syndrome

Hardly anyone these days recommends punching and slapping as a   1
way of settling marital disputes. On the daytime talk shows, audiences go into frenzies of outrage over batterers and any batterees who dawdle before calling the hotline. In California and Massachusetts, Governors who are feverishly cutting programs that aid women in poverty are proposing actual increases in funds to combat domestic violence. Thanks to Nicole Brown Simpson's sad fate, we tell ourselves, we're all painfully aware of the problem. So why, a rational observer might inquire, are we simultaneously hell-bent on policies that will lock millions of women into violent and abusive relationships?

Because this will be one undeniable effect of welfare reform, as   2
passed by the House and contemplated in many states. One of the first things a woman is likely to do when fleeing an abusive relationship is apply for welfare; officials at some battered-women's shelters report that 60% to 95% of the women they help go on welfare, at least for the short term. These are such women as the San Antonio mother of three profiled in the Houston *Chronicle,* who fled when her otherwise straight-living, Baptist, teetotaler husband took to slapping her in front of the children. She fled to a shelter, got on welfare and eventually became single and self-sufficient.

Reforms that make welfare harder to get and worth less when you   3
get it will leave this escape hatch a lot narrower. Residency requirements, for example, effectively bar women from fleeing their abusers from one state to another, and work requirements will discourage the woman with no child care from escaping her—and possibly her children's—tormentor.

No one knows exactly what portion of the welfare rolls is made up [4] of refugees from domestic violence, but knowledgeable estimates are startlingly high. In preliminary research on a small sample of Chicago welfare recipients, Susan Lloyd at Northwestern University found nearly half mentioned abusive relationships as a factor in their need for welfare. Arlene McAtee, associate director of Mid-Iowa Community Action, estimates three-quarters of the women she sees come to welfare as a way out of domestic violence. And in some surveys of women in homeless shelters, half the respondents say they're homeless because they fled from a violent mate.

In fact, abuse at any point in a woman's life appears to increase the [5] odds for future welfare enrollment. A recent study by the Washington State Institute for Public Policy found that 60% of women on public assistance had experienced some form of abuse, physical or sexual, as adults. Abuse experienced in childhood was, if anything, even more damaging—predisposing girls to early sexual activity, teenage mother-hood and, again, the eventual need for welfare.

All this suggests the "cycle of dependency" that needs to be cured [6] is not so much one of the dependency on government "handouts" as one of dependency on abusive men. Abuse, even of the verbal kind, saps self-esteem; physical abuse can imprison a woman at home, too ashamed to show up for work with a black eye or cigarette burns. No matter where they start out in the socioeconomic spectrum, victims of abuse are especially vulnerable to poverty and—to round out the cycle—poor women are especially vulnerable to abuse.

Welfare can and sometimes does free women from dependency on [7] predatory males, as plenty of welfare alumnae can testify. But welfare benefits have been shrinking for two decades, to a level—a little less than $400 a month per family, on average—that forces many recipients into financial reliance on any man who can help pay for the groceries. This, according to the researchers, is why one recent study found that 58% of the women enrolled in a Chicago welfare-to-work-training pro-gram were *current* victims of domestic violence.

Some women, of course, can escape their abusers with no help from [8] welfare, and plenty of women who go on welfare have been battered by poverty alone. But only a fool, or a smug male legislator, could think of crafting welfare policy as if domestic violence doesn't exist. The closer you look at the real narratives of women's lives, the more you realize that there is a war going on, a hidden war of men against women— fought with fists and blunt objects, over such issues as why the baby makes so much noise or dinner wasn't ready on time. In this war the wounded don't get much help; they're often stigmatized and reviled for seeking it.

Enter, stage right, the welfare reformers, full of helpful advice for [9] downtrodden women. Get a job, they say, not noticing that some batter-ers will do anything to prevent that, including stalking their victims at job sites. Get married, they say, not noticing that the potential bridegroom may be a practicing sadist. Even a reasonable-sounding "reform," such as requiring recipients to identify the father of their children, can be enough to trigger his rage and precipitate a new round of abuse.

The fact is that domestic violence, ugly as we pretend to find it, 10 seems to be becoming part of our national policy. Despite our pious concern for the battered, the message from the welfare reformers is clear and cold: stand by your man, they're saying, even when he's knocked you to the floor.

COMPREHENSION

1. What is the meaning of the title of this piece? What popular term is it adapted from?
2. In paragraph 9, Ehrenreich says, "Enter, stage right, the welfare reformers." What pun is intended in this remark?
3. On which group of individuals does Ehrenreich most clearly place the blame for the threat to the welfare system?

RHETORIC

1. In paragraphs 2, 3, and 4, Ehrenreich uses three tools of argumentation to support her views. What are they? Are they effective?
2. In paragraphs 8 and 9, Ehrenreich describes two ways "a hidden war of men against women" manifests itself. How does the author make the transition from describing one battle in this war to another?
3. A common rule in essay writing is to capture the reader's attention in the first paragraph. What rhetorical devices does Ehrenreich employ to pique your interest? Is she successful? Why, or why not?
4. In the final paragraph, the author states, "domestic violence, ugly as we pretend to find it, seems to be becoming part of our national policy." Does this conclusion follow from her argument, or is it a leap in logic? Explain your view.
5. Study the topic sentences of each paragraph. Do they fulfill their function of introducing the subject matter for the information that follows?
6. Study the introductory paragraph and the concluding paragraph. What similarities in style, tone, and content can you find that help "frame" Ehrenreich's main argument? How do they help lend structural cohesiveness to the essay as a whole?

WRITING

1. Write an argumentative essay entitled, "If Women Were in Charge of Welfare Legislation."
2. Arrange a visit to a local community-based organization or welfare office, and interview a social worker concerning the profile of the typical welfare recipient. Explain that you are writing a college paper based upon your reading of the Ehrenreich article. Write an informative report based on your primary research.

3. Write a satirical essay entitled, "If Men Were the Sole Recipients of Welfare Benefits."

ELLEN GOODMAN   Ellen Holtz Goodman (b. 1941) is an award-winning journalist who writes a syndicated column for the *Boston Globe.* She is the author of *Close to Home* (1979) and *At Large* (1981) and has been a commentator on television and radio. Goodman is an adept practitioner of the personal essay. In the following selection, her celebrated penchant for irony and satire finds a perfect focus in the working lives of women.

ELLEN GOODMAN

Being a Secretary
Can Be Hazardous to Your Health

They used to say it with flowers or celebrate it with a somewhat liquid lunch. National Secretaries Week was always good for at least a token of appreciation. But the way the figures add up now, the best thing a boss can do for a secretary this week is cough up for her cardiogram.

"Stress and the Secretary" has become the hottest new syndrome on the heart circuit.

It seems that it isn't those Daring Young Women in their Dress-for-Success Suits who are following men down the cardiovascular trail to ruin. Nor is it the female professionals who are winning their equal place in intensive care units.

It is powerlessness and not power that corrupts women's hearts. And clerical workers are the number one victims.

In the prestigious Framingham study, Dr. Suzanne Haynes, an epidemiologist with the National Heart, Lung and Blood Institute, found that working women as a whole have no higher rate of heart disease than housewives. But women employed in clerical and sales occupations do. Their coronary disease rates are twice that of other women.

"This is not something to ignore," says Dr. Haynes, "since such a high percent of women work at clerical jobs." In fact, 35 percent of all working women, or 18 million of us, hold these jobs.

When Dr. Haynes looked into their private lives, she found the women at greatest risk—with a one in five chance of heart disease—were clerical workers with blue-collar husbands, and three or more children. When she then looked at their work lives, she discovered that the ones who actually developed heart disease were those with nonsupportive bosses who hadn't changed jobs very often and who had trouble letting their anger out.

In short, being frustrated, dead-ended, without a feeling of control over your life is bad for your health. 8

The irony in all the various and sundry heart statistics is that we now have a weird portrait of the Cardiovascular Fun Couple of the Office: The Type A Boss and his secretary. The male heart disease stereotype is, after all, the Type A aggressive man who always needs to be in control, who lives with a great sense of time urgency . . . and is likely to be a white-collar boss. 9

"The Type A man is trying to be in control. But given the way most businesses are organized there are, in fact, few ways for them to be in control of their jobs," says Dr. Haynes. The only thing the Type A boss can be in control of is his secretary who in turn feels . . . well you get the picture. He's not only getting heart disease, he's giving it. 10

As if all this weren't enough to send you out for the annual three martini lunch, clerical workers are increasingly working for a new Type A boss: the computer. 11

These days fewer women are sitting in front of bosses with notepads and more are sitting in front of Visual Display Terminals. Word processors, data processors, microprocessors . . . these are the demanding, time-conscious, new automatons of automation. 12

There is nothing intrinsically evil about computers. I am writing this on a VDT and if you try to take it away from me, I will break your arm. But as Working Women, the national association of office workers, puts it in their release this week, automation is increasingly producing clerical jobs that are de-skilled, down-graded, dead-ended and dissatisfying. 13

As Karen Nussbaum of the Cleveland office described it, the office of the future may well be the factory of the past. Work on computers is often reduced to simple, repetitive, monotonous tasks. Workers are often expected to produce more for no more pay, and there are also reports of a disturbing trend to processing speed-ups and piece-rate pay, and a feeling among clerical workers that their jobs are computer controlled. 14

"It's not the machine, but the way it's used by employers," says Working Women's research director, Judith Gregory. Too often, automation's most important product is stress. 15

Groups, like Working Women, are trying to get clerical workers to organize in what they call "a race against time" so that computers will become their tools instead of their supervisors. 16

But in the meantime, if you are (1) a female clerical worker, (2) with a blue-collar husband, (3) with three or more children, (4) in a dead-end job, (5) without any way to express anger, (6) with a Type A boss, (7) or a Type A computer controlling your work day . . . *you better start jogging.* 17

COMPREHENSION

1. What slogan does the author's title play upon? How does it prepare us for Goodman's thesis? What is her thesis?

2. What major problem does Goodman discuss in this essay? What are the causes of the problem?

3. How does the author describe the Type A boss and the Type A female employee?

RHETORIC

1. How does Goodman use colloquial language to help establish the tone of her essay?

2. List examples of comic language. What is Goodman's purpose? Comment on the relationship of Goodman's use of comic language to her thesis.

3. What technique does Goodman use to establish the topic of her essay?

4. What types of examples does Goodman use to reinforce her generalizations? Do any of the examples qualify as expert testimony? Explain.

5. Where does Goodman state her thesis? How does her conclusion reinforce this thesis?

6. What patterns of comparison and contrast do you find? Why does the author employ this technique?

WRITING

1. Does Goodman's range of humor work for or against the seriousness of her topic? Explain your response in an evaluative essay.

2. Analyze the varieties of stress that you have felt while employed at a particular job.

3. Argue for or against the proposition that working women do not experience any more stress than working men.

4. Describe the Type A worker or professional, and propose solutions to his or her problems.

E. M. FORSTER   Edward Morgan Forster (1879–1970), English essayist, novelist, biographer, and literary critic, wrote several notable works of fiction dealing with the constricting effects of social and national conventions upon human relationships. These novels include *A Room with a View* (1908), *Howards End* (1910), and *A Passage to India* (1924). In addition, his lectures on fiction, collected as *Aspects of the Novel* (1927), remain graceful elucidations of the genre. In "My Wood," taken from his essay collection *Abinger Harvest* (1936), Forster writes with wit and wisdom about the effect of property upon human behavior—notably his own.

E. M. FORSTER

My Wood

A few years ago I wrote a book which dealt in part with the difficulties   1
of the English in India. Feeling that they would have had no difficulties
in India themselves, the Americans read the book freely. The more they
read it the better it made them feel, and a cheque to the author was the
result. I bought a wood with the cheque. It is not a large wood—it contains scarcely any trees, and it is intersected, blast it, by a public footpath. Still, it is the first property that I have owned, so it is right that
other people should participate in my shame, and should ask themselves, in accents that will vary in horror, this very important question:
What is the effect of property upon the character? Don't let's touch
economics; the effect of private ownership upon the community as a
whole is another question—a more important question, perhaps, but
another one. Let's keep to psychology. If you own things, what's their
effect on you? What's the effect on me of my wood?

In the first place, it makes me feel heavy. Property does have this   2
effect. Property produces men of weight, and it was a man of weight
who failed to get into the Kingdom of Heaven. He was not wicked, that
unfortunate millionaire in the parable, he was only stout; he stuck out
in front, not to mention behind, and as he wedged himself this way and
that in the crystalline entrance and bruised his well-fed flanks, he saw
beneath him a comparatively slim camel passing through the eye of a
needle and being woven into the robe of God. The Gospels all through
couple stoutness and slowness. They point out what is perfectly obvious, yet seldom realized: that if you have a lot of things you cannot
move about a lot, that furniture requires dusting, dusters require servants, servants require insurance stamps, and the whole tangle of them
makes you think twice before you accept an invitation to dinner or go
for a bathe in the Jordan. Sometimes the Gospels proceed further and
say with Tolstoy that property is sinful; they approach the difficult
ground of asceticism here, where I cannot follow them. But as to the
immediate effects of property on people, they just show straightforward
logic. It produces men of weight. Men of weight cannot, by definition,
move like the lightning from the East unto the West, and the ascent of
a fourteen-stone bishop into a pulpit is thus the exact antithesis of the
coming of the Son of Man. My wood makes me feel heavy.

In the second place, it makes me feel it ought to be larger.   3

The other day I heard a twig snap in it. I was annoyed at first, for I   4
thought that someone was blackberrying, and depreciating the value of
the undergrowth. On coming nearer, I saw it was not a man who had
trodden on the twig and snapped it, but a bird, and I felt pleased. My

bird. The bird was not equally pleased. Ignoring the relation between us, it took fright as soon as it saw the shape of my face, and flew straight over the boundary hedge into a field, the property of Mrs. Henessy, where it sat down with a loud squawk. It had become Mrs. Henessy's bird. Something seemed grossly amiss here, something that would not have occurred had the wood been larger. I could not afford to buy Mrs. Henessy out, I dared not murder her, and limitations of this sort beset me on every side. Ahab did not want that vineyard—he only needed it to round off his property, preparatory to plotting a new curve—and all the land around my wood has become necessary to me in order to round off the wood. A boundary protects. But—poor little thing—the boundary ought in its turn to be protected. Noises on the edge of it. Children throw stones. A little more, and then a little more, until we reach the sea. Happy Canute! Happier Alexander! And after all, why should even the world be the limit of possession? A rocket containing a Union Jack, will, it is hoped, be shortly fired at the moon. Mars. Sirius. Beyond which. . . . But these immensities ended by saddening me. I could not suppose that my wood was the destined nucleus of universal dominion—it is so very small and contains no mineral wealth beyond the blackberries. Nor was I comforted when Mrs. Henessy's bird took alarm for the second time and flew clean away from us all, under the belief that it belonged to itself.

In the third place, property makes its owner feel that he ought to do something to it. Yet he isn't sure what. A restlessness comes over him, a vague sense that he has a personality to express—the same sense which, without any vagueness, leads the artist to an act of creation. Sometimes I think I will cut down such trees as remain in the wood, at other times I want to fill up the gaps between them with new trees. Both impulses are pretentious and empty. They are not honest movements towards money-making or beauty. They spring from a foolish desire to express myself and from an inability to enjoy what I have got. Creation, property, enjoyment form a sinister trinity in the human mind. Creation and enjoyment are both very, very good, yet they are often unattainable without a material basis, and at such moments property pushes itself in as a substitute, saying, "Accept me instead—I'm good enough for all three." It is not enough. It is, as Shakespeare said of lust, "The expense of spirit in a waste of shame": it is "Before, a joy proposed; behind, a dream." Yet we don't know how to shun it. It is forced on us by our economic system as the alternative to starvation. It is also forced on us by an internal defect in the soul, by the feeling that in property may lie the germs of self-development and of exquisite or heroic deeds. Our life on earth is, and ought to be, material and carnal. But we have not yet learned to manage our materialism and carnality properly; they are still entangled with the desire for ownership, where (in the words of Dante) "Possession is one with loss."

And this brings us to our fourth and final point: the blackberries.

Blackberries are not plentiful in this meager grove, but they are easily seen from the public footpath which traverses it, and all too easily

337

gathered. Foxgloves, too—people will pull up the foxgloves, and ladies of an educational tendency even grub for toadstools to show them on the Monday in class. Other ladies, less educated, roll down the bracken in the arms of their gentlemen friends. There is paper, there are tins. Pray, does my wood belong to me or doesn't it? And, if it does, should I not own it best by allowing no one else to walk there? There is a wood near Lyme Regis, also cursed by a public footpath, where the owner has not hesitated on this point. He had built high stone walls each side of the path, and has spanned it by bridges, so that the public circulate like termites while he gorges on the blackberries unseen. He really does own his wood, this able chap. Dives in Hell did pretty well, but the gulf dividing him from Lazarus could be traversed by vision, and nothing traverses it here. And perhaps I shall come to this in time. I shall wall in and fence out until I really taste the sweets of property. Enormously stout, endlessly avaricious, pseudo-creative, intensely selfish, I shall weave upon my forehead the quadruple crown of possession until those nasty Bolshies come and take it off again and thrust me aside into the outer darkness.

COMPREHENSION

1. What sort of essay is Forster writing for his audience? What is his purpose? How do you know?
2. List the four effects that property ownership has upon the author. How serious is he in describing these effects? Explain.
3. Describe the persona that emerges from the essay. What is the relationship of the last sentence to this persona?

RHETORIC

1. What words and phrases does the author use to create a conversational style in the essay?
2. Analyze biblical, historical, and literary allusions in the essay. What is their function?
3. What is the purpose of Forster's reference to Americans at the outset of the essay?
4. How is the thesis reinforced in the first paragraph? How are essay clarity and proper sequence achieved through the placement of topic sentences?
5. Analyze the manner in which Forster integrates the analysis of effects with a personal definition of *property*.
6. Explain the shift in tone, and the movement from concrete to abstract, in paragraph 5.

WRITING

1. Do you agree with Forster that property ownership is as difficult as he declares it to be? Give the basis of your response, and elucidate in an essay.

2. Write an essay of definition in which you explain an abstract term in personal, concrete, and carefully organized terms.

3. Write a comparative essay on the theme of property and nature as developed by Forster in "My Wood" and Thoreau in "Economy," in Chapter 11.

JONATHAN SWIFT   Jonathan Swift (1667–1745) is best known as the author of three satires: *A Tale of a Tub* (1704), *Gulliver's Travels* (1726), and *A Modest Proposal* (1729). In these satires, Swift pricks the balloon of many of his contemporaries' and our own most cherished prejudices, pomposities, and delusions. He was also a famous churchman, an eloquent spokesman for Irish rights, and a political journalist. The following selection, perhaps the most famous satiric essay in the English language, offers modest advice to a nation suffering from poverty, overpopulation, and political injustice.

JONATHAN SWIFT

A Modest Proposal

For Preventing the Children of Poor People in Ireland From Being a Burden to Their Parents or Country, and for Making Them Beneficial to the Public

It is a melancholy object to those who walk through this great town or travel in the country, when they see the streets, the roads, and cabin doors, crowded with beggars of the female-sex, followed by three, four, or six children, all in rags and importuning every passenger for an alms. These mothers, instead of being able to work for their honest livelihood, are forced to employ all their time in strolling to beg sustenance for their helpless infants, who, as they grow up, either turn thieves for want of work, or leave their dear native country to fight for the Pretender in Spain, or sell themselves to the Barbadoes.

I think it is agreed by all parties that this prodigious number of children in the arms, or on the backs, or at the heels of their mothers, and frequently of their fathers, is in the present deplorable state of the kingdom a very great additional grievance; and therefore whoever could find out a fair, cheap, and easy method of making these children sound, useful members of the commonwealth would deserve so well of the public as to have his statue set up for a preserver of the nation.

But my intention is very far from being confined to provide only for the children of professed beggars; it is of a much greater extent, and shall take in the whole number of infants at a certain age who are born of parents in effect as little able to support them as those who demand our charity in the streets.

As to my own part, having turned my thoughts for many years upon this important subject, and maturely weighted the several schemes of other projectors, I have always found them grossly mistaken in their computation. It is true, a child just dropped from its dam may be supported by her milk for a solar year, with little other nourishment; at most not above the value of two shillings, which the mother may certainly get, or the value in scraps, by her lawful occupation of begging; and it is exactly at one year old that I propose to provide for them in such a manner as instead of being a charge upon their parents or the parish, or wanting food and raiment for the rest of their lives, they shall on the contrary contribute to the feeding, and partly to the clothing, of many thousands.

There is likewise another great advantage in my scheme, that it will prevent those voluntary abortions, and that horrid practice of women murdering their bastard children, alas, too frequent among us, sacrificing the poor innocent babes, I doubt, more to avoid the expense than the shame, which would move tears and pity in the most savage and inhuman breast.

The number of souls in this kingdom being usually reckoned one million and a half, of these I calculate there may be about two hundred thousand couples whose wives are breeders; from which number I subtract thirty thousand couples who are able to maintain their own children, although I apprehend there cannot be so many under the present distresses of the kingdom; but this being granted, there will remain an hundred and seventy thousand breeders. I again subtract fifty thousand for those women who miscarry, or whose children die by accident or disease within the year. There only remain an hundred and twenty thousand children of poor parents annually born. The question therefore is, how this number shall be reared and provided for, which, as I have already said, under the present situation of affairs, is utterly impossible by all the methods hitherto proposed. For we can neither employ them in handicraft or agriculture; we neither build houses (I mean in the country) nor cultivate land. They can very seldom pick up a livelihood by stealing till they arrive at six years old, except where they are of towardly parts; although I confess they learn the rudiments much earlier, during which time they can however be looked upon only as probationers, as I have been informed by a principal gentlemen in the county of Cavan, who protested to me that he never knew above one or two instances under the age of six, even in a part of the kingdom so renowned for the quickest proficiency in that art.

I am assured by our merchants that a boy or girl before twelve years old is no salable commodity; and even when they come to this age they will not yield above three pounds, or three pounds and half a crown at most on the Exchange; which cannot turn to account either to the parents or the kingdom, the charge of nutriment and rags having been at least four times that value.

I shall now therefore humbly propose my own thoughts, which I hope will not be liable to the least objection.

I have been assured by a very knowing American of my acquaintance in London, that a young healthy child well nursed is at a year old a most delicious, nourishing, and wholesome food, whether stewed, roasted, baked or boiled; and I make no doubt that it will equally serve in a fricassee or a ragout.

I do therefore humbly offer it to public consideration that of the hundred and twenty thousand children, already computed, twenty thousand may be reserved for breed, whereof only one fourth part to be males, which is more than we allow to sheep, black cattle, or swine; and my reason is that these children are seldom the fruits of marriage, a circumstance not much regarded by our savages, therefore one male will be sufficient to serve four females. That the remaining hundred thousand may at a year old be offered in sale to the persons of quality and fortune through the kingdom, always advising the mother to let them suck plentifully in the last month, so as to render them plump and fat for a good table. A child will make two dishes at an entertainment for friends; and when the family dines alone, the fore or hind quarter will make a reasonable dish, and seasoned with a little pepper or salt will be very good boiled on the fourth day, especially in winter.

I have reckoned upon a medium that a child just born will weigh twelve pounds, and in a solar year if tolerably nursed increaseth to twenty-eight pounds.

I grant this food will be somewhat dear, and therefore very proper for landlords, who, as they have already devoured most of the parents, seem to have the best title to the children.

Infant's flesh will be in season throughout the year, but more plentiful in March, and a little before and after. For we are told by a grave author, an eminent French physician, that fish being a prolific diet, there are more children born in Roman Catholic countries about nine months after Lent than at any other season: therefore, reckoning a year after Lent, the markets will be more glutted than usual, because the number of popish infants is at least three to one in this kingdom; and therefore it will have one other collateral advantage, by lessening the number of Papists among us.

I have already computed the charge of nursing a beggar's child (in which list I reckon all cottagers, laborers, and four fifths of the farmers) to be about two shillings per annum, rags included: and I believe no gentleman would repine to give ten shillings for the carcass of a good fat child, which, as I have said, will make four dishes of excellent nutritive meat, when he hath only some particular friend or his own family to dine with him. Thus the squire will learn to be a good landlord, and grow popular among the tenants; the mother will have eight shillings net profit, and be fit for work till she produces another child.

Those who are more thrifty (as I must confess the times require) may flay the carcass; the skin of which artificially dressed will make admirable gloves for ladies, and summer boots for fine gentlemen.

As to our city of Dublin, shambles may be appointed for this pur- 16
pose in the most convenient parts of it, and butchers we may be
assured will not be wanting; although I rather recommend buying the
children alive, and dressing them hot from the knife as we do roasting
pigs.

A very worthy person, a true lover of his country, and whose virtues 17
I highly esteem, was lately pleased in discoursing on this matter to offer
a refinement upon my scheme. He said that many gentlemen of this
kingdom, having of late destroyed their deer, he conceived that the
want of venison might be well supplied by the bodies of young lads and
maidens, not exceeding fourteen years of age nor under twelve, so great
a number of both sexes in every county being now ready to starve for
want of work and service; and these to be disposed of by their parents,
if alive, or otherwise by their nearest relations. But with due deference
to so excellent a friend and so deserving a patriot, I cannot be altogether in his sentiments; for as to the males, my American acquaintance
assured me from frequent experience that their flesh was generally
tough and lean, like that of our schoolboys, by continual exercise, and
their taste disagreeable; and to fatten them would not answer the
charge. Then as to the females, it would, I think with humble submission, be a loss to the public, because they soon would become breeders
themselves: and besides, it is not improbable that some scrupulous people might be apt to censure such a practice (although indeed very
unjustly) as a little bordering upon cruelty; which, I confess, hath
always been with me the strongest objection against any project, how
well so ever intended.

But in order to justify my friend, he confessed that this expedient 18
was put into his head by the famous Psalmanazar, a native of the
island Formosa, who came from thence to London above twenty years
ago, and in conversation told my friend that in his country when any
young person happened to be put to death, the executioner sold the
carcass to persons of quality as a prime dainty; and that in his time
the body of a plump girl of fifteen, who was crucified for an attempt
to poison the emperor, was sold to his Imperial Majesty's prime minister of state, and other great mandarins of the court, in joints from
the gibbet, at four hundred crowns. Neither indeed can I deny that if
the same use were made of several plump young girls in this town,
who without one single groat to their fortunes cannot stir abroad
without a chair, and appear at the playhouse and assemblies in foreign
fineries which they never will pay for, the kingdom would not be the
worse.

Some persons of a desponding spirit are in great concern about that 19
vast number of poor people who are aged, diseased, or maimed, and I
have been desired to employ my thoughts what course may be taken to
ease the nation of so grievous an encumbrance. But I am not in the
least pain upon that matter, because it is very well known that they are
every day dying and rotting by cold and famine, and filth and vermin,
as fast as can be reasonably expected. And as to the younger laborers,

they are now in almost as hopeful a condition. They cannot get work, and consequently pine away for want of nourishment to a degree that if at any time they are accidentally hired to common labor, they have not strength to perform it; and thus the country and themselves are happily delivered from the evils to come.

I have too long digressed, and therefore shall return to my subject. [20] I think the advantages by the proposal which I have made are obvious and many, as well as of the highest importance.

For first, as I have already observed, it would greatly lessen the [21] number of Papists, with whom we are yearly overrun, being the principal breeders of the nation as well as our most dangerous enemies; and who stay at home on purpose to deliver the kingdom to the Pretender, hoping to take their advantage by the absence of so many good Protestants, who have chosen rather to leave their country than to stay at home and pay tithes against their conscience to an Episcopal curate.

Secondly, the poorer tenants will have something valuable of their [22] own, which by law may be made liable to distress, and help to pay their landlord's rent, their corn and cattle being already seized and money a thing unknown.

Thirdly, whereas the maintenance of an hundred thousand chil- [23] dren, from two years old and upwards, cannot be computed at less than ten shillings a piece per annum, the nation's stock will be thereby increased fifty thousand pounds per annum, besides the profit of a new dish introduced to the tables of all gentlemen of fortune in the kingdom who have any refinement in taste. And the money will circulate among ourselves, the goods being entirely of our own growth and manufacture.

Fourthly, the constant breeders, besides the gain of eight shillings [24] sterling per annum by the sale of their children, will be rid of the charge of maintaining them after the first year.

Fifthly, this food would likewise bring great custom to taverns, [25] where the vintners will certainly be so prudent as to procure the best receipts for dressing it to perfection, and consequently have their houses frequented by all the fine gentlemen, who justly value themselves upon their knowledge in good eating; and a skillful cook, who understands how to oblige his guests, will contrive to make it as expensive as they please.

Sixthly, this would be a great inducement to marriage, which all [26] wise nations have either encouraged by rewards or enforced by laws and penalties. It would increase the care and tenderness of mothers toward their children, when they were sure of a settlement for life to the poor babes, provided in some sort by the public, to their annual profit instead of expense. We should see an honest emulation among the married women, which of them could bring the fattest child to the market. Men would become as fond of their wives during the time of their pregnancy as they are now of their mares in foal, their cows in calf, or sows when they are ready to farrow; nor offer to beat or kick them (as is too frequent a practice) for fear of a miscarriage.

Many other advantages might be enumerated. For instance, the addition of some thousand carcasses in our exportation of barreled beef, the propagation of swine's flesh, and improvement in the art of making good bacon, so much wanted among us by the great destruction of pigs, too frequent at our tables, which are no way comparable in taste or magnificence to a well-grown, fat yearling child, which roasted whole will make a considerable figure at a lord mayor's feast or any other public entertainment. But this and many others I omit, being studious of brevity. 27

Supposing that one thousand families in this city would be constant customers for infants' flesh, besides others who might have it at merry meetings, particularly weddings and christenings, I compute that Dublin would take off annually about twenty thousand carcasses, and the rest of the kingdom (where probably they will be sold somewhat cheaper) the remaining eighty thousand. 28

I can think of no one objection that will possibly be raised against this proposal, unless it should be urged that the number of people will be thereby much lessened in the kingdom. This I freely own, and it was indeed one principal design in offering it to the world. I desire the reader will observe, that I calculate my remedy for this one individual kingdom of Ireland and for no other that ever was, is, or I think ever can be upon earth. Therefore let no man talk to me of other expedients: of taxing our absentees at five shillings a pound: of using neither clothes nor household furniture except what is of our own growth and manufacture: of utterly rejecting the materials and instruments that promote foreign luxury: of curing the expensiveness of pride, vanity, idleness, and gaming in our women: of introducing a vein of parsimony, prudence, and temperance: of learning to love our country, in the want of which we differ even from Laplanders and the inhabitants of Topinamboo: of quitting our animosities and factions, nor acting any longer like the Jews, who were murdering one another at the very moment their city was taken: of being a little cautious not to sell our country and conscience for nothing: of teaching landlords to have at least one degree of mercy toward their tenants: lastly, of putting a spirit of honesty, industry, and skill into our shopkeepers; who, if a resolution could be now taken to buy only our native goods, would immediately unite to cheat and exact upon us in the price, the measure and the goodness, nor could ever yet be brought to make one fair proposal of just dealing, though often and earnestly invited to it. 29

Therefore I repeat, let no man talk to me of these and the like expedients, till he hath at least some glimpse of hope that there will ever be some hearty and sincere attempt to put them in practice. 30

But as to myself, having been wearied out for many years with offering vain, idle, visionary thoughts, and at length utterly despairing of success, I fortunately fell upon this proposal, which, as it is wholly new, so it hath something solid and real, of no expense and little trouble, full in our own power, and whereby we can incur no danger in dis- 31 obliging England. For this kind of commodity will not bear exportation, the flesh being of too tender a consistence to admit a long continuance in salt, although perhaps I could name a country which would be glad to eat up our whole nation without it.

After all, I am not so violently bent upon my own opinion as to reject any offer proposed by wise men, which shall be found equally innocent, cheap, easy, and effectual. But before something of that kind shall be advanced in contradiction to my scheme, and offering a better, I desire the author or authors will be pleased maturely to consider two points. First, as things now stand, how they will be able to find food and raiment for an hundred thousand useless mouths and backs. And secondly, there being a round million of creatures in human figure throughout this kingdom, whose sole subsistence put into a common stock would leave them in debt two millions of pounds sterling, adding those who are beggars by profession to the bulk of farmers, cottagers, and laborers, with their wives and children who are beggars in effect; I desire those politicians who dislike my overture, and may perhaps be so bold to attempt an answer, that they will first ask the parents of these mortals whether they would not at this day think it a great happiness to have been sold for food at a year old in the manner I prescribe, and thereby have avoided such a perpetual scene of misfortunes as they have since gone through by the oppression of landlords, the impossibility of paying rent without money or trade, the want of common sustenance, with neither house nor clothes to cover them from the inclemencies of the weather, and the most inevitable prospect of entailing the like or greater miseries upon their breed forever.

I profess, in the sincerity of my heart, that I have not the least personal interest in endeavoring to promote this necessary work, having no other motive than the public good of my country, by advancing our trade, providing for infants, relieving the poor, and giving some pleasure to the rich. I have no children by which I can propose to get a single penny; the youngest being nine years old, and my wife past childbearing.

COMPREHENSION

1. Who is Swift's audience for this essay? Defend your answer.
2. Describe the persona in this essay. How is the unusual narrative personality (as distinguished from Swift's personality) revealed by the author in degrees? How can we tell that the speaker's opinions are not shared by Swift?
3. What are the major propositions behind Swift's modest proposal? What are the minor propositions?

RHETORIC

1. Explain the importance of the word *modest* in the title. What stylistic devices does this "modesty" contrast with?

2. What is the effect of Swift's persistent reference to people as "breeders," "dams," "carcass," and the like? Why does he define *children* in economic terms? Find other words that contribute to this motif.

3. Analyze the purpose of the relatively long introduction, consisting of paragraphs 1 to 7. How does Swift establish his ironic-satiric tone in this initial section?

4. What contrasts and discrepancies are at the heart of Swift's ironic statement in paragraphs 9 and 10? Explain both the subtlety and savagery of the satire in paragraph 12.

5. Paragraphs 13 to 20 develop six advantages of Swift's proposal, while paragraphs 21 to 26 list them in enumerative manner. Analyze the progression of these propositions. What is the effect of the listing? Why is Swift parodying argumentative techniques?

6. How does the author both sustain and suspend the irony in paragraph 29? How is the strategy repeated in paragraph 32? How does the concluding paragraph cap his satiric commentary on human nature?

WRITING

1. Write a modest proposal—on, for example, how to end the drug problem—advancing an absurd proposition through various argumentative techniques.

2. Discuss Swift's social, political, religious, and economic views as they are revealed in the essay.

3. Write a comprehensive critique of America's failure to address the needs of its poor.

JEREMY RIFKIN   Jeremy Rifkin was born in 1935 in Denver, Colorado. He received his B.A. degree from the University of Pennsylvania and his M.A. degree from the Fletcher School of Law and Diplomacy. As a lecturer, activist, and author, he advocates total interrogation of our most basic institutions, such as business, politics, and the law. His belief that humans must radically redefine themselves as political, social, and economic beings has polarized critics. His book *Beyond Beef* took a critical look at the American agriculture industry and called for a revolution in the way it operates. Other of his books include *Time Wars: The Primary Conflict in Human History* (1987); *Declaration of a Heretic* (1985); and *A New World View* (1980), the latter coauthored with Ted Howard.

JEREMY RIFKIN

African-Americans and Automation

The story of automation's impact on African-Americans may be prophetic of what lies ahead for the rest of the workforce. In the early years of the 20th century more than 90 percent of the black population of the United States still lived below the Mason-Dixon Line, and the vast majority was tied to agriculture.

Then, in 1944, an event took place in the rural Mississippi delta that was to change the circumstances of African-Americans forever. On October 2 an estimated 3,000 people crowded onto a cotton field just outside of Clarksdale, Mississippi, to watch the first successful demonstration of a mechanical cotton picker. The onlookers were awed by the sight. Each machine could do the work of 50 people. For the first time since blacks had been brought over as slaves to work the agricultural fields in the South, their hands and backs were no longer needed.

The push of mechanization in Southern agriculture combined with 3 the pull of jobs and less overt discrimination in the industrial cities of the North to create what Nicholas Lemann called "one of the largest and most rapid mass internal movements of people in history." More than 5 million black men, women, and children migrated north in search of work between 1940 and 1970.

Although most African-Americans were unaware of it at the time of 4 their trek north, a second technological revolution had already begun in the manufacturing industries of Chicago, Detroit, Cleveland, and New York that once again would lock many of them out of gainful employment. In the mid-1950s, automation began to take a toll in the nation's factories. Hardest hit were unskilled jobs in the very industries where black workers were concentrated. Between 1953 and 1962, 1.6 million blue-collar manufacturing jobs were lost. In *The Problem of the Negro Movement*, published in 1964, civil rights activist Tom Kahn quipped, "It is as if racism, having put the Negro in his economic place, stepped aside to watch technology destroy that place."

Companies started to build more automated manufacturing plants 5 in the newly emerging suburban industrial parks. Automation and suburban relocation created a crisis of tragic dimensions for unskilled black workers in the inner cities. The newly laid interstate highway system and the ring of metropolitan expressways being built around cities favored truck over train transport of goods, providing a further incentive to relocate plants to the suburbs. Finally, employers anxious to reduce labor costs and weaken unions saw relocation as a way to create distance between plants and militant union concentrations in urban neighborhoods. Eventually these same anti-union feelings pushed companies to locate plants in the South, in Mexico, and overseas.

The corporate drive to automate and relocate manufacturing jobs 6 split the black community into two distinct economic groups. While many blacks were able to take advantage of the loosening grip of outright discrimination and join the middle-class mainstream of American life, millions of unskilled African-American workers and their families became part of what social historians now call an underclass—a permanently unemployed part of the population whose

unskilled labor is no longer required and who live a marginal existence, often as welfare recipients or in the underground economy of
drugs and crime.

COMPREHENSION

1. What is the major thesis of this essay?
2. Some knowledge of American geography and technology is necessary for a full appreciation of this essay. Identify the Mason-Dixon line, the Missis-sippi delta, suburban industrial parks, and manufacturing industries.
3. In the final paragraph, Rifkin refers to a group of specialists as "social histo-rians." What are social historians? What do they do, and how do they do it?

RHETORIC

1. Note the opening sentence of paragraph 2. How does it achieve its dra-matic effect?
2. In paragraph 5, the author suggests that companies took advantage of tech-nology to further their own agendas. Identify the two transitions in the para-graph where Rifkin demonstrates shifts in company policies.
3. In the final paragraph, Rifkin uses definition to hammer home one of his points. How clear is his definition? Why has he saved it for the final sen-tence of the essay?
4. In paragraph 1, the author states that "automation's impact on African-Americans may be prophetic of what lies ahead for the rest of the work-force." Yet he does not refer back to this prophecy in the rest of the essay. Is this faulty argumentation, or is the prophecy simply implied in the description of the changing economic landscape Rifkin describes? Explain your view. In a similar vein, Rifkin chooses to cite from a book written in 1964. How prophetic is the direct quotation from this book regarding the American workplace? How effective is it from the standpoint of advancing the author's argument?
5. A key image in this essay is one of movement. Consider, for example, the following terms: *lies ahead, push of mechanization, newly emerging, relo-cate,* and *corporate drive.* To what extent does this theme of movement serve to make the final paragraph particularly poignant?
6. To whom is the essay implicitly addressed? What assumptions does the author have about the level of knowledge or education of his readership? Explain your view.

WRITING

1. Argue for or against the proposition that the "story of automation's impact on African-Americans" is *not* prophetic; it is already a reality for *all* Amer-icans.
2. For a research paper, study the industrial trends in your hometown, city, or region. How have they changed over the last fifty years?

3. Argue for or against the proposition that since it is the goal of a corporation to make money, cost-cutting practices are a legitimate form of company policy.

RICHARD RODRIGUEZ   Richard Rodriguez, born in 1944 in San Francisco, received degrees from both Stanford University and Columbia University. He also did graduate study at the University of California, Berkeley, and at the War-burg Institute, London. Rodriguez became a nationally known writer with the publication of his autobiography, *Hunger of Memory: The Education of Richard Rodriguez* (1982). In it, he describes the struggles of growing up biculturally—feeling alienated from his Spanish-speaking parents yet not wholly comfortable in the dominant culture of the United States. He opposes bilingualism and affir-mative action as they are now practiced in the United States, and his stance has caused much controversy in educational and intellectual circles. Rodriguez continues to write about social issues such as acculturation, education, and lan-guage. In "Los Pobres," Rodriguez shows us how what starts off as a summer job ends with a personal revelation about social and personal identity.

RICHARD RODRIGUEZ

Los Pobres

It was at Stanford, one day near the end of my senior year, that a friend   1
told me about a summer construction job he knew was available. I was quickly alert. Desire uncoiled within me. My friend said that he knew I had been looking for summer employment. He knew I needed some money. Almost apologetically he explained: It was something I proba-bly wouldn't be interested in, but a friend of his, a contractor, needed someone for the summer to do menial jobs. There would be lots of shoveling and raking and sweeping. Nothing too hard. But nothing more interesting either. Still, the pay would be good. Did I want it? Or did I know someone who did?

I did. Yes, I said, surprised to hear myself say it.   2

In the weeks following, friends cautioned that I had no idea how   3
hard physical labor really is. ("You only *think* you know what it is like to shovel for eight hours straight.") Their objections seemed to me challenges. They resolved the issue. I became happy with my plan. I decided, however, not to tell my parents. I wouldn't tell my mother because I could guess her worried reaction. I would tell my father only after the summer was over, when I could announce that, after all, I did know what "real work" is like.

The day I met the contractor (a Princeton graduate, it turned out),   4
he asked me whether I had done any physical labor before. "In high

school, during the summer," I lied. And although he seemed to regard me with skepticism, he decided to give me a try. Several days later, expectant, I arrived at my first construction site. I would take off my shirt to the sun. And at last grasp desired sensation. No longer afraid. At last become like a *bracero*. "We need those tree stumps out of here by tomorrow," the contractor said. I started to work.

I labored with excitement that first morning—and all the days after. The work was harder than I could have expected. But it was never as tedious as my friends had warned me it would be. There was too much physical pleasure in the labor. Especially early in the day, I would be most alert to the sensations of movement and straining. Beginning around seven each morning (when the air was still damp but the scent of weeds and dry earth anticipated the heat of the sun), I would feel my body resist the first thrusts of the shovel. My arms, tightened by sleep, would gradually loosen; after only several minutes, sweat would gather in beads on my forehead and then—a short while later—I would feel my chest silky with sweat in the breeze. I would return to my work. A nervous spark of pain would fly up my arm and settle to burn like an ember in the thick of my shoulder. An hour, two passed. Three. My whole body would assume regular movements. Even later in the day, my enthusiasm for primitive sensation would survive the heat and the dust and the insects pricking my back. I would strain wildly for sensation as the day came to a close. At three-thirty, quitting time, I would stand upright and slowly let my head fall back, luxuriating in the feeling of tightness relieved.

Some of the men working nearby would watch me and laugh. Two or three of the older men took the trouble to teach me the right way to use a pick, the correct way to shovel. "You're doing it wrong, too fucking hard," one man scolded. Then proceeded to show me—what persons who work with their bodies all their lives quickly learn—the most economical way to use one's body in labor.

"Don't make your back do so much work," he instructed. I stood impatiently listening, half listening, vaguely watching, then noticed his work-thickened fingers clutching the shovel. I was annoyed. I wanted to tell him that I enjoyed shoveling the wrong way. And I didn't want to learn the right way. I wasn't afraid of back pain. I liked the way my body felt sore at the end of the day.

I was about to, but, as it turned out, I didn't say a thing. Rather it was at that moment I realized that I was fooling myself if I expected a few weeks of labor to gain me admission to the world of the laborer. I would not learn in three months what my father had meant by "real work." I was not bound to this job; I could imagine its rapid conclusion. For me the sensations of exertion and fatigue could be savored. For my father or uncle, working at comparable jobs when they were my age, such sensations were to be feared. Fatigue took a different toll on their bodies—and minds.

It was, I know, a simple insight. But it was with this realization that I took my first step that summer toward realizing something even more important about the "worker." In the company of carpenters, electricians, plumbers, and painters at lunch, I would often sit quietly, observant. I was not shy in such company. I felt easy, pleased by the knowledge that I was casually accepted, my presence taken for granted by men (exotics) who worked with their hands. Some days the younger men would talk and talk about sex, and they would howl at women who drove by in cars. Other days the talk at lunchtime was subdued; men gathered in separate groups. It depended on who was around. There were rough, good-natured workers. Others were quiet. The more I remember that summer, the more I realize that there was no single *type* of worker. I am embarrassed to say I had not expected such diversity. I certainly had not expected to meet, for example, a plumber who was an abstract painter in his off hours and admired the work of Mark Rothko. Nor did I expect to meet so many workers with college diplomas. (They were the ones who were not surprised that I intended to enter graduate school in the fall.) I suppose what I really want to say here is painfully obvious, but I must say it nevertheless: The men of that summer were middle-class Americans. They certainly didn't constitute an oppressed society. Carefully completing their work sheets; talking about the fortunes of local football teams; planning Las Vegas vacations; comparing the gas mileage of various makes of campers—they were not *los pobres* my mother had spoken about.

On two occasions, the contractor hired a group of Mexican aliens. 10 They were employed to cut down some trees and haul off debris. In all, there were six men of varying age. The youngest in his late twenties; the oldest (his father?) perhaps sixty years old. They came and they left in a single old truck. Anonymous men. They were never introduced to the other men at the site. Immediately upon their arrival, they would follow the contractor's directions, start working—rarely resting—seemingly driven by a fatalistic sense that work which had to be done was best done as quickly as possible.

I watched them sometimes. Perhaps they watched me. The only time 11 I saw them pay me much notice was one day at lunchtime when I was laughing with the other men. The Mexicans sat apart when they ate, just as they worked by themselves. Quiet. I rarely heard them say much to each other. All I could hear were their voices calling out sharply to one another, giving directions. Otherwise, when they stood briefly resting, they talked among themselves in voices too hard to overhear.

The contractor knew enough Spanish, and the Mexicans—or at 12 least the oldest of them, their spokesman—seemed to know enough English to communicate. But because I was around, the contractor decided one day to make me his translator. (He assumed I could speak Spanish.) I did what I was told. Shyly I went over to tell the Mexicans that the patrón wanted them to do something else before they left for the day. As I started to speak, I was afraid with my old fear that I would be unable to pronounce the Spanish words. But it was a simple instruction I had to convey. I could say it in phrases.

The dark sweating faces turned toward me as I spoke. They stopped 13
their work to hear me. Each nodded in response. I stood there. I wanted
to say something more. But what could I say in Spanish, even if I could
have pronounced the words right? Perhaps I just wanted to engage in
small talk, to be assured of their confidence, our familiarity. I thought
for a moment to ask them where in Mexico they were from. Something
like that. And maybe I wanted to tell them (a lie, if need be) that my
parents were from the same part of Mexico.

I stood there. 14

Their faces watched me. The eyes of the man directly in front of me 15
moved slowly over my shoulder, and I turned to follow his glance
toward *el patrón* some distance away. For a moment I felt swept up by
that glance into the Mexicans' company. But then I heard one of them
returning to work. And then the others went back to work. I left them
without saying anything more.

When they had finished, the contractor went over to pay them in 16
cash. (He later told me that he paid them collectively—"for the job,"
though he wouldn't tell me their wages. He said something quickly
about the good rate of exchange "in their own country.") I can still hear
the loudly confident voice he used with the Mexicans. It was the sound
of the *gringo* I had heard as a very young boy. And I can still hear the
quiet, indistinct sounds of the Mexican, the oldest who replied. At hearing that voice I was sad for the Mexicans. Depressed by their vulnerability. Angry at myself. The adventure of the summer seemed suddenly
ludicrous. I would not shorten the distance I felt from *los pobres* with a
few weeks of physical labor. I would not become like them. They were
different from me. . . .

In the end, my father was right—though perhaps he did not know 17
how right or why—to say that I would never know what real work is.
I will never know what he felt at his last factory job. If tomorrow I
worked at some kind of factory, it would go differently for me. My
long education would favor me. I could act as a public person—able
to defend my interests, to unionize, to petition, to speak up—to challenge and demand. (I will never know what real work is.) I will never
know what the Mexicans knew, gathering their shovels and ladders
and saws.

Their silence stays with me now. The wages those Mexicans 18
received for their labor were only a measure of their disadvantaged
condition. Their silence is more telling. They lack a public identity.
They remain profoundly alien. Persons apart. People lacking a union
obviously, people without grounds. They depend upon the relative
good will or fairness of their employers each day. For such people, lacking a better alternative, it is not such an unreasonable risk.

Their silence stays with me. I have taken these many words to 19
describe its impact. Only: the quiet. Something uncanny about it. Its
compliance. Vulnerability. Pathos. As I heard their truck rumbling away,
I shuddered, my face mirrored with sweat. I had finally come face to
face with *los pobres*.

COMPREHENSION

1. How does Rodriguez set the scene for his narrative? What contrasts does he develop in the course of the essay?
2. What are the chief revelations Rodriguez receives from his work experience?
3. Why does Rodriguez focus on the silence of the Mexicans in the final two paragraphs? What is the relationship between this silence and the "real work" his father knows?

RHETORIC

1. In paragraph 9, Rodriguez puts quotes around *worker;* parentheses around *exotics;* and italicizes *type.* What is the purpose of each choice of punctuation?
2. There are several fragments in each of the final two paragraphs. What is the effect of using this sentence structure? Where else are fragments employed in the essay?
3. Why are paragraphs 2 and 14 so short? How does the length of these paragraphs help delineate Rodriguez's mood?
4. What sensations does Rodriguez focus on in paragraph 5? Which words contribute most to evoking them?
5. In what way do the first three paragraphs prepare or fail to prepare you for the narrative that follows?
6. The opening sentence of paragraph 19 repeats that of paragraph 18. What is the purpose of this repetition?

WRITING

1. Imagine yourself in the same situation as Rodriguez. Would your presumptions about "hard work" and your coworkers have been the same? Would you be more or less naive than Rodriguez? Explain in a brief essay.
2. What are the major differences between the Mexican workers and the American workers in the essay? Write an essay focusing on these differences.
3. Write an essay explaining why Rodriguez feels excluded from each of the two groups.
4. Have you ever felt like an outsider in a social situation? Describe a time in your life when you were confronted with the desire to be accepted. How were you different from the others? How did you try to transcend this difference?

JESSICA MITFORD Jessica Mitford (b. 1917) is an English-born American writer whose lifelong devotion to social justice and civil rights has spurred her into taking on institutions. Most notably, Mitford brought her sharp journalistic skills to bear on the American funeral industry in her scathing, witty, and informative exposé, *The American Way of Death* (1963). In her most recent book,

The American Way of Birth (1992), Mitford does battle with obstetrical and gynecological care in America. Mitford has also written two autobiographical books, *Daughters and Rebels* (1960) and *A Fine Old Conflict* (1977), in which she gives a lively account of her family, including her sister Nancy, also a respected writer. In this excerpt from *The American Way of Death*, Mitford explains how funeral directors manipulate the American public with sophisticated marketing techniques that play on their vulnerability in their time of grief.

JESSICA MITFORD

The American Way of Death

How long, I would ask, are we to be subjected to the tyranny of custom and undertakers? Truly, it is all vanity and vexation of spirit—a mere mockery of woe, costly to all, far, far beyond its value; and ruinous to many; hateful, and an abomination to all; yet submitted to by all, because none have the moral courage to speak against it and act in defiance of it.   —Lord Essex

O death, where is they sting? O grave, where is they victory? Where, indeed. Many a badly stung survivor, faced with the aftermath of some relative's funeral, has ruefully concluded that the victory has been won hands down by a funeral establishment—in disastrously unequal battle.

Much has been written of late about the affluent society in which we live, and much fun poked at some of the irrational "status symbols" set out like golden snares to trap the unwary consumer at every turn. Until recently, little has been said about the most irrational and weirdest of the lot, lying in ambush for all of us at the end of the road—the modern American funeral.

If the Dismal Traders (as an eighteenth-century English writer calls them) have traditionally been cast in a comic role in literature, a universally recognized symbol of humor from Shakespeare to Dickens to Evelyn Waugh, they have successfully turned the tables in recent years to perpetrate a huge, macabre and expensive practical joke on the American public. It is not consciously conceived of as a joke, of course; on the contrary, it is hedged with admirably contrived rationalizations.

Gradually, almost imperceptibly, over the years the funeral men have constructed their own grotesque cloud-cuckoo-land where the trappings of Gracious Living are transformed, as in a nightmare, into the trappings of Gracious Dying. The same familiar Madison Avenue language, with its peculiar adjectival range designed to anesthetize sales resistance to all sorts of products, has seeped into the funeral industry in a new and bizarre guise. The emphasis is on the same desirable qualities that we have all been schooled to look for in our daily search for excellence: comfort, durability, beauty, craftsmanship. The attuned ear will recognize too the convincing quasi-scientific language, so reassuring even if unintelligible.

So that this too, too solid flesh might not melt, we are offered "solid copper—a quality casket which offers superb value to the client seeking long-lasting protection," or "the Colonial Classic Beauty—18 gauge lead coated steel, seamless top, lap-jointed welded body construction." Some are equipped with foam rubber, some with innerspring mattresses. Elgin offers "the revolutionary 'Perfect-Posture' bed." Not every casket need have a silver lining, for one may choose between "more than 60 color matched shades, magnificent and unique masterpieces" by the Cheney casket-lining people. Shrouds no longer exist. Instead, you may patronize a grave-wear couturière who promises "handmade original fashions—styles from the best in life for the last memory—dresses, men's suits, negligees, accessories." For the final, perfect grooming: "Nature-Glo—the ultimate in cosmetic embalming." And, where have we heard that phrase "peace of mind protection" before? No matter. In funeral advertising, it is applied to the Wilbert Burial Vault, with its ⅜-inch precast asphalt inner liner plus extra-thick, reinforced concrete—all this "guaranteed by Good Housekeeping." Here again the Cadillac, status symbol par excellence, appears in all its gleaming glory, this time transformed into a pastel-colored funeral hearse.

You, the potential customer for all this luxury, are unlikely to read the lyrical descriptions quoted above, for they are culled from *Mortuary Management* and *Casket and Sunnyside,* two of the industry's eleven trade magazines. For you there are ads in your daily newspaper, generally found on the obituary page, stressing dignity, refinement, high-caliber professional service and that intangible quality, *sincerity.* The trade advertisements are, however, instructive, because they furnish an important clue to the frame of mind into which the funeral industry has hypnotized itself.

A new mythology, essential to the twentieth-century American funeral rite, has grown up—or rather has been built up step by step—to justify the peculiar customs surrounding the disposal of our dead. And, just as the witch doctor must be convinced of his own infallibility in order to maintain a hold over his clientele, so the funeral industry has had to "sell itself" on its articles of faith in the course of passing them along to the public.

The first of these is the tenet that today's funeral procedures are founded in "American tradition." The story comes to mind of a sign on the freshly sown lawn of a brand-new Midwest college: "There is a tradition on this campus that students never walk on this strip of grass. This tradition goes into effect next Tuesday." The most cursory look at American funerals of past times will establish the parallel. Simplicity to the point of starkness, the plain pine box, the laying out of the dead by friends and family who also bore the coffin to the grave—these were the hallmarks of the traditional funeral until the end of the nineteenth century.

Secondly, there is the myth that the American public is only being 9 given what it wants—an opportunity to keep up with the Joneses to the end. "In keeping with our high standard of living, there should be an equally high standard of dying," says the past president of the Funeral Directors of San Francisco. "The cost of a funeral varies according to individual taste and the niceties of living the family has been accustomed to." Actually, choice doesn't enter the picture for the average individual, faced, generally for the first time, with the necessity of buying a product of which he is totally ignorant, at a moment when he is least in a position to quibble. In point of fact the cost of a funeral almost always varies, not "according to individual taste" but according to what the traffic will bear.

Thirdly, there is an assortment of myths based on half-digested psy- 10 chiatric theories. The importance of the "memory picture" is stressed— meaning the last glimpse of the deceased in open casket, done up with the latest in embalming techniques and finished off with a dusting of makeup. A newer one, impressively authentic-sounding, is the need for "grief therapy," which is beginning to go over big in mortuary circles. A historian of American funeral directing hints at the grief-therapist idea when speaking of the new role of the undertaker—"the dramaturgic role, in which the undertaker becomes a stage manager to create an appropriate atmosphere and to move the funeral party through a drama in which social relationships are stressed and an emotional catharsis or release is provided through ceremony."

Lastly, a whole new terminology, as ornately shoddy as the satin 11 rayon casket liner, has been invented by the funeral industry to replace the direct and serviceable vocabulary of former times. Undertaker has been supplanted by "funeral director" or "mortician." (Even the classified section of the telephone directory gives recognition of this; in its pages you will find "Undertakers—see Funeral Directors.") Coffins are "caskets"; hearses are "coaches," or "professional cars"; flowers are "floral tributes"; corpses generally are "loved ones," but mortuary etiquette dictates that a specific corpse be referred to by name only—as, "Mr. Jones"; cremated ashes are "cremains." Euphemisms such as "slumber room," "reposing room," and "calcination—the *kindlier* heat" abound in the funeral business.

If the undertaker is the stage manager of the fabulous production 12 that is the modern American funeral, the stellar role is reserved for the occupant of the open casket. The decor, the stagehands, the supporting cast are all arranged for the most advantageous display of the deceased, without which the rest of the paraphernalia would lose its point—*Hamlet* without the Prince of Denmark. It is to this end that a fantastic array of costly merchandise and services is pyramided to dazzle the mourners and facilitate the plunder of the next of kin.

Grief therapy, anyone? But it's going to come high. According to 13 the funeral industry's own figures, the *average* undertaker's bill in 1961 was $708 for casket and "services," to which must be added the cost of a burial vault, flowers, clothing, clergy and musician's honorarium, and cemetery charges. When these costs are added to the undertaker's bill, the total average cost for an adult's funeral is, as we shall see, closer to $1,450.

The question naturally arises, *is* this what most people want for themselves and their families? For several reasons, this has been a hard one to answer until recently. It is a subject seldom discussed. Those who have never had to arrange for a funeral frequently shy away from its implications, preferring to take comfort in the thought that sufficient unto the day is the evil thereof. Those who have acquired personal and painful knowledge of the subject would often rather forget about it. Pioneering "Funeral Societies" or "Memorial Associations," dedicated to the principle of dignified funerals at reasonable cost, have existed in a number of communities throughout the country, but their membership has been limited for the most part to the more sophisticated element in the population—university people, liberal intellectuals—and those who, like doctors and lawyers, come up against problems in arranging funerals for their clients.

Some indication of the pent-up resentment felt by vast numbers of people against the funeral interests was furnished by the astonishing response to an article by Roul Tunley, titled "Can You Afford to Die?" in *The Saturday Evening Post* of June 17, 1961. As though a dike had burst, letters poured in from every part of the country to the *Post,* to the funeral societies, to local newspapers. They came from clergymen, professional people, old-age pensioners, trade unionists. Three months after the article appeared, an estimated six thousand had taken pen in hand to comment on some phase of the high cost of dying. Many recounted their own bitter experiences at the hands of funeral directors; hundreds asked for advice on how to establish a consumer organization in communities where none exists; others sought information about pre-need plans. The membership of the funeral societies skyrocketed. The funeral industry, finding itself in the glare of public spotlight, has begun to engage in serious debate about its own future course—as well it might.

Is the funeral inflation bubble ripe for bursting? A few years ago, the United States public suddenly rebelled against the trend in the auto industry towards ever more showy cars, with their ostentatious and nonfunctional fins, and a demand was created for compact cars patterned after European models. The all-powerful auto industry, accustomed to *telling* the customer what sort of car he wanted, was suddenly forced to *listen* for a change. Overnight, the little cars became for millions a new kind of status symbol. Could it be that the same cycle is working itself out in the attitude towards the final return of dust to dust, that the American public is becoming sickened by ever more ornate and costly funerals, and that a status symbol of the future may indeed be the simplest kind of "funeral without fins"?

COMPREHENSION

1. According to the essay, what role does consumerism play in the funeral industry?
2. What image does the funeral industry want to advance?
3. What does Mitford mean by "a new mythology" in paragraph 7?

RHETORIC

1. To what end does Mitford use the Lord Essex quote at the beginning of her essay?
2. What is Mitford's thesis? What is her tone? Cite evidence from the essay to support your view.
3. Mitford quotes Shakespeare in a few places. Locate one of these instances, and explain why it's an effective device.
4. Which paragraphs rely on classification and division? What is the purpose of this rhetorical strategy?
5. Find some examples of what Mitford calls "Madison Avenue language," and explain how they work to strengthen her thesis.
6. Assess Mitford's use of illustrations and evidence. How effective do you find it?

WRITING

1. In an analytical essay, examine the attitudes of Americans toward death and burial. How do their attitudes make them more susceptible to the practices cited in Mitford's essay?
2. In an essay, describe in detail how you would like your own funeral to be arranged and by whom. Be specific: Include instructions regarding guests, flowers, music, and the eulogy.

CLASSIC AND CONTEMPORARY

VIRGINIA WOOLF Virginia Woolf (1882–1941), novelist and essayist, was the daughter of Sir Leslie Stephen, a famous critic and writer on economics. An experimental novelist, Woolf attempted to portray consciousness through a poetic, symbolic, and concrete style. Her novels include *Jacob's Room* (1922), *Mrs. Dalloway* (1925), *To the Lighthouse* (1927), and *The Waves* (1931). She was also a perceptive reader and critic; her criticism appears in *The Common Reader* (1925) and *The Second Common Reader* (1933). In the following essay, which was delivered originally as a speech to The Women's

Service League in 1931, Woolf argues that women must overcome several "angels," or phantoms, in order to succeed in professional careers.

VIRGINIA WOOLF

Professions for Women

When your secretary invited me to come here, she told me that your Society is concerned with the employment of women and she suggested that I might tell you something about my own professional experiences. It is true I am a woman; it is true I am employed; but what professional experiences have I had? It is difficult to say. My profession is literature; and in that profession there are fewer experiences for women than in any other, with the exception of the stage—fewer, I mean, that are peculiar to women. For the road was cut many years ago—by Fanny Burney, by Aphra Behn, by Harriet Martineau, by Jane Austen, by George Eliot—many famous women, and many more unknown and forgotten, have been before me, making the path smooth, and regulating my steps. Thus, when I came to write, there were very few material obstacles in my way. Writing was a reputable and harmless occupation. The family peace was not broken by the scratching of a pen. No demand was made upon the family purse. For ten and sixpence one can buy paper enough to write all the plays of Shakespeare—if one has a mind that way. Pianos and models, Paris, Vienna and Berlin, masters and mistresses, are not needed by a writer. The cheapness of writing paper is, of course, the reason why women have succeeded as writers before they have succeeded in the other professions.

But to tell you my story—it is a simple one. You have only got to figure to yourselves a girl in a bedroom with a pen in her hand. She had only to move that pen from left to right—from ten o'clock to one. Then it occurred to her to do what is simple and cheap enough after all—to slip a few of those pages into an envelope, fix a penny stamp in the corner, and drop the envelope into the red box at the corner. It was thus that I became a journalist; and my effort was rewarded on the first day of the following month—a very glorious day it was for me—by a letter from an editor containing a cheque for one pound ten shillings and sixpence. But to show you how little I deserve to be called a professional woman, how little I know of the struggles and difficulties of such lives, I have to admit that instead of spending that sum upon bread and butter, rent, shoes and stockings, or butcher's bills, I went out and bought a cat—a beautiful cat, a Persian cat, which very soon involved me in bitter disputes with my neighbors.

What could be easier than to write articles and to buy Persian cats with the profits? But wait a moment. Articles have to be about something. Mine, I seem to remember, was about a novel by a famous man. And while I was writing this review, I discovered that if I were going to review books I should need to do battle with a certain phantom. And the phantom was a woman, and when I came to know her better I called her after the heroine of a famous poem, The Angel in the House. It was she who used to come between me and my paper when I was writing reviews. It was she who bothered me and wasted my time and so tormented me that at last I killed her. You who come of a younger and happier generation may not have heard of her—you may not know what I mean by the Angel in the House. I will describe her as shortly as I can. She was intensely sympathetic. She was immensely charming. She was utterly unselfish. She excelled in the difficult arts of family life. She sacrificed herself daily. If there was chicken, she took the leg; if there was a draught she sat in it—in short she was so constituted that she never had a mind or a wish of her own, but preferred to sympathize always with the minds and wishes of others. Above all—I need not say it—she was pure. Her purity was supposed to be her chief beauty—her blushes, her great grace. In those days—the last of Queen Victoria—every house had its Angel. And when I came to write I encountered her with the very first words. The shadow of her wings fell on my page; I heard the rustling of her skirts in the room. Directly, that is to say, I took my pen in hand to review that novel by a famous man, she slipped behind me and whispered: "My dear, you are a young woman. You are writing about a book that has been written by a man. Be sympathetic; be tender; flatter; deceive; use all the arts and wiles of our sex. Never let anybody guess that you have a mind of your own. Above all, be pure." And she made as if to guide my pen. I now record the one act for which I take some credit to myself, though the credit rightly belongs to some excellent ancestors of mine who left me a certain sum of money—shall we say five hundred pounds a year?—so that it was not necessary for me to depend solely on charm for my living. I turned upon her and caught her by the throat. I did my best to kill her. My excuse, if I were to be had up in a court of law, would be that I acted in self-defense. Had I not killed her she would have killed me. She would have plucked the heart out of my writing. For, as I found, directly I put pen to paper, you cannot review even a novel without having a mind of your own, without expressing what you think to be the truth about human relations, morality, sex. And all these questions, according to the Angel in the House, cannot be dealt with freely and openly by women; they must charm, they must conciliate, they must—to put it bluntly—tell lies if they are to succeed. Thus, whenever I felt the shadow of her wing or the radiance of her halo upon my page, I took up the inkpot and flung it at her. She died hard. Her fictitious nature was of great assistance to her. It is far harder to kill a phantom than a reality. She was always creeping back when I thought I had dispatched her. Though I flatter myself that I killed her in the end, the struggle was severe; it took much time that had better have been spent upon learning Greek grammar; or in roaming the world in search of adventures. But it was a real experience; it was an experience that was bound to befall all women writers at that time. Killing the Angel in the House was part of the occupation of a woman writer.

But to continue my story. The Angel was dead; what then remained? You may say that what remained was a simple and common object—a young woman in a bedroom with an inkpot. In other words, now that she had rid herself of falsehood, that young woman had only to be herself. Ah, but what is "herself"? I mean, what is a woman? I assure you, I do not know. I do not believe that you know. I do not believe that anybody can know until she has expressed herself in all the arts and professions open to human skill. That indeed is one of the reasons why I have come here—out of respect for you, who are in process of showing us by your experiments what a woman is, who are in process of providing us, by your failures and successes, with that extremely important piece of information.

But to continue the story of my professional experiences. I made one pound ten and six by my first review; and I bought a Persian cat with the proceeds. Then I grew ambitious. A Persian cat is all very well, I said; but a Persian cat is not enough. I must have a motor car. And it was thus that I became a novelist—for it is a very strange thing that people will give you a motor car if you will tell them a story. It is a still stranger thing that there is nothing so delightful in the world as telling stories. It is far pleasanter than writing reviews of famous novels. And yet, if I am to obey your secretary and tell you my professional experiences as a novelist, I must tell you about a very strange experience that befell me as a novelist. And to understand it you must try first to imagine a novelist's state of mind. I hope I am not giving away professional secrets if I say that a novelist's chief desire is to be as unconscious as possible. He has to induce in himself a state of perpetual lethargy. He wants life to proceed with the utmost quiet and regularity. He wants to see the same faces, to read the same books, to do the same things day after day, month after month, while he is writing, so that nothing may break the illusion in which he is living—so that nothing may disturb or disquiet the mysterious nosings about, feelings round, darts, dashes and sudden discoveries of that very shy and illusive spirit, the imagination. I suspect that this state is the same both for men and women. Be that as it may, I want you to imagine me writing a novel in a state of trance. I want you to figure to yourselves a girl sitting with a pen in her hand, which for minutes, and indeed for hours, she never dips into the inkpot. The image that comes to my mind when I think of this girl is the image of a fisherman lying sunk in dreams on the verge of a deep lake with a rod held out over the water. She was letting her imagination sweep unchecked round every rock and cranny of the world that lies submerged in the depths of our unconscious being. Now came the experience, the experience that I believe to be far commoner with women writers than with men. The line raced through the girl's fingers. Her imagination had rushed away. It had sought the pools, the depths, the dark places where the largest fish slumber. And then there was a smash. There was an explosion. There was foam and confusion. The imagination had dashed itself against something hard. The girl was roused from her dream. She was indeed in a state of the most acute and difficult distress. To speak without figure she had thought of something, something about the body, about the passions which it was unfitting for her as a woman to say. Men, her reason told her, would be shocked. The consciousness of what men will say of a woman who speaks the truth about her passions had roused her from her artist's state of unconsciousness. She could write no more. The trance was over. Her imagination could work no longer. This I believe to be a very common experience with women writers—they are impeded by the extreme conventionality of the other sex. For though men sensibly allow themselves great freedom in these respects, I doubt that they realize or can control the extreme severity with which they condemn such freedom in women.

These then were two very genuine experiences of my own. These were two of the adventures of my professional life. The first—killing the Angel in the House—I think I solved. She died. But the second, telling the truth about my own experiences as a body, I do not think I solved. I doubt that any woman has solved it yet. The obstacles against her are still immensely powerful—and yet they are very difficult to define. Outwardly, what is simpler than to write books? Outwardly, what obstacles are there for a woman rather than for a man? Inwardly, I think, the case is very different; she has still many ghosts to fight, many prejudices to overcome. Indeed it will be a long time still, I think, before a woman can sit down to write a book without finding a phantom to be slain, a rock to be dashed against. And if this is so in literature, the freest of all professions for women, how is it in the new professions which you are now for the first time entering?

Those are the questions that I should like, had I time, to ask you. And indeed, if I have laid stress upon these professional experiences of mine, it is because I believe that they are, though in different forms, yours also. Even when the path is nominally open—when there is nothing to prevent a woman from being a doctor, a lawyer, a civil servant—there are many phantoms and obstacles, as I believe, looming in her way. To discuss and define them is I think of great value and importance; for thus only can the labour be shared, the difficulties be solved. But besides this, it is necessary also to discuss the ends and the aims for which we are fighting, for which we are doing battle with these formidable obstacles. Those aims cannot be taken for granted; they must be perpetually questioned and examined. The whole position, as I see it—here in this hall surrounded by women practising for the first time in history I know not how many different professions—is one of extraordinary interest and importance. You have won rooms of your own in the house hitherto exclusively owned by men. You are able, though not without great labour and effort, to pay the rent. You are earning your five hundred pounds a year. But this freedom is only a beginning; the room is your own, but it is still bare. It has to be furnished; it has to be decorated; it has to be shared. How are you going to furnish it, how are you going to decorate it? With whom are you going to share it, and upon what terms? These, I think, are questions of the utmost importance and interest. For the first time in history you are able to ask for them; for the first time you are able to decide for yourselves what the answers should be. Willingly would I stay and discuss those questions and answers—but not tonight. My time is up; and I must cease.

COMPREHENSION

1. This essay was presented originally as a speech. What internal evidence indicates that it was intended as a talk? How do you respond to it today as a reader?
2. Who or what is the "angel" that Woolf describes in this essay? Why must she kill it? What other obstacles does a professional woman encounter?
3. Paraphrase the last two paragraphs of this essay. What is the essence of Woolf's argument?

RHETORIC

1. There is a significant amount of figurative language in the essay. Locate and explain examples. What does the figurative language contribute to the tone of the essay? Compare and contrast the figurative language in this essay and in Woolf's "The Death of the Moth" in Chapter 10.
2. How do we know that Woolf is addressing an audience of women? Why does she pose so many questions, and what does this strategy contribute to the rapport that she wants to establish? Explain the effect of the last two sentences.
3. How does Woolf use analogy to structure part of her argument?
4. Why does Woolf rely on personal narration? How does it affect the logic of her argument?
5. Evaluate Woolf's use of contrast to advance her argument.
6. Where does Woolf place her main proposition? How emphatic is it, and why?

WRITING

1. How effectively does Woolf use her own example as a professional writer to advance a broader proposition concerning all women entering professional life? Answer this question in a brief essay.
2. Explain the value of Woolf's essay for women today.

3. Discuss the problems and obstacles that you anticipate when you enter your chosen career.
4. Compare and contrast the essays by Goodman and Woolf.

HENRY LOUIS GATES, JR.   Henry Louis Gates (b. 1950) is an educator, writer, and editor. He was born in West Virginia and educated at Yale and at Clare College in Cambridge. Gates has had a varied career, working as a general anesthetist in Tanzania and as a staff correspondent for *Time* magazine in London. His essays have appeared in such diverse publications as *Black American Literature Forum, Yale Review, The New York Times Book Review,* and *Sports Illustrated.* He is also the author of *Figures in Black: Words, Signs, and the Racial Self* (1987) and *The Signifying Monkey: A Theory of Afro-American Literary Criticism* (1988). In this article from *Sports Illustrated,* Gates turns his attention to the limited career choices presented as viable to African-American youth and to public misconceptions about blacks in sports.

HENRY LOUIS GATES, JR.

Delusions of Grandeur

Standing at the bar of an all-black VFW post in my hometown of 1 Piedmont, W.Va., I offered five dollars to anyone who could tell me how many African-American professional athletes were at work today. There are 35 million African-Americans, I said.

"Ten million!" yelled one intrepid soul, too far into his cups. 2

"No way . . . more like 500,000," said another. 3

"You mean *all* professional sports," someone interjected, "including 4 golf and tennis, but not counting the brothers from Puerto Rico?" Everyone laughed.

"Fifty thousand, minimum," was another guess. 5

Here are the facts: 6

There are 1,200 black professional athletes in the U.S.

There are 12 times more black lawyers than black athletes.

There are 2½ times more black dentists than black athletes.

There are 15 times more black doctors than black athletes.

Nobody in my local VFW believed these statistics; in fact, few peo- 7 ple would believe them if they weren't reading them in the pages of *Sports Illustrated.* In spite of these statistics, too many African-American youngsters still believe that they have a much better chance of becoming another Magic Johnson or Michael Jordan than they do of matching the achievements of Baltimore Mayor Kurt Schmoke or neurosurgeon Dr. Benjamin Carson, both of whom, like Johnson and Jordan, are black.

In reality, an African-American youngster has about as much 8 chance of becoming a professional athlete as he or she does of winning the lottery. The tragedy for our people, however, is that few of us accept that truth.

Let me confess that I love sports. Like most black people of my generation—I'm 40—I was raised to revere the great black athletic heroes, and I never tired of listening to the stories of triumph and defeat that, for blacks, amount to a collective epic much like those of the ancient Greeks: Joe Louis's demolition of Max Schmeling; Satchel Paige's dazzling repertoire of pitches; Jesse Owens's in-your-face performance in Hitler's 1936 Olympics; Willie Mays's over-the-shoulder basket catch; Jackie Robinson's quiet strength when assaulted by racist taunts; and a thousand other grand tales.

Nevertheless, the blind pursuit of attainment in sports is having a 10 devastating effect on our people. Imbued with a belief that our principal avenue to fame and profit is through sport, and seduced by a win-at-any-cost system that corrupts even elementary school students, far too many black kids treat basketball courts and football fields as if they were classrooms in an alternative school system. "O.K., I flunked English," a young athlete will say. "But I got an A plus in slamdunking."

The failure of our public schools to educate athletes is part and 11 parcel of the schools' failure to educate almost everyone. A recent survey of the Philadelphia school system, for example, stated that "more than half of all students in the third, fifth and eighth grades cannot perform minimum math and language tasks." One in four middle school students in that city fails to pass to the next grade each year. It is a sad truth that such statistics are repeated in cities throughout the nation. Young athletes—particularly young black athletes—are especially ill-served. Many of them are functionally illiterate, yet they are passed along from year to year for the greater glory of good old Hometown High. We should not be surprised to learn, then, that only 26.6% of black athletes at the collegiate level earn their degrees. For every successful educated black professional athlete, there are thousands of dead and wounded. Yet young blacks continue to aspire to careers as athletes, and it's no wonder why; when the University of North Carolina recently commissioned a sculptor to create archetypes of its student body, guess which ethnic group was selected to represent athletes?

Those relatively few black athletes who do make it in the profes- 12 sional ranks must be prevailed upon to play a significant role in the education of all of our young people, athlete and nonathlete alike. While some have done so, many others have shirked their social obligations: to earmark small percentages of their incomes for the United Negro College Fund; to appear on television for educational purposes rather than merely to sell sneakers; to let children know the message that becoming a lawyer, a teacher or a doctor does more good for our people than winning the Super Bowl; and to form productive liaisons with educators to help forge solutions to the many ills that beset the black community. These are merely a few modest proposals.

A similar burden falls upon successful blacks in all walks of life. ₁₃
Each of us must strive to make our young people understand the
realities. Tell them to cheer Bo Jackson but to emulate novelist Toni
Morrison or businessman Reginald Lewis or historian John Hope
Franklin or Spelman College president Johnetta Cole—the list is
long.

Of course, society as a whole bears responsibility as well. Until col- ₁₄
leges stop using young blacks as cannon fodder in the big-business
wars of so-called nonprofessional sports, until training a young black's
mind becomes as important as training his or her body, we will continue to perpetuate a system akin to that of the Roman gladiators, sacrificing a class of people for the entertainment of the mob.

COMPREHENSION

1. What is the general assumption made about African Americans in sports?
2. Why do American schools continue to perpetuate this myth?
3. According to Gates, what should successful African-American athletes do
   to help guide the career choices of young black males?

RHETORIC

1. What is Gates's thesis? Where does it appear?
2. How does the introductory paragraph work to set up the writer's focus?
3. State Gates's purpose in using statistics in his essay.
4. What is the tone of Gates's essay? Cite specific sections where this tone
   seems strongest.
5. Examine the accumulation of facts in paragraph 11. How does this technique underscore Gates's point?
6. Explain Gates's allusion to Roman gladiators in his conclusion. How does
   it aid in emphasizing his main point?

WRITING

1. Write a brief essay in which you analyze your personal reaction to Gates's
   statistics. Were you surprised by them? What assumptions did you have
   about the number of black athletes? Why do you think most Americans
   share these assumptions?
2. Pretend you are addressing a group of young African Americans at an elementary school. What will you tell them about sports, their career choices,
   and education?
3. Write a biographical research paper on the life and career of an African-
   American athlete.

1. Examine the argumentative styles of Woolf and Gates. What is their main proposition? What are their minor propositions? What evidence do they provide?

2. Woolf first presented her paper as a speech before an audience of women. Gates wrote his essay as an opinion piece for *Sports Illustrated.* Write a comparative audience analysis of the two selections. Analyze purpose, tone, style, and any other relevant aspects of the two essays.

3. Argue for or against the proposition that white women and African-American men face the same barriers to employment in today's professions. Refer to the essays by Woolf and Gates to support your position.

Chapter Seven
Work, Business,
and Economics

1. Using the essays of Quindlen and Rodriguez, compare the effects of work on human relationships.

2. Using the essays of Rifkin and Goodman, consider the impact that technological progress has had on the American work landscape.

3. Write an essay about "real" work (as defined by Rodriguez) versus "unreal" work (for example, Woolf's writing). Use any relevant writer in this section to explore this issue.

4. Using the works of any of the writers in this section for support, write an essay that equates money and power.

5. Compare the writings of Swift, Rodriguez, and Gates in terms of the work options of the poor in Western society.

6. Using the writings of Ehrenreich, Woolf, and Goodman, consider the role of women in the job market.

7. Write a definition essay entitled "What Is Work?" Refer to any of the selections in this section to substantiate your opinions.

8. Write an essay that establishes a link between money and power, using the work of any writer in this section whose ideas support your views.

9. Compare the analysis of work presented by Rifkin and Rodriguez.

10. Compare the essays of Mitford and Swift in the writer's use of humor and satire to convey their points. How does the period in which each essay was written affect the type of humor used? Cite specific examples of satire and humor in both essays, and compare them as to effectiveness and audience response.

CHAPTER EIGHT

Language and Communication

*A*t the outset of his classic essay "Politics and the English Language," George Orwell asserts that English "is in a bad way." Yet Orwell's essay and the others in this chapter suggest that the English language is in a good way when we are alert and responsive to its many dimensions, careful and precise in our usage of it. As you know from political campaigns, advertising, and ordinary conversations, language is a powerful weapon. It can be used creatively or destructively. Through the power of language, we make sense of our culture, our values, and ourselves.

We all know that language—spoken, written, and nonverbal—is the vehicle whereby we communicate with each other, but language is also the means whereby we communicate our understanding of culture—both our own and the culture of others. English is spoken and written as a primary language by almost 400 million people in five nations; another 700 million nonnative speakers employ the language worldwide. With more than a billion people professing knowledge of English, we might be tempted to call it our "universal" language. However, as several writers in this chapter attest—among them Amy Tan and Rosario Ferré—ethnic diversity and the global movement of populations highlight language differences. These cross-cultural influences alert us to the ways in which language informs our economic and social condition, empowering certain groups and blocking others from full participation in society.

Language molds our social, ethnic, racial, and cultural identity. It can liberate or enslave us, place us at an advantage or at a disadvantage. If we can communicate in more than one language, for example, we probably have an advantage over those who command only one language. From the name we are given to our most powerful convictions, language is primordial and powerful. Through language we constantly create and return to a sense of ourselves.

Previewing the Chapter

As you read the essays in this chapter and respond to them in discussion and writing, consider the following questions:

• Does the author deal with spoken language or written language, or both?

• What is the author's attitude toward language? Is it positive or negative? Why?

• What are some of the misunderstandings about language that are raised by the writer?

• How does language reveal the writer's sense of herself or himself?

• In what way does language reveal certain cultural conflicts?

• According to the author, how does language relate to one's ethnic, racial, and cultural identity?

• What political dimensions to language do the writers explore?

• How can language be used to enforce the codes and values of a majority culture?

• Do you agree or disagree with the assumptions that the author makes about language and communication?

• What cross-cultural problems with language do you encounter in these essays?

JOAN DIDION   Joan Didion (b. 1934) grew up in California and graduated from the University of California at Berkeley in 1956. She began her career writing for national magazines such as *Mademoiselle, Saturday Evening Post,* and *Life.* Didion published her first novel, *Run River,* in 1963. Although she has continued to write novels and has written several screenplays, her most acclaimed work is in nonfiction. This work includes *Slouching Towards Bethlehem* (1968), *The White Album* (1979), *Salvador* (1983), *Democracy* (1984), *Miami* (1987), and her latest collection, *After Henry* (1992). Didion, an intensely introspective writer, attempts, in her essays, to draw significance from the particulars of her own life. In this essay, she describes one of the sources of her work—her own notebooks.

JOAN DIDION

On Keeping a Notebook

" 'That woman Estelle,' " the note reads, " 'is partly the reason why   1
George Sharp and I are separated today.' *Dirty crepe-de-Chine wrapper,
hotel bar, Wilmington RR, 9:45 a.m. August Monday morning."*

Since the note is in my notebook, it presumably has some meaning   2
to me. I study it for a long while. At first I have only the most general
notion of what I was doing on an August Monday morning in the bar
of the hotel across from the Pennsylvania Railroad station in Wilmington, Delaware (waiting for a train? missing one? 1960? 1961? why
Wilmington?), but I do remember being there. The woman in the dirty
crepe-de-Chine wrapper had come down from her room for a beer,
and the bartender had heard before the reason why George Sharp and
she were separated today. "Sure," he said, and went on mopping the
floor. "You told me." At the other end of the bar is a girl. She is talking,
pointedly, not to the man beside her but to a cat lying in the triangle of
sunlight cast through the open door. She is wearing a plaid silk dress
from Peck & Peck, and the hem is coming down.

Here is what it is: the girl has been on the Eastern Shore, and now she   3
is going back to the city, leaving the man beside her, and all she can see
ahead are the viscous summer sidewalks and the 3 a.m. long-distance
calls that will make her lie awake and then sleep drugged through all the
steaming mornings left in August (1960? 1961?). Because she must go
directly from the train to lunch in New York, she wishes that she had a
safety pin for the hem of the plaid silk dress, and she also wishes that she
could forget about the hem and the lunch and stay in the cool bar that
smells of disinfectant and malt and make friends with the woman in the
crepe-de-Chine wrapper. She is afflicted by a little self-pity, and she
wants to compare Estelles. That is what that was all about.

Why did I write it down? In order to remember, of course, but exactly what was it I wanted to remember? How much of it actually happened? Did any of it? Why do I keep a notebook at all? It is easy to deceive oneself on all those scores. The impulse to write things down is a peculiarly compulsive one, inexplicable to those who do not share it, useful only accidentally, only secondarily, in the way that any compulsion tries to justify itself. I suppose that it begins or does not begin in the cradle. Although I have felt compelled to write things down since I was five years old, I doubt that my daughter ever will, for she is a singularly blessed and accepting child, delighted with life exactly as life presents itself to her, unafraid to go to sleep and unafraid to wake up. Keepers of private notebooks are a different breed altogether, lonely and resistant rearrangers of things, anxious malcontents, children afflicted apparently at birth with some presentiment of loss.

My first notebook was a Big Five tablet, given to me by my mother with the sensible suggestion that I stop whining and learn to amuse myself by writing down my thoughts. She returned the tablet to me a few years ago; the first entry is an account of a woman who believed herself to be freezing to death in the Arctic night, only to find, when day broke, that she had stumbled onto the Sahara Desert, where she would die of the heat before lunch. I have no idea what turn of a five-year-old's mind could have prompted so insistently "ironic" and exotic a story, but it does reveal a certain predilection for the extreme which has dogged me into adult life; perhaps if I were analytically inclined I would find it a truer story than any I might have told about Donald Johnson's birthday party or the day my cousin Brenda put Kitty Litter in the aquarium.

So the point of my keeping a notebook has never been, nor is it now, to have an accurate factual record of what I have been doing or thinking. That would be a different impulse entirely, an instinct for reality which I sometimes envy but do not possess. At no point have I ever been able successfully to keep a diary; my approach to daily life ranges from the grossly negligent to the merely absent, and on those few occasions when I have tried dutifully to record a day's events, boredom has so overcome me that the results are mysterious at best. What is this business about "shopping, typing piece, dinner with E, depressed"? Shopping for what? Typing what piece? Who is E? Was this "E" depressed, or was I depressed? Who cares?

In fact I have abandoned altogether that kind of pointless entry; instead I tell what some would call lies. "That's simply not true," the members of my family frequently tell me when they come up against my memory of a shared event. "The party was *not* for you, the spider was *not* a black widow, *it wasn't that way at all.*" Very likely they are right, for not only have I always had trouble distinguishing between what happened and what merely might have happened, but I remain unconvinced that the distinction, for my purposes, matters. The cracked crab that I recall having for lunch the day my father came home from Detroit in 1945 must certainly be embroidery, worked into the day's pattern to lend verisimilitude; I was ten years old and would not now remember the cracked crab. The day's events did not turn on cracked crab. And yet it is precisely that fictitious crab that makes me see the afternoon all over again, a home movie run all too often, the father bearing gifts, the child weeping, an exercise in family love and guilt. Or that is what it was to me. Similarly, perhaps it never did snow that August in Vermont; perhaps there never were flurries in the night wind, and maybe no one else felt the ground hardening and summer already dead even as we pretended to bask in it, but that was how it felt to me, and it might as well have snowed, could have snowed, did snow.

How it felt to me: that is getting closer to the truth about a notebook. I sometimes delude myself about why I keep a notebook, imagine that some thrifty virtue derives from preserving everything observed. See enough and write it down, I tell myself, and then some morning when the world seems drained of wonder, some day when I am only going through the motions of doing what I am supposed to do, which is write—on that bankrupt morning I will simply open my notebook and there it will all be, a forgotten account with accumulated interest, paid passage back to the world out there: dialogue overheard in hotels and elevators and at the hatcheck counter in Pavillon (one middle-aged man shows his hatcheck to another and says, "That's my old football number"); impressions of Bettina Aptheker and Benjamin Sonnenberg and Teddy ("Mr. Acapulco") Stauffer; careful *apercus* about tennis bums and failed fashion models and Greek shipping heiresses, one of whom taught me a significant lesson (a lesson I could have learned from F. Scott Fitzgerald, but perhaps we all must meet the very rich for ourselves) by asking, when I arrived to interview her in her orchid-filled sitting room on the second day of a paralyzing New York blizzard, whether it was snowing outside.

I imagine, in other words, that the notebook is about other people. But of course it is not. I have no real business with what one stranger said to another at the hatcheck counter in Pavillon; in fact I suspect that the line "That's my old football number" touched not my own imagination at all, but merely some memory of something once read, probably "The Eighty-Yard Run." Nor is my concern with a woman in a dirty crepe-de-Chine wrapper in a Wilmington bar. My stake is always, of course, in the unmentioned girl in the plaid silk dress. *Remember what it was to be me:* that is always the point.

It is a difficult point to admit. We are brought up in the ethic that others, any others, all others, are by definition more interesting than ourselves; taught to be diffident, just this side of self-effacing. ("You're the least important person in the room and don't forget it," Jessica Mitford's governess would hiss in her ear on the advent of any social occasion; I copied that into my notebook because it is only recently that I have been able to enter a room without hearing some such phrase in my inner ear.) Only the very young and the very old may recount their dreams at breakfast, dwell upon self, interrupt with memories of beach picnics and favorite Liberty lawn dresses and the rainbow trout in a creek near Colorado Springs. The rest of us are expected, rightly, to affect absorption in other people's favorite dresses, other people's trout.

And so we do. But our notebooks give us away, for however duti- 11 fully we record what we see around us, the common denominator of all we see is always, transparently, shamelessly, the implacable "I." We are not talking here about the kind of notebook that is patently for public consumption, a structural conceit for binding together a series of graceful *pensées;* we are talking about something private, about bits of the mind's string too short to use, an indiscriminate and erratic assemblage with meaning only for its maker.

And sometimes even the maker has difficulty with the meaning. 12 There does not seem to be, for example, any point in my knowing for the rest of my life that, during 1964, 720 tons of soot fell on every square mile of New York City, yet there it is in my notebook, labeled "FACT." Nor do I really need to remember that Ambrose Bierce liked to spell Leland Stanford's name "£eland $tanford" or that "smart women almost always wear black in Cuba," a fashion hint without much potential for practical application. And does not the relevance of these notes seem marginal at best?

> In the basement museum of the Inyo County Courthouse in Indepen-
> dence, California, sign pinned to a mandarin coat: "This MANDARIN
> COAT was often worn by Mrs. Minnie S. Brooks when giving lectures
> on her TEAPOT COLLECTION." Redhead getting out of car in front of
> Beverly Wilshire Hotel, chinchilla stole, Vuitton bags with tags reading:
>
> MRS. LOU FOX
> HOTEL SAHARA
> VEGAS

Well, perhaps not entirely marginal. As a matter of fact, Mrs. Min- 13 nie S. Brooks and her MANDARIN COAT pull me back into my own child-hood, for although I never knew Mrs. Brooks and did not visit Inyo County until I was thirty, I grew up in just such a world, in houses cluttered with Indian relics and bits of gold ore and ambergris and the souvenirs my Aunt Mercy Farnsworth brought back from the Orient. It is a long way from that world to Mrs. Lou Fox's world, where we all live now, and is it not just as well to remember that? Might not Mrs. Minnie S. Brooks help me to remember what I am? Might not Mrs. Lou Fox help me to remember what I am not?

But sometimes the point is harder to discern. What exactly did I 14 have in mind when I noted down that it cost the father of someone I know $650 a month to light the place on the Hudson in which he lived before the Crash? What use was I planning to make of this line by Jimmy Hoffa: "I may have my faults, but being wrong ain't one of them"? And although I think it interesting to know where the girls who travel with the Syndicate have their hair done when they find themselves on the West Coast, will I ever make suitable use of it? Might I not be better off just passing it on to John O'Hara? What is a recipe for sauerkraut doing in my notebook? What kind of magpie keeps this notebook? *"He was born the night the Titanic went down."* That seems a nice enough line, and I even recall who said it, but is it not really a better line in life than it could ever be in fiction?

But of course that is exactly it: not that I should ever use the line, but that I should remember the woman who said it and the afternoon I heard it. We were on her terrace by the sea, and we were finishing the wine left from lunch, trying to get what sun there was, a California winter sun. The woman whose husband was born the night the *Titanic* went down wanted to rent her house, wanted to go back to her children in Paris. I remember wishing that I could afford the house, which cost $1,000 a month. "Someday you will," she said lazily. "Someday it all comes." There in the sun on her terrace it seemed easy to believe in someday, but later I had a low-grade afternoon hangover and ran over a black snake on the way to the supermarket and was flooded with inexplicable fear when I heard the checkout clerk explaining to the man ahead of me why she was finally divorcing her husband. "He left me no choice," she said over and over as she punched the register. "He has a little seven-month-old baby by her, he left me no choice." I would like to believe that my dread then was for the human condition, but of course it was for me, because I wanted a baby and did not then have one and because I wanted to own the house that cost $1,000 a month to rent and because I had a hangover.

It all comes back. Perhaps it is difficult to see the value in having 16 one's self back in that kind of mood, but I do see it; I think we are well advised to keep on nodding terms with the people we used to be whether we find them attractive company or not. Otherwise they turn up unannounced and surprise us, come hammering on the mind's door at 4 a.m. of a bad night and demand to know who deserted them, who betrayed them, who is going to make amends. We forget all too soon the things we thought we could never forget. We forget the loves and the betrayals alike, forget what we whispered and what we screamed, forget who we were. I have already lost touch with a couple of people I used to be; one of them, a seventeen-year-old, presents little threat, although it would be of some interest to me to know again what it feels like to sit on a river levee drinking vodka-and-orange-juice and listening to Les Paul and Mary Ford and their echoes sing "How High the Moon" on the car radio. (You see I still have the scenes, but I no longer perceive myself among those present, no longer could even improvise the dialogue.) The other one, a twenty-three-year-old, bothers me more. She was always a good deal of trouble, and I suspect she will reappear when I least want to see her, skirts too long, shy to the point of aggravation, always the injured party, full of recriminations and little hurts and stories I do not want to hear again, at once saddening me and angering me with her vulnerability and ignorance, an apparition all the more insistent for being so long banished.

It is a good idea, then, to keep in touch, and I suppose that keeping 17 in touch is what notebooks are all about. And we are all on our own when it comes to keeping those lines open to ourselves: your notebook will never help me, nor mine you. *"So what's new in the whiskey business?"* What could that possibly mean to you? To me it means a blonde in a Pucci bathing suit sitting with a couple of fat men by the pool at the Beverly Hills Hotel. Another man approaches, and they all regard one another in silence for a while. "So what's new in the whiskey business?" one of the fat men finally says by way of welcome, and the blonde stands up, arches one foot and dips it in the pool, looking all the while at the cabana where Baby Pignatari is talking on the telephone. That is all there is to that, except that several years later I saw the blonde coming out of Saks Fifth Avenue in New York with her California complexion and a voluminous mink coat. In the harsh wind that day she looked old and irrevocably tired to me, and even the skins in the mink coat were not worked the way they were doing them that year, not the way she would have wanted them done, and there is the point of the story. For a while after that I did not like to look in the mirror, and my eyes would skim the newspapers and pick out only the deaths, the cancer victims, the premature coronaries, the suicides, and I stopped riding the Lexington Avenue IRT because I noticed for the first time that all the strangers I had seen for years—the man with the seeing-eye dog, the spinster who read the classified pages every day, the fat girl who always got off with me at Grand Central—looked older than they once had.

It all comes back. Even that recipe for sauerkraut: even that brings 18 it back. I was on Fire Island when I first made that sauerkraut, and it was raining, and we drank a lot of bourbon and ate the sauerkraut and went to bed at ten, and I listened to the rain and the Atlantic and felt safe. I made the sauerkraut again last night and it did not make me feel any safer, but that is, as they say, another story.

COMPREHENSION

1. Why does Didion mention "keeping" a notebook in her title? How is her essay about keeping rather than writing a notebook?
2. What sort of entries does Didion make in her notebooks? How and why does Didion alter the reality of the events she described in her notebooks?
3. What are the various reasons Didion explores for keeping a notebook? What is her purpose in examining so many possible reasons?

RHETORIC

1. What is the function of the numerous rhetorical questions in the essay?
2. How does the style of Didion's notebooks differ from her regular writing style?
3. How do the introductory quote and other quotes from her notebook help Didion develop the theme of her essay?
4. Repetition is a key device used to unify the essay. Identify examples of important repetitions.

5. Identify topic sentences in the essay. How does Didion prepare us for the thesis through her topic sentences?
6. Analyze causal patterns of development that appear in the essay.

WRITING

1. If you were to keep a notebook, what would you record in it? Why would you keep it? Write a brief essay on this topic.
2. Write an essay about some events that have occurred in your own past that you feel were significant to your growth.
3. Didion speaks of "lying" or "embroidery" in recounting events. Write an essay about an episode in your life that you like to embellish.

MORTIMER ADLER   Mortimer Jerome Adler was born in 1902 in New York City and received his Ph.D. from Columbia University in 1928. A staunch advocate for classical philosophy, Adler believes that there are unshakable truths—an idea rejected by most contemporary philosophers. For this reason, Adler has not been taken seriously by the academic establishment. He is a champion of knowledge, believing that philosophy should be a part of everyone's life and that access to the great ideas in philosophy can be of value to everyone. Many of his over seventy-five books attempt to edify the general reader by explaining basic philosophical concepts in everyday language. He is also chairman of the editorial board of the *Encyclopaedia Britannica.* To make knowledge more accessible to everyone, he also assumed editorship of the Encyclopedia Britannica's Great Books project, partly sponsored by the University of Chicago. This project, which has put 443 of the world's "classics" into a 54-volume set, graces the bookcases of many dens and studies in middle-class American homes. Despite his advancing years, Adler continues to work on many projects to promote his goal of universal education and enlightenment. "How to Mark a Book" is typical of his didactic, pragmatic approach to education.

MORTIMER J. ADLER

How to Mark a Book

You know you have to read "between the lines" to get the most out of anything. I want to persuade you to do something equally important in the course of your reading. I want to persuade you to "write between the lines." Unless you do, you are not likely to do the most efficient kind of reading.

I contend, quite bluntly, that marking up a book is not an act of mutilation but of love.

You shouldn't mark up a book which isn't yours. Librarians (or ₃ your friends) who lend you books expect you to keep them clean, and you should. If you decide that I am right about the usefulness of marking books, you will have to buy them. Most of the world's great books are available today, in reprint editions, at less than a dollar.

There are two ways in which one can own a book. The first is the ₄ property right you establish by paying for it, just as you pay for clothes and furniture. But this act of purchase is only the prelude to possession. Full ownership comes only when you have made it a part of yourself, and the best way to make yourself a part of it is by writing in it. An illustration may make the point clear. You buy a beefsteak and transfer it from the butcher's ice-box to your own. But you do not own the beefsteak in the most important sense until you consume it and get it into your bloodstream. I am arguing that books, too, must be absorbed in your bloodstream to do you any good.

Confusion about what it means to own a book leads people to a ₅ false reverence for paper, binding, and type—a respect for the physical thing—the craft of the printer rather than the genius of the author. They forget that it is possible for a man to acquire the idea, to possess the beauty, which a great book contains, without staking his claim by pasting his bookplate inside the cover. Having a fine library doesn't prove that its owner has a mind enriched by books; it proves nothing more than that he, his father, or his wife, was rich enough to buy them.

There are three kinds of book owners. The first has all the standard ₆ sets and best-sellers—unread, untouched. (This deluded individual owns woodpulp and ink, not books.) The second has a great many books—a few of them read through, most of them dipped into, but all of them as clean and shiny as the day they were bought. (This person would probably like to make books his own, but is restrained by a false respect for their physical appearance.) The third has a few books or many—every one of them dog-eared and dilapidated, shaken and loosened by continual use, marked and scribbled in from front to back. (This man owns books.)

Is it false respect, you may ask, to preserve intact and unblemished ₇ a beautifully printed book, an elegantly bound edition? Of course not. I'd no more scribble all over the first edition of *Paradise Lost* than I'd give my baby a set of crayons and an original Rembrandt! I wouldn't mark up a painting or a statue. Its soul, so to speak, is inseparable from its body. And the beauty of a rare edition or of a richly manufactured volume is like that of a painting or a statue.

But the soul of a book *can* be separated from its body. A book is ₈ more like the score of a piece of music than it is like a painting. No great musician confuses a symphony with the printed sheets of music. Arturo Toscanini reveres Brahms, but Toscanini's score of the C-minor Symphony is so thoroughly marked up that no one but the maestro himself can read it. The reason why a great conductor makes notations on his musical scores—marks them up again and again each time he returns to study them—is the reason why you should mark up your books. If your respect for magnificent binding or typography gets in the way, buy yourself a cheap edition and pay your respects to the author.

Why is marking up a book indispensable to reading it? First, it keeps you awake. (And I don't mean merely conscious; I mean wide awake.) In the second place, reading, if it is active, is thinking, and thinking tends to express itself in words, spoken or written. The marked book is usually the thought-through book. Finally, writing helps you remember the thoughts you had, or the thoughts the author expressed. Let me develop these three points.

If reading is to accomplish anything more than passing time, it must 10 be active. You can't let your eyes glide across the lines of a book and come up with an understanding of what you have read. Now an ordinary piece of light fiction, like say, *Gone with the Wind*, doesn't require the most active kind of reading. The books you read for pleasure can be read in a state of relaxation, and nothing is lost. But a great book, rich in ideas and beauty, a book that raises and tries to answer great fundamental questions, demands the most active reading of which you are capable. You don't absorb the ideas of John Dewey the way you absorb the crooning of Mr. Vallee. You have to reach for them. That you cannot do while you're asleep.

If, when you've finished reading a book, the pages are filled with 11 your notes, you know that you read actively. The most famous *active* reader of great books I know is President Hutchins, of the University of Chicago. He also has the hardest schedule of business activities of any man I know. He invariably reads with a pencil, and sometimes, when he picks up a book and pencil in the evening, he finds himself, instead of making intelligent notes, drawing what he calls "caviar factories" on the margins. When that happens, he puts the book down. He knows he's too tired to read, and he's just wasting time.

But, you may ask, why is writing necessary? Well, the physical act of 12 writing, with your own hand, brings words and sentences more sharply before your mind and preserves them better in your memory. To set down your reaction to important words and sentences you have read, and the questions they have raised in your mind, is to preserve those reactions and sharpen those questions.

Even if you wrote on a scratch pad, and threw the paper away when 13 you had finished writing, your grasp of the book would be surer. But you don't have to throw the paper away. The margins (top and bottom, as well as side), the end-papers, the very space between the lines, are all available. They aren't sacred. And, best of all, your marks and notes become an integral part of the book and stay there forever. You can pick up the book the following week or year, and there are all your points of agreement, disagreement, doubt, and inquiry. It's like resuming an interrupted conversation with the advantage of being able to pick up where you left off.

And that is exactly what reading a book should be: a conversation 14 between you and the author. Presumably he knows more about the subject than you do; naturally, you'll have the proper humility as you approach him. But don't let anybody tell you that a reader is supposed to be solely on the receiving end. Understanding is a two-way operation; learning doesn't consist in being an empty receptacle. The learner has to question himself and question the teacher. He even has to argue with the teacher, once he understands what the teacher is saying. And marking a book is literally an expression of your differences, or agreements of opinion, with the author.

There are all kinds of devices for marking a book intelligently and 15 fruitfully. Here's the way I do it:

1. Underlining: Of major points, of important or forceful state- 16 ments.

2. Vertical lines at the margin: To emphasize a statement already 17 underlined.

3. Star, asterisk, or other doo-dad at the margin: To be used spar- 18 ingly, to emphasize the ten or twenty most important statements in the book. (You may want to fold the bottom corner of each page on which you use such marks. It won't hurt the sturdy paper on which most modern books are printed, and you will be able to take the book off the shelf at any time and, by opening it at the folded-corner page, refresh your recollection of the book.)

4. Numbers in the margin: To indicate the sequence of points the 19 author makes in developing a single argument.

5. Numbers of other pages in the margin: To indicate where else in 20 the book the author made points relevant to the point marked; to tie up the ideas in a book, which, though they may be separated by many pages, belong together.

6. Circling of key words or phrases. 21

7. Writing in the margin, or at the top or bottom of the page, for 22 the sake of: Recording questions (and perhaps answers) which a passage raised in your mind; reducing a complicated discussion to a simple statement; recording the sequence of major points right through the book. I use the end-papers at the back of the book to make a personal index of the author's points in the order of their appearance.

The front end-papers are, to me, the most important. Some people 23 reserve them for a fancy bookplate. I reserve them for fancy thinking. After I have finished reading the book and making my personal index on the back end-papers, I turn to the front and try to outline the book, not page by page, or point by point (I've already done that at the back), but as an integrated structure, with a basic unity and an order of parts. This outline is, to me, the measure of my understanding of the work.

If you're a die-hard and anti-book-marker, you may object that the 24 margins, the space between the lines, and the end-papers don't give you room enough. All right. How about using a scratch pad slightly smaller than the page-size of the book—so that the edges of the sheets won't protrude? Make your index, outlines, and even your notes on the pad, and then insert these sheets permanently inside the front and back covers of the book.

Or, you may say that this business of marking books is going to slow 25 up your reading. It probably will. That's one of the reasons for doing it. Most of us have been taken in by the notion that speed of reading is a measure of our intelligence. There is no such thing as the right speed for intelligent reading. Some things should be read quickly and effortlessly, and some should be read slowly and even laboriously. The sign of intelligence in reading is the ability to read different things differently according to their worth. In the case of good books, the point is not to see how many of them you can get through, but rather how many can get through you—how many you can make your own. A few friends are better than a thousand acquaintances. If this be your aim, as it should be, you will not be impatient if it takes more time and effort to read a great book than it does a newspaper.

You may have one final objection to marking books. You can't lend 26 them to your friends because nobody else can read them without being distracted by your notes. Furthermore, you won't want to lend them because a marked copy is a kind of intellectual diary, and lending it is almost like giving your mind away.

If your friend wishes to read your *Plutarch's Lives,* "Shakespeare," or 27 *The Federalist Papers,* tell him gently but firmly, to buy a copy. You will lend him your car or your coat—but your books are as much a part of you as your head or your heart.

COMPREHENSION

1. Summarize what Adler means by "marking up a book."
2. In your own words, explain how you believe Adler would define the word *book.*
3. Adler mentions books throughout the essay. What particular type of book is he referring to?

RHETORIC

1. What is the tone of the essay? What can you infer from this tone about Adler's emotional relationship to books?
2. Paragraphs 16 through 22 list devices for marking a book. What is the function of enumerating them in this way? How would the tone of this section have been altered if he had summarized these devices in paragraph form?
3. The author makes reference to various intellectual and artistic figures and works in the essay. How does this help determine for whom the essay has been targeted?

4. Study the relationship between paragraph 9 and paragraphs 10, 11, and 12. What is the rhetorical format of this section? What is the method of argumentation he is employing?
5. Adler uses the analogy that "reading a book should be: a conversation between you and the author." What other analogies can you find in the essay?
6. Adler raises objections to his argument and then refutes the objections. Where does he make use of this rhetorical device? How effective is it in advancing his argument?
7. Adler calls *Gone with the Wind* "light fiction." Is this opinion or fact? Is it a mere observation or a criticism of the book?

WRITING

1. Mark up Adler's essay in the same manner he recommends that you mark up any good piece of writing. Then write an essay using process analysis to summarize the different methods you used.
2. Argue for or against the proposition that this essay has lost its relevance owing to the introduction of new forms of educational media.
3. Compare and contrast two books: one that Adler would regard as "light reading" and one that he would regard as worthy of marking up. Indicate the primary differences between these books in terms of their diction, level of discourse, insight, purpose, and scholarship.

DEBORAH TANNEN   Deborah Tannen was born in 1945 in Brooklyn, New York. She holds a Ph.D. in linguistics from the University of California at Berkeley. Tannen published numerous specialized articles and books on language and linguistics before becoming nationally known as a best-selling author. She publishes regularly in such magazines as *Vogue* and *New York,* and her book *That's Not What I Meant: How Conversational Style Makes or Breaks Your Relations with Others* (1986) drew national attention to her work on interpersonal communication. The following summary of her work was published in *The Washington Post* in 1990.

DEBORAH TANNEN

Sex, Lies and Conversation:

Why Is It So Hard for Men and Women to Talk to Each Other?

I was addressing a small gathering in a suburban Virginia living   1
room—a women's group that had invited men to join them. Throughout the evening, one man had been particularly talkative, frequently

offering ideas and anecdotes, while his wife sat silently beside him on the couch. Toward the end of the evening, I commented that women frequently complain that their husbands don't talk to them. This man quickly concurred. He gestured toward his wife and said, "She's the talker in our family." The room burst into laughter; the man looked puzzled and hurt. "It's true," he explained. "When I come home from work I have nothing to say. If she didn't keep the conversation going, we'd spend the whole evening in silence."

This episode crystallizes the irony that although American men tend to talk more than women in public situations, they often talk less at home. And this pattern is wreaking havoc with marriage.

The pattern was observed by political scientist Andrew Hacker in the late '70s. Sociologist Catherine Kohler Riessman reports in her new book *Divorce Talk* that most of the women she interviewed—but only a few of the men—gave lack of communication as the reason for their divorces. Given the current divorce rate of nearly 50 percent, that amounts to millions of cases in the United States every year—a virtual epidemic of failed conversation.

In my own research, complaints from women about their husbands most often focused not on tangible inequities such as having given up the chance for a career to accompany a husband to his, or doing far more than their share of daily life-support work like cleaning, cooking, social arrangements and errands. Instead, they focused on communication: "He doesn't listen to me," "He doesn't talk to me." I found, as Hacker observed years before, that most wives want their husbands to be, first and foremost, conversational partners, but few husbands share this expectation of their wives.

In short, the image that best represents the current crisis is the stereotypical cartoon scene of a man sitting at the breakfast table with a newspaper held up in front of his face, while a woman glares at the back of it, wanting to talk.

Linguistic Battle of the Sexes

How can women and men have such different impressions of communication in marriage? Why the widespread imbalance in their interests and expectations?

In the April [1990] issue of *American Psychologist*, Stanford University's Eleanor Maccoby reports the results of her own and others' research showing that children's development is most influenced by the social structure of peer interactions. Boys and girls tend to play with children of their own gender, and their sex-separate groups have different organizational structures and interactive norms.

I believe these systematic differences in childhood socialization make talk between women and men like cross-cultural communication, heir to all the attraction and pitfalls of that enticing but difficult enterprise. My research on men's and women's conversations uncovered patterns similar to those described for children's groups.

For women, as for girls, intimacy is the fabric of relationships, and 9 talk is the thread from which it is woven. Little girls create and maintain friendships by exchanging secrets; similarly, women regard conversation as the cornerstone of friendship. So a woman expects her husband to be a new and improved version of a best friend. What is important is not the individual subjects that are discussed but the sense of closeness, of a life shared, that emerges when people tell their thoughts, feelings, and impressions.

Bonds between boys can be as intense as girls', but they are based 10 less on talking, more on doing things together. Since they don't assume talk is the cement that binds a relationship, men don't know what kind of talk women want, and they don't miss it when it isn't there.

Boy's groups are larger, more inclusive, and more hierarchical, so 11 boys must struggle to avoid the subordinate position in the group. This may play a role in women's complaints that men don't listen to them. Some men really don't like to listen, because being the listener makes them feel one-down, like a child listening to adults or an employee to a boss.

But often when women tell men, "You aren't listening," and the 12 men protest, "I am," the men are right. The impression of not listening results from misalignments in the mechanics of conversation. The misalignment begins as soon as a man and a woman take physical positions. This became clear when I studied videotapes made by psychologist Bruce Dorval of children and adults talking to their same-sex best friends. I found that at every age, the girls and women faced each other directly, their eyes anchored on each other's faces. At every age, the boys and men sat at angles to each other and looked elsewhere in the room, periodically glancing at each other. They were obviously attuned to each other, often mirroring each other's movements. But the tendency of men to face away can give women the impression they aren't listening even when they are. A young woman in college was frustrated: Whenever she told her boyfriend she wanted to talk to him, he would lie down on the floor, close his eyes, and put his arm over his face. This signaled to her, "He's taking a nap." But he insisted he was listening extra hard. Normally, he looks around the room, so he is easily distracted. Lying down and covering his eyes helped him concentrate on what she was saying.

Analogous to the physical alignment that women and men take in 13 conversation is their topical alignment. The girls in my study tended to talk at length about one topic, but the boys tended to jump from topic to topic. The second-grade girls exchanged stories about people they knew. The second-grade boys teased, told jokes, noticed things in the room and talked about finding games to play. The sixth-grade girls talked about problems with a mutual friend. The sixth-grade boys talked about 55 different topics, none of which extended over more than a few turns.

Listening to Body Language

Switching topics is another habit that gives women the impression men aren't listening, especially if they switch to a topic about themselves. But the evidence of the 10th-grade boys in my study indicates otherwise. The 10th-grade boys sprawled across their chairs with bodies parallel and eyes straight ahead, rarely looking at each other. They looked as if they were riding in a car, staring out the windshield. But they were talking about their feelings. One boy was upset because a girl had told him he had a drinking problem, and the other was feeling alienated from all his friends.

Now, when a girl told a friend about a problem, the friend responded by asking probing questions and expressing agreement and understanding. But the boys dismissed each other's problems. Todd assured Richard that his drinking was "no big problem" because "sometimes you're funny when you're off your butt." And when Todd said he felt left out, Richard responded, "Why should you? You know more people than me." 15

Women perceived such responses as belittling and unsupportive. But the boys seemed satisfied with them. Whereas women reassure each other by implying, "You shouldn't feel bad because I've had similar experiences," men do so by implying, "You shouldn't feel bad because your problems aren't so bad." 16

There are even simpler reasons for women's impression that men don't listen. Linguist Lynette Hirschman found that women make more listener-noise, such as "mhm," "uhuh," and "yeah," to show "I'm with you." Men, she found, more often give silent attention. Women who expect a stream of listener-noise interpret silent attention as no attention at all. 17

Women's conversational habits are as frustrating to men as men's are to women. Men who expect silent attention interpret a stream of listener-noise as overreaction or impatience. Also, when women talk to each other in a close, comfortable setting, they often overlap, finish each other's sentences and anticipate what the other is about to say. This practice, which I call "participatory listenership," is often perceived by men as interruption, intrusion and lack of attention. 18

A parallel difference caused a man to complain about his wife, "She just wants to talk about her own point of view. If I show her another view, she gets mad at me." When most women talk to each other, they assume a conversationalist's job is to express agreement and support. But many men see their conversational duty as pointing out the other side of an argument. This is heard as disloyalty by women, and refusal to offer the requisite support. It is not that women don't want to see other points of view, but that they prefer them phrased as suggestions and inquiries rather than as direct challenges. 19

In his book *Fighting for Life*, Walter Ong points out that men use "agonistic" or warlike, oppositional formats to do almost anything; thus discussion becomes debate, and conversation a competitive sport. In 20 contrast, women see conversation as a ritual means of establishing rapport. If Jane tells a problem and June says she has a similar one, they walk away feeling closer to each other. But this attempt at establishing rapport can backfire when used with men. Men take too literally women's ritual "troubles talk," just as women mistake men's ritual challenges for real attack.

The Sounds of Silence

These differences begin to clarify why women and men have such [21] different expectations about communication in marriage. For women, talk creates intimacy. Marriage is an orgy of closeness: you can tell your feelings and thoughts, and still be loved. Their greatest fear is being pushed away. But men live in a hierarchical world, where talk maintains independence and status. They are on guard to protect themselves from being put down and pushed around.

This explains the paradox of the talkative man who said of his silent [22] wife, "She's the talker." In the public setting of a guest lecture, he felt challenged to show his intelligence and display his understanding of the lecture. But at home, where he has nothing to prove and no one to defend against, he is free to remain silent. For his wife, being home means she is free from the worry that something she says might offend someone, or spark disagreement, or appear to be showing off; at home she is free to talk.

The communication problems that endanger marriage can't be [23] fixed by mechanical engineering. They require a new conceptual framework about the role of talk in human relationships. Many of the psychological explanations that have become second nature may not be helpful, because they tend to blame either women (for not being assertive enough) or men (for not being in touch with their feelings). A sociolinguistic approach by which male-female conversation is seen as cross-cultural communication allows us to understand the problem and forge solutions without blaming either party.

Once the problem is understood, improvement comes naturally, as [24] it did to the young woman and her boyfriend who seemed to go to sleep when she wanted to talk. Previously, she had accused him of not listening, and he had refused to change his behavior, since that would be admitting fault. But then she learned about and explained to him the differences in women's and men's habitual ways of aligning themselves in conversation. The next time she told him she wanted to talk, he began, as usual, by lying down and covering his eyes. When the familiar negative reaction bubbled up, she reassured herself that he really was listening. But then he sat up and looked at her. Thrilled she asked why. He said, "You like me to look at you when we talk, so I'll try to do it." Once he saw their differences as cross-cultural rather than right and wrong, he independently altered his behavior.

Women who feel abandoned and deprived when their husbands [25] won't listen to or report daily news may be happy to discover their husbands trying to adapt once they understand the place of small talk in women's relationships. But if their husbands don't adapt, the women may still be comforted that for men, this is not a failure of intimacy. Accepting the difference, the wives may look to their friends or family for that kind of talk. And husbands who can't provide it shouldn't feel their wives have made unreasonable demands. Some couples will still decide to divorce, but at least their decisions will be based on realistic expectations.

In these times of resurgent ethnic conflicts, the world desperately needs cross-cultural understanding. Like charity, successful cross-cultural communication should begin at home. 26

COMPREHENSION

1. What is the thesis of this essay? Where does the author most clearly articulate it?
2. To advance her argument, the author cites political scientists and sociologists, while she, herself, is a linguist. What exactly is the nature of these three professions? What do professionals in the first two fields do? Why does the author use their observations in developing her argument?
3. Why does the author employ a question in her title? What other device does she employ in her title to capture the reader's attention? (*Hint:* It is a reference to the title of a movie.)

RHETORIC

1. The author begins her essay with an anecdote. Is this an effective way of opening this particular essay? Why, or why not?
2. Besides anecdotes, the author uses statistics, social science research, appeals to authority, and definition in advancing her argument. Find at least one example of these devices. Explain their effectiveness or lack thereof.
3. Where and how does the author imply that she is an authority on the subject? How does this contribute or detract from her ability to win the reader's confidence?
4. The author divides her essay into four sections: one untitled and three with headings. How does each section relate to the others structurally and thematically?
5. The author dramatically states that "Given the current divorce rate of nearly 50 percent" the United States has a "virtual epidemic of failed conversation." Is this fact or opinion? Does it serve to heighten or weaken the import of her thesis?
6. Concerning the lack of proper communication between men and women, the author states "Once the problem is understood, improvement comes naturally." Is this statement substantiated or backed up with evidence? Explain.
7. Explain the analogy the author employs in the final paragraph. Is it a good or poor analogy? Explain.

1. Another linguist has written an essay entitled, "The Communication Panacea," which argues that much of what is blamed on lack of communication actually has economic and political causes. Argue for or against this proposition in the light of the ideas advanced in Tannen's essay.
2. Using some of the observational methods described in the essay, conduct your own "ethnographic" research by observing a couple communicating. Write a report discussing your findings.
3. The author states, "Once the problem is understood, improvement comes naturally." Argue for or against this proposition.

AMY TAN   Amy Tan (b. 1952) is the daughter of a minister/electrical engineer and a vocational nurse. She was born in California and educated at San Jose State and the University of California, Berkeley. Tan has worked as a reporter and as a technical writer; her fiction focuses on the lives of Chinese-American women seeking to reconcile their traditional Chinese heritage with modern American culture. Her novels are *The Joy Luck Club* (1989), *The Kitchen God's Wife* (1991), and a children's book, *The Moon Lady* (1992). In this narrative essay, from *The State of the Language,* Tan writes with both emotion and clarity about growing up with two languages, and attacks some linguists who make hasty assumptions.

AMY TAN

The Language of Discretion

At a recent family dinner in San Francisco, my mother whispered to me: "Sau-sau [Brother's Wife] pretends too hard to be polite! Why bother? In the end, she always takes everything."   1

My mother thinks like a *waixiao*, an expatriate, temporarily away   2
from China since 1949, no longer patient with ritual courtesies. As if to prove her point, she reached across the table to offer my elderly aunt from Beijing the last scallop from the Happy Family seafood dish.

Sau-sau scowled. *"B'yao, zhen b'yao!"* (I don't want it, really I   3
don't!) she cried, patting her plump stomach.

"Take it! Take it!" scolded my mother in Chinese.   4

"Full, I'm already full," Sau-sau protested weakly, eyeing the   5
beloved scallop.

"Ai!" exclaimed my mother, completely exasperated. "Nobody else   6
wants it. If you don't take it, it will only rot!"

At this point, Sau-sau sighed, acting as if she were doing my mother   7
a big favor by taking the wretched scrap off her hands.

My mother turned to her brother, a high-ranking communist official who was visiting her in California for the first time: "In America a Chinese person could starve to death. If you say you don't want it, they won't ask you again forever."

My uncle nodded and said he understood fully: Americans take things quickly because they have no time to be polite.

I thought about this misunderstanding again—of social contexts failing in translation—when a friend sent me an article from the *New York Times Magazine* (24 April 1988). The article, on changes in New York's Chinatown, made passing reference to the inherent ambivalence of the Chinese language.

Chinese people are so "discreet and modest," the article stated, there aren't even words for "yes" and "no."

That's not true, I thought, although I can see why an outsider might think that. I continued reading.

If one is Chinese, the article went on to say, "One compromises, one doesn't hazard a loss of face by an overemphatic response."

My throat seized. Why do people keep saying these things? As if we truly were those little dolls sold in Chinatown tourist shops, heads bobbing up and down in complacent agreement to anything said!

I worry about the effect of one-dimensional statements on the unwary and guileless. When they read about this so-called vocabulary deficit, do they also conclude that Chinese people evolved into a mildmannered lot because the language only allowed them to hobble forth with minced words?

Something enormous is always lost in translation. Something insidious seeps into the gaps, especially when amateur linguists continue to compare, one-for-one, language differences and then put forth notions wide open to misinterpretation: that Chinese people have no direct linguistic means to make decisions, assert or deny, affirm or negate, just say no to drug dealers, or behave properly on the witness stand when told, "Please answer yes or no."

Yet one can argue, with the help of renowned linguists, that the Chinese are indeed up a creek without "yes" and "no." Take any number of variations on the old language-and-reality theory stated years ago by Edward Sapir: "Human beings . . . are very much at the mercy of the particular language which has become the medium for their society. . . . The fact of the matter is that the 'real world' is to a large extent built up on the language habits of the group."[1]

This notion was further bolstered by the famous Sapir-Whorf hypothesis, which roughly states that one's perception of the world and how one functions in it depends a great deal on the language used. As Sapir, Whorf, and new carriers of the banner would have us believe, language shapes our thinking, channels us along certain patterns embedded in words, syntactic structures, and intonation patterns. Lan-

[1] Edward Sapir, *Selected Writings,* ed. D. G. Mandelbaum (Berkeley and Los Angeles, 1949).

guage has become the peg and the shelf that enables us to sort out and categorize the world. In English, we see "cats" and "dogs"; what if the language had also specified *glatz,* meaning "animals that leave fur on the sofa," and *glotz,* meaning "animals that leave fur and drool on the sofa"? How would language, the enabler, have changed our perceptions with slight vocabulary variations?

And if this were the case—of language being the master of destined thought—think of the opportunities lost from failure to evolve two little words, *yes* and *no,* the simplest of opposites! Ghenghis Khan could have been sent back to Mongolia. Opium wars might have been averted. The Cultural Revolution could have been sidestepped.

There are still many, from serious linguists to pop psychology cultists, who view language and reality as inextricably tied, one being the consequence of the other. We have traversed the range from the Sapir-Whorf hypothesis to est and neurolinguistic programming, which tell us "you are what you say."

I too have been intrigued by the theories. I can summarize, albeit badly, ages-old empirical evidence: of Eskimos and their infinite ways to say "snow," their ability to *see* the differences in snowflake configurations, thanks to the richness of their vocabulary, while non-Eskimo speakers like myself founder in "snow," "more snow," and "lots more where that came from."

I too have experienced dramatic cognitive awakenings via the word. Once I added "mauve" to my vocabulary I began to see it everywhere. When I learned how to pronounce *prix fixe,* I ate French food at prices better than the easier-to-say *à la carte* choices.

But just how seriously are we supposed to take this?

Sapir said something else about language and reality. It is the part that often gets left behind in the dot-dot-dots of quotes: ". . . No two languages are ever sufficiently similar to be considered as representing the same social reality. The worlds in which different societies live are distinct worlds, not merely the same world with different labels attached."

When I first read this, I thought, Here at last is validity for the dilemmas I felt growing up in a bicultural, bilingual family! As any child of immigrant parents knows, there's a special kind of double bind attached to knowing two languages. My parents, for example, spoke to me in both Chinese and English; I spoke back to them in English.

"Amy-ah!" they'd call to me.

"What?" I'd mumble back.

"Do not question us when we call," they scolded me in Chinese. "It is not respectful."

"What do you mean?"

"Ai! Didn't we just tell you not to question?"

To this day, I wonder which parts of my behavior were shaped by Chinese, which by English. I am tempted to think, for example, that if I am of two minds on some matter it is due to the richness of my linguistic experiences, not to any personal tendencies toward wishy-washiness. But which mind says what?

Was it perhaps patience—developed through years of deciphering my mother's fractured English—that had me listening politely while a woman announced over the phone that I had won one of five valuable prizes? Was it respect—pounded in by the Chinese imperative to accept convoluted explanations—that had me agreeing that I might find it worthwhile to drive seventy-five miles to view a time-share resort? Could I have been at a loss for words when asked, "Wouldn't you like to win a Hawaiian cruise or perhaps a fabulous Star of India designed exclusively by Carter and Van Arpels?"

And when this same woman called back a week later, this time complaining that I had missed my appointment, obviously it was my type A language that kicked into gear and interrupted her. Certainly, my blunt denial—"Frankly I'm not interested"—was as American as apple pie. And when she said, "But it's in Morgan Hill," and I shouted, "Read my lips. I don't care if it's Timbuktu," you can be sure I said it with the precise intonation expressing both cynicism and disgust.

It's dangerous business, this sorting out of language and behavior. Which one is English? Which is Chinese? The categories manifest themselves: passive and aggressive, tentative and assertive, indirect and direct. And I realize they are just variations of the same theme: that Chinese people are discreet and modest.

Reject them all!

If my reaction is overly strident, it is because I cannot come across as too emphatic. I grew up listening to the same lines over and over again, like so many rote expressions repeated in an English phrasebook. And I too almost came to believe them.

Yet if I consider my upbringing more carefully, I find there was nothing discreet about the Chinese language I grew up with. My parents made everything abundantly clear. Nothing wishy-washy in their demands, no compromises accepted: "Of course you will become a famous neurosurgeon," they told me. "And yes, a concert pianist on the side."

In fact, now that I remember, it seems that the more emphatic outbursts always spilled over into Chinese: "Not that way! You must wash rice so not a single grain spills out."

I do not believe that my parents—both immigrants from mainland China—are an exception to the modest-and-discreet rule. I have only to look at the number of Chinese engineering students skewing minority ratios at Berkeley, MIT, and Yale. Certainly they were not raised by passive mothers and fathers who said, "It is up to you, my daughter. Writer, welfare recipient, masseuse, or molecular engineer—you decide."

And my American mind says, See, those engineering students weren't able to say no to their parents' demands. But then my Chinese mind remembers: Ah, but those parents all wanted their sons and daughters to be *pre-med.*

Having listened to both Chinese and English, I also tend to be suspicious of any comparisons between the two languages. Typically, one

391

language—that of the person doing the comparing—is often used as the standard, the benchmark for a logical form of expression. And so the language being compared is always in danger of being judged deficient or superfluous, simplistic or unnecessarily complex, melodious or cacophonous. English speakers point out that Chinese is extremely difficult because it relies on variations in tone barely discernible to the human ear. By the same token, Chinese speakers tell me English is extremely difficult because it is inconsistent, a language of too many broken rules, of Mickey Mice and Donald Ducks.

Even more dangerous to my mind is the temptation to compare both language and behavior *in translation.* To listen to my mother speak English, one might think she has no concept of past or future tense, that she doesn't see the difference between singular and plural, that she is gender blind because she calls my husband "she." If one were not careful, one might also generalize that, based on the way my mother talks, all Chinese people take a circumlocutory route to get to the point. It is, in fact, my mother's idiosyncratic behavior to ramble a bit.

Sapir was right about differences between two languages and their realities. I can illustrate why word-for-word translation is not enough to translate meaning and intent. I once received a letter from China which I read to non-Chinese speaking friends. The letter, originally written in Chinese, had been translated by my brother-in-law in Beijing. One portion described the time when my uncle at age ten discovered his widowed mother (my grandmother) had remarried—as a number three concubine, the ultimate disgrace for an honorable family. The translated version of my uncle's letter read in part:

> In 1925, I met my mother in Shanghai. When she came to me, I didn't have greeting to her as if seeing nothing. She pull me to a corner secretly and asked me why didn't have greeting to her. I couldn't control myself and cried, "Ma! Why did you leave us? People told me: one day you ate a beancake yourself. Your sister-in-law found it and sweared at you, called your names. So . . . is it true?" She clasped my hand and answered immediately, "It's not true, don't say what like this." After this time, there was a few chance to meet her.

"What!" cried my friends. "Was eating a beancake so terrible?"

Of course not. The beancake was simply a euphemism; a ten-year-old boy did not dare question his mother on something as shocking as concubinage. Eating a beancake was his equivalent for committing this selfish act, something inconsiderate of all family members, hence, my grandmother's despairing response to what seemed like a ludicrous charge of gluttony. And sure enough, she was banished from the family, and my uncle saw her only a few times before her death.

While the above may fuel people's argument that Chinese is indeed a language of extreme discretion, it does not mean that Chinese people speak in secrets and riddles. The contexts are fully understood. It is only to those on the *outside* that the language seems cryptic, the behavior inscrutable.

I am, evidently, one of the outsiders. My nephew in Shanghai, who recently started taking English lessons, has been writing me letters in English. I had told him I was a fiction writer, and so in one letter he wrote, "Congratulate to you on your writing. Perhaps one day I should like to read it." I took it in the same vein as "Perhaps one day we can get together for lunch." I sent back a cheery note. A month went by and another letter arrived from Shanghai. "Last one perhaps I hadn't writing distinctly," he said. "In the future, you'll send a copy of your works for me."

I try to explain to my English-speaking friends that Chinese language use is more *strategic* in manner, whereas English tends to be more direct; an American business executive may say, "Let's make a deal," and the Chinese manager may reply, "Is your son interested in learning about your widget business?" Each to his or her own purpose, each with his or her own linguistic path. But I hesitate to add more to the pile of generalizations, because no matter how many examples I provide and explain, I fear that it appears defensive and only reinforces the image: that Chinese people are "discreet and modest"—and it takes an American to explain what they really mean. 48

Why am I complaining? The description seems harmless enough (after all, the *New York Times Magazine* writer did not say "slippery and evasive"). It is precisely the bland, easy acceptability of the phrase that worries me. 49

I worry that the dominant society may see Chinese people from a limited—and limiting—perspective. I worry that seemingly benign stereotypes may be part of the reason there are few Chinese in top management positions, in mainstream political roles. I worry about the power of language: that if one says anything enough times—in *any* language—it might become true. 50

Could this be why Chinese friends of my parents' generation are willing to accept the generalization? 51

"Why are you complaining?" one of them said to me. "If people think we are modest and polite, let them think that. Wouldn't Americans be pleased to admit they are thought of as polite?" 52

And I do believe anyone would take the description as a compliment—at first. But after a while, it annoys, as if the only things that people heard one say were phatic remarks: "I'm so pleased to meet you. I've heard many wonderful things about you. For me? You shouldn't have!" 53

These remarks are not representative of new ideas, honest emotions, or considered thought. They are what is said from the polite distance of social contexts: of greetings, farewells, wedding thank-you notes, convenient excuses, and the like. 54

It makes me wonder though. How many anthropologists, how many sociologists, how many travel journalists have documented so-called 55

393

"natural interactions" in foreign lands, all observed with spiral notebook in hand? How many other cases are there of the long-lost primitive tribe, people who turned out to be sophisticated enough to put on the stone-age show that ethnologists had come to see?

And how many tourists fresh off the bus have wandered into Chinatown expecting the self-effacing shopkeeper to admit under duress that the goods are not worth the price asked? I have witnessed it. 56

"I don't know," the tourist said to the shopkeeper, a Cantonese woman in her fifties. "It doesn't look genuine to me. I'll give you three dollars." 57

"You don't like my price, go somewhere else," said the shopkeeper. 58

"You are not a nice person," cried the shocked tourist, "not a nice person at all!" 59

"Who say I have to be nice," snapped the shopkeeper. 60

"So how does one say 'yes' and 'no' in Chinese?" ask my friends a bit warily. 61

And here I do agree in part with the *New York Times Magazine* article. There is no one word for "yes" or "no"—but not out of necessity to be discreet. If anything, I would say the Chinese equivalent of answering "yes" or "no" is dis*crete*, that is, specific to what is asked. 62

Ask a Chinese person if he or she has eaten, and he or she might say *chrle* (eaten already) or perhaps *meiyou* (have not). 63

Ask, "So you had insurance at the time of the accident?" and the response would be *dwei* (correct) or *meiyou* (did not have). 64

Ask, "Have you stopped beating your wife?" and the answer refers directly to the proposition being asserted or denied: stopped already, still have not, never beat, have no wife. 65

What could be clearer? 66

As for those who are still wondering how to translate the language of discretion, I offer this personal example. 67

My aunt and uncle were about to return to Beijing after a three-month visit to the United States. On their last night I announced I wanted to take them out to dinner. 68

"Are you hungry?" I asked in Chinese. 69

"Not hungry," said my uncle promptly, the same response he once gave me ten minutes before he suffered a low-blood-sugar attack. 70

"Not too hungry," said my aunt. "Perhaps you're hungry?" 71

"A little," I admitted. 72

"We can eat, we can eat," they both consented. 73

"What kind of food?" I asked. 74

"Oh, doesn't matter. Anything will do. Nothing fancy, just some simple food is fine." 75

"Do you like Japanese food? We haven't had that yet," I suggested. 76

They looked at each other. 77

"We can eat it," said my uncle bravely, this survivor of the Long March. 78

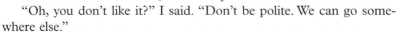
"We have eaten it before," added my aunt. "Raw fish."

"Oh, you don't like it?" I said. "Don't be polite. We can go somewhere else."

"We are not being polite. We can eat it," my aunt insisted.

So I drove them to Japantown and we walked past several restaurants featuring colorful plastic displays of sushi.   82

"Not this one, not this one either," I continued to say, as if searching for a Japanese restaurant similar to the last. "Here it is," I finally said, turning into a restaurant famous for its Chinese fish dishes from Shandong.   83

"Oh, Chinese food!" cried my aunt, obviously relieved.   84

My uncle patted my arm. "You think Chinese."   85

"It's your last night here in America," I said. "So don't be polite. Act like an American."   86

And that night we ate a banquet.   87

COMPREHENSION

1. Why is the writer suspicious of any comparisons made between Chinese and English? What dangerous generalizations may be drawn?
2. What is meant by "the double bind attached to knowing two languages"?
3. In your own words, define Sapir's language theory.

RHETORIC

1. What tone does Tan use in her essay? Is her approach objective or subjective? Justify your response.
2. What is Tan's thesis? Is it implied or stated explicitly?
3. How do the anecdotes at the beginning and conclusion of the essay help frame what happens in between? How well do they illustrate or support the essay's body?
4. Cite specific examples of irony or humor in the essay. Is it used consistently throughout the piece? How does its use advance Tan's main ideas?
5. How does Tan employ comparison and contrast to structure this essay?
6. How many sections are there in this essay? What principles of writing and coherence govern each section?

WRITING

1. Tan writes about the generalizations made by "outsiders" about Chinese culture based on the language. Write an essay in which you explore this topic by focusing on misconceptions others may have about you or you may have about others based on language.
2. Linguistic theories are presented by both Tan and Tannen in their essays. Using support from either or both writers, consider the dangers of linking

behavior to language. Can these theories be used to further racist or sexist notions? Are they valid, scientific attempts to study human behavior?

SAMUEL ICHIZE HAYAKAWA   Samuel Ichize Hayakawa (1906–1992) began his career as a professor of linguistics and was the author of numerous books on languages, such as *Language in Thought and Action* (1941), *Our Language and Our World* (1959), and *Symbol, Status, and Personality* (1963). When Hayakawa became president of San Francisco State College, student unrest was at its height. By defending traditional values and, indeed, authority itself, Hayakawa became a national and controversial figure. His notoriety propelled him into the U.S. Senate. The present essay reflects his original career as a semanticist.

S. I. HAYAKAWA

Words and Children

Those who still believe, after all the writing that semanticists have done, that semantics is a science of words, may be surprised to learn that semantics has the effect—at least, it has had on me and on many others—of reducing rather than increasing one's preoccupation with words. First of all, there is that vast area of nonverbal communication with children that we accomplish through holding, touching, rocking, caressing our children, putting food in their mouths, and all of the little attentions that we give them. These are all communication, and we communicate in this way for a long time before the children even start to talk.

Then, after they start to talk, there is always the problem of interpretation. There is a sense in which small children are recent immigrants in our midst. They have trouble both in understanding and in using the language, and they often make errors. Many people (you can notice this in the supermarkets, especially with parents of two- and three-year-old children) get angry at their children when they don't seem to mind. Anyone standing within earshot of one of these episodes can tell that the child just hasn't understood what the mother said. But the mother feels, "Well, I said it, didn't I? What's wrong with the child that he doesn't understand? It's English, isn't it?" But, as I say, the child is a recent immigrant in our midst and there are things that the child doesn't understand.

There are curious instances. Once, when our daughter was three years old, she found the bath too hot and she said, "Make it warmer." It took me a moment to figure out that she meant, "Bring the water more nearly to the condition we call warm." It makes perfectly good sense looked at that way. Confronted with unusual formulations such as these which children constantly make, many of us react with incredible lack of imagination. Sometimes children are laughed at for making "silly statements," when it only requires understanding their way of abstracting and their way of formulating their abstractions to see that they are not silly at all.

Children are newcomers to the language. Learning a language isn't just learning words; rules of the language are learned at the same time. Prove this? Very simple. Little children use a past tense like "I runned all the way to the park and I swimmed in the pool." "Runned" and "swimmed" are words they did not hear. They made them up by analogy from other past tenses they had heard. This means that they learned not only the vocabulary, they learned the rule for making the past tense—except that the English language doesn't follow its own rules. And when the child proves himself to be more logical than the English language, we take it out on the child—which is nonsense. Children's language should be listened to with great attentiveness and respect.

Again, when our daughter was three years old, I was pounding away at my typewriter in my study and she was drawing pictures on the floor when she suddenly said, "I want to go see the popentole."

I kept typing.

Then I stopped and said, "What?!"

She said, "I want to see the popentole."

"Did you say *popentole?*"

I just stopped. It was a puzzle to figure out, but I did. In a few seconds I said, "You mean like last Saturday, you want to go to Lincoln Park and see the totem pole?"

She said, "Yes."

And what was so warm about this, so wonderful about it, was that having got her point across she played for another twenty minutes singing to herself, happy that she had communicated. I didn't say to her, "Okay, I'll take you next Sunday to see the popentole." The mere fact that she'd made her point and got it registered was a source of satisfaction to her. And I felt very proud of myself at the time for having understood.

One of the things we tend to overlook in our culture is the tremendous value of the acknowledgment of message. Not, "I agree with you" or "I disagree with you" or "That's a wonderful idea" or "That's a silly idea," but just the acknowledgment, "I know exactly what you've said. It goes on the record. You said that." She said, "I want to go see the totem pole." I said, "Okay, you want to go see the totem pole." The acknowledgment of message says in effect, "I know you're around. I know what you're thinking. I acknowledge your presence."

There is also a sense in which a child understands far more than we suspect. Because a child doesn't understand words too well (and also because his nervous system is not yet deadened by years spent as a lawyer, accountant, advertising executive, or professor of philosophy), a child attends not only to what we say but to everything about us as we say it—tone of voice, gesture, facial expression, bodily tensions, and so on. A child attends to a conversation between grown-ups with the same amazing absorption. Indeed, a child listening is, I hope, like a good psychiatrist listening—or like a good semanticist listening—because she watches not only the words but also the nonverbal events to which words bear, in all too many cases, so uncertain a relationship. Therefore a child is in some matters quite difficult to fool, especially on the subject of one's true attitude toward her. For this reason many parents, without knowing it, are to a greater or lesser degree in the situation of the worried mother who said to the psychiatrist to whom she brought her child, "I tell her a dozen times a day that I love her, but the brat still hates me. Why, doctor?"

"Life in a big city is dangerous," a mother once said to me. "You hear so often of children running thoughtlessly out in the street and being struck by passing cars. They will never learn unless you keep telling them and telling them." This is the communication theory that makes otherwise pleasant men and women into nagging parents: You've got to keep telling them; then you've got to remind them; then tell 'em again. Are there no better ways to teach children not to run out into the street? Of course there are. I think it was done in our family without words.

Whenever my wife crossed the street with our boy Alan—he was then about three—she would come to a stop at the curb whether there was any traffic in sight or not, and look up and down the boulevard before crossing. It soon became a habit. One day I absentmindedly started crossing the street without looking up and down—the street was empty. Alan grabbed my coat and pulled me back on the curb to look up and down before we started out again. Children love to know the right way to do things. They learn by imitation far more than by precept.

The uncritical confidence that many people place in words is a matter of constant amazement to me. When we were living in Chicago there was a concrete courtyard behind our apartment house. I heard a great deal of noise and shouting out there one day, and I looked out and saw a father teaching his boy to ride a bicycle. The father was shouting instructions: "Keep your head up. Now push down with your left foot. Now look out, you're running into the wall. Steer away from it. *Steer away from it!* Now push down with your right foot. Don't fall down!" and so on and so on. The poor boy was trying to keep his balance, manage the bicycle, obey his father's instructions all at the same time, and he looked about as totally confused as it is possible for a little boy to get. One thing we learn from general semantics, if we haven't learned it some other way already, is that there are limits to what can be accomplished in words. Learning to ride a bicycle is beyond those limits. Having sensed those limits, we become content to let many things take care of themselves without words. All this makes for a quieter household.

The anthropologist Ray Birdwhistell has undertaken a study that he calls "kinesics"* which is the systematic examination of gesture and body motion in communication; this is a rich area of concern about which many students of human behavior have been much excited. But there is a danger in going too far in this direction—in going overboard to the extent of saying that words are of *no* importance. There are thousands of things children must know and enjoy that it is not possible for them to get *without* words.

The sense of what one misses through the lack of words has been brought home to us by the fact that our second boy, Mark, now twenty-nine, is seriously mentally retarded. At the age of six he was hardly able to talk at all. Now he talks quite a bit, but his speech is very difficult to understand; members of the family can understand it about half the time. He was always able to understand words with direct physical referents—watch, glass of water, orange juice, record player, television, and so on. But there are certain things that exist only in words, like the concept of the future. I remember the following incident when he was six years old. He came across a candy bar at ten minutes to twelve when lunch was just about to be served. I tried to take it away from him and said, "Look, Mark, you can have it right after lunch. Don't eat it now. You can have it right after lunch." Well, when he was six all he could understand was that it was being taken away from him *now,* and the idea that there was a future in which he'd have it back was something he just couldn't get at the time. Of course, the concept of futurity developed later, but it took him much longer to develop it than it took the other children.

For human beings, the future, which exists *only in language,* is a wonderful dimension in which to live. That is, human beings can readily endure and even enjoy postponement; the anticipation of future pleasures is itself a pleasure. But futurity is something that has no physical referent like "a glass of water." It exists only in language. Mark's frequent frustrations and rage when he was younger were a constant reminder to us that all the warmth and richness of nonverbal communication, all that we could communicate by holding him and feeding him and patting his head and playing on the floor with him, were not enough for the purpose of human interaction. Organized games of any kind all have linguistically formulated rules. Take an organized game like baseball. Can there be a baseball without language? No, there can't. What's the difference between a ball and a strike? There are linguistically formulated rules by which we define the difference. All systematic games, even much simpler games that children play, have to have a language to formulate the rules. An enormous amount of human life is possible only with language, and without it one is very much impoverished.

*Ray Birdwhistell, *Kinesics and Context*. Philadelphia: University of Pennsylvania Press, 1970.

COMPREHENSION

1. How does the author encourage readers to understand what *semantics* means? Cite examples.
2. Hayakawa says that as a semanticist he has learned that we don't communicate only through words. What other ways of communication does he mention?
3. Hayakawa also points out some of the advantages of language as a communicative skill. What are they?

RHETORIC

1. Hayakawa uses two metaphors to explain a child's relation to language. What are they?
2. Cite examples of Hayakawa's use of scientific jargon. What does this suggest about the audience for which he is writing?
3. Explain how Hayakawa uses process to develop his essay.
4. Hayakawa makes several statements about communication. What are they? How does he use examples to illustrate these points?
5. Where does Hayakawa use personal examples? How do they contribute to the development of the essay?
6. Explain the importance of paragraphs 3, 14, and 18 to the development of the essay.

WRITING

1. Write an essay describing how we use nonverbal forms of communication, such as signals in sports or streetlights. Consider how we communicate through arts such as music, ballet, and painting.
2. Write an essay about the language of children based on your personal experience.
3. Imagine yourself an immigrant or a newcomer to a language. In what ways would you be like a child? Describe the situation in an essay.

ROSARIO FERRÉ   Rosario Ferré (b. 1942) is a poet as well as the founder and director of *Zona de cargo y descargos,* a Latin-American journal devoted to Puerto-Rican writers. Ferré was born in Ponce, Puerto Rico, and received her Ph.D. from the University of Maryland in 1986. Her poetry collections include *Arbor y sombras* (1989) and *Sonatinas* (1989); Ferré's verse also appears in various anthologies, including *Contemporary Latin American Literature: 1960–1984.* In the essay below, Ferré describes the process of freeing herself from ghostly mentors in order to develop as a woman writer.

ROSARIO FERRÉ

The Writer's Kitchen

Throughout time, women narrators have written for many reasons: 1
Emily Brontë wrote to prove the revolutionary nature of passion; Virginia Woolf wrote to exorcise her terror of madness and death; Joan Didion writes to discover what and how she thinks; Clarice Lispector discovered in her writing a reason to love and be loved. In my case, writing is simultaneously a constructive and a destructive urge, a possibility for growth and change. I write to build myself word by word, to banish my terror of silence; I write as a speaking, human mask. With respect to words, I have much for which to be grateful. Words have allowed me to forge for myself a unique identity, one that owes its existence only to my efforts. For this reason, I place more trust in the words I use than perhaps I ever did in my natural mother. When all else fails, when life becomes an absurd theater, I know words are there, ready to return my confidence to me. This need to reconstruct which moves me to write is closely tied to my need for love: I write so as to reinvent myself, to convince myself that what I love will endure.

But my urge to write is also destructive, an attempt to annihilate 2
myself and the world. Words are infinitely wise and, like all mothers, they know when to destroy what is worn out or corrupt so that life may be rebuilt on new foundations. To the degree that I take part in the corruption of the world, I turn my instrument against myself. I write because I am poorly adjusted to reality; because the deep disillusionment within me has given rise to a need to re-create life, to replace it with a more compassionate, tolerable reality. I carry within me a utopian person, a utopian world.

This destructive urge that moves me to write is tied to my need for 3
hate, my need for vengeance. I write so as to avenge myself against reality and against myself; I write to give permanence to what hurts me and to what tempts me. I believe that deep wounds and harsh insults might someday release within me all the creative forces available to human expression, a belief that implies, after all, that I love the word passionately.

Now I would like to address these constructive and destructive 4
forces with relation to my work. The day I finally sat down at my typewriter to write my first story, I knew from experience how hard it was for a woman to obtain her own room with a lock on the door, as well as those metaphorical five hundred pounds a year that assure her independence. I had gotten divorced and had suffered many changes because of love, or because of what I had then thought was love: the

*Chapter Eight
Language and
Communication*

renouncing of my own intellectual and spiritual space for the sake of the relationship with the one I loved. What made me turn against myself was the determination to become the perfect wife. I wanted to be as they were telling me I should be, so I had ceased to exist; I had renounced my soul's private obligations. It has always seemed to me that living intensely was the most important of these obligations. I did not like the protected existence I had led until then in the sanctuary of my home, free from all danger but also from any responsibilities. I wanted to live, to enjoy firsthand knowledge, art, adventure, danger, without waiting for someone else to tell me about them. In fact, what I wanted was to dispel my fear of death. We all fear death, but I had a special terror of it, the terror of those who have not lived. Life tears us apart, making us become partners to its pleasures and terrors, yet in the end it consoles us; it teaches us to accept death as a necessary and natural end. But to see myself forced to face death without having known life—without passing through its apprenticeship—seemed to me unforgivable cruelty. I would tell myself that that was why children who die without having lived, without having to account for their own acts, all went to Limbo. I was convinced that Heaven was for the good, and Hell for the evil, for those men who had arduously earned either salvation or damnation. But in Limbo there were only women and children, unaware of how we had gotten there.

The day of my debut as a writer, I sat at my typewriter for a long time, mulling over these thoughts. Inevitably, writing my first story meant taking my first step toward Heaven or Hell, and that made me vacillate between a state of euphoria and a state of depression. It was as if I were about to be born, peering timidly through the doors of Limbo. If my voice rings false or my will fails me, I said to myself, all my sacrifices will have been in vain. I will have foolishly given up the protection that despite its disadvantages, at least allowed me to be a good wife and mother, and I will have justly fallen from the frying pan into the fire.

In those days, Virginia Woolf and Simone de Beauvoir were my mentors; I wanted them to show me how to write well, or at least how not to write poorly. I would read everything they had written like a person who takes several spoonfuls of a health potion nightly before retiring. The potion would prevent death from a host of plagues and ills that had killed off the majority of women writers before them, as well as some of their contemporaries. I must admit that those readings didn't do much to strengthen my as yet newborn and fragile identity as a writer. My hand's instinctive reflex was still to hold the frying pan patiently over the fire—not to brandish my pen aggressively through the flames—and Simone and Virginia, while recognizing the achievements that women writers had attained up to that time, criticized them quite severely. Simone was of the opinion that women too frequently insisted on themes traditionally considered feminine, the preoccupation with love, for example, or the denunciation of training and customs that had irreparably limited their existence. Justifiable though these themes were, to reduce oneself to them meant that the capacity for freedom had not been adequately internalized. "Art, literature, and philosophy," Simone would say to me, "are attempts to base the world on a new human freedom, the freedom of the individual creator, and to achieve this goal a woman must, above all, assume the status of a being who already has freedom."

In her opinion, a woman should be constructive in her literature, 7 not of interior realities, but of exterior realities, principally of those of a historical and social nature. For Simone, the intuitive capacity, the contact with irrational forces, the capacity for emotion, were all important talents, but they were also of secondary importance. "The functioning of the world, the order of political and social events which determine the course of our lives, are in the hands of those who make their decisions in the light of knowledge and reason," Simone would say to me, "and not in the light of intuition and emotion," and it was with those themes that women should henceforth occupy themselves in their literature.

Virginia Woolf, for her part, was obsessed with the need for an objec- 8 tivity and distance which, she thought, had seldom been found in the writings of women. Of the writers of the past, Virginia excluded only Jane Austen and Emily Brontë, because only they had managed to write, like Shakespeare, "with a mind incandescent, unimpeded." "It is deadly for a writer to think about his or her gender," Virginia would say to me, and "it is deadly for a woman to register a complaint, however mild, to advocate a cause, however justifiably—deadly, then, to speak consciously as a woman. In Virginia's opinion, the books of a woman writer who doesn't free herself from rage will contain distortions, deviations. She will write with anger instead of with sensitivity. She will speak of herself, instead of about her characters. At war with her fate, how can she avoid dying young, frustrated, always at odds with the world? Clearly, for Virginia, women's literature should never be destructive or irate, but rather harmonious and translucid as was her own.

I had, then, chosen my subject—nothing less than the world—as 9 well as my style—nothing less than an absolutely neutral and serene language, which could let the truth of the material emerge, exactly as Simone and Virginia had advised. Now I had only to find my starting point, that most personal window, from among the thousands that Henry James says fiction possesses, through which I would gain access to my theme, the window to my story. I thought it best to select a historical anecdote, perhaps something related to how our Puerto Rican bourgeois culture changed from an agrarian one based on sugar cane and ruled by a rural oligarchy to an urban or industrial one ruled by a new professional class, an anecdote that would convey how this change brought about a shift in values at the turn of the century—the abandonment of the land and the replacement of a patriarchal code of behavior, based on exploitation but also on certain ethical principles and on Christian charity, with a new utilitarian code that came to us from the United States.

A story centered on this series of events seemed excellent to me in every way. There was no possibility whatever that I might be accused of useless constructions or destructions; there was nothing further from the boring feminine conflicts than that kind of plot. With the context of my plot finally chosen, I raised my hands to the typewriter, ready to begin writing. Under my fingers, ready to leap to the fore, trembled the twenty-six letters of the Latin alphabet, like the chords of a powerful instrument. An hour passed, two, then three, without a single idea crossing the frighteningly limpid horizon of my mind. There was so much information, so many writable events in that moment of our historical becoming, that I had not the faintest idea where to begin. Everything seemed worthy, not just of the clumsy and amateurish story I might write, but of a dozen novels yet to be written.

I decided to be patient and not to despair, to spend the whole night keeping vigil if necessary. Maturity is everything, I told myself, and this was, after all, my first story. If I concentrated hard enough, I would at last find the starting point of my story. It was dawn and a purple light washed over my study windows. Surrounded by full ashtrays and abandoned cups of cold coffee, I fell into a deep sleep, draped over my typewriter's silent keyboard.

Fortunately, I have since learned that the setbacks we must face don't matter, for life keeps right on living us. That night's defeat, after all, had nothing to do with my love for short stories. If I couldn't write stories I could at least listen to them, and in daily life I have always been an avid listener of stories. Verbal tales, the ones people tell me in the street, are the ones that always interest me the most, and I marvel at the fact that those who tell them tend to be unaware that what they are telling me is a story. Something like this took place a few days later, when I was invited to lunch at my aunt's house.

Sitting at the head of the table, dropping a slow spoonful of honey into her tea, my aunt began to tell a story while I listened. It had taken place at a sugarcane plantation some distance away, at the beginning of the century, she said, and its heroine was a distant cousin of hers who made dolls filled with honey. The strange woman had been the victim of her husband, a ne'er-do-well and a drunkard who had wasted away her fortune, kicked her out of the house, and taken up with another woman. My aunt's family, out of respect for the customs of the time, had offered her room and board, despite the fact that by that time the cane plantation on which they lived was on the verge of ruin. To reciprocate for their generosity she had dedicated herself to making honey-filled dolls for the girls in the family.

Soon after her arrival at the plantation, my aunt's cousin, who was still young and beautiful, had developed a strange ailment: her right leg began to swell with no apparent cause, and her relatives sent for the doctor from the nearby town so he could examine her. The doctor, an unscrupulous young man recently graduated from a university in the United States, made the young woman fall in love with him, then falsely diagnosed her ailment as being incurable. Applying plasters like a quack, he condemned her to live like an invalid in an armchair while he dispassionately relieved her of the little money the unfortunate woman had managed to save from her marriage. The doctor's behavior seemed reprehensible to me, of course, but what moved me most about the story were not his despicable acts but the absolute resignation with which, in the name of love, that woman had let herself be exploited for twenty years.

I am not going to repeat here the rest of the story my aunt told me that afternoon because it appears in "La muñeca menor," my first story. True, I didn't tell it with the words my aunt used, nor did I repeat her naive praises to a world fortunately gone by, a world in which day-laborers in the cane fields died of malnutrition while the daughters of plantation owners played with honey-filled dolls. But the story I listened to, in its broad outlines, fulfilled the requirements I had imposed on myself: it dealt with the ruin of one social class and its replacement by another, with the metamorphosis of a value system based on the concept of family into one based on profit and personal gain, a value system implanted among us by strangers from the United States.

The flame was lit. That very afternoon I locked myself in my study and didn't stop until the spark that danced before my eyes stopped right at the heart of what I wanted to say. With my story finished, I leaned back in my chair to read the whole thing, sure of having written a story with an objective theme, a story absolutely free of feminine conflicts, a story with transcendence. Then I realized that all my care had been in vain. That strange relative, victim of a love that subjected her twice to exploitation by her loved one, had appropriated my story; she reigned over it like a tragic, implacable vestal. My theme, while framed in the historical and sociopolitical context I had outlined, was still love, complaint, and—oh! I had to admit it—even vengeance. The image of that woman, hovering for years on end at the edge of the cane field with her broken heart, had touched me deeply. It was she who had finally opened the window for me, the window that had been so hermetically sealed, the window to my story.

I had betrayed Simone, writing once again about the interior reality of women; and I had betrayed Virginia, letting myself get carried away by my anger, by the fury the story produced in me. I confess that I was on the verge of throwing my story into the trash so as to rid myself of the evidence that, in the opinion of my mentors, identified me with all the women writers past and present who had tragically wasted themselves. Luckily I didn't do it; I kept it in a desk drawer to await better times, to await a day when I would perhaps arrive at a better understanding of myself.

Ten years have passed since I wrote, "La muñeca menor," and I have written many stories since then; I think now I can objectively analyze the lessons I learned that day with more maturity. I feel less guilt toward Simone and Virginia because I have discovered that, when one tries to write a story (or a poem or novel), stopping to listen to advice, even from those masters whom one most admires, almost always has negative consequences. Today I know from experience that it is no use to write by setting out beforehand to construct exterior realities or to deal with universal and objective themes if one doesn't first create one's own interior reality. It is no use to try to write in a neutral, harmonious, distant way if one doesn't first have the courage to destroy one's own interior reality. When writing about her characters, a writer is always writing about herself, or about possible versions of herself because, as with all human beings, no virtue or vice is alien to her.

By identifying with the strange relative from "La muñeca menor" I   19 had made possible both processes. On the one hand I had reconstructed, in her misfortune, my own amorous misfortune; and on the other hand, by realizing where her weaknesses and failings were—her passivity, her acceptance, her terrifying resignation—I had destroyed her in my name. Although I may also have saved her. In subsequent stories, my heroines have managed to be braver, freer, more energetic and positive, perhaps because they were born from the ashes of "La muñeca menor." Her betrayal was, in any case, what brought about my fall from the frying pan into the fire of literature.

COMPREHENSION

1. In your own words, explain why Ferré writes. What forces govern her writing?
2. What advice about writing and women did Ferré receive from her literary mentors? Why did she finally discard this advice?
3. Why is Ferré unsuccessful in her initial attempt to write about "external realities"?

RHETORIC

1. What is Ferré's point in writing this essay? Justify your response.
2. Find examples of figurative language in Ferré's essay. How do they enrich the author's thesis?
3. Comment on Ferré's use of extended metaphor in paragraphs 5 and 6 and at the end of paragraph 9. Does it resonate anywhere else in the essay?
4. How is Ferré's concept about the destructive and constructive forces in her writing carried through in the body of the essay?
5. Examine the vocabulary Ferré uses in paragraph 9. How do words like *oligarchy, exploitation,* and *utilitarian code* illustrate the point of that paragraph?
6. What is the point of the narrative in paragraphs 13 and 14? Why does the writer choose not to finish it?

WRITING

1. Write an essay that considers these questions: Is there any connection between gender and writing? What assumptions are made about feminine

versus masculine writers (external versus internal)? Which is considered more legitimate?

2. Ferré uses the word *kitchen* in her title. Write an essay exploring the way in which the writer uses the word and the connections she makes between the word and her life as a woman and a writer.

3. Agree or disagree with Ferré's contention that "a writer is always writing about herself." Is this true of all writers, male and female? In what situations might this *not* be true, or at least not obvious?

ANNIE DILLARD   Annie Dillard was born in 1945 in Pittsburgh and received her B.A. and M.A. degrees from Hollins College in Roanoke, Virginia. Her first book, *Pilgrim at Tinker Creek,* won the 1975 Pulitzer Prize for general nonfiction. Other published works of nonfiction include *Teaching a Stone to Talk* (1982) and *An American Childhood* (1987). She has received awards from the National Endowment for the Arts and the Guggenheim Foundation as well as many other sources. As an essayist, poet, memoirist, and literary critic, her themes focus on the relationships among the self, nature, religion, and faith. Her writing is recognizable by its observations on the minutia of life and its search for meaning in such unlikely places as a stone or an insect. Dillard expanded her range of writing with the publication of her first novel, *The Living* (1992). In this excerpt from *The Writing Life* (1989), the author offers a striking analogy for the creative process.

ANNIE DILLARD

The Writing Life

When you write, you lay out a line of words. The line of words is a 1
miner's pick, a woodcarver's gouge, a surgeon's probe. You wield it, and it digs a path you follow. Soon you find yourself deep in new territory. Is it a dead end, or have you located the real subject? You will know tomorrow, or this time next year.

You make the path boldly and follow it fearfully. You go where the 2
path leads. At the end of the path, you find a box canyon. You hammer out reports, dispatch bulletins.

The writing has changed, in your hands, and in a twinkling, from 3
an expression of your notions to an epistemological tool. The new place interests you because it is not clear. You attend. In your humility, you lay down the words carefully, watching all the angles. Now the earlier writing looks soft and careless. Process is nothing; erase your tracks. The path is not the work. I hope your tracks have grown over; I hope birds ate the crumbs; I hope you will toss it all and not look back.

The line of words is a hammer. You hammer against the walls of ⁴
your house. You tap the walls, lightly, everywhere. After giving many
years' attention to these things, you know what to listen for. Some of
the walls are bearing walls; they have to stay, or everything will fall
down. Other walls can go with impunity; you can hear the difference.
Unfortunately, it is often a bearing wall that has to go. It cannot be
helped. There is only one solution, which appalls you, but there it is.
Knock it out. Duck.

Courage utterly opposes the bold hope that this is such fine stuff ⁵
the work needs it, or the world. Courage, exhausted, stands on bare
reality: this writing weakens the work. You must demolish the work and
start over. You can save some of the sentences, like bricks. It will be a
miracle if you can save some of the paragraphs, no matter how excellent in themselves or hard-won. You can waste a year worrying about it,
or you can get it over with now. (Are you a woman, or a mouse?)

The part you must jettison is not only the best-written part; it is also, ⁶
oddly, that part which was to have been the very point. It is the original key passage, the passage on which the rest was to hang, and from
which you yourself drew the courage to begin. Henry James knew it
well, and said it best. In his preface to *The Spoils of Poynton*, he pities
the writer, in a comical pair of sentences that rises to a howl: "Which is
the work in which he hasn't surrendered, under dire difficulty, the best
thing he meant to have kept? In which indeed, before the dreadful *done,*
doesn't he ask himself what has become of the thing all for the sweet
sake of which it was to proceed to that extremity?"

So it is that a writer writes many books. In each book, he intended ⁷
several urgent and vivid points, many of which he sacrificed as the
book's form hardened. "The youth gets together his materials to build
a bridge to the moon," Thoreau noted mournfully, "or perchance a
palace or temple on the earth, and at length the middle-aged man concludes to build a wood-shed with them." The writer returns to these
materials, these passionate subjects, as to unfinished business, for they
are his life's work.

COMPREHENSION

1. What is the central metaphor Dillard uses in describing the act of writing?
2. According to the author, what should a writer's attitude be toward her or
his work?
3. Explain the meaning of the quotation taken from Thoreau.
4. Explain the meaning of the quotation taken from James.

RHETORIC

1. How does paragraph 1 prepare you for the tone and diction of what is to
follow? How would you describe this tone and diction?
2. The essay is unusual in that it is written in the form of the second-person
singular. To whom does *you* refer?

3. What is the intended audience of this essay: writers, would-be writers, the general public, a highly educated public? Explain by providing examples of grammar and sentence structure.

4. Paragraph 4 is distinct in its use of semicolons and short sentences. In fact, the final sentence is only one word. Assuming that good writers try to correlate the meaning of their writing with the style of their writing, how can you find a relationship between meaning and style in this paragraph?

5. What unifying image about the act of writing does the author create in paragraphs 1 and 2? Consider the number of one-syllable words in this section. How does the rhythm of these monosyllabic words complement the overriding image?

6. What is the chief purpose of this essay? Explain your view.

*Chapter Eight
Language and
Communication*

WRITING

1. Imitate Dillard's introductory sentence with one of your own, using the pattern, "When you ———, you ———." Follow the topic sentence with analogies that support your central image. For example, "When you ski, you launch yourself from the Earth" or "When you enter the Internet, you enter distant galaxies," and so on.

2. Describe a time in your life when you overcame tremendous obstacles to accomplish a difficult task. Explain how you achieved your goal.

3. Develop a series of interview questions in preparation for interviewing a master craftsman, artist, or scientist. Interview your subject and write an essay employing process analysis. Explore and explain the way your subject proceeds with his or her work.

LEWIS THOMAS Lewis Thomas (1913–1994), physician, educator, and author, was born in New York City. He received a B.S. from Princeton in 1933, an M.D. from Harvard in 1937, and an M.A. from Yale in 1969. In addition to a monthly column in *Nature,* Thomas authored *Lives of a Cell* (1974), which won the National Book Award; *Medusa and the Snail* (1979); *The Youngest Science* (1983); and *The Fragile Species* (1992). Dr. Thomas also published extensively in scientific and medical journals. Although best known for his ability to explain the life sciences to lay persons, in this essay he takes up the subject of punctuation in a unique and amusing way.

LEWIS THOMAS

Notes on Punctuation

There are no precise rules about punctuation (Fowler lays out some ₁ general advice (as best as he can under the complex circumstances of

409

English prose (he points out, for example, that we possess only four stops (the comma, the semicolon, the colon and the period (the question mark and exclamation point are not, strictly speaking, stops; they are indicators of tone (oddly enough, the Greeks employed the semicolon for their question mark (it produces a strange sensation to read a Greek sentence which is a straightforward question: Why weepest thou; (instead of Why weepest thou? (and, of course, there are parentheses (which are surely a kind of punctuation making this whole matter much more complicated by having to count up the left-handed parentheses in order to be sure of closing with the right number (but if the parentheses were left out, with nothing to work with but the stops, we would have considerably more flexibility in the deploying of layers of meaning than if we tried to separate all the clauses by physical barriers (and in the latter case, while we might have more precision and exactitude for our meaning, we would lose the essential flavor of language, which is its wonderful ambiguity)))))))))))).

The commas are the most useful and usable of all the stops. It is highly important to put them in place as you go along. If you try to come back after doing a paragraph and stick them in the various spots that tempt you you will discover that they tend to swarm like minnows into all sorts of crevices whose existence you hadn't realized and before you know it the whole long sentence becomes immobilized and lashed up squirming in commas. Better to use them sparingly, and with affection, precisely when the need for each one arises, nicely, by itself.

I have grown fond of semicolons in recent years. The semicolon tells you that there is still some question about the preceding full sentence; something needs to be added; it reminds you sometimes of the Greek usage. It is almost always a greater pleasure to come across a semicolon than a period. The period tells you that that is that; if you didn't get all the meaning you wanted or expected, anyway you got all the writer intended to parcel out and now you have to move along. But with a semicolon there you get a pleasant little feeling of expectancy; there is more to come; read on; it will get clearer.

Colons are a lot less attractive, for several reasons: firstly, they give you the feeling of being rather ordered around, or at least having your nose pointed in a direction you might not be inclined to take if left to yourself, and, secondly, you suspect you're in for one of those sentences that will be labeling the points to be made: firstly, secondly and so forth, with the implication that you haven't sense enough to keep track of a sequence of notions without having them numbered. Also, many writers use this system loosely and incompletely, starting out with number one and number two as though counting off on their fingers but then going on and on without the succession of labels you've been led to expect, leaving you floundering about searching for the ninethly or seventeenthly that ought to be there but isn't.

Exclamation points are the most irritating of all. Look! they say, look at what I just said! How amazing is my thought! It is like being forced to watch someone else's small child jumping up and down crazily in the center of the living room shouting to attract attention. If a sentence really has something of importance to say, something quite remarkable, it doesn't need a mark to point it out. And if it is really, after all, a banal sentence needing more zing, the exclamation point simply emphasizes its banality!

Quotation marks should be used honestly and sparingly, when there is a genuine quotation at hand, and it is necessary to be very rigorous about the words enclosed by the marks. If something is to be quoted, the *exact* words must be used. If part of it must be left out because of space limitations, it is good manners to insert three dots to indicate the omission, but it is unethical to do this if it means connecting two thoughts which the original author did not intend to have tied together. Above all, quotation marks should not be used for ideas that you'd like to disown, things in the air so to speak. Nor should they be put in place around clichés; if you want to use a cliché you must take full responsibility for it yourself and not try to fob it off on anon., or on society. The most objectionable misuse of quotation marks, but one which illustrates the dangers of misuse in ordinary prose, is seen in advertising, especially in advertisements for small restaurants, for example "just around the corner," or "a good place to eat." No single, identifiable, citable person ever really said, for the record, "just around the corner," much less "a good place to eat," least likely of all for restaurants of the type that use this type of prose.

The dash is a handy device, informal and essentially playful, telling you that you're about to take off on a different tack but still in some way connected with the present course—only you have to remember that the dash is there, and either put a second dash at the end of the notion to let the reader know that he's back on course, or else end the sentence, as here, with a period.

The greatest danger in punctuation is for poetry. Here it is necessary to be as economical and parsimonious with commas and periods as with the words themselves, and any marks that seem to carry their own subtle meanings, like dashes and little rows of periods, even semicolons and question marks, should be left out altogether rather than inserted to clog up the thing with ambiguity. A single exclamation point in a poem, no matter what else the poem has to say, is enough to destroy the whole work.

The things I like best in T. S. Eliot's poetry, especially in the *Four Quartets,* are the semicolons. You cannot hear them, but they are there, laying out the connections between the images and the ideas. Sometimes you get a glimpse of a semicolon coming, a few lines farther on, and it is like climbing a steep path through woods and seeing a wooden bench just at a bend in the road ahead, a place where you can expect to sit for a moment, catching your breath.

Commas can't do this sort of thing; they can only tell you how the different parts of a complicated thought are to be fitted together, but you can't sit, not even take a breath, just because of a comma,

411

COMPREHENSION

1. Does a formal definition of *punctuation* appear in the essay? Why, or why not?
2. What is Thomas's purpose in writing "Notes on Punctuation"? What is his thesis?
3. What is Thomas's favorite form of punctuation? What about it does he like? What about it does he find irritating?

RHETORIC

1. What stylistic technique does Thomas use to illustrate punctuation? What is his purpose in doing it this way?
2. Is Thomas's style subjective or objective? Why?
3. Carefully analyze the author's introductory paragraph. How does it set up the rest of the essay?
4. How does Thomas use classification to develop the essay? What is the basis of his classification scheme?
5. In which paragraphs is illustration used? What is its purpose?
6. What use of transitional devices does Thomas make? Why does he organize his paragraphs in this way?

WRITING

1. Write a brief, amusing essay on your favorite form of punctuation.
2. Analyze and evaluate the approach to language taken by Thomas in his essay.
3. In an essay entitled "Language and Evolution," Thomas marvels over the common root for the words *human, humane,* and *humble.* Develop a paper on these related words or any other set of related words that interests you.

CLASSIC AND CONTEMPORARY

GEORGE ORWELL   George Orwell (1903–1950) was the pseudonym of Eric Arthur Blair, an English novelist, essayist, and journalist. Orwell served with the Indian Imperial Police from 1922 to 1927 in Burma, fought in the Spanish Civil War, and acquired from his experience a disdain of totalitarian and imperialistic systems. This attitude is reflected in the satiric fable *Animal Farm* (1945) and in the bleak, futuristic novel *1984* (1949). This essay, one of the more famous of the twentieth century, relates sloppy thinking and writing with political oppression.

Politics and the English Language

Most people who bother with the matter at all would admit that the
English language is in a bad way, but it is generally assumed that we
cannot by conscious action do anything about it. Our civilisation is
decadent, and our language—so the argument runs—must inevitably
share in the general collapse. It follows that any struggle against the
abuse of language is a sentimental archaism, like preferring candles to
electric light or hansom cabs to aeroplanes. Underneath this lies the
half-conscious belief that language is a natural growth and not an
instrument which we shape for our own purposes.

Now, it is clear that the decline of a language must ultimately have
political and economic causes: it is not due simply to the bad influence
of this or that individual writer. But an effect can become a cause, reinforcing the original cause and producing the same effect in an intensified form, and so on indefinitely. A man may take to drink because he
feels himself to be a failure, and then fail all the more completely
because he drinks. It is rather the same thing that is happening to the
English language. It becomes ugly and inaccurate because our thoughts
are foolish, but the slovenliness of our language makes it easier for us
to have foolish thoughts. The point is that the process is reversible.
Modern English, especially written English, is full of bad habits which
spread by imitation and which can be avoided if one is willing to take
the necessary trouble. If one gets rid of these habits one can think more
clearly, and to think clearly is a necessary first step towards political
regeneration: so that the fight against bad English is not frivolous and
is not the exclusive concern of professional writers. I will come back to
this presently, and I hope that by that time the meaning of what I have
said here will have become clearer. Meanwhile, here are five specimens
of the English language as it is now habitually written.

These five passages have not been picked out because they are especially bad—I could have quoted far worse if I had chosen—but because
they illustrate various of the mental vices from which we now suffer.
They are a little below the average, but are fairly representative samples.
I number them so that I can refer back to them when necessary:

> *1.* I am not, indeed, sure whether it is not true to say the Milton
> who once seemed not unlike a seventeenth-century Shelley had not
> become, out of an experience even more bitter in each year, more alien
> (sic) to the founder of that Jesuit sect which nothing could induce him
> to tolerate.
>
> —Professor Harold Laski (essay in *Freedom of Expression)*

> *2.* Above all, we cannot play ducks and drakes with a native battery
> of idioms which prescribes such egregious collocations of vocables as
> the Basic *put up with* for *tolerate* or *put at a loss* for *bewilder.*
>
> —Professor Lancelot Hogben *(Interglossa)*

3. On the one side we have the free personality: by definition it is not neurotic, for it has neither conflict nor dream. Its desires, such as they are, are transparent, for they are just what institutional approval keeps in the forefront of consciousness; another institutional pattern would alter their number and intensity; there is little in them that is natural, irreducible, or culturally dangerous. But on the other side, the social bond itself is nothing but the mutual reflection of these self-secure integrities. Recall the definition of love. Is not this the very picture of a small academic? Where is there a place in this hall of mirrors for either personality or fraternity?

—Essay on psychology in *Politics* (New York)

4. All the "best people" from the gentlemen's clubs, and all the frantic Fascist captains, united in common hatred of Socialism and bestial horror of the rising tide of the mass revolutionary movement, have turned to acts of provocation, to foul incendiarism, to medieval legends of poisoned wells, to legalise their own destruction to proletarian organisations, and rouse the agitated petty-bourgeoisie to chauvinistic fervour on behalf of the fight against the revolutionary way out of the crisis. —Communist pamphlet

5. If a new spirit is to be infused into this old country, there is one thorny and contentious reform which must be tackled, and that is the humanisation and galvanisation of the BBC. Timidity here will bespeak canker and atrophy for the soul. The heart of Britain may be sound and of strong beat, for instance, but the British lion's roar at present is like that of Bottom in Shakespeare's Midsummer Night's Dream—as gentle as any sucking dove. A virile new Britain cannot continue indefinitely to be traduced in the eyes, or rather ears, of the world by the effete languors of Langham Place, brazenly masquerading as "standard English." When the Voice of Britain is heard at nine o'clock, better far and infinitely less ludicrous to hear aitches honestly dropped than the present priggish, inflated, inhibited, school-ma'amish braying of blameless bashful mewing maidens! —Letter in *Tribune*

Each of these passages has faults of its own, but, quite apart from avoidable ugliness, two qualities are common to all of them. The first is staleness of imagery: the other is lack of precision. The writer either has a meaning and cannot express it, or he inadvertently says something else, or he is almost indifferent as to whether his words mean anything or not. This mixture of vagueness and sheer incompetence is the most marked characteristic of modern English prose, and especially of any kind of political writing. As soon as certain topics are raised, the concrete melts into the abstract and no one seems able to think of turns of speech that are not hackneyed: prose consists less and less of *words* chosen for the sake of their meaning, and more of *phrases* tacked together like the sections of a prefabricated henhouse. I list below, with notes and examples, various of the tricks by means of which the work of prose construction is habitually dodged:

Dying Metaphors

A newly invented metaphor assists thought by evoking a visual image, while on the other hand a metaphor which is technically "dead" (e.g., *iron resolution*) has in effect reverted to being an ordinary word and can generally be used without loss of vividness. But in between these two classes there is a huge dump of worn-out metaphors which have lost all evocative power and are merely used because they save people the trouble of inventing phrases for themselves. Examples are: *Ring the changes on, take up the cudgels for, toe the line, ride roughshod over, stand shoulder to shoulder with, play into the hands of, no axe to grind, grist to the mill, fishing in troubled waters, rift within the lute, on the order of the day, Achilles' heel, swan song, hotbed.* Many of these are used without knowledge of their meaning (what is a "rift," for instance?), and incompatible metaphors are frequently mixed, a sure sign that the writer is not interested in what he is saying. Some metaphors now current have been twisted out of their original meaning without those who use them even being aware of the fact. For example, *toe the line* is sometimes written *tow the line.* Another example is *the hammer and the anvil,* now always used with the implication that the anvil gets the worst of it. In real life it is always the anvil that breaks the hammer, never the other way about: a writer who stopped to think what he was saying would be aware of this, and would avoid perverting the original phrase.

Operators, or Verbal False Limbs

These save the trouble of picking out appropriate verbs and nouns, and at the same time pad each sentence with extra syllables which give it an appearance of symmetry. Characteristic phrases are: *render inoperative, militate against, prove unacceptable, make contact with, be subjected to, give rise to, give grounds for, have the effect of, play a leading part (rôle) in, make itself felt, take effect, exhibit a tendency to, serve the purpose of,* etc. etc. The keynote is the elimination of simple verbs. Instead of being a single word, such as *break, stop, spoil, mend, kill,* a verb becomes a *phrase,* made up of a noun or adjective tacked on to some general-purposes verb such as *prove, serve, form, play, render.* In addition, the passive voice is wherever possible used in preference to the active, and noun constructions are used instead of gerunds *(by examination of* instead of *by examining).* The range of verbs is further cut down by means of the *-ise* and *de-* formations, and banal statements are given an appearance of profundity by means of the *not un-* formation. Simple conjunctions and prepositions are replaced by such phrases as *with respect to, having regard to, the fact that, by dint of, in view of, in the interests of, on the hypothesis that;* and the ends of sentences are saved from anticlimax by such resounding commonplaces as *greatly to be desired, cannot be left out of account, a development to be expected in the near future, deserving of serious consideration, brought to a satisfactory conclusion,* and so on and so forth.

Pretentious Diction

Words like *phenomenon, element, individual* (as noun), *objective, categorical, effective, virtual, basic, primary, promote, constitute, exhibit, exploit, utilise, eliminate, liquidate,* are used to dress up simple statements and give an air of scientific impartiality to biassed judgements. Adjectives like *epoch-making, epic, historic, unforgettable, triumphant, age-old, inevitable, inexorable, veritable,* are used to dignify the sordid processes of international politics, while writing that aims at glorifying war usually takes on an archaic colour, its characteristic words being: *realm, throne, chariot, mailed fist, trident, sword, shield, buckler, banner, jackboot, clarion.* Foreign words and expressions such as *cul de sac, ancien régime, deus ex machina, mutatis mutandis, status quo, Gleichschaltung, Weltanschauung,* are used to give an air of culture and elegance. Except for the useful abbreviations *i.e., e.g.,* and *etc.,* there is no real need for any of the hundreds of foreign phrases now current in English. Bad writers, and especially scientific, political and sociological writers, are nearly always haunted by the notion that Latin or Greek words are grander than Saxon ones, and unnecessary words like *expedite, ameliorate, predict, extraneous, deracinated, clandestine, subaqueous* and hundreds of others constantly gain ground from their Anglo-Saxon opposite numbers.[1] The jargon peculiar to Marxist writing (*hyena, hangman, cannibal, petty bourgeois, these gentry, lacquey, flunkey, mad dog, White Guard,* etc.) consists largely of words and phrases translated from Russian, German or French; but the normal way of coining a new word is to use a Latin or Greek root with the appropriate affix and, where necessary, the -*ise* formation. It is often easier to make up words of this kind (*deregionalise, impermissible, extramarital, non-fragmentatory* and so forth) than to think up the English words that will cover one's meaning. The result, in general, is an increase in slovenliness and vagueness.

Meaningless Words

In certain kinds of writing, particularly in art criticism and literary criticism, it is normal to come across long passages which are almost

---

[1]An interesting illustration of this is the way in which the English flower names which were in use till very recently are being ousted by Greek ones, *snapdragon* becoming *antirrhinum, forget-me-not* becoming *myosotis,* etc. It is hard to see any practical reason for this change of fashion: it is probably due to an instinctive turning-away from the more homely word and a vague feeling that the Greek word is scientific.

completely lacking in meaning.[2] Words like *romantic, plastic, values, human, dead, sentimental, natural, vitality,* as used in art criticism, are strictly meaningless, in the sense that they not only do not point to any discoverable object, but are hardly even expected to do so by the reader. When one critic writes, "The outstanding features of Mr X's work is its living quality," while another writes, "The immediately striking thing about Mr X's work is its peculiar deadness," the reader accepts this as a simple difference of opinion. If words like *black* and *white* were involved, instead of the jargon words *dead* and *living,* he would see at once that language was being used in an improper way. Many political words are similarly abused. The word *Fascism* has now no meaning except in so far as it signifies "something not desirable." The words *democracy, socialism, freedom, patriotic, realistic, justice,* have each of them several different meanings which cannot be reconciled with one another. In the case of a word like *democracy,* not only is there no agreed definition, but the attempt to make one is resisted from all sides. It is almost universally felt that when we call a country democratic we are praising it: consequently the defenders of every kind of régime claim that it is a democracy, and fear that they might have to stop using the word if it were tied down to any one meaning. Words of this kind are often used in a consciously dishonest way. That is, the person who uses them has his own private definition, but allows his hearer to think he means something quite different. Statements like *Marshal Pétain was a true patriot, The Soviet press is the freest in the world, The Catholic Church is opposed to persecution,* are almost always made with intent to deceive. Other words used in variable meanings, in most cases more or less dishonestly, are: *class, totalitarian, science, progressive, reactionary, bourgeois, equality.*

Now that I have made this catalogue of swindles and perversions, 9 let me give another example of the kind of writing that they lead to. This time it must of its nature be an imaginary one. I am going to translate a passage of good English into modern English of the worst sort. Here is a well-known verse from *Ecclesiastes:*

I returned, and saw under the sun, that the race is not to the swift, nor the battle to the strong, neither yet bread to the wise, nor yet riches to men of understanding, not yet favour to men of skill; but time and chance happeneth to them all.

Here it is in modern English: 10

Objective consideration of contemporary phenomena compels the conclusion that success or failure in competitive activities exhibits no ten-

---

[2]*Example:* "Comfort's catholicity of perception and image, strangely Whitmanesque in range, almost the exact opposite in aesthetic compulsion, continues to evoke that trembling atmospheric accumulative hinting at a cruel, an inexorably serene timelessness. . . . Wrey Gardiner scores by aiming at simple bullseyes with precision. Only they are not so simple, and through this contented sadness runs more than the surface bitter-sweet of resignation." *(Poetry Quarterly).*

dency to be commensurate with innate capacity, but that a considerable element of the unpredictable must invariably be taken into account.

This is a parody, but not a very gross one. Exhibit 3, above, for instance, contains several patches of the same kind of English. It will be seen that I have not made a full translation. The beginning and ending of the sentence follow the original meaning fairly closely, but in the middle the concrete illustrations—race, battle, bread—dissolve into the vague phrase "success or failure in competitive activities." This had to be so, because no modern writer of the kind I am discussing—no one capable of using phrases like "objective consideration of contemporary phenomena"—would ever tabulate his thoughts in that precise and detailed way. The whole tendency of modern prose is away from concreteness. Now analyse these two sentences a little more closely. The first contains 49 words but only 60 syllables, and all its words are those of everyday life. The second contains 38 words of 90 syllables: 18 of its words are from Latin roots, and one from Greek. The first sentence contains six vivid images, and only one phrase ("time and chance") that could be called vague. The second contains not a single fresh, arresting phrase, and in spite of its 90 syllables it gives only a shortened version of the meaning contained in the first. Yet without a doubt it is the second kind of sentence that is gaining ground in modern English. I do not want to exaggerate. This kind of writing is not yet universal, and outcrops of simplicity will occur here and there in the worst-written page. Still, if you or I were told to write a few lines on the uncertainty of human fortunes, we should probably come much nearer to my imaginary sentence than to the one from *Ecclesiastes*.

As I have tried to show, modern writing at its worst does not consist in picking out words for the sake of their meaning and inventing images in order to make the meaning clearer. It consists in gumming together long strips of words which have already been set in order by someone else, and making the results presentable by sheer humbug. The attraction of this way of writing is that it is easy. It is easier—even quicker, once you have the habit—to say *In my opinion it is a not unjustifiable assumption that* than to say *I think*. If you use ready-made phrases, you not only don't have to hunt about for words; you also don't have to bother with the rhythms of your sentences, since these phrases are generally so arranged as to be more or less euphonious. When you are composing in a hurry—when you are dictating to a stenographer, for instance, or making a public speech—it is natural to fall into a pretentious, latinised style. Tags like *a consideration which we should do well to bear in mind or a conclusion to which all of us would readily assent* will save many a sentence from coming down with a bump. By using stale metaphors, similes and idioms, you save much mental effort, at the cost of leaving your meaning vague, not only for your reader but for yourself. This is the significance of mixed metaphors. The sole aim of a metaphor is to call up a visual image. When these images clash—as in *The Fascist octopus has sung its swan*

418

song, *the jackboot is thrown into the melting-pot*—it can be taken as certain that the writer is not seeing a mental image of the objects he is naming; in other words he is not really thinking. Look again at the examples I gave at the beginning of this essay. Professor Laski (1) uses five negatives in 53 words. One of these is superfluous, making nonsense of the whole passage, and in addition there is the slip *alien* for akin, making further nonsense, and several avoidable pieces of clumsiness which increase the general vagueness. Professor Hogben (2) plays ducks and drakes with a battery which is able to write prescriptions, and, while disapproving of the everyday phrase *put up with,* is unwilling to look *egregious* up in the dictionary and see what it means. In (3), if one takes an uncharitable attitude towards it, is simply meaningless: probably one could work out its intended meaning by reading the whole of the article in which it occurs. In (4) the writer knows more or less what he wants to say, but an accumulation of stale phrases chokes him like tea-leaves blocking a sink. In (5) words and meaning have almost parted company. People who write in this manner usually have a general emotional meaning—they dislike one thing and want to express solidarity with another—but they are not interested in the detail of what they are saying. A scrupulous writer, in every sentence that he writes, will ask himself at least four questions, thus: What am I trying to say? What words will express it? What image or idiom will make it clearer? Is this image fresh enough to have an effect? And he will probably ask himself two more: Could I put it more shortly? Have I said anything that is avoidably ugly? But you are not obliged to go to all this trouble. You can shirk it by simply throwing your mind open and letting the ready-made phrases come crowding in. They will construct your sentences for you—even think your thoughts for you, to a certain extent—and at need they will perform the important service of partially concealing your meaning even from yourself. It is at this point that the special connection between politics and the debasement of language becomes clear.

In our time it is broadly true that political writing is bad writing. Where it is not true, it will generally be found that the writer is some kind of rebel, expressing his private opinions, and not a "party line." Orthodoxy, of whatever colour, seems to demand a lifeless, imitative style. The political dialects to be found in pamphlets, leading articles, manifestos, White Papers and the speeches of Under-Secretaries do, of course, vary from party to party, but they are all alike in that one almost never finds in them a fresh, vivid, home-made turn of speech. When one watches some tired hack on the platform mechanically repeating the familiar phrases—*bestial atrocities, iron heel, blood-stained tyranny, free peoples of the world, stand shoulder to shoulder*—one often has a curious feeling that one is not watching a live human being but some kind of dummy: a feeling which suddenly becomes stronger at moments when the light catches the speaker's spectacles and turns them into blank discs which seem to have no eyes behind them. And this is not altogether fanciful. A speaker who uses that kind of phrase-

13

ology has gone some distance towards turning himself into a machine. The appropriate noises are coming out of his larynx, but his brain is not involved as it would be if he were choosing his words for himself. If the speech he is making is one that he is accustomed to make over and over again, he may be almost unconscious of what he is saying, as one is when one utters the responses in church. And this reduced state of consciousness, if not indispensable, is at any rate favourable to political conformity.

In our time, political speech and writing are largely the defence of the indefensible. Things like the continuance of British rule in India, the Russian purges and deportations, the dropping of the atom bombs on Japan, can indeed be defended, but only by arguments which are too brutal for most people to face, and which do not square with the professed aims of political parties. Thus political language has to consist largely of euphemism, question-begging and sheer cloudy vagueness. Defenceless villages are bombarded from the air, the inhabitants driven out into the countryside, the cattle machine-gunned, the huts set on fire with incendiary bullets: this is called *pacification*. Millions of peasants are robbed of their farms and sent trudging along the roads with no more than they can carry: this is called *transfer of population or rectification of frontiers*. People are imprisoned for years without trial, or shot in the back of the neck or sent to die of scurvy in Arctic lumber camps: this is called *elimination of unreliable elements*. Such phraseology is needed if one wants to name things without calling up mental pictures of them. Consider for instance some comfortable English professor defending Russian totalitarianism. He cannot say outright, "I believe in killing off your opponents when you can get good results by doing so." Probably, therefore, he will say something like this:

> While freely conceding that the Soviet régime exhibits certain features which the humanitarian may be inclined to deplore, we must, I think, agree that a certain curtailment of the right to political opposition is an unavoidable concomitant of transitional periods, and that the rigours which the Russian people have been called upon to undergo have been amply justified in the sphere of concrete achievement.

The inflated style is itself a kind of euphemism. A mass of Latin words falls upon the facts like soft snow, blurring the outlines and covering up all the details. The great enemy of clear language is insincerity. When there is a gap between one's real and one's declared aims, one turns as it were instinctively to long words and exhausted idioms, like a cuttlefish squirting out ink. In our age there is no such thing as "keeping out of politics." All issues are political issues, and politics itself is a mass of lies, evasions, folly, hatred and schizophrenia. When the general atmosphere is bad, language must suffer. I should expect to find—this is a guess which I have not sufficient knowledge to verify—that the German, Russian and Italian languages have all deteriorated in the last ten or fifteen years, as a result of dictatorship.

But if thought corrupts language, language can also corrupt thought. A bad usage can spread by tradition and imitation, even among people who should and do know better. The debased language that I have been discussing is in some ways very convenient. Phrases like *a not unjustifiable assumption, leaves much to be desired, would serve no good purpose, a consideration which we should do well to bear in mind,* are a continuous temptation, a packet of aspirins always at one's elbow. Look back through this essay, and for certain you will find that I have again and again committed the very faults I am protesting against. By this morning's post I have received a pamphlet dealing with conditions in Germany. The author tells me that he "felt impelled" to write it. I open it at random, and here is almost the first sentence that I see: "(The Allies) have an opportunity not only of achieving a radical transformation of Germany's social and political structure in such a way as to avoid a nationalistic reaction in Germany itself, but at the same time of laying the foundations of a co-operative and unified Europe." You see, he "feels impelled" to write—feels, presumably, that he has something new to say—and yet his words, like cavalry horses answering the bugle, group themselves automatically into the familiar dreary pattern. This invasion of one's mind by ready-made phrases *(lay the foundations, achieve a radical transformation)* can only be prevented if one is constantly on guard against them, and every such phrase anaesthetises a portion of one's brain.

I said earlier that the decadence of our language is probably curable. Those who deny this would argue, if they produced an argument at all, that language merely reflects existing social conditions, and that we cannot influence its development by any direct tinkering with words and constructions. So far as the general tone or spirit of a language goes, this may be true, but it is not true in detail. Silly words and expressions have often disappeared, not through any evolutionary process but owing to the conscious action of a minority. Two recent examples were *explore every avenue* and *leave no stone unturned,* which were killed by the jeers of a few journalists. There is a long list of fly-blown metaphors which could similarly be got rid of if enough people would interest themselves in the job; and it should also be possible to laugh the *not un-* formation out of existence,[3] to reduce the amount of Latin and Greek in the average sentence, to drive out foreign phrases and strayed scientific words, and, in general, to make pretentiousness unfashionable. But all these are minor points. The defence of the English language implies more than this, and perhaps it is best to start by saying what it does *not* imply.

To begin with, it has nothing to do with archaism, with the salvaging of obsolete words and turns of speech, or with the setting up of a "standard English" which must never be departed from. On the

---

[3]One can cure oneself of the *not un-* formation by memorising this sentence: *A not unblack dog was chasing a not unsmall rabbit across a not ungreen field.*

contrary, it is especially concerned with the scrapping of every word or idiom which has outworn its usefulness. It has nothing to do with correct grammar and syntax, which are of no importance so long as one makes one's meaning clear, or with the avoidance of Americanisms, or with having what is called a "good prose style." On the other hand it is not concerned with fake simplicity and the attempt to make written English colloquial. Nor does it even imply in every case preferring the Saxon word to the Latin one, though it does imply using the fewest and shortest words that will cover one's meaning. What is above all needed is to let the meaning choose the word, and not the other way about. In prose, the worst thing one can do with words is to surrender to them. When you think of a concrete object, you think wordlessly, and then, if you want to describe the thing you have been visualising, you probably hunt about till you find the exact words that seem to fit it. When you think of something abstract you are more inclined to use words from the start, and unless you make a conscious effort to prevent it, the existing dialect will come rushing in and do the job for you, at the expense of blurring or even changing your meaning. Probably it is better to put off using words as long as possible and get one's meaning as clear as one can through pictures or sensations. Afterwards one can choose—not simply *accept*—the phrases that will best cover the meaning, and then switch around and decide what impression one's words are likely to make on another person. This last effort of the mind cuts out all stale or mixed images, all prefabricated phrases, needless repetitions, and humbug and vagueness generally. But one can often be in doubt about the effect of a word or a phrase, and one needs rules that one can rely on when instinct fails. I think the following rules will cover most cases:

i. Never use a metaphor, simile or other figure of speech which you are used to seeing in print.

ii. Never use a long word where a short one will do.

iii. If it is possible to cut a word out, always cut it out.

iv. Never use the passive where you can use the active.

v. Never use a foreign phrase, a scientific word or a jargon word if you can think of an everyday English equivalent.

vi. Break any of these rules sooner than say anything outright barbarous.

These rules sound elementary, and so they are, but they demand a deep change of attitude in anyone who has grown used to writing in the style now fashionable. One could keep all of them and still write bad English, but one could not write the kind of stuff that I quoted in those five specimens at the beginning of this article.

I have not here been considering the literary use of language, but merely language as an instrument for expressing and not for conceal- 19

422

ing or preventing thought. Stuart Chase and others have come near to claiming that all abstract words are meaningless, and have used this as a pretext for advocating a kind of political quietism. Since you don't know what Fascism is, how can you struggle against Fascism? One need not swallow such absurdities as this, but one ought to recognise that the present political chaos is connected with the decay of language, and that one can probably bring about some improvement by starting at the verbal end. If you simplify your English, you are freed from the worst follies of orthodoxy. You cannot speak any of the necessary dialects, and when you make a stupid remark its stupidity will be obvious, even to yourself. Political language—and with variations this is true of all political parties, from Conservatives to Anarchists—is designed to make lies sound truthful and murder respectable, and to give an appearance of solidity to pure wind. One cannot change this all in a moment, but one can at least change one's own habits, and from time to time one can even, if one jeers loudly enough, send some worn-out and useless phrase—some *jackboot, Achilles' heel, hotbed, melting pot, acid test, veritable inferno* or other lump of verbal refuse—into the dustbin where it belongs.

COMPREHENSION

1. What is Orwell's purpose? For what type of audience is he writing? Where does he summarize his concerns for readers?
2. According to Orwell, "thought corrupts language" and "language can also corrupt thought." Give examples of these assertions in the essay.
3. In what ways does Orwell believe that politics and language are related?

RHETORIC

1. Orwell himself uses similes and metaphors. Locate five of them, and explain their relationship to the author's analysis.
2. Orwell claims that concrete language is superior to abstract language. Give examples of Orwell's attempt to write concretely.
3. One of the most crucial rhetorical devices in this essay is definition. What important concepts does Orwell define? What methods of definition does he tend to use?
4. Identify an example of hypothetical reasoning in the essay. How does it contribute to the thesis of the essay?
5. After having given five examples of bad English, why does Orwell, in paragraph 10, give another example? How does this example differ from the others? What does it add to the essay?
6. Explain the use of extended analogy in paragraph 14.

1. In an analytical essay, assess the state of language in politics today. Cite examples from newspapers and television reports.
2. Apply Orwell's advice on language to "Shooting an Elephant" in Chapter 2.
3. Prepare an essay analyzing the use and abuse of any word that sparks controversy today—for example, *abortion, AIDS,* or *greed.*

CASEY MILLER AND KATE SWIFT Casey Miller (b. 1919) and Kate Swift (b. 1923) work as a writing team, focusing on issues addressing women and language. Swift received her A.B. degree from Smith College. Miller received her A.B. degree from the University of North Carolina. Their book *Words and Women* is an extensive look at the impact language has on the perception and identity of women. Both authors have worked in other areas. Miller has served as an educational curriculum editor; Swift, as a public relations writer. The following essay is an adaptation of a talk given at the Association of American University Professors in 1990.

CASEY MILLER AND KATE SWIFT

Who's in Charge
of the English Language?

In order to encourage the use of language that is free of gender bias, it's 1
obviously necessary to get authors to *recognize* gender bias in their writing. The reason that's so difficult is that our culture is steeped in unconscious attitudes and beliefs about gender characteristics, a condition reflected in our use of words.

Every human society has recognized the relationship between 2
power and naming: that the *act of naming* confers power over the thing named. In the Book of Genesis, Adam named all the animals and was given dominion over them, and then, later, the story says "Adam called his wife's name Eve." Those who have the power to name and define other things—animals, wives, whatever—inevitably take themselves as the norm or standard, the measure of all things.

English is androcentric because for centuries it has been evolving in 3
a society where men have been dominant. They were the ones in charge of the major social institutions: government, law, commerce, education, religion. They shaped the course of history and were the subjects of history. It's natural that the languages of patriarchal societies should come to express a male-centered view. That's basic anthropology. Anthropologists know that the single best way to understand the culture of any society is to study the lexicon of its language: a people's words reflect their reality. But the question is: whose reality? The English language still reflects a world in which the power to define gender characteristics is a male prerogative.

We all know that English contains a variety of words that identify and emphasize difference between the sexes. A number of English words actually express polarization of the sexes. Never mind that beyond having one or the other set of biological features necessary for reproduction, every individual is distinct in personality, combining in a unique way those polarized qualities called "masculine" and "feminine." Never mind that virtually no one fits the mold at either pole. It remains a cherished precept of our culture, semantically underlined in our lexicon and embraced by the purveyors of every commodity imaginable, that the sexes must be thought of as opposite.

Female-Negative-Trivial

This linguistic syndrome can be described as "female-negative-trivial" on the one hand, and "male-positive-important" on the other. If that strikes you as overly exaggerated, consider for a moment a group of people who are *not* in charge of the English language—that is, lexicographers—and the definitions they have come up with for a pair of words which relate to gender—the words *manly* and *womanly*. These definitions are from the most recently updated edition of *Webster's Third New International Dictionary* (copyright 1986).

> **Manly** 1. a: having qualities appropriate to a man: not effeminate or timorous: bold, resolute, and open in conduct or bearing . . . b. (1): belonging to or appropriate in character to man [*and they give as examples*] "manly sports," "beer is a manly drink," and "a big booming manly voice." (2): of undaunted courage: gallant, brave [*and among the quotations they give as examples*] "it seemed a big manly thing to say" and "a manly disregard of his enemies" . . .

Now compare the same dictionary's definition of *womanly*, remembering that lexicographers base their definitions on hundreds of examples of usage that have appeared in print.

> **Womanly** 1: marked by qualities characteristic of a woman, esp. marked by qualities becoming a well-balanced adult woman [*and their examples are*] "womanly manners" and "womanly advice." 2: possessed of the character or behavior befitting a grown woman: no longer childish or girlish: becoming to a grown woman [*and their example is from Charles Dickens*] "a little girl wearing a womanly sort of bonnet much too large for her" 3: characteristic of, belonging to, or suitable to women: conforming to or motivated by a woman's nature and attitudes rather than a man's. [*The first example here is*] "convinced that drawing was a waste of time, if not downright womanly, like painting on China." [*And another example*] "her usual womanly volubility."

What are these two supposedly parallel entries telling us? They're saying that in addition to defining characteristics appropriate to a man, like vocal pitch, *manly* is synonymous with admirable qualities that all of us might wish we had. "Bold, resolute, open in conduct or

425

bearing; of undaunted courage, gallant, brave." And where is the list of comparable synonyms for *womanly?* There aren't any. Instead, *womanly* is defined only in a circular way—through characteristics seen to be appropriate or inappropriate to women, not to human beings in general. And the examples of usage cited give a pretty good picture of what is considered appropriate to, or characteristic of, a well-balanced adult woman: she's concerned with manners, advice, and hat styles (as distinguished from sports and beer, which are felt to be manly); she wastes time in trivial pursuits like painting on china; and she talks too much.

The Slippery Slope

Most writers and editors today recognize that the female-negative-trivial syndrome is clearly evident in the use of so-called feminine suffixes with nouns of common gender. In 1990 no publishable author would identify someone as "a poetess," except in ridicule. (Adrienne Rich says the word brings out the "terroristress" in her.) But respectable writers are still using *heroine, suffragette,* and *executrix* when referring to a hero, a suffragist, or an executor who is a woman. [7]

These words illustrate what Douglas Hofstadter calls "the slippery slope" of meaning. In his book *Metamagical Themas,* Hofstadter shows diagramatically how the slippery slope works. A triangle represents the idea of, let's say, a heroic person. At one base angle of this triangle is the word *heroine,* representing the female heroic person. At the other base angle is the word *hero,* representing the male heroic person. And at the apex is the generic word, again *hero,* encompassing both. But because the *hero* at the apex and the *hero* at one base angle are identical in name, their separate meanings slip back and forth along one side of the triangle, the slippery slope. The meanings blend and absorb each other. They bond together on the slope. And *heroine,* at the other base angle, remains outside that bond. [8]

Another word that comes to mind in this connection is *actress*. It's our impression that women performers in the theater and films today are tending more and more to refer to themselves and one another as "actors." It may be deliberate, conscious usage on the part of some. Considering that their union is called Actors Equity, and that they may have trained at Actors Studio, and performed at Actors Playhouse, they simply accept that the generic word for their profession is *actor*. But when this word appears in juxtaposition with *actress,* the generic meaning of *actor* is absorbed into the gender-specific meaning, and women are identified as nonactors, as being outside or marginal, in de Beauvoir's phrase, as "the other." [9]

Many people will undoubtedly go on feeling that *actress* is a term without bias, but we would like to suggest that it is on its way to becoming archaic, or at least quaint, simply because people it has [10] identified are abandoning it by a process that may be more visceral than cerebral. In a sense it's their word, it has defined them, and, whether intentionally or not, they are taking charge of it, perhaps dumping it. We'll see.

Because linguistic changes reflect changes in our ways of thinking, a living language is constantly being created and re-created by the people who speak it. Linguistic changes spring from nothing less than new perceptions of the world and of ourselves.

Obviously we all know that over time the "rules" of grammar have 12
changed, and we know that words themselves change their meanings: they lose some and acquire others; new words come into existence and old ones disappear into that word heaven, the *Oxford English Dictionary*. Nevertheless, most people resist change, especially, it seems, changes in grammar and the meanings of words. What we tend to forget—or choose to forget—is that the only languages which don't change are the ones no one speaks any more, like classical Greek and Latin.

Take the narrowing process that turned the Old English word *man* 13
into a synonym for "adult male human being." As long ago as 1752 the philosopher David Hume recognized how ambiguous that word had already become: "All men," he wrote, and then added, "both male and female." And you are probably familiar with the numerous experimental studies done in the last few years, primarily by psychologists and sociologists rather than linguists, which show that most native speakers of English simply do not conceptualize women and girls when they encounter *man* and *mankind* used generically. In fact the narrowing process is felt so strongly, at least at an existential level, that a growing number of women today strongly object to being subsumed under those male-gender terms. "We aren't men," they're saying; "we're women, and we're tired of being made invisible."

Yet despite women's objections, and despite the slippery, ambigu- 14
ous nature of generic *man,* lots of people, especially formally educated people, have a hard time giving it up. They forget, it seems, that words have a power of their own—the power of taking over meaning. A writer starts out talking about the species as a whole and, more often than we'll ever know, ends up talking about males. Listen to this well-known author, for example, who was discussing aggressive behavior in human beings—all of us, *Homo sapiens*. "[M]an," he wrote, "can do several things which the animal cannot do. . . . Eventually, his vital interests are not only life, food, access to females, etc., but also values, symbols, institutions."

Resistance to Change and the Problem of Precision

It's probably helpful, once in a while, to look back at the way some 15
of the most familiar and accepted words in use today were greeted when they were newcomers.

Back in 1619, for example, the London schoolmaster Alexander Gil 16
described what he called "the new mange in speaking and writing."
What he was deploring was the introduction of newly coined, Latin-
derived words to replace older English ones. According to him, the
"new mange" included such terms as *virtue, justice, pity, compassion,*
and *grace.* And he asked, "Whither have you banished those words our
forefathers used for these new-fangled ones?" Alexander Gil was head-
master of St. Paul's school at the time, and it might be noted that one
of his students was an eleven-year-old named John Milton who—fortunately—was not persuaded to reject Gil's "new-fangled" words.

And how about old terms that have lost favor, like the once- 17
accepted use of the pronoun *they* with a singular referent, as in "If a
person is born of a gloomy temper, they cannot help it." That was written in 1759 by none other than the very correct, well-educated British
statesman, Lord Chesterfield. However, since most academics are not
yet ready to revive that convenient usage—despite precedents ranging
from Shakespeare to Shaw—it still isn't surprising to come across a
recently published book about, let's say, the psychology of children, in
which the distinguished author uses *he* and its inflected forms as all-
purpose pronouns, leaving readers to guess whether a particular problem or development applies to boys only or to children of both sexes.
We submit that such writing is not just unfortunate. It's inexcusable.

These days more and more writers acknowledge that *he* used gener- 18
ically is, like *man* used generically, both ambiguous and insidious, and
they take the time and trouble to write more precisely. But sometimes,
even after several polite but probably exhausting battles between author
and editor, all the author will agree to do is add a disclaimer. Dis-
claimers can be helpful, of course (for example, those providing guidance as to what a writer of some previous century may have meant by
a now-ambiguous term). More often, however, they are nothing but
excuses for sloppiness.

There is also an element here which we don't think should be 19
ignored: the deep if often unacknowledged *psychological* impact of the
grammatical "rule" mandating masculine-gender pronouns for indefinite referents. As long ago as the 1950s, Lynn White, Jr., then the president of Mills College, described with great perception the harm that
rule can do to children when he wrote:

> The penetration of this habit of language into the minds of little girls as
> they grow up to be women is more profound than most people, includ-
> ing most women, have recognized; for it implies that personality is
> really a male attribute, and that women are a human subspecies. . . . It
> would be a miracle if a girl-baby, learning to use the symbols of our
> tongue, could escape some unverbalized wound to her self-respect;
> whereas a boy-baby's ego is bolstered by the pattern of our language.

Obviously many literate men (and some literate women) must find 20
the truth of White's perception difficult to accept, or we wouldn't still

428

be battling the generic use of masculine-gender pronouns. But since accuracy and precision are what we're talking about today, let us ask this question: what is one to make of a scholar—a professor of communications with a special interest in semantics, as a matter of fact—who dismissed the problem of sexist language as follows: "I tend to avoid 'gender-exclusive' words," he wrote, "except when in so doing, I would injure the rhythm of a sentence."

Has it never occurred to him that in writing a sentence, any sentence, he must choose both its words and the way those words, in their infinite variety, are put together? That the choice isn't between exclusionary language on the one hand and rhythm on the other? (Surely it's possible to write with style and still communicate accurately what it is you want to say.) The choice is between settling for an ambiguous or inaccurate term because it "sounds good"—and finding the exact combination of words to convey one's message with clarity and precision. It seems to us that editors have every right to expect nothing less than the latter.

English is a vigorously alive tongue, and it reflects a vigorously alive, dynamic society that is capable of identifying its ills and thereby trying to cope with them. Neither the term *sexism* nor the term *racism* existed fifty years ago—which, as you know, isn't the same as saying that the attitudes and practices they define didn't exist before; of course they did. But those attitudes and practices came to be widely examined and questioned, and finally to be widely acknowledged within the dominant culture, only after they were put into words.

Without precision, language can betray everything we stand for. As George Orwell put it in his essay "Politics and the English Language," we must "Let the meaning choose the word and not the other way about." And Orwell went on, "In prose the worst thing you can do with words is surrender to them."

With George Orwell giving us courage, may we be so bold, in closing, as to adapt his wisdom to the occasion by adding this final thought? In publishing, the worst thing you can do is surrender to some tyrannical author who lets the *word* choose the *meaning* rather than the other way about.

COMPREHENSION

1. The authors pose a question in their title. Where, if at all, do they answer it in the essay?

2. In your own words, explain what is meant by "the slippery slope."

3. Define these specialized words: *androcentric, lexicon, lexicographer, generic,* and *inflected.*

4. What overriding issues—issues that transcend matters solely pertaining to the English language—concern the authors?

1. The authors devote one section to each of three major reasons for the resistance to altering gender-biased language. Does this method create a solid foundation for their argument? Explain.
2. Identify at least two cases of each of the following methods of argumentation: example, definition, explanation, and appeal to authority.
3. The authors place quotation marks around the expressions "masculine," "feminine," and "rules of grammar." What is the function of these quotation marks?
4. Describe the intended audience for this essay. Where do they fit in the social, political, and educational scale of society? Explain your view.
5. The authors refer to the historical record in making a case for altering sexist language in writing. For what type of audience would this be a particularly strong argument?
6. In paragraph 16, the authors state: "And you are probably familiar with the numerous experimental studies done in the last few years, primarily by psychologists and sociologists rather than linguists." To whom does the *you* in this sentence refer? Is this a fair assumption on the part of the writers? What, if anything, does it imply about the relationship of the writers to their audience?
7. A final section is set off by space. What is the purpose of this division? How does it distinguish the final section from the rest of the essay?

WRITING

1. Write an argumentative essay entitled, "Why Gender Writing Bias Bothers Me" or the alternative, "Why So-Called Gender Writing Bias Doesn't Bother Me."
2. As a research assignment, compare and contrast a chapter from a book on child development written in the 1950s and one written in the 1990s. Compare and contrast the chapters in terms of gender-biased language.
3. For a creative writing project, write two identical short mystery stories. In one, use feminine-inflected words for the major character; in the other, use masculine-inflected ones. When you are finished, read each, and note the differences in your psychological reactions to the hero.

CLASSIC AND CONTEMPORARY:
QUESTIONS FOR COMPARISON

1. Miller, Swift, and Orwell believe that bad language habits often do not change because they serve to hide unconscious truths that writers and readers do not want to face. Compare and contrast the truths that Miller and Swift attempt to uncover with those that Orwell refers to.
2. Compare and contrast the solutions to the problems addressed in each essay. Does one essay articulate a clearer solution than another? Does one essay address a more significant issue than another? Explain.

3. Orwell admits that even he probably breaks his own dictates about writing clear English. One of his rules is "Never use a foreign phrase, a scientific word or a jargon word if you can think of an everyday English equivalent." Do Miller and Swift break this rule in their essay? If so, where? And what would be an alternative means of expressing what they mean to say?

4. It is clear that Miller and Swift have read Orwell because they quote him in their conclusion. Are there any other signs of Orwell's influence in their essay?

CONNECTIONS

1. Compare the attitudes of Tan and Ferré regarding the connection between language and cultural or ethnic identity.

2. Write an essay exploring Tannen's analysis of communication. How would Tan and coauthors Miller and Swift respond to that analysis? Would they agree or disagree? Use evidence from their writing to support your opinions.

3. Some of the writers in this section mention specific literary influences on their writing. What have these writers learned from their mentors? Use examples from their essays.

4. Compare the views of Hayakawa and Tan regarding the value of linguistic theories and their possible effect on developing the identities of immigrant children.

5. Expand on the theme of Miller and Swift, using Ferré's struggles with gender as a writer. Use any other writers whose work may apply.

6. Write an essay on the effects of a dominant culture and language on the creative development of a writer. How does an artist escape "speechlessness" in a racist society? Support your opinion with quotes from any writer in this section.

7. Explore the theme of "language as refuge," using the work of Tan and Dillard.

CHAPTER NINE

Media and the Arts

*I*magine a world without fiction, poetry, or drama; music, art, or dance; radio, television, or film. We are so accustomed to taking "the arts" in their totality for granted that it is hard for us to conceive of contemporary culture without them. Our fondness for stories or paintings or any other creative form might help us to understand our culture or might even move us to action. Yet the value of various artistic forms doesn't derive exclusively from their ability to tell us something about life. The arts can also take us into an imaginative realm offering perhaps more intense experiences than anything we encounter in the "ordinary" world.

Think of media and the arts as an exercise in imaginative freedom. You are free to select the books you read, the movies you see, the exhibitions and concerts you attend. Some of your decisions—for example, to look more deeply into the work of John Updike or Alice Walker after reading their essays in this chapter—might be serious and consequential to your education. Other decisions, perhaps to watch a few soaps on a rainy afternoon or to buy something you see in a commercial, are less important. The way you view the arts—whether as a temporary escape from conventional reality or as a way to learn something about the temper of civilization—is entirely a matter of taste. Regardless of your purpose or intent, you approach the arts initially for the sheer exhilaration and pleasure they provide. Art, as Plato observed, is a dream for awakened minds.

The arts awaken you to the power and intensity of the creative spirit. At the same time, you make judgments and evaluations of the nature of your creative encounter. When you assert that you "like" this painting or "dislike" that movie, you are assessing the worth or value of the artistic experience. As Marya Mannes states in her essay "How Do You Know It's Good?" it is clear that "the more you read and see and hear, the more equipped you'll be to practice that art of association which is at the basis of all understanding and judgment."

Perhaps you prefer to keep your experience of literature and the arts a pleasurable pastime or escape from reality. Or you may wish to participate in them as a creative writer, musician, painter, or dancer. Ultimately, you may come to view the arts as a transformational experience, a voyage of discovery in which you encounter diverse peoples and cultures, learn to see the world in creative terms, and begin to perceive your own creative potential in a new light.

Previewing the Chapter

As you read the essays in this chapter and respond to them in discussion and writing, consider the following questions:

• According to the author, what is the value of the art or literary form under discussion?

• What function does literature or art serve?

• Is the writer's perspective subjective or objective, and why?

• How does the author define his or her subject—whether it is poetry, fiction, art, or advertising?

• Is the writer's experience of literature or art similar to or different from your own?

• In what ways do gender and race influence the writer's perspective on the subject?

• What is the nature of the creative process under discussion?

• In what specific cultural context does the writer place his or her subject?

• What is the main idea that the author wants to present about literature, advertising, or the arts? Do you agree or disagree with this key concept?

• What have you learned about the importance of literature, media, and the arts from reading these essays?

MARIE WINN   Marie Winn was born in the mid-1930s in Prague, Czecho-slovakia, and came to the United States in 1939. She has been a prolific author of books for children. She has contributed many articles to publications such as *The New York Times Magazine, The New York Times Book Review,* and *Parade.* But she gained national fame with her book about the hazards of tele-vision, *The Plug-In Drug,* in 1977, followed by *Children without Childhood* in 1983. The following excerpt is from her book on television, one of the first to alert parents to the effects of the mass media on their children.

MARIE WINN

Television Addiction

The word "addiction" is often used loosely and wryly in conversation. People will refer to themselves as "mystery book addicts" or "cookie addicts." E. B. White writes of his annual surge of interest in gardening: "We are hooked and are making an attempt to kick the habit." Yet nobody really believes that reading mysteries or ordering seeds by cat-alogue is serious enough to be compared with addictions to heroin or alcohol. The word "addiction" is here used jokingly to denote a ten-dency to overindulge in some pleasurable activity.

People often refer to being "hooked on TV." Does this, too, fall into the lighthearted category of cookie eating and other pleasures that peo-ple pursue with unusual intensity, or is there a kind of television view-ing that falls into the more serious category of destructive addiction?

When we think about addiction to drugs or alcohol, we frequently focus on negative aspects, ignoring the pleasures that accompany drinking or drug-taking. And yet the essence of any serious addiction is a pursuit of pleasure, a search for a "high" that normal life does not supply. It is only the inability to function without the addictive sub-stance that is dismaying, the dependence of the organism upon a cer-tain experience and an increasing inability to function normally without it. Thus a person will take two or three drinks at the end of the day not merely for the pleasure drinking provides, but also because he "doesn't feel normal" without them.

An addict does not merely pursue a pleasurable experience and need to experience it in order to function normally. He needs to *repeat* it again and again. Something about that particular experience makes life without it less than complete. Other potentially pleasurable experi-ences are no longer possible, for under the spell of the addictive expe-rience, his life is peculiarly distorted. The addict craves an experience and yet he is never really satisfied. The organism may be temporarily sated, but soon it begins to crave again.

Finally a serious addiction is distinguished from a harmless pursuit ₅ of pleasure by its distinctly destructive elements. A heroin addict, for instance, leads a damaged life: his increasing need for heroin in increasing doses prevents him from working, from maintaining relationships, from developing in human ways. Similarly an alcoholic's life is narrowed and dehumanized by his dependence on alcohol.

Let us consider television viewing in the light of the conditions that ₆ define serious addictions.

Not unlike drugs or alcohol, the television experience allows the ₇ participant to blot out the real world and enter into a pleasurable and passive mental state. The worries and anxieties of reality are as effectively deferred by becoming absorbed in a television program as by going on a "trip" induced by drugs or alcohol. And just as alcoholics are only inchoately aware of their addiction, feeling that they control their drinking more than they really do ("I can cut it out any time I want—I just like to have three or four drinks before dinner"), people similarly overestimate their control over television watching. Even as they put off other activities to spend hour after hour watching television, they feel they could easily resume living in a different, less passive style. But somehow or other while the television set is present in their homes, the click doesn't sound. With television pleasures available, those other experiences seem less attractive, more difficult somehow.

A heavy viewer (a college English instructor) observes: ₈

"I find television almost irresistible. When the set is on, I cannot ₉ ignore it. I can't turn it off. I feel sapped, will-less, enervated. As I reach out to turn off the set, the strength goes out of my arms. So I sit there for hours and hours."

The self-confessed television addict often feels he "ought" to do ₁₀ other things—but the fact that he doesn't read and doesn't plant his garden or sew or crochet or play games or have conversations means that those activities are no longer as desirable as television viewing. In a way a heavy viewer's life is as imbalanced by his television "habit" as a drug addict's or an alcoholic's. He is living in a holding pattern, as it were, passing up the activities that lead to growth or development or a sense of accomplishment. This is one reason people talk about their television viewing so ruefully, so apologetically. They are aware that it is an unproductive experience, that almost any other endeavor is more worthwhile by any human measure.

Finally it is the adverse effect of television viewing on the lives of so ₁₁ many people that defines it as a serious addiction. The television habit distorts the sense of time. It renders other experiences vague and curiously unreal while taking on a greater reality for itself. It weakens relationships by reducing and sometimes eliminating normal opportunities for talking, for communicating.

And yet television does not satisfy, else why would the viewer con- ₁₂ tinue to watch hour after hour, day after day? "The measure of health," writes Lawrence Kubie, "is flexibility . . . and especially the freedom to cease when sated."[1] But the television viewer can never be sated with his television experiences—they do not provide the true nourishment that satiation requires—and thus he finds that he cannot stop watching.

COMPREHENSION

1. Why does Winn consider television watching a true addiction?
2. Why does Winn consider television viewing hazardous to one's well-being?
3. What implicit assumption does Winn make concerning the purpose of human experience that leads her to conclude that television watching is harmful?

RHETORIC

1. What function does the question Winn poses in paragraph 2 serve in setting up her argument?
2. Study the introductory paragraph. Is it truly needed? Does it add strength to the author's argument? What is its function, if any?
3. In paragraph 3, Winn refers to a person as "the organism." From what branch of learning is she borrowing this term? What is the purpose of using this word within the context of her argument?
4. In paragraph 11, the author states several effects of television viewing. Are these based on fact or opinion? Does it matter for the sake of her argument?
5. What does paragraph 6 contribute to the structure and coherence of the essay?
6. In her concluding paragraph the author cites the work of a psychologist. Does this support her main argument? Explain.
7. The author presents "television addiction" as a serious issue. How does the tone of her essay communicate how seriously she regards the subject?

WRITING

1. Argue for against the view that watching television "critically" can be a positive educational experience.
2. Develop a manual for people who want to cut down on their television viewing. Model it after a weight-loss or smoking-cessation program.
3. It seems these days as though television is blamed for everything. Argue for the proposition that watching television is good for you.

[1]Lawrence Kubie, *Neurotic Distortion and the Creative Process* (Lawrence: University of Kansas Press, 1958).

JOHN CORRY John Corry was born in Brooklyn, New York. He has been a Nieman Fellow at Harvard and a contributing writer for *The New York Times* and *Harper's* magazine. Corry is the author of *The Manchester Affair* (1967), *TV News and the Dominant Culture* (1986), and *My Times* (1994). Currently a columnist for *The American Spectator*—where the following essay appeared in 1994—Corry is an astute critic of media culture and American politics.

JOHN CORRY

Medea and the O. J. Media

Say now that the O. J. Simpson case is gripping, and that there has never been anything quite like it before: a double murder and its aftermath played out in real time on television. When Simpson finally gave himself up at his house in California, all the network anchors went on air in New York, not adding much with their commentary, but exalting the event by their presence. There was a hint of what was to come right there. Even Peter Jennings began musing about "the enormous pressure of the media on every inch of the story."

And indeed the pressure was enormous, although it was on the media as much as it was on the story. How could the press, especially television, justify all the attention it was paying to O. J. Simpson? A redemptive reason had to be found, and almost immediately one was. Simpson was picked up on a Friday, and two days later Cokie Roberts could explain on "This Week With David Brinkley" that the story was focusing our attention on spouse abuse. A consensus began to form. On the "MacNeil/Lehrer NewsHour" the next night, the essayist Anne Taylor Fleming said there might even be an "analogue to the Anita Hill thing." The Simpson case could draw attention to the absence of women in power.

There may have been a point there. After Nicole Simpson's piteous 911 call was disclosed, the network news programs and major publications all ran pieces on domestic violence. The larger questions, though, were about race and the nature of victims, and they troubled the press from the start. Surely Simpson had to be suffering from secret afflictions. The day after he was taken into custody, William C. Rhoden, a sports columnist at *The New York Times*, wrote about the burdens on famous black athletes:

> Money and notoriety based on physical prowess can never fully fill certain voids, heal old scars, change skin tone, straighten hair, change any of those intrinsic qualities. The money is a temporary salve—a pain killer that allows the athlete to get through a day, a life, a career. Even-

tually the troubled soul must stop to confront the demons that have been in pursuit.

Perhaps Simpson had never been able to fill the voids, much less change his skin tone, or confront the demons. The truth was obscure, but the reference to skin tone was prophetic. *Newsweek* said Simpson had transcended race: "His genial, race-neutral style went down easily with white audiences." Rival *Time,* however, innocently reminded everyone he was black. It darkened the mug shot of Simpson that had been released by the Los Angeles Police Department, and used it on its cover.

This was a mistake. In a sensitive age such as ours, political cor- 5 rectness takes precedence over aesthetics. Frank Rich wrote on the op-ed page of the *Times* that by darkening Simpson's face, *Time* had sent him "back to the ghetto." Benjamin Chavis of the NAACP was more vitriolic. He said *Time* had tried to portray Simpson as "some kind of animal." The head of the nation's largest civil-rights organization was attaching a moral stigma to an ebony, as opposed to café-au-lait, color. This seemed bizarre, although in the ensuing argument, no prominent journalist or news organization joined in to take *Time'* s side. Presumably they were afraid to. Responding to "the storm of controversy," James Gaines, the managing editor, had to explain in a full-page letter "to our readers" in the next issue why *Time* darkened the mug shot. A photo-illustrator, he said, had used computer imaging for artistic effect:

> The harshness of the mug shot—the merciless bright light, the stubble on Simpson's face, the cold specificity of the picture—had been shaped into an icon of tragedy. The expression on his face was not merely blank now; it was bottomless. This cover, with the simple nonjudgmental headline "An American Tragedy," seemed the right choice.

And probably it was the right choice, and surely "An American 6 Tragedy" was meant to be nonjudgmental. Indeed, the idea that the Simpson case was a "tragedy" would go on to suffuse much of the press coverage. A *Times* editorial even declared that it was precisely because the case was a tragedy that it had gripped the national interest. "The fall of the mighty was a central theme of classical Greek tragedy . . . and it became the spine of Elizabethan tragedy," the *Times* said. "O. J. Simpson may or may not be a 'hero' to individual citizens, but as one who was given great gifts and has been brought to a grim pass by either fate or frailty, he fits the pattern that lurks in our ancestral memory."

The *Times,* however, was reaching. The characters of classical 7 tragedy accepted their grim passes. Medea howled out her pain, and took responsibility for murdering her children. Simpson wrote a self-pitying letter, and then fled in a Ford Bronco. If innocent he is badly muddled, and if guilty he is beneath contempt. Either way, he is not a tragic figure. In her column in the *Times,* Anna Quindlen chided those who felt sorry for him, and said the real victim was Nicole

Brown Simpson. Quindlen was right about that, although in her feminist zeal to turn the murder into a plea for battered wives, she forgot about Robert Goldman, who had been left as dead as Nicole Simpson.

Implicit in Quindlen's column, meanwhile, was the notion that 8 Simpson was guilty. In fact, although prominent columnists, correspondents, and anchors do not admit it—nor should they—it is likely that most agree: Simpson has committed two murders. Nonetheless, as professional participants in the drama—"the live electronic drama," Tom Brokaw called it—they have been able to cloak their feelings. Posturing defense attorneys and other sympathizers to the contrary, Simpson has not had a bad press. The tone of the coverage has been more elegiac than censorious, and "An American Tragedy" suggests that the guilt is shared, diffuse, and not anyone's in particular.

Certainly there have been exceptions, and Simpson is not necessarily pictured as nice. *People* magazine ran a notable cover story—"The O. J. Nobody Knew: All his life he worked hard to be loved. But behind the smile and the charm was a dangerous temper and a desperate need to get what he wanted"—that insisted he was nasty. Then, the day after Judge Kathleen Kennedy-Powell ruled that Simpson must face trial, the enterprising *New York Post* published the findings of two experts who had studied his handwriting. They found, the *Post* said, that he was "cowardly, oversexed, immature, tenacious, unpredictable and surly." But no other publication seemed to pick up the story, and probably that was just as well.

The defense team is claiming, of course, that the press already has 10 convicted Simpson, and that it is impossible for him to get a fair trial. Obviously we will continue to hear this. Robert L. Shapiro, Simpson's lead counsel, once wrote an article entitled "Using the Media for Your Advantage." F. Lee Bailey, another celebrated member of the team, first became famous when he was successful in overturning the conviction of Sam Sheppard, the Cleveland osteopath who had been found guilty of murdering his wife. The case is cited in law schools as the classic example in which pretrial publicity was used to reverse a conviction. Bailey may be seen on CNN now, arguing that he has never seen pretrial publicity this bad, and preparing the ground for an appeal if his client is convicted.

But contrast the press treatment of Simpson with its treatment of 11 Mike Tyson, another gifted athlete who also was born poor and black. He was never seen as ambiguous, interesting, or worthy of much pity. The press was hostile toward him from the start, in part because in a sensitive age, it finds rape less socially acceptable than murder. Murder may be explained—diminished capacity, temporary insanity, disadvantaged circumstances—but rape has no alleviating factors. Attempted or alleged, it is always heinous. Moreover, Tyson practiced a brutal profession, and hit other men with his fists. Prominent journalists could not find much to empathize with there, and although

Tyson was convicted on the most slender evidence, few thought of it as a tragedy. He is serving a three-year sentence, and will not be released until next year.

Tyson had a further disadvantage. He was, by almost anyone's reckoning, ill-favored and homely, while Simpson, either in café au lait or *Time*'s ebony, is extremely good-looking. The cameras linger on the one in a way that would have been unthinkable with the other. There is no contest between Simpson's sculpted cheekbones and Tyson's beetling brows. The media are susceptible to conventional beauty, and do what they can to promote it. They may pretend it does not influence their coverage, but given the chance they extol it. When Jacqueline Kennedy Onassis died at age 64, she was eulogized for having lived the last years of her life with dignity, grace and discretion, and successfully raising two children. But *Time, Newsweek,* and *U.S. News & World Report* all ran cover photos of Mrs. Onassis at approximately age 30, while *People* filled a "commemorative issue" with similar glamorous pictures. An older, more interesting woman gave way to an ephemeral Jackie.

Obviously, Simpson has some advantages. Bailey and his colleagues notwithstanding, the press has been fair, or as fair as it probably can be, to their client. Polls by both *Newsweek* and CNN found that most black Americans believe Simpson cannot get a fair trial; but that depressing finding reflects cultural paranoia more than anything real, and it is to be devoutly hoped that Chavis, as well as the Rev. Jesse Jackson and the Rev. Joseph Lowery, the head of the Southern Christian Leadership Conference, who also have joined in the argument, will in the future stay silent. *Newsweek* was right when it called Simpson "race neutral." Even the cheesiest publications have been hesitant to exploit the fact that he had a mixed marriage. Colin Powell aside, it is hard to think of another male black celebrity who has so transcended race other than, perhaps, Bryant Gumbel.

Certainly the trial will be a circus, but there is no reason to think that will be to Simpson's disadvantage. More likely it will work in his favor. Alan Dershowitz, who zipped into Los Angeles in his Lear jet, and then was uncharacteristically quiet, will emerge from hiding, and anchors and correspondents will scrupulously report all the defense arguments, while priding themselves on their balance and fairness. The preliminary hearing could be seen on ten channels in New York, while the national news programs led with it more often than not, and only "MacNeil/Lehrer" had the audacity to sometimes ignore it. Meanwhile, the old rationale of spouse abuse was dropped; the new idea was that we could see the criminal-justice system at work. Former Attorney General Richard Thornburg even told Larry King that the whole world was watching. It probably was, and you wonder what it made of it.

COMPREHENSION

1. What is the thesis of this essay?
2. The title of the essay is a play on words. What is the relevance of using the words *Medea* and *Media* together other than that they are similar in spelling and pronunciation?
3. In paragraph 6, the author says "political correctness takes precedence over aesthetics." What specifically does this refer to in the case of O. J. Simpson? What is its general implication about our society?
4. Who was the mythical figure Medea? What is her relevance to the original Greek concept of tragedy?

RHETORIC

1. Study the opening sentence of the essay. Why is its rhetorical effect and structure unusual for an introduction?
2. In paragraph 1, the author ironically comments that the network anchors were "exalting the event by their presence." What irony does this imply concerning the power of the media? Where else does the author use irony to convey the same idea?
3. To what overall purpose do you attribute the author's numerous and various references to media sources regarding the O. J. Simpson case?
4. Study the topic sentence of each of the four sections of the essay. How do they lead into the substance of the sections that follow, and how do they lend coherence to the essay as a whole?
5. Consider the final sentence of the essay. What is its relevance to the major rhetorical thrust of the entire work? How does it extend the major issues raised by the author?
6. Locate all references in the essay to how Simpson is being displayed by the media in a distorted light, either positive or negative. Then study the way in which the author attempts to defuse these portraits. Explain the methods he uses.
7. The author discusses a range of media perspectives concerning his subject matter in this essay. How does his use of transitional devices help lead the reader from one example to the next?

WRITING

1. Argue for or against the proposition that it was the media on trial in the O. J. Simpson case and not the defendant.
2. Write a conjectural essay entitled, "If O. J. Simpson Were White and Poor . . ."
3. Argue for or against the proposition that a heroic, beloved figure in American culture will always be given special privileges, regardless of his or her race.

JOHN UPDIKE John Updike was born in Shillington, Pennsylvania, in 1932 and educated at Harvard University, where he received his A.B. degree in 1954. His first career goal was to become an artist, and so he attended the Ruskin School of Drawing and Fine Art in England. However, upon his return to the United States, he embarked on a career as a writer, working first as an essayist for *The New Yorker Magazine*. A prolific writer, he has published more than twenty volumes of poetry, thirty novels or collections of short stories, and ten essay anthologies. Many of his book reviews have appeared in the *New Yorker* over the past forty years. Updike writes about the middle-class repressions of contemporary life and the ways in which modern Americans deal with family, work, and sexuality. He has won numerous awards for his work, and, in 1982, his novel *Rabbit Is Rich* won the Pulitzer Prize for fiction, the American Book Award, and the National Book Critics Circle Award for fiction. Updike's output remains undiminished as he continues to explore new thematic and stylistic territories. The following essay appeared originally in *The Art of Mickey Mouse* (1991).

JOHN UPDIKE

The Mystery of Mickey Mouse

It's all in the ears. When Mickey Mouse was born, in 1927, the world of early cartoon animation was filled with two-legged zoomorphic humanoids, whose strange half-black faces were distinguished one from another chiefly by the ears. Felix the Cat had pointed triangular ears and Oswald the Rabbit—Walt Disney's first successful cartoon creation, which he abandoned when his New York distributor, Charles Mintz, attempted to swindle him—had long floppy ears, with a few notches in the end to suggest fur. Disney's Oswald films, and the Alice animations that preceded them, had mice in them, with linear limbs, wiry tails, and ears that are oblong, not yet round. On the way back to California from New York by train, having left Oswald enmeshed for good in the machinations of Mr. Mintz, Walt and his wife Lillian invented another character based—the genesis legend claims—on the tame field mice that used to wander into Disney's old studio in Kansas City. His first thought was to call the mouse Mortimer; Lillian proposed instead the less pretentious name Mickey. Somewhere between Chicago and Los Angeles, the young couple concocted the plot of Mickey's first cartoon short, *Plane Crazy*, costarring Minnie and capitalizing on 1927's Lindbergh craze. The next short produced by Disney's fledgling studio—which included, besides himself and Lillian, his brother Roy and his old Kansas City associate Ub Iwerks—was *Gal-*

lopin' Gaucho, and introduced a fat and wicked cat who did not yet wear the prosthesis that would give him his name of Pegleg Pete. The third short, *Steamboat Willie,* incorporated that brand-new novelty a sound track, and was released first, in 1928. Mickey Mouse entered history, as the most persistent and pervasive figment of American popular culture in this century.

His ears are two solid black circles, no matter the angle at which he holds his head. Three-dimensional images of Mickey Mouse—toy dolls, or the papier-mâché heads the grotesque Disneyland Mickeys wear— make us uneasy, since the ears inevitably exist edgewise as well as frontally. These ears properly belong not to three-dimensional space but to an ideal realm of notation, of symbolization, of cartoon resilience and indestructibility. In drawings, when Mickey is in profile, one ear is at the back of his head like a spherical ponytail, or like a secondary bubble in a computer-generated Mandelbrot set. We accept it, as we accepted Li'l Abner's hair always being parted on the side facing the viewer. A surreal optical consistency is part of the cartoon world, halfway between our world and the plane of pure signs, of alphabets and trademarks.

In the sixty-four years since Mickey Mouse's image was promulgated, the ears, though a bit more organically irregular and flexible than the classic 1930s appendages, have not been essentially modified. Many other modifications have, however, overtaken that first crude cartoon, born of an era of starker stylizations. White gloves, like the gloves worn in minstrel shows, appeared after those first, to cover the black hands. The infantile bare chest and shorts with two buttons were phased out in the forties. The eyes have undergone a number of changes, most drastically in the late thirties, when, some historians mistakenly claim, they acquired pupils. Not so: the old eyes, the black oblongs that acquired a nick of reflection in the sides, *were* the pupils; the eye whites filled the entire space beneath Mickey's cap of black, its widow's peak marking the division between these enormous oculi. This can be seen clearly in the face of the classic Minnie; when she bats her eyelids, their lashed shades cover over the full width of what might be thought to be her brow. But all the old animated animals were built this way from Felix the Cat on; Felix had lower lids, and the Mickey of *Plane Crazy* also. So it was an evolutionary misstep that, beginning in 1938, replaced the shiny black pupils with entire oval eyes, containing pupils of their own. No such mutation has overtaken Pluto, Goofy, or Donald Duck. The change brought Mickey closer to us humans, but also took away something of his vitality, his alertness, his bug-eyed cartoon readiness for adventure. It made him less abstract, less iconic, more merely cute and dwarfish. The original Mickey, as he scuttles and bounces through those early animated shorts, was angular and wiry, with much of the impudence and desperation of a true rodent. He was gradually rounded to the proportions of a child, a regression sealed by his fifties manifestation as the genius of the children's television show *The Mickey Mouse Club,* with its live Mouseketeers. Most of the artists who depict

Mickey today, though too young to have grown up, as I did, with his old form, have instinctively reverted to it; it is the bare-chested basic Mickey, with his yellow shoes and oval buttons on his shorts, who is the icon, beside whom his modified later version is a mere mousy trousered pipsqueak.

His first, iconic manifestation had something of Chaplin to it; he was the little guy, just over the border of the respectable. His circular ears, like two minimal cents, bespeak the smallest economic unit, the overlookable democratic man. His name has passed into the language as a byword for the small, the weak—a "Mickey Mouse operation" means an undercapitalized company or minor surgery. Children of my generation—wearing our Mickey Mouse watches, prying pennies from our Mickey Mouse piggy banks (I won one in a third-grade spelling bee, my first intellectual triumph), following his running combat with Pegleg Pete in the daily funnies, going to the local movie-house movies every Saturday afternoon and cheering when his smiling visage burst onto the screen to introduce a cartoon—felt Mickey was one of us, a bridge to the adult world of which Donald Duck was, for all of his childish sailor suit, an irascible, tyrannical member. Mickey didn't seek trouble, and he didn't complain; he rolled with the punches, and surprised himself as much as us when, as in *The Little Tailor,* he showed warrior resourcefulness and won, once again, a blushing kiss from dear, all but identical Minnie. His minimal, decent nature meant that he would yield, in the Disney animated cartoons, the starring role to combative, sputtering Donald Duck and even to Goofy, with his "gawshes" and Gary Cooper–like gawkiness. But for an occasional comeback like the "Sorcerer's Apprentice" episode of *Fantasia,* and last year's rather souped-up *The Prince and the Pauper,* Mickey was through as a star by 1940. But as with Marilyn Monroe when her career was over, his life as an icon gathered strength. The America that is not symbolized by that imperial Yankee Uncle Sam is symbolized by Mickey Mouse. He is America as it feels to itself—plucky, put-on, inventive, resilient, good-natured, game.

Like America, Mickey has a lot of black blood. This fact was revealed to me in conversation by Saul Steinberg, who, in attempting to depict the racially mixed reality of New York streets for the supersensitive and race-blind *New Yorker* of the sixties and seventies, hit upon scribbling numerous Mickeys as a way of representing what was jauntily and scruffily and unignorably there. From just the way Mickey swings along in his classic, trademark pose, one three-fingered gloved hand held on high, he is jiving. Along with round black ears and yellow shoes, Mickey has soul. Looking back to such early animations as the early Looney Tunes' Bosko and Honey series (1930–36) and the Arab figures in Disney's own *Mickey in Arabia* of 1932, we see that blacks were drawn much like cartoon animals, with round button noses and great white eyes creating the double arch of the curious peaked skull-caps. Cartoon characters' rubberiness, their jazziness, their cheerful buoyancy and idleness, all chimed with popular images of African

Americans, earlier embodied in minstrel shows and in Joel Chandler Harris's tales of Uncle Remus, which Disney was to make into an animated feature, *Song of the South,* in 1946.

Up to 1950, animated cartoons, like films in general, contained caricatures of blacks that would be unacceptable now; in fact, *Song of the South* raised objections from the NAACP when it was released. In recent reissues of *Fantasia,* two Nubian centaurettes and a pickaninny centaurette who shines the others' hooves have been edited out. Not even the superb crows section of *Dumbo* would be made now. But there is a sense in which all animated cartoon characters are more or less black. Steven Spielberg's hectic tribute to animation, *Who Framed Roger Rabbit?,* has them all, from the singing trees of Silly Symphonies to Daffy Duck and Woody Woodpecker, living in a Los Angeles ghetto, Toonville. As blacks were second-class citizens with entertaining qualities, so the animated shorts were second-class movies, with unreal actors who mocked and illuminated from underneath the real world, the live-actor cinema. Of course, even in a ghetto there are class distinctions. Porky Pig and Bugs Bunny have homes that they tend and defend, whereas Mickey started out, like those other raffish stick figures and dancing blots from the twenties, as a free spirit, a wanderer. As Richard Schickel has pointed out, "The locales of his adventures throughout the 1930s ranged from the South Seas to the Alps to the deserts of Africa. He was, at various times, a gaucho, teamster, explorer, swimmer, cowboy, fireman, convict, pioneer, taxi driver, castaway, fisherman, cyclist, Arab, football player, inventor, jockey, storekeeper, camper, sailor, Gulliver, boxer," and so forth. He was, in short, a rootless vaudevillian who would play any part that the bosses at Disney Studios assigned him. And though the comic strip, which still persists, has fitted him with all of a white man's household comforts and headaches, it is as an unencumbered drifter whistling along on the road of hard knocks, ready for whatever adventure waits at the next turning, that he lives in our minds.

Cartoon characters have soul as Carl Jung defined it in his *Archetypes and the Collective Unconscious:* "soul is a life-giving demon who plays his elfin game above and below human existence." Without the "leaping and twinkling of the soul," Jung says, "man would rot away in his greatest passion, idleness." The Mickey Mouse of the thirties shorts was a whirlwind of activity, with a host of unsuspected skills and a reluctant heroism that rose to every occasion. Like Chaplin and Douglas Fairbanks and Fred Astaire, he acted out our fantasies of endless nimbleness, of perfect weightlessness. Yet withal, there was nothing aggressive or self-promoting about him, as there was about Popeye. Disney, interviewed in the thirties, said, "Sometimes I've tried to figure out why Mickey appealed to the whole world. Everybody's tried to figure it out. So far as I know, nobody has. He's a pretty nice fellow who never does anybody any harm, who gets into scrapes through no fault of his own, but always manages to come up grinning." This was perhaps Disney's image of himself: for twenty years he did Mickey's voice in the films, and would often say, "There's a lot of the Mouse in me." Mickey was a character created with his own pen, and nurtured on Disney's memories of his mouse-ridden Kansas City studio and of the Missouri farm where his struggling father tried for a time to make a living. Walt's humble, scrambling beginnings remained embodied in the mouse, whom the Nazis, in a fury against the Mickey-inspired Allied legions (the Allied code word on D-Day was "Mickey Mouse"), called "the most miserable ideal ever revealed . . . mice are dirty."

But was Disney, like Mickey, just "a pretty nice fellow"? He was 8 until crossed in his driving perfectionism, his Napoleonic capacity to marshal men and take risks in the service of an artistic and entrepreneurial vision. He was one of those great Americans, like Edison and Henry Ford, who invented themselves in terms of a new technology. The technology—in Disney's case, film animation—would have been there anyway, but only a few driven men seized the full possibilities and made empires. In the dozen years between *Steamboat Willie* and *Fantasia,* the Disney studios took the art of animation to heights of ambition and accomplishment it would never have reached otherwise, and Disney's personal zeal was the animating force. He created an empire of the mind, and its emperor was Mickey Mouse.

The thirties were Mickey's conquering decade. His image circled 9 the globe. In Africa, tribesmen painfully had tiny mosaic Mickey Mouses inset into their front teeth, and a South African tribe refused to buy soap unless the cakes were embossed with Mickey's image, and a revolt of some native bearers was quelled when the safari masters projected some Mickey Mouse cartoons for them. Nor were the high and mighty immune to Mickey's elemental appeal—King George V and Franklin Roosevelt insisted that all film showings they attended include a dose of Mickey Mouse. But other popular phantoms, like Felix the Cat, have faded, where Mickey has settled into the national collective consciousness. The television program revived him for my children's generation, and the theme parks make him live for my grandchildren's. Yet survival cannot be imposed through weight of publicity; Mickey's persistence springs from something unhyped, something timeless in the image that has allowed it to pass in status from a fad to an icon.

To take a bite out of our imaginations, an icon must be simple. The 10 ears, the wiggly tail, the red shorts, give us a Mickey. Donald Duck and Goofy, Bugs Bunny and Woody Woodpecker are inextricably bound up with the draftsmanship of the artists who make them move and squawk, but Mickey floats free. It was Claes Oldenburg's pop art that first alerted me to the fact that Mickey Mouse had passed out of the realm of commercially generated image into that of artifact. A new Disney gadget, advertised on television, is a camera-like box that spouts bubbles when a key is turned; the key consists of three circles, two mounted on a larger one, and the image is unmistakably Mickey. Like yin and yang, like the Christian cross and the star of Israel, Mickey can be seen everywhere—a sign, a rune, a hieroglyphic trace of a secret power, an electricity we want to plug into. Like totem poles, like African masks, Mickey stands at that intersection of abstraction and representation where magic connects.

Usually cartoon figures do not age, and yet their audience does age, 11 as generation succeeds generation, so that a weight of allusion and sentimental reference increases. To the movie audiences of the early thirties, Mickey Mouse was a piping-voiced live wire, the latest thing in entertainment; by the time of *Fantasia* he was already a sentimental figure, welcomed back. *The Mickey Mouse Club,* with its slightly melancholy pack leader, Jimmie Dodd, created a Mickey more removed and marginal than in his first incarnation. The generation that watched it grew up into the rebels of the sixties, to whom Mickey became camp, a symbol of U.S. cultural fast food, with a touch of the old rodent raffishness. Politically, Walt, stung by the studio strike of 1940, moved to the right, but Mickey remains one of the thirties proletariat, not uncomfortable in the cartoon-rickety, cheerfully verminous crash pads of the counterculture. At the Florida and California theme parks, Mickey manifests himself as a short real person wearing an awkward giant head, costumed as a ringmaster; he is in danger, in these nineties, of seeming not merely venerable kitsch but part of the great trash problem, one more piece of visual litter being moved back and forth by the bulldozers of consumerism.

But never fear, his basic goodness will shine through. Beyond recall, 12 perhaps, is the simple love felt by us of the generation that grew up with him. He was five years my senior and felt like a playmate. I remember crying when the local newspaper, cutting down its comic pages to help us win World War II, eliminated the Mickey Mouse strip. I was old enough, nine or ten, to write an angry letter to the editor. In fact, the strips had been eliminated by the votes of a readership poll, and my indignation and sorrow stemmed from my incredulous realization that not everybody loved Mickey Mouse as I did. In an account of my boyhood written over thirty years ago, "The Dogwood Tree," I find these sentences concerning another boy, a rival: "When we both collected Big Little Books, he outbid me for my supreme find (in the attic of a third boy), the first Mickey Mouse. I can still see that book. I wanted it so badly, its paper tan with age and its drawings done in Disney's primitive style, when Mickey's black chest is naked like a child's and his eyes are two nicked oblongs." And I once tried to write a short story called "A Sensation of Mickey Mouse," trying to superimpose on adult experience, as a shiver-inducing revenant, that indescribable childhood sensation—a rubbery taste, a licorice smell, a feeling of supernatural clarity and close-in excitation that Mickey Mouse gave me, and gives me, much dimmed by the years, still. He is a "genius" in the primary dictionary sense of "an attendant spirit," with his vulnerable bare black chest, his touchingly big yellow shoes, the mysterious place at the back of his shorts where his tail came out, the little cleft cushion of a tongue, red as a valentine and glossy as candy, always peeping through the catenary curves of his undiscourageable smile. Not to mention his ears.

COMPREHENSION

1. What is the primary reason for Updike referring to Mickey Mouse as a "mystery"?
2. The author describes Mickey Mouse in complex, arcane fashion through much of the essay. For example, in paragraph 10, he refers to Mickey as "a sign, a rune, a hieroglyphic trace of a secret power, an electricity we want to plug into. Like totem poles, like African masks, Mickey stands at that intersection of abstraction and representation where magic connects." Carefully review each descriptor, and explain in your own words these various aspects of Mickey.
3. According to the author, why has Mickey Mouse survived so long while other cartoon characters have lost their appeal and popularity?

RHETORIC

1. This excerpt from an Updike book appeared in the magazine *Art & Antiques.* Is there a relationship between the tone and level of discourse in the essay and the magazine it which it appeared?
2. Describe the implied audience for this essay: Is it for children, young adults, cartoon aficionados, or some other group?
3. What is the significance of the opening sentence? How does it capture the attention of the reader?
4. In paragraph 4, Updike states that "Mickey was one of us." To whom does the word *us* refer? What methods of description—such as metaphor, simile, anthropomorphism, and so on—does the author use to support this statement?
5. Updike is famous for his use of unique and playful imagery to enliven his prose. Explain the originality behind the use of language in the sentence "cartoon-rickety, cheerfully verminous crash pads of the counterculture" in paragraph 11. Find at least two other sentences with unique characteristics, and explain their oddities in terms of style, language, and meaning.
6. Why has the author divided his essay into two major parts? How do the parts differ in terms of content? Why does the second part logically devolve from the first?
7. In the final paragraph, the author switches to recollections of his own boyhood experiences of Mickey. Why has he saved this for last?

WRITING

1. Select a public icon, such as E.T. or Michael Jackson, and explain the mass appeal of this icon.
2. Argue for or against the proposition that contemporary life has robbed us of our innocence and so characters like Mickey Mouse will never have the prestige or appeal they once had.
3. Describe your personal attachment to and feelings toward a public figure—real or imaginary. Include what it is that appeals to you and causes you to identify with the figure.

JOAN DIDION Joan Didion (b. 1934) grew up in California and graduated from the University of California at Berkeley in 1956. She began by writing for national magazines such as *Mademoiselle, Saturday Evening Post,* and *Life* and published her first novel, *Run River,* in 1963. Although she has continued to write novels and has written several screenplays, her most acclaimed work is in nonfiction. This work includes *Slouching towards Bethlehem* (1968), *The White Album* (1979), *Salvador* (1983), *Democracy* (1984), *Miami* (1987), and *After Henry* (1992). "Georgia O'Keeffe" paints a portrait of a highly irreverent and independent woman who challenged the status quo at a time when "the men" were supposed to dictate artistic style.

JOAN DIDION

Georgia O'Keeffe

"Where I was born and where and how I have lived is unimportant," 1
Georgia O'Keeffe told us in the book of paintings and words published in her ninetieth year on earth. She seemed to be advising us to forget the beautiful face in the Stieglitz photographs. She appeared to be dismissing the rather condescending romance that had attached to her by then, the romance of extreme good looks and advanced age and deliberate isolation. "It is what I have done with where I have been that should be of interest." I recall an August afternoon in Chicago in 1973 when I took my daughter, then seven, to see what Georgia O'Keeffe had done with where she had been. One of the vast O'Keeffe "Sky Above Clouds" canvases floated over the back stairs in the Chicago Art Institute that day, dominating what seemed to be several stories of empty light, and my daughter looked at it once, ran to the landing, and kept on looking. "Who drew it," she whispered after a while. I told her. "I need to talk to her," she said finally.

My daughter was making, that day in Chicago, an entirely uncon- 2
scious but quite basic assumption about people and the work they do. She was assuming that the glory she saw in the work reflected a glory in its maker, that the painting was the painter as the poem is the poet, that every choice one made alone—every word chosen or rejected, every brush stroke laid or not laid down—betrayed one's character. *Style is character.* It seemed to me that afternoon that I had rarely seen so instinctive an application of this familiar principle, and I recall being pleased not only that my daughter responded to style as character but that it was Georgia O'Keeffe's particular style to which she responded: this was a hard woman who had imposed her 192 square feet of clouds on Chicago.

"Hardness" has not been in our century a quality much admired in 3
women, nor in the past twenty years has it even been in official favor

for men. When hardness surfaces in the very old we tend to transform it into "crustiness" or eccentricity, some tonic pepperiness to be indulged at a distance. On the evidence of her work and what she has said about it, Georgia O'Keeffe is neither "crusty" nor eccentric. She is simply hard, a straight shooter, a woman clean of received wisdom and open to what she sees. This is a woman who could early on dismiss most of her contemporaries as "dreamy," and would later single out one she liked as "a very poor painter." (And then add, apparently by way of softening the judgment: "I guess he wasn't a painter at all. He had no courage and I believe that to create one's own world in any of the arts takes courage.") This is a woman who in 1939 could advise her admirers that they were missing her point, that their appreciation of her famous flowers was merely sentimental. "When I paint a red hill," she observed coolly in the catalogue for an exhibition that year, "you say it is too bad that I don't always paint flowers. A flower touches almost everyone's heart. A red hill doesn't touch everyone's heart." This is a woman who could describe the genesis of one of her most well-known paintings—the "Cow's Skull: Red, White and Blue" owned by the Metropolitan—as an act of quite deliberate and derisive orneriness. "I thought of the city men I had been seeing in the East," she wrote. "They talked so often of writing the Great American Novel—the Great American Play—the Great American Poetry. . . . So as I was painting my cow's head on blue I thought to myself, 'I'll make it an American painting. They will not think it great with the red stripes down the sides—Red, White and Blue—but they will notice it.'"

The city men. The men. They. The words crop up again and again as 4 this astonishingly aggressive woman tells us what was on her mind when she was making her astonishingly aggressive paintings. It was those city men who stood accused of sentimentalizing her flowers: "I made you take time to look at what I saw and when you took time to really notice my flower you hung all your associations with flowers on my flower and you write about my flower as if I think and see what you think and see— and I don't." *And I don't.* Imagine those words spoken, and the sound you hear is *don't tread on me*. "The men" believed it impossible to paint New York, so Georgia O'Keeffe painted New York. "The men" didn't think much of her bright color, so she made it brighter. The men yearned toward Europe so she went to Texas, and then New Mexico. The men talked about Cézanne, "long involved remarks about the 'plastic quality' of his form and color," and took one another's long involved remarks, in the view of this angelic rattlesnake in their midst, altogether too seriously. "I can paint one of those dismal-colored paintings like the men," the woman who regarded herself always as an outsider remembers thinking one day in 1922, and she did: a painting of a shed "all low-toned and dreary with the tree beside the door." She called this act of rancor "The Shanty" and hung it in her next show. "The men seemed to approve of it," she reported fifty-four years later, her contempt undimmed. "They seemed to think that maybe I was beginning to paint. That was my only low-toned dismal-colored painting."

Some women fight and others do not. Like so many successful guer-   5
rillas in the war between the sexes, Georgia O'Keeffe seems to have been
equipped early with an immutable sense of who she was and a fairly
clear understanding that she would be required to prove it. On the surface her upbringing was conventional. She was a child on the Wisconsin
prairie who played with china dolls and painted watercolors with cloudy
skies because sunlight was too hard to paint and, with her brother and
sisters, listened every night to her mother read stories of the Wild West,
of Texas, of Kit Carson and Billy the Kid. She told adults that she wanted
to be an artist and was embarrassed when they asked what kind of artist
she wanted to be: she had no idea "what kind." She had no idea what
artists did. She had never seen a picture that interested her, other than a
pen-and-ink Maid of Athens in one of her mother's books, some Mother
Goose illustrations printed on cloth, a tablet cover that showed a little
girl with pink roses, and the painting of Arabs on horseback that hung in
her grandmother's parlor. At thirteen, in a Dominican convent, she was
mortified when the sister corrected her drawing. At Chatham Episcopal
Institute in Virginia she painted lilacs and sneaked time alone to walk out
to where she could see the line of the Blue Ridge Mountains on the horizon. At the Art Institute in Chicago she was shocked by the presence of
live models and wanted to abandon anatomy lessons. At the Art Students
League in New York one of her fellow students advised her that, since he
would be a great painter and she would end up teaching painting in a
girls' school, any work of hers was less important than modeling for him.
Another painted over her work to show her how the Impressionists did
trees. She had not before heard how the Impressionists did trees and she
did not much care.

At twenty-four she left all those opinions behind and went for the   6
first time to live in Texas, where there were no trees to paint and no one
to tell her how not to paint them. In Texas there was only the horizon
she craved. In Texas she had her sister Claudia with her for a while, and
in the late afternoons they would walk away from town and toward the
horizon and watch the evening star come out. "That evening star fascinated me," she wrote. "It was in some way very exciting to me. My sister had a gun, and as we walked she would throw bottles into the air
and shoot as many as she could before they hit the ground. I had nothing but to walk into nowhere and the wide sunset space with the star.
Ten watercolors were made from that star." In a way one's interest is
compelled as much by the sister Claudia with the gun as by the painter
Georgia with the star, but only the painter left us this shining record.
Ten watercolors were made from that star.

COMPREHENSION

1. Does this essay have an explicit or implied thesis? Explain.
2. What does Didion suggest is O'Keeffe's greatest attribute as an artist? Compare her approach to O'Keeffe to Walker's approach to the artists in her life
in this chapter.

3. Didion refers to specific paintings, museums, and artists in the essay. List them. What assumptions is she making about the cultural and educational background of her reading audience?

RHETORIC

1. What is the purpose of the repetition of the word *men* in paragraph 4? Why is the word italicized and quoted?
2. What do Didion's phrases "ninetieth year on earth" (paragraph 1) and "imposed her 192 square feet of clouds" (paragraph 2) suggest about her attitude toward her subject?
3. Didion begins the essay with a quote from the artist. How does this strategy help set the tone of the essay?
4. In paragraph 3, Didion begins three sentences with the words, "This is a woman . . ."; how do they contribute to the unity and rhetorical effect of the paragraph?
5. Why has Didion included detailed biographical material in paragraph 5? Why has she included this information *after* she discusses O'Keeffe's life as a painter? Which of the facts help us understand O'Keeffe's development as "a woman clean of received wisdom and open to what she sees" (paragraph 3)?
6. Why does Didion's conclusion include a commentary about O'Keeffe's sister? Where and for what purpose does Didion make an implied comparison between O'Keeffe's personality and her sister's habit of firing a gun?

WRITING

1. In what way can O'Keeffe's outlook and behavior be considered existential? Write a brief essay on the topic.
2. Select a woman whom you admire, and write an essay describing how her professional life reflects her values, attitude, and character.
3. Consider one of your own pursuits, for example, a hobby, sport, pastime, or interest. Write an essay in which you explain how this activity reflects an aspect of your personality.

HENRY LOUIS GATES, JR.   Henry Louis Gates, Jr., was born in 1950 in Keyser, West Virginia, and educated at Yale University and Clare College, Cambridge, where he received his Ph.D. in 1979. He now teaches at Harvard University. Gates has edited numerous books addressing the issues of race, identity, and African-American history and has contributed to over a dozen periodicals and journals, including *Critical Inquiry, Black World, Yale Review,* and *Antioch Review,* among others. His work attempts to apply contemporary literary theories, such as structuralism and poststructuralism, to African and African-American literature so that readers can develop a deep understanding of the structure, significance, methods, and meanings of this body of work. Much of his theoretical insights are summed up in his book *The Signifying Monkey:*

Towards a Theory of Afro-American Literary Criticism (1988). Among his awards and honors have been a Carnegie Foundation fellowship, a MacArthur Prize fellowship, and a Mellon fellowship from Yale University. In the following essay, Gates offers a keen analysis of the rap-music phenomenon.

HENRY LOUIS GATES, JR.

2 Live Crew, Decoded

The rap group 2 Live Crew and their controversial hit recording, "As Nasty as They Wanna Be," may well earn a signal place in the history of First Amendment rights. But just as important is how these lyrics will be interpreted and by whom.

For centuries, African-Americans have been forced to develop coded ways of communicating to protect them from danger. Allegories and double meanings, words redefined to mean their opposites ("bad" meaning "good," for instance), even neologisms ("bodacious") have enabled blacks to share messages only the initiated understand.

Many blacks were amused by the transcripts of Marion Barry's sting operation which reveals that he used the traditional black expression about one's "nose being opened." This referred to a love affair and not, as Mr. Barry's prosecutors have suggested, to the inhalation of drugs. Understanding this phrase could very well spell the difference (for the Mayor) between prison and freedom.

2 Live Crew is engaged in heavy-handed parody, turning the stereotypes of black and white American culture on their heads. These young artists are acting out, to lively dance music, a parodic exaggeration of the age-old stereotypes of the oversexed black female and male. Their exuberant use of hyperbole (phantasmagoric sexual organs, for example) undermines—for anyone fluent in black cultural codes—a too literal-minded hearing of the lyrics.

This is the street tradition called "signifying" or "playing the dozens," which has generally been risqué, and where the best signifier or "rapper" is the one who invents the most extravagant images, the biggest "lies," as the culture says. (H. "Rap" Brown earned his nickname in just this way.) In the face of racist stereotypes about black sexuality, you can do one of two things: you can disavow them or explode them with exaggeration.

2 Live Crew, like many "hip-hop" groups, is engaged in sexual carnivalesque. Parody reigns supreme, from a take-off of standard blues to a spoof of the black power movement, their off-color nursery rhymes are part of a venerable Western tradition. The group even satirizes the culture of commerce when it appropriates popular advertising slogans ("Tastes great!" "Less filling!") and puts them in a bawdy context.

2 Live Crew must be interpreted within the context of black culture generally and of signifying specifically. Their novelty, and that of other adventuresome rap groups, is that their defiant rejection of euphemism now voices for the mainstream what before existed largely in the "race record" market—where the records of Redd Foxx and Rudy Ray Moore once were forced to reside.

Rock songs have always been about sex but have used elaborate subterfuges to convey that fact. 2 Live Crew uses Anglo-Saxon words and is self-conscious about it: a parody of a white voice in one song refers to "private personal parts," as a coy counterpart to the group's bluntness.

Much more troubling than its so-called obscenity is the group's overt sexism. Their sexism is so flagrant, however, that it almost cancels itself out in a hyperbolic war between the sexes. In this, it recalls the inter-sexual jousting in Zora Neale Hurston's novels. Still, many of us look toward the emergence of more female rappers to redress sexual stereotypes. And we must not allow ourselves to sentimentalize street culture: the appreciation of verbal virtuosity does not lessen one's obligation to critique bigotry in all of its pernicious forms.

Is 2 Live Crew more "obscene" than, say, the comic Andrew Dice Clay? Clearly, this rap group is seen as more threatening than others that are just as sexually explicit. Can this be completely unrelated to the specter of the young black male as a figure of sexual and social disruption, the very stereotypes 2 Live Crew seem determined to undermine?

This question—and the very large question of obscenity and the First Amendment—cannot even be addressed until those who would answer them become literate in the vernacular traditions of African Americans. To do less is to censor through the equivalent of intellectual prior restraint—and censorship is to art what lynching is to justice.

COMPREHENSION

1. What is the author's thesis?

2. According to Gates, what must one know before engaging in a critique of 2 Live Crew?

3. Does Gates consider 2 Live Crew's music obscene? Why, or why not?

RHETORIC

1. The paragraphs in this essay are fairly short. How does this affect Gates's argument?

2. How does the author use definition to "decode" certain aspects of African-American culture? Why is definition an important strategy in his argument?

3. Gates uses the word *hyperbole* in paragraph 4 and the word *hyperbolic* in paragraph 9. Why is it necessary for him to emphasize this concept to develop his argument?

4. Does the author appear to use a particular tone toward his subject matter? Does he appear to support the art of his subject, condemn it, explain it, or provide a mixture of all three?

5. For whom is this essay written? What is its intended purpose? Explain your view.

6. Examine the final sentence of the essay. Does it provide an effective closure? Why is it particularly pertinent considering 2 Live Crew is an African-American music group? Explain your view.

WRITING

1. Argue for or against the proposition that only after informed study and consideration can one legitimately judge the quality of a work of art or determine if something *is* art.

2. Argue for or against the proposition that 2 Live Crew is obscene, basing your argument on the points raised in the article by Gates.

3. For a research project, write a paper entitled "The Arts and Obscenity during the Twentieth Century."

ALICE WALKER   Alice Walker, born in Eatonton, Georgia, in 1944, now lives in San Francisco and Mendocino County, California. A celebrated poet, short-story writer, and novelist, she is the author of *Revolutionary Petunias and Other Poems, In Love and Trouble: Stories of Black Women,* and *Meridian,* among other works. Her 1983 novel, *The Color Purple,* won the American Book Award and the Pulitzer Prize. The following essay, from *In Search of Our Mothers' Gardens* (1983), offers a highly personalized and perceptive analysis of the importance of influence in both art and life.

ALICE WALKER

Saving the Life That Is Your Own:
The Importance of Models in the Artist's Life

There is a letter Vincent Van Gogh wrote to Emile Bernard that is very meaningful to me. A year before he wrote the letter, Van Gogh had had a fight with his domineering friend Gauguin, left his company, and cut off, in desperation and anguish, his own ear. The letter was written in Saint-Remy, in the South of France, from a mental institution to which Van Gogh had voluntarily committed himself.

I imagine Van Gogh sitting at a rough desk too small for him, looking out at the lovely Southern light, and occasionally glancing critically next to him at his own paintings of the landscape he loved so much. The date of the letter is December 1889. Van Gogh wrote:

> However hateful painting may be, and however cumbersome in the times we are living in, if anyone who has chosen this handicraft pursues it zealously, he is a man of duty, sound and faithful.
>
> Society makes our existence wretchedly difficult at times, hence our impotence and the imperfection of our work.
>
> . . . I myself am suffering under an absolute lack of models.
>
> But on the other hand, there are beautiful spots here. I have just done five size 30 canvasses, olive trees. And the reason I am staying on here is that my health is improving a great deal.
>
> What I am doing is hard, dry, but that is because I am trying to gather new strength by doing some rough work, and I'm afraid abstractions would make me soft.

Six months later, Van Gogh—whose health was "improving a great deal"—committed suicide. He had sold one painting during his lifetime. Three times was his work noticed in the press. But these are just details.

The real Vincent Van Gogh is the man who has "just done five size 30 canvasses, olive trees." To me, in context, one of the most moving and revealing descriptions of how a real artist thinks. And the knowledge that when he spoke of "suffering under an absolute lack of models" he spoke of that lack in terms of both the intensity of his commitment and the quality and singularity of his work, which was frequently ridiculed in his day.

The absence of models, in literature as in life, to say nothing of painting, is an occupational hazard for the artist, simply because models in art, in behavior, in growth of spirit and intellect—even if rejected—enrich and enlarge one's view of existence. Deadlier still, to the artist who lacks models, is the curse of ridicule, the bringing to bear on an artist's best work, especially his or her most original, most strikingly deviant, only a fund of ignorance and the presumption that, as an artist's critic, one's judgment is free of the restrictions imposed by prejudice, and is well informed, indeed, about all the art in the world that really matters.

What is always needed in the appreciation of art, or life, is the larger perspective. Connections made, or at least attempted, where none existed before, the straining to encompass in one's glance at the varied world the common thread, the unifying theme through immense diversity, a fearlessness of growth, of search, of looking, that enlarges the private and the public world. And yet, in our particular society, it is the narrowed and narrowing view of life that often wins.

Recently, I read at a college and was asked by one of the audience what I considered the major difference between the literature written by black and by white Americans. I had not spent a lot of time considering this question, since it is not the difference between them that interests me, but, rather, the way black writers and white writers seem to me to be writing one immense story—the same story, for the most part—with different parts of this immense story coming from a multitude of different perspectives. Until this is generally recognized, literature will always be broken into bits, black and white, and there will always be questions, wanting neat answers, such as this.

Still, I answered that I thought, for the most part, white American 8
writers tended to end their books and their characters' lives as if there were no better existence for which to struggle. The gloom of defeat is thick.

By comparison, black writers seem always involved in a moral 9
and/or physical struggle, the result of which is expected to be some kind of larger freedom. Perhaps this is because our literary tradition is based on the slave narratives, where escape for the body and freedom for the soul went together, or perhaps this is because black people have never felt themselves guilty of global, cosmic sins.

This comparison does not hold up in every case, of course, and 10
perhaps does not really hold up at all. I am not a gatherer of statistics, only a curious reader, and this has been my impression from reading many books by black and white writers.

There are, however, two books by American women that illustrate 11
what I am talking about: *The Awakening,* by Kate Chopin, and *Their Eyes Were Watching God,* by Zora Neale Hurston.

The plight of Mme Pontellier is quite similar to that of Janie Craw- 12
ford. Each woman is married to a dull, society-conscious husband and living in a dull, propriety-conscious community. Each woman desires a life of her own and a man who loves her and makes her feel alive. Each woman finds such a man.

Mme Pontellier, overcome by the strictures of society and the exis- 13
tence of her children (along with the cowardice of her lover), kills herself rather than defy the one and abandon the other. Janie Crawford, on the other hand, refuses to allow society to dictate behavior to her, enjoys the love of a much younger, freedom-loving man, and lives to tell others of her experience.

When I mentioned these two books to my audience, I was not sur- 14
prised to learn that only one person, a young black poet in the first row, had ever heard of *Their Eyes Were Watching God* (*The Awakening* they had fortunately read in their "Women in Literature" class), primarily because it was written by a black woman, whose experience—in love and life—was apparently assumed to be unimportant to the students (and the teachers) of a predominantly white school.

Certainly, as a student, I was not directed toward this book, which 15
would have urged me more toward freedom and experience than toward comfort and security, but was directed instead toward a plethora of books by mainly white male writers who thought most women worthless if they didn't enjoy bullfighting or hadn't volunteered for the trenches in World War I.

Loving both these books, knowing each to be indispensable to my 16
own growth, my own life, I choose the model, the example, of Janie

Crawford. And yet this book, as necessary to me and to other women as air and water, is again out of print.[1] But I have distilled as much as I could of its wisdom in this poem about its heroine, Janie Crawford:

> I love the way Janie Crawford
> left her husbands
> the one who wanted to change her
> into a mule
> and the other who tried to interest her
> in being a queen.
> A woman, unless she submits,
> is neither a mule
> nor a queen
> though like a mule she may suffer
> and like a queen pace the floor.

It has been said that someone asked Toni Morrison why she writes the kind of books she writes, and that she replied: Because they are the kind of books I want to read. 17

This remains my favorite reply to that kind of question. As if anyone reading the magnificent, mysterious *Sula* or the grim, poetic *The Bluest Eye* would require more of a reason for their existence than for the brooding, haunting *Wuthering Heights,* for example, or the melancholy, triumphant *Jane Eyre.* (I am not speaking here of the most famous short line of that book, "Reader, I married him," as the triumph, but, rather, of the triumph of Jane Eyre's control over her own sense of morality and her own stout will, which are but reflections of her creator's, Charlotte Brontë, who no doubt wished to write the sort of books *she* wished to read.) 18

Flannery O'Connor has written that more and more the serious novelist will write, not what other people want, and certainly not what other people expect, but whatever interests her or him. And that the direction taken, therefore, will be away from sociology, away from the "writing of explanation," of statistics, and further into mystery, into poetry, and into prophecy. I believe this is true, *fortunately true;* especially for "Third World Writers"; Morrison, Marquez, Ahmadi, Camara Laye make good examples. And not only do I believe it is true for serious writers in general, but I believe, as firmly as did O'Connor, that this is our only hope—in a culture so in love with flash, with trendiness, with superficiality, as ours—of acquiring a sense of essence, of timelessness, and of vision. Therefore, to write the books one wants to read is both to point in the direction of vision and, at the same time, to follow it. 19

When Toni Morrison said she writes the kind of books she wants to read, she was acknowledging the fact that in a society in which 20

---

[1]Reissued by the University of Illinois Press, 1979.

459

"accepted literature" is so often sexist and racist and otherwise irrelevant or offensive to so many lives, she must do the work of two. She must be her own model as well as the artist attending, creating, learning from, realizing the model, which is to say, herself.

(It should be remembered that, as a black person, one cannot completely identify with a Jane Eyre, or with her creator, no matter how much one admires them. And certainly, if one allows history to impinge on one's reading pleasure, one must cringe at the thought of how Heathcliff, in the New World far from Wuthering Heights, amassed his Cathy-dazzling fortune.) I have often been asked why, in my own life and work, I have felt such a desperate need to know and assimilate the experiences of earlier black women writers, most of them unheard of by you and by me, until quite recently; why I felt a need to study them and to teach them. 21

I don't recall the exact moment I set out to explore the works of black women, mainly those in the past, and certainly, in the beginning, I had no desire to teach them. Teaching being for me, at that time, less rewarding than star-gazing on a frigid night. My discovery of them— most of them out of print, abandoned, discredited, maligned, nearly lost—came about, as many things of value do, almost by accident. As it turned out—and this should not have surprised me—I found I was in need of something that only one of them could provide. 22

Mindful that throughout my four years at a prestigious black and then a prestigious white college I had heard not one word about early black women writers, one of my first tasks was simply to determine whether they had existed. After this, I could breathe easier, with more assurance about the profession I myself had chosen. 23

But the incident that started my search began several years ago: I sat down at my desk one day, in a room of my own, with key and lock, and began preparations for a story about voodoo, a subject that had always fascinated me. Many of the elements of this story I had gathered from a story my mother several times told me. She had gone, during the Depression, into town to apply for some government surplus food at the local commissary, and had been turned down, in a particularly humiliating way, by the white woman in charge. 24

My mother always told this story with a most curious expression on her face. She automatically raised her head higher than ever—it was always high—and there was a look of righteousness, a kind of holy *heat* coming from her eyes. She said she had lived to see this same white woman grow old and senile and so badly crippled she had to get about on *two* sticks. 25

To her, this was clearly the working of God, who, as in the old spiritual, ". . . may not come when you want him, but he's right on time!" To me, hearing the story for about the fiftieth time, something else was discernible: the possibilities of the story, for fiction. 26

What, I asked myself, would have happened if, after the crippled old lady died, it was discovered that someone, my mother perhaps (who would have been mortified at the thought, Christian that she is), had voodooed her? 27

Then, my thoughts sweeping me away into the world of hexes and conjurings of centuries past, I wondered how a larger story could be created out of my mother's story; one that would be true to the magnitude of her humiliation and grief, and to the white woman's lack of sensitivity and compassion.

My third quandary was: How could I find out all I needed to know in order to write a story that used *authentic* black witchcraft?

Which brings me back, almost, to the day I became really interested in black women writers. I say "almost" because one other thing, from my childhood, made the choice of black magic a logical and irresistible one for my story. Aside from my mother's several stories about root doctors she had heard of or known, there was the story I had often heard about my "crazy" Walker aunt.

Many years ago, when my aunt was a meek and obedient girl growing up in a strict, conventionally religious house in the rural South, she had suddenly thrown off her meekness and had run away from home, escorted by a rogue of a man permanently attached elsewhere.

When she was returned home by her father, she was declared quite mad. In the backwoods South at the turn of the century, "madness" of this sort was cured not by psychiatry but by powders and by spells. (One can see Scott Joplin's *Treemonisha* to understand the role voodoo played among black people of that period.) My aunt's madness was treated by the community conjurer, who promised, and delivered, the desired results. His treatment was a bag of white powder, bought for fifty cents, and sprinkled on the ground around her house, with some of it sewed, I believe, into the bodice of her nightgown.

So when I sat down to write my story about voodoo, my crazy Walker aunt was definitely on my mind.

But she had experienced her temporary craziness so long ago that her story had all the excitement of a might-have-been. I needed, instead of family memories, some hard facts about the *craft* of voodoo, as practiced by Southern blacks in the nineteenth century. (It never once, fortunately, occurred to me that voodoo was not worthy of the interest I had in it, or was too ridiculous to study seriously.)

I began reading all I could find on the subject of "The Negro and His Folkways and Superstitions." There were Botkin and Puckett and others, all white, most racist. How was I to believe anything they wrote, since at least one of them, Puckett, was capable of wondering, in his book, if "The Negro" had a large enough brain?

Well, I thought, where are the *black* collectors of folklore? Where is the *black* anthropologist? Where is the *black* person who took the time to travel the back roads of the South and collect the information I need: how to cure heat trouble, treat dropsy, hex somebody to death, lock bowels, cause joints to swell, eyes to fall out, and so on. Where was this black person?

And that is when I first saw, in a *footnote* to the white voices of authority, the name Zora Neale Hurston.

Folklorist, novelist, anthropologist, serious student of voodoo, also 38
all-around black woman, with guts enough to take a slide rule and measure random black heads in Harlem; not to prove their inferiority, but
to prove that whatever their size, shape, or present condition of servitude, those heads contained all the intelligence anyone could use to get
through this world.

Zora Hurston, who went to Barnard to learn how to study what she 39
really wanted to learn: the ways of her own people, and what ancient
rituals, customs, and beliefs had made them unique.

Zora, of the sandy-colored hair and the daredevil eyes, a girl who 40
escaped poverty and parental neglect by hard work and a sharp eye for
the main chance.

Zora, who left the South only to return to look at it again. Who went 41
to root doctors from Florida to Louisiana and said, "Here I am. I want
to learn your trade."

Zora, who had collected all the black folklore I could ever use. 42
That Zora. 43

And having found *that Zora* (like a golden key to a storehouse of 44
varied treasure), I was hooked.

What I had discovered, of course, was a model. A model, who, as it 45
happened, provided more than voodoo for my story, more than one of
the greatest novels America had produced—though, being America, it
did not realize this. She had provided, as if she knew someday I would
come along wandering in the wilderness, a nearly complete record of
her life. And though her life sprouted an occasional wart, I am eternally
grateful for that life, warts and all.

It is not irrelevant, nor is it bragging (except perhaps to gloat a lit- 46
tle on the happy relatedness of Zora, my mother and me), to mention
here that the story I wrote, called "the Revenge of Hannah Kemhuff,"
based on my mother's experiences during the Depression, and on Zora
Hurston's folklore collection of the 1920s, and on my own response to
both out of a contemporary existence, was immediately published and
was later selected, by a reputable collector of short stories, as one of the
Best Short Stories of 1974.

I mention it because this story might never have been written, 47
because the very bases of its structure, authentic black folklore, viewed
from a black perspective, might have been lost.

Had it been lost, my mother's story would have had no historical 48
underpinning, none I could trust, anyway. I would not have written the
story, which I enjoyed writing as much as I've enjoyed writing anything
in my life, had I not known that Zora had already done a thorough job
of preparing the ground over which I was then moving.

In that story I gathered up the historical and psychological threads 49
of the life my ancestors lived, and in the writing of it I felt joy and
strength and my own continuity. I had that wonderful feeling writers
get sometimes, not very often, of being *with* a great many people,
ancient spirits, all very happy to see me consulting and acknowledging

them, and eager to let me know, through the joy of their presence, that, indeed, I am not alone.

To take Toni Morrison's statement further, if that is possible, in my own work I write not only what I want to read—understanding fully and indelibly that if I don't do it no one else is so vitally interested, or capable of doing it to my satisfaction—I write all the things *I should have been able to read*. Consulting, as belatedly discovered models, those writers—most of whom, not surprisingly, are women—who understood that their experience as ordinary human beings was also valuable, and in danger of being misrepresented, distorted, or lost:

Zora Hurston—novelist, essayist, anthropologist, autobiographer;

Jean Toomer—novelist, poet, philosopher, visionary, a man who cared what women felt;

Colette—whose crinkly hair enhances her French, part-black face; novelist, playwright, dancer, essayist, newspaperwoman, lover of women, men, small dogs; fortunate not to have been born in America;

Anaïs Nin—recorder of everything, no matter how minute;

Tillie Olson—a writer of such generosity and honesty, she literally saves lives;

Virginia Woolf—who has saved so many of us.

It is, in the end, the saving of lives that we writers are about. 51 Whether we are "minority" writers or "majority." It is simply in our power to do this.

We do it because we care. We care that Vincent Van Gogh mutilated 52 his ear. We care that behind a pile of manure in the yard he destroyed his life. We care that Scott Joplin's music *lives!* We care because we know this: *the life we save is our own*.

COMPREHENSION

1. Explain the significance of Walker's title. How does it serve her purpose and guide readers to her thesis? What is her thesis?

2. According to the author, what is the importance of models in art? What is the relationship of models to life? List the models in Walker's life. Which of them stand out?

3. Paraphrase Walker's remarks on the relationship between black American and white American writing.

RHETORIC

1. Walker uses many allusions in this essay. Identify as many as you can. What is the allusion in the title? Comment on the general effectiveness of her allusions.

2. Is the author's style and choice of diction suitable to her subject matter and to her audience? Why, or why not?

3. Why does the author personalize her treatment of the topic? What does she gain? Is there anything lost?

4. Walker employs several unique structuring devices in this essay. Cite at least three, and analyze their utility.
5. Explain Walker's use of examples to reinforce her generalizations and to organize the essay.
6. Which paragraphs constitute Walker's conclusion? What is their effect?

WRITING

1. Discuss the meaning of Walker's remark, "What is always needed in the appreciation of art, or life, is the larger perspective."
2. If you were planning on a career as a writer, artist, actor, or musician, who would your models be, and why?

DAVE BARRY   Dave Barry was born in Armonk, New York, in 1947. He graduated from Haverford College in 1969 and was a reporter and editor at the *Daily Local News* from 1971 to 1975. Since 1983, he has been a columnist for *The Miami Herald.* Besides writing his columns, Barry has written numerous books, all with his unique, amusing point of view. His books include *Stay Fit and Healthy Until You're Dead* (1985), *Dave Barry's Greatest Hits* (1988), *Dave Barry Turns 40* (1990), and *Dave Barry's Only Travel Guide You'll Ever Need* (1991). Barry won the 1988 Pulitzer Prize for commentary. In the piece below, he comments on the relation between television commercials and patriotism.

DAVE BARRY

Red, White, and Beer

Lately I've been feeling very patriotic, especially during commercials.   1
Like, when I see those strongly pro-American Chrysler commercials, the ones where the winner of the Bruce Springsteen Sound-Alike Contest sings about how The Pride Is Back, the ones where Lee Iacocca himself comes striding out and practically challenges the president of Toyota to a knife fight, I get this warm, proud feeling inside, the same kind of feeling I get whenever we hold routine naval maneuvers off the coast of Libya.

But if you want to talk about *real* patriotism, of course, you have to   2
talk about beer commercials. I would have to say that Miller is the most patriotic brand of beer. I grant you it tastes like rat saliva, but we are not talking about taste here. What we are talking about, according to the commercials, is that Miller is by God an *American* beer, "born and brewed in the U.S.A.," and the men who drink it are American men, the kind of men who aren't afraid to perspire freely and shake a man's

hand. That's mainly what happens in Miller commercials: Burly American men go around, drenched in perspiration, shaking each other's hands in a violent and patriotic fashion.

You never find out exactly why these men spend so much time shaking hands. Maybe shaking hands is just their simple straightforward burly masculine American patriotic way of saying to each other: "Floyd, I am truly sorry I drank all that Miller beer last night and went to the bathroom in your glove compartment." Another possible explanation is that, since there are never any women in the part of America where beer commercials are made, the burly men have become lonesome and desperate for any form of physical contact. I have noticed that sometimes, in addition to shaking hands, they hug each other. Maybe very late at night, after the David Letterman show, there are Miller commercials in which the burly men engage in slow dancing. I don't know.

I do know that in one beer commercial, I think this is for Miller— 4 although it could be for Budweiser, which is also a very patriotic beer— the burly men build a house. You see them all getting together and pushing up a brand-new wall. Me, I worry some about a house built by men drinking beer. In my experience, you run into trouble when you ask a group of beer-drinking men to perform any task more complex than remembering not to light the filter ends of cigarettes.

For example, in my younger days, whenever anybody in my circle 5 of friends wanted to move, he'd get the rest of us to help, and, as an inducement, he'd buy a couple of cases of beer. This almost always produced unfortunate results, such as the time we were trying to move Dick "The Wretch" Curry from a horrible fourth-floor walk-up apartment in Manhattan's Lower East Side to another horrible fourth-floor walk-up apartment in Manhattan's Lower East Side, and we hit upon the labor-saving concept of, instead of carrying The Wretch's possessions manually down the stairs, simply dropping them out the window, down onto the street, where The Wretch was racing around, gathering up the broken pieces of his life and shrieking at us to stop helping him move, his emotions reaching a fever pitch when his bed, which had been swinging wildly from a rope, entered the apartment two floors below his through what had until seconds earlier been a window.

This is the kind of thinking you get, with beer. So I figure what hap- 6 pens, in the beer commercial where the burly men are building the house, is they push the wall up so it's vertical, and then, after the camera stops filming them, they just keep pushing, and the wall crashes down on the other side, possibly onto somebody's pickup truck. And then they all shake hands.

But other than that, I'm in favor of the upsurge in retail patriotism, 7 which is lucky for me because the airwaves are saturated with pro-American commercials. Especially popular are commercials in which the newly restored Statue of Liberty—and by the way, I say Lee Iacocca should get some kind of medal for that, or at least be elected president— appears to be endorsing various products, as if she were Mary Lou Retton or somebody. I saw one commercial strongly suggesting that the Statue of Liberty uses Sure brand underarm deodorant.

I have yet to see a patriotic laxative commercial, but I imagine it's 8 only a matter of time. They'll show some actors dressed up as hardworking country folk, maybe at a church picnic, smiling at each other and eating pieces of pie. At least one of them will be a black person. The Statue of Liberty will appear in the background. Then you'll hear a country-style singer singing:

> Folks 'round here they love this land;
> They stand by their beliefs;
> An' when they git themselves stopped up;
> They want some quick relief.

Well, what do you think? Pretty good commercial concept, huh? 9

Nah, you're right. They'd never try to pull something like that. 10 They'd put the statue in the *foreground*.

COMPREHENSION

1. What does Barry mean by "retail patriotism"? How does the essay's title illustrate this concept?

2. According to Barry, what makes beer commercials, especially those for Miller, patriotic?

3. In Barry's opinion, what do sexism, patriotism, and beer have in common?

RHETORIC

1. Barry doesn't explicitly state his thesis anywhere in the essay. In your own words, what is his implied thesis? Use evidence from the essay to support your view.

2. Barry uses irony and humor very effectively in this piece. Cite some examples of his humor, and analyze how he achieves the desired effect.

3. The writer uses specific brand names in his essay. How does this device help to strengthen his argument? Would eliminating them make the essay less persuasive? Why, or why not?

4. Barry seems to digress from his point in paragraphs 4, 5, and 6. Why does he do this? How does this digression serve the purpose of the piece?

5. Does the anecdote Barry uses in paragraph 5 ring true? Why, or why not? What purpose does it serve in the essay? Does its plausibleness affect the strength of Barry's argument?

6. How does paragraph 10 function as a conclusion? Is it in keeping with the essay's tone and style? Is it an effective device? Justify your response.

WRITING

1. Barry's essay examines how television sells patriotism. Write an essay analyzing how television sells other abstract ideas, such as success, love, freedom, democracy. Pattern your essay after Barry's, using humor. Also, use specific television commercials you have seen as examples.

2. Write an essay entitled "Patriotism," using both denotative and connotative definitions of the word.

3. In an essay, examine the impact that television advertising has had on American consumers and its repercussions.

MARYA MANNES Marya Mannes (1904–1990), wrote several novels and some light verse, but she is best known for her essays, which appeared in *Vogue, McCall's, Harper's,* and *The New Republic.* She collected her essays in *More in Anger* (1958) and in *The New York I Know* (1961). Mannes also wrote on such subjects as suicide and euthanasia in *Last Rights* (1974) and television in *Who Owns the Air?* (1960). In this essay from *But Will It Sell?* (1964), she establishes standards for judging excellence in the arts.

MARYA MANNES

How Do You Know It's Good?

Suppose there were no critics to tell us how to react to a picture, a play, or a new composition of music. Suppose we wandered innocent as the dawn into an art exhibition of unsigned paintings. By what standards, by what values would we decide whether they were good or bad, talented or untalented, successes or failures? How can we ever know that what we think is right?

For the last fifteen or twenty years the fashion in criticism or appreciation of the arts has been to deny the existence of any valid criteria and to make the words "good" or "bad" irrelevant, immaterial, and inapplicable. There is no such thing, we are told, as a set of standards, first acquired through experience and knowledge and later imposed on the subject under discussion. This has been a popular approach, for it relieves the critic of the responsibility of judgment and the public of the necessity of knowledge. It pleases those resentful of disciplines, it flatters the empty-minded by calling them open-minded, it comforts the confused. Under the banner of democracy and the kind of equality which our forefathers did *not* mean, it says, in effect, "Who are you to tell us what *is* good or bad?" This is the same cry used so long and so effectively by the producers of mass media who insist that it is the public, not they, who decides what it wants to hear and see, and that for a critic to say that *this* program is bad and *this* program is good is purely a reflection of personal taste. Nobody recently has expressed this philosophy more succinctly than Dr. Frank Stanton, the highly intelligent president of CBS television. At a hearing before the Federal Communications Commission, this phrase escaped him under questioning: "One man's mediocrity is another man's good program."

There is no better way of saying "No values are absolute." There is another important aspect to this philosophy of *laissez faire:* It is the fear, in all observers of all forms of art, of guessing wrong. This fear is well come by, for who has not heard of the contemporary outcries against artists who later were called great? Every age has its arbiters who do not grow with their times, who cannot tell evolution from revolution or the difference between frivolous faddism, amateurish experimentation, and profound and necessary change. Who wants to be caught *flagrante delicto* with an error of judgment as serious as this? It is far safer, and certainly easier, to look at a picture or a play or a poem and to say "This is hard to understand, but it may be good," or simply to welcome it as a new form. The word "new"—in our country especially—has magical connotations. What is new must be good; what is old is probably bad. And if a critic can describe the new in language that nobody can understand, he's safer still. If he has mastered the art of saying nothing with exquisite complexity, nobody can quote him later as saying anything.

But all these, I maintain, are forms of abdication from the responsibility of judgment. In creating, the artist commits himself; in appreciating, you have a commitment of your own. For after all, it is the audience which makes the arts. A climate of appreciation is essential to its flowering, and the higher the expectations of the public, the better the performance of the artist. Conversely, only a public ill-served by its critics could have accepted as art and as literature so much in these last years that has been neither. If anything goes, everything goes; and at the bottom of the junkpile lie the discarded standards too.

But what are these standards? How do you get them? How do you know they're the right ones? How can you make a clear pattern out of so many intangibles, including that greatest one, the very private I?

Well for one thing, it's fairly obvious that the more you read and see and hear, the more equipped you'll be to practice that art of association which is at the basis of all understanding and judgment. The more you live and the more you look, the more aware you are of a consistent pattern—as universal as the stars, as the tides, as breathing, as night and day—underlying everything. I would call this pattern and this rhythm an order. Not order—*an* order. Within it exists an incredible diversity of forms. Without it lies chaos—the wild cells of destruction—sickness. It is in the end up to you to distinguish between the diversity that is health and the chaos that is sickness, and you can't do this without a process of association that can link a bar of Mozart with the corner of a Vermeer painting, or a Stravinsky score with a Picasso abstraction; or that can relate an aggressive act with a Franz Kline painting and a fit of coughing with a John Cage composition.

There is no accident in the fact that certain expressions of art live for all time and that others die with the moment, and although you may not always define the reasons, you can ask the questions. What does an artist say that is timeless; how does he say it? How much is fashion, how much is merely reflection? Why is Sir Walter Scott so hard to read now, and Jane Austen not? Why is baroque right for one age and too effulgent for another?

Can a standard of craftsmanship apply to art of all ages, or does each have its own, and different, definitions? You may have been aware, inadvertently, that craftsmanship has become a dirty word these years because, again, it implies standards—something done well or done badly. The result of this convenient avoidance is a plentitude of actors who can't project their voices, singers who can't phrase their songs, poets who can't communicate emotion, and writers who have no vocabulary—not to speak of painters who can't draw. The dogma now is that craftsmanship gets in the way of expression. You can do better if you don't know *how* you do it, let alone *what* you're doing.

I think it is time you helped reverse this trend by trying to redis- 9 cover craft: the command of the chosen instrument, whether it is a brush, a word, or a voice. When you begin to detect the difference between freedom and sloppiness, between serious experimentation and egotherapy, between skill and slickness, between strength and violence, you are on your way to separating the sheep from the goats, a form of segregation denied us for quite a while. All you need to restore it is a small bundle of standards and a Geiger counter that detects fraud, and we might begin our tour of the arts in an area where both are urgently needed: contemporary painting.

I don't know what's worse: to have to look at acres of bad art to find 10 the little good, or to read what the critics say about it all. In no other field of expression has so much double-talk flourished, so much confusion prevailed, and so much nonsense been circulated: further evidence of the close interdependence between the arts and the critical climate they inhabit. It will be my pleasure to share with you some of this double-talk so typical of our times.

Item one: preface for a catalogue of an abstract painter: 11

"Time-bound meditation experiencing a life; sincere with plastic 12 piety at the threshold of hallowed arcana; a striving for pure ideation giving shape to inner drive; formalized patterns where neural balances reach a fiction." End of quote. Know what this artist paints like now?

Item two: a review in the *Art News:* 13

". . . a weird and disparate assortment of material, but the mon- 14 strosity which bloomed into his most recent cancer of aggregations is present in some form everywhere. . . ." Then, later, "A gluttony of things and processes terminated by a glorious constipation."

Item three, same magazine, review of an artist who welds automo- 15 bile fragments into abstract shapes:

"Each fragment . . . is made an extreme of human exasperation, 16 torn at and fought all the way, and has its rightness of form as if by accident. *Any technique that requires order or discipline would just be the human ego.* No, these must be egoless, uncontrolled, undesigned and different enough to give you a bang—fifty miles an hour around a telephone pole. . . ."

"Any technique that requires order or discipline would just be the 17 human ego." What does he mean—"just be"? What are they really talking about? Is this journalism? Is it criticism? Or is it that other convenient abdication from standards of performance and judgment practiced by so many artists and critics that they, like certain writers who deal only in sickness and depravity, "reflect the chaos about them"? Again, whose chaos? Whose depravity?

I had always thought that the prime function of art was to create 18 order *out* of chaos—again, not the order of neatness or rigidity or convention or artifice, but the order of clarity by which one will and one vision could draw the essential truth out of apparent confusion. I still do. It is not enough to use parts of a car to convey the brutality of the machine. This is as slavishly representative, and just as easy, as arranging dried flowers under glass to convey nature.

Speaking of which, i.e., the use of real materials (burlap, old gloves, 19 bottletops) in lieu of pigment, this is what one critic had to say about an exhibition of Assemblage at the Museum of Modern Art last year:

> Spotted throughout the show are indisputable works of art, accounting for a quarter or even a half of the total display. But the remainder are works of non-art, anti-art, and art substitutes that are the aesthetic counterparts of the social deficiencies that land people in the clink on charges of vagrancy. These aesthetic bankrupts . . . have no legitimate ideological roof over their heads and not the price of a square intellectual meal, much less a spiritual sandwich, in their pockets.

I quote these words of John Canaday of *The New York Times* as an 20 example of the kind of criticism which puts responsibility to an intelligent public above popularity with an intellectual coterie. Canaday has the courage to say what he thinks and the capacity to say it clearly: two qualities notably absent from his profession.

Next to art, I would say that appreciation and evaluation in the field 21 of music is the most difficult. For it is rarely possible to judge a new composition at one hearing only. What seems confusing or fragmented at first might well become clear and organic a third time. Or it might not. The only salvation here for the listener is, again, an instinct born of experience and association which allows him to separate intent from accident, design from experimentation, and pretense from conviction. Much of contemporary music is, like its sister art, merely a reflection of the composer's own fragmentation: an absorption in self and symbols at the expense of communication with others. The artist, in short, says to the public: If you don't understand this, it's because you're dumb. I maintain that you are not. You may have to go part way or even halfway to meet the artist, but if you must go the whole way, it's his fault, not yours. Hold fast to that. And remember it too when you read new poetry, that estranged sister of music.

A multitude of causes, unknown to former times, are now acting with a 22 combined force to blunt the discriminating powers of the mind, and, unfitting it for all voluntary exertion, to reduce it to a state of almost savage torpor. The most effective of these causes are the great national events which are daily taking place and the increasing accumulation of men in cities, where the uniformity of their occupations produces a craving for extraordinary incident, which the rapid communication of intelligence hourly gratifies. To this tendency of life and manners, the literature and theatrical exhibitions of the country have conformed themselves.

This startlingly applicable comment was written in the year 1800 by [23] William Wordsworth in the preface to his "Lyrical Ballads"; and it has been cited by Edwin Muir in his recently published book "The Estate of Poetry." Muir states that poetry's effective range and influence have diminished alarmingly in the modern world. He believes in the inherent and indestructible qualities of the human mind and the great and permanent objects that act upon it, and suggests that the audience will increase when "poetry loses what obscurity is left in it by attempting greater themes, for great themes have to be stated clearly." If you keep that firmly in mind and resist, in Muir's words, "the vast dissemination of secondary objects that isolate us from the natural world," you have gone a long way toward equipping yourself for the examination of any work of art.

When you come to theatre, in this extremely hasty tour of the arts, [24] you can approach it on two different levels. You can bring to it anticipation and innocence, giving yourself up, as it were, to the life on the stage and reacting to it emotionally, if the play is good, or listlessly, if the play is boring; a part of the audience organism that expresses its favor by silence or laughter and its disfavor by coughing and rustling. Or you can bring to it certain critical faculties that may heighten, rather than diminish, your enjoyment.

You can ask yourselves whether the actors are truly in their parts or [25] merely projecting themselves; whether the scenery helps or hurts the mood; whether the playwright is honest with himself, his characters, and you. Somewhere along the line you can learn to distinguish between the true creative art and the false arbitrary gesture; between fresh observation and stale cliché; between the avant-garde play that is pretentious drivel and the avant-garde play that finds new ways to say old truths.

Purpose and craftsmanship—end and means—these are the keys to [26] your judgment in all the arts. What is this painter trying to say when he slashes a broad band of black across a white canvas and lets the edges dribble down? Is it a statement of violence? Is it a self-portrait? If it is *one* of these, has he made you believe it? Or is this a gesture of the ego or a form of therapy? If it shocks you, what does it shock you into?

And what of this tight little painting of bright flowers in a vase? Is [27] the painter saying anything new about flowers? Is it different from a million other canvases of flowers? Has it any life, any meaning, beyond its statement? Is there any pleasure in its forms or texture? The question is not whether a thing is abstract or representational, whether it is "modern" or conventional. The question, inexorably, is whether it is good. And this is a decision which only you, on the basis of instinct, experience, and association, can make for yourself. It takes independence and courage. It involves, moreover, the risk of wrong decision and the humility, after the passage of time, of recognizing it as such. As we grow and change and learn, our attitudes can change too, and what we once thought obscure or "difficult" can later emerge as coherent and illuminating. Entrenched prejudices, obdurate opinions are as sterile as no opinions at all.   28

Yet standards there are, timeless as the universe itself. And when you have committed yourself to them, you have acquired a passport to that elusive but immutable realm of truth. Keep it with you in the forests of bewilderment. And never be afraid to speak up.

COMPREHENSION

1. What is the author's thesis? Where does she state it most emphatically?

2. What examples does Mannes provide of the "abdication from the responsibility of judgment" (paragraph 4)?

3. Explain Mannes's criteria, or standards, for judging excellence in the arts.

RHETORIC

1. Account for the author's use of the pronoun *you* in addressing her audience. How does it affect tone, notably at the end of the essay?

2. Explain Mannes's strategy of formulating questions, starting with the title and moving consistently through the essay to the conclusion.

3. Where does the author's introduction end? Analyze the material presented in the introduction and the rhetorical strategies involved. What paragraphs constitute the conclusion of the essay? Describe the nature of the conclusion.

4. Explain the function of paragraphs 5 to 9.

5. How does Mannes employ illustration to structure paragraphs 10 to 25? Analyze the main stages in the organization of this section.

6. Explain the author's use of process and causal analysis in the essay.

WRITING

1. Mannes maintains that standards are absolutely necessary in distinguishing good from bad work in the arts. Do you agree or disagree with her premise? Why? What standards do you employ in determining whether an artistic product is good or bad?

2. Write your own essay entitled "How Do You Know It's Good?" Focus on some aspect of music, art, literature, or film that you know well.

3. Evaluate one literary, artistic, or media work, making clear the standards you are applying.

4. Analyze the various models—personal, cultural, and artistic—in your own life.

5. Explore the types of literature, art, film, and music that you like. How do these varieties of art influence your life?

CLASSIC AND CONTEMPORARY

ROBERT WARSHOW   Robert Warshow (1917–1955) attended the University of Michigan and worked for the U.S. Army Security Agency from 1942 to 1946. After the war, he served as an editor of *Commentary,* writing film criticism for this magazine and also for *Partisan Review.* Before his untimely death from a heart attack, Warshow had written several brilliant essays on film and on popular culture. Writing of Warshow, Lionel Trilling observed, "I believe that certain of his pieces establish themselves in the line of Hazlitt, a tradition in which I would place only one other writer of our time, George Orwell." One of these brilliant essays, focusing on the interrelation of film and society, is "The Gangster as Tragic Hero," which appeared in *The Immediate Experience: Movies, Games, Theatre and Other Aspects of Popular Culture* (1962).

ROBERT WARSHOW

The Gangster as Tragic Hero

America, as a social and political organization, is committed to a cheerful view of life. It could not be otherwise. The sense of tragedy is a luxury of aristocratic societies, where the fate of the individual is not conceived of as having a direct and legitimate political importance, being determined by a fixed and supra-political—that is, non-controversial—moral order or fate. Modern equalitarian societies, however, whether democratic or authoritarian in their political forms, always base themselves on the claim that they are making life happier; the avowed function of the modern state, at least in its ultimate terms, is not only to regulate social relations, but also to determine the quality and possibilities of human life in general. Happiness thus becomes the chief political issue—in a sense, the only political issue—and for that reason it can never be treated as an issue at all. If an American or a Russian is unhappy, it implies a certain reprobation of his society, and therefore, by a logic of which we can all recognize the necessity, it becomes an obligation of citizenship to be cheerful; if the authorities find it necessary, the citizen may even be compelled to make a public display of his cheerfulness on important occasions, just as he may be conscripted into the army in time of war.

Naturally, this civic responsibility rests most strongly upon the ₂
organs of mass culture. The individual citizen may still be permitted his
private unhappiness so long as it does not take on political significance,
the extent of this tolerance being determined by how large an area of
private life the society can accommodate. But every production of mass
culture is a public act and must conform with accepted notions of the
public good. Nobody seriously questions the principle that it is the
function of mass culture to maintain public morale, and certainly
nobody in the mass audience objects to having his morale maintained.[1]
At a time when the normal condition of the citizen is a state of anxiety,
euphoria spreads over our culture like the broad smile of an idiot. In
terms of attitudes towards life, there is very little difference between a
"happy" movie like *Good News,* which ignores death and suffering, and
a "sad" movie like *A Tree Grows in Brooklyn,* which uses death and suffering as incidents in the service of a higher optimism.

But, whatever its effectiveness as a source of consolation and a ₃
means of pressure for maintaining "positive" social attitudes, this optimism is fundamentally satisfying to no one, not even to those who
would be most disoriented without its support. Even within the area of
mass culture, there always exists a current of opposition, seeking to
express by whatever means are available to it that sense of desperation
and inevitable failure which optimism itself helps to create. Most often,
this opposition is confined to rudimentary or semi-literate forms: in
mob politics and journalism, for example, or in certain kinds of religious enthusiasm. When it does enter the field of art, it is likely to be
disguised or attenuated: in an unspecific form of expression like jazz, in
the basically harmless nihilism of the Marx Brothers, in the continually
reasserted strain of hopelessness that often seems to be the real meaning of the soap opera. The gangster film is remarkable in that it fills the
need for disguise (though not sufficiently to avoid arousing uneasiness)
without requiring any serious distortion. From its beginnings, it has
been a consistent and astonishingly complete presentation of the modern sense of tragedy.[2]

In its initial character, the gangster film is simply one example of ₄
the movies' constant tendency to create fixed dramatic patterns that
can be repeated indefinitely with a reasonable expectation of profit.
One gangster film follows another as one musical or one Western follows another. But this rigidity is not necessarily opposed to the require-

---

[1]In her testimony before the House Committee on Un-American Activities, Mrs. Leila
Rogers said that the movie *None But the Lonely Heart* was un-American because it was
gloomy. Like so much else that was said during the unhappy investigation of Hollywood,
this statement was at once stupid and illuminating. One knew immediately what Mrs.
Rogers was talking about; she had simply been insensitive enough to carry her philistinism to its conclusion.

[2]Efforts have been made from time to time to bring the gangster film into line with the
prevailing optimism and social constructiveness of our culture; *Kiss of Death* is a recent
example. These efforts are usually unsuccessful; the reasons for their lack of success are
interesting in themselves, but I shall not be able to discuss them here.

ments of art. There have been very successful types of art in the past which developed such specific and detailed conventions as almost to make individual examples of the type interchangeable. This is true, for example, of Elizabethan revenge tragedy and Restoration comedy.

For such a type to be successful means that its conventions have imposed themselves upon the general consciousness and become the accepted vehicles of a particular set of attitudes and a particular aesthetic effect. One goes to any individual example of the type with very definite expectations, and originality is to be welcomed only in the degree that it intensifies the expected experience without fundamentally altering it. Moreover, the relationship between the conventions which go to make up such a type and the real experience of its audience or the real facts of whatever situation it pretends to describe is of only secondary importance and does not determine its aesthetic force. It is only in an ultimate sense that the type appeals to its audience's experience of reality; much more immediately, it appeals to previous experience of the type itself: it creates its own field of reference.

Thus the importance of the gangster film, and the nature and intensity of its emotional and aesthetic impact, cannot be measured in terms of the place of the gangster himself or the importance of the problem of crime in American life. Those European movie-goers who think there is a gangster on every corner in New York are certainly deceived, but defenders of the "positive" side of American culture are equally deceived if they think it relevant to point out that most Americans have never seen a gangster. What matters is that the experience of the gangster *as an experience of art* is universal to Americans. There is almost nothing we understand better or react to more readily or with quicker intelligence. The Western film, though it seems never to diminish in popularity, is for most of us no more than the folklore of the past, familiar and understandable only because it has been repeated so often. The gangster film comes much closer. In ways that we do not easily or willingly define, the gangster speaks for us, expressing that part of the American psyche which rejects the qualities and the demands of modern life, which rejects "Americanism" itself.

The gangster is the man of the city, with the city's language and knowledge, with its queer and dishonest skills and its terrible daring, carrying his life in his hands like a placard, like a club. For everyone else, there is at least the theoretical possibility of another world—in that happier American culture which the gangster denies, the city does not really exist; it is only a more crowded and more brightly lit country—but for the gangster there is only the city; he must inhabit it in order to personify it: not the real city, but that dangerous and sad city of the imagination which is so much more important, which is the modern world. And the gangster—though there are real gangsters—is also, and primarily, a creature of the imagination. The real city, one might say, produces only criminals; the imaginary city produces the gangster: he is what we want to be and what we are afraid we may become.

Thrown into the crowd without background or advantages, with only 8 those ambiguous skills which the rest of us—the real people of the real city—can only pretend to have, the gangster is required to make his way, to make his life and impose it on others. Usually, when we come upon him, he has already made his choice or the choice has already been made for him, it doesn't matter which: we are not permitted to ask whether at some point he could have chosen to be something else than what he is.

The gangster's activity is actually a form of rational enterprise, 9 involving fairly definite goals and various techniques for achieving them. But this rationality is usually no more than a vague background; we know, perhaps, that the gangster sells liquor or that he operates a numbers racket; often we are not given even that much information. So his activity becomes a kind of pure criminality: he hurts people. Certainly our response to the gangster film is most consistently and most universally a response to sadism; we gain the double satisfaction of participating vicariously in the gangster's sadism and then seeing it turned against the gangster himself.

But on another level the quality of irrational brutality and the qual- 10 ity of rational enterprise become one. Since we do not see the rational and routine aspects of the gangster's behavior, the practice of brutality—the quality of unmixed criminality—becomes the totality of his career. At the same time, we are always conscious that the whole meaning of this career is a drive for success: the typical gangster film presents a steady upward progress followed by a very precipitate fall. Thus brutality itself becomes at once the means to success and the content of success—a success that is defined in its most general terms, not as accomplishment or specific gain, but simply as the unlimited possibility of aggression. (In the same way, film presentations of businessmen tend to make it appear that they achieve their success by talking on the telephone and holding conferences and that success *is* talking on the telephone and holding conferences.)

From this point of view, the initial contact between the film and its 11 audience is an agreed conception of human life: that man is a being with the possibilities of success or failure. This principle, too, belongs to the city; one must emerge from the crowd or else one is nothing. On that basis the necessity of the action is established, and it progresses, by inalterable paths to the point where the gangster lies dead and the principle has been modified: there is really only one possibility—failure. The final meaning of the city is anonymity and death.

In the opening scene of *Scarface*, we are shown a successful man; we 12 know he is successful because he has just given a party of opulent proportions and because he is called Big Louie. Through some monstrous lack of caution, he permits himself to be alone for a few moments. We understand from this immediately that he is about to be killed. No convention of the gangster film is more strongly established than this: it is dangerous to be alone. And yet the very conditions of success make it impossible not to be alone, for success is always the establishment of an *individual* pre-eminence that must be imposed on others, in whom it automatically arouses hatred; the successful man is an outlaw. The gangster's whole life is an effort to assert himself as an individual, to draw himself out of the crowd, and he always dies *because* he is an individual; the final bullet thrusts him back, makes him, after all, a failure. "Mother of God," says the dying Little Caesar, "is this the end of Rico?"—speaking of himself thus in the third person because what has been brought low is not the undifferentiated *man,* but the individual with a name, the gangster, the success; even to himself he is a creature of the imagination. (T. S. Eliot has pointed out that a number of Shakespeare's tragic heroes have this trick of looking at themselves dramatically; their true identity, the thing that is destroyed when they die, is something outside themselves—not a man, but a style of life, a kind of meaning.)

At bottom, the gangster is doomed because he is under the obligation to succeed, not because the means he employs are unlawful. In the deeper layers of the modern consciousness, *all* means are unlawful, every attempt to succeed is an act of aggression, leaving one alone and guilty and defenseless among enemies: one is *punished* for success. This is our intolerable dilemma; that failure is a kind of death and success is evil and dangerous, is—ultimately—impossible. The effect of the gangster film is to embody this dilemma in the person of the gangster and resolve it by his death. The dilemma is resolved because it is *his* death, not ours. We are safe; for the moment, we can acquiesce in our failure, we can choose to fail. 13

COMPREHENSION

1. What are the "organs of mass culture"? What properties do they all have in common?
2. Define the term "tragic hero" as Warshow uses it in his title.
3. Compare and contrast Warhow's concepts of the "real city" with those of the "imaginary city" as they relate to modern life and mass culture.

RHETORIC

1. Although the ultimate focus of the essay is on the "gangster," the subject is not referred to until paragraph 4. Why does the author need so much exposition before focusing on his main topic?
2. What do terms such as "supra-political" (paragraph 1), "harmless nihilism," (paragraph 3), and "general consciousness" (paragraph 5) suggest about the tone of the essay? What do they imply concerning the target audience for the essay?
3. Study the topic sentence of each paragraph. Are they successful in setting up the subject matter for the material which follows? How does this enhance or detract from the coherence of the author's argument?
4. Essayists usually provide their thesis at the beginning of their essays. Where is the thesis provided in Warshow's essay? What is the purpose and effect of placing it where it is?

5. The author explains the nature of the gangster film genre—its function, characters, themes, plots, meanings, and so on—*before* he cites specific films. Is this a rhetorical weakness in the essay, or does it give the essay particular potency? Explain.

6. Does the conclusion summarize the main points of the essay, bolster them, provide new insights into them, or does it do a combination of these things? Explain.

7. Study the introductory paragraph and the conclusion. What themes are reiterated or complemented? How do these two paragraphs serve to provide both thematic and structural coherence?

WRITING

1. Select a genre of television show or movie. Analyze its conventions and to what degree these conventions transgress the implicit values of our society.

2. Select a contemporary gangster movie. Using Warshow's criteria, demonstrate—via reference to its characters, plot, and theme—how your selection reinforces the author's thesis.

3. Argue for or against the proposition that genre movies are escapism that distorts the individual's concept of true society and its citizens.

RON ROSENBAUM   Ron Rosenbaum is a novelist and journalist who has written cover stories for *Harper's, The New Republic, Esquire, Vanity Fair,* and other publications. He grew up in Brightwaters, New York; graduated from Yale University; and currently lives in lower Manhattan. He is the author of the novel, *Murder at Elaine's* (1978), *Manhattan Passions* (1987), and *Travels with Dr. Death* (1991). Rosenbaum is known for his witty and intelligent perspectives on the values of our age. The following is an excerpt from an article published in the *New York Times Magazine* in 1995.

RON ROSENBAUM

The Theology of Pulp Fiction

Perhaps it's understandable that so much of the crit-chat discussion   1
about "Pulp Fiction" has missed the point: the flashy violence, trashy language and bloody brain spatterings are red herrings that easily distract.

In fact, in its own sly but serious way, "Pulp Fiction" is engaged in   2
a sustained inquiry into the theological problem of the relativity of good and evil. What I love about Quentin Tarantino's screenplay is how apparently throwaway time-passing dialogue often embodies tricky theological questions.

Consider the much-discussed but little-understood "mindless chit-   3
chat" about the French names for Big Macs and Quarter Pounders with cheese that preoccupies the hit men, Vincent and Jules, as they

478

cruise through L.A. on the way to commit a contract hit for their big-time drug-dealer boss.

Just two bored "thick-witted hit men" (as the jacket copy for the published version of the screenplay inaccurately describes them) filling time. No, wrong: the Quarter Pounder exchange is one of the key poles of the sophisticated philosophic argument underlying "Pulp Fiction."

Like the discussion of the contextual legality of hash bars in Amsterdam ("It's legal, but it ain't a hundred percent legal") and the gender-based framework for judging the transgressiveness of giving the boss's wife a foot massage ("You're sayin' a foot massage don't mean nothin' and I'm sayin' it does. . . . We act like they don't, but they do"), the exchange about Quarter Pounders is ultimately about the relativity of systems of value. 5

They have to call a Quarter Pounder with cheese a "Royale with cheese" in Paris, Vincent explains to Jules. 6

"You know why they call it that?" Jules later asks one of the small-time dealers he and Vincent are about to murder. 7

"Because of the metric system?" the dealer guesses correctly. Jules praises his intelligence before shooting him. The grams of the metric system, the pounds and ounces of the Anglo-Saxon avoirdupois system are systems of value, yes, but still just different names for the same thing, different ways of expressing the weight and value of the same greasy slab of meat, a suggestion that all systems of values, categories like good and evil are just names given to behavior, names that carry no real weight themselves but merely reflect the different linguistic and cultural frameworks of the namer—of whoever holds the power or the franchise to give the name. A multiculturalist, relativistic vision of burgers. One that is challenged, however, by the introduction of the Big Kahuna Burger into this conversation—and the manifestation of the Big Kahuna himself. 8

Big Kahuna is the Hawaiian phrase for high priest, and Big Kahuna Burger is from "that Hawaiian burger joint," the one that has supplied the burger that the doomed small-timer is eating when the hit men call. "That's a tasty burger," says Jules, taking a bite out of his victim's meal. He offers one to Vincent, who declines, saying, "I ain't hungry"—the division between them over Big Kahuna Burgers foreshadowing the division between them over the imminent manifestation of the Big Kahuna, the "divine intervention," as Jules comes to call it, that ensues. A hidden confederate of the doomed small-time dealer emerges from the bathroom, firing point-blank at Jules and Vincent. All the bullets miss. ("God came down from heaven and stopped the bullets," Jules insists. It "was a [expletive] miracle. . . . I felt God's touch.") 9

The invocation of the Big Kahuna challenges the ironies of nominalism (it's all in the name) and ethical relativism (it's all in the frame) that have been flickering back and forth in the Quarter Pounder dialogue. Challenges them by posing absolutism beyond (or beneath) frameworks, points of view and eyes-of-beholders, forcing Jules to question his own comfortable framework, something Vincent never does. 10

Jules is a guy who has previously been discussing the fine points of 11
the ethics of foot massages while killing time before executing a contract murder for a crime boss. Within his framework, murder is not a
violation of any code but a fulfillment of the ethics of loyalty and justice. (He's carrying out a sentence.) Before the Big Kahuna, we are in,
with Jules, the ethically relative framework of the "Godfather" movies,
where family values can include coldblooded murder and still seem like
virtues. But suddenly he rejects the "tyranny of the evil man" for a
transcendent framework.

Still, the film doesn't blindly junk relativism for absolutism about 12
good and evil; it's intelligent and self-conscious enough to see the problem in accepting the Big Kahuna's presentation.

"*You* witnessed" a miracle, Vincent tells Jules. "*I* witnessed a freak 13
occurrence."

"You don't judge [expletive] like this based on merit," Jules says. 14
"Whether or not what we experienced was an according-to-Hoyle miracle is insignificant. What is significant is I felt God's touch. God got
involved."

Which is an answer, but is it the answer to the $64,000 question, the 15
problem of how to get back beyond relative frameworks to some
absolute shared sense of evil?

Leaving it up to whether one feels "God's touch" can be dicey: the 16
people who murder abortion doctors claim to feel God's touch; terror
bombers say they feel God's touch. In the search for absolutes we may
be back to personal frameworks again. Perhaps it's comforting that
philosophers have as much difficulty as hit men in deciding what's the
Big Kahuna and what's just another Whopper.

COMPREHENSION

1. The author refers to *Pulp Fiction* as a "sustained inquiry into the theological problem of the relativity of good and evil." Explain this phrase in your
   own words.
2. The author uses some specialized terminology from the discipline of philosophy, terms such as *absolutism, nominalism,* and *ethical relativism.*
   Refer to a dictionary or an encyclopedia of philosophy to make sure you
   understand the meanings of these terms.
3. The author suggests that *Pulp Fiction* challenges the viewer to reflect on a
   major argument concerning ethics. What is this argument?

RHETORIC

1. The essay infuses a playful, contemporary tone into the framework of a
   classic argument. How does this blend reflect the writer's unique voice?
2. Study the following sentence from paragraph 2 in terms of syntax and
   sound. "What I love about Quentin Tarantino's screenplay is how apparently throwaway time-passing dialogue often embodies tricky theological
   questions." Does it have a particular aesthetic ring to it? Why, or why not?

3. The author claims that the film has a "sly but serious way." What examples does he provide to support this contention? How does the style of the essay itself mirror the style of the film?

4. What do you think the author assumes about his audience, particularly regarding its entertainment habits, level of education, breadth of education, and ability to "decode" various forms of diction? What does this implicitly suggest about the contemporary reading public?

5. Locate the numerous use of parenthetical phrases in the essay. Why are they used so frequently? What are some of the various functions they serve?

6. How would you best "label" this essay: film review, critique, interpretation, summary? Explain your view.

7. The conclusion—like much of the essay—mixes humor, informal language, and pop-culture references with profound questions of human existence. How does the author use language to combine all these elements in order to resolve these seemingly disparate domains?

WRITING

1. The poet William Blake said that you could find "the universe in a grain of sand." Argue for or against the proposition that everyday occurrences can lend themselves to profound questions of existence.

2. Write an account of a time in your life when something occurred to you that defied rational explanation.

3. Argue for or against the proposition that concerns over the nature and meaning of popular culture are far too prevalent today considering the more pressing issues that need to be addressed, issues such as hunger, homelessness, genocide, injustice, and so on.

CLASSIC AND CONTEMPORARY: QUESTIONS FOR COMPARISON

1. Compare the rhetorical strategies and levels of language used by Warshow and Rosenbaum in their essays, as well as the main points each is making. Pay special attention to the vocabulary and diction used by the writers.

2. Using Warshow's conception of the gangster as "tragic hero," consider how he would evaluate *Pulp Fiction*. Would he concur with Rosenbaum's analysis of good and evil? Why, or why not?

3. Select your own gangster film, and write an assessment of it incorporating the ideas of both Warshow and Rosenbaum.

CONNECTIONS

1. Examine the role of the media in society and the responsibilities or duties to humanity of individuals associated with the media. Use at least three essays from this section to illustrate or support your thesis.

2. Define *popular culture,* using the essays of Updike and Gates as reference points, along with any additional essays that you consider relevant.

3. Judging from her essay, how do you think that Mannes would respond to the work of Georgia O'Keeffe? How do you think Didion knows O'Keeffe's work is good?

4. Write an essay exploring the importance of role models in literature, media, and the arts, especially for women and minorities. Use the writing of Didion and Walker to address this issue.

5. Write an essay comparing and contrasting the essays by Winn and Barry. What merits do their respective arguments have? Are there any limitations to their approaches? Which essay do you find more convincing, and why?

6. Use the essays of Updike, Warshow, and Rosenbaum to explore the connections of American film to national experience. What strategies do these writers use? Are their goals similar?

7. In their essays, Gates and Walker refer to the African-American experience in music and literature. Do they have similar theses or differing points of view? Refer specifically to segments of both essays to support your position.

CHAPTER TEN

Philosophy, Ethics, and Religion

You do not have to be an academician in an ivory tower to think about religion and the destiny of humankind or about questions of right and wrong. All of us possess beliefs about human nature and conduct, about "rival conceptions of God" (to use C. S. Lewis's phrase), about standards of behavior and moral duty. In fact, as Robert Coles argues in an essay appearing in this chapter, even children make ethical choices every day and are attuned to the "moral currents and issues in the larger society."

Most of us have a system of ethical and religious beliefs, a philosophy of sorts, although it may not be a fully logical and systematic philosophy. This system of beliefs and values is transmitted to us by family members, friends, educators, religious figures, and representatives of social groups. Such a philosophical system is not unyielding or unchanging because our typical conflicts and the choices that we make often force us to test our ethical assumptions and our values. For example, you may believe in nonviolence, but what would you do if someone threatened physical harm to you or a loved one? Or you may support the death penalty but encounter an essay—perhaps Coretta Scott King's—that causes you to reassess your position. Our beliefs about nonviolence, capital punishment, abortion, cheating, equality, and so on are often paradoxical and place us in a universe of ethical dilemmas.

Your ability to resolve such dilemmas and make complex ethical decisions depends on your storehouse of knowledge and experience and on how well formulated your philosophy or system of belief is. When you know what is truly important in your life, you can make choices and decisions carefully and responsibly. Yet as Plato observes in his classic "The Allegory of the Cave," the idea of what is truly good and correct never appears without wisdom and effort.

In this context, religion is also intrinsically connected to our sense of morality and ethics. Our personal code of ethics often has a religious grounding. Our religion often determines the way in which we apply our ethics—for instance, it may determine our attitude toward contraception, equality of the races or the sexes, and evolution. In all instances, competing religious and secular values may force us to make hard decisions about our positions on significant cultural issues.

At the end of this section, Virginia Woolf and Annie Dillard contemplate a seemingly insignificant creature—a moth—that tells them (and us) a great deal about life and death. They seek the "essence" of existence in the moth's struggle. We, too, engage in a life struggle; and the values and ideas that we develop during our brief moment on this planet are what lend meaning and vitality to our lives.

Previewing the Chapter

As you read the essays in this chapter and respond to them in discussion and writing, consider the following questions:

• On what ethical or religious problem or conflict does the author focus?

• Is the author's view of life optimistic or pessimistic? Why?

• Do you agree or disagree with the philosophical or religious perspective that the author adopts?

• Is there a clear solution to the issue the author investigates?

• Does the author present rational arguments or engage in emotional appeals and weak reasoning?

• Does the author approach ethical, theological, and philosophical issues in an objective or in a subjective way?

• How significant is the ethical or philosophical subject addressed by the author?

• What social, political, or racial issues are raised by the author?

• Are there religious dimensions to the essay? If so, how does religion reinforce the author's philosophical inquiry?

• How do these essays encourage you to examine your own attitudes and values? In reading them, what do you discover about your own system of beliefs and the beliefs of society at large?

H. L. MENCKEN H(enry) L(ouis) Mencken (1880–1956) was an American editor, author, and critic. Born in Baltimore, he served as an editor for three Baltimore newspapers: the *Morning Herald, Evening Herald,* and *The Baltimore Sun.* Noted for his pungent and iconoclastic criticism, he regaled in satirizing the middle classes. He was also a student of philology and published *The American Language,* which went through several editions with added supplements. The topics for his many books ranged from studies of dramatists to the defense of women's rights. He was also a champion for a whole generation of American realist fiction writers, including Theodore Dreiser, Sherwood Anderson, Sinclair Lewis, and Eugene O'Neill. The following well-known essay reveals the hypocrisy behind the rationale many people give for supporting the death penalty and the true reason they support it.

H. L. MENCKEN

The Penalty of Death

Of the arguments against capital punishment that issue from uplifters, two are commonly heard most often, to wit:

1. That hanging a man (or frying him or gassing him) is a dreadful business, degrading to those who have to do it and revolting to those who have to witness it.

2. That it is useless, for it does not deter others from the same crime.

The first of these arguments, it seems to me, is plainly too weak to need serious refutation. All it says, in brief, is that the work of the hangman is unpleasant. Granted. But suppose it is? It may be quite necessary to society for all that. There are, indeed, many other jobs that are unpleasant, and yet no one thinks of abolishing them—that of the plumber, that of the soldier, that of the garbage-man, that of the priest hearing confessions, that of the sand-hog, and so on. Moreover, what evidence is there that any actual hangman complains of his work? I have heard none. On the contrary, I have known many who delighted in their ancient art, and practised it proudly.

In the second argument of the abolitionists there is rather more force, but even here, I believe, the ground under them is shaky. Their fundamental error consists in assuming that the whole aim of punishing criminals is to deter other (potential) criminals—that we hang or electrocute A simply in order to so alarm B that he will not kill C. This, I believe, is an assumption which confuses a part with the whole. Deterence, obviously, is *one* of the aims of punishment, but it is surely not the only one. On the contrary, there are at least half a dozen, and some are probably quite as important. At least one of them, practically considered, is *more* important. Commonly, it is described as revenge, but revenge is really not the word for it. I borrow a better term from the late Aristotle: *katharsis*. *Katharsis,* so used, means a salubrious discharge of emotions, a healthy letting off of steam. A school-boy, disliking his teacher, deposits a tack upon the pedagogical chair; the teacher jumps and the boy laughs. This is *katharsis*. What I contend is that one of the prime objects of all judicial punishments is to afford the same grateful relief *(a)* to the immediate victims of the criminal punished, and *(b)* to the general body of moral and timorous men.

These persons, and particularly the first group, are concerned only indirectly with deterring other criminals. The thing they crave primarily is the satisfaction of seeing the criminal actually before them suffer as he made them suffer. What they want is the peace of mind that goes with the feeling that accounts are squared. Until they get that satisfaction they are in a state of emotional tension, and hence unhappy. The instant they get it they are comfortable. I do not argue that this yearning is noble; I simply argue that it is almost universal among human beings. In the face of injuries that are unimportant and can be borne without damage it may yield to higher impulses; that is to say, it may yield to what is called Christian charity. But when the injury is serious, Christianity is adjourned, and even saints reach for their sidearms. It is plainly asking too much of human nature to expect it to conquer so natural an impulse. A keeps a store and has a bookkeeper, B. B steals $700, employs it in playing at dice or bingo, and is cleaned out. What is A to do? Let B go? If he does so he will be unable to sleep at night. The sense of injury, of injustice, of frustration will haunt him like pruritus. So he turns B over to the police, and they hustle B to prison. Thereafter A can sleep. More, he has pleasant dreams. He pictures B chained to the wall of a dungeon a hundred feet underground, devoured by rats and scorpions. It is so agreeable that it makes him forget his $700. He has got his *katharsis*.

This same thing precisely takes place on a larger scale when there is a crime which destroys a whole community's sense of security. Every law-abiding citizen feels menaced and frustrated until the criminals have been struck down—until the communal capacity to get even with them, and more than even, has been dramatically demonstrated. Here, manifestly, the business of deterring others is no more than an afterthought. The main thing is to destroy the concrete scoundrels whose act has alarmed everyone, and thus made everyone unhappy. Until they are brought to book that unhappiness continues; when the law has been executed upon them there is a sigh of relief. In other words, there is *katharsis*.

I know of no public demand for the death penalty for ordinary crimes, even for ordinary homicides. Its infliction would shock all men of normal decency of feeling. But for crimes involving the deliberate and inexcusable taking of human life, by men openly defiant of all civilized order—for such crimes it seems, to nine men out of ten, a just and proper punishment. Any lesser penalty leaves them feeling that the criminal has got the better of society—that he is free to add insult to injury by laughing. That feeling can be dissipated only by a recourse to *katharsis,* the invention of the aforesaid Aristotle. It is more effectively and economically achieved, as human nature now is, by wafting the criminal to realms of bliss.

The real objection to capital punishment doesn't lie against the actual extermination of the condemned, but against our brutal American habit of putting it off so long. After all, every one of us must die soon or late, and a murderer, it must be assumed, is one who makes that sad fact the cornerstone of his metaphysic. But it is one thing to die, and quite another thing to lie for long months and even years under the shadow of death. No sane man would choose such a finish. All of us, despite the Prayer Book, long for a swift and unexpected end. Unhappily, a murderer, under the irrational American system, is tortured for what, to him, must seem a whole series of eternities. For months on end he sits in prison while his lawyers carry on their idiotic buffoonery with writs, injunctions, mandamuses, and appeals. In order to get his money (or that of his friends) they have to feed him with hope. Now and then, by the imbecility of a judge or some trick of juridic science, they actually justify it. But let us say that, his money all gone, they finally throw up their hands. Their client is now ready for the rope or the chair. But he must still wait for months before it fetches him.

That wait, I believe, it horribly cruel. I have seen more than one man sitting in the death-house, and I don't want to see any more. Worse, it is wholly useless. Why should he wait at all? Why not hang him the day after the last court dissipates his last hope? Why torture him as not even cannibals would torture their victims? The common answer is that he must have time to make his peace with God. But how long does that take? It may be accomplished, I believe, in two hours quite as comfortably as in two years. There are, indeed, no temporal limitations upon God. He could forgive a whole herd of murderers in a millionth of a second. More, it has been done.

COMPREHENSION

1. Based upon your reading of Mencken's essay, is the author for or against capital punishment? Explain.
2. Study the last three lines of the essay. Explain what they mean in your own words.
3. The author's facility with language is due partly to his impressive vocabulary. Define words such as *salubrious, timorous,* and *manifestly.*

RHETORIC

1. The author uses symbolic logic, classification, and definition as devices in paragraphs 1 through 4. Cite examples of each of these rhetorical methods. What is each one's function?

2. What is the author's purpose in using rather droll means of argument in discussing a subject that usually elicits emotional responses?

3. In paragraph 3, the author defines *katharsis* as "a healthy letting off of steam." In the light of the author's view that carrying out the death penalty results in a societal *katharsis,* what is the implicit irony in the definition?

4. What is the author's purpose in using both the placement of a tack on a teacher's seat and the execution of a human being as examples of *katharsis.*

5. What tone does the author use in describing humankind's desire for revenge? Does he support or deride this sentiment? Explain your conclusion by citing particular clues the author provides in his writing.

6. In paragraph 4, the author states, "But when the injury is serious, Christianity is adjourned, and even saints reach for their sidearms." How does this statement relate to the theme of the essay?

WRITING

1. For a creative writing project, pretend you are a legislator. Write an essay wherein you describe a crime and what its proper particular punishment should be. Be sure to fit the punishment to the crime.

2. Argue for or against the use of the death penalty in crimes other than murder.

3. There is some evidence to suggest that the death penalty may actually *increase* the murder rate. Study this line of inquiry, and write a research paper based upon your findings that either supports or rejects the thesis.

CORETTA SCOTT KING   Coretta Scott King (b. 1927) is a civil-rights activist, free-lance journalist, and, since 1980, writer and commentator for CNN. Born in Alabama, she graduated from Antioch College and the New England Conservatory of Music. She first gained international prominence as the wife of Martin Luther King, Jr., whom she married in 1953. She wrote about her experiences with the revered civil-rights leader and orator in a book entitled *My Life with Martin Luther King, Jr.* (1969). The following essay states in clear, thoughtful prose her feelings about the death penalty, which she considers both racist and immoral.

CORETTA SCOTT KING

The Death Penalty Is a Step Back

When Steven Judy was executed in Indiana [in 1981] America took another step backwards towards legitimizing murder as a way of dealing with evil in our society.

Although Judy was convicted of four of the most horrible and brutal murders imaginable, and his case is probably the worst in recent memory for opponents of the death penalty, we still have to face the real issue squarely: Can we expect a decent society if the state is allowed to kill its own people?

In recent years, an increase of violence in America, both individual and political, has prompted a backlash of public opinion on capital punishment. But however much we abhor violence, legally sanctioned executions are no deterrent and are, in fact, immoral and unconstitutional.

Although I have suffered the loss of two family members by assassination, I remain firmly and unequivocally opposed to the death penalty for those convicted of capital offenses.

An evil deed is not redeemed by an evil deed of retaliation. Justice is never advanced in the taking of a human life.

Morality is never upheld by legalized murder. Morality apart, there are a number of practical reasons which form a powerful argument against capital punishment.

First, capital punishment makes irrevocable any possible miscarriage of justice. Time and again we have witnessed the specter of mistakenly convicted people being put to death in the name of American criminal justice. To those who say that, after all, this doesn't occur too often, I can only reply that if it happens just once, that is too often. And it has occurred many times.

Second, the death penalty reflects an unwarranted assumption that the wrongdoer is beyond rehabilitation. Perhaps some individuals cannot be rehabilitated; but who shall make that determination? Is any amount of academic training sufficient to entitle one person to judge another incapable of rehabilitation?

Third, the death penalty is inequitable. Approximately half of the 711 persons now on death row are black. From 1930 through 1968, 53.5% of those executed were black Americans, all too many of whom were represented by court-appointed attorneys and convicted after hasty trials.

The argument that this may be an accurate reflection of guilt, and homicide trends, instead of a racist application of laws lacks credibility in light of a recent Florida survey which showed that persons convicted of killing whites were four times more likely to receive a death sentence than those convicted of killing blacks.

Proponents of capital punishment often cite a "deterrent effect" as the main benefit of the death penalty. Not only is there no hard evidence that murdering murderers will deter other potential killers, but even the "logic" of this argument defies comprehension.

Numerous studies show that the majority of homicides committed in this country are the acts of the victim's relatives, friends and acquaintances in the "heat of passion."

What this strongly suggests is that rational consideration of future consequences are seldom a part of the killer's attitude at the time he commits a crime.

The only way to break the chain of violent reaction is to practice nonviolence as individuals and collectively through our laws and institutions.

489

COMPREHENSION

1. On what grounds does King oppose capital punishment?
2. King calls the death penalty "immoral" and "unconstitutional." What does she mean by this?
3. Does King offer any solutions to the problem of crime and violence? What are they?

RHETORIC

1. Where in the essay does King place her thesis statement? In your own words, what is this thesis?
2. What function do paragraphs 1 to 5 have in the essay?
3. What impact do the words *practical* and *powerful* (in paragraph 6) have on the reader? Who is King's intended audience?
4. Comment on the use of language in King's essay. Is it concrete or abstract? How would you characterize her writing style?
5. Trace King's use of transitions in paragraphs 7, 8, and 9.
6. Where does the writer use refutation in her essay? How does she use it to strengthen her argument? How effective are her responses?
7. Is King's ordering of ideas inductive or deductive? Justify your answer.

WRITING

1. Write an essay for or against capital punishment, using quotes from King's essay either as support or as refutation. Provide examples and your own observations as proof.
2. If capital punishment doesn't deter crime, what will? Write an essay in which you offer detailed solutions to the problem of crime and violence. How can society take a step forward in its treatment of criminals?
3. King's essay makes a connection between the death penalty and racism. Develop this theme in an essay. Consider the issues of class, race, legal representation, and political empowerment in determining who goes to prison and who gets executed.

ROBERT COLES   Robert Coles (b. 1929), author and psychologist, won the Pulitzer Prize in general nonfiction for volumes 1 and 2 of *Children of Crisis,* in which he examines with compassion and intelligence the effects of the controversy over integration on children in the South. Walker Percy has praised Coles because he "spends his time listening to people and trying to understand them." In its final form, *Children of Crisis* has five volumes, and Coles has widened its focus to include the children of the wealthy and the poor, the exploited and the exploiters. In collaboration with Jane Coles, he completed *Women of Crisis II* (1980). Below, Coles demonstrates his capacity to listen to and to understand children.

ROBERT COLES

I Listen to My Parents and I Wonder What They Believe

Not so long ago children were looked upon in a sentimental fashion as "angels," or as "innocents." Today, thanks to Freud and his followers, boys and girls are understood to have complicated inner lives; to feel love, hate, envy and rivalry in various and subtle mixtures; to be eager participants in the sexual and emotional politics of the home, neighborhood and school. Yet some of us parents still cling to the notion of childhood innocence in another way. We do not see that our children also make ethical decisions every day in their own lives, or realize how attuned they may be to moral currents and issues in the larger society.

In Appalachia I heard a girl of eight whose father owns coal fields (and gas stations, a department store and much timberland) wonder about "life" one day: "I'll be walking to the school bus, and I'll ask myself why there's some who are poor and their daddies can't find a job, and there's some who are lucky like me. Last month there was an explosion in a mine my daddy owns, and everyone became upset. Two miners got killed. My daddy said it was their own fault, because they'll be working and they get careless. When my mother asked if there was anything wrong with the safety down in the mine, he told her no and she shouldn't ask questions like that. Then the Government people came and they said it was the owner's fault—Daddy's. But he has a lawyer and the lawyer is fighting the Government and the union. In school, kids ask me what I think, and I sure do feel sorry for the two miners and so does my mother—I know that. She told me it's just not a fair world and you have to remember that. Of course, there's no one who can be sure there won't be trouble; like my daddy says, the rain falls on the just and the unjust. My brother is only six and he asked Daddy awhile back who are the 'just' and the 'unjust,' and Daddy said there are people who work hard and they live good lives, and there are lazy people and they're always trying to sponge off others. But I guess you have to feel sorry for anyone who has a lot of trouble, because it's poured-down, heavy rain."

Listening, one begins to realize that an elementary-school child is no stranger to moral reflection—and to ethical conflict. This girl was torn between her loyalty to her particular background, its values and assumptions, and to a larger affiliation—her membership in the nation, the world. As a human being whose parents were kind and decent to her, she was inclined to be thoughtful and sensitive with respect to others, no matter what their work or position in society. But her father was among other things a mineowner, and she had already learned to shape her concerns to suit that fact of life. The result: a moral oscillation of sorts, first toward nameless others all over the world and then toward her own family. As the girl put it later, when she was a year older: "You should try to have 'good thoughts' about everyone, the minister says, and our teacher says that too. But you should honor your father and mother most of all; that's why you should find out what they think and then sort of copy them. But sometimes you're not sure if you're on the right track."

Sort of copy them. There could be worse descriptions of how chil- 4 dren acquire moral values. In fact, the girl understood how girls and boys all over the world "sort of" develop attitudes of what is right and wrong, ideas of who the just and the unjust are. And they also struggle hard and long, and not always with success, to find out where the "right track" starts and ends. Children need encouragement or assistance as they wage that struggle.

In home after home that I have visited, and in many classrooms, I 5 have met children who not only are growing emotionally and intellectually but also are trying to make sense of the world morally. That is to say, they are asking themselves and others about issues of fair play, justice, liberty, equality. Those last words are abstractions, of course—the stuff of college term papers. And there are, one has to repeat, those in psychology and psychiatry who would deny elementary-school children access to that "higher level" of moral reflection. But any parent who has listened closely to his or her child knows that girls and boys are capable of wondering about matters of morality, and knows too that often it is their grown-up protectors (parents, relatives, teachers, neighbors) who are made uncomfortable by the so-called "innocent" nature of the questions children may ask or the statements they may make. Often enough the issue is not the moral capacity of children but the default of us parents who fail to respond to inquiries put to us by our daughters and sons—and fail to set moral standards for both ourselves and our children.

Do's and don't's are, of course, pressed upon many of our girls and 6 boys. But a moral education is something more than a series of rules handed down, and in our time one cannot assume that every parent feels able—sure enough of her own or his own actual beliefs and values—to make even an initial explanatory and disciplinary effect toward a moral education. Furthermore, for many of us parents these days it is a child's emotional life that preoccupies us.

In 1963, when I was studying school desegregation in the South, I 7 had extended conversations with Black and white elementary-school children caught up in a dramatic moment of historical change. For longer than I care to remember, I concentrated on possible psychiatric troubles, on how a given child was managing under circumstances of extreme stress, on how I could be of help—with "support," with reassurance, with a helpful psychological observation or interpretation. In many instances I was off the mark. These children weren't "patients"; they weren't even complaining. They were worried, all right, and often enough they had things to say that were substantive—that had to do not so much with troubled emotions as with questions of right and wrong in the real-life dramas taking place in their worlds.

Here is a nine-year-old white boy, the son of ardent segregationists, telling me about his sense of what desegregation meant to Louisiana in the 1960s: "They told us it wouldn't happen—never. My daddy said none of us white people would go into schools with the colored. But then it did happen, and when I went to school the first day I didn't know what would go on. Would the school stay open or would it close up? We didn't know what to do; the teacher kept telling us that we should be good and obey the law, but my daddy said the law was wrong. Then my mother said she wanted me in school even if there were some colored kids there. She said if we all stayed home she'd be a 'nervous wreck.' So I went.

"After a while I saw that the colored weren't so bad. I saw that there are different kinds of colored people, just like with us whites. There was one of the colored who was nice, a boy who smiled, and he played real good. There was another one, a boy, who wouldn't talk with anyone. I don't know if it's right that we all be in the same school. Maybe it isn't right. My sister is starting school next year, and she says she doesn't care if there's 'mixing of the races.' She says they told her in Sunday school that everyone is a child of God, and then a kid asked if that goes for the colored too and the teacher said yes, she thought so. My daddy said that it's true, God made everyone—but that doesn't mean we all have to be living together under the same roof in the home or the school. But my mother said we'll never know what God wants of us but we have to try to read His mind, and that's why we pray. So when I say my prayers I ask God to tell me what's the right thing to do. In school I try to say hello to the colored, because they're kids, and you can't be mean or you'll be 'doing wrong,' like my grandmother says."

Children aren't usually long-winded in the moral discussions they have with one another or with adults, and in quoting this boy I have pulled together comments he made to me in the course of several days. But everything he said was of interest to me. I was interested in the boy's changing racial attitudes. It was clear he was trying to find a coherent, sensible moral position too. It was also borne in on me that if one spends days, weeks in a given home, it is hard to escape a particular moral climate just as significant as the psychological one.

In many homes parents establish moral assumptions, mandates, priorities. They teach children what to believe in, what not to believe in. They teach children what is permissible or not permissible—and why. They may summon up the Bible, the flag, history, novels, aphorisms, philosophical or political sayings, personal memories—all in an effort to teach children how to behave, what and whom to respect and for which reasons. Or they may neglect to do so, and in so doing teach their children *that*—a moral abdication, of sorts—and in this way fail their children. Children need and long for words of moral advice, instruction, warning, as much as they need words of affirmation or criticism from their parents about other matters. They must learn how to dress and what to wear, how to eat and what to eat; and they must also learn how to behave under X or Y or Z conditions, and why.

All the time, in 20 years of working with poor children and rich children, Black children and white children, children from rural areas and urban areas and in every region of this country, I have heard questions—thoroughly intelligent and discerning questions—about social and historical matters, about personal behavior, and so on. But most striking is the fact that almost all those questions, in one way or another, are moral in nature: Why did the Pilgrims leave England? Why didn't they just stay and agree to do what the king wanted them to do? . . . Should you try to share all you've got or should you save a lot for yourself? . . . What do you do when you see others fighting—do you try to break up the fight, do you stand by and watch or do you leave as fast as you can? . . . Is it right that some people haven't got enough to eat? . . . I see other kids cheating and I wish I could copy the answers too; but I won't cheat, though sometimes I feel I'd like to and I get all mixed up. I go home and talk with my parents, and I ask them what should you do if you see kids cheating—pay no attention, or report the kids or do the same thing they are doing?

Those are examples of children's concerns—and surely millions of American parents have heard versions of them. Have the various "experts" on childhood stressed strongly enough the importance of such questions—and the importance of the hunger we all have, no matter what our age or background, to examine what we believe in, are willing to stand up for, and what we are determined to ask, likewise, of our children?

Children not only need our understanding of their complicated emotional lives; they also need a constant regard for the moral issues that come their way as soon as they are old enough to play with others and take part in the politics of the nursery, the back yard and the schoolroom. They need to be told what they must do and what they must not do. They need control over themselves and a sense of what others are entitled to from them—cooperation, thoughtfulness, an attentive ear and eye. They need discipline not only to tame their excesses of emotion but discipline also connected to stated and clarified moral values. They need, in other words, something to believe in that is larger than their own appetites and urges and, yes, bigger than their "psychological drives." They need a larger view of the world, a moral context, as it were—a faith that addresses itself to the meaning of this life we all live and, soon enough, let go of.

Yes, it is time for us parents to begin to look more closely at what ideas our children have about the world; and it would be well to do so before they become teenagers and young adults and begin to remind us, as often happens, of how little attention we did pay to their moral development. Perhaps a nine-year-old girl from a well-off suburban home in Texas put it better than anyone else I've met:

I listen to my parents, and I wonder what they believe in more than anything else. I asked my mom and my daddy once: What's the thing that means most to you? They said they didn't know but I shouldn't worry my head too hard with questions like that. So I asked my best friend, and she said she wonders if there's a God and how do you know Him and what does He want you to do—I mean, when you're in school or out playing with your friends. They talk about God in church, but is it only in church that He's there and keeping an eye on you? I saw a kid steal in a store, and I know her father has a lot of money—because I hear my daddy talk. But stealing's wrong. My mother said she's a 'sick girl,' but it's still wrong what she did. Don't you think?

There was more—much more—in the course of the months I came   16
to know that child and her parents and their neighbors. But those observations and questions—a "mere child's"—reminded me unforgettably of the aching hunger for firm ethical principles that so many of us feel. Ought we not begin thinking about this need? Ought we not all be asking ourselves more intently what standards we live by—and how we can satisfy our children's hunger for moral values?

COMPREHENSION

1. How does the author's title capture the substance of his essay? What is his thesis?
2. According to Coles, why do parents have difficulty explaining ethics to their children? On what aspects of their children's development do they tend to concentrate? Why?
3. There is an implied contrast between mothers' and fathers' attitudes toward morality in Coles's essay. Explain this contrast, and cite examples for your explanation.

RHETORIC

1. What point of view does Coles use here? How does that viewpoint affect the tone of the essay?
2. Compare Coles's sentence structure with the sentence structure of the children he quotes. How do they differ?
3. Does this essay present an inductive or a deductive argument? Give evidence for your answer.
4. How does paragraph 13 differ from paragraphs 3, 10, and 16? How do all four paragraphs contribute to the development of the essay?
5. Explain the line of reasoning in the first paragraph. Why does Coles allude to Freud? How is that allusion related to the final sentence of the paragraph?
6. What paragraphs constitute the conclusion of the essay? Why? How do they summarize Coles's argument?

1. Coles asserts the need for clear ethical values. How have your parents provided such values? What kind of values will you give your children?
2. Write an essay describing conflict between your parents' ethical views and your own.
3. Gather evidence, from conversations with your friends and relatives, about an ethical issue such as poverty, world starvation, abortion, or capital punishment. Incorporate their opinions in your essay through direct and indirect quotation.
4. Compare Coles's observations in this essay with those of Hayakawa in "Words and Children" (Chapter 8).

PLATO   Plato (427?–347 B.C.), pupil and friend of Socrates, was one of the greatest philosophers of the ancient world. Plato's surviving works are all dialogues and epistles, many of the dialogues purporting to be conversations of Socrates and his disciples. Two key aspects of his philosophy are the dialectical method—represented by the questioning and probing of the particular event to reveal the general truth—and the existence of Forms. Plato's best-known works include the *Phaedo, Symposium, Phaedrus,* and *Timaeus.* The following selection, from the *Republic,* is an early description of the nature of Forms.

PLATO

The Allegory of the Cave

And now, I said, let me show in a figure how far our nature is enlightened or unenlightened: Behold! human beings living in an underground den, which has a mouth open towards the light and reaching all along the den; here they have been from their childhood, and have their legs and necks chained so that they cannot move, and can only see before them, being prevented by the chains from turning round their heads. Above and behind them a fire is blazing at a distance, and between the fire and the prisoners there is a raised way; and you will see, if you look, a low wall built along the way, like the screen which marionette players have in front of them, over which they show the puppets.

I see.

And do you see, I said, men passing along the wall carrying all sorts of vessels, and statues and figures of animals made of wood and stone and various materials, which appear over the wall? Some of them are talking, others silent.

You have shown me a strange image, and they are strange prisoners.

Like ourselves, I replied; and they see only their own shadows, or
the shadows of one another, which the fire throws on the opposite wall
of the cave?

True, he said; how could they see anything but the shadows if they
were never allowed to move their heads?

And of the objects which are being carried in like manner they
would only see the shadows?

Yes, he said.

And if they were able to converse with one another, would they not
suppose that they were naming what was actually before them?

Very true.

10

And suppose further that the prison had an echo which came from
the other side, would they not be sure to fancy when one of the passers-
by spoke that the voice which they heard came from the passing
shadow?

No question, he replied.

To them, I said, the truth would be literally nothing but the shadows
of the images.

That is certain.

And now look again, and see what will naturally follow if the prisoners are released and disabused of their error. At first, when any of
them is liberated and compelled suddenly to stand up and turn his neck
round and walk and look towards the light, he will suffer sharp pains;
the glare will distress him and he will be unable to see the realities of
which in his former state he had seen the shadows; and then conceive
some one saying to him, that what he saw before was an illusion, but
that now, when he is approaching nearer to being and his eye is turned
towards more real existence, he has a clearer vision—what will be his
reply? And you may further imagine that his instructor is pointing to
the objects as they pass and requiring him to name them—will he not
be perplexed? Will he not fancy that the shadows which he formerly
saw are truer than the objects which are now shown to him?

Far truer.

And if he is compelled to look straight at the light, will he not have
a pain in his eyes which will make him turn away to take refuge in the
objects of vision which he can see, and which he will conceive to be in
reality clearer than the things which are now being shown to him?

True, he said.

And suppose once more, that he is reluctantly dragged up a steep
and rugged ascent, and held fast until he is forced into the presence of
the sun himself, is he not likely to be pained and irritated? When he
approaches the light his eyes will be dazzled and he will not be able to
see anything at all of what are now called realities.

Not all in a moment, he said.

20

He will require to grow accustomed to the sight of the upper world.
And first he will see the shadows best, next the reflections of men and
other objects in the water, and then the objects themselves; then he will
gaze upon the light of the moon and the stars and the spangled heaven;

and he will see the sky and the stars by night better than the sun or the light of the sun by day?

Certainly. 22

Last of all he will be able to see the sun, and not mere reflections of 23 him in the water, but he will see him in his own proper place, and not in another; and he will contemplate him as he is.

Certainly. 24

He will then proceed to argue that this is he who gives the season 25 and the years, and is the guardian of all that is in the visible world, and in a certain way the cause of all things which he and his fellows have been accustomed to behold?

Clearly, he said, he would first see the sun and then reason about 26 him.

And when he remembered his old habitation, and the wisdom of the 27 den and his fellow-prisoners, do you not suppose that he would felicitate himself on the change, and pity them?

Certainly, he would. 28

And if they were in the habit of conferring honors among them- 29 selves on those who were quickest to observe the passing shadows and to remark which of them went before, and which followed after, and which were together; and who were therefore best able to draw conclusions as to the future, do you think that he would care for such honors and glories, or envy the possessors of them? Would he not say with Homer, Better to be the poor servant of a poor master, and to endure anything, rather than think as they do and live after their manner?

Yes, he said, I think that he would rather suffer anything than enter- 30 tain these false notions and live in this miserable manner.

Imagine once more, I said, such as one coming suddenly out of the 31 sun to be replaced in his old situation; would he not be certain to have his eyes full of darkness?

To be sure, he said. 32

And if there were a contest, and he had to compete in measuring 33 the shadows with the prisoners who had never moved out of the den, while his sight was still weak, and before his eyes had become steady (and the time which would be needed to acquire this new habit of sight might be very considerable) would he not be ridiculous? Men would say of him that up he went and down he came without his eyes; and that it was better not even to think of ascending; and if any one tried to loose another and lead him up to the light, let them only catch the offender, and they would put him to death.

No question, he said. 34

This entire allegory, I said, you may now append, dear Glaucon, to 35 the previous argument; the prison-house is the world of sight, the light of fire is the sun, and you will not misapprehend me if you interpret the journey upwards to be the ascent of the soul into the intellectual world according to my poor belief, which, at your desire, I have expressed—whether rightly or wrongly God knows. But, whether true or false, my opinion is that in the world of knowledge the idea of good appears last of all, and is seen only with an effort; and, when seen, is also inferred to be the universal author of all things beautiful and right, parent of light and of the lord of light in this visible world, and the immediate source of reason and truth in the intellectual; and that this is the power upon which he who would act rationally either in public or private life must have his eye fixed.

I agree, he said, as far as I am able to understand you. 36

Moreover, I said, you must not wonder that those who attain to this 37 beautiful vision are unwilling to descend to human affairs; for their souls are ever hastening into the upper world where they desire to dwell; which desire of theirs is very natural, if our allegory may be trusted.

Yes, very natural. 38

And is there anything surprising in one who passes from divine 39 contemplations to the evil state of man, misbehaving himself in a ridiculous manner; if, while his eyes are blinking and before he has become accustomed to the surrounding darkness, he is compelled to fight in courts of law, or in other places, about the images or the shadows of images of justice, and is endeavouring to meet the conceptions of those who have never yet seen absolute justice?

Anything but surprising, he replied. 40

Any one who has common sense will remember that the bewilder- 41 ments of the eyes are of two kinds, and arise from two causes, either from coming out of the light or from going into the light, which is true of the mind's eye, quite as much as of the bodily eye; and he who remembers this when he sees any one whose vision is perplexed and weak, will not be too ready to laugh; he will first ask whether that soul of man has come out of the brighter light, and is unable to see because unaccustomed to the dark, or having turned from darkness to the day is dazzled by excess of light. And he will count the one happy in his condition and state of being, and he will pity the other; or, if he have a mind to laugh at the soul which comes from below into the light, there will be more reason in this than in the laugh which greets him who returns from above out of the light into the den.

That, he said, is a very just distinction. 42

COMPREHENSION

1. What does Plato hope to convey to readers of his allegory?
2. According to Plato, do human beings typically perceive reality? To what does he compare the world?
3. According to Plato, what often happens to people who develop a true idea of reality? How well do they compete with others? Who is usually considered superior? Why?

RHETORIC

1. Is the conversation portrayed here realistic? How effective is this conversational style at conveying information?

2. How do you interpret such details of this allegory as the chains, the cave, and the fire? What connotations do such symbols have?

3. How does Plato use conversation to develop his argument? What is Glaucon's role in the conversation?

4. Note examples of transition words that mark contrasts between the real and the shadow world. How does Plato use contrast to develop his idea of the true real world?

5. Plato uses syllogistic reasoning to derive human behavior from his allegory. Trace his line of reasoning, noting transitional devices and the development of ideas in paragraphs 5 to 14. Find and describe a similar line of reasoning.

6. In what paragraph does Plato explain his allegory? Why do you think he locates his explanation where he does?

WRITING

1. Are Plato's ideas still influencing contemporary society? How do his ideas affect our evaluation of materialism, sensuality, sex, and love?

2. Write an allegory based upon a sport, business, or space flight to explain how we act in the world.

3. Imagine an encounter with Plato. Report briefly on your conversation.

JOSEPH WOOD KRUTCH   Joseph Wood Krutch (1893–1970), American journalist, naturalist, and literary critic, is best known for *The Desert Year* (1952) and *The Modern Temper* (1929). The following essay, first published in 1960, reflects Krutch's concern for the contemporary condition. In it, he argues against an immoral society and criticizes what he terms "the paradox of our age."

JOSEPH WOOD KRUTCH

The New Immorality

The provost of one of our largest and most honored institutions told   1
me not long ago that a questionnaire was distributed to his undergraduates and that 40 percent refused to acknowledge that they believed cheating on examinations to be reprehensible.

Recently a report for a New York newspaper stopped six people on   2
the street and asked them if they would consent to take part in a rigged television quiz for money. He reported that five of the six said yes. Yet most of these five, like most of the college cheaters, would probably profess a strong social consciousness. They may cheat, but they vote for foreign aid and for enlightened social measures.

These two examples exhibit a paradox of our age. It is often said, 3
and my observation leads me to believe it true, that our seemingly
great growth in social morality has oddly enough taken place in a
world where private morality—a sense of the supreme importance of
purely personal honor, honesty, and integrity—seems to be declining.
Beneficent and benevolent social institutions are administered by men
who all too frequently turn out to be accepting "gifts." The world of
popular entertainment is rocked by scandals. College students, put on
their honor, cheat on examinations. Candidates for the Ph.D. hire
ghost writers to prepare their theses.

But, one may object, haven't all these things always been true? Is 4
there really any evidence that personal dishonesty is more prevalent
than it always was?

I have no way of making a historical measurement. Perhaps these 5
things are not actually more prevalent. What I do know is that there is an
increasing tendency to accept and take for granted such personal dishonesty. The bureaucrat and disk jockey say, "Well, yes, I took presents,
but I assure you that I made just decisions anyway." The college student
caught cheating does not even blush. He shrugs his shoulders and comments: "Everybody does it, and besides, I can't see that it really hurts
anybody."

Jonathan Swift once said: "I have never been surprised to find men 6
wicked, but I have often been surprised to find them not ashamed." It
is my conviction that though men may be no more wicked than they
always have been, they seem less likely to be ashamed. If anybody does
it, it must be right. Honest, moral, decent mean only what is usual. This
is not really a wicked world, because morality means mores or manners
and usual conduct is the only standard.

The second part of the defense, "it really doesn't hurt anybody," is 7
equally revealing. "It doesn't hurt anybody" means it doesn't do that
abstraction called society any harm. The harm it did the bribe-taker
and the cheater isn't important; it is purely personal. And personal as
opposed to social decency doesn't count for much. Sometimes I am
inclined to blame sociology for part of this paradox. Sociology has
tended to lay exclusive stress upon social morality, and tended too often
to define good and evil as merely the "socially useful" or its reverse.

What social morality and social conscience leave out is the narrower 8
but very significant concept of honor—as opposed to what is sometimes called merely "socially desirable conduct." The man of honor is
not content to ask merely whether this or that will hurt society, or
whether it is what most people would permit themselves to do. He asks,
and he asks first of all, would it hurt him and his self-respect? Would it
dishonor him personally?

It was a favorite and no doubt sound argument among early twentieth- 9
century reformers that "playing the game" as the gentleman was supposed to play it was not enough to make a decent society. They were right:
it is not enough. But the time has come to add that it is indeed inevitable

that the so-called social conscience unsupported by the concept of personal honor will create a corrupt society. But suppose that it doesn't? Suppose that no one except the individual suffers from the fact that he sees nothing wrong in doing what everybody else does? Even so, I still insist that for the individual himself nothing is more important than this personal, interior sense of right and wrong and his determination to follow that rather than to be guided by what everybody does or merely the criterion of "social usefulness." It is impossible for me to imagine a good society composed of men without honor.

We hear it said frequently that what present-day men most desire is security. If that is so, then they have a wrong notion of what the real, the ultimate, security is. No one who is dependent on anything outside himself, upon money, power, fame, or whatnot, is or ever can be secure. Only he who possesses himself and is content with himself is actually secure. Too much is being said about the importance of adjustment and "participation in the group." Even cooperation, to give this thing its most favorable designation, is no more important than the ability to stand alone when the choice must be made between the sacrifice of one's own integrity and adjustment to or participation in group activity.

No matter how bad the world may become, no matter how much the mass man of the future may lose such of the virtues as he still has, one fact remains. If one person alone refuses to go along with him, if one person alone asserts his individual and inner right to believe in and be loyal to what his fellow men seem to have given up, then at least he will still remain what is perhaps the most important part of humanity.

COMPREHENSION

1. How do you know that Krutch is writing for a general audience rather than a specialized one?

2. According to Krutch, what is the paradox of our age? What is unique about this paradox in terms of history?

3. What are the standard defenses and assumptions concerning the new immorality? How does Krutch respond to them?

RHETORIC

1. Krutch employs highly connotative language in this essay. What are some of these words? How does the author both control and exploit connotative language in advancing his analysis and argument?

2. Why is the allusion to Jonathan Swift especially appropriate?

3. Explain the patterns of development in paragraphs 1 to 4, 5 to 7, and 8 to 11.

4. Does Krutch present an inductive or a deductive argument in this essay? Explain your answer by reference to the text.

5. In what ways do causal analysis and extended definition enter into the development of the essay?
6. Analyze the last paragraph of the essay and evaluate its effectiveness.

WRITING

1. Do you accept Krutch's premise that a good society depends on people of honor? Why, or why not? Cite examples to support your contention.
2. Write an analytical essay on cheating on your campus. Is it a problem or not?
3. Argue for or against the proposition that personal morality in the United States is declining.

RUTH BENEDICT   Ruth Benedict (1887–1948), an anthropologist and educator, began her career as a poet. Later, she studied anthropology under Franz Boas and succeeded him as chairman of the department of anthropology at Columbia University (1936–1939). In 1934, she wrote *Patterns of Culture;* in 1940, *Race: Science and Politics.* In her work, Benedict attempted to study anthropology through sociology, psychology, and philosophy, of which this examination of Zuñi life and worship is an excellent example.

RUTH BENEDICT

Periodic Worship of the Zuñis

The Zuñis are a ceremonious people, a people who value sobriety and inoffensiveness above all other virtues. Their interest is centered upon their rich and complex ceremonial life. Their cults of the masked gods, of healing, of the sun, of the sacred fetishes, of war, of the dead, are formal and established bodies of ritual with priestly officials and calendric observances. No field of activity competes with ritual for foremost place in their attention. Probably most grown men among the western Pueblos give to it the greater part of their waking life. It requires the memorizing of an amount of word-perfect ritual that our less trained minds find staggering, and the performance of neatly dovetailed ceremonies that are charted by the calendar and complexly interlock all the different cults and the governing body in endless formal procedure.

The ceremonial life not only demands their time; it preoccupies their attention. Not only those who are responsible for the ritual and those who take part in it, but all the people of the pueblo, women and families who "have nothing," that is, that have no ritual possessions, centre their daily conversation about it. While it is in progress, they

503

stand all day as spectators. If a priest is ill, or if no rain comes during his retreat, village gossip runs over and over his ceremonial missteps and the implications of his failure. Did the priest of the masked gods give offence to some supernatural being? Did he break his retreat by going home to his wife before the days were up? These are the subjects of talk in the village for a fortnight. If an impersonator wears a new feather on his mask, it eclipses all talk of sheep or gardens or marriage or divorce.

This preoccupation with detail is logical enough. Zuñi religious practices are believed to be supernaturally powerful in their own right. At every step of the way, if the procedure is correct, the costume of the masked god traditional to the last detail, the offerings unimpeachable, the words of the hours-long prayers letter-perfect, the effect will follow according to man's desires. One has only, in the phrase they have always on their tongues, to "know how." According to all the tenets of their religion, it is a major matter if one of the eagle feathers of a mask has been taken from the shoulder of the bird instead of from the breast. Every detail has magical efficacy.

Zuñis place great reliance upon imitative magic. In the priests' retreats for rain they roll round stones across the floor to produce thunder, water is sprinkled to cause the rain, a bowl of water is placed upon the altar that the springs may be full, suds are beaten up from a native plant that clouds may pile in the heavens, tobacco smoke is blown out that the gods "may not withhold their misty breath." In the masked-god dances mortals clothe themselves with the "flesh" of the supernaturals, that is, their paint and their masks, and by this means gods are constrained to grant their blessings. Even the observances that are less obviously in the realm of magic partake in Zuñi thought of the same mechanistic efficacy. One of the obligations that rest upon every priest or official during the time when he is actively participating in religious observances is that of feeling no anger. But anger is not tabu in order to facilitate communication with a righteous god who can only be approached by those with a clean heart. Its absence is a sign of concentration upon supernatural affairs, a state of mind that constrains the supernaturals and makes it impossible for them to withhold their share of the bargain. It has magical efficacy.

Their prayers also are formulas, the effectiveness of which comes from their faithful rendition. The amount of traditional prayer forms of this sort in Zuñi can hardly be exaggerated. Typically they describe in ritualistic language the whole course of the reciter's ceremonial obligations leading up to the present culmination of the ceremony. They itemize the appointment of the impersonator, the gathering of willow shoots for prayer-sticks, the binding of the bird feathers to them with cotton string, the painting of the sticks, the offering to the gods of the finished plume wands, the visits to sacred springs, the periods of retreat. No less than the original religious act, the recital must be meticulously correct.

Seeking yonder along the river courses
The ones who are our fathers,
Male willow,
Female willow,
Four times cutting the straight young shoots,
To my house
I brought my road.
This day
With my warm human hands
I took hold of them.
I gave my prayer-sticks human form.
With the striped cloud tail
Of the one who is my grandfather,
With eagle's thin cloud tail,
With the striped cloud wings
And massed cloud tails
Of all the birds of summer,
With these four times I gave my prayer-sticks human form.
With the flesh of the one who is my mother,
Cotton woman,
Even a poorly made cotton thread,
Four times encircling them and tying it about their bodies.
I gave my prayer-sticks human form.
With the flesh of the one who is our mother,
Black paint woman,
Four times covering them with flesh,
I gave my prayer-sticks human form.

Prayer in Zuñi is never an outpouring of the human heart. There are some ordinary prayers that can be slightly varied, but this means little more than that they can be made longer or shorter. And the prayers are never remarkable for their intensity. They are always mild and ceremonious in form, asking for orderly life, pleasant days, shelter from violence. Even war priests conclude their prayer:

I have sent forth my prayers.
Our children,
Even those who have erected their shelters
At the edge of the wilderness,
May their roads come in safely,
May the forests
And the brush
Stretch out their water-filled arms
To shield their hearts;
May their roads come in safely;
May their roads all be fulfilled,
May it not somehow become difficult for them
When they have gone but a little way.

505

May all the little boys,
All the little girls,
And those whose roads are ahead,
May they have powerful hearts,
Strong spirits;
On roads reaching to Dawn Lake
May you grow old;
May your roads be fulfilled;
May you be blessed with life.
Where the life-giving road of your sun father comes out,
May your roads reach;
May your roads be fulfilled.

If they are asked the purpose of any religious observance, they have
a ready answer. It is for rain. This is of course a more or less conventional answer. But it reflects a deep-seated Zuñi attitude. Fertility is
above all else the blessing within the bestowal of the gods and in the
desert country of the Zuñi plateau, rain is the prime requisite for the
growth of crops. The retreats of the priests, the dances of the masked
gods, even many of the activities of the medicine societies are judged by
whether or not there has been rain. To "bless with water" is the synonym of all blessing. Thus, in the prayers, the fixed epithet the gods
apply in blessing to the rooms in Zuñi to which they come, is "water-
filled," their ladders are "water ladders," and the scalp taken in warfare
is "the water-filled covering." The dead, too, come back in the rain
clouds, bringing the universal blessing. People say to the children when
the summer afternoon rain clouds come up the sky, "Your grandfathers
are coming," and the reference is not to individual dead relatives, but
applies impersonally to all forbears. The masked gods also are the rain
and when they dance they constrain their own being—rain—to descend
upon the people. The priests, again, in their retreat before their altars sit
motionless and withdrawn for eight days, summoning the rain.

From wherever you abide permanently
You will make your roads come forth.
Your little wind blown clouds,
Your thin wisp of clouds
Replete with living waters,
You will send forth to stay with us.
Your fine rain caressing the earth,
Here at Itiwana,★
The abiding place of our fathers,
Our mothers,
The ones who first had being,
With your great pile of waters
You will come together.

★"The Middle," the ceremonial name of Zuñi, the center of the world.

Rain, however, is only one of the aspects of fertility for which 8
prayers are constantly made in Zuñi. Increase in the gardens and
increase in the tribe are thought of together. They desire to be blessed
with happy women:

> Even those who are with child,
> Carrying one child on the back,
> Holding another on a cradle board,
> Leading one by the hand,
> With yet another going before.

Their means of promoting human fertility are strongly symbolic and
impersonal, as we shall see, but fertility is one of the recognized objects
of religious observances.

This ceremonial life that preoccupies Zuñi attention is organized 9
like a series of interlocking wheels. The priesthoods have their sacred
objects, their retreats, their dances, their prayers, and their year-long
programme is annually initiated by the great winter solstice ceremony
that makes use of all the different groups and sacred things and focuses
all their functions. The tribal masked-god society has similar possessions and calendric observances, and these culminate in the great winter tribal masked-god ceremony, the Shalako. In like fashion the medicine societies, with their special relation to curing, function throughout
the year, and have their annual culminating ceremony for tribal health.
These three major cults of Zuñi ceremonial life are not mutually exclusive. A man may be, and often is, for the greater part of his life, a member of all three. They each give him sacred possessions "to live by" and
demand of him exacting ceremonial knowledge.

The priesthoods stand on the highest level of sanctity. There are 10
four major and eight minor priesthoods. They "hold their children[2]
fast." They are holy men. Their sacred medicine bundles, in which their
power resides, are, as Dr. Bunzel says, of "indescribable sanctity." They
are kept in great covered jars, in bare, inner rooms of the priests'
houses, and they consist of pairs of stoppered reeds, one filled with
water, in which there are miniature frogs, and the other with corn. The
two are wrapped together with yards and yards of unspun native cotton. No one ever enters the holy room of the priests' medicine bundle
except the priests when they go in for their rituals, and an elder woman
of the household or the youngest girl child, who go in before every
meal to feed the bundle. Anyone entering, for either purpose, removes
his moccasins.

The priests, as such, do not hold public ceremonies, though in great 11
numbers of the rites their presence is necessary or they initiate essential first steps in the undertaking. Their retreats before their sacred bundle are secret and sacrosanct. In June, when rain is needed for the corn,
at that time about a foot above the ground, the series of retreats begins.

[2]That is, the people of Zuñi.

In order, each new priesthood going "in" as the preceding one comes out, they "make their days." The heads of the sun cult and of the war cult are included also in this series of the priests' retreats. They must sit motionless, with their thoughts fixed upon ceremonial things. Eight days for the major priesthoods, four for the lesser. All Zuñis await the granting of rain during these days, and priests blessed with rain are greeted and thanked by everyone upon the street after their retreat is ended. They have blessed their people with more than rain. They have upheld them in all their ways of life. Their position as guardians of their people has been vindicated. The prayers they have prayed during their retreat have been answered:

> All my ladder-descending children,
> All of them I hold in my hands,
> May no one fall from my grasp
> After going but a little way.
> Even every little beetle,
> Even every dirty little beetle
> Let me hold them all fast in my hands,
> Let none of them fall from my grasp.
> May my children's roads all be fulfilled;
> May they grow old;
> May their roads reach all the way to Dawn Lake;
> May their roads be fulfilled;
> In order that your thoughts may bend to this
> Your days are made.

The heads of the major priesthoods, with the chief priest of the sun cult and the two chief priests of the war cult, constitute the ruling body, the council, of Zuñi. Zuñi is a theocracy to the last implication. Since priests are holy men and must never during the prosecution of their duties feel anger, nothing is brought before them about which there will not be unanimous agreement. They initiate the great ceremonial events of the Zuñi calendar, they make ritual appointments, and they give judgment in cases of witchcraft. To our sense of what a governing body should be, they are without jurisdiction and without authority.

If the priesthoods stand on the level of greatest sanctity, the cult of the masked gods is most popular. It has first claim in Zuñi affection, and it flourishes today like the green bay tree.

There are two kinds of masked gods: the masked gods proper, the kachinas; and the kachina priests. These kachina priests are the chiefs of the supernatural world and are themselves impersonated with masks by Zuñi dancers. Their sanctity in Zuñi eyes makes it necessary that their cult should be quite separate from that of the dancing gods proper. The dancing gods are happy and comradely supernaturals who live at the bottom of a lake far off in the empty desert south of

Zuñi. There they are always dancing. But they like best to return to
Zuñi to dance. To impersonate them, therefore, is to give them the
pleasure they most desire. A man, when he puts on the mask of the
gods, becomes for the time being the supernatural himself. He has no
longer human speech, but only the cry which is peculiar to that god.
He is tabu, and must assume all the obligations of anyone who is for
the time being sacred. He not only dances, but he observes an esoteric
retreat before the dance, and plants prayer-sticks and observes conti-
nence.

There are more than a hundred different masked gods of the
Zuñi pantheon, and many of these are dance groups that come in
sets, thirty or forty of a kind. Others come in sets of six, coloured
for the six directions—for Zuñi counts up and down as cardinal
points. Each of these gods has individual details of costuming, an
individual mask, an individual place in the hierarchy of the gods,
myths that recount his doings, and ceremonies during which he is
expected.

The dances of the masked gods are administered and carried out by
a tribal society of all adult males. Women too may be initiated "to save
their lives," but it is not customary. They are not excluded because of
any tabu, but membership for a woman is not customary, and there are
today only three women members. As far back as tradition reaches
there seem not to have been many more at any one time. The men's
tribal society is organized in six groups, each with its kiva or ceremonial chamber. Each kiva has its officials, its dances that belong to it, and
its own roll of members.

Membership in one or the other of these kivas follows from the
choice of a boy's ceremonial father at birth, but there is no initiation
till the child is between five and nine years old. It is his first attainment of ceremonial status. This initiation, as Dr. Bunzel points out,
does not teach him esoteric mysteries; it establishes a bond with
supernatural forces. It makes him strong, and, as they say, valuable.
The "scare kachinas," the punitive masked gods, come for the initiation, and they whip the children with their yucca whips. It is a rite of
exorcism, "to take off the bad happenings," and to make future events
propitious. In Zuñi whipping is never used as a corrective of children.
The fact that white parents use it in punishment is a matter for
unending amazement. In the initiation children are supposed to be
very frightened, and they are not shamed if they cry aloud. It makes
the rite the more valuable.

15

16

17

COMPREHENSION

1. What is the importance of ritual and ceremony to the Zuñi people?
2. What are the major levels of the Zuñi religion?
3. What role does rain play in the beliefs and rituals of the Zuñi religion?

RHETORIC

1. Explain the purpose of definition in the introduction. Cite other paragraphs where Benedict uses definition as an expository technique.

2. Does Benedict approach the subject as a scientist or as a practitioner? What about the tone or language in the essay support your opinion?

3. What function does the prayer in paragraph 5 serve? How is it reflective of the Zuñi religion? Would the essay be just as effective without it? Justify your response.

4. Does Benedict use abstract or concrete language in her essay? Cite examples from the writing.

5. Where does the writer use classification in her essay? How does it serve the purpose of the writing?

6. Why does Benedict choose not to elaborate on the role of the "medicine societies" mentioned in paragraph 9? Does this detract from her exposition?

WRITING

1. Research in more detail a particular area of Zuñi religious practices—for example, the role of women in rituals, the function of medicine societies, or children's rite-of-passage ceremonies.

2. Benedict mentions that the Zuñis are baffled by the practice of using physical punishment on children. Write a brief essay using information given in the essay, about other customs in the Judeo-Christian world that they might find confusing.

3. Write an essay arguing that non-Native Americans could learn a great deal from the Zuñis. What do you find especially interesting or reasonable about them? How could their beliefs or practices be used in other contexts to enrich humanity?

JOHN DONNE   John Donne (1572–1631), English poet and priest, was a master of wit and devotion. Ben Jonson called him "the first poet in the world in some things." Donne's early career was threatened constantly by poverty, until he became dean of St. Paul's in 1621. He wrote richly complex poetry and sermons. Most of his works were published after his death by his son. Collections of his sermons appeared in 1640, 1649, and 1661; a collection of his poetry appeared in 1633. Donne was a superb inventor of metaphors, as the following essay, called a *meditation,* indicates.

JOHN DONNE

No Man Is an Island

Perchance he for whom this bell tolls may be so ill, as that he knows not
it tolls for him; and perchance I may think myself so much better than
I am, as that they who are about me, and see my state, may have caused
it to toll for me, and I know not that. The church is Catholic, universal,
so are all her actions; all that she does belongs to all. When she baptizes
a child, that action concerns me; for that child is thereby connected to
that body which is my head too, and ingrafted into that body whereof
I am a member. And when she buries a man, that action concerns me:
all mankind is of one author, and is one volume; when one man dies,
one chapter is not torn out of the book, but translated into a better language; and every chapter must be so translated; God employs several
translators; some pieces are translated by age, some by sickness, some
by war, some by justice; but God's hand is in every translation, and his
hand shall bind up all our scattered leaves again for that library where
every book shall lie open to one another. As therefore the bell that rings
to a sermon calls not upon the preacher only, but upon the congregation to come, so this bell calls us all; but how much more me, who am
brought so near the door by this sickness. There was a contention as far
as a suit (in which both poetry and dignity, religion and estimation,
were mingled), which of the religious orders should ring to prayers first
in the morning; and it was determined, that they should ring first that
rose earliest. If we understand aright the dignity of this bell that tolls for
our evening prayer, we would be glad to make it ours by rising early, in
that application, that it might be ours as well as his, whose indeed it is.
The bell doth toll for him that thinks it doth; and though it intermit
again, yet from that minute that that occasion wrought upon him, he is
united to God. Who casts not up his eye to the sun when it rises? But
who takes off his eye from a comet when that breaks out? Who bends
not his ear to any bell which upon any occasion rings? but who can
remove it from that bell which is passing a piece of himself out of this
world? No man is an island, entire of itself; every man is a piece of the
continent, a part of the main. If a clod be washed away by the sea,
Europe is the less, as well as if a promontory were, as well as if a manor
of thy friend's or of thine own were: any man's death diminishes me,
because I am involved in mankind, and therefore never send to know
for whom the bell tolls; it tolls for thee. Neither can we call this a begging of misery, or a borrowing of misery, as though we were not miserable enough of ourselves, but must fetch in more from the next
house, in taking upon us the misery of our neighbors. Truly it were an

excusable covetousness if we did, for affliction is a treasure, and scarce any man hath enough of it. No man hath affliction enough that is not matured and ripened by it, and made fit for God by that affliction. If a man carry treasure in bullion, or in a wedge of gold, and have none coined into current money, his treasure will not defray him as he travels. Tribulation is treasure in the nature of it, but it is not current money in the use of it, except we get nearer and nearer our home, heaven, by it. Another man may be sick too, and sick to death, and this affliction may lie in his bowels, as gold in a mine, and be of no use to him; but this bell, that tells me of his affliction, digs out and applies that gold to me: if by this consideration of another's danger I take mine own into contemplation, and so secure myself, by making my recourse to my God, who is our only security.

COMPREHENSION

1. What is the theme of this essay?

2. The central metaphor in this essay is "bells." What do they signify?

3. Donne referred to his sermons as *meditations*. Upon what subject is this work a meditation?

RHETORIC

1. Standard punctuation has changed dramatically since the time this essay was written. Select one semicolon from each of five sentences in the essay. Explain the function of each semicolon within its context.

2. Read the essay aloud. What clues exist in the essay that it was meant to be recited rather than merely read?

3. The entire essay (or meditation) is one paragraph long. Many religions rely on repetitive prayer or chants to help the believer enter a "sanctified" state of mind. Discuss how the form of the essay can be considered part of the "rhetoric of the spiritual."

4. The author often joins ideas with coordinating conjunctions *(for, and, yet, but, so).* However there are few connecting words with more than one syllable—*nevertheless, however, because, moreover*—in the essay. How does this stylistic device contribute toward the tone of the writing?

5. A portion of one sentence reads, "Neither can we call this a begging of misery or a borrowing of misery, as though we were not miserable enough of ourselves." Locate three other sentences with repetition of sounds and words. What is the effect of repetition as a rhetorical device?

6. Identify at least four other uses of metaphor besides the word *bells* in the essay. How does the author's frequent use of metaphor contribute to the effect of the essay?

7. Consider the statement, "The bell doth toll for him that thinks it doth." What aspects of this make it resemble poetry rather than prose?

1. Argue for or against the proposition that no man is an island.

2. Write an imaginative essay in which you assume the persona of John Donne and examine today's society in terms of his philosophy.

3. Have a friend read the essay aloud. Afterward, write an essay describing the response you had while listening to the meditation.

C. S. LEWIS   Clive Staples Lewis (1898–1963) was born in Belfast, Ireland, but spent the most important years of his life as a lecturer in English at Oxford. His first book, *Dymer,* was published in 1926, but it was not until the publication of *The Pilgrim's Regress* in 1933 that he addressed the central work of his life: a passionate defense of the Christian faith. Lewis's immense output embraced science fiction, fantasy, children's books, theology, and literary criticism. Among his best-known works are *The Screwtape Letters* (1942); *The Lion, the Witch, and the Wardrobe* (1950); and *The Narnia Chronicle* (1956). In this essay, Lewis describes the reasoning that led to his conversion.

C. S. LEWIS

The Rival Conceptions of God

I have been asked to tell you what Christians believe, and I am going to 1
begin by telling you one thing that Christians do not need to believe. If you are a Christian you do not have to believe that all the other religions are simply wrong all through. If you are an atheist you do have to believe that the main point in all the religions of the whole world is simply one huge mistake. If you are a Christian, you are free to think that all these religions, even the queerest ones, contain at least some hint of the truth. When I was an atheist I had to try to persuade myself that most of the human race have always been wrong about the question that mattered to them most; when I became a Christian I was able to take a more liberal view. But, of course, being a Christian does mean thinking that where Christianity differs from other religions, Christianity is right and they are wrong. As in arithmetic—there is only one right answer to a sum, and all other answers are wrong: but some of the wrong answers are much nearer being right than others.

The first big division of humanity is into the majority, who 2
believe in some kind of God or gods, and the minority who do not. On this point, Christianity lines up with the majority—lines up with ancient Greeks and Romans, modern savages, Stoics, Platonists, Hindus, Mohammedans, etc., against the modern Western European materialist.

Now I go on to the next big division. People who all believe in God ₃
can be divided according to the sort of God they believe in. There are
two very different ideas on this subject. One of them is the idea that He
is beyond good and evil. We humans call one thing good and another
thing bad. But according to some people that is merely our human
point of view. These people would say that the wiser you become the
less you would want to call anything good or bad, and the more clearly
you would see that everything is good in one way and bad in another,
and that nothing could have been different. Consequently, these people
think that long before you got anywhere near the divine point of view
the distinction would have disappeared altogether. We call a cancer bad,
they would say, because it kills a man; but you might just as well call a
successful surgeon bad because he kills a cancer. It all depends on the
point of view. The other and opposite idea is that God is quite definitely
"good" or "righteous," a God who takes sides, who loves love and hates
hatred, who wants us to behave in one way and not in another. The first
of these views—the one that thinks God beyond good and evil—is
called Pantheism. It was held by the great Prussian philosopher Hegel
and, as far as I can understand them, by the Hindus. The other view is
held by Jews, Mohammedans and Christians.

And with this big difference between Pantheism and the Christian ₄
idea of God, there usually goes another. Pantheists usually believe that
God, so to speak, animates the universe as you animate your body: that
the universe almost *is* God, so that if it did not exist He would not exist
either, and anything you find in the universe is a part of God. The
Christian idea is quite different. They think God invented and made
the universe—like a man making a picture or composing a tune. A
painter is not a picture, and he does not die if his picture is destroyed.
You may say, "He's put a lot of himself into it," but you only mean that
all its beauty and interest has come out of his head. His skill is not in
the picture in the same way that it is in his head, or even in his hands.
I expect you see how this difference between Pantheists and Christians
hangs together with the other one. If you do not take the distinction
between good and bad very seriously, then it is easy to say that anything you find in this world is a part of God. But, of course, if you think
some things really bad, and God really good, then you cannot talk like
that. You must believe that God is separate from the world and that
some of the things we see in it are contrary to His will. Confronted with
a cancer or a slum the Pantheist can say, "If you could only see it from
the divine point of view, you would realize that this also is God." The
Christian replies, "Don't talk damned nonsense."[1] For Christianity is a
fighting religion. It thinks God made the world—that space and time,
heat and cold, and all the colours and tastes, and all the animals and
vegetables, are things that God "made up out of His head" as a man

---

[1]One listener complained of the word *damned* as frivolous swearing. But I mean exactly
what I say—nonsense that is *damned* is under God's curse, and will (apart from God's
grace) lead those who believe it to eternal death.

makes up a story. But it also thinks that a great many things have gone wrong with the world that God made and that God insists, and insists very loudly, on our putting them right again.

And, of course, that raises a very big question. If a good God made ₅ the world why has it gone wrong? And for many years I simply refused to listen to the Christian answers to this question, because I kept on feeling "whatever you say, and however clever your arguments are, isn't it much simpler and easier to say that the world was not made by any intelligent power? Aren't all your arguments simply a complicated attempt to avoid the obvious?" But then that threw me back into another difficulty.

My argument against God was that the universe seemed so cruel ₆ and unjust. But how had I got this idea of *just* and *unjust?* A man does not call a line crooked unless he has some idea of a straight line. What was I comparing this universe with when I called it unjust? If the whole show was bad and senseless from A to Z, so to speak, why did I, who was supposed to be part of the show, find myself in such violent reaction against it? A man feels wet when he falls into water, because man is not a water animal: a fish would not feel wet. Of course I could have given up my idea of justice by saying it was nothing but a private idea of my own. But if I did that, then my argument against God collapsed too—for the argument depended on saying that the world was really unjust, not simply that it did not happen to please my private fancies. Thus in the very act of trying to prove that God did not exist—in other words, that the whole of reality was senseless—I found I was forced to assume that one part of reality—namely my idea of justice—was full of sense. Consequently atheism turns out to be too simple. If the whole universe has no meaning, we should never have found out that it has no meaning: just as, if there were no light in the universe and therefore no creature with eyes, we should never know it was dark. *Dark* would be without meaning.

COMPREHENSION

1. Who is Lewis's audience? What is his purpose? How do you know?
2. Lewis divides humanity into a number of distinct categories. Name them, and discuss his purpose in establishing these categories.
3. What is Lewis's purpose in likening Christianity to arithmetic? In what sense is this apt? Where does he use a similar image?

RHETORIC

1. Look up the following words in paragraph 2 in a dictionary or an encyclopedia: *Stoics, Platonists, Hindus,* and *Mohammedans.* What are the major tenets of their beliefs?
2. Explain Lewis's use of the word *damned* (paragraph 4). What is specific about his use of this word? Is it appropriate?

3. How does Lewis develop his argument? What line of reasoning does he follow? What transition markers does Lewis use?
4. How does Lewis use definition to structure certain parts of his argument?
5. In which paragraph is Lewis making what he considers the one irrefutable argument in favor of the existence of God? Is this paragraph coherently reasoned in terms of the whole essay? Explain.
6. Why is Lewis's idea of justice critical to the evaluation of his thought? Is his use of the word *justice* idiosyncratic or objective? How does accepting his definition make an important difference to the response that a reader would give to this piece?

WRITING

1. The Western tradition is based, in large part, on the belief that "Christianity is right" and other religions are wrong. Is this belief as strong today as it was in the past? Does it still cohere as an argument?
2. Write an essay describing your religious beliefs and how they originated.
3. Argue for or against atheism.

CLASSIC AND CONTEMPORARY

VIRGINIA WOOLF Virginia Woolf (1882–1941), English novelist and essayist, was the daughter of Sir Leslie Stephen, a famous critic and writer on economics. An experimental novelist, Woolf attempted to portray consciousness through a poetic, symbolic, and concrete style. Her novels include *Jacob's Room* (1922), *Mrs. Dalloway* (1925), *To the Lighthouse* (1927), and *The Waves* (1931). She was also a perceptive reader and critic, and her criticism appears in *The Common Reader* (1925) and *The Second Common Reader* (1933). The following essay, which demonstrates Woolf's capacity to find profound meaning even in commonplace events, appeared in *The Death of the Moth and Other Essays* (1942).

VIRGINIA WOOLF

The Death of the Moth

Moths that fly by day are not properly to be called moths; they do not   1
excite that pleasant sense of dark autumn nights and ivy-blossom which the commonest yellow-underwing asleep in the shadow of the curtain never fails to rouse in us. They are hybrid creatures, neither gay like butterflies nor sombre like their own species. Nevertheless the

present specimen, with his narrow hay-coloured wings, fringed with a tassel of the same colour, seemed to be content with life. It was a pleasant morning, mid-September, mild, benignant, yet with a keener breath than that of the summer months. The plough was already scoring the field opposite the window, and where the share had been, the earth was pressed flat and gleamed with moisture. Such vigour came rolling in from the fields and the down beyond that it was difficult to keep the eyes strictly turned upon the book. The rooks too were keeping one of their annual festivities; soaring round the tree tops until it looked as if a vast net with thousands of black knots in it had been cast up into the air; which, after a few moments sank slowly down upon the trees until every twig seemed to have a knot at the end of it. Then, suddenly, the net would be thrown into the air again in a wider circle this time, with the utmost clamour and vociferation, as though to be thrown into the air and settle down upon the tree tops were a tremendously exciting experience.

The same energy which inspired the rooks, the ploughmen, the 2 horses, and even, it seemed, the lean bare-backed downs, sent the moth fluttering from side to side of his square of the windowpane. One could not help watching him. One was, indeed, conscious of a queer feeling of pity for him. The possibilities of pleasure seemed that morning so enormous and so various that to have only a moth's part in life, and a day moth's at that, appeared a hard fate, and his zest in enjoying his meagre opportunities to the full, pathetic. He flew vigorously to one corner of his compartment, and, after waiting there a second, flew across to the other. What remained for him but to fly to a third corner and then to a fourth? That was all he could do, in spite of the size of the downs, the width of the sky, the far-off smoke of houses, and the romantic voice, now and then, of a steamer out at sea. What he could do he did. Watching him, it seemed as if a fibre, very thin but pure, of the enormous energy of the world had been thrust into his frail and diminutive body. As often as he crossed the pane, I could fancy that a thread of vital light became visible. He was little or nothing but life.

Yet, because he was so small, and so simple a form of the energy that 3 was rolling in at the open window and driving its way through so many narrow and intricate corridors in my own brain and in those of other human beings, there was something marvellous as well as pathetic about him. It was as if someone had taken a tiny bead of pure life and decking it as lightly as possible with down and feathers, had set it dancing and zigzagging to show us the true nature of life. Thus displayed one could not get over the strangeness of it. One is apt to forget all about life, seeing it humped and bossed and garnished and cumbered so that it has to move with the greatest circumspection and dignity. Again, the thought of all that life might have been had he been born in any other shape caused one to view his simple activities with a kind of pity.

After a time, tired by his dancing apparently, he settled on the win- 4 dow ledge in the sun, and, the queer spectacle being at an end, I forgot about him. Then, looking up, my eye was caught by him. He was trying to resume his dancing, but seemed either so stiff or so awkward that he could only flutter to the bottom of the windowpane; and when he tried to fly across it he failed. Being intent on other matters I watched these futile attempts for a time without thinking, unconsciously waiting for him to resume his flight, as one waits for a machine, that has stopped momentarily, to start again without considering the reason of its failure. After perhaps a seventh attempt he slipped from the wooden ledge and fell, fluttering his wings, on to his back on the window sill. The helplessness of his attitude roused me. It flashed upon me that he was in difficulties; he could no longer raise himself; his legs struggled vainly. But, as I stretched out a pencil, meaning to help him to right himself, it came over me that the failure and awkwardness were the approach of death. I laid the pencil down again.

The legs agitated themselves once more. I looked as if for the enemy 5 against which he struggled. I looked out of doors. What had happened there? Presumably it was midday, and work in the fields had stopped. Stillness and quiet had replaced the previous animation. The birds had taken themselves off to feed in the brooks. The horses stood still. Yet the power was there all the same, massed outside, indifferent, impersonal, not attending to anything in particular. Somehow it was opposed to the little hay-coloured moth. It was useless to try to do anything. One could only watch the extraordinary efforts made by those tiny legs against an oncoming doom which could, had it chosen, have submerged an entire city, not merely a city, but masses of human beings; nothing, I knew, had any chance against death. Nevertheless after a pause of exhaustion the legs fluttered again. It was superb this last protest, and so frantic that he succeeded at last in righting himself. One's sympathies, of course, were all on the side of life. Also, when there was nobody to care or to know, this gigantic effort on the part of an insignificant little moth, against a power of such magnitude, to retain what no one else valued or desired to keep, moved one strangely. Again, somehow, one saw life, a pure bead. I lifted the pencil again, useless though I knew it to be. But even as I did so, the unmistakable tokens of death showed themselves. The body relaxed, and instantly grew stiff. The struggle was over. The insignificant little creature now knew death. As I looked at the dead moth, this minute wayside triumph of so great a force over so mean an antagonist filled me with wonder. Just as life had been strange a few minutes before, so death was now as strange. The moth having righted himself now lay most decently and uncomplainingly composed. O yes, he seemed to say, death is stronger than I am.

COMPREHENSION

1. Why is Woolf so moved by the moth's death? Why does she call the moth's protest (paragraph 5) "superb"?
2. What, according to Woolf, is the "true nature of life"?
3. What paradox is inherent in the death of the moth?

1. Examine Woolf's use of simile in paragraph 1. Where else in the essay does she use similes? Are any of them similar to the similes used in paragraph 1?
2. Why does the author personify the moth?
3. What sentences constitute the introduction of this essay? What rhetorical device do they use?
4. Divide the essay into two parts. Now explain why you divided the essay where you did. How are the two parts different? How are they similar?
5. Explain the importance of description in this essay. Where, particularly, does Woolf describe the setting of her scene? How does that description contribute to the development of her essay? How does she describe the moth, and how does this description affect tone?
6. How is narration used to structure the essay?

WRITING

1. Woolf implicitly connects insect and human life. What else can we learn about human development by looking at other forms of life? Analyze this connection in an essay.
2. Write a detailed description of a small animal. Try to invest it with the importance that Woolf gives her moth.
3. Give an analysis of Woolf's use of figurative language in "The Death of the Moth."

ANNIE DILLARD   Annie Dillard, whose writings include poems, autobiographies, and novels, was born in Pennsylvania in 1945. Her books include *Pilgrim at Tinker Creek* (1974), for which she won the 1975 Pulitzer Prize in general nonfiction, *Teaching a Stone to Talk* (1982), and *The Living* (1992), a novel that celebrates the spirit of pioneer women. Dillard's work has been published in *Harper's, Atlantic Monthly, Cosmopolitan,* and *Sports Illustrated.* In the essay below, Dillard uses evocative sensory images to examine the process of creating and the nature of solitude.

ANNIE DILLARD

Death of a Moth

I live alone with two cats, who sleep on my legs. There is a yellow one, and a black one whose name is Small. In the morning I joke to the black one, Do you remember last night? Do you remember? I throw them both out before breakfast, so I can eat.

There is a spider, too, in the bathroom, of uncertain lineage, bulbous at the abdomen and drab, whose six-inch mess of web works, works somehow, works miraculously, to keep her alive and me amazed. The web is in a corner behind the toilet, connecting tile wall to tile wall. The house is new, the bathroom immaculate, save for the spider, her web, and the sixteen or so corpses she's tossed to the floor.

The corpses appear to be mostly sow bugs, those little armadillo creatures who live to travel flat out in houses, and die round. In addition to sow-bug husks, hollow and sipped empty of color, there are what seem to be two or three wingless moth bodies, one new flake of earwig, and three spider carcasses crinkled and clenched.

I wonder on what fool's errand an earwig, or a moth, or a sow bug, would visit that clean corner of the house behind the toilet; I have not noticed any blind parades of sow bugs blundering into corners. Yet they do hazard there, at a rate of more than one a week, and the spider thrives. Yesterday she was working on the earwig, mouth on gut; today he's on the floor. It must take a certain genius to throw things away from there, to find a straight line through that sticky tangle to the floor.

Today the earwig shines darkly, and gleams, what there is of him: a dorsal curve of thorax and abdomen, and a smooth pair of pincers by which I knew his name. Next week, if the other bodies are any indication, he'll be shrunk and gray, webbed to the floor with dust. The sow bugs beside him are curled and empty, fragile, a breath away from brittle fluff. The spiders lie on their sides, translucent and ragged, their legs drying in knots. The moths stagger against each other, headless, in a confusion of arcing strips of chitin like peeling varnish, like a jumble of buttresses for cathedral vaults, like nothing resembling moths, so that I would hesitate to call them moths, except that I have had some experience with the figure Moth reduced to a nub.

Two summers ago I was camped alone in the Blue Ridge Mountains of Virginia. I had hauled myself and gear up there to read, among other things, *The Day on Fire*, by James Ullman, a novel about Rimbaud that had made me want to be a writer when I was sixteen; I was hoping it would do it again. So I read every day sitting under a tree by my tent, while warblers sang in the leaves overhead and bristle worms trailed their inches over the twiggy dirt at my feet; and I read every night by candlelight, while barred owls called in the forest and pale moths seeking mates massed round my head in the clearing, where my light made a ring.

Moths kept flying into the candle. They would hiss and recoil, reeling upside down in the shadows among my cooking pans. Or they would singe their wings and fall, and their hot wings, as if melted, would stick to the first thing they touched—a pan, a lid, a spoon—so that the snagged moths could struggle only in tiny arcs, unable to flutter free. These I could release by a quick flip with a stick; in the morning I would find my cooking stuff decorated with torn flecks of moth wings, ghostly triangles of shiny dust here and there on the aluminum. So I read, and boiled water, and replenished candles, and read on.

One night a moth flew into the candle, was caught, burnt dry, and held. I must have been staring at the candle, or maybe I looked up when a shadow crossed my page; at any rate, I saw it all. A golden female moth, a biggish one with a two-inch wingspread, flapped into the fire, dropped abdomen into the wet wax, stuck, flamed, and frazzled in a second. Her moving wings ignited like tissue paper, like angels' wings, enlarging the circle of light in the clearing and creating out of the darkness the sudden blue sleeves of my sweater, the green leaves of jewelweed by my side, the ragged red trunk of a pine; at once the light contracted again and the moth's wings vanished in a fine, foul smoke. At the same time, her six legs clawed, curled, blackened, and ceased, disappearing utterly. And her head jerked in spasms, making a spattering noise; her antennae crisped and burnt away and her heaving mouthparts cracked like pistol fire. When it was all over, her head was, so far as I could determine, gone, gone the long way of her wings and legs. Her head was a hole lost to time. All that was left was the glowing horn shell of her abdomen and thorax—a fraying, partially collapsed gold tube jammed upright in the candle's round pool.

And then this moth-essence, this spectacular skeleton, began to act as a wick. She kept burning. The wax rose in the moth's body from her soaking abdomen to her thorax to the shattered hole where her head should have been, and widened into flame, a saffron-yellow flame that robed her to the ground like an immolating monk. That candle had two wicks, two winding flames of identical light, side by side. The moth's head was fire. She burned for two hours, until I blew her out.

She burned for two hours without changing, without swaying or kneeling—only glowing within, like a building fire glimpsed through silhouetted walls, like a hollow saint, like a flame-faced virgin gone to God, while I read by her light, kindled, while Rimbaud in Paris burnt out his brain in a thousand poems, while night pooled wetly at my feet.

So. That is why I think those hollow shreds on the bathroom floor are moths. I believe I know what moths look like, in any state.

I have three candles here on the table which I disentangle from the plants and light when visitors come. The cats avoid them, although Small's tail caught fire once; I rubbed it out before she noticed. I don't mind living alone. I like eating alone and reading. I don't mind sleeping alone. The only time I mind being alone is when something is funny; then, when I am laughing at something funny, I wish someone were around. Sometimes I think it is pretty funny that I sleep alone.

COMPREHENSION

1. What is the link between the moth, its death, and Dillard's writing?
2. What is the significance of Dillard's reading material (paragraph 6) to the moth? What associations does it have?
3. Do we learn anything of Dillard's emotional response to the death of the moth? Why, or why not?

RHETORIC

1. Why do you think Dillard has written this essay?
2. How do images like "moth-essence" and "immolating monk" (in paragraph 9) help to enrich the meaning of the paragraph? What are other examples of Dillard's figurative language?
3. Comment on the use of transitions in paragraph 10 and the beginning of paragraph 11. How is repetition used effectively here? What impact does it have on the tone?
4. Note Dillard's use of similes in paragraph 10. What mood is the writer trying to evoke? How does the rest of the paragraph set off these images?
5. Dillard organizes this essay in three sections. What is the relationship of these sections to each other?
6. How well does Dillard's conclusion work? Does it serve to frame the essay? How does it relate to the paragraphs preceding it?

WRITING

1. In a brief essay, explore what the moth represents to Dillard. Use support or examples from her piece to develop your theme.
2. Dillard explores the nature of solitude and introspection. In an essay, consider how the former can facilitate the latter. How do you feel about solitude? What do you think about when you're alone? Are your powers of observation and perception heightened by solitude? Is solitude at night different?
3. Have you ever witnessed the death of an insect or a small animal? How did you respond physically, emotionally? In a descriptive narrative, relate the experience and its effect on you.

CLASSIC AND CONTEMPORARY: QUESTIONS FOR COMPARISON

1. Why is the moth so central to the essays of Dillard and Woolf? Do the two writers use a moth to symbolize the same thing? How does the article in Dillard's title affect her focus? Why does Woolf use the definite article? Do the two writers respond similarly to the event?
2. How do the writers use setting and mood in their essays? How do these enrich the essays? What role does solitude play in establishing the writer's theme?

3. Analyze the levels of language used by Woolf and Dillard. Cite examples of their use of figurative language to enhance their narratives. How do they use language to set the tone of the essays? Who is the intended audience, and how does their language reflect this?

4. In a brief essay, compare the writers' attitudes toward the event. Does the fact that Woolf personifies the moth in her essay and attempts to rescue it reveal anything about her sensibilities? Does Dillard's reactions to the moth show a lack of compassion? Respond to these questions, using the writers' work as a foundation for your responses.

CONNECTIONS

1. How do you think Coretta Scott King would respond to Mencken's essay advocating capital punishment? Do you believe she defines her terms adequately in her argument? Do you think she offers a convincing rebuttal?

2. How do writers like Plato, Donne, and Woolf use figurative language to make philosophical points? Use support from the above-mentioned authors to form your answer.

3. Are people "wicked," as Krutch infers in his essay? Left to their own devices, without the regulations of church and state, would most people behave morally? Use the ideas of Coles, Lewis, or King to develop your theme.

4. Explore the connection between Plato, the philosopher, and Donne, the theologian. How do their essays complement each other? How does Donne's attitude toward existence reflect Plato's philosophy of the cave?

5. Coles argues that the moral education of children is essential to a well-functioning society. How would Krutch respond to Coles's argument? What might Krutch advise parents to teach their children?

6. What is *morality?* What is its origin? Use the work of King, Mencken, and others to respond to this question. How would these writers define the word?

7. Consider the differences between *public religion* and *private religion*. Refer to the essays by Benedict, Lewis, and others to develop this comparative essay.

8. What is the difference between philosophy and religion? Is it merely a matter of belief? Address this question in an essay, using support from writers in this section.

9. Write an essay entitled "The Purpose of Life." Using examples and evidence from their works, choose three writers in this section to develop this theme.

CHAPTER ELEVEN

Nature and the Environment

We are at a point in the history of civilization where consciousness of our fragile relationship to nature and the environment is high. Even as you spend an hour reading a few of the essays in this chapter, it is estimated that we are losing 3,000 acres of rain forest around the world and four species of plants or animals. From pollution to the population explosion to the depletion of the ozone layer, we seem to be confronted with ecological catastrophe. Nevertheless, as Rachel Carson reminds us, we have "an obligation to endure," to survive potential natural catastrophe by understanding and managing our relationship with the natural world.

Ecology, or the study of nature and the environment, as many of the essayists in this chapter attest, involves us in the conservation of the earth. It moves us to suppress our suicidally rapacious destruction of the planet. Clearly, the biological stability of the planet is increasingly precarious. More plants, insects, birds, and animals are becoming extinct in the twentieth century than in any era since the Cretaceous catastrophe more than 65 million years ago that led to the extinction of the dinosaurs. Within this ecological context, writers like Thoreau and Carson become our literary conscience, reminding us of how easily natural processes can break down unless we insist on a degree of ecological "economy."

Of course, any modification of human behavior in an effort to conserve nature is a complex matter. To save the spotted owl in the Pacific Northwest, we must sacrifice the jobs of people in the timber industry. To reduce pollution, we must forsake gas and oil for alternate energy sources that are costly to develop. To reduce the waste stream, we must shift from a consumption to a conservation society. The ecological debate is complicated, but it is clear that the preservation of the myriad life cycles on earth is crucial, for we, too, could become an endangered species.

The language of nature is as enigmatic as the sounds of dolphins and whales communicating with their respective species. Writers like Loren Eiseley, Gretel Ehrlich, and John Steinbeck, who appear in this chapter, help us to decipher the language of our environment. They encourage us to converse with nature, learn from it, and even revere it. All of us are guests on this planet; the natural world is our host. If we do not protect the earth, how can we guarantee the survival of global civilization?

Previewing the Chapter

As you read the essays in this chapter and respond to them in discussion and writing, consider the following questions:

• According to the author, what should our relationship to the natural world be?

• What claims or arguments does the author make about the importance of nature? Do you agree or disagree with these claims and arguments?

• What specific ecological problem does the author investigate?

• How does the author think that nature influences human behavior?

• What cultural factors are involved in our approach to the environment?

• Is the writer optimistic, pessimistic, or neutral in the assessment of our ability to conserve nature?

• Do you find that the author is too idealistic or sentimental in the depiction of nature? Why?

• Based on the author's essay, how does he or she qualify as a "nature writer"?

• How have you been challenged or changed by the essays in this section?

RACHEL CARSON   Rachel Carson (1907–1964) was a seminal figure in the environmental movement. Born in Pennsylvania, she awakened public consciousness to environmental issues through her writing. Her style was both literary and scientific as she described nature's riches in such books as *The Sea Around Us* (1951) and *The Edge of the Sea* (1954). Her last book, *Silent Spring* (1962), aroused controversy and concern with its indictment of insecticides. In the following excerpt from that important book, Carson provides compelling evidence of the damage caused by indiscriminate use of insecticides and the danger of disturbing the earth's delicate balance.

RACHEL CARSON

The Obligation to Endure

The history of life on earth has been a history of interaction between living things and their surroundings. To a large extent, the physical form and the habits of the earth's vegetation and its animal life have been molded by the environment. Considering the whole span of earthly time, the opposite effect, in which life actually modifies its surroundings, has been relatively slight. Only within the moment of time represented by the present century has one species—man—acquired significant power to alter the nature of his world.

During the past quarter century this power has not only increased to one of disturbing magnitude but it has changed in character. The most alarming of all man's assaults upon the environment is the contamination of air, earth, rivers, and sea with dangerous and even lethal materials. This pollution is for the most part irrecoverable; the chain of evil it initiates not only in the world that must support life but in living tissues is for the most part irreversible. In this now universal contamination of the environment, chemicals are the sinister and little-recognized partners of radiation in changing the very nature of the world—the very nature of its life. Strontium 90, released through nuclear explosions into the air, comes to earth in rain or drifts down as fallout, lodges in soil, enters into the grass or corn or wheat grown there, and in time takes up its abode in the bones of a human being, there to remain until his death. Similarly, chemicals sprayed on croplands or forests or gardens lie long in soil, entering into living organisms, passing from one to another in a chain of poisoning and death. Or they pass mysteriously by underground streams until they emerge and, through the alchemy of air and sunlight, combine into new forms that kill vegetation, sicken cattle, and work unknown harm on those who drink from once pure wells. As Albert Schweitzer has said, "Man can hardly even recognize the devils of his own creation."

It took hundreds of millions of years to produce the life that now ₃ inhabits the earth—eons of time in which that developing and evolving and diversifying life reached a state of adjustment and balance with its surroundings. The environment, rigorously shaping and directing the life it supported, contained elements that were hostile as well as supporting. Certain rocks gave out dangerous radiation; even within the light of the sun, from which all life draws its energy, there were short-wave radiations with power to injure. Given time—time not in years but in millennia—life adjusts, and a balance has been reached. For time is the essential ingredient; but in the modern world there is no time.

The rapidity of change and the speed with which new situations are ₄ created follow the impetuous and heedless pace of man rather than the deliberate pace of nature. Radiation is no longer merely the background radiation of rocks, the bombardment of cosmic rays, the ultraviolet of the sun that have existed before there was any life on earth; radiation is now the unnatural creation of man's tampering with the atom. The chemicals to which life is asked to make its adjustment are no longer merely the calcium and silica and copper and all the rest of the minerals washed out of the rocks and carried in rivers to the sea; they are the synthetic creations of man's inventive mind, brewed in his laboratories, and having no counterparts in nature.

To adjust to these chemicals would require time on the scale that is ₅ nature's; it would require not merely the years of a man's life but the life of generations. And even this, were it by some miracle possible, would be futile, for the new chemicals come from our laboratories in an endless stream; almost five hundred annually find their way into actual use in the United States alone. The figure is staggering and its implications are not easily grasped—500 new chemicals to which the bodies of men and animals are required somehow to adapt each year, chemicals totally outside the limits of biologic experience.

Among them are many that are used in man's war against nature. ₆ Since the mid-1940's over 200 basic chemicals have been created for use in killing insects, weeds, rodents, and other organisms described in the modern vernacular as "pests"; and they are sold under several thousand different brand names.

These sprays, dusts, and aerosols are now applied almost univer- ₇ sally to farms, gardens, forests, and homes—nonselective chemicals that have the power to kill every insect, the "good" and the "bad," to still the song of birds and the leaping of fish in the streams, to coat the leaves with a deadly film, and to linger on in soil—all this though the intended target may be only a few weeds or insects. Can anyone believe it is possible to lay down such a barrage of poisons on the surface of the earth without making it unfit for all life? They should not be called "insecticides," but "biocides."

The whole process of spraying seems caught up in an endless spi- ₈ ral. Since DDT was released for civilian use, a process of escalation has been going on in which ever more toxic materials must be found. This has happened because insects, in a triumphant vindication of Darwin's principle of the survival of the fittest, have evolved super races immune to the particular insecticide used, hence a deadlier one has always to be developed—and then a deadlier one than that. It has happened also because, for reasons to be described later, destructive insects often undergo a "flareback," or resurgence, after spraying in numbers greater than before. Thus the chemical war is never won, and all life is caught in its violent crossfire.

Along with the possibility of the extinction of mankind by nuclear war, the central problem of our age has therefore become the contamination of man's total environment with such substances of incredible potential for harm—substances that accumulate in the tissues of plants and animals and even penetrate the germ cells to shatter or alter the very material of heredity upon which the shape of the future depends.

Some would-be architects of our future look toward a time when it will be possible to alter the human germ plasm by design. But we may easily be doing so now by inadvertence, for many chemicals, like radiation, bring about gene mutations. It is ironic to think that man might determine his own future by something so seemingly trivial as the choice of an insect spray.

All this has been risked—for what? Future historians may well be amazed by our distorted sense of proportion. How could intelligent beings seek to control a few unwanted species by a method that contaminated the entire environment and brought the threat of disease and death even to their own kind? Yet this is precisely what we have done. We have done it, moreover, for reasons that collapse the moment we examine them. We are told that the enormous and expanding use of pesticides is necessary to maintain farm production. Yet is our real problem not one of *overproduction?* Our farms, despite measures to remove acreages from production and to pay farmers *not* to produce, have yielded such a staggering excess of crops that the American taxpayer in 1962 is paying out more than one billion dollars a year as the total carrying cost of the surplus-food storage program. And is the situation helped when one branch of the Agriculture Department tries to reduce production while another states, as it did in 1958, "It is believed generally that reduction of crop acreages under provisions of the Soil Bank will stimulate interest in use of chemicals to obtain maximum production on the land retained in crops."

All this is not to say there is no insect problem and no need of control. I am saying, rather, that control must be geared to realities, not to mythical situations, and that the methods employed must be such that they do not destroy us along with the insects.

The problem whose attempted solution has brought such a train of disaster in its wake is an accompaniment of our modern way of life. Long before the age of man, insects inhabited the earth—a group of extraordinarily varied and adaptable beings. Over the course of time since man's advent, a small percentage of the more than half a million species of insects have come into conflict with human welfare in two principal ways: as competitors for the food supply and as carriers of human disease.

Disease-carrying insects become important where human beings 14 are crowded together, especially under conditions where sanitation is poor, as in time of natural disaster or war or in situations of extreme poverty and deprivation. Then control of some sort becomes necessary. It is a sobering fact, however, as we shall presently see, that the method of massive chemical control has had only limited success, and also threatens to worsen the very conditions it is intended to curb.

Under primitive agricultural conditions the farmer had few insect 15 problems. These arose with the intensification of agriculture—the devotion of immense acreages to a single crop. Such a system set the stage for explosive increases in specific insect populations. Single-crop farming does not take advantage of the principles by which nature works; it is agriculture as an engineer might conceive it to be. Nature has introduced great variety into the landscape, but man has displayed a passion for simplifying it. Thus he undoes the built-in checks and balances by which nature holds the species within bounds. One important natural check is a limit on the amount of suitable habitat for each species. Obviously then, an insect that lives on wheat can build up its population to much higher levels on a farm devoted to wheat than on one in which wheat is intermingled with other crops to which the insect is not adapted.

The same thing happens in other situations. A generation or more 16 ago, the towns of large areas of the United States lined their streets with the noble elm tree. Now the beauty they hopefully created is threatened with complete destruction as disease sweeps through the elms, carried by a beetle that would have only limited chance to build up large populations and to spread from tree to tree if the elms were only occasional trees in a richly diversified planting.

Another factor in the modern insect problem is one that must be 17 viewed against a background of geologic and human history: the spreading of thousands of different kinds of organisms from their native homes to invade new territories. This worldwide migration has been studied and graphically described by the British ecologist Charles Elton in his recent book *The Ecology of Invasions*. During the Cretaceous Period, some hundred million years ago, flooding seas cut many land bridges between continents and living things found themselves confined in what Elton calls "colossal separate nature reserves." There, isolated from others of their kind, they developed many new species. When some of the land masses were joined again, about 15 million years ago, these species began to move out into new territories—a movement that is not only still in progress but is now receiving considerable assistance from man.

The importation of plants is the primary agent in the modern 18 spread of species, for animals have almost invariably gone along with the plants, quarantine being a comparatively recent and not completely effective innovation. The United States Office of Plant Introduction alone has introduced almost 200,000 species and varieties of plants

from all over the world. Nearly half of the 180 or so major insect enemies of plants in the United States are accidental imports from abroad,
and most of them have come as hitchhikers on plants.

In new territory, out of reach of the restraining hand of the natural
enemies that kept down its numbers in its native land, an invading plant
or animal is able to become enormously abundant. Thus it is no accident that our most troublesome insects are introduced species.

These invasions, both the naturally occurring and those dependent
on human assistance, are likely to continue indefinitely. Quarantine and
massive chemical campaigns are only extremely expensive ways of buying time. We are faced, according to Dr. Elton, "with a life-and-death
need not just to find new technological means of suppressing this plant
or that animal"; instead we need the basic knowledge of animal populations and their relations to their surroundings that will "promote an
even balance and damp down the explosive power of outbreaks and
new invasions." 20

Much of the necessary knowledge is now available but we do not
use it. We train ecologists in our universities and even employ them in
our governmental agencies but we seldom take their advice. We allow
the chemical death rain to fall as though there were no alternative,
whereas in fact there are many, and our ingenuity could soon discover
many more if given opportunity. 21

Have we fallen into a mesmerized state that makes us accept as
inevitable that which is inferior or detrimental, as though having lost
the will or the vision to demand that which is good? Such thinking, in
the words of the ecologist Paul Shepard, "idealizes life with only its
head out of water, inches above the limits of toleration of the corruption of its own environment. . . . Why should we tolerate a diet of
weak poisons, a home in insipid surroundings, a circle of acquaintances
who are not quite our enemies, the noise of motors with just enough
relief to prevent insanity? Who would want to live in a world which is
just not quite fatal?" 22

Yet such a world is pressed upon us. The crusade to create a chem-
ically sterile, insect-free world seems to have engendered a fanatic zeal
on the part of many specialists and most of the so-called control agencies. On every hand there is evidence that those engaged in spraying
operations exercise a ruthless power. "The regulatory entomologists . . .
function as prosecutor, judge and jury, tax assessor and collector and
sheriff to enforce their own orders," said Connecticut entomologist
Neely Turner. The most flagrant abuses go unchecked in both state and
federal agencies. 23

It is not my contention that chemical insecticides must never be
used. I do contend that we have put poisonous and biologically potent
chemicals indiscriminately into the hands of persons largely or wholly
ignorant of their potentials for harm. We have subjected enormous
numbers of people to contact with these poisons, without their consent
and often without their knowledge. If the Bill of Rights contains no
guarantee that a citizen shall be secure against lethal poisons distributed 24

either by private individuals or by public officials, it is surely only because our forefathers, despite their considerable wisdom and foresight, could conceive of no such problem.

I contend, furthermore, that we have allowed these chemicals to be used with little or no advance investigation of their effect on soil, water, wildlife, and man himself. Future generations are unlikely to condone our lack of prudent concern for the integrity of the natural world that supports all life.

There is still very limited awareness of the nature of the threat. This is an era of specialists, each of whom sees his own problem and is unaware of or intolerant of the larger frame into which it fits. It is also an era dominated by industry, in which the right to make a dollar at whatever cost is seldom challenged. When the public protests, confronted with some obvious evidence of damaging results of pesticide applications, it is fed little tranquilizing pills of half truth. We urgently need an end to these false assurances, to the sugar coating of unpalatable facts. It is the public that is being asked to assume the risks that the insect controllers calculate. The public must decide whether it wishes to continue on the present road, and it can do so only when in full possession of the facts. In the words of Jean Rostand, "The obligation to endure gives us the right to know."

COMPREHENSION

1. What does Carson mean by "the obligation to endure"?
2. What reasons does the author cite for the overpopulation of insects?
3. What remedies does Carson propose?

RHETORIC

1. What tone does Carson use in her essay? Does she seem to be a subjective or an objective speaker? Give specific support for your response.
2. How does the use of words such as *dangerous, evil, irrevocable,* and *sinister* help to shape the reader's reaction to the piece?
3. Examine the ordering of ideas in paragraph 4, and consider how such an order serves to reinforce Carson's argument.
4. Paragraph 9 consists of only one sentence. What is its function in the essay's scheme?
5. Examine Carson's use of expert testimony. How does it help to strengthen her thesis?
6. How effectively does the essay's conclusion help to tie up Carson's points? What is the writer's intent in this final paragraph? How does she accomplish this aim?

WRITING

1. Write an essay in which you suggest solutions to the problems brought up in Carson's piece. You may want to suggest measures that the average citi-

zen can take to eliminate the casual use of insecticides to control the insect population.

2. Write an essay entitled "Insects Are Not the Problem; Humanity Is." In this essay, argue that it is humanity's greed that has caused such an imbalance in nature as to threaten the planet's survival.

3. Write a biographical research paper on Rachel Carson that focuses on her involvement with nature and environmental issues.

GREGG EASTERBROOK   Gregg Easterbrook was born in Buffalo, New York, in 1953. He received his B.A. degree from Colorado College in 1976 and an M.S.J. degree from Northwestern University in 1987. He has served as a contributing editor for the *Washington Monthly,* the *Atlantic Monthly,* and *Newsweek.* In addition, he published a novel entitled *A Love Story for People Who Want the World to Make Sense.* His nonfiction has also been published in book form. Much of his writing reflects his concern both for the environment and for morality, such as this essay published in *The New Yorker* in 1995.

GREGG EASTERBROOK

Here Comes the Sun

Few ideas are more deeply entrenched in our political culture than that of impending ecological doom. Beginning in 1962, when Rachel Carson warned readers of this magazine that pollution was a threat to all human and animal life on the planet, pessimistic appraisals of the health of the environment have been issued with increasing urgency. And yet, thanks in large part to her warnings, a powerful political movement was born—its coming-out party, the first Earth Day demonstration, took place on April 22nd, twenty-five years ago—and a series of landmark environmental bills became law: the Clean Air Act (1970), the Clean Water Act (1972), and the Endangered Species Act (1973). These laws and their equivalents in Western Europe, along with a vast array of private efforts spurred by the environmental consciousness that Carson helped raise, have been a stunning success. In both the United States and Europe, environmental trends are, for the most part, positive; and environmental regulations, far from being burdensome and expensive, have proved to be strikingly effective, have cost less than was anticipated, and have made the economies of the countries that have put them into effect stronger, not weaker.

Nevertheless, the vocabulary of environmentalism has continued to be dominated by images of futility, crisis, and decline. In 1988, Thomas Berry, an essayist popular among ecologists, wrote that "the planet cannot long endure present modes of human exploitation." In 1990, Gaylord Nelson, the former senator from Wisconsin, who was a prime mover behind the first Earth Day, said that environmental problems "are a greater threat to Earth's life-sustaining systems than a nuclear war." And in 1993 Vice-President Al Gore said that the planet now was suffering "grave and perhaps irreparable damage." But, at least insofar as the Western world is concerned, this line of thought is an anachronism, rendered obsolete by its own success. Nor are environmentalists the only people reluctant to acknowledge the good news; advocates at both ends of the political spectrum, each side for its own reasons, seem to have tacitly agreed to play it down. The left is afraid of the environmental good news because it undercuts stylish pessimism; the right is afraid of the good news because it shows that government regulations might occasionally amount to something other than wickedness incarnate, and actually produce benefits at an affordable cost.

This is a bad bargain—for liberals especially. Their philosophy is under siege on many fronts—crime, welfare, medical care, and education, among others. So why not trumpet the astonishing, and continuing, record of success in environmental protection?

Consider some of what has been accomplished in this country in the quarter century since the first Earth Day. Thanks to legislation, technical advances, and lawsuits that have forced polluters to pay liability costs, America's air and water are getting cleaner, forests are expanding, and many other environmental indicators are on the upswing.

Smog has declined by about a third, though there are now eighty-five per cent more vehicles being driven a hundred and five per cent more miles a year. In Los Angeles, the decline has been particularly dramatic: smog has decreased by almost fifty per cent, during a time when the city's vehicle population has risen sixty-five per cent. Since 1970, airborne levels of lead have declined ninety-eight per cent nationwide; annual emissions of carbon monoxide are down twenty-four per cent; emissions of sulfur dioxide, the chief cause of acid rain, have fallen thirty per cent, even as the use of coal, the main source of sulfur, has almost doubled; and emissions of fine soot, which causes respiratory disease, have fallen seventy-eight per cent. Air-quality trends are sufficiently positive so that several urban areas, such as Detroit and Kansas City, have been removed from the federal smog-watch list, and none have been added.

Signs of improved water quality are equally in evidence. In 1972, only a third of the bodies of water in the United States were safe for fishing and swimming. Today, almost two-thirds are safe, and the proportion continues to rise. Excessive phosphorus, a barometer of pollution, peaked in the Great Lakes around fifteen years ago; readings now are between forty and seventy per cent lower. Boston Harbor, Chesapeake Bay, Long Island Sound, Puget Sound, and other bodies of water that were once on the verge of biological death are showing steady improvement.

Another sign of progress is the decline of toxic hazards. Quarrels over the final disposition of old chemical-waste dumps continue to bedevil courts and politicians, but, because of tight regulations and industrial liability, the creation of new toxic dumps has nearly stopped, and is unlikely ever to resume. One of the largest chemical-waste sites, the Rocky Mountain Arsenal, near Denver, where nerve gases, pesticides, and firebombs were once manufactured, used to be described as the deadliest place on earth. In 1992, it was designated a National Wildlife Refuge; a number of rare species now thrive there. Their presence hardly proves that chemical wastes are somehow good for birds and animals, of course, but it does show that toxic wastes can be and are being contained. Just between 1988 and 1992, American industry's toxic emissions fell thirty-five per cent, even as petrochemical production expanded. Thanks to tight regulation of the dangerous compound dioxin, an estimated thirty pounds of this substance will be emitted in 1995 by all known United States sources combined, which suggests that the problem is almost certainly under control. 7

In recent years, several worrisome environmental trends have either declined from their peak or ended altogether. The amount of household trash dumped in landfills, for example, has been diminishing since the late nineteen-eighties, when recycling began to take hold. Recycling, which was a fringe idea a decade ago, is now a major growth industry, and is converting more than twenty per cent of America's municipal wastes into useful products. Despite start-up problems, many municipal recycling programs now pay for themselves. Emissions of chlorofluorocarbons, which deplete the ozone layer, have been declining since 1987. Studies now suggest that ozone-layer replenishment may begin within a decade. Dozens of American cities once dumped raw sludge into the ocean. This category of pollution passed into history in 1992, when the final load of New York City sludge slithered off a barge imaginatively named Spring Brook. Today, instead of being dumped into the ocean, municipal sludge is either disposed of in regulated landfills or, increasingly, put to good use as fertilizer. 8

It may be hard to believe, but efficient new manufacturing techniques, recycling, and other technological advances are allowing us to consume some natural resources at lower rates. Eric Larson, of Princeton University, and his colleagues have shown that American per-capita use of ammonia, cement, aluminum, chlorine, and steel has been flat or falling for a decade or more. 9

Even though Americans use more paper than they did a decade ago, this country is increasingly covered by a canopy of trees. It is commonly assumed that America is undergoing deforestation, but reforestation has been the trend for at least half a century. Everyone knows that in some parts of the United States urban acreage is expanding; what is much less widely recognized is that, in some areas, forest acreage is expanding rapidly, too. (For example, in the mid-eighteen-hundreds about a third of Massachusetts was wooded; today, though the state has six times the population, three-fifths of its area is forest- 10 land.) High-yield agriculture allows farmers to produce more food from the same or less land, and much of the acreage that is withdrawn from agriculture ends up reverting to woodland or prairie. The supposed crisis of the vanishing American farm, which has been regularly bemoaned throughout the postwar era, has in fact been a blessing to nature. And acid rain has proved less damaging to trees than was once projected, and is in decline. At the same time, the acreage of America held in preservation has risen steadily through this century and now amounts to more than two times the area of California. Last year alone, 7.4 million acres of ancient forest in the Pacific Northwest were put into reserves by President Clinton, and nearly ten million acres of Southwestern desert were declared off limits by Congress—a combined area larger than the state of West Virginia.

America's record of protecting species threatened with extinction,   11
which is often depicted as dismal, is in truth enviable. Since 1973, when the Endangered Species Act took effect, seven animal species in North America have disappeared, but several hundred others once considered certain to die out continue to exist in the wild. A number of species, including the bald eagle and the Arctic peregrine falcon, are doing so well that they have been or are being taken off the priority-protection list.

Even more extraordinary than America's environmental progress of   12
the past generation is the fact that these advances have been achieved in affordable and practical ways. When pollution controls for cars were first proposed, in 1970, automakers predicted that the required systems would cost about three thousand dollars per car in today's dollars. Instead, controls now add between five hundred and a thousand dollars to the price of a new vehicle, and they work amazingly well: current models emit an average of eighty per cent less pollution per mile than was emitted by new cars in 1970. Moreover, fuel-efficiency gains have reduced the typical car's annual gasoline consumption by around three hundred gallons. The fuel savings offset the equipment costs, with the result that for motorists the environmental features on new cars are essentially free of charge.

Nor is this an isolated example. In 1990, when new acid-rain con-   13
trols were imposed on power plants, they were expected to cost about seven hundred and fifty dollars per ton of pollution avoided; instead, the price today is a hundred and fifty dollars per ton. Monsanto, the chemical and pharmaceutical giant, has been able to cut toxic-air emissions by ninety per cent without excessive expense, at least in part because savings from the recycling of chemicals have offset the costs of pollution-reduction technology. The installation of high-efficiency commercial-lighting systems—inspired in part by the 1990 version of the Clean Air Act—is saving business tens of millions of dollars a year in expenses.

Solar power and wind power, disappointments in the past, appear   14
to be on the verge of a takeoff. Last fall, the energy conglomerate

Enron announced plans to break ground in Nevada for the first unsubsidized, commercial-scale solar-electric array. The array will be built for profit, at a cost competitive with that of fossil-fuelled generators. Though fossil fuels today seem indispensable, they may be supplanted by renewable-energy sources in the near future. Today, the energy economy of the Western world is closer to operation on a renewable-power basis than it was a century ago to operation on the basis of the headlong combustion of petroleum. Should fossil-fuel use wane, in historic terms, as quickly as it arose, the greenhouse problem could almost solve itself.

It's true, of course, that some environmental programs are muddled. For instance, the Endangered Species Act can have the unfair effect of penalizing landholders who discover rare creatures on their property, by prohibiting use of the land. In the main, though, conservation has been an excellent investment for society. Environmental initiatives worked well even in their early years, when they were driven by top-heavy federal edicts. They work even better as new regulations have centered on market mechanisms and voluntary choice; new acid-rain reductions, for example, are being achieved at unexpectedly affordable rates, thanks to a free-market program under which companies trade pollution "allowances" with each other. Western market economies excel at producing what they are asked to produce, and, increasingly, the market is being asked to produce conservation. Environmental reform should be seen as a boon to Western industry, impelling it toward efficiencies that enhance its long-term competitiveness; indeed, environmentalism may be saving the consumer society from itself.   15

The unmistakable trend toward environmental progress in the West should not delude us into supposing that from now on the global environment will somehow take care of itself. Throughout much of the Third World, basic water sanitation is awful, the air is thick with pollutants, and wildlife loss is rampant. Nor can we afford to be complacent about the domestic environment. Though most indicators in the West are positive, danger signs nevertheless remain, including the decline of the Pacific salmon and the unresolved problem of how to deal with the nuclear detritus of the Cold War. The bewildering array of environmental statutes in the Western world (there are sixteen major laws in the United States alone) needs to be streamlined with a simplified general conservation law that would focus on habitat preservation, for this is likely to be the primary ecological issue of the coming century.   16

Environmentalism has become a core American political value, close to unassailable even among conservatives. A recent Times Mirror survey is typical. A majority of the respondents agreed with the statement that "government regulation of business usually does more harm than good," yet seventy-eight per cent of the same respondents also think that "this country should do whatever it takes to protect the environment."   17

Poll numbers of this kind suggest that Speaker Newt Gingrich may 18
come to regret the anti-environmentalist aspects of his Contract with
America. In February, House Republicans rushed through a measure
designed to weaken anti-pollution regulations by making them very difficult to enforce. The bill prompted Dick Zimmer, of New Jersey, a
conservative who is the leading House Republican thinker on regulatory reform, to criticize it for substituting "bumper-sticker slogans" for
considered judgments. The House Republican anti-environment initiative—which may fail in the Senate—has become an indiscriminate
attack on all conservation rules, including the ones that have proved
themselves effective and affordable.

In the nineteen-eighties, Gingrich was a frequent supporter of envi- 19
ronmental legislation, but now that he has become Speaker he sees red
when he hears green. Recently, for example, he attacked the ripping of
asbestos out of walls as an "absurdly irrational" expense and danger for
which the Environmental Protection Agency is to blame. This is a convenient rewriting of history, and not just because as a backbencher
Gingrich himself cast at least two votes in favor of asbestos removal:
since 1990, the Environmental Protection Agency has been urging that
most asbestos *not* be ripped out, on the ground that removal can cause
more harm than good. Who, then, mandates asbestos removal? State
and local governments. That is, the drive to get asbestos out of walls
comes from the local officials whom Gingrich seems to revere, while
the federal bureaucrats he disdains have been urging moderation.

The ecological recovery in progress in the West has many heroes: 20
pioneers such as Rachel Carson; environmental activists who carried
on the fight; scientists and engineers who have increasingly made clean
technology viable; even some business leaders who have become con-
verts to conservation. Political liberalism, which provided the legislative
muscle, deserves a large share of the credit, too. Yet liberalism resists the
glad tidings of ecological rebound. When liberal intellectuals and
Democratic politicians talk about nature in the vocabulary of fashionable defeatism, they sell themselves and their philosophy short.

A telling example of liberal discomfort with environmental opti- 21
mism came in the 1988 Presidential campaign. Candidate George Bush
began his comeback from a deep deficit in the polls with a memorable
TV commercial that pronounced the waters of Boston Harbor the dirt-
iest in America, and pinned the blame on his opponent, Governor
Michael Dukakis. After the commercial ran, Dukakis was silent about
the harbor, seeming to accede to the charge. Many analysts consider
the Boston Harbor spot to have been the turning point in the 1988
campaign. Yet the commercial was shot so as to frame out of the picture a four-billion-dollar complex rising in the background—the largest
water-treatment system in United States history. Its construction had
already begun, at regional expense. At the time Bush made his commercial, there was every reason to hope that the new system would
clean Boston Harbor rapidly; it has, and the harbor is now safe again

for swimming. So why didn't Dukakis respond to Bush immediately by pointing out that a solution was at hand? Because doing so would have required Dukakis to talk about the environment in upbeat tones.

More recently, Carol Browner, the current head of the Environmental Protection Agency, fell victim to the same syndrome. In 1994, Browner, a lifelong liberal Democrat, gave a series of speeches pointing out that there were many signs of environmental progress. She proposed a "common-sense initiative" and revisions that would improve conservation law by adding cost-benefit analysis, simplifying rules for cleanups, and eliminating regulatory overkill. And she did this long before anyone had heard the words "Contract with America." In 1994, Browner's hopeful declarations sank without a trace into the abyss of conventional opinion. Her effort fizzled because Democrats, then still in control of Congress, were put off by the suggestion of environmental good news, and also because White House support was faint.

Liberalism is on the defensive today because, as a philosophy, it 23 concentrates almost entirely on what has failed—about America, about public policy, about daily life. Obviously, there are failures aplenty, but there are successes as well. In the West, environmental protection is the leading postwar triumph of progressive government. Because of this, the notion of impending doomsday is about to expire. We are about to become environmental optimists.

COMPREHENSION

1. What is the thesis of the essay?
2. According to the author, which political group has celebrated the improvement in environmental conditions that began in the 1970s? Explain.
3. The author states, "Environmentalism has become a core American political value." What does this mean? What does it signify in terms of the evolution of American politics?

RHETORIC

1. What is the reference to pop culture in the essay's title? What is the purpose of choosing a title that has reader recognition? What can you infer about the age group to which the author is addressing his essay?
2. Examine the opening sentences of the first two paragraphs. How do they serve as topic sentences for the paragraphs they introduce?
3. The essay is divided into four sections. Discuss the relationship of each section to the others. How does the opening sentence of each section contribute to establishing the content of the section it introduces?
4. What forms of evidence does the author use to persuade the reader that he is an expert in his subject matter? What is the cumulative effect of providing this evidence?
5. The author uses the terms *environmentalism* and *environmentalist* frequently in the essay, but he never defines the terms. What is your defin-

ition of these terms? What elements of the essay helped to define them for you?

6. The final sentence of the essay is a prediction. Why has the author chosen to end his essay with this device? Try reading the conclusion without this sentence. How does its absence change the tone of the conclusion and the essay as a whole?

7. What assumptions is the author making about his readership? How meaningful would the essay be to someone unfamiliar with the individual and historical references made in it?

WRITING

1. Rachel Carson is mentioned several times during the essay. For a research project, study the works of Rachel Carson, and write a cause-and-effect essay describing her influence upon today's environmental movement.

2. Write a 400-word précis, or summary, of the essay. Include enough details to make the author's theme and topic clear to someone who had not read the essay.

3. Using the rhetoric of process analysis, write an essay in which you describe ten ways to make your school, neighborhood, or workplace more environmentally sound.

LOREN EISELEY   Loren Eiseley (1907–1977) was an educator, anthropologist, poet, and author. He is best known for his books *The Immense Journey* (1957), *Darwin's Century* (1958), *The Firmament of Time* (rev. ed., 1960), and *The Night Country* (1971). His books wonderfully combine poetic imagination with scientific objectivity. In the following essay, Eiseley shows his capacity for seeing profoundly into the most common scenes.

LOREN EISELEY

How Natural Is Natural?

In the more obscure scientific circles which I frequent there is a legend circulating about a late distinguished scientist who, in his declining years, persisted in wearing enormous padded boots much too large for him. He had developed, it seems, what to his fellows was a wholly irrational fear of falling through the interstices of that largely empty molecular space which common men in their folly speak of as the world. A stroll across his living-room floor had become, for him, something as dizzily horrendous as the activities of a window washer on the Empire State Building. Indeed, with equal reason he could have passed a ghostly hand through is own ribs.

The quivering network of his nerves, the awe-inspiring movement of his thought had become a vague cloud of electrons interspersed with the light-year distances that obtain between us and the farther galaxies. This was the natural world which he had helped to create, and in which, at last, he had found himself a lonely and imprisoned occupant. All around him the ignorant rushed on their way over the illusion of substantial floors, leaping, though they did not see it, from particle to particle, over a bottomless abyss. There was even a question as to the reality of the particles which bore them up. It did not, however, keep insubstantial newspapers from being sold, or insubstantial love from being made.

Not long ago I became aware of another world perhaps equally nat- ural and real, which man is beginning to forget. My thinking began in New England under a boat dock. The lake I speak of has been pre-empted and civilized by man. All day long in the vacation season high-speed motorboats, driven with the reckless abandon common to the young Apollos of our society, speed back and forth, carrying loads of equally attractive girls. The shores echo to the roar of powerful motors and the delighted screams of young Americans with uncounted horse-power surging under their hands. In truth, as I sat there under the boat dock, I had some desire to swim or to canoe in the older ways of the great forest which once lay about this region. Either notion would have been folly. I would have been gaily chopped to ribbons by teen-age youngsters whose eyes were always immutably fixed on the far horizons of space, or upon the dials which indicated the speed of their passing. There was another world, I was to discover, along the lake shallows and under the boat dock, where the motors could not come.

As I sat there one sunny morning when the water was peculiarly translucent, I saw a dark shadow moving swiftly over the bottom. It was the first sign of life I had seen in this lake, whose shores seemed to yield little but washed-in beer cans. By and by the gliding shadow ceased to scurry from stone to stone over the bottom. Unexpectedly, it headed almost directly for me. A furry nose with gray whiskers broke the sur-face. Below the whiskers green water foliage trailed out in an inverted V as long as his body. A muskrat still lived in the lake. He was bringing in his breakfast.

I sat very still in the strips of sunlight under the pier. To my surprise the muskrat came almost to my feet with his little breakfast of greens. He was young, and it rapidly became obvious to me that he was labor-ing under an illusion of his own, and that he thought animals and men were still living in the Garden of Eden. He gave me a friendly glance from time to time as he nibbled his greens. Once, even, he went out into the lake again and returned to my feet with more greens. He had not, it seemed, heard very much about men. I shuddered. Only the evening before I had heard a man describe with triumphant enthusiasm how he had killed a rat in the garden because the creature had dared to nibble his petunias. He had even showed me the murder weapon, a sharp-edged brick.

On this pleasant shore a war existed and would go on until nothing 6
remained but man. Yet this creature with the gray, appealing face
wanted very little: a strip of shore to coast up and down, sunlight and
moonlight, some weeds from the deep water. He was an edge-of-the-
world dweller, caught between a vanishing forest and a deep lake pre-
empted by unpredictable machines full of chopping blades. He eyed
me near-sightedly, a green leaf posed in his mouth. Plainly he had come
with some poorly instructed memory about the lion and the lamb.

"You had better run away now," I said softly, making no move- 7
ment in the shafts of light. "You are in the wrong universe and must
not make this mistake again. I am really a very terrible and cunning
beast. I can throw stones." With this I dropped a little pebble at his
feet.

He looked at me half blindly, with eyes much better adjusted to the 8
wavering shadows of his lake bottom than to sight in the open air. He
made almost as if to take the pebble up into his forepaws. Then a
thought seemed to cross his mind—a thought perhaps telepathically
received, as Freud once hinted, in the dark world below and before
man, a whisper of ancient disaster heard in the depths of a burrow. Perhaps after all this was not Eden. His nose twitched carefully; he edged
toward the water.

As he vanished in an oncoming wave, there went with him a natural 9
world, distinct from the world of girls and motorboats, distinct from the
world of the professor holding to reality by some great snowshoe effort
in his study. My muskrat's shore-line universe was edged with the dark
wall of hills on one side and the waspish drone of motors farther out,
but it was a world of sunlight he had taken down into the water weeds.
It hovered there, waiting for my disappearance. I walked away,
obscurely pleased that darkness had not gained on life by any act of
mine. In so many worlds, I thought, how natural is "natural"—and is
there anything we can call a natural world at all?

COMPREHENSION

1. State in your own words the thesis of this essay.
2. Describe the three "worlds" mentioned in this essay by Eiseley.
3. Why is Eiseley surprised that a muskrat still lives in the lake? Cite specific
   details that might threaten a muskrat in the lake's world.

RHETORIC

1. The phrases "world of sunlight" and "darkness" (paragraph 9) are meant to
   be taken figuratively. What do they mean?
2. Explain the allusions to "Apollos" (paragraph 3); "the Garden of Eden"
   (paragraph 5); and Freud (paragraph 8).
3. Explain the relation between paragraphs 1 to 2 and 3 to 9. What rhetorical
   technique do both groups use?

4. How does Eiseley use narration and description in his essay? Cite examples of both.
5. What details does Eiseley use in contrasting the muskrat's world to the typical American's world?
6. Analyze the way Eiseley develops his concluding paragraph.

WRITING

1. Why does Eiseley despair at the disappearance of the other world? Why should we protect wildlife and wilderness if it means limiting our own growth?
2. Write an essay in which you contrast aspects of the natural world with the artificial world. Use details to support your contrast: For example, you can describe the life of a bird in the city, of a raccoon in the suburbs, or a deer or bear in a state park.
3. Both Eiseley and E. B. White (in "Once More to the Lake," Chapter 1) focus on specific bodies of water in order to develop insights into human nature and the natural world. In a comparative essay, explain their purpose and how they develop it.
4. Analyze the writing styles of Eiseley and Carson. Examine sentence structure, descriptive techniques, use of evidence, and figurative language.

GRETEL EHRLICH   Gretel Ehrlich was born in California in 1949 and educated at Bennington College, UCLA, and The New School for Social Research. She currently lives on a ranch in Shell, Wyoming. She has worked as a professional documentary filmmaker. Her essays have appeared in *The New York Times, The Atlantic, Harper's,* and the *New Age Journal.* She has also published two books of poetry and a story collection, *City tales, Wyoming Stories.* Ehrlich has received awards from the National Endowment for the Arts and the Wyoming Council for the Arts. In the following selection, with the eyes and ears of an anthropologist and the knowledge of a historian, Ehrlich provides us with a comprehensive view of a life most Americans are no longer familiar with.

GRETEL EHRLICH

Wyoming: The Solace of Open Spaces

It's May, and I've just awakened from a nap, curled against sagebrush the way my dog taught me to sleep—sheltered from wind. A weather front is pulling the huge sky over me, and from the dark a hailstone has hit me on the head.

I'm trailing a band of 2000 sheep across a stretch of Wyoming bad- 2
land, a 50-mile trip that takes five days because sheep shade up in the
hot sun and won't budge until it cools. Bunched together now, and
excited into a run by the storm, they drift across dry land, tumbling
into draws like water and surging out again onto the rugged, choppy
plateaus that are the building blocks of this state.

The name "Wyoming" comes from an Indian word meaning "at the 3
great plains," but the plains are really valleys, great arid valleys, 1600
square miles' worth of them, with the horizon bending up on all sides
into mountain ranges. This gives the vastness a sheltering look.

Winter lasts six months here. Prevailing winds spill snowdrifts to 4
the east, and new storms from the northwest replenish them. This white
bulk is sometimes dizzying, even nauseating, to look at. At 20, 30, 40
degrees below zero, it is not only your car that doesn't work but also
your mind and body.

The landscape hardens into a dungeon of space. During the winter, 5
while I was riding to find a new calf, my legs half froze to the saddle,
and in the silence that such cold creates, I felt like the first person on
earth, or the last.

Today the sun is out—only a few clouds billowing. In the east, where 6
the sheep have started off without me, the benchland tilts up in a series
of red-earthed, eroded mesas, planed flat on top by a million years of
water. Behind them, a bold line of muscular scraps rears up 10,000 feet
to become the Big Horn Mountains. A tidal pattern is engraved into the
ground, as if left by the sea that once covered this state. Canyons curve
down like galaxies to meet the oncoming rush of flat land.

To live and work in this kind of open country, with its 100-mile 7
views, is to lose the distinction between background and foreground.
When I asked an older ranch hand to describe Wyoming's openness, he
said, "It's all a bunch of nothing—wind and rattlesnakes—and so much
of it you can't tell where you're going or where you've been and it don't
make much difference."

John, a sheepman I know, is tall and handsome and has an explosive 8
temperament. He has a perfect intuition about people and sheep. They
call him "Highpockets" because he's so long-legged; his graceful stride
matches the distances he has to cover.

"Open space hasn't affected me at all. It's all the people moving in 9
on it," he said. The huge ranch he was born on takes up much of one
county and spreads into another state. For him to put 100,000 miles on
his pickup in three years and never leave home is not unusual.

Most of Wyoming has a "lean-to" look. Instead of big, roomy barns 10
and Victorian houses, there are dugouts, low sheds, log cabins, sheep
camps and fence lines that look like driftwood blown haphazardly into
place. People in Wyoming still feel pride because they live in such a
harsh place, part of the glamorous cowboy past, and they are determined not to be the victims of a mining-dominated future.

Most characteristic of the state's landscape is what a developer 11
euphemistically describes as "indigenous growth right up to your front

door"—a reference to waterless stands of salt sage, snakes, jack-rabbits, deerflies, red dust, a brief respite of wildflowers, dry washes and no trees.

Sagebrush covers 58,000 square miles of Wyoming. The biggest city has a population of 50,000, and there are only five settlements that could be called cities in the whole state. The rest are towns, scattered across the expanse with as much as 60 miles between them, their populations 2000, 50 or 10. They are fugitive-looking, perched on a barren, windblown bench, or tagged onto a river or a railroad, or laid out straight in a farming valley with implement stores and a block-long Mormon church.

In the eastern part of the state, which slides down into the Great Plains, the new mining settlements are boomtowns, trailer cities, metal knots on flat land. 13

Despite the desolate look, there's a coziness to living in this state. 14

There are so few people (only 470,000) that ranchers who buy and sell cattle know each other statewide. The kids who choose to go to college usually go to the state's one university, in Laramie. Hired hands work their way around Wyoming in a lifetime of hirings and firings. And, despite the physical separation, people stay in touch, often driving two or three hours to another ranch for dinner. 15

Seventy-five years ago, when travel was by buckboard or horseback, cowboys who were temporarily out of work rode the grub line—drifting from ranch to ranch, mending fences or milking cows, and receiving in exchange a bed and meals. Gossip and messages traveled this slow circuit with them, creating an intimacy among ranchers who were three and four weeks' ride apart. 16

One old-time couple I know, whose turn-of-the-century homestead was used by an outlaw gang as a relay station for stolen horses, recall that if you were traveling, desperado or not, any lighted ranch house was a welcome sign. 17

Even now, for someone who lives in a remote spot, arriving at a ranch or coming to town for supplies is cause for celebration. To emerge from isolation can be disorienting. Everything looks bright, new, vivid. After I had been herding sheep for only three days, the sound of the camp-tender's pickup flustered me. Longing for human company, I felt a foolish grin take over my face, yet I had to resist an urgent temptation to run and hide. 18

Things happen suddenly in Wyoming: the change of seasons and weather; for people, the violent swings into and out of isolation. But goodnaturedness goes hand in hand with severity. Friendliness is a tradition. Strangers passing on the road wave hello. 19

A common sight is two pickups stopped side by side far out on a range, on a dirt track winding through the sage. The drivers will share a cigarette, uncap their Thermos bottles, and pass a battered cup, steaming with coffee, between windows. These meetings summon up the details of several generations, because in Wyoming private histories are largely public knowledge. 20

In most parts of Wyoming, the human population is visibly outnumbered by the animal. Not far from my town of 50, I rode into a 21 narrow valley and startled a herd of 200 elk. Eagles look like small people as they eat car-killed deer by the road. Antelope, moving in small, graceful bands, travel at 60 m.p.h., their mouths open as if drinking in the space.

The solitude in which Westerners live makes them quiet. They telegraph thoughts and feelings by the way they tilt their heads and listen; pulling their Stetsons into a steep dive over their eyes or pigeon-toeing one boot over the other, they lean against a fence and take the whole scene in. These detached looks of quiet amusement are sometimes cynical, but they can also come from a dry-eyed humility as lucid as the air is clear. 22

Conversation goes on in what sounds like a private code. A few phrases imply a complex of meanings. Asking directions you get a curious list of details. While trailing sheep, I was told to "ride up to that kinda upturned rock, follow the pin wash, turn left at the dump, and then you'll see the waterhole. 23

I've spent hours riding to sheep camp at dawn in a pickup when nothing was said and eaten meals in the cookhouse when the only words spoken were a mumbled "Thank you, ma'am" at the end of dinner. The silence is profound. Instead of talking, we seem to share one eye. The landscape is engorged with detail, every movement on it chillingly sharp. The air between people is charged. 24

Spring weather is capricious and mean. It snows, then blisters with heat. There have been tornadoes. They lay their elephant trunks out in the sage until they find houses, then slurp everything up and leave. I've noticed that melting snowbanks hiss and rot, viperous, then drip into calm pools where ducklings hatch and livestock, being trailed to summer range, drink. 25

With the ice cover gone, rivers churn a milkshake brown, taking culverts and small bridges with them. Water in such an arid place (the average annual rainfall where I live is less than eight inches) is like blood. It festoons drab land with green veins: a line of cottonwoods following a stream; a strip of alfalfa, and on ditchbanks, wild asparagus growing. 26

I try to imagine a world of uncharted land, in which one could look over an uncompleted map and ride a horse past where all the lines have stopped. There is no real wilderness left; wilderness, yes, but true wilderness has been gone on this continent since the time of Lewis and Clark's overland journey. 27

Two hundred years ago, the Crow, Shoshone, Arapaho, Cheyenne, and Sioux roamed the intermountain West, orchestrating their movements according to hunger, season, and warfare. Once they acquired horses, they traversed the spines of all the big Wyoming ranges—the Absarokas, the Wind Rivers, the Tetons, the Big Horns—and wintered on the unprotected plains that fan out from them. Space was life. The word was their home. 28

What was life-giving to native Americans was often nightmarish to sod-busters who arrived encumbered with families and ethnic pasts to 29 be transplanted in nearly uninhabitable land. The great distances, the shortage of water and trees, and the loneliness created unexpected hardships for them.

In her book *O Pioneers!* Willa Cather gives a settler's version of the bleak landscape: "The little town behind them had vanished as if it had never been, had fallen behind the swell of the prairie, and the stern frozen country received them into its bosom. The homesteads were few and far apart; here and there a windmill gaunt against the sky, a sod house crouching in a hollow."

The emptiness of the West was for others a geography of possibility. Men and women who amassed great chunks of land and struggled to preserve unfenced empires were, despite their self-serving motives, unwitting geographers. They understood the lay of the land.

But by the 1850s, the Oregon and Mormon trails sported bumper-to-bumper traffic. Wealthy landowners, many of them aristocratic absentee landlords, known as remittance men because they were paid to come West and get out of their families' hair, overstocked the range with more than a million head of cattle. By 1885, the feed and water were desperately short, and the winter of 1886 laid out the gaunt bodies of dead animals so closely together that when the thaw came, one rancher from Kaycee claimed to have walked on cowhide all the way to Crazy Woman Creek, 20 miles away.

Territorial Wyoming was a boy's world. The land was generous with everything but water. At first there was room enough and food enough for everyone. And, as with all beginnings, an expansive mood set in. The young cowboys, drifters, shopkeepers, and schoolteachers were heroic, lawless, generous, rowdy, and tenacious. The individualism and optimism generated during those times have endured.

Cattle barons tried to control all the public grazing land by restricting membership in the Wyoming Stock Growers Association, as if it were a country club. They ostracized from roundups and brandings cowboys and ranchers who were not members, then denounced them as rustlers.

One cold-blooded murder of a small-time stockman kicked off the Johnson County cattle war, which was no simple good guy–bad guy shootout but a complicated class struggle between landed gentry and less affluent settlers—a shocking reminder that the West was not an egalitarian sanctuary after all.

Fencing ultimately enforced boundaries, but barbed wire abolished space. It was stretched across the beautiful valleys, into mountains, over desert badlands, through buffalo grass.

The "anything is possible" fever—the lure of any place—was constricted. The integrity of the land as a geographical body, and the freedom to ride anywhere on it, was lost.

I punched cows with a young man named Martin, who is the great-grandson of John Tisdale. His inheritance is not the open land that Tisdale knew and prematurely lost but a rage against restraint.

In all this open space, values crystalize quickly. People are strong on scruples but tenderhearted about quirky behavior. A friend and I found one ranch hand, who's "not right in the head," sitting in front of the badly decayed carcass of a cow, shaking his finger and saying, "Now, I don't want you to do this ever again!"

When I asked what was wrong with him, I was told, "He's goofier than hell, just like the rest of us." 40

Perhaps because the West is historically new, conventional morality is still felt to be less important than rock-bottom truths. Though there's always a lot of teasing and sparring around, people are blunt with each other, sometimes even cruel, believing honesty is stronger medicine than sympathy, which may console but often conceals. 41

The formality that goes hand in hand with the rowdiness is known as "the Western Code." It's a list of practical do's and don'ts, faithfully observed. A friend, Cliff, who runs a trapline in the winter, cut off half his foot while axing a hole in the ice. Alone, he dragged himself to his pickup and headed for town, stopping to open the ranch gate as he left, and getting out to close it again, thus losing, in his observance of rules, precious time and blood. 42

Later, he commented, "How would it look, them having to come to the hospital to tell me their cows had gotten out?" 43

The roominess of the state has affected political attitudes. Ranchers keep up with world politics and the convulsions of the economy but are basically isolationists. Used to running their own small empires of land and livestock, they're suspicious of big government. 44

It's a "don't fence me in" holdover from a century ago. They still want the elbow room their grandfathers had, so they're strongly conservative, but with a populist twist. 45

Summer is the season when we get our "cowboy tans"—on the lower parts of our faces and on three fourths of our arms. Excessive heat, in the 90s and higher, sends us outside with the mosquitoes. 46

After the brief lushness of summer, the sun moves south. The range grass is brown. Livestock has been trailed back down from the mountains. Waterholes begin to frost over at night. Last fall Martin asked me to accompany him on a pack trip. With five horses, we followed a river into the mountains behind the tiny Wyoming town of Meeteetse. Groves of aspen, red and orange, gave off a light that made us look toasted. 47

One of our evening entertainments was to watch the night sky. My dog, who also came on the trip, a dingo bred to herd sheep, is so used to the silence and empty skies that when an airplane flies over he always looks up and eyes the distant intruder quizzically. 48

The sky, lately, seems to be much more crowded than it used to be. Satellites make their silent passes in the dark with great regularity. We counted 18 in one hour's viewing. How odd to think that while they circumnavigated the planet, Martin and I had moved only six miles into our local wilderness, and had seen no other human for the two weeks we stayed there. 49

At night, by moonlight, the land is whittled to slivers—a ridge, a river, a strip of grassland stretching to the mountains, then the huge 50 sky. One morning a full moon was setting in the west just as the sun was rising. I felt precariously balanced between the two as I loped across a meadow. For a moment, I could believe that the stars, which were still visible, work like cooper's bands, holding everything above Wyoming together.

Space has a spiritual equivalent, and can heal what is divided and burdensome in us. My grandchildren will probably use space shuttles for a honeymoon trip or to recover from heart attacks, but closer to home we might also learn how to carry space inside ourselves in the effortless way we carry our skins. Space represents sanity, not a life purified, dull, or "spaced out" but one that might accommodate intelligently any idea or situation.

COMPREHENSION

1. What is Wyoming's predominant appeal to the author? Why has she chosen to live in its rather inhospitable climate?
2. Explain the ways in which Wyoming, for Ehrlich, symbolizes the American West.
3. In the concluding paragraph, Ehrlich says, "Space has a spiritual equivalent." What does she mean by this? How do the Wyoming natives display this spirituality? How has it affected the author?

RHETORIC

1. How do the following descriptions help create the nature of Wyoming space: "This gives the vastness a sheltering look" (paragraph 3); "The landscape hardens into a dungeon of space" (paragraph 5); and "Canyons curve down like galaxies" (paragraph 6)?
2. None of the direct speech in this essay is in the form of dialogue. How is this indicative of the Westerner's attitude toward speech? How does it support the idea that "A few phrases imply a complex of meanings" (paragraph 23)?
3. How does Ehrlich's introductory comment that "my dog taught me to sleep" (paragraph 1) set the general tone for the bond between humans and nature in Wyoming? What other evidence is there in the essay of this special relationship?
4. Paragraphs 28 through 37 describe Wyoming's history. What function does this serve in the essay? How does it explain life in present-day Wyoming?
5. In the conclusion, Ehrlich suggests that the relationship of humans to space as it exists in Wyoming may be dying out. What references are there in the essay that seem to move toward this conclusion?

WRITING

1. How can one's environment affect the nature of one's relationship with others? How can it affect one's "communicative style"? For example, do city dwellers speak differently from rural ones? Do people from one region—for

549

example, the South—relate differently toward one another than do people from another region? Explore these issues in an essay, focusing on a locale you are familiar with. Your topics don't have to be limited to speech but may include body language, dress, jewelry, and so forth.

2. Compare and contrast the sense of space in this essay with that in Orwell's "Shooting an Elephant" in Chapter 2.

3. Think about some quality that is important to you—for example, solitude or brightness—and then write an essay about a place or environment that captures this quality.

MARK TWAIN   Mark Twain (1835–1910) was the pseudonym of Samuel Langhorne Clemens, perhaps America's most famous humorist, narrator, and social observer. Many critics consider his book *The Adventures of Huckleberry Finn* (1884) the most significant and influential American novel ever written. Apprenticed to a printer in Hannibal, Missouri, at the age of 13, Twain quickly turned to life on the river, eventually becoming a pilot on riverboats. This job required him to measure and announce the depth of the river at each point so as to avoid accidents. After the Civil War put an end to river traffic, Twain went to Nevada, where he attempted and failed at several get-rich-quick schemes before turning to work as a newspaperman. His tales and anecdotes soon won him fame as a writer. His more famous books include *The Adventures of Tom Sawyer* (1876), *The Prince and the Pauper* (1882), and *A Connecticut Yankee in King Arthur's Court* (1889). His later life had bitter and tragic aspects, including heavy debt and the sad death of two of his daughters. His keen powers of observation and natural ability to create metaphors are evident in the following excerpt from *Life on the Mississippi.*

MARK TWAIN

Two Views of the Mississippi

The face of the water, in time, became a wonderful book—a book that was a dead language to the uneducated passenger, but which told its mind to me without reserve, delivering its most cherished secrets as clearly as if it uttered them with a voice. And it was not a book to be read once and thrown aside, for it had a new story to tell every day. Throughout the long twelve hundred miles there was never a page that was void of interest, never one that you could leave unread without loss, never one that you would want to skip, thinking you could find higher enjoyment in some other thing. There never was so wonderful a book written by man; never one whose interest was so absorbing, so unflagging, so sparklingly renewed with every re-perusal. The passenger who could not read it was charmed with a peculiar sort of faint dimple on its surface (on the rare occasions when he did not overlook it alto-gether); but to the pilot that was an *italicized* passage; indeed, it was more than that, it was a legend of the largest capitals, with a string of shouting exclamation points at the end of it; for it meant that a wreck or a rock was buried there that could tear the life out of the strongest vessel that ever floated. It is the faintest and simplest expression the water ever makes, and the most hideous to a pilot's eye. In truth, the passenger who could not read this book saw nothing but all manner of pretty pictures in it, painted by the sun and shaded by the clouds, whereas to the trained eye these were not pictures at all, but the grimmest and most dead-earnest of reading-matter.

Now when I had mastered the language of this water and had come 2 to know every trifling feature that bordered the great river as familiarly as I knew the letters of the alphabet, I had made a valuable acquisition. But I had lost something, too. I had lost something which could never be restored to me while I lived. All the grace, the beauty, the poetry had gone out of the majestic river! I still keep in mind a certain wonderful sunset which I witnessed when steamboating was new to me. A broad expanse of the river was turned to blood; in the middle distance the red hue brightened into gold, through which a solitary log came floating, black and conspicuous; in one place a long, slanting mark lay sparkling upon the water; in another the surface was broken by boiling, tumbling rings, that were as many-tinted as an opal; where the ruddy flush was faintest, was a smooth spot that was covered with graceful circles and radiating lines, ever so delicately traced; the shore on our left was densely wooded, and the sombre shadow that fell from this forest was broken in one place by a long, ruffled trail that shone like silver; and high above the forest wall a clean-stemmed dead tree waved a single leafy bough that glowed like a flame in the unobstructed splendor that was flowing from the sun. There were graceful curves, reflected images, woody heights, soft distances; and over the whole scene, far and near, the dissolving lights drifted steadily, enriching it, every passing moment, with new marvels of coloring.

I stood like one bewitched. I drank it in, in a speechless rapture. The 3 world was new to me, and I had never seen anything like this at home. But as I have said, a day came when I began to cease from noting the glories and the charms which the moon and the sun and the twilight wrought upon the river's face; another day came when I ceased alto-gether to note them. Then, if that sunset scene had been repeated, I should have looked upon it without rapture, and should have com-mented upon it, inwardly, after this fashion: This sun means that we are going to have wind to-morrow; that floating log means that the river is rising, small thanks to it; that slanting mark on the water refers to a bluff reef which is going to kill somebody's steamboat one of these nights, if it keeps on stretching out like that; those tumbling "boils" show a dissolving bar and a changing channel there; the lines and cir-cles in the slick water over yonder are a warning that that troublesome place is shoaling up dangerously; that silver streak in the shadow of the forest is the "break" from a new snag, and he has located himself in the very best place he could have found to fish for steamboats; that tall dead tree, with a single living branch, is not going to last long, and then how is a body ever going to get through this blind place at night without the friendly old landmark?

No, the romance and the beauty were all gone from the river. All the ⁴ value any feature of it had for me now was the amount of usefulness it could furnish toward compassing the safe piloting of a steamboat. Since those days, I have pitied doctors from my heart. What does the lovely flush in a beauty's cheek mean to a doctor but a "break" that ripples above some deadly disease? Are not all her visible charms sown thick with what are to him the signs and symbols of hidden decay? Does he ever see her beauty at all, or doesn't he simply view her professionally, and comment upon her unwholesome condition all to himself? And doesn't he sometimes wonder whether he has gained most or lost most by learning his trade?

COMPREHENSION

1. According to the author, what are the two Mississippis?
2. What is the author's attitude toward the "uneducated passenger"?
3. What does the author mean when he writes that he had "mastered the language" of the river (paragraph 2)?

RHETORIC

1. What is the central metaphor the author uses to describe the river? How does he divide the central metaphor into components?
2. From what time perspective is the author musing on the river? How does this perspective influence the tone of the essay?
3. Study the number and placement of semicolons in paragraphs 2 and 3. What is their rhetorical function? How would the mood of the paragraphs change if the semicolons were replaced with periods?
4. In general, the sentences in this essay are much longer than the standard English sentence. How does this alter the overall coherence of the essay? Why are long sentences uniquely suited for the subject matter?
5. The author uses descriptive passages such as "graceful curves, reflected images, woody heights, soft distances," and many other descriptors denoting and suggesting space and visual imagery. How do they contribute to the tone of the essay?
6. What is the author's purpose in posing four questions in the concluding paragraph of the essay? What is the rhetorical effect of ending the essay with a question?
7. The author paints a mental picture of the Mississippi in the following sentence: "A broad expanse of the river was turned to blood; in the middle distance the red hue brightened into gold, through which a solitary log came floating, black and conspicuous." What function does color serve in this

sentence? Cite other instances of Twain's use of color. How do they affect the relationship between you, the reader, and the subject matter?

WRITING

1. Write an essay comparing and contrasting your emotions and perceptual responses on your first day of college with your current perceptions and emotions.

2. Create a central metaphor out of a familiar place; for example, "school is a jail," "the street is a jungle," "the library is a house of ghosts," or "the park is an oasis." Describe the place you have selected, using vocabulary that reflects your central metaphor.

3. Write a critical essay on the subject of Twain's use of metaphor in this selection.

BARRY LOPEZ   Barry Lopez (b. 1945) was educated at the University of Notre Dame, where he received an A.B. degree in 1966 and an M.A.T. degree in 1968. He turned quickly to writing about nature, folklore, and the environment. His explorations of these subjects have led him to travel into wildernesses, including the Arctic and remote regions of the American Northwest. Among his books on nature are *Arctic Dreams: Imagination and Desire in a Northern Landscape* (1986), *Crossing Open Ground* (1988), and *The Rediscovery of North America* (1991). Lopez does not attempt to romanticize nature. Rather, he takes a long, hard look at the natural forces around us and reaches many original insights that have been praised by numerous reviewers. In addition, his lyrical style has brought him a faithful following of readers. He has received many awards and honors, including the National Book Award in nonfiction and the John Burroughs medal for distinguished natural history writing. In a recent interview, Lopez stated that he wanted his writing to create a continuous sense of wonder and hope in a world filled with chicanery and subterfuge.

BARRY LOPEZ

Renegotiating the Contracts

In an essay in *Harper's* magazine several years ago, Lewis Lapham wrote that democracy was an experiment, a flawed enterprise that required continued human attention if it was going to serve us well. The philosophy behind our relationship with animals in the Western world is also flawed, and in need of continued attention.

To put this in the most basic terms, our relationships with wild animals were once contractual—principled agreements, established and maintained in a spirit of reciprocity and mythic in their pervasiveness. Among hunting peoples in general in the northern hemisphere, these agreements derived from a sense of mutual obligation and courtesy.

Over the past two decades, in particular, our contemporary relationships with wild animals have been energetically scrutinized by anthropologists, moral philosophers, and field biologists. A renewed interest in the mythologies and values of hunting peoples has caused us to question the moral basis for a continuation of hunting by industrialized cultures. Tests to determine the lethal dosages of consumer products and the corrosiveness of cosmetics in animal laboratories, the commercial harvest of infant harp seals, and research on cetacean brains have all provoked heated debate over animal rights. A proliferation of animal images in advertising, and their dominant presence in children's stories, have brought thinkers such as Paul Shepard to wonder how animals affect the very way we conceptualize.

We once thought of animals as not only sentient but as congruent with ourselves in a world beyond the world we can see, one structured by myth and moral obligation, and activated by spiritual power. The departure from the original conception was formalized in Cartesian dualism—the animal was a soulless entity with which people could not have a moral relationship—and in Ruskin's belief that to find anything but the profane and mechanistic in the natural world was to engage in a pathetic fallacy. Both these ideas seem short-sighted and to have not served us well.

Today, commerce raises perhaps the most strenuous objection to the interference of animals—their mere presence, their purported rights—in human activity. Wilderness areas the world over, the only places where animals are free of the social and economic schemes of men, are consistently violated for their wealth of timber, minerals, and hydrocarbons; and to fill zoos. Fundamentalist religions and reductionist science deny—or persist in regarding as "outdated"—the aboriginal aspects of our relationships with animals; and deny that animals themselves have any spiritual dimension.

If we have embarked on a shared path in reevaluating this situation as humanists and scientists, it has been to inquire how we are going to repair the original contracts. These agreements were abrogated during the agricultural, scientific, and industrial revolutions with a determined degradation of the value of animal life. Acts once indefensible became, over the centuries, only what was acceptable or expeditious. Such a reconsideration bears sharply on the fate of zoos and the future of animal experimentation, but it is also fundamentally important to us as creatures. Whatever wisdom we have shown in deriving a science of ecology, whatever insight we have gained from quantum mechanics into the importance of *relationships* (rather than the mere existence of *things*), urges us to consider these issues without calculation and passionately. We must examine a deep and long-lived insult.

I believe there are two failures to face. I speak with the view of someone who regards human beings as a Pleistocene species rather than a twentieth-century phenomenon; and who also believes that to set aside our relationships with wild animals as inconsequential is to undermine our regard for the other sex, other cultures, other universes. Animals exist apart from us, and the balance here between self-esteem and a prejudice directed toward what is different is one of the most rarefied and baffling issues in anthropology. Our own direction as a culture has been to enhance self-esteem *and* to dismantle prejudice by eradicating ignorance. No culture, however, including our own, with its great admiration for compassion and the high value it places on a broad education, has erased prejudice. (No one for that matter has proved it a worthless aspect of cultural evolution and survival.) What is required— or our Western venture is for naught—is to rise above prejudice to a position of respectful regard toward everything that is different from ourselves and not innately evil.

The two ways we have broken with animals are clear and could easily be the focus of our repair. One is that we have simply lost contact with them. Our notions of animal life are highly intellectualized, and no longer checked by daily contact with their environs. Our conceptions of them are not only bookish but stagnant, for, once discovered, we do not permit them to evolve as cultures. We allow them very little grace, enterprise, or individual variation. On the basis of even my own meager field experience—with wolves in Alaska, with mountain lion in Arizona, and with muskoxen, polar bear, and narwhal in the Canadian Arctic—this is a major blind spot in our efforts to erase ignorance. By predetermining categories of relevant information, by dismissing what cannot be easily quantified, by designing research to flatter the predilection of sponsors or defeat the political aims of a special interest group—field biologists have complained to me of both—we have produced distorted and incomplete images of animals. 8

We have created, further, mathematical models of ecosystems we only superficially grasp and then set divisions of government to managing the lives of the affected animals on the basis of these abstractions. We come perilously close in this to the worst moments of our history, to events we regret most deeply: the subjugation of races, the violent persecution of minority beliefs, the waging of war. With animals, all that saves us here is Descartes' convenience. Of course, some believe him right and regard this as firm ethical ground. But we skirt such imperious condescension here, such hubris, that we cannot help but undermine our principles of behavior toward ourselves, toward each other. 9

Some doubt the validity or the pertinence of these themes. But I have often heard, at grave and hopeful meetings, eloquent talk of the intellectual and social crises of our times—suppression of personality in a patriarchal society; the inhumane thrust of industry; the colonial designs of Russian or American foreign policy. With the change of only a word or two people could have been speaking of animals. The prejudices inform each other. 10

If the first failure is one of principle, where our attitudes toward animals have become those of owners and our knowledge skewed because 11 we no longer meet with them and rarely enter their landscapes, the second is a failure of imagination. We have largely lost our understanding of where in an adult life to fit the awe and mystery that animals excite. This sensibility is still maintained in some fashion, however, by many aboriginal peoples and I would suggest, again on the basis of my own short time with Eskimos, that to step beyond a superficial acquaintance with such people is to enter a realm of understanding where what has meant human survival for the past 40,000 years remains clear. Here the comprehension of fundamental human needs and their application— how to live a successful life—is revealed continuously in story, often in stories of human encounters with animals. These stories employ the prosaic to announce the profound, the profound to reveal the ineffable. They balance reassuringly the unfathomable and the concrete. In our age we prefer analysis, not awe; but historically, human beings have subsisted as much on the mystery and awe inspired by animals as they have on the actual flesh of the caribou or the salmon. They have actively sought them in the hunting experience and have preserved them in their oral literatures.

The cultivation of mystery and awe keeps the human capacity for metaphor alive. And a capacity for metaphor allows us to perceive several layers of meaning in a story about, say, a polar bear; to perceive animals not only as complex physiological organisms but as part of a coherent and shared landscape. 12

Our second failure with animals, then, has been to banish them from our minds, as though they were not capable of helping us with our predicaments, the myriad paradoxes of our existence. It is as though we had told the polar bear that his solitary life and the implacable hunger that makes him a persistent and resourceful hunter have no meaning for us. I believe this is a false sophistication of mind, and ultimately destructive. 13

A convenience of rational thought allows me to say there are but two places where our relationships with animals have been severed; audacity perhaps moves me to state that we must repair these breaks. I say so out of years of coming and going in a world inhabited largely by animals and aboriginal peoples, and out of repeated contact with human despair and loneliness in my own culture. What we do to animals troubles us—the horror of laboratory experiment, trophy shooting, factory farming; and our loss of contact with them leaves us mysteriously bereaved. If we could establish an atmosphere of respect in our relationships, simple awe for the complexities of animals' lives, I think we would feel revived as a species. And we would know more, deeply more, about what we are fighting for when we raise our voices against tyranny of any sort. 14

I am aware of having written here without reference to the incidents of day-to-day life by which most of us corroborate our beliefs. I think of several images. There is a group of sea ducks called scoters. They are dark, thick-bodied birds. With the exception of the males, who have bright, oddly shaped bills, they are of undistinguished coloration. The 15 casual spring visitor to Cape Cod or to Cape Flattery would very likely see a few, but we know little about them. Like the ribbon seal and the narwhal, we cannot easily find them again once they leave these accustomed meeting places. So they are not really known to us.

Taxonomists took years to finally differentiate the spotted seal *(Phoca largha)* from the harbor seal *(Phoca vitulina).* They distrusted the statements of Eskimos in the same Bering Sea region who had always separated the two seals on the basis of their ice-related behavior. Now the scientists speak like Yup'ik men about the matter. 16

A marine biologist, armed with a prestigious grant, went to Hawaii to study a certain crab. The animal's behavior was so utterly different from what he had imagined it would be (from reading the literature) that his research proposal made no sense. To maintain his credibility he abandoned the experiment rather than restructure his conception of the animal. 17

One morning, walking through fresh snow, looking for mountain lion tracks on the north rim of the Grand Canyon, a biologist with years of this behind him said to me suddenly, "It's not in the data." I looked at him. "It's not in the data," he reiterated. With his hands he made a motion to indicate his head, his chest. "It's here. What I know is here." We went on in silence. "But as a field biologist," I said, "you must offer data or——." "We are not biologists," he answered. "We are historians." 18

A final moment. In the Sea of Labrador one summer a sperm whale approached our ship head-on. I was standing in the bow with a retired Danish master mariner. The calm green sea broke over the whale's brow as he closed on us at ten or twelve knots. His approach was unwavering. I wondered out loud to my companion if they were aware on the bridge of our collision course. The whale surged past suddenly to port, crashing across our bow wave. I turned around—the mate shrugged from the superstructure several hundred feet away: who knows? The retired captain had not moved. He had not loosened the tenacious grip he had on the ship's rail. He slowly began to tell me a story about a convoy in the North Atlantic in 1942, the night they were torpedoed. 19

If we are to locate animals again at the complicated ethical and conceptual level of our ancestors, where they seem to have such a bearing on our state of mental health, we must decide what obligations and courtesies we will be bound by. The hunting contracts of our ancestors are no longer appropriate, just as their insight into natural history is no longer superior to our own at every point. These are to be new contracts. They must represent a new decorum, born of our aboriginal attachment to ancestral landscapes, our extraordinary learning, and the evolution of our culture from Altamira and Lascaux to the chambers of Washington, D.C. and the corridors of the Metropolitan Museum of Art. 20

Enormous as these steps are to contemplate, we seem in diverse ways to have firm hold of a beginning. The best of our books and films reflect a wider-than-Western, wider-than-purely scientific, more-than-utilitarian view of animals. Moral philosophers are at work in a scholarly remodeling of Western philosophy in this area. And some people 21

557

Chapter Eleven
Nature and the
Environment

choose now to vacation among snow geese in northern California or among egrets and roseate spoonbills in Florida, as well as among the pyramids, or creations of the Medici.

However new agreements are drawn up, they must reflect as the old ones did an atmosphere of mutual regard, some latitude for mystery, and a sense of hope. As a European people we have taken great intellectual risks and made at various times penetrating insights—Leibnitz's calculus, Darwin's theory of natural selection, Heisenberg's uncertainty principle, Levi-Strauss's anthropology. We have in common with all other people in the world an understanding of how animals inform our intellectual, physical, aesthetic, and spiritual lives. From this reservoir of knowledge and sensitivity we could hope to forge a new covenant, fiercely honest, with other creatures. 22

In the time I have spent with native peoples in North America I have observed a deceptively simple event—how superstition, a slight, seemingly irrational prohibition, will be used to undercut arrogance in a young, headstrong hunter. To see it once is to be reminded forever that all life is a great gamble; wisdom is not simply erudition; and to behave in an irrational manner can, in fact, be life-enhancing. We tore up the animal contracts when the animals got in the way of our agriculture, our husbandry, and our science. We are now tearing up and rewriting our contracts with native peoples, because they block our political and industrial development. We cannot keep doing this. We will find ourselves with a false and miserable existence, a hollow probity, isolated far from our roots. 23

We will never find a way home until we find a way to look the caribou, the salmon, the lynx, and the white-throated sparrow in the face, without guile, with no plan of betrayal. We have to decide, again, after a long hiatus, how we are going to behave. We have to decide again to be impeccable in our dealings with the elements of our natural history. 24

COMPREHENSION

1. What is the thesis of this essay?
2. In your own words, explain the two "failures" the author sees as contributing to our alienation from the animal kingdom.
3. When the biologist referred to in paragraph 18 states, "We are not biologists. . . . We are historians," what does he mean?

RHETORIC

1. This essay was originally published in *Parabola,* a magazine noted for its erudite essays, particularly in the areas of myth and religion. What evidence, in terms of level of discourse and vocabulary, can you find to demonstrate that this essay was not written for the general reader?
2. Most textbooks claim that essays have a three-part structure: introduction, body, and conclusion. Where do the body and the conclusion in this essay begin? What clues in the essay lead you to this opinion?

3. From paragraphs 15 through 18, the author employs a particular rhetorical mode. What is it, and does it strengthen the thrust of his argument? Explain.
4. The author uses some rather abstract terms in this essay, terms such as *mythic,* (paragraph 2), *awe* and *mystery* (paragraph 11) and *aesthetic* and *spiritual* (paragraph 22). How does the use of these terms contribute to the tone of the essay?
5. In paragraph 22, the author cites some intellectual giants of the past. What assumptions is the author making about the educational level of his audience when he cites these individuals without explaining who they are?
6. How does the author imply that he is an expert in the subject area and topic of his essay?
7. As do many professional essayists, Lopez often uses long sentences—sentences far longer than those used in other forms of writing. Identify at least three such sentences, and examine and explain their structure.

WRITING

1. Argue for or against the proposition that society should concern itself with the plight of humans before it tackles the plight of animals.
2. Argue for or against the morality or immorality of eating meat.
3. Write a personal essay describing a relationship you had with a pet that brought you insight and understanding.

JOYCE CAROL OATES   Joyce Carol Oates (b. 1938) is a poet, novelist, short-story writer, and essayist. She received her B.A. in 1960 from Syracuse University, where she was class valedictorian; and her M.A. in 1961 from the University of Wisconsin. Her first book, *By the North Gate* (1963), is a collection of short stories. Since then, Oates's life has been "more or less dedicated to promoting and exploring literature," both as a university professor and as the author of many works, including *Wonderland* (1971), *Do with Me What You Will* (1973), *Solstice* (1985), and *Because It Is Bitter, and It Is My Heart* (1990). In this piece, written in 1986, Oates finds discrepancies between the bucolic images presented by some nature writers and the often unpleasant realities.

JOYCE CAROL OATES

Against Nature

We soon get through with Nature. She excites an expectation which she cannot satisfy.   —Thoreau, *Journal,* 1854
Sir, if a man has experienced the inexpressible, he is under no obligation to attempt to express it.   —Samuel Johnson

The writer's resistance to Nature.   1

It has no sense of humor: In its beauty, as in its ugliness, or its neutrality, there is no laughter.

It lacks a moral purpose.

It lacks a satiric dimension, registers no irony.

Its pleasures lack resonance, being accidental; its horrors, even when premeditated, are equally perfunctory, "red in tooth and claw" et cetera.

It lacks a symbolic subtext—excepting that provided by man.

It has no (verbal) language.

It has no interest in ours.

It inspires a painfully limited set of responses in "nature-writers"—REVERENCE, AWE, PIETY, MYSTICAL ONENESS.

It eludes us even as it prepares to swallow us up, books and all.

I was lying on my back in the dirt-gravel of the towpath beside the   2
Delaware-Raritan Canal, Titusville, New Jersey, staring up at the sky and trying, with no success, to overcome a sudden attack of tachycardia that had come upon me out of nowhere—such attacks are always "out of nowhere," that's their charm—and all around me Nature thrummed with life, the air smelling of moisture and sunlight, the canal reflecting the sky, red-winged blackbirds testing their spring calls—the usual. I'd become the jar in Tennessee, a fictitious center, or parenthesis, aware beyond my erratic heartbeat of the numberless heartbeats of the earth, its pulsing pumping life, sheer life, incalculable. Struck down in the midst of motion—I'd been jogging a minute before—I was "out of time" like a fallen, stunned boxer, privileged (in an abstract manner of speaking) to be an involuntary witness to the random, wayward, nameless motion on all sides of me.

Paroxysmal tachycardia is rarely fatal, but if the heartbeat acceler-   3
ates to 250–270 beats a minute you're in trouble. The average attack is about 100–150 beats and mine seemed so far to be about average; the trick now was to prevent it from getting worse. Brainy people try brainy strategies, such as thinking calming thoughts, pseudo-mystic thoughts, *If I die now it's a good death,* that sort of thing, *if I die this is a good place and a good time,* the idea is to deceive the frenzied heartbeat that, really, you don't care: You hadn't any other plans for the afternoon. The important thing with tachycardia is to prevent panic! you must prevent panic! otherwise you'll have to be taken by ambulance to the closest emergency room, which is not so very nice a way to spend the afternoon, really. So I contemplated the blue sky overhead. The earth beneath my head. Nature surrounding me on all sides, I couldn't quite see it but I could hear it, smell it, sense it—there is something *there,* no mistake about it. Completely oblivious to the predicament of the individual but that's only "natural" after all, one hardly expects otherwise.

When you discover yourself lying on the ground, limp and unre-   4
sisting, head in the dirt, and helpless, the earth seems to shift forward as a presence; hard, emphatic, not mere surface but a genuine force—

there is no other word for it but *presence*. To keep in motion is to keep in time and to be stopped, stilled, is to be abruptly out of time, in another time-dimension perhaps, an alien one, where human language has no resonance. Nothing to be said about it expresses it, nothing touches it, it's an absolute against which nothing human can be measured. . . . Moving through space and time by way of your own volition you inhabit an interior consciousness, a hallucinatory consciousness, it might be said, so long as breath, heartbeat, the body's autonomy hold; when motion is stopped you are jarred out of it. The interior is invaded by the exterior. The outside wants to come in, and only the self's fragile membrane prevents it.

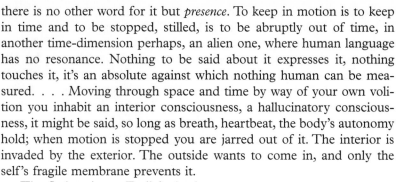
The fly buzzing at Emily's death.   5

Still, the earth *is* your place. A tidy grave-site measured to your size.   6
Or, from another angle of vision, one vast democratic grave.

Let's contemplate the sky. Forget the crazy hammering heartbeat,   7
don't listen to it, don't start counting, remember that there is a clever way of breathing that conserves oxygen as if you're lying below the surface of a body of water breathing through a very thin straw but you *can* breathe through it if you're careful, if you don't panic, one breath and then another and then another, isn't that the story of all lives? careers? Just a matter of breathing. Of course it is. But contemplate the sky, it's there to be contemplated. A mild shock to see it so blank, blue, a thin airy ghostly blue, no clouds to disguise its emptiness. You are beginning to feel not only weightless but near-bodiless, lying on the earth like a scrap of paper about to be blown off. Two dimensions and you'd imagined you were there! And there's the sky rolling away forever, into infinity—if "infinity" can be "rolled into"—and the forlorn truth is, that's where you're going too. And the lovely blue isn't even blue, is it? isn't even there, is it? a mere optical illusion, isn't it? no matter what art has urged you to believe.

Early Nature memories. Which it's best not to suppress.   8

. . . Wading, as a small child, in Tonawanda Creek near our house, and afterward trying to tear off, in a frenzy of terror and revulsion, the sticky fat black bloodsuckers that had attached themselves to my feet, particularly between my toes.

. . . Coming upon a friend's dog in a drainage ditch, dead for several days, evidently the poor creature had been shot by a hunter and left to die, bleeding to death, and we're stupefied with grief and horror but can't resist sliding down to where he's lying on his belly, and we can't resist squatting over him, turning the body over. . . .

. . . The raccoon, mad with rabies, frothing at the mouth and tearing at his own belly with his teeth, so that his intestines spilled out onto the ground . . . a sight I seem to remember though in fact I did not see. I've been told I did not see.

Consequently, my chronic uneasiness with Nature-mysticism; Nature-   9
adoration; Nature-as-(moral)-instruction-for-mankind. My doubt that one can, with philosophical validity, address "Nature" as a single coher-

ent noun, anything other than a Platonic, hence discredited, isness. My resistance to "Nature-writing" as a genre, except when it is brilliantly fictionalized in the service of a writer's individual vision—Thoreau's books and *Journal,* of course—but also, less known in this country, the miniaturist prose-poems of Colette *(Flowers and Fruit)* and Ponge *(Taking the Side of Things)*—in which case it becomes yet another, and ingenious, form of storytelling. The subject is *there* only by the grace of the author's language.

Nature has no instructions for mankind except that our poor belea- 10 guered humanist-democratic way of life, our fantasies of the individual's high worth, our sense that the weak, no less than strong, have a right to survive, are absurd.

In any case, where *is* Nature? one might (skeptically) inquire. Who 11 has looked upon her/its face and survived?

But isn't this all exaggeration, in the spirit of rhetorical contentious- 12 ness? Surely Nature is, for you, as for most reasonably intelligent people, a "perennial" source of beauty, comfort, peace, escape from the delirium of civilized life; a respite from the ego's ever-frantic strategies of self-promotion, as a way of insuring (at least in fantasy) some small measure of immortality? Surely Nature, as it is understood in the usual slapdash way, as human, if not dilettante, *experience* (hiking in a national park, jogging on the beach at dawn, even tending, with the usual comical frustrations, a suburban garden), is wonderfully consoling; a place where, when you go there, it has to take you in?—a palimpsest of sorts you choose to read, layer by layer, always with care, always cautiously, in proportion to your psychological strength?

Nature: as in Thoreau's upbeat Transcendentalist mode ("The inde- 13 scribable innocence and beneficence of Nature,—such health, such cheer, they afford forever! and such sympathy have they ever with our race, that all Nature would be affected . . . if any man should ever for a just cause grieve"), and not in Thoreau's grim mode ("Nature is hard to be overcome but she must be overcome").

Another way of saying, not *Nature-in-itself* but *Nature-as-experience*. 14

The former, Nature-in-itself, is, to allude slantwise to Melville, a 15 blankness ten times blank; the latter is what we commonly, or perhaps always, mean when we speak of Nature as a noun, a single entity—something of ours. Most of the time it's just an activity, a sort of hobby, a weekend, a few days, perhaps a few hours, staring out of the window at the mind-dazzling autumn foliage of, say, Northern Michigan, being rendered speechless—temporarily—at the sight of Mt. Shasta, the Grand Canyon, Ansel Adams's West. Or Nature writ small, contained in the back yard. Nature filtered through our optical nerves, our "sense," our fiercely romantic expectations. Nature that pleases us because it mirrors our souls, or gives the comforting illusion of doing so. As in our first mother's awakening to the self's fatal beauty—

> I thither went
> With unexperienc't thought, and laid me down
> On the green bank, to look into the clear
> Smooth Lake, that to me seem'd another Sky.
> As I bent down to look, just opposite,
> A Shape within the watr'y gleam appear'd
> Bending to look on me, I started back,
> It started back, but pleas'd I soon return'd,
> Pleas'd it return'd as soon with answering looks
> Of sympathy and love; there I had fixt
> Mine eyes till now, and pin'd with vain desire.

—in these surpassingly beautiful lines from Book IV of Milton's *Paradise Lost.*

Nature as the self's (flattering) mirror, but not ever, no never, [16] Nature-in-itself.

Nature is mouths, or maybe a single mouth. Why glamorize it, [17] romanticize it, well yes but we must, we're writers, poets, mystics (of a sort) aren't we, precisely what else are we to do but glamorize and romanticize and generally exaggerate the significance of anything we focus the white heat of our "creativity" upon . . . ? And why not Nature, since it's there, common property, mute, can't talk back, allows us the possibility of transcending the human condition for a while, writing prettily of mountain ranges, white-tailed deer, the purple crocuses outside this very window, the thrumming dazzling "life-force" we imagine we all support. Why not.

Nature *is* more than a mouth—it's a dazzling variety of mouths. [18] And it pleases the senses, in any case, as the physicists' chill universe of numbers certainly does not.

Oscar Wilde, on our subject: [19]

> Nature is no great mother who has borne us. She is our creation. It is in our brain that she quickens to life. Things are because we see them, and what we see, and how we see it, depends on the Arts that have influenced us. To look at a thing is very different from seeing a thing. . . . At present, people see fogs, not because there are fogs, but because poets and painters have taught them the mysterious loveliness of such effects. There may have been fogs for centuries in London. I dare say there were. But no one saw them. They did not exist until Art had invented them. . . . Yesterday evening Mrs. Arundel insisted on my going to the window and looking at the glorious sky, as she called it. And so I had to look at it. . . . And what was it? It was simply a very second-rate Turner, a Turner of a bad period, with all the painter's worst faults exaggerated and over-emphasized.

(If we were to put it to Oscar Wilde that he exaggerates, his reply [20] might well be: "Exaggeration? I don't know the meaning of the word.")

Walden, that most artfully composed of prose fictions, concludes, in ²¹ the rhapsodic chapter "Spring," with Henry David Thoreau's contemplation of death, decay, and regeneration as it is suggested to him, or to his protagonist, by the spectacle of vultures feeding off carrion. There is a dead horse close by his cabin and the stench of its decomposition, in certain winds, is daunting. Yet:

> The assurance it gave me of the strong appetite and inviolable health of Nature was my compensation. I love to see that Nature is so rife with life that myriads can be afforded to be sacrificed and suffered to prey upon one another; that tender organizations can be so serenely squashed out of existence like pulp,—tadpoles which herons gobble up, and tortoises and toads run over in the road; and that sometimes it has rained flesh and blood! . . . The impression made on a wise man is that of universal innocence.

Come off it, Henry David. You've grieved these many years for your ²² elder brother John, who dies a ghastly death of lockjaw, you've never wholly recovered from the experience of watching him die. And you know, or must know, that you're fated too to die young of consumption. . . . But this doctrinaire Transcendentalist passage ends *Walden* on just the right note. It's as impersonal, as coolly detached, as the Oversoul itself: A "wise man" filters his emotions through his brain.

Or through his prose. ²³

Nietzsche: "We all pretend to ourselves that we are more simple- ²⁴ minded than we are: That is how we get a rest from our fellow men."

> Once out of nature I shall never take ²⁵
> My bodily form from any natural thing,
> But such a form as Grecian goldsmiths make
> Of hammered gold and gold enamelling
> To keep a drowsy Emperor awake;
> Or set upon a golden bough to sing
> To lords and ladies of Byzantium
> Of what is past, or passing, or to come.
> —William Butler Yeats, "Sailing to Byzantium"

Yet even the golden bird is a "bodily form taken from [a] natural ²⁶ thing." No, it's impossible to escape!

The writer's resistance to Nature.

Wallace Stevens: "In the presence of extraordinary actuality, con- ²⁷ sciousness takes the place of imagination."

Once, years ago, in 1972 to be precise, when I seemed to have been ²⁸ another person, related to the person I am now as one is related, tangentially, sometimes embarrassingly, to cousins not seen for decades,— once, when we were living in London, and I was very sick, I had a mystical vision. That is, I "had" a "mystical vision"—the heart sinks: such pretension—or something resembling one. A fever-dream, let's call it. It impressed me enormously and impresses me still, though I've long since lost the capacity to see it with my mind's eye, or even, I suppose, to believe in it. There is a statute of limitations on "mystical visions" as on romantic love.

I was very sick, and I imagined my life as a thread, a thread of [29] breath, or heartbeat, or pulse, or light, yes it was light, radiant light, I was burning with fever and I ascended to that plane of serenity that might be mistaken for (or *is*, in fact) Nirvana, where I had a waking dream of uncanny lucidity—

My body is a tall column of light and heat.

My body is not "I" but "it."

My body is not one but many.

My body, which "I" inhabit, is inhabited as well by other creatures, [30] unknown to me, imperceptible—the smallest of them mere sparks of light.

My body, which I perceive as substance, is in fact an organization [31] of infinitely complex, overlapping, imbricated structures, radiant light their manifestation, the "body" a tall column of light and blood-heat, a temporary agreement among atoms, like a high-rise building with numberless rooms, corridors, corners, elevator shafts, windows. . . . In this fantastical structure the "I" is deluded as to its sovereignty, let alone its autonomy in the (outside) world; the most astonishing secret is that the "I" doesn't exist!—but it behaves as if it does, as if it were one and not many.

In any case, without the "I" the tall column of light and heat would [32] die, and the microscopic life-particles would die with it . . . will die with it. The "I," which doesn't exist, is everything.

But Dr. Johnson is right, the inexpressible need not be expressed. [33] And what resistance, finally? There is none.

This morning, an invasion of tiny black ants. One by one they appear, [34] out of nowhere—that's their charm too!—moving single file across the white Parsons table where I am sitting, trying without much success to write a poem. A poem of only three or four lines is what I want, something short, tight, mean. I want it to hurt like a white-hot wire up the nostrils, small and compact and turned in upon itself with the density of a hunk of rock from the planet Jupiter. . . .

But here come the black ants: harbingers, you might say, of [35] spring. One by one they appear on the dazzling white table and one by one I kill them with a forefinger, my deft right forefinger, mashing each against the surface of the table and then dropping it into a wastebasket at my side. Idle labor, mesmerizing, effortless, and I'm curious as to how long I can do it, sit here in the brilliant March sunshine killing ants with my right forefinger, how long I, and the ants, can keep it up.

After a while I realize that I can do it a long time. And that I've writ- [36] ten my poem.

COMPREHENSION

1. What event precipitates the writer's contemplation of nature?
2. According to Oates, what is the artist's relationship to nature? Why does she object to nature writers?
3. What associations or memories does Oates have while lying on the grass? How may they have influenced her opinion of nature?

RHETORIC

1. What is the purpose of the introductory section? How does it aid in setting up Oates's argument? Why does she capitalize the words *reverence, awe, pity,* and *mystical oneness?*
2. How does the narrative part of the essay contribute to the development of Oates's argument? Could the essay have succeeded without it? Why, or why not?
3. To what end does Oates use quotes from other writers? What does she assume about her readers? Do the quotes help to illustrate her points?
4. What is the significance of paragraph 5? To what does it refer, and how does its use help advance the ideas of the writer?
5. Closely examine the language and punctuation used in paragraph 7. How do these elements strengthen the author's argument?
6. Why does Oates refute her own observations in paragraph 12? What is her aim? Does this help or hurt her argument?

WRITING

1. Write an essay about your own response to nature. What formed this relationship? When was the last time you felt close to nature? How does nature affect your everyday life and actions?
2. In a brief essay, define Oates's concept of "Nature-in-itself" versus "Nature-as-experience." Use your own observations and examples.
3. Write a definition essay on *nature* that explores the connotations and denotations of the word.

JOHN STEINBECK   John Steinbeck (1902–1968) was born in California, the setting for some of his best fiction. Steinbeck's fiction of the 1930s, including *The Pastures of Heaven* (1932), *Tortilla Flat* (1935), *In Dubious Battle* (1936), *Of Mice and Men* (1937), and the Pulitzer Prize-winning epic *The Grapes of Wrath* (1939), offers one of the best imaginative presentations of the American Depression. Steinbeck won the Nobel Prize in Literature in 1962 for "realistic and imaginative writings, distinguished as they are by a sympathetic humor and a social perception." In this section from *America and Americans* (1966), Steinbeck offers a probing, critical appraisal of American social development.

JOHN STEINBECK

Americans and the Land

I have often wondered at the savagery and thoughtlessness with which our early settlers approached this rich continent. They came at it as though it were an enemy, which of course it was. They burned the forests and changed the rainfall; they swept the buffalo from the plains, blasted the streams, set fire to the grass, and ran a reckless scythe through the virgin and noble timber. Perhaps they felt that it was limitless and could never be exhausted and that a man could move on to new wonders endlessly. Certainly there are many examples to the contrary, but to a large extent the early people pillaged the country as though they hated it, as though they held it temporarily and might be driven off at any time.

This tendency toward irresponsibility persists in very many of us today; our rivers are poisoned by reckless dumping of sewage and toxic industrial wastes, the air of our cities is filthy and dangerous to breathe from the belching of uncontrolled products from combustion of coal, coke, oil, and gasoline. Our towns are girdled with wreckage and the debris of our toys—our automobiles and our packaged pleasures. Through uninhibited spraying against one enemy we have destroyed the natural balances our survival requires. All these evils can and must be overcome if America and Americans are to survive; but many of us still conduct ourselves as our ancestors did, stealing from the future for our clear and present profit.

Since the river-polluters and the air-poisoners are not criminal or even bad people, we must presume that they are heirs to the early conviction that sky and water are unowned and that they are limitless. In the light of our practices here at home it is very interesting to me to read of the care taken with the carriers of our probes into space to make utterly sure that they are free of pollution of any kind. We would not think of doing to the moon what we do every day to our own dear country.

When the first settlers came to America and dug in on the coast, they huddled in defending villages hemmed in by the sea on one side and by endless forests on the other, by Red Indians and, most frightening, the mystery of an unknown land extending nobody knew how far. And for a time very few cared or dared to find out. Our first Americans organized themselves and lived in a state of military alertness; every community built its blockhouse for defense. By law the men went armed and were required to keep their weapons ready and available. Many of them wore armor, made here or imported; on the East Coast, they wore the cuirass and helmet, and the Spaniards on the West Coast wore both steel armor and heavy leather to turn arrows.

On the East Coast, and particularly in New England, the colonists farmed meager lands close to their communities and to safety. Every man was permanently on duty for the defense of his family and his village; even the hunting parties went into the forest in force, rather like raiders than hunters, and their subsequent quarrels with the Indians, resulting in forays and even massacres, remind us that the danger was very real. A man took his gun along when he worked the land, and the women stayed close to their thick-walled houses and listened day and night for the signal of alarm. The towns they settled were permanent, and most of them exist today with their records of Indian raids, of slaughter, of scalpings, and of punitive counter-raids. The military leader of the community became the chief authority in time of trouble, and it was a long time before danger receded and the mystery could be explored.

After a time, however, brave and forest-wise men drifted westward to hunt, to trap, and eventually to bargain for the furs which were the first precious negotiable wealth America produced for trade and export. Then trading posts were set up as centers of collection and the exploring men moved up and down the rivers and crossed the mountains, made friends for mutual profit with the Indians, learned the wilderness techniques, so that these explorer-traders soon dressed, ate, and generally acted like the indigenous people around them. Suspicion lasted a long time, and was fed by clashes sometimes amounting to full-fledged warfare; but by now these Americans attacked and defended as the Indians did.

For a goodly time the Americans were travelers, moving about the country collecting its valuables, but with little idea of permanence; their roots and their hearts were in the towns and the growing cities along the eastern edge. The few who stayed, who lived among the Indians, adopted their customs and some took Indian wives and were regarded as strange and somehow treasonable creatures. As for their half-breed children, while the tribe sometimes adopted them they were unacceptable as equals in the eastern settlements.

Then the trickle of immigrants became a stream, and the population began to move westward—not to grab and leave but to settle and live, they thought. The newcomers were of peasant stock, and they had their roots in a Europe where they had been landless, for the possession of land was the requirement and the proof of a higher social class than they had known. In America they found beautiful and boundless land for the taking—and they took it.

It is little wonder that they went land-mad, because there was so much of it. They cut and burned the forests to make room for crops; they abandoned their knowledge of kindness to the land in order to maintain its usefulness. When they had cropped out a piece they moved on, raping the country like invaders. The topsoil, held by roots and freshened by leaffall, was left helpless to the spring freshets, stripped and eroded with the naked bones of clay and rock exposed. The destruction of the forests changed the rainfall, for the searching clouds could find no green and beckoning woods to draw them on and milk them. The merciless nineteenth century was like a hostile expedition for loot that seemed limitless. Uncountable buffalo were killed, stripped of their hides, and left to rot, a reservoir of permanent food supply eliminated. More than that, the land of the Great Plains was robbed of the manure of the herds. Then the plows went in and ripped off the protection of the buffalo grass and opened the helpless soil to quick water and slow drought and the mischievous winds that roamed through the Great Central Plains. There has always been more than enough desert in America; the new settlers, like overindulged children, created even more.

The railroads brought new hordes of land-crazy people, and the 10 new Americans moved like locusts across the continent until the western sea put a boundary to their movements. Coal and copper and gold drew them on; they savaged the land, gold-dredged the rivers to skeletons of pebbles and debris. An aroused and fearful government made laws for the distribution of public lands—a quarter section, one hundred and sixty acres, per person—and a claim had to be proved and improved; but there were ways of getting around this, and legally. My own grandfather proved out a quarter section for himself, one for his wife, one for each of his children, and, I suspect, acreage for children he hoped and expected to have. Marginal lands, of course, suitable only for grazing, went in larger pieces. One of the largest land-holding families in California took its richest holdings by a trick: By law a man could take up all the swamp or water-covered land he wanted. The founder of this great holding mounted a scow on wheels and drove his horses over thousands of acres of the best bottom land, then reported that he had explored it in a boat, which was true, and confirmed his title. I need not mention his name; his descendants will remember.

Another joker with a name still remembered in the West worked out 11 a scheme copied many times in after years. Proving a quarter section required a year of residence and some kind of improvement—a fence, a shack—but once the land was proved the owner was free to sell it. This particular princely character went to the stews and skid rows of the towns and found a small army of hopeless alcoholics who lived for whiskey and nothing else. He put these men on land he wanted to own, grubstaked them and kept them in cheap liquor until the acreage was proved, then went through the motions of buying it from his protégés and moved them and their one-room shacks on sled runners to new quarter sections. Bums of strong constitution might prove out five or six homesteads for this acquisitive hero before they died of drunkenness.

It was full late when we began to realize that the continent did not 12 stretch out to infinity; that there were limits to the indignities to which we could subject it. Engines and heavy mechanical equipment were allowing us to ravage it even more effectively than we had with fire, dynamite, and gang plows. Conservation came to us slowly, and much of it hasn't arrived yet. Having killed the whales and wiped out the sea otters and most of the beavers, the market hunters went to work on game birds; ducks and quail were decimated, and the passenger pigeon eliminated. In my youth I remember seeing a market hunter's gun, a three-gauge shotgun bolted to a frame and loaded to the muzzle with shingle nails. Aimed at a lake and the trigger pulled with a string, it slaughtered every living thing on the lake. The Pacific Coast pilchards were once the raw material for a great and continuing industry. We hunted them with aircraft far at sea until they were gone and the canneries had to be closed. In some of the valleys of the West, where the climate makes several crops a year available, which the water supply will not justify, wells were driven deeper and deeper for irrigation, so that in one great valley a million acre feet more of water was taken out than rain and melting snow could replace, and the water table went down and a few more years may give us a new desert.

The great redwood forests of the western mountains early attracted 13 attention. These ancient trees, which once grew everywhere, now exist only where the last Ice Age did not wipe them out. And they were found to have value. The Sempervirens and the Gigantea, the two remaining species, make soft, straight-grained timber. They are easy to split into planks, shakes, fenceposts, and railroad ties, and they have a unique virtue: they resist decay, both wet and dry rot, and an inherent acid in them repels termites. The loggers went through the great groves like a barrage, toppling the trees—some of which were two thousand years old— and leaving no maidens, no seedlings or saplings on the denuded hills.

Quite a few years ago when I was living in my little town on the 14 coast of California a stranger came in and bought a small valley where the Sempervirens redwoods grew, some of them three hundred feet high. We used to walk among these trees, and the light colored as though the great glass of the Cathedral at Chartres had strained and sanctified the sunlight. The emotion we felt in this grove was one of awe and humility and joy; and then one day it was gone, slaughtered, and the sad wreckage of boughs and broken saplings left like nonsensical spoilage of the battle-ruined countryside. And I remember that after our rage there was sadness, and when we passed the man who had done this we looked away, because we were ashamed for him.

From early times we were impressed and awed by the fantastic acci- 15 dents of nature, like the Grand Canyon and Yosemite and Yellowstone Park. The Indians had revered them as holy places, visited by the gods, and all of us came to have somewhat the same feeling about them. Thus we set aside many areas of astonishment as publicly owned parks; and though this may to a certain extent have been because there was no other way to use them as the feeling of preciousness of the things we had been destroying grew in Americans, more and more areas were set aside as national and state parks, to be looked at but not injured. Many people loved and were in awe of the redwoods; societies and individuals bought groves of these wonderful trees and presented them to the state for preservation.

No longer do we Americans want to destroy wantonly, but our new- 16 found sources of power—to take the burden of work from our shoulders, to warm us, and cool us, and give us light, to transport us quickly, and to make the things we use and wear and eat—these power sources spew pollution on our country, so that the rivers and streams are becoming poisonous and lifeless. The birds die for the lack of food; a noxious cloud hangs over our cities that burns our lungs and reddens our eyes. Our ability to conserve has not grown with our power to create, but this slow and sullen poisoning is no longer ignored or justified. Almost daily, the pressure of outrage among Americans grows. We are no longer content to destroy our beloved country. We are slow to learn; but we learn. When a superhighway was proposed in California which would trample the redwood trees in its path, an outcry arose all over the land, so strident and fierce that the plan was put aside. And we no longer believe that a man, by owning a piece of America, is free to outrage it.

But we are an exuberant people, careless and destructive as active 17 children. We make strong and potent tools and then have to use them to prove that they exist. Under the pressure of war we finally made the atom bomb, and for reasons which seemed justifiable at the time we dropped it on two Japanese cities—and I think we finally frightened ourselves. In such things, one must consult himself because there is no other point of reference. I did not know about the bomb, and certainly I had nothing to do with its use, but I am horrified and ashamed; and nearly everyone I know feels the same thing. And those who loudly and angrily justify Hiroshima and Nagasaki—why, they must be the most ashamed of all.

Chapter Eleven
Nature and the
Environment

COMPREHENSION

1. What is Steinbeck's purpose in writing this essay? State his thesis in your own words.
2. According to Steinbeck, how did the American attitude toward the land evolve?
3. Does Steinbeck think that the American attitude toward the land can be changed? Cite evidence from the essay to support your answer.

RHETORIC

1. Analyze Steinbeck's use of figurative language in paragraphs 1, 2, 9, and 14.
2. Locate images and vocabulary relating to "rape" and destruction in the essay. What is the relevance of this motif to the development of Steinbeck's thesis?
3. How does Steinbeck use examples in paragraphs 1 and 2 to establish the subject and thesis of his essay?
4. Analyze the relationship between the patterns of description and example in the essay. What types of illustration does Steinbeck employ? How does he achieve concreteness through examples? Where does he employ extended example? Does he use examples subjectively or objectively? Explain.
5. How does Steinbeck employ process analysis to highlight his thesis?
6. Explain the relationship between paragraph 16 and paragraph 17 in the essay.

1. Analyze the way in which description and figurative language advance Steinbeck's thesis.

2. Write an essay entitled "Americans and the Land," using examples to support your thesis.

3. Write an essay on the relationship between ecology and the state of civilization.

CLASSIC AND CONTEMPORARY

HENRY DAVID THOREAU   Henry David Thoreau (1817–1862), author of the masterpiece *Walden* (1854), is one of the most important figures in American thought and literature. A social and political activist, he opposed the Mexican War, protested slavery, and refused to pay his poll taxes. As a naturalist, he believed in the preeminence of individualism and nature over technology, materialism, and nationalism. In 1845, Thoreau went to live at Walden Pond, "living deep and sucking out all the marrow of life." *Walden,* describing his life at the pond, is one of the most challenging, exuberant, and innovative works of American literature. This account from Thoreau's masterpiece, tracing the construction of his dwelling, reflects his preoccupation with economy, natural process, and self-reliance.

HENRY DAVID THOREAU

Economy

Near the end of March, 1845, I borrowed an axe and went down to the woods by Walden Pond, nearest to where I intended to build my house, and began to cut down some tall arrowy white pines, still in their youth, for timber. It is difficult to begin without borrowing, but perhaps it is the most generous course thus to permit your fellow-men to have an interest in your enterprise. The owner of the axe, as he released his hold on it, said that it was the apple of his eye; but I returned it sharper than I received it. It was a pleasant hillside where I worked, covered with pine woods, through which I looked out on the pond, and a small open field in the woods where pines and hickories were springing up. The ice in the pond was not yet dissolved, though there were some open spaces, and it was all dark colored and saturated with water. There were some slight flurries of snow during the days that I worked there; but for the most part when I came out onto the railroad, on my way home, its yellow sand heap stretched away gleaming in the hazy atmosphere, and the rails shone in the spring sun, and I heard the lark and pewee and other birds already come to commence another year with us. They were pleasant spring days, in which the winter of man's discontent was thawing as well as the earth, and the life that had lain torpid began to stretch itself. One day, when my axe had come off and I had cut a green hickory for a wedge, driving it with a stone, and had placed the whole to soak in a pond hole in order to swell the wood, I saw a striped snake run into the water, and he lay on the bottom, apparently without inconvenience, as long as I stayed there, or more than a quarter of an hour; perhaps because he had not yet fairly come out of the torpid state. It appeared to me that for a like reason men remain in their present low and primitive condition; but if they should feel the influence of the spring of springs arousing them, they would of necessity rise to a higher and more ethereal life. I had previously seen the snakes in frosty mornings in my path with portions of their bodies still numb and inflexible, waiting for the sun to thaw them. On the 1st of April it rained and melted the ice, and in the early part of the day, which was very foggy, I heard a stray goose groping about over the pond and cackling as if lost, or like the spirit of the fog.

So I went on for some days cutting and hewing timber, and also   2
studs and rafters, all with my narrow axe, not having many communicable or scholar-like thoughts, singing to myself.

> Men say they know many things;
> But lo! they have taken wings—
> The arts and sciences,
> And a thousand appliances;
> The wind that blows
> Is all that anybody knows.

I hewed the main timber six inches square, most of the studs on two sides only, and the rafters and floor timbers on one side, leaving the rest of the bark on, so that they were just as straight and much stronger than sawed ones. Each stick was carefully mortised or tenoned by its stump, for I had borrowed other tools by this time. My days in the woods were not very long ones; yet I usually carried my dinner of bread and butter, and read the newspaper in which it was wrapped, at noon, sitting amid the green pine boughs which I had cut off, and to my bread was imparted some of their fragrance, for my hands were covered with a thick coat of pitch. Before I had done I was more the friend than the foe of the pine tree, though I had cut down some of them, having become better acquainted with it. Sometimes a rambler in the wood was attracted by the sound of my axe, and we chatted pleasantly over the chips which I had made.

By the middle of April, for I made no haste in my work, but rather   3
made the most of it, my house was framed and ready for the raising. I had already bought the shanty of James Collins, an Irishman who worked on the Fitchburg Railroad, for boards. James Collins' shanty was considered an uncommonly fine one. When I called to see it he was not at home. I walked about the outside, at first unobserved from within, the window was so deep and high. It was of small dimensions, with a peaked

cottage roof, and not much else to be seen, the dirt being raised five feet all around as if it were a compost heap. The roof was the soundest part, though a good deal warped and made brittle by the sun. Doorsill there was none, but a perennial passage for the hens under the door board. Mrs. C. came to the door and asked me to view it from the inside. The hens were driven in by my approach. It was dark, and had a dirt floor for the most part, dank, clammy, and aguish, only here a board and there a board which would not bear removal. She lighted a lamp to show me the inside of the roof and the walls, and also that the board floor extended under the bed, warning me not to step into the cellar, a sort of dust hole two feet deep. In her own words, they were "good boards overhead, good boards all around, and a good window"—of two whole squares origi-nally, only the cat had passed out that way lately. There was a stove, a bed, and a place to sit, an infant in the house where it was born, a silk parasol, gilt-framed looking-glass, and a patent new coffee-mill nailed to an oak sapling, all told. The bargain was soon concluded, for James had in the meanwhile returned. I to pay four dollars and twenty-five cents tonight, he to vacate at five tomorrow morning, selling to nobody else meanwhile: I to take possession at six. It were well, he said, to be there early, and anticipate certain indistinct but wholly unjust claims on the score of ground rent and fuel. This he assured me was the only encum-brance. At six I passed him and his family on the road. One large bundle held their all—bed, coffee-mill, looking-glass, hens—all but the cat; she took to the woods and became a wild cat and, as I learned afterward, trod in a trap set for woodchucks, and so became a dead cat at last.

I took down this dwelling the same morning, drawing the nails, and removed it to the pond side by small cartloads, spreading the boards on the grass there to bleach and warp back again in the sun. One early thrush gave me a note or two as I drove along the woodland path. I was informed treacherously by a young Patrick that neighbor Seeley, an Irishman, in the intervals of the carting, transferred the still tolerable, straight, and dri-vable nails, staples, and spikes to his pocket, and then stood when I came back to pass the time of day, and look freshly up, unconcerned, with spring thoughts, at the devastation; there being a dearth of work, as he said. He was there to represent spectatordom, and help make this seem-ingly insignificant event one with the removal of the gods of Troy. 4

I dug my cellar in the side of a hill sloping to the south, where a woodchuck had formerly dug his burrow, down through sumach and blackberry roots, and the lowest stain of vegetation, six feet square by seven deep, to a fine sand where potatoes would not freeze in any win-ter. The sides were left shelving, and not stoned; but the sun having never shone on them, the sand still keeps its place. It was but two hours' work. I took particular pleasure in this breaking of ground, for in almost all latitudes men dig into the earth for an equable temperature. Under the most splendid house in the city is still to be found the cellar where they store their roots as of old, and long after the superstructure had disappeared posterity remark its dent in the earth. The house is still but a sort of porch at the entrance of a burrow. 5

At length, in the beginning of May, with the help of some of my acquaintances, rather to improve so good an occasion for neighborliness than from any necessity, I set up the frame of my house. No man was ever more honored in the character of his raisers than I. They are destined, I trust, to assist at the raising of loftier structures one day. I began to occupy my house on the 4th of July, as soon as it was boarded and roofed, for the boards were carefully feather-edged and lapped, so that it was perfectly impervious to rain, but before boarding I laid the foundation of a chimney at one end, bringing two cartloads of stones up the hill from the pond in my arms. I built the chimney after my hoeing in the fall, before a fire became necessary for warmth, doing my cooking in the meanwhile out of doors on the ground, early in the morning: which mode I still think is in some respects more convenient and agreeable than the usual one. When it stormed before my bread was baked, I fixed a few boards over the fire, and sat under them to watch my loaf, and passed some pleasant hours in that way. In those days, when my hands were much employed, I read but little, but the least scraps of paper which lay on the ground, my holder, or tablecloth, afforded me as much entertainment, in fact answered the same purpose as the Iliad.

COMPREHENSION

1. Explain the process by which Thoreau builds his house. What are the main steps in this process?
2. What is Thoreau's attitude toward economy in this selection? Which of the details Thoreau has included most successfully reveal this attitude?
3. Compare Thoreau's evocation of place in this essay with Ehrlich's presentation of place in "Wyoming: The Solace of Open Spaces." Are the two authors addressing readers in the same way? Justify your response.

RHETORIC

1. In paragraph 1, what connotation does the author develop for the word *borrowing?* How do words related to economics serve as a motif in the essay?
2. What is the analogy in paragraph 1?
3. How does Thoreau use process analysis? Why is this rhetorical technique reinforced by the natural processes depicted in the essay?
4. How does Thoreau particularize the generalizations he makes in the essay?
5. What is the tone of the essay? Does an implied thesis for the essay emerge? Justify your answer.
6. What is the relationship of the last two sentences in paragraph 6 to the rest of the selection?

WRITING

1. Analyze Thoreau's poem in paragraph 2. Identify the poem's theme. Then write a brief essay explaining its relevance to "Economy."

2. Using Thoreau's method, write an essay in which you trace the process of building or creating something that was important to you.
3. Write a letter to the editor of your college newspaper arguing the need to economize in some aspect of personal or public life. Refer to Thoreau in this letter.

SUE HUBBELL   Sue Hubbell (b. 1935) once managed a bookstore in New York. She has also worked as a librarian and as a commercial beekeeper, an occupation from which she still makes a living. Hubbell was born in Michigan, attended Swarthmore College and the University of Michigan, and earned her M.S. from Drexel University in 1963. In 1986 she published *A Country Year: Living the Questions,* in which she reflects on her experiences with nature in the Ozarks, where she lives. In a selection from that work, Hubbell recounts her struggle to live self-sufficiently in nature without alienating her neighbors.

SUE HUBBELL

Felling Trees

I was out in the woods early in the morning cutting firewood for the winter. I do that every day this time of year. For an hour or two I cut wood, load it into the pickup and carry it back to my cabin and stack it. It isn't such a tiring job when I do a bit of it each day, before it gets hot, and I like being out there at that hour, when the woods are fresh and fragrant.

This morning I finished sawing up a tree from the place where I had been cutting for the past week. In the process I lost my screwrench, part screwdriver, part wrench, that I use to make adjustments on my chain saw. I shouldn't carry it in my pocket, but the chain had been loose; I had tightened it and had not walked back to the truck to put the wrench away. Scolding myself for being so careless, I began looking for another tree to cut and found a big one that had recently died.

I like to cut the dead trees from my woodlot, leaving the ones still alive to flourish, but this one was bigger than I feel comfortable about felling. I've been running a chain saw and cutting my own firewood for six years now, but I am still awed by the size and weight of a tree as it crashes to the ground. I have to nerve myself to cut the really big ones. I wanted this tree to fall onto a stretch of open ground that was free of other trees and brush, so I cut a wedge-shaped notch on that side of it. The theory is that the tree, thus weakened, will fall slowly on the side of the notch when the serious cut, slightly above the notch on the other side, is made. The trouble is that trees, particularly dead ones that may have rot on the inside, do not know the theory and may fall in an unexpected direction. That is the way accidents happen.

I was aware of that and was scared, besides, to be cutting down such a big tree; as a result, perhaps, I cut too timid a wedge. I started sawing

576

through on the other side, keeping an eye on the treetop to detect the characteristic tremble of a tree about to fall. I did not have time to jam the plastic wedge in my back pocket into the cut to hold it open because the tree began to sway and started to fall in my direction. I killed the engine on the saw and jumped out of the way.

There was no danger, however. Directly in back of where I had been standing were a number of other trees, which was why I had wanted to have the dead one fall the other way, and as it started down, its top branches snagged. I had sawed completely through the tree, but now the butt end had trapped the saw against the stump. I had cut what is descriptively called a widow maker. If I had been cutting with someone else, we could have used the second saw to free mine and perhaps brought the tree down, but it is dangerous and I don't like to do it. I couldn't even free my saw by taking it apart, for I had lost my screwrench, so I drove back to the barn, gathered up the tools I needed, a socket wrench, chains and a portable winch known as a come-along.

The day was warming and I was sweating by the time I got back to the woods, but I was determined to repair the botch I had made. Using the socket wrench, I removed the bar and chain from the saw and set the saw body aside. The weight of the saw gone, I worked the bar and chain free from under the butt of the tree. Then I spat and drank ice water from my thermos and figured out how I was going to pull down the tree with chain and winch.

The come-along is a cheery, sensible tool for a woman. It has a big hook at one end and a hook connected to a steel cable at the other. The cable is wound around a ratchet gear operated by a long handle to give leverage. It divides a heavy job into small, manageable bits that require no more than female strength, and I have used it many times to pull my pickup free from a mudhole. I decided that if I wound a chain around the butt of the widow maker and another chain around a nearby standing tree and connected the two with the come-along, I might be able to winch the felled tree to the ground. I attached the chains and come-along appropriately and began. Slowly, with each pump of the handle against the ratchet gear, the tree sank to the ground. The sun was high, the heat oppressive, and my sweatshirt was soaked with sweat, so I decided to leave the job of cutting up the tree to firewood lengths until tomorrow. I gathered up my tools and, in the process, found the screwrench almost hidden in leaf mold.

I am good friends with a woman who lives across the hollow. She and her husband sell cordwood to the charcoal factory in town. Her husband cuts the logs because a chain saw, in the Ozarks, is regarded as a man's tool, and she helps him load and unload the logs. Even though the wood is going to be turned into charcoal, it is traditional to cut it to four-foot lengths. A four-foot oak log is heavy; a strong man can lift it, but a woman has to use all her strength to do her part. My friend returns from her mornings sick with exhaustion, her head throbbing. She and I talk sometimes about how it would be if women were the woodcutters: the length would be less than four feet. Having to do

6

7

8

work beyond her strength makes my friend feel weak, ineffectual, dependent and cross.

My friend, and other Ozark women, often ask me curiously about my chain saw. Most people out here heat with wood, and if families in the suburbs quarrel about taking out the garbage, here the source of squabbles is getting enough firewood cut early in the year so that it can season. Women usually help by carrying the cut wood to the truck, but it is the men who cut the wood, and since the women think they cannot cut it, they frequently worry and sometimes nag about it.

My female Ozark friends envy me having my firewood supply under my own control, and they are interested when I tell them that they have had the hardest part of the job anyway, carrying the wood to the trucks. Cutting the wood into lengths with the chain saw is not hard work, although it does require some skill. So far, however, my friends have not taken up my offer to come over so that I can give them a lesson in using a chain saw. Forty years ago chain saws were heavy and certainly beyond the strength of a woman to use; today they are much improved and light. My saw is a small, light one, but with its 16-inch bar it is big enough to cut any tree I want to fell.

I know that feeling of helplessness and irritation that my friends have, for that is the way I used to be. Like many women my age, I would stand back and let a man change a flat tire. I could press a button on a washing machine but not fix the machine if something failed. I felt uneasy with tools other than a needle, a typewriter or kitchen utensils.

When I began living here alone I had to learn how to break down work into parcels that I could perform with my strength and I had to learn to use tools that I had never used and use them easily. Either that, or I would have had to leave. It was the hardest schooling I've ever taken but the most exhilarating. When there were Things in the world too heavy to move where I wanted them to be and too mysterious to be kept doing what I wanted them to do, I was filled with dissatisfaction and petulance. Those Things controlled me.

I prefer it the other way around.

COMPREHENSION

1. What does felling trees represent to the writer?
2. What points does Hubbell make about outdoor life? What is of particular concern to her Ozark community?
3. What do we learn about the division of labor between men and women in the essay? Does it seem to be traditional or modern in nature? How does Hubbell relate to the other women in the community?

RHETORIC

1. What is the main idea of the essay? At what point does it become clear? What does she accomplish in the sections that precede her thesis? Is this an effective technique? Why, or why not?

2. Does Hubbell employ abstract or concrete language in her piece? Why is this a good choice for her subject and audience?

3. How does the writer's language help set up a mood and evoke a sense of place? Cite specific words or phrases that are especially powerful.

4. What is the tone of the essay? What in the writer's style indicates this?

5. How does the author use process analysis in her essay? How does it work with the narration to strengthen her point?

6. Why does Hubbell end her essay as she does? What point is she making with her final sentence? Is this indicative of her attitude? How does the conclusion reinforce the rest of the piece?

WRITING

1. Write a process analysis essay describing, in detail, a difficult task you have accomplished. Consider why the task was so hard, why it had to be done, and how you felt after it was finished.

2. Consider "women's work" in a rural community. Does the nature of the work itself dictate the division of labor, or are there other factors to consider? How does city life affect the nature of working women? Consider these questions in an essay, using your own observations or research.

3. How does city living blunt people's perceptions of and responses to nature? Use Hubbell's essay to answer this question.

CLASSIC AND CONTEMPORARY: QUESTIONS FOR COMPARISON

1. Compare and contrast Thoreau's and Hubbell's essays considering these factors: the work they're undertaking, their relationship to others in the community, the way they choose to tell their stories. What conclusions can we form about the writers' lives and priorities based on the information and ideas expressed in their essays?

2. Define what Thoreau meant by *economy*, and explain its relevance to Hubbell's lifestyle and opinions. How do you think Hubbell might respond to Thoreau's ideas and circumstances?

3. Compare the language used by the writers. Is there anything about Thoreau's syntax that dates his essay? How modern does Hubbell's language appear in comparison? How do they evoke a sense of place through their writing? How is humor used or not used in both essays? How do the writers reveal their attitudes toward nature by their words?

CONNECTIONS

1. Using support from the works of Steinbeck, Carson, and others, write a causal-analysis essay tracing our relationship to the land. To what extent has history, greed, and fear helped to shape our attitude? Can this attitude be changed? How?

2. Compare the essays of Thoreau and Oates. Considering her objections to nature writers, how would Oates respond to his work? How would she critique his tone, content, and language? What about his essay might she applaud? Use the works of both writers to support your view.

3. Write a letter to the Op-Ed page of a newspaper objecting to a governmental ruling harmful to the environment. State the nature of the policy, its possible dangers, and your reasons for opposing it. Use support from any of the writers in this section. Extra reading or research may be necessary.

4. Consider why we fear nature. Why do we consider it an enemy, alien, something to be controlled or destroyed? How would Steinbeck, Oates, and Easterbrook respond to this question? Do you agree or disagree with them?

5. Both Steinbeck and Ehrlich use historical data and description to explore our relationship to the land. How do they approach their subject in terms of language, attitude, and style?

6. Choose an author in this section whose essay, in your opinion, romanticizes nature. Compare his or her attitude to that of a writer with a more pragmatic approach to the subject. Compare the two views, and specify the elements in their writing that contribute to the overall strength of their arguments.

7. Thoreau and Hubbell both use process analysis in their essays to convey their messages. Which essay do you feel makes a stronger, more effective point? What about the language and content make it relevant in today's world?

8. Write an essay entitled "Nature's Revenge" in which you examine the consequences of environmental abuse. Consider the short- as well as the long-term effects on the quality of life. Use support from any writer in this section to support your opinion.

9. Write specifically about our relationship to other living creatures on our planet. Is it one of exploitation, cooperation, tyranny? How does this relationship influence how we treat each other? Explore the answers to these questions in an essay. Use the works of Lopez, Oates, Steinbeck, and Eiseley to support your thesis.

CHAPTER TWELVE

Science, Medicine, and Mathematics

Contrary to popular assumptions, contemporary science and mathematics are not dry subjects but, rather, bodies of specialized knowledge concerned with the great "how" and "why" questions of our time. In fact, we are currently in the midst of a whole series of scientific revolutions that will radically transform our lives as we move toward the twenty-first century. The essential problem for humankind is to make sense of all this revolutionary scientific and mathematical knowledge, invest it with value, and make it serve our cultural and global needs.

As you will see in the essays assembled for this chapter, human beings are always the ultimate subject of scientific investigation. Science and mathematics attempt to understand the physical, biological, and chemical events that shape our lives. Whenever we switch on a light or turn on a computer, take an aspirin or start the car, we see that science has intervened effectively in our lives. Often the specialized knowledge of science forces us to make painful decisions. As Deborah Salazar admits in her highly personal essay, "My Abortion," science can provide powerful options for us, but it doesn't simplify the ethical choices that we continually have to make.

The technology of science thus affects everyday decisions as well as the larger contours of culture. Nowhere is the impact of science more apparent than in medicine. As Isaac Asimov and Stephen Jay Gould observe in their essays on cholesterol and AIDS, medical science exists to serve us, to help us with our common dilemmas. At the same time, medical science reminds us that despite advances, we are still mortal. Even as knowledge flows from research laboratories, these mortal paradoxes tend to perplex and goad us as we seek scientific solutions to the complex problems of our era.

Science and mathematics, as specialized bodies of knowledge, can send contradictory messages (for example, Bertrand Russell tells us that there is "supreme beauty" in mathematics, while we learn from another author that women are often denied access to this body of knowledge) because science and mathematics are socially constructed and reflect the contours of culture. How we manage the revolution in science—how we harness nuclear weapons or solve the ravages of AIDS—will determine the health of civilization in the next century.

Previewing the Chapter

As you read the essays in this chapter and respond to them in discussion and writing, consider the following questions:

• Does the author take a personal or an objective approach to the subject? What is the effect?

• What area of scientific or mathematical inquiry does the writer focus on?

• What scientific conflicts arise in the course of the essay?

• Is the writer a specialist, a lay person, a journalist, or a commentator? How does the background of the writer affect the tone of the essay?

• What assumptions does the author make about his or her audience? How much specialized knowledge must you bring to the essay?

• How do social issues enter into the author's presentation?

• What gender issues are raised by the author?

• How have your perceptions of the author's topic been changed or enhanced? What new knowledge have you gained? Does the writer contradict any of your assumptions or beliefs?

• Is the writer optimistic or pessimistic about the state of mathematics or science? How do you know?

DEBORAH SALAZAR   Deborah Salazar was born in Ecuador but grew up in Denhem Springs, Louisiana, and attended Louisiana State University, where she received her master of fine arts degree. Salazar's poetry has been published in many literary magazines. In this essay, which appeared in *Harper's* in 1990, Salazar offers an ostensibly objective account of her abortion, describing a medical procedure that readers themselves must make final judgments upon.

DEBORAH SALAZAR

My Abortion

The procedure itself was the easiest part. A friend had told me to close   ₁
my eyes and think about anything, think about Donald Duck—sweet and useless advice, I thought at the time—but when I heard the machine come on and the doctor say, "The cervix is slanted at a right angle, this could be a problem; okay, honey, *relax*," I thought, Donald Duck, Donald Duck, Donald Duck, Donald Duck. I will never be able to watch another Donald Duck cartoon without thinking about my abortion, but I went through the experience feeling pretty calm and entitled. Twenty-seven years old and pregnant for the first time in my life. God bless America, I thought, I sure as hell want a cheap, legal, safe abortion.

After I learned that I was pregnant, I started practicing a necessary   ₂
detachment. The Supreme Court was due to hand down its *Webster* decision any day, and the usual mobs of protesters around women's clinics were doubling in size. I got up before dawn on the fifteenth of June and packed a paper bag with a sweater and socks (because the receptionist said it would be cold inside the clinic) and maxi pads. I wanted to get there as soon as the doors opened, before most of the cross-waving, sign-carrying, chanting, singing protesters showed up. When I pulled into the clinic parking lot with my friend Beth, I saw only two people standing on the curb: a woman, dressed all in black, and a man. As we got closer, I saw that the woman was about my age, with straight black hair and pale eyes turned skyward. She was moaning the words, "Don't kill me, Mommy, don't kill me."

The man and the woman followed our car until it stopped at the   ₃
door. I stepped out, and the man stood in front of me. He was tall, wearing a suit and tie and singing, "Jesus loves the little children." I laughed in his face. Strange. Three years ago I had worked as a volunteer escort at this very clinic, and I'd always been so solemn with these people. I never would've expected to laugh today. The man obviously hadn't expected me to laugh either. He got angry. "Lesbian!" he called

after me as I walked into the clinic. "You're a lesbian. That's why you hate babies!" A tall young man wearing an official clinic-escort T-shirt was standing at the threshold. "Sorry about this," he muttered as I passed by. I was still laughing. "I wish I were a lesbian," I said a little hysterically. "I wouldn't be pregnant." And then I was inside the clinic.

I knew the routine. I took my forms and my plastic cup. I went directly to the bathroom. I could hear the protesters while I was in the bathroom. I could hear them the whole time I was in the clinic. The chanting was discontinuous, but it was louder every time it started up. "Murderers! Murderers!" I could hear them in the dressing room, in the weigh-in room, in counseling, in recovery, although I don't remember if I heard them in the procedure room itself. I was told later that my encounter with the protesters had been relatively undramatic: one escort said that these days he was seeing protesters trying to hold car doors shut while women fought to get out.

After I turned in my urine cup, I sat back in the waiting room and started filling out forms. One of them was a personal questionnaire that included the question, "What method of birth control were you using at the time you got pregnant?" I thought about lying for a second before I checked the box beside "none." One of the protesters outside had started playing a tape of a baby crying. I signed my name over and over. Yes, I understand the risks involved, yes, I understand that the alternatives to abortion are birth and adoption. I wanted to do more—I wanted to fill out a page or so explaining why I had chosen to do this. I wanted to explain to someone that I was a responsible person; you see, ladies and gentlemen, I never had sex without condoms unless I was having my period; I got pregnant during my period, isn't there something I could sign swearing to that? I had a three-day affair with a friend, I'm broke and unemployed, I can't give up a baby for adoption, I can't afford to be pregnant while I look for a job.

In counseling, I was asked why I'd gone off the pill, and I didn't hesitate to respond, "I can get rid of an accidental pregnancy. I can't get rid of cancer." In the lounge room where I sat in my dressing gown before going in to see the doctor, there was a tiny television (Pee-wee Herman was on) and a table with magazines *(Cosmopolitan, Vogue, American Baby)*. The room was already filled to capacity, all twelve chairs taken, when the little bowhead came in. She couldn't have been more than seventeen, wearing only her gown and a very big white satin bow in her hair. She was a beauty. She looked like she belonged on a homecoming float. She had been crying. "I hate them," she announced, dropping her shopping bag of clothes on the floor. "They don't have to say the things they say. Makes me want to go out there and shoot them with a gun."

"You can't hear them that well in here, honey," one of the older women said. "You can watch the cartoons."

"You know what one of them called my mama?" the beauty said. "Called her a slut, an unchristian woman. My mama yelled back that I got raped by a priest, that's how come I'm here." Stares. The bowhead picked up her shopping bag and leaned against the wall. She spoke again in a quieter voice. "I didn't really get raped by a priest. My mama just said that."

The doctor was late that morning. Outside, the chants were getting louder, competing with Pee-wee Herman, who was on full blast. The protesters were singing a hymn when my name was called. I walked down a short hallway in my bare feet, and then liquid Valium injected directly into my left arm made everything after that feel like it was taking place on another planet. I remember that the doctor was wearing a dark red surgical outfit and that it looked pretty gruesome—I wished he'd worn the traditional pale blue or green. I remember that the Valium made me want to laugh and I didn't want to laugh because I was afraid I'd wiggle, and I'd been warned *not* to wiggle unless I wanted my uterus perforated. I'd been at the clinic six hours already, preparing for this little operation that would take only five minutes. I remember that after the machine came on, it seemed like less than five minutes. I remember that it hurt and that I was amazed at how empty, relieved, and not pregnant I felt as soon as it was over. The cramps that followed were painful but not terribly so; I could feel my uterus contracting, trying to collapse back to its former size. I was led by a nurse into a dark room, where I sat on a soft mat in a soft chair and bled for a while. I closed my eyes. The woman in the next seat was sobbing softly. I knew it was the blond with the white bow in her hair. I reached over and took her hand in mine. The Valium made me feel as though we were both wearing gloves. Her hand was so still I wondered if she knew I was there, but the sobbing grew softer and softer and eventually it just stopped.

COMPREHENSION

1. How would you describe the writer's state of mind during the abortion procedure?
2. Why does the narrator choose to have an abortion?
3. How would you describe the atmosphere outside the clinic?

RHETORIC

1. How would you describe the author's tone in the essay? Are there any indications of Salazar's feelings about the event?
2. Why does Salazar use dialogue in her essay? What impact does its use have on the narrative? Find especially powerful uses of dialogue in the essay to support your views.
3. Cite specific use of descriptive details and figurative language. How does their use enrich the atmosphere in the story?
4. Why has the writer chosen narrative to explore her topic? What makes it an effective choice?
5. How does Salazar organize her essay? What transitional words contribute to the structure of the piece?

6. Examine Salazar's final paragraph. How does it function as a conclusion? How does it serve to unify the essay?

WRITING

1. Pretend to be one of the protesters outside the abortion clinic. If you had a chance to approach Salazar quietly and discuss her decision with her, how would you do it? What would you say to her about the morality of her actions? Develop this idea in a brief essay.
2. Write a descriptive narrative about a visit you made to a clinic. What was your medical problem? What procedure did you have done? What was the experience like? Describe the atmosphere and the people around you in detail to evoke a sense of place.
3. In an argumentation essay, express your own views on abortion. Do you consider it immoral? Necessary in certain cases? What are the alternatives to abortion? Be sure to include opposing viewpoints in your argument.

DAVID QUAMMEN David Quammen was born in Cincinnati, Ohio, in 1948. He received a B.A. degree from Yale University in 1970 and a B. Litt. degree from Oxford University, which he attended as a Rhodes scholar. Quammen published his first novel, *To Walk the Line,* an exploration of his experiences working in a Chicago ghetto, when he was just 22. Since then, he has divided his writing time between fiction and nonfiction. His fiction output has included a political thriller, *The Soul of Viktor Tronko* (1987), and his nonfiction writing includes a regular column about nature and the environment for the magazine *Outside.* Although not a professional scientist, Quammen is able to use science as a way to reflect unsentimentally on other subjects, such as politics and philosophy. He was a Guggenheim recipient in 1988.

DAVID QUAMMEN

The Man with the Metal Nose

Tycho Brahe and the Olfactory Dimension of Science

A very good friend of mine claims—among other matters of wild and ornery personal ethic—that he chooses his friends strictly by smell. I'm not sure what this says about my own aromaticity but I do understand, and endorse, his point in principle: The ineffable qualities are the ones that count, not the objective characteristics that can be capsulized in an introduction or on a resumé or during two hours' conversation over cocktails. Those ineffable qualities will answer the more crucial questions upon which a friendship is based, like *Would this person instinctively step between me and a charging wart hog?* or *Could I trust him to borrow a book without turning the page corners down?* And the nose, being humanity's most underdeveloped sensory organ, is perhaps the only apt emblem for our groping and sniffling efforts to register the ineffable. Which is why I can't stop wondering about one particular nose that occupies an intriguingly prominent place in the history of scientific inquiry.

It was an artificial one, this nose, a prosthesis made of gold and silver alloy. It was worn by an aristocratic Danish astronomer of the sixteenth century, a portly and sybaritic man named Tycho Brahe, who had lost his own God-given schnozzle in a duel. History does not record whether the replacement was held in position by a leather thong (as was that suspiciously similar one worn by Lee Marvin in *Cat Ballou*), or if not then how; but we do know that all his life Tycho carried a small snuffbox full of ointment, with which he constantly kept his metal nose lubricated, like one of those people compulsive about Chapstick. There is likewise no evidence as to what purpose this cold piece of technology might have served. The surviving portraits of Tycho suggest that its role was not to support eyeglasses. Did it smell? Did it run? Could it be turned up? Was it often out of joint? We'll never know. In fact Tycho himself, with or without his peculiar nose, would probably be forgotten completely by history if it weren't for two important considerations. The second of these was a set of notebooks full of numbers, and we'll come to that in a moment. The first was a galactic event of literally the greatest magnitude.

Step outside on a summer night and look off toward the northeastern part of the sky. Not far below the Little Dipper you'll see the constellation Cassiopeia, easily recognizable in the shape of a W. Back in early November of 1572, when Tycho Brahe was still a young amateur stargazer of twenty-five, a bright new star appeared suddenly in that constellation. It was shining with more brilliance than any other star, more brilliance than the planet Venus, so bright that it could be seen faintly even during daylight. Furthermore it was gleaming out from a spot where, just a week earlier and throughout the centuries before, no star at all had ever been visible. This phenomenon posed a serious philosophic problem in the late sixteenth century, when Aristotelean cosmology as sanctioned by the Catholic Church decreed that the upper celestial spheres—everything out there beyond the moon—were absolutely immutable. On the fourth day of Genesis, God had created the lights in the firmament, then left them alone, and that was that. Now suddenly here was a big brand new dot of fire flaunting its power in Cassiopeia. The star attracted attention, and concern, not just among theologians and astronomers. It was a popular event of mythic resonance. And it made the reputation of Tycho Brahe.

Tycho wasn't the first knowledgeable watcher to spot the new star, but he noticed it for himself one night before the news had gone public, and it left him agape. Over the next sixteen months, while the star

587

changed color and rapidly dimmed, he performed a continuous sequence of very precise measurements, using a fine sextant he had crafted from walnut wood (the best available technology, the telescope not yet having been invented), that allowed him to speak about this new star more authoritatively than anyone else in Europe. It was immobile relative to Cassiopeia, Tycho stated; it was not in the sublunary atmosphere, but far beyond amid the other stars; it was not a comet without a tail, as some thought, but a true star. Tycho's book, *De Nova Stella,* made him internationally famous. He had charted all apparent aspects of the star with surpassing accuracy; but he had no idea what in the devil it was.

Today we know: It was a supernova explosion. Only five such cataclysmic events have been visible from Earth during the past thousand years, and of those, Tycho's in 1572 was the fourth. Some thousands of years earlier a gigantic star (much larger than our sun) had come to the end of its lifespan—the hydrogen nuclei at its core all "burnt" by fusion to form helium nuclei, and the helium further fused into still bigger nuclei. The star had then fallen into a terminal sequence of convulsions, alternately expanding and contracting, gravitational compaction seething down against rising internal pressures, which led to a final incredible thermonuclear explosion. That explosion flared out perhaps one billion times brighter than the star itself had shone. And the flash, having traveled across all those light-years between, eventually showed itself to Earth from the direction of Cassiopeia. Then by 1574 it was gone. No one knew why. Not even Tycho Brahe.

But Tycho, who had so faithfully measured and plotted the thing, was now a national hero in Denmark. The king gave him his own island, as well as lavish financial support with which to construct there a great astronomical observatory that would be Tycho's private scientific demesne. Tycho built a castle in Gothic Renaissance style, with spires and gables and cornices, and at the apex an onion dome topped by a gilt vane in the shape of Pegasus. There were guest rooms and aviaries and fountains, formal gardens and neat orchards laid out within a great perimeter wall, fish ponds, English mastiffs to stand guard, a paper mill, a print shop for his publications, and from ceiling to floor in the main workroom an oversized mural of Tycho himself. He called the place Uraniborg. The various chambers and towers he furnished with all the best astronomical instruments a king's money could order up: sextants of walnut, quadrants of brass and steel, armillary spheres ornamented with his own portrait, triquetrums and azimuth circles and astrolabiums—who knows what they all did. In this setting Tycho commanded his many assistants, threw grand parties for visiting nobility, rubbed ointment on his metal nose, and tossed scraps of meat to his attending dwarf Jeppe, who served as official court fool. Tycho, in other words, was not a scientist in the ascetic vein.

But during the next twenty years at Uraniborg he also performed the most precise and potentially useful collection of continuous astronomical observations that mankind up to that date had achieved. Where other astronomers (including most recently Copernicus) had been casual and sporadic about their own observations, Tycho was thorough, punctilious, indefatigable. Where others had tracked the planets with only their unaided eyes, occasionally a primitive sextant, Tycho devised his ingenious new instruments. Where others watched for a few nights or a few months, then went inside to dream up more or less misguided theories, Tycho kept watch relentlessly for over two decades, all the while recording his careful notes. The large quarto volumes containing those notes were his treasure. His contribution to science lay in recognizing that serious astronomy *required* data-gathering of such precision and continuity, and in marshalling the financial resources, the elaborate equipment, the patience, to make it possible. But again, as with the star of 1572, Tycho never knew what he had.

He was unpersuaded by the Copernican theory of celestial organization (which had been published quietly about fifty years earlier) and dissatisfied with the old Ptolemaic view. So in 1588 Tycho announced his own version. Earth, according to Tycho, was stationary in space, as Ptolemy had thought. The other planets, he said, moved in uniform circular motion around the sun. And the sun in turn orbited, pulling its satellites along, in a great graceful circle around Earth. This Tychonic system supposedly explained all the complex planetary motions that Tycho's skywatching, over the years, had so accurately mapped. It was mathematically sweet and theologically acceptable. Its only drawback was that it was wrong.

After two decades at Uraniborg, where Tycho was a greedy and irresponsible landlord to the island's peasants, putting himself gradually into disfavor with the new Danish king, those munificent cash subsidies ended. So Tycho felt obliged to pack up his gear, his entourage, and leave. He went shopping across Europe for another royal patron willing to support him in similar high style, and two years later he found one: Tycho settled into a new castle just outside Prague, on the River Iser, under sponsorship of the Emperor Rudolph. Again there was money enough to pay for lordly living and a staff of assistants, among whom now was a twenty-nine-year-old German who had already earned modest recognition as an astronomer in his own right. This man's name was Johannes Kepler, and he had some ideas about celestial organization himself.

Kepler had abandoned everything to join Tycho in Prague, for a single ulterior reason: He hungered to see the data in those precious notebooks. But Tycho let him go hungry, assigning Kepler to some demeaning lesser chores, while refusing to share information with him as a colleague. Then in October of 1601, Tycho Brahe quite suddenly died. And Kepler got hold of the notebooks.

Within eight years, using Tycho's data, Johannes Kepler had formulated and published two laws that for the first time accurately explained the dynamics of our solar system, and thereby began the modern age in astronomy. The laws were as simple, once recognized, as they had been ineffable before. First, said Kepler, the planets (including Earth) travel

589

around the sun not in circles but in ellipses, great oval orbits with the sun nearer one end. Second, each planet moves not at uniform speed but at a velocity that changes according to its distance from the sun. Today those statements might seem unexceptional. But in 1609, how many minds could have guessed that God would design a universe using *ovals* and *irregular motion?*

Something more was at work here than just astronomical training, hard thinking, and Tycho Brahe's data. What else? In many of the great scientific discoveries there seems to have been an additional mode of percipience that took up in the shadowy zone where pure rationality ended, a further faculty that helped point the way to the particular revolutionary idea. The word *intuition* is sometimes applied but, like a paper label on a bottle, only obscures what's inside. Arthur Koestler in his intriguing book on the early astronomers calls it "sleep-walking." Einstein spoke in his own case of "the gift of fantasy." As a young man of twenty-three, Isaac Newton suddenly glimpsed his law of gravity in little more time than an apple would take to fall from a tree. Alfred Russel Wallace came across natural selection with the same suddenness, supposedly during an attack of fever, after Darwin had labored over the problem for half a lifetime. Watson and Crick found the structure of DNA using tinkertoys, youthful cockiness, and another lab's x-ray photographs—photographs which until then had failed to be correctly interpreted. 12

In each of these entries upon the ineffable, something more was at work than mere cerebration. 13

And Kepler shaped his inherited Tychonic data into a vision of cosmological order that was ingeniously simple, drastically unorthodox, and true. But Tycho himself, evidently, just did not have the nose for it. 14

COMPREHENSION

1. What is the thesis of the essay?
2. What is the irony implicit in the title? What is the irony implicit in the fact that Brahe wore a metal nose? How is this irony reinforced in the final sentence of the essay?
3. According to the author, what personal quality did Kepler have that was lacking in Brahe?

RHETORIC

1. Although the essay explores an important historical and scientific circumstance, the introduction is written with quite a bit of levity. What function does this strategy serve in setting the tone of the essay?
2. Topic sentences are important for introducing paragraphs. However, final sentences in paragraphs must serve as bridges to the next paragraph. Examine the final sentences in the paragraphs in this essay, and explain how the author uses them to create coherence between the paragraphs.

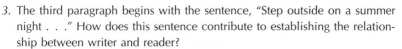
3. The third paragraph begins with the sentence, "Step outside on a summer night . . ." How does this sentence contribute to establishing the relationship between writer and reader?

4. Paragraph 5 offers a process analysis of a supernova explosion. How well does the author describe this event? What knowledge does the author assume the reader has in order to fully appreciate it?

5. In paragraph 6, the author describes Tycho's lifestyle after he became a national hero. Is this significant in terms of understanding the astronomer's contribution to scientific knowledge? What *is* the purpose of describing his personal proclivities?

6. In paragraph 12, the author uses example and appeals to authority to support his thesis. How do they strengthen his argument? Why has he reserved them for the latter part of the essay?

7. Compare the style and tone of this essay to the style and tone of a college textbook on astronomy or history. How do they differ? To what degree does this difference support the author's thesis about scientific discovery?

WRITING

1. Interview a member of the science faculty at your college about his or her views on intuition and scientific discovery. Transform your interview notes into an essay.

2. Argue for or against the proposition that students who major in science should also take courses in the liberal arts.

3. For a research assignment, compare and contrast the concepts of "science" and "technology."

LEWIS THOMAS   Lewis Thomas (1913–1994) was president of the Memorial Sloan-Kettering Cancer Center. He first came to public attention when his collection of essays, *Lives of a Cell* (1974), appeared. Because of his eloquent capacity to extract metaphors from the discoveries of modern biology and because of his optimism, Thomas's essays have attracted a large and enthusiastic following. Another collection of his essays, *The Medusa and the Snail*, was published in 1979. Thomas can discover an almost magical value in the most humble activities, as the essay below demonstrates.

LEWIS THOMAS

On Societies as Organisms

Viewed from a suitable height, the aggregating clusters of medical scientists in the bright sunlight of the boardwalk at Atlantic City, swarmed there from everywhere for the annual meetings, have the look of assemblages of social insects. There is the same vibrating, ionic movement, interrupted by the darting back and forth of jerky individuals to touch antennae and exchange small bits of information; periodically, the mass casts out, like a trout-line, a long single file unerringly toward Child's. If the boards were not fastened down, it would not be a surprise to see them put together a nest of sorts.

It is permissible to say this sort of thing about humans. They do resemble, in their most compulsively social behavior, ants at a distance. It is, however, quite bad form in biological circles to put it the other way round, to imply that the operation of insect societies has any relation at all to human affairs. The writers of books on insect behavior generally take pains, in their prefaces, to caution that insects are like creatures from another planet, that their behavior is absolutely foreign, totally unhuman, unearthly, almost unbiological. They are more like perfectly tooled but crazy little machines, and we violate science when we try to read human meanings in their arrangements.

It is hard for a bystander not to do so. Ants are so much like human beings as to be an embarrassment. They farm fungi, raise aphids as livestock, launch armies into wars, use chemical sprays to alarm and confuse enemies, capture slaves. The families of weaver ants engage in child labor, holding their larvae like shuttles to spin out the thread that sews the leaves together for their fungus gardens. They exchange information ceaselessly. They do everything but watch television.

What makes us most uncomfortable is that they, and the bees and termites and social wasps, seem to live two kinds of lives: they are individuals, going about the day's business without much evidence of thought for tomorrow, and they are at the same time component parts, cellular elements, in the huge, writhing, ruminating organism of the Hill, the nest, the hive. It is because of this aspect, I think, that we most wish for them to be something foreign. We do not like the notion that there can be collective societies with the capacity to behave like organisms. If such things exist, they can have nothing to do with us.

Still, there it is. A solitary ant, afield, cannot be considered to have much of anything on his mind; indeed, with only a few neurons strung together by fibers, he can't be imagined to have a mind at all, much less a thought. He is more like a ganglion on legs. Four ants together, or ten, encircling a dead moth on a path, begin to look more like an idea. They fumble and shove, gradually moving the food toward the Hill, but as though by blind chance. It is only when you watch the dense mass of thousands of ants, crowded together around the Hill, blackening the ground, that you begin to see the whole beast, and now you observe it thinking, planning, calculating. It is an intelligence, a kind of live computer, with crawling bits for its wits.

At a stage in the construction, twigs of certain size are needed, and all the members forage obsessively for twigs of just this size. Later, when outer walls are to be finished, thatched, the size must change, and as though given new orders by telephone, all the workers shift the search to the new twigs. If you disturb the arrangement of a part of the Hill, hundreds of ants will set it vibrating, shifting, until it is put right again. Distant sources of food are somehow sensed, and long lines, like tentacles, reach out over the ground, up over walls, behind boulders, to fetch it in.

Termites are even more extraordinary in the way they seem to accumulate intelligence as they gather together. Two or three termites in a chamber will begin to pick up pellets and move them from place to place, but nothing comes of it; nothing is built. As more join in, they seem to reach a critical mass, a quorum, and the thinking begins. They place pellets atop pellets, then throw up columns and beautiful, curving, symmetrical arches, and the crystalline architecture of vaulted chambers is created. It is not known how they communicate with each other, how the chains of termites building one column know when to turn toward the crew on the adjacent column, or how, when the time comes, they manage the flawless joining of the arches. The stimuli that set them off at the outset, building collectively instead of shifting things about, may be pheromones released when they reach committee size. They react as if alarmed. They become agitated, excited, and then they begin working, like artists.

Bees live lives of organisms, tissues, cells, organelles, all at the same time. The single bee, out of the hive retrieving sugar (instructed by the dancer: "south-southeast for seven hundred meters, clover—mind you make corrections for the sundrift") is still as much a part of the hive as if attached by a filament. Building the hive, the workers have the look of embryonic cells organizing a developing tissue; from a distance they are like the viruses inside of a cell, running off row after row of symmetrical polygons as though laying down crystals. When the time for swarming comes, and the old queen prepares to leave with her part of the population, it is as though the hive were involved in mitosis. There is an agitated moving of bees back and forth, like granules in cell sap. They distribute themselves in almost precisely equal parts, half to the departing queen, half to the new one. Thus, like an egg, the great, hairy, black and golden creature splits in two, each with an equal share of the family genome.

The phenomenon of separate animals joining up to form an organism is not unique in insects. Slime-mold cells do it all the time, of course, in each life cycle. At first they are single amebocytes swimming around, eating bacteria, aloof from each other, untouching, voting straight Republican. Then, a bell sounds, and acrasin is released by special cells toward which the others converge in stellate ranks, touch, fuse together, and construct the slug, solid as a trout. A splendid stalk is raised, with a fruiting body on top, and out of this comes the next generation of amebocytes, ready to swim across the same moist ground, solitary and ambitious.

Herring and other fish in schools are at times so closely integrated, their actions so coordinated, that they seem to be functionally a great multi-fish organism. Flocking birds, especially the seabirds nesting on the slopes of offshore islands in Newfoundland, are similarly attached, connected, synchronized.

Although we are by all odds the most social of all social animals— more interdependent, more attached to each other, more inseparable in our behavior than bees—we do not often feel our conjoined intelligence. Perhaps, however, we are linked in circuits for the storage, processing, and retrieval of information, since this appears to be the most basic and universal of all human enterprises. It may be our biological function to build a certain kind of Hill. We have access to all the information of the biosphere, arriving as elementary units in the stream of solar photons. When we have learned how these are rearranged against randomness, to make, say, springtails, quantum mechanics, and the late quartets, we may have a clearer notion how to proceed. The circuitry seems to be there, even if the current is not always on.

The system of communications used in science should provide a   12
neat, workable model for studying mechanisms of information-building in human society. Ziman, in a recent *Nature* essay, points out, "the invention of a mechanism for the systematic publication of *fragments* of scientific work may well have been the key event in the history of modern science." He continues:

> A regular journal carries from one research worker to another the various . . . observations which are of common interest. . . . A typical scientific paper has never pretended to be more than another little piece in a larger jigsaw—not significant in itself but as an element in a grander scheme. *This technique, of soliciting many modest contributions to the store of human knowledge, has been the secret of Western science since the seventeenth century, for it achieves a corporate, collective power that is far greater than any one individual can exert.* [italics mine]

With some alteration of terms, some toning down, the passage   13
could describe the building of a termite nest.

It is fascinating that the word "explore" does not apply to the   14
searching aspect of the activity, but has its origins in the sounds we make while engaged in it. We like to think of exploring in science as a lonely, meditative business, and so it is in the first stages, but always, sooner or later, before the enterprise reaches completion, as we explore, we call to each other, communicate, publish, send letters to the editor, present papers, cry out on finding.

COMPREHENSION

1. In this essay, does Thomas write for a specialized or for a general audience? Explain your answer.
2. Describe the insects that Thomas says have humanlike behavior. What is his thesis?
3. Why do writers of books about insects avoid using personification in their descriptions? Why does Thomas purposely use it?

RHETORIC

1. Thomas tends to use words that are not generally used. Define *genome, ionic, amebocytes, mitosis, acrasin, ganglion, stellate,* and *organism.*
2. Thomas uses metaphors frequently and imaginatively. List seven metaphors

in the essay, and describe how they are used. Compare his use of metaphor to that of Virginia Woolf in "The Death of the Moth" (Chapter 10).

3. Paragraph 4 is crucial to the organization of the essay. What two methods of classification does it introduce?

4. What is the difference between solitary and collective behavior among the social insects? Thomas compares this behavior to certain kinds of human behavior. What are the details of this comparison?

5. According to your dictionary, what is the etymology of the word *explore?* How does Thomas use this etymology?

6. Thomas extends his discussion in paragraph 9 beyond insects. What effect does he achieve by doing this?

WRITING

1. Do you find it reassuring or disturbing to compare human behavior to insect behavior? Do you find it difficult to consider human society an organism? Why do you think Thomas finds this encouraging?

2. Divide human behavior into groups (school, sports, business), and compare solitary and collective behavior within one or more groups.

3. Write an essay comparing your pet's behavior to human behavior.

4. Thomas has complained about "how awful the prose is in scientific papers." Evaluate the author's own prose in this essay. Argue for or against its effectiveness.

RICHARD SELZER   Richard Selzer (b. 1928), a surgeon with a full-time practice in New Haven, Connecticut, began writing several hours each night after already establishing a successful medical career. His first book of essays, *Mortal Lessons: Notes on the Art of Surgery* (1974), established him as a prominent essayist specializing in the world of medicine and surgery. Selzer employs his elegant prose style in describing the often tragic, unpleasant, and painful world of medical patients. He is a contributor to popular magazines, and his essays have been collected in several books, among them *Confessions of a Knife* (1979) and *Letters to a Young Doctor* (1982). The following essay demonstrates Selzer's experience and expertise as a surgeon as well as his unique ability to describe the world of medicine in poetic and graceful terms.

RICHARD SELZER

Sarcophagus

We are six who labor here in the night. No . . . seven! For the man horizontal upon the table strives as well. But we do not acknowledge his struggle. It is our own that preoccupies us.

595

I am the surgeon. 2

David is the anesthesiologist. You will see how kind, how soft he is. 3
Each patient is, for him, a preparation respectfully controlled. Blood
pressure, pulse, heartbeat, flow of urine, loss of blood, temperature,
whatever is measurable, David measures. And he is a titrator, adding a
little gas, drug, oxygen, fluid, blood in order to maintain the dynamic
equilibrium that is the only state compatible with life. He is in the very
center of the battle, yet he is one step removed; he has not known the
patient before this time, nor will he deal with the next of kin. But for
him, the occasion is no less momentous.

Heriberto Paz is an assistant resident in surgery. He is deft, tiny, 4
mercurial. I have known him for three years. One day he will be the
best surgeon in Mexico.

Evelyn, the scrub nurse, is a young Irish woman. For seven years we 5
have worked together. Shortly after her immigration, she led her young
husband into my office to show me a lump on his neck. One year ago he
died of Hodgkin's disease. For the last two years of his life, he was paralyzed from the waist down. Evelyn has one child, a boy named Liam.

Brenda is a black woman of forty-five. She is the circulating nurse, 6
who will conduct the affairs of this room, serving our table, adjusting the
lights, counting the sponges, ministering to us from the unsterile world.

Roy is a medical student who is beginning his surgical clerkship. He 7
has been assigned to me for the next six weeks. This is his first day, his
first operation.

David is inducing anesthesia. In cases where the stomach is not 8
empty through fasting, the tube is passed into the windpipe while the
patient is awake. Such an "awake" intubation is called crashing. It is
done to avoid vomiting and the aspiration of stomach contents into the
lungs while the muscles that control coughing are paralyzed.

We stand around the table. To receive a tube in the windpipe while 9
fully awake is a terrifying thing.

"Open your mouth wide," David says to the man. The man's mouth 10
opens slowly to its fullest, as though to shriek. But instead, he yawns.
We smile down at him behind our masks.

"OK. Open again. Real wide." 11

David sprays the throat of the man with a local anesthetic. He does this 12
three times. Then, into the man's mouth, David inserts a metal tongue
depressor which bears a light at the tip. It is called a laryngoscope. It is to
light up the throat, reveal the glottic chink through which the tube must be
shoved. All this while, the man holds his mouth agape, submitting to the
hard pressure of the laryngoscope. But suddenly, he cannot submit. The
man on the table gags, struggles to free himself, to spit out the instrument.
In his frenzy his lip is pinched by the metal blade.

There is little blood. 13

"Suction," says David. 14

Secretions at the back of the throat obscure the view. David suctions 15
them away with a plastic catheter.

"Open," commands David. More gagging. Another pass with the 16
scope. Another thrust with the tube. Violent coughing informs us that

the tube is in the right place. It has entered the windpipe. Quickly the balloon is inflated to snug it against the wall of the trachea. A bolus of Pentothal is injected into a vein in the man's arm. It takes fifteen seconds for the drug to travel from his arm to his heart, then on to his brain. I count them. In fifteen seconds, the coughing stops, the man's body relaxes. He is asleep.

"All set?" I ask David. 17

"Go ahead," he nods. 18

A long incision. You do not know how much room you will need. This part of the operation is swift, tidy. Fat . . . muscle . . . fascia . . . the peritoneum is snapped open and a giant shining eggplant presents itself. It is the stomach, black from the blood it contains and that threatens to burst it. We must open that stomach, evacuate its contents, explore. 19

Silk sutures are placed in the wall of the stomach as guidelines between which the incision will be made. They are like the pitons of a mountaineer. I cut again. No sooner is the cavity of the stomach achieved, than a columnar geyser of blood stands from the small opening I have made. Quickly, I slice open the whole front of the stomach. We scoop out handfuls of clot, great black gelatinous masses that shimmy from the drapes to rest against our own bellies as though, having been evicted from one body, they must find another in which to dwell. Now and then we step back to let them slither to the floor. They are under our feet. We slip in them. "Jesus," I say. "He is bleeding all over North America." Now my hand is inside the stomach, feeling, pressing. There! A tumor spreads across the back wall of this stomach. A great hard craterous plain, the dreaded linitis plastica (leather bottle) that is not content with seizing one area, but infiltrates between the layers until the entire organ is stiff with cancer. It is that, of course, which is bleeding. I stuff wads of gauze against the tumor. I press my fist against the mass of cloth. The blood slows. I press harder. The bleeding stops. 20

A quick glance at Roy. His gown and gloves, even his mask, are sprinkled with blood. Now is he dipped; and I, his baptist. 21

David has opened a second line into the man's veins. He is pumping blood into both tubings. 22

"Where do we stand?" I ask him. 23

"Still behind. Three units." He checks the blood pressure. 24

"Low, but coming up," he says. 25

"Shall I wait 'til you catch up?" 26

"No. Go ahead. I'll keep pumping." 27

I try to remove my fist from the stomach, but as soon as I do, there is a fresh river of blood. 28

"More light," I say. "I need more light." 29

Brenda stands on a platform behind me. She adjusts the lamps. 30

"More light," I say, like a man going blind. 31

"That's it," she says. "There is no more light." 32

"We'll go around from the outside," I say. Heriberto nods agreement. "Free up the greater curvature first, then the lesser, lift the stomach up and get some control from behind." 33

597

I must work with one hand. The other continues as the compressor. ₃₄
It is the tiredest hand of my life. One hand, then, inside the stomach,
while the other creeps behind. Between them . . . a ridge of tumor. The
left hand fumbles, gropes toward its mate. They swim together. I lift the
stomach forward to find that *nothing* separates my hands from each
other. The wall of the stomach has been eaten through by the tumor.
One finger enters a large tubular structure. It is the aorta. The incision
in the stomach has released the tamponade of blood and brought us to
this rocky place.

"Curved aortic clamp." ₃₅

A blind grab with the clamp, high up at the diaphragm. The bleed- ₃₆
ing slackens, dwindles. I release the pressure warily. A moment later
there is a great bang of blood. The clamp has bitten through the can-
cerous aorta.

"Zero silk on a big Mayo needle." ₃₇

I throw the heavy sutures, one after the other, into the pool of blood, ₃₈
hoping to snag with my needle some bit of tissue to close over the rent in
the aorta, to hold back the blood. There is no tissue. Each time, the needle pulls through the crumble of tumor. I stop. I repack the stomach.
Now there is a buttress of packing both outside and inside the stomach.
The bleeding is controlled. We wait. Slowly, something is gathering here,
organizing. What had been vague and shapeless before is now declaring
itself. All at once, I know what it is. There is nothing to do.

For what tool shall I ask? With what device fight off this bleeding? ₃₉
A knife? There is nothing here to cut. Clamps? Where place the jaws of
a hemostat? A scissors? Forceps? Nothing. The instrument does not
exist that knows such deep red jugglery. Not all my clever picks, my
rasp . . . A miner's lamp, I think, to cast a brave glow.

David has been pumping blood steadily. ₄₀

"He is stable at the moment," he says. "Where do we go from ₄₁
here?"

"No place. He's going to die. The minute I take away my pressure, ₄₂
he'll bleed to death."

I try to think of possibilities, alternatives. I cannot; there are none. ₄₃
Minutes pass. We listen to the cardiac monitor, the gassy piston of the
anesthesia machine.

"More light!" I say. "Fix the light." ₄₄

The light seems dim, aquarial, a dilute beam slanting through a green ₄₅
sea. At such a fathom the fingers are clumsy. There is pressure. It is cold.

"Dave," I say, "stop the transfusion." I hear my voice coming as ₄₆
from a great distance. "Stop it," I say again.

David and I look at each other, standing among the drenched rags, ₄₇
the smeared equipment.

"I can't," he says. ₄₈

"Then I will," I say, and with my free hand I reach across the ₄₉
boundary that separates the sterile field from the outside world, and I
close the clamp on the intravenous tubing. It is the act of an outlaw,

someone who does not know right from wrong. But I know. I know that this is right to do.

"The oxygen," I say. "Turn it off."

"You want it turned off, you do it," he says.

"Hold this," I say to Heriberto, and I give over the packing to him. I step back from the table, and go to the gas tanks.

"This one?" I have to ask him. 53

"Yes," David nods. 54

I turn it off. We stand there, waiting, listening to the beeping of 55 the electrocardiograph. It remains even, regular, relentless. Minutes go by, and the sound continues. The man will not die. At last, the intervals on the screen grow longer, the shape of the curve changes, the rhythm grows wild, furious. The line droops, flattens. The man is dead.

It is silent in the room. Now we are no longer a team, each with his 56 circumscribed duties to perform. It is Evelyn who speaks first.

"It is a blessing," she says. I think of her husband's endless dying. 57

"No," says Brenda. "Better for the family if they have a few days 58 . . . to get used to the idea of it."

"But, look at all the pain he's been spared." 59

"Still, for the ones that are left, it's better to have a little time." 60

I listen to the two women murmuring, debating without rancor, 61 speaking in hushed tones of the newly dead as women have done for thousands of years.

"May I have the name of the operation?" It is Brenda, picking up 62 her duties. She is ready with pen and paper.

"Exploratory laparotomy. Attempt to suture malignant aorto-gastric 63 fistula."

"Is he pronounced?" 64

"What time is it?" 65

"Eleven-twenty." 66

"Shall I put that down?" 67

"Yes." 68

"Sew him up," I say to Heriberto. "I'll talk to the family." 69

To Roy I say, "You come with me." 70

Roy's face is speckled with blood. He seems to me a child with the 71 measles. What, in God's name, is he doing here?

From the doorway, I hear the voices of the others, resuming. 72

"Stitch," says Heriberto. 73

Roy and I go to change our bloody scrub suits. We put on long white 74 coats. In the elevator, we do not speak. For the duration of the ride to the floor where the family is waiting, I am reasonable. I understand that in its cellular wisdom, the body of this man had sought out the murderous function of my scalpel, and stretched itself upon the table to receive the final stabbing. For this little time, I know that it is not a murder committed but a mercy bestowed. Tonight's knife is no assassin, but the kind scythe of time.

We enter the solarium. The family rises in unison. There are so many! How ruthless the eyes of the next of kin.

"I am terribly sorry . . . ," I begin. Their faces tighten, take guard. "There was nothing we could do."

I tell them of the lesion, tell of how it began somewhere at the back of the stomach; how, long ago, no one knows why, a cell lost the rhythm of the body, fell out of step, sprang, furious, into rebellion. I tell of how the cell divided and begat two of its kind, which begat four more and so on, until there was a whole race of lunatic cells, which is called cancer.

I tell of how the cancer spread until it had replaced the whole back of the stomach, invading, chewing until it had broken into the main artery of the body. Then it was, I tell them, that the great artery poured its blood into the stomach. I tell of how I could not stop the bleeding, how my clamps bit through the crumbling tissue, how my stitches would not hold, how there was nothing to be done. All of this I tell.

A woman speaks. She has not heard my words, only caught the tone of my voice.

"Do you mean he is dead?"

Should I say "passed away" instead of "died"? No. I cannot.

"Yes," I tell her, "he is dead."

Her question and my answer unleash their anguish. Roy and I stand among the welter of bodies that tangle, grapple, rock, split apart to form new couplings. Their keening is exuberant, wild. It is more than I can stand. All at once, a young man slams his fist into the wall with great force.

"Son of a bitch!" he cries.

"Stop that!" I tell him sharply. Then, more softly, "Please try to control yourself."

The other men crowd about him, patting, puffing, grunting. They are all fat, with huge underslung bellies. Like their father's. A young woman in a nun's habit hugs each of the women in turn.

"Shit!" says one of the men.

The nun hears, turns away her face. Later, I see the man apologizing to her.

The women, too, are fat. One of them has a great pile of yellowish hair that has been sprayed and rendered motionless. All at once, she begins to whine. A single note, coming louder and louder. I ask a nurse to bring tranquilizer pills. She does, and I hand them out, one to each, as though they were the wafers of communion. They urge the pills upon each other.

"Go on, Theresa, take it. Make her take one."

Roy and I are busy with cups of water. Gradually it grows quiet. One of the men speaks.

"What's the next step?"

"Do you have an undertaker in mind?"

They look at each other, shrug. Someone mentions a name. The rest nod.

"Give the undertaker a call. Let him know. He'll take care of everything."

I turn to leave.

"Just a minute," one of the men calls. "Thanks, Doc. You did what you could."

"Yes," I say.

Once again in the operating room. Blood is everywhere. There is a wild smell, as though a fox had come and gone. The others, clotted about the table, work on. They are silent, ravaged. 99

"How did the family take it?" 100

"They were good, good." 101

Heriberto has finished reefing up the abdomen. The drapes are 102 peeled back. The man on the table seems more than just dead. He seems to have gone beyond that, into a state where expression is possible— reproach and scorn. I study him. His baldness had advanced beyond the halfway mark. The remaining strands of hair had been gallantly dyed. They are, even now, neatly combed and crenellated. A stripe of black moustache rides his upper lip. Once, he had been spruce!

We all help lift the man from the table to the stretcher. 103

"On three," says David. "One . . . two . . . three." 104

And we heft him over, using the sheet as a sling. My hand brushes 105 his shoulder. It is cool. I shudder as though he were infested with lice. He has become something that I do not want to touch.

More questions from the women. 106

"Is a priest coming?" 107

"Does the family want to view him?" 108

"Yes. No. Don't bother me with these things." 109

"Come on," I say to Roy. We go to the locker room and sit together 110 on a bench. We light cigarettes.

"Well?" I ask him. 111

"When you were scooping out the clots, I thought I was going to 112 swoon."

I pause over the word. It is too quaint, too genteel for this time. I 113 feel, at that moment, a great affection for him.

"But you fought it." 114

"Yes. I forced it back down. But, almost . . ." 115

"Good," I say. Who knows what I mean by it? I want him to know 116 that I count it for something.

"And you?" he asks me. The students are not shy these days. 117

"It was terrible, his refusal to die." 118

I want him to say that it was right to call it quits, that I did the best 119 I could. But he says nothing. We take off our scrub suits and go to the shower. There are two stalls opposite each other. They are curtained. But we do not draw the curtains. We need to see each other's healthy bodies. I watch Roy turn his face directly upward into the blinding fall of water. His mouth is open to receive it. As though it were milk flowing from the breasts of God. For me, too, this water is like a well in a wilderness.

In the locker room, we dress in silence. 120

"Well, goodnight." 121

Awkwardly our words come out in unison. 122

"In the morning . . ." 123

"Yes, yes, later." 124

"Goodnight." 125

I watch him leave through the elevator door. 126

For the third time I go to that operating room. The others have long 127
since finished and left. It is empty, dark. I turn on the great lamps above
the table that stands in the center of the room. The pediments of the
table and the floor have been scrubbed clean. There is no sign of the
struggle. I close my eyes and see again the great pale body of the man,
like a white bullock, bled. The line of stitches on his abdomen is a
hieroglyph. Already, the events of this night are hidden from me by
these strange untranslatable markings.

COMPREHENSION

1. What has the author implied by choosing his title for the essay? How is the title reinforced by the final paragraph?

2. Based upon Selzer's description of the surgeon's work, to what other profession does the author draw analogies? Explain.

3. Why do the other members of the operating team refuse to tamper with the medical apparatus, even after being ordered to do so by the surgeon?

RHETORIC

1. What is the dramatic effect of telling the story in the present tense?

2. The author often eschews conventional sentence structure. For example in paragraph 16, he employs fragments: "Another pass with the scope. Another thrust with the tube." In paragraph 21, he uses odd syntax, "Now is he dipped; and I, his baptist." And some sentences are extremely short, such as paragraph 96: "I turn to leave." What is the cumulative effect of using such innovative sentence structure?

3. Why has the author divided his essay into six parts? What is the function of each part? How does the author create drama via the juxtaposition of one section to the next?

4. Dialogue is used frequently in the essay. What is the function and effect of the dialogue?

5. Selzer's imagery is often vivid and original. How do the following excerpts contribute to the tone of the essay:

   "I understand that in its cellular wisdom, the body of this man had sought out the murderous function of my scalpel"; "Tonight's knife is no assassin, but the kind scythe of time" (paragraph 74).

   "There is a wild smell, as though a fox had come and gone" (paragraph 99).

6. There are several references to religion in the essay. Locate them, and explain what their cumulative effect is on the tone of the essay.

7. The role of mystery plays a significant part in the author's mood; for example, the final sentence reads, "Already, the events of this night are hidden

from me by these strange untranslatable markings." What other passages reflect this mood of mystery in the essay? How does this mood affect the description of the essay's events, which are supposedly based on science?

WRITING

1. We take for granted many things which are mysterious to us; for example, the act of reading, writing, and breathing. Write a descriptive essay of 500 words in which you reflect upon some basic activity that you have never analyzed before.
2. Write a 400-word critique of Selzer's essay, entitling it "Religious Imagery in Selzer's 'Sarcophagus.'"
3. Create a metaphor or simile for a particular profession, such as "a professional athlete is superhuman" or "a rock star is like a god (or goddess)." Extend your metaphor in a 400-word essay, using analogies to fit your central metaphor.

ISAAC ASIMOV   Isaac Asimov (1920–1992), a writer and scientist, taught biochemistry at Boston University. He was born in Russia and educated in America. Asimov's works included both scientific textbooks and science fiction, most notably *The Foundation Trilogy* (1951–1953). Asimov was extraordinarily productive, the author of more than a hundred books; his texts on popular science helped to explain difficult concepts for the lay reader. In the essay below, Asimov uses a clear, straightforward style to explain the function of cholesterol.

ISAAC ASIMOV

Cholesterol

Cholesterol is a dirty word these days, and every report that comes out seems to make it worse. A government study of more than 350,000 American men between 35 and 37 years old was reported last month and 80% of them had cholesterol levels of more than 180 milligrams per 100 milliliters of blood. Anything over the 180 mark indicates an increased probability of an early death from heart disease. The higher the measurement the higher the probability.

And yet this grinning death mask is not the only face that cholesterol bears. Cholesterol happens to be absolutely essential to animal life. Every animal from the amoeba to the whale (including human beings, of course) possesses cholesterol. The human body is about one-third of 1% cholesterol.

The portion of the animal body that is richest in cholesterol is the nervous system. There we encounter masses of nerve cells which, in bulk, have a grayish appearance and are therefore referred to as "gray matter."

603

Each nerve cell has fibers extending from it, including a particularly ₄ long one called the "axon" along which electrical impulses travel from nerve cell to nerve cell, coordinating the body and making it possible for us to receive sense-impressions, to respond appropriately and, above all (for human beings), to think.

The axon is surrounded by a fatty sheath, which presumably acts as ₅ an insulating device that enables the electrical impulse to travel faster and more efficiently. Without its insulating powers, it is possible that nerve cells would "short-circuit" and that the nervous system would not function.

The fatty sheath has a whitish appearance so that those portions of ₆ the nervous system that are made up of masses of axons are called the "white matter."

As it happens, two out of every five molecules in the fatty sheath are ₇ cholesterol. Why that should be, we don't know, but the cholesterol cannot be dispensed with. Without it, we would have no nervous system, and without a nervous system, we could neither think nor live.

So important is cholesterol that the body has the full power to man- ₈ ufacture it from simpler materials. Cholesterol does not need to be present in the diet at all.

The trouble is, though, that if, for any reason, the body has more ₉ cholesterol than it needs, there is a tendency to get rid of it by storing it on the inner surface of the blood vessels—especially the coronary vessels that feed the heart. This is "atherosclerosis," and it occurs in men more often than in women. The cholesterol deposits narrow the blood vessels, stiffen and roughen them, make internal clotting easier and, in general, tend to produce heart attacks, strokes and death.

Why is that? Why should such a vital substance, without which we ₁₀ could not live, present such a horrible other face? Why haven't we evolved in such a way as not to experience such dangerous cholesterol deposits?

One possible answer is that until the coming of modern medicine, ₁₁ human beings did not have a long life span, on the average. Most people, even in comparatively good times, were dead of violence or infectious disease before they were 40, and by that time atherosclerosis had not had time to become truly dangerous.

It is only since the average human life span has reached 75, in many ₁₂ parts of the world, that atherosclerosis and other "degenerative diseases" have become of overwhelming importance.

What to do? There is the matter of diet, for one thing. Apparently, ₁₃ flooding the body with high-cholesterol items of diet (eggs, bacon, butter and other fatty foods of animal origin) encourages a too-high level of cholesterol in the blood and consequently atherosclerosis.

As it happens, plants do not contain cholesterol. They have related ₁₄ compounds, but not cholesterol. Therefore, to cut down on fatty animal food in the diet (the cholesterol is in the fat) and to increase plant food lower the chance of atherosclerosis.

In fact, since most primates (apes and monkeys) are much more ₁₅ vegetarian in their diet than human beings, can it be that we have not yet had time to fully adapt to the kind of carnivorous diet we have grown accustomed to? This is particularly so in prosperous Western countries. People of the Third World countries eat far less meat than Westerners do. They may have troubles of their own, but atherosclerosis, at least, is a minor problem.

We may also develop drugs that interfere with the body's ability to deposit cholesterol in the blood vessels. A new drug called lovastatin has been recently reported to show promising effectiveness in this direction. There is hope.

COMPREHENSION

1. What is cholesterol? Where is it found? What is its function?
2. According to Asimov, what are some of the reasons that humans may have problems with cholesterol?
3. What solutions does Asimov offer?

RHETORIC

1. Comment on Asimov's first sentence. What tone does it establish for the essay? How does the rest of the paragraph support the topic sentence?
2. Does this essay contain a thesis statement? Is it implied or explicit? Where does it appear?
3. What level of language does Asimov use? Is it aimed at the general reader or at a specialized one? Justify your response.
4. How does Asimov use definition in his piece?
5. What technique does Asimov employ in paragraph 10? What is the effect on the structure of the essay? How does it relate to subsequent paragraphs?
6. Critique Asimov's conclusion. How does it serve to unify the information preceding it?

WRITING

1. Write an essay defining another biological or medical term. Consider your intended audience and how technical you want to make the language. Some research will be necessary.
2. Asimov mentions diet in his essay. Write an essay in which you emphasize the importance of diet in maintaining a healthy body. What diet would you recommend? What kinds of food do you eat? What other factors, such as physical exercise, affect health?
3. Research the latest findings about cholesterol. How does this new information disprove or support Asimov's theories? Compare and contrast what you discover with Asimov's essay.

CARL SAGAN   Carl Edward Sagan (b. 1934) received his A.B., B.S., M.A., and Ph.D. degrees from the University of Chicago. Probably the most popular scientist in America, he has been the host of several television series on science and has written a number of best-selling books on science, including *The Dragons of Eden* (1977) and *Broca's Brain* (1979). The former earned him a Pulitzer Prize for general nonfiction in 1978. He has also contributed hundreds of papers to scientific journals. Besides writing, Sagan has served as a full-time professor at Cornell University and a visiting professor at dozens of other institutions of higher learning in the United States and abroad. He is also an activist for many philanthropic causes, serving as an adviser to groups such as the Council for a Livable World Education Fund, the Children's Health Fund, and the American Committee on U.S.–Soviet Relations. Despite controversies surrounding the speculative nature of his work, Carl Sagan continues to be one of modern science's most popular spokespersons. Sagan's philosophy may be summed up in a statement he made in a *Time* magazine interview: "We make our world significant by the courage of our questions and by the depth of our answers."

CARL SAGAN

Can We Know the Universe?
Reflections on a Grain of Salt

Nothing is rich but the inexhaustible wealth of nature. She shows us only surfaces, but she is a million fathoms deep. —Ralph Waldo Emerson

Science is a way of thinking much more than it is a body of knowledge. Its goal is to find out how the world works, to seek what regularities there may be, to penetrate to the connections of things—from subnuclear particles, which may be the constituents of all matter, to living organisms, the human social community, and thence to the cosmos as a whole. Our intuition is by no means an infallible guide. Our perceptions may be distorted by training and prejudice or merely because of the limitations of our sense organs, which, of course, perceive directly but a small fraction of the phenomena of the world. Even so straightforward a question as whether in the absence of friction a pound of lead falls faster than a gram of fluff was answered incorrectly by Aristotle and almost everyone else before the time of Galileo. Science is based on experiment, on a willingness to challenge old dogma, on an openness to see the universe as it really is. Accordingly, science sometimes requires courage—at the very least the courage to question the conventional wisdom.

Beyond this the main trick of science is to *really* think of something: the shape of clouds and their occasional sharp bottom edges at the same altitude everywhere in the sky; the formation of a dewdrop on a leaf; the origin of a name or a word—Shakespeare, say, or "philanthropic"; the reason for human social customs—the incest taboo, for example; how it is that a lens in sunlight can make paper burn; how a "walking stick" got to look so much like a twig; why the Moon seems to follow us as we walk; what prevents us from digging a hole down to the center of the Earth; what the definition is of "down" on a spherical Earth; how it is possible for the body to convert yesterday's lunch into today's muscle and sinew; or how far is up—does the universe go on forever, or if it does not, is there any meaning to the question of what lies on the other side? Some of these questions are pretty easy. Others, especially the last, are mysteries to which no one even today knows the answer. They are natural questions to ask. Every culture has posed such questions in one way or another. Almost always the proposed answers are in the nature of "Just So Stories," attempted explanations divorced from experiment, or even from careful comparative observations.

But the scientific cast of mind examines the world critically as if many alternative worlds might exist, as if other things might be here which are not. Then we are forced to ask why what we see is present and not something else. Why are the Sun and the Moon and the planets spheres? Why not pyramids, or cubes, or dodecahedra? Why not irregular, jumbly shapes? Why so symmetrical, worlds? If you spend any time spinning hypotheses, checking to see whether they make sense, whether they conform to what else we know, thinking of tests you can pose to substantiate or deflate your hypotheses, you will find yourself doing science. And as you come to practice this habit of thought more and more you will get better and better at it. To penetrate into the heart of the thing—even a little thing, a blade of grass, as Walt Whitman said—is to experience a kind of exhilaration that, it may be, only human beings of all the beings on this planet can feel. We are an intelligent species and the use of our intelligence quite properly gives us pleasure. In this respect the brain is like a muscle. When we think well, we feel good. Understanding is a kind of ecstasy.

But to what extent can we *really* know the universe around us? Sometimes this question is posed by people who hope the answer will be in the negative, who are fearful of a universe in which everything might one day be known. And sometimes we hear pronouncements from scientists who confidently state that everything worth knowing will soon be known—or even is already known—and who paint pictures of a Dionysian or Polynesian age in which the zest for intellectual discovery has withered, to be replaced by a kind of subdued languor, the lotus eaters drinking fermented coconut milk or some other mild hallucinogen. In addition to maligning both the Polynesians, who were intrepid explorers (and whose brief respite in paradise is now sadly ending), as well as the inducements to intellectual discovery provided by some hallucinogens, this contention turns out to be trivially mistaken.

Let us approach a much more modest question: not whether we can know the universe or the Milky Way Galaxy or a star or a world. Can we know, ultimately and in detail, a grain of salt? Consider one microgram of table salt, a speck just barely large enough for someone with keen eyesight to make out without a microscope. In that grain of salt there are about 10^{16} sodium and chlorine atoms. This is a 1 followed by 16 zeros, 10 million billion atoms. If we wish to know a grain of salt, we must know at least the three-dimensional positions of each of these atoms. (In fact, there is much more to be known—for example, the nature of the forces between the atoms—but we are making only a modest calculation.) Now, is this number more or less than the number of things which the brain can know?

How much *can* the brain know? There are perhaps 10^{11} neurons in the brain, the circuit elements and switches that are responsible in their electrical and chemical activity for the functioning of our minds. A typical brain neuron has perhaps a thousand little wires, called dendrites, which connect it with its fellows. If, as seems likely, every bit of information in the brain corresponds to one of these connections, the total number of things knowable by the brain is no more than 10^{14}, one hundred trillion. But this number is only one percent of the number of atoms in our speck of salt.

So in this sense the universe is intractable, astonishingly immune to any human attempt at full knowledge. We cannot on this level understand a grain of salt, much less the universe.

But let us look a little more deeply at our microgram of salt. Salt happens to be a crystal in which, except for defects in the structure of the crystal lattice, the position of every sodium and chlorine atom is predetermined. If we could shrink ourselves into this crystalline world, we would see rank upon rank of atoms in an ordered array, a regularly alternating structure—sodium, chlorine, sodium, chlorine, specifying the sheet of atoms we are standing on and all the sheets above us and below us. An absolutely pure crystal of salt could have the position of every atom specified by something like 10 bits of information.[1] This would not strain the information-carrying capacity of the brain.

If the universe had natural laws that governed its behavior to the same degree of regularity that determines a crystal of salt, then, of course, the universe would be knowable. Even if there were many such laws, each of considerable complexity, human beings might have the capability to understand them all. Even if such knowledge exceeded the information-carrying capacity of the brain, we might store the additional information outside our bodies—in books, for example, or in computer memories—and still, in some sense, know the universe.

Human beings are, understandably, highly motivated to find regularities, natural laws. The search for rules, the only possible way to understand such a vast and complex universe, is called science. The universe forces those who live in it to understand it. Those creatures who find everyday experience a muddled jumble of events with no predictability, no regularity, are in grave peril. The universe belongs to those who, at least to some degree, have figured it out.

It is an astonishing fact that there *are* laws of nature, rules that summarize conveniently—not just qualitatively but quantitatively—how the

---

[1]Chlorine is a deadly poison gas employed on European battlefields in World War I. Sodium is a corrosive metal which burns upon contact with water. Together they make a placid and unpoisonous material, table salt. Why each of these substances has the properties it does is a subject called chemistry, which requires more than 10 bits of information to understand.

world works. We might imagine a universe in which there are no such laws, in which the 10^{80} elementary particles that make up a universe like our own behave with utter and uncompromising abandon. To understand such a universe we would need a brain at least as massive as the universe. It seems unlikely that such a universe could have life and intelligence, because beings and brains require some degree of internal stability and order. But even if in a much more random universe there were such beings with an intelligence much greater than our own, there could not be much knowledge, passion or joy.

Fortunately for us, we live in a universe that has at least important parts that are knowable. Our common-sense experience and our evolutionary history have prepared us to understand something of the workaday world. When we go into other realms, however, common sense and ordinary intuition turn out to be highly unreliable guides. It is stunning that as we go close to the speed of light our mass increases indefinitely, we shrink toward zero thickness in the direction of motion, and time for us comes as near to stopping as we would like. Many people think that this is silly, and every week or two I get a letter from someone who complains to me about it. But it is a virtually certain consequence not just of experiment but also of Albert Einstein's brilliant analysis of space and time called the Special Theory of Relativity. It does not matter that these effects seem unreasonable to us. We are not in the habit of traveling close to the speed of light. The testimony of our common sense is suspect at high velocities.

Or consider an isolated molecule composed of two atoms shaped something like a dumbbell—a molecule of salt, it might be. Such a molecule rotates about an axis through the line connecting the two atoms. But in the world of quantum mechanics, the realm of the very small, not all orientations of our dumbbell molecule are possible. It might be that the molecule could be oriented in a horizontal position, say, or in a vertical position, but not at many angles in between. Some rotational positions are forbidden. Forbidden by what? By the laws of nature. The universe is built in such a way as to limit, or quantize, rotation. We do not experience this directly in everyday life; we would find it startling as well as awkward in sitting-up exercises, to find arms outstretched from the sides or pointed up to the skies permitted but many intermediate positions forbidden. We do not live in the world of the small, on the scale of 10^{-13} centimeters, in the realm where there are twelve zeros between the decimal place and the one. Our common-sense intuitions do not count. What does count is experiment—in this case observations from the far infrared spectra of molecules. They show molecular rotation to be quantized.

The idea that the world places restrictions on what humans might do is frustrating. Why *shouldn't* we be able to have intermediate rotational positions? Why *can't* we travel faster than the speed of light? But so far as we can tell, this is the way the universe is constructed. Such prohibitions not only press us toward a little humility; they also make the world more knowable. Every restriction corresponds to a law of nature, a regularization of the universe. The more restrictions there are on what matter and energy can do, the more knowledge human beings can attain. Whether in some sense the universe is ultimately knowable depends not only on how many natural laws there are that encompass widely divergent phenomena, but also on whether we have the openness and the intellectual capacity to understand such laws. Our formulations of the regularities of nature are surely dependent on how the brain is built, but also, and to a significant degree, on how the universe is built.

For myself, I like a universe that includes much that is unknown 15 and, at the same time, much that is knowable. A universe in which everything is known would be static and dull, as boring as the heaven of some weak-minded theologians. A universe that is unknowable is no fit place for a thinking being. The ideal universe for us is one very much like the universe we inhabit. And I would guess that this is not really much of a coincidence.

COMPREHENSION

1. What is the thesis of the essay? In what paragraph is this thesis most clearly expressed?
2. Why does the author say, in paragraph 12, that in many circumstances, "common sense and ordinary intuition turn out to be highly unreliable guides"?
3. Why does Sagan say, in his conclusion, that "The ideal universe for us is one very much like the universe we inhabit"?

RHETORIC

1. What is the function of the epigram by Emerson? How does it relate to the essay proper?
2. Many of the paragraphs in the essay begin with coordinating conjunctions (a structure frowned upon by many high school English teachers). What is Sagan's rhetorical purpose in using them as connecting devices?
3. What specific clues are there in the essay that Sagan's tone is one of excitement and celebration regarding science?
4. Sagan refers often to what he calls "a law of nature." Where and how in the essay does he explain, describe, or define this term?
5. The essay begins abruptly with an explanation of the concept of science. What purpose is served by diving into the subject so dramatically?
6. What is the intended effect of combining the terms "universe" and "grain of salt" in the title and subtitle? How does the author exploit this juxtaposition in his essay?
7. Examine the italicized words in the essay. Why has Sagan chosen to italicize these words? Explain.

WRITING

1. Argue for or against the proposition that scientific knowledge takes the mystery out of life.

2. For a research paper, select one of the items Sagan enumerates in paragraph 2, such as "the formation of a dewdrop on a leaf," the origin of the name *Shakespeare* or the word *philanthropic*, "the incest taboo," or "how a 'walking stick' got to look so much like a twig." Write a 500- to 600-word expository essay on your topic.

3. Write a personal essay in which you describe how you felt when you suddenly understood a particular topic in school that had previously eluded you.

STEPHEN JAY GOULD   Stephen Jay Gould (b. 1941), an acclaimed contemporary science writer, teaches biology, geology, and the history of science at Harvard University. He also writes a monthly column, "This View of Life," for *Natural History* and is the author of *Ever Since Darwin* (1977), *Ontogeny and Phylogeny* (1977), *The Panda's Thumb* (1980), *Wonderful Life* (1989), and *Bully for Brontosaurus* (1991). In this 1987 essay, Gould explains in clear, precise language why AIDS is a "natural phenomenon" and warns against viewing it in moral terms.

STEPHEN JAY GOULD

The Terrifying Normalcy of AIDS

Disney's Epcot Center in Orlando, Fla., is a technological tour de force 1
and a conceptual desert. In this permanent World's Fair, American industrial giants have built their versions of an unblemished future. These masterful entertainments convey but one message, brilliantly packaged and relentlessly expressed: progress through technology is the solution to all human problems. G.E. proclaims from Horizons: "If we can dream it, we can do it." A.T.&T. speaks from on high within its giant golf ball: We are now "unbounded by space and time." United Technologies bubbles from the depths of Living Seas: "With the help of modern technology, we feel there's really no limit to what can be accomplished."

Yet several of these exhibits at the Experimental Prototype Commu- 2
nity of Tomorrow, all predating last year's space disaster, belie their stated message from within by using the launch of the shuttle as a visual metaphor for technological triumph. The Challenger disaster may represent a general malaise, but it remains an incident. The AIDS pandemic, an issue that may rank with nuclear weaponry as the greatest danger of our era, provides a more striking proof that mind and technology are not omnipotent and that we have not canceled our bond to nature.

In 1984, John Platt, a biophysicist who taught at the University of 3
Chicago for many years, wrote a short paper for private circulation. At a time when most of us were either ignoring AIDS, or viewing it as a

contained and peculiar affliction of homosexual men, Platt recognized that the limited data on the origin of AIDS and its spread in America suggested a more frightening prospect: we are all susceptible to AIDS, and the disease has been spreading in a simple exponential manner.

Exponential growth is a geometric increase. Remember the old kiddy problem: if you place a penny on square one of a checkerboard and double the number of coins on each subsequent square—2, 4, 8, 16, 32 . . . —how big is the stack by the sixty-fourth square? The answer: about as high as the universe is wide. Nothing in the external environment inhibits this increase, thus giving to exponential processes their relentless character. In the real, noninfinite world, of course, some limit will eventually arise, and the process slows down, reaches a steady state, or destroys the entire system: the stack of pennies falls over, the bacterial cells exhaust their supply of nutrients.

Platt noticed that data for the initial spread of AIDS fell right on an exponential curve. He then followed the simplest possible procedure of extrapolating the curve unabated into the 1990's. Most of us were incredulous, accusing Platt of the mathematical gamesmanship that scientists call "curve fitting." After all, aren't exponential models unrealistic? Surely we are not all susceptible to AIDS. Is it not spread only by odd practices to odd people? Will it not, therefore, quickly run its short course within a confined group?

Well, hello 1987—worldwide data still match Platt's extrapolated curve. This will not, of course, go on forever. AIDS has probably already saturated the African areas where it probably originated, and where the sex ratio of afflicted people is 1-to-1, male-female. But AIDS still has far to spread, and may be moving exponentially, through the rest of the world. We have learned enough about the cause of AIDS to slow its spread, if we can make rapid and fundamental changes in our handling of that most powerful part of human biology—our own sexuality. But medicine, as yet, has nothing to offer as a cure and precious little even for palliation.

This exponential spread of AIDS not only illuminates its, and our, biology, but also underscores the tragedy of our moralistic misperception. Exponential processes have a definite time and place of origin, an initial point of "inoculation"—in this case, Africa. We didn't notice the spread at first. In a population of billions, we pay little attention when one increases to two, or eight to sixteen, but when one million becomes two million, we panic, even though the *rate* of doubling has not increased.

The infection has to start somewhere, and its initial locus may be little more than an accident of circumstance. For a while, it remains confined to those in close contact with the primary source, but only by accident of proximity, not by intrinsic susceptibility. Eventually, given the power and lability of human sexuality, it spreads outside the initial group and into the general population. And now AIDS has begun its march through our own heterosexual community.

What a tragedy that our moral stupidity caused us to lose precious time, the greatest enemy in fighting an exponential spread, by downplaying the danger because we thought that AIDS was a disease of three irregular groups of minorities: minorities of life style (needle users), of sexual preference (homosexuals) and of color (Haitians). If AIDS had first been imported from Africa into a Park Avenue apartment, we would not have dithered as the exponential march began.

The message of Orlando—the inevitability of technological solutions— is wrong, and we need to understand why. 10

Our species has not won its independence from nature, and we can- not do all that we can dream. Or at least we cannot do it at the rate required to avoid tragedy, for we are not unbounded from time. Viral diseases are preventable in principle, and I suspect that an AIDS vac- cine will one day be produced. But how will this discovery avail us if it takes until the millennium, and by then AIDS has fully run its expo- nential course and saturated our population, killing a substantial per- centage of the human race? A fight against an exponential enemy is pri- marily a race against time. 11

We must also grasp the perspective of ecology and evolutionary biology and recognize, once we reinsert ourselves properly into nature, that AIDS represents the ordinary workings of biology, not an irrational or diabolical plague with a moral meaning. Disease, including epidemic spread, is a natural phenomenon, part of human history from the beginning. An entire subdiscipline of my profession, paleopathology, studies the evidence of ancient diseases preserved in the fossil remains of organisms. Human history has been marked by episodic plagues. More native peoples died of imported disease than ever fell before the gun during the era of colonial expansion. Our memories are short, and we have had a respite, really, only since the influenza pandemic at the end of World War I, but AIDS must be viewed as a virulent expression of an ordinary natural phenomenon. 12

I do not say this to foster either comfort or complacency. The evolu- tionary perspective is correct, but utterly inappropriate for our human scale. Yes, AIDS is a natural phenomenon, one of a recurring class of pandemic diseases. Yes, AIDS may run through the entire population, and may carry off a quarter or more of us. Yes, it may make no *biological* difference to Homo sapiens in the long run: there will still be plenty of us left and we can start again. Evolution cares as little for its agents— organisms struggling for reproductive success—as physics cares for individual atoms of hydrogen in the sun. But we care. These atoms are our neighbors, our lovers, our children and ourselves. AIDS is both a natural phenomenon and, potentially, the greatest natural tragedy in human history. 13

The cardboard message of Epcot fosters the wrong attitudes: we must both reinsert ourselves into nature and view AIDS as a natural phe- nomenon in order to fight properly. If we stand above nature and if technology is all-powerful, then AIDS is a horrifying anomaly that must be trying to tell us something. If so, we can adopt one of two atti- tudes, each potentially fatal. We can either become complacent, because 14 we believe the message of Epcot and assume that medicine will soon generate a cure, or we can panic in confusion and seek a scapegoat for something so irregular that it must have been visited upon us to teach us a moral lesson.

But AIDS is not irregular. It is part of nature. So are we. This should galvanize us and give us hope, not prompt the worst of all responses: a kind of "new-age" negativism that equates natural with what we must accept and cannot, or even should not, change. When we view AIDS as natural, and when we recognize both the exponential property of its spread and the accidental character of its point of entry into America, we can break through our destructive tendencies to blame others and to free ourselves of concern.

If AIDS is natural, then there is no message in its spread. But by all that science has learned and all that rationality proclaims, AIDS works by a *mechanism*—and we can discover it. Victory is not ordained by any principle of progress, or any slogan of technology, so we shall have to fight like hell, and be watchful. There is no message, but there is a mechanism.

COMPREHENSION

1. What does Gould mean when he defines AIDS as a "natural phenomenon"? How does the title support this definition?
2. What does Gould mean by "our moral stupidity" in paragraph 9?
3. What connection does Gould make between our reaction to the AIDS crisis and our alienation from nature?

RHETORIC

1. What is Gould's main idea? Where in the essay is it stated?
2. What is the purpose of paragraphs 1 and 2? How do they contribute to Gould's argument? How do they help establish the tone of the essay? What *is* the tone? What is the importance of Epcot Center to Gould's thesis?
3. Gould uses scientific terminology in his essay. Define the words *exponential* in paragraph 3 and *pandemic* and *phenomenon* in paragraph 13. Is this essay intended for a specialized audience? Justify your response.
4. Trace the progression of ideas in paragraphs 2, 3, 4, and 5. What transitions does Gould employ?
5. Does Gould use rhetorical strategies besides argument in his essay? Cite evidence of this.
6. Explain the final sentence in Gould's conclusion. What is its relation to the total paragraph?

WRITING

1. Write an essay in which you expand on Gould's belief that "our moral stupidity" has not only hindered society's recognition of the AIDS threat but continues to impede AIDS research and treatment.

2. Gould states that we must "reinstate ourselves into nature." What does he mean by this? How would this affect the way in which we deal with disease and death in our society? Explore this issue in a brief essay.

J. B. S. HALDANE John Burdon Sanderson Haldane (1892–1964) was a geneticist, biologist, and writer of science books for the lay reader. His best-known work is *Animal Biology* (1927), written in collaboration with John S. Huxley. He also wrote *Adventures of a Biologist* (1940) and *Everything Has a History* (1951), a collection of essays. Haldane was famous for his ability to explain the abstract, often abstruse, ideas of modern science with concrete examples. "On Being the Right Size," which mixes mathematics and physics with insects and elephants, exemplifies Haldane's skill.

J. B. S. HALDANE

On Being the Right Size

The most obvious differences between different animals are differences ₁ of size, but for some reason the zoologists have paid singularly little attention to them. In a large textbook of zoology before me I find no indication that the eagle is larger than the sparrow, or the hippopotamus bigger than the hare, though some grudging admissions are made in the case of the mouse and the whale. But yet it is easy to show that a hare could not be as large as a hippopotamus, or a whale as small as a herring. For every type of animal there is a most convenient size, and a large change in size inevitably carries with it a change of form.

Let us take the most obvious of possible cases, and consider a giant ₂ man sixty feet high—about the height of Giant Pope and Giant Pagan in the illustrated *Pilgrim's Progress* of my childhood. These monsters were not only ten times as high as Christian, but ten times as wide and ten times as thick, so that their total weight was a thousand times his, or about eighty to ninety tons. Unfortunately the cross sections of their bones were only a hundred times those of Christian, so that every square inch of giant bone had to support ten times the weight borne by a square inch of human bone. As the human thighbone breaks under about ten times the human weight, Pope and Pagan would have broken their thighs every time they took a step. This was doubtless why they were sitting down in the picture I remember. But it lessens one's respect for Christian and Jack the Giant Killer.

To turn to zoology, suppose that a gazelle, a graceful little creature ₃ with long thin legs, is to become large, it will break its bones unless it does one of two things. It may make its legs short and thick, like the rhinoceros, so that every pound of weight has still about the same area of bone to support it. Or it can compress its body and stretch out its legs obliquely to gain stability, like the giraffe. I mention these two beasts because they happen to belong to the same order as the gazelle, and both are quite successful mechanically, being remarkably fast runners.

Gravity, a mere nuisance to Christian, was a terror to Pope, Pagan, and Despair. To the mouse and any smaller animal it presents practically no dangers. You can drop a mouse down a thousand-yard mine shaft; and, on arriving at the bottom, it gets a slight shock and walks away, provided that the ground is fairly soft. A rat is killed, a man is broken, a horse splashes. For the resistance presented to movement by the air is proportional to the surface of the moving object. Divide an animal's length, breadth, and height each by ten; its weight is reduced to a thousandth, but its surface only to a hundredth. So the resistance to falling in the case of the small animal is relatively ten times greater than the driving force.

An insect, therefore, is not afraid of gravity; it can fall without danger, and can cling to the ceiling with remarkably little trouble. It can go in for elegant and fantastic forms of support like that of the daddy-longlegs. But there is a force which is as formidable to an insect as gravitation to a mammal. This is surface tension. A man coming out of a bath carries with him a film of water of about one-fiftieth of an inch in thickness. This weighs roughly a pound. A wet mouse has to carry about its own weight of water. A wet fly has to lift many times its own weight and, as everyone knows, a fly once wetted by water or any other liquid is in a very serious position indeed. An insect going for a drink is in as great danger as a man leaning out over a precipice in search of food. If it once falls into the grip of the surface tension of the water—that is to say, gets wet—it is likely to remain so until it drowns. A few insects, such as waterbeetles, contrive to be unwettable; the majority keep well away from their drink by means of a long proboscis.

Of course tall land animals have other difficulties. They have to pump their blood to greater heights than a man, and therefore, require a larger blood pressure and tougher blood-vessels. A great many men die from burst arteries, especially in the brain, and this danger is presumably still greater for an elephant or a giraffe. But animals of all kinds find difficulties in size for the following reason. A typical small animal, say a microscopic worm or rotifer, has a smooth skin through which all the oxygen it requires can soak in, a straight gut with sufficient surface to absorb its food, and a single kidney. Increase its dimensions tenfold in every direction, and its weight is increased a thousand times, so that if it is to use its muscles as efficiently as its miniature counterpart, it will need a thousand times as much food and oxygen per day and will excrete a thousand times as much of waste products.

Now if its shape is unaltered its surface will be increased only a hundredfold, and ten times as much oxygen must enter per minute through each square millimetre of skin, ten times as much food through each square millimetre of intestine. When a limit is reached to their absorptive powers their surface has to be increased by some special device. For example, a part of the skin may be drawn out into tufts to make gills or pushed in to make lungs, thus increasing the oxygen-absorbing surface in proportion to the animal's bulk. A man, for example, has a hundred square yards of lung. Similarly, the gut, instead of being smooth and straight, becomes coiled and develops a velvety surface, and other organs increase in complication. The higher animals are not larger than the lower because they are more complicated. They are more complicated because they are larger. Just the same is true of plants. The simplest plants, such as the green algae growing in stagnant water or on the bark of trees, are mere round cells. The higher plants increase their surface by putting out leaves and roots. Comparative anatomy is largely the story of the struggle to increase surface in proportion to volume.

Some of the methods of increasing the surface are useful up to a point, but not capable of a very wide adaptation. For example, while vertebrates carry the oxygen from the gills or lungs all over the body in the blood, insects take air directly to every part of their body by tiny blind tubes called tracheae which open to the surface at many different points. Now, although by their breathing movements they can renew the air in the outer part of the tracheal system, the oxygen has to penetrate the finer branches by means of diffusion. Gases can diffuse easily through very small distances, not many times larger than the average length travelled by a gas molecule between collisions with other molecules. But when such vast journeys—from the point of view of a molecule—as a quarter of an inch have to be made, the process becomes slow. So the portions of an insect's body more than a quarter of an inch from the air would always be short of oxygen. In consequence hardly any insects are much more than half an inch thick. Land crabs are built on the same general plan as insects, but are much clumsier. Yet like ourselves they carry oxygen around in their blood, and are therefore able to grow far larger than any insects. If the insects had hit on a plan for driving air through their tissues instead of letting it soak in, they might well have become as large as lobsters, though other considerations would have prevented them from becoming as large as man.

Exactly the same difficulties attach to flying. It is an elementary principle of aeronautics that the minimum speed needed to keep an aeroplane of a given shape in the air varies as the square root of its length. If its linear dimensions are increased four times, it must fly twice as fast. Now the power needed for the minimum speed increases more rapidly than the weight of the machine. So the larger aeroplane, which weighs sixty-four times as much as the smaller, needs one hundred and twenty-eight times its horsepower to keep up. Applying the same principle to the birds, we find that the limit to their size is soon reached. An angel whose muscles developed no more power weight for weight than those of an eagle or a pigeon would require a breast projecting for about four feet to house the muscles engaged in working its wings, while to economize its weight, its legs would have to be reduced to mere stilts. Actually a large bird such as an eagle or kite does not keep in the air mainly by moving its wings. It is generally to be seen soaring, that is to say balanced on a rising column of air. And even soaring becomes more and more difficult with increasing size. Were this not the case eagles might be as large as tigers and as formidable to man as hostile aeroplanes.

But it is time that we pass to some of the advantages of size. One of the most obvious is that it enables one to keep warm. All warm-blooded animals at rest lose the same amount of heat from a unit area of skin, for which purpose they need a food-supply proportional to their surface and not to their weight. Five thousand mice weigh as much as a man. Their combined surface and food or oxygen consumption are about seventeen times a man's. In fact a mouse eats about one quarter its own weight of food every day, which is mainly used in keeping it warm. For the same reason small animals cannot live in cold countries. In the arctic regions there are no reptiles or amphibians, and no small mammals. The smallest mammal in Spitzbergen is the fox. The small birds fly away in winter, while the insects die, though their eggs can survive six months or more of frost. The most successful mammals are bears, seals, and walruses.

Similarly, the eye is a rather inefficient organ until it reaches a large size. The back of the human eye on which an image of the outside world is thrown, and which corresponds to the film of a camera, is composed of a mosaic of "rods and cones" whose diameter is little more than a length of an average light wave. Each eye has about a half a million, and for two objects to be distinguishable their images must fall on separate rods or cones. It is obvious that with fewer but larger rods and cones we should see less distinctly. If they were twice as broad two points would have to be twice as far apart before we could distinguish them at a given distance. But if their size were diminished and their number increased we should see no better. For it is impossible to form a definite image smaller than a wave-length of light. Hence a mouse's eye is not a small-scale model of a human eye. Its rods and cones are not much smaller than ours, and therefore there are far fewer of them. A mouse could not distinguish one human face from another six feet away. In order that they should be of any use at all the eyes of small animals have to be much larger in proportion to their bodies than our own. Large animals on the other hand only require relatively small eyes, and those of the whale and elephant are little larger than our own.

For rather more recondite reasons the same general principle holds true of the brain. If we compare the brain-weights of a set of very similar animals such as the cat, cheetah, leopard, and tiger, we find that as we quadruple the body-weight the brain-weight is only doubled. The larger animal with proportionately larger bones can economize on brain, eyes, and certain other organs.

Such are a very few of the considerations which show that for every type of animal there is an optimum size. Yet although Galileo demonstrated the contrary more than three hundred years ago, people still believe that if a flea were as large as a man it could jump a thousand feet into the air. As a matter of fact the height to which an animal can jump is more nearly independent of its size than proportional to it. A flea can jump about two feet, a man about five. To jump a given height, if we neglect the resistance of the air, requires an expenditure of energy proportional to the jumper's weight. But if the jumping muscles form a constant fraction of the animal's body, the energy developed per ounce of muscle is independent of the size, provided it can be developed quickly enough in the small animal. As a matter of fact an insect's muscles, although they can contract more quickly than our own, appear to be less efficient; as otherwise a flea or grasshopper could rise six feet into the air.

COMPREHENSION

1. According to Haldane, how do people adapt to the problems of their size?
2. What are the effects of size on insects and mice?
3. Explain Haldane's thesis in your own words.

RHETORIC

1. Cite examples of personification in the essay. Why does Haldane use them?
2. Haldane is an adept practitioner of parallel structure. Cite examples of parallel structure in paragraphs 4 and 5.
3. Describe the simple dichotomy Haldane uses to organize his essay.
4. Because Haldane is describing neither a scene nor an event, he can use neither temporal nor spatial transitional devices to make his essay coherent. Identify the transitional devices he employs.
5. Many of Haldane's explanations involve mathematical formulas. Give specific examples of how he helps his reader understand his math.
6. Where does Haldane use hypothetical examples? Why are they effective?

WRITING

1. Based on Haldane's discussion of size, speculate on how the size of a country, of a business, of a family, or of a college might have limits.
2. Write an essay on the effect of size on a human institution.
3. Although explaining mathematical and physical laws is difficult, Haldane is successful. Write an essay in which you try to explain a physical law.

CLASSIC AND CONTEMPORARY

BERTRAND RUSSELL Bertrand Arthur William Russell (1872–1970) was one of the great philosophers, mathematicians, liberal political theorists, and authors of the twentieth century. His works are legion. From his early *Princi-*

ples of Mathematics* (1903) to *An Inquiry into Meaning and Truth* (1940) and, finally, his three-volume *Autobiography* (1967–1969), Russell demonstrated his multivarious talents as a writer and thinker. He was awarded the Nobel Prize in Literature in 1950. One aspect of Russell's career—his desire to explain science to lay people—is represented in the following essay.

BERTRAND RUSSELL

The Study of Mathematics

In regard to every form of human activity it is necessary that the question should be asked from time to time, What is its purpose and ideal? In what way does it contribute to the beauty of human existence? As respects those pursuits which contribute only remotely, by providing the mechanism of life, it is well to be reminded that not the mere fact of living is to be desired, but the art of living in the contemplation of great things. Still more in regard to those avocations which have no end outside themselves, which are to be justified, if at all, as actually adding to the sum of the world's permanent possessions, it is necessary to keep alive a knowledge of their aims, a clear prefiguring vision of the temple in which creative imagination is to be embodied.

Although tradition has decreed that the great bulk of educated men shall know at least the elements of the subject [of mathematics], the reasons for which the tradition arose are forgotten, buried beneath a great rubbish-heap of pedantries and trivialities. To those who inquire as to the purpose of mathematics, the usual answer will be that it facilitates the making of machines, the travelling from place to place, and the victory over foreign nations, whether in war or commerce. If it be objected that these ends—all of which are of doubtful value—are not furthered by the merely elementary study imposed upon those who do not become expert mathematicians, the reply, it is true, will probably be that mathematics trains the reasoning faculties. Yet the very men who make this reply are, for the most part, unwilling to abandon the teaching of definite fallacies, known to be such, and instinctively rejected by the unsophisticated mind of every intelligent learner. And the reasoning faculty itself is generally conceived, by those who urge its cultivation, as merely a means for the avoidance of pitfalls and a help in the discovery of rules for the guidance of practical life. All these are undeniably important achievements to the credit of mathematics; yet it is none of these that entitles mathematics to a place in every liberal education.

Mathematics, rightly viewed, possesses not only truth, but supreme beauty—a beauty cold and austere, like that of sculpture, without appeal to any part of our weaker nature, without the gorgeous trappings of painting or music, yet sublimely pure, and capable of a stern perfection such as only the greatest art can show. The true spirit of delight, the exaltation, the sense of being more than man, which is the touchstone of the highest excellence, is to be found in mathematics as surely as in poetry. What is best in mathematics deserves not merely to be learnt as a task, but to be assimilated as a part of daily thought, and brought again and again before the mind with ever-renewed encouragement. Real life is, to most men, a long second-best, a perpetual compromise between the ideal and the possible; but the world of pure reason knows no compromise, no practical limitations, no barrier to the creative activity embodying in splendid edifices the passionate aspiration after the perfect from which all great work springs. Remote from human passions, remote even from the pitiful facts of nature, the generations have gradually created an ordered cosmos, where pure thought can dwell as in its natural home, and where one, at least, of our nobler impulses can escape from the dreary exile of the actual world.

So little, however, have mathematicians aimed at beauty, that hardly anything in their work has had this conscious purpose. Much, owing to irrepressible instincts, which were better than avowed beliefs, has been moulded by an unconscious taste; but much also has been spoilt by false notions of what was fitting. The characteristic excellence of mathematics is only to be found where the reasoning is rigidly logical: the rules of logic are to mathematics what those of structure are to architecture. In the most beautiful work, a chain of argument is presented in which every link is important on its own account, in which there is an air of ease and lucidity throughout, and the premises achieve more than would have been thought possible, by means which appear natural and inevitable. Literature embodies what is general in particular circumstances whose universal significance shines through their individual dress; but mathematics endeavours to present whatever is most general in its purity, without any irrelevant trappings.

COMPREHENSION

1. What is Russell's thesis?
2. In this essay, Russell compares and contrasts several disciplines or vocations with mathematics. Of which one does he approve? Of which ones does he disapprove?
3. According to Russell, what are the reasons for studying mathematics?

RHETORIC

1. Identify examples of connotative language in this essay.
2. How many specific details appear in this essay? How does this affect the style of the essay?
3. Describe the structure of this four-paragraph essay.
4. Why does Russell compare mathematics to the arts? How is mathematics superior?
5. What assumptions about the world of nature and human beings and of the mind underlie the essay?

6. In paragraph 4, what method of definition does Russell use?

WRITING

1. How would you define *beauty,* as Russell uses the word? Does your own idea of beauty differ from Russell's? How is mathematics "beautiful"? Write a brief essay on this topic.
2. Imitate the structure of this essay to organize your definition of *engineering, science,* or *medicine.* Use specific details and examples from the field to clarify your extended definition.
3. Write your own personal essay entitled "My Study of Mathematics."

SUSAN JACOBY   Susan Jacoby has worked as an educator and as a reporter for *The Washington Post.* As a free-lance journalist in the Soviet Union (from 1969 to 1971), she produced two books about her experiences. Jacoby now contributes to *The Nation* and *McCall's;* her books include *The Possible She* (1979), a collection of autobiographical essays. In this essay from *The New York Times,* Jacoby examines the reasons why girls are often deficient in math and science.

SUSAN JACOBY

When Bright Girls Decide
That Math Is "a Waste of Time"

Susannah, a 16-year-old who has always been an A student in every   1
subject from algebra to English, recently informed her parents that she intended to drop physics and calculus in her senior year of high school and replace them with a drama seminar and a work-study program. She expects a major in art or history in college, she explained, and "any more science or math will just be a waste of my time."

Her parents were neither concerned by nor opposed to her decision.   2
"Fine, dear," they said. Their daughter is, after all, an outstanding student. What does it matter if, at age 16, she has taken a step that may limit her understanding of both machines and the natural world for the rest of her life?

This kind of decision, in which girls turn away from studies that   3
would give them a sure footing in the world of science and technology, is a self-inflicted female disability that is, regrettably, almost as common today as it was when I was in high school. If Susannah had announced that she had decided to stop taking English in her senior year, her mother and father would have been horrified. I also think they would have been a good deal less sanguine about her decision if she were a boy.

In saying that scientific and mathematical ignorance is a self-   4
inflicted female wound, I do not, obviously, mean that cultural expecta-

622

tions play no role in the process. But the world does not conspire to deprive modern women of access to science as it did in the 1930's, when Rosalyn S. Yalow, the Nobel Prize-winning physicist, graduated from Hunter College and was advised to go to work as a secretary because no graduate school would admit her to its physics department. The current generation of adolescent girls—and their parents, bred on old expectations about women's interests—are active conspirators in limiting their own intellectual development.

It is true that the proportion of young women in science-related graduate and professional schools, most notably medical schools, has increased significantly in the past decade. It is also true that so few women were studying advanced science and mathematics before the early 1970's that the percentage increase in female enrollment does not yet translate into large numbers of women actually working in science.

The real problem is that so many girls eliminate themselves from any serious possibility of studying science as a result of decisions made during the vulnerable period of midadolescence, when they are most likely to be influenced—on both conscious and subconscious levels—by the traditional belief that math and science are "masculine" subjects.

During the teen-age years the well-documented phenomenon of "math anxiety" strikes girls who never had any problem handling numbers during earlier schooling. Some men, too, experience this syndrome—a form of panic, akin to a phobia, at any task involving numbers—but women constitute the overwhelming majority of sufferers. The onset of acute math anxiety during the teen-age years is, as Stalin was fond of saying, "not by accident."

In adolescence girls begin to fear that they will be unattractive to boys if they are typed as "brains." Science and math epitomize unfeminine braininess in a way that, say, foreign languages do not. High-school girls who pursue an advanced interest in science and math (unless they are students at special institutions like the Bronx High School of Science where everyone is a brain) usually find that they are greatly outnumbered by boys in their classes. They are, therefore, intruding on male turf at a time when their sexual confidence, as well as that of the boys, is most fragile.

A 1981 assessment of female achievement in mathematics, based on research conducted under a National Institute for Education grant, found significant differences in the mathematical achievements of 9th and 12th graders. At age 13 girls were equal to or slightly better than boys in tests involving algebra, problem solving and spatial ability; four years later the boys had outstripped the girls.

It is not mysterious that some very bright high-school girls suddenly decide that math is "too hard" and "a waste of time." In my experience, self-sabotage of mathematical and scientific ability is often a conscious process. I remember deliberately pretending to be puzzled by geometry problems in my sophomore year in high school. A male teacher called me in after class and said, in a baffled tone, "I don't see how you can

5

6

7

8

9

10

be having so much trouble when you got straight A's last year in my algebra class."

The decision to avoid advanced biology, chemistry, physics and cal- 11 culus in high school automatically restricts academic and professional choices that ought to be wide open to anyone beginning college. At all coeducational universities women are overwhelmingly concentrated in the fine arts, social sciences and traditionally female departments like education. Courses leading to degrees in science- and technology-related fields are filled mainly by men.

In my generation, the practical consequences of mathematical and 12 scientific illiteracy are visible in the large number of special programs to help professional women overcome the anxiety they feel when they are promoted into jobs that require them to handle statistics.

The consequences of this syndrome should not, however, be viewed 13 in narrowly professional terms. Competence in science and math does not mean one is going to become a scientist or mathematician any more than competence in writing English means one is going to become a professional writer. Scientific and mathematical illiteracy—which has been cited in several recent critiques by panels studying American education from kindergarten through college—produces an incalculably impoverished vision of human experience.

Scientific illiteracy is not, of course, the exclusive province of 14 women. In certain intellectual circles it has become fashionable to proclaim a willed, aggressive ignorance about science and technology. Some female writers specialize in ominous, uninformed diatribes against genetic research as a plot to remove control of childbearing from women, while some well-known men of letters proudly announce that they understand absolutely nothing about computers, or, for that matter, about electricity. This lack of understanding is nothing in which women or men ought to take pride.

Failure to comprehend either computers or chromosomes leads to a 15 terrible sense of helplessness, because the profound impact of science on everyday life is evident even to those who insist they don't, won't, can't understand why the changes are taking place. At this stage of history women are more prone to such feelings of helplessness than men because the culture judges their ignorance less harshly and because women themselves acquiesce in that indulgence.

Since there is ample evidence of such feelings in adolescence, it is 16 up to parents to see that their daughters do not accede to the old stereotypes about "masculine" and "feminine" knowledge. Unless we want our daughters to share our intellectual handicaps, we had better tell them no, they can't stop taking mathematics and science at the ripe old age of 16.

COMPREHENSION

1. What reasons does Jacoby give for girls' deficiency in math and science?

2. Why does she call it a "self-inflicted disability"?

3. What are the consequences of being math and science illiterate?

RHETORIC

1. Explain the main idea of Jacoby's essay in your own words.
2. Does the writer use abstract or concrete language in her essay? Cite examples to support your response.
3. What technique does Jacoby use in paragraphs 1 and 2? How does it aid in setting up her argument?
4. What rhetorical strategies does the writer use in her essay?
5. How does the use of dialogue aid in developing paragraph 10? What effect does the general use of dialogue have on the writer's point?
6. How is Jacoby's conclusion consistent in tone with the rest of the essay? Does it supply a sense of unity? Why, or why not?

WRITING

1. Write an essay describing a school-related phobia you once had, or continue to have (for example, in math, writing, physical education, biology). Explain where you think that fear came from, how it affected your performance in school, and what you did (or are doing) to cope with the problem.
2. Write an argumentation essay proposing that math and science phobia is not "self-inflicted" but caused primarily by the continued presence of sexism in society.
3. Write an essay about the need for math and science literacy in today's world. Use support from Jacoby's essay.

CLASSIC AND CONTEMPORARY: QUESTIONS FOR COMPARISON

1. How do Russell and Jacoby approach the subject of math? Do they have different priorities? Are they writing for a similar audience? Use examples from both writers to support your ideas.
2. Analyze the language used in the two essays. What is similar or different about the style and diction of the two pieces? Which uses figurative language? Is one essay more accessible to the modern reader? If so, why? How do they each use details?
3. Would Russell's essay inspire the modern young women Jacoby writes about? Why, or why not? What advice would Russell give today's young women about studying math? Do you think in his day Russell advocated the study of math for both boys and girls? Do you think Russell would find fault with Jacoby's pragmatic approach to mathematics?

CONNECTIONS

1. Using the essays of Salazar and Selzer, compare and contrast the settings, the patients, and the doctors.

2. How does Haldane's essay on size illustrate the usefulness of mathematics in explaining the world? How does his essay reinforce what Russell calls the "beauty" of mathematics?

3. Compare the essays of Salazar, Quammen, and Selzer in their use of figurative language and details to convey the atmosphere of a clinical environment.

4. Using any of the essays in this section, write an essay advancing the need for literacy in math and science. What will society lose if its young people continue to rate low in these subjects?

5. Compare the essays of Thomas and Haldane. What does each have to say about the life and functions of different organisms? How does each use personification, figurative language, and humor to convey information?

6. Consider the treatment of AIDS patients in hospitals today. How might "moral stupidity" affect the way doctors, nurses, and other workers cope with these patients? How might doctor arrogance manifest itself in that situation? Use the works of Selzer and Gould to explore this issue.

7. Make a connection between Thomas's views on societies (both human and insect) and Gould's view that "Our species has not won its independence from nature." How alienated are we from other animal societies? What do we share with them? How can we use this knowledge to save ourselves and our planet?

CHAPTER THIRTEEN

Civilization

*A*t the end of the twentieth century, the paroxysms caused by con-flicts among peoples, nations, and cultures continue to shake con-tinents. The United States might have emerged from the cold war as the dominant superpower, but numerous local and global threats remain. We seem to be at a crossroads in civilization, but does the future hold great promise or equally great danger?

The future of civilization assuredly holds significant peril as well as promise. If by *civilization* we mean the complete absence of barbarism and nonrational behavior in human affairs, coupled with a commitment to harmonious or "civil" conduct within various social realms, then it is clear that we have not attained this ideal state of cultural or world development. At the same time, we have advanced beyond the point in primitive civilization where someone chipped at a stone in order to make a better tool. The *process* of civilization whereby we harness our physical, creative, scientific, political, philosophical, and spiritual resources is well advanced. However, the current state of civilization, as many writers in this final chapter testify, remains ambiguous.

As we consider the course of contemporary civilization, we must contend with the interplay of contradictory forces. We have become increasingly what V. S. Naipaul terms one "universal civilization," but we still have rampant nationalism to deal with. Indeed, we have entered an era of renewed ethnic strife, where a preoccupation with cultural difference seems stronger than the desire for universal civilization. The writers assembled here grapple with these contradictions; they move from the United States, to Canada, to Europe, to Asia as they search for those constituents of culture that might hasten a civilized world.

The idea of civilization suggests a pluralistic ethos whereby people of diverse backgrounds can maintain cultural identities but also coexist with other cultural representatives in a spirit of tolerance and mutual respect. The wars, upheavals, and catastrophes of this century were spawned by a narrower consciousness, rooted in the various "ism's" that J. B. Priestley alluded to in an earlier essay. Hopefully, as we prepare for a new century, all of us can advance the goal of a universal civilization based on the best that we have been able to create for humankind.

Previewing the Chapter

As you read the essays in this chapter and respond to them in discussion and writing, consider the following questions:

• How does the author define *civilization*? Is this definition stated or implied? Is it broad or narrow? Explain.

• Is the writer hopeful or pessimistic about the state of civilization?

• What values does the author seem to think are necessary to advance the idea of civilization?

• Do you find the author's tone to be objective or subjective?

• Which areas of knowledge—for example, history, philosophy, political science—does the author bring to bear on the subject?

• Do you agree or disagree with the author's view of the contemporary state of civilization?

• What essays in previous chapters inform your understanding of the selections in this chapter?

• Based on your reading of these essays, how would you define *civilization*? Are you hopeful about the current state of civilization?

PICO IYER   Pico Iyer was born in Oxford, England, in 1957 and educated at both Oxford and Harvard universities. Born to Indian parents, he has traveled extensively in the East. He is a writer for *Time* and has written three books on his experiences as a world traveler: *Video Night in Kathmandu* (1988); *The Lady and the Monk* (1991); and *Falling Off the Map* (1993). About writing, he has stated, "Writing should be an act of communication more than of mere self-expression—a telling of a story rather than a flourishing of skills. . . . Writing is, in the end, that oddest of anomalies: an intimate letter to a stranger."

PICO IYER

Strangers in a Small World

The global village is one of those ideas to which almost everyone can give assent: it rhymes with all the notions with which we buoy and congratulate ourselves—the family of man, the brotherhood of souls, the replacement of walls with bridges. The global village tells us, in powerful, palpable ways, that we're all one race under the skin and that, beneath all the superficial differences of custom and fashion and tongue, the fears and fantasies of that villager in, say, Mali are not so different from our own: he, too, after all, is moved by Michael Jackson rhythms and transfixed by *Dallas* archetypes. Small wonder companies try to concoct slogans like the United Colors of Benetton: one touch of nurture makes the whole world kin.

We accept, of course, that with proximity come problems, and problems for which the old world order scarcely prepared us; that, in the absence of external divisions, we are obliged to create and consolidate our own new and artificial ones; that more and more countries, in this time of mass migration, may seem as factionalized as Lebanon; and that now, when any country sneezes (to extend the age-old axiom), the whole world catches a cold. Yet, at bottom, we are still ready to applaud the virtues of this new multiculturalism and its resuscitation of all our *e pluribus unum* hopes. We know that we are enriched and educated by having Thai children in the classroom and Salvadoran refugees down the street; that choices—the great luxury of a diverse consumer society—can now multiply. We know too that the globe is our oyster in ways that before only the rich could enjoy; we can fly around the world, and the world can fly around us.

Yet it is precisely the blessings of this order—evident and indisputable as they are—that can blind us to its dangers, and they are dangers for which we are as unguarded as children in first love: we have no precedents to stay us or to guide us. When a stranger comes knocking on our door, we have no sense of his needs and expectations. If he is a smiling and exotic stranger, we may be doubly disarmed. And the very charms that his foreignness confers may lead us into places where we are soon quite lost.

The dangers of the global village begin, not surprisingly, with the problems of mobility: to put it simply, our vices are now global. Italians go to Prague and Havana to get cheap dates, and Germans can hop on a plane to Sri Lanka to find underage sex partners. Nigerians regularly get caught in Bangkok Airport with balloons of heroin in their stomachs, and the "economic miracle" in Japan is often, in small ways, subverted by the tens of thousands of immigrants from Iran and Israel who set up their own stalls and deals on the streets of Tokyo. Prostitution, to take one specific example, now takes unprecedented forms: Ghanaian girls in Antwerp, Russians throughout the Middle East, Dominicans in Spain. The menace of these freely moving bodies has gained an almost concrete meaning in the age of AIDS; now we have an all too literal metaphor for the danger of getting too close to a stranger, as the deadly virus is passed, like a kiss almost, from Africa to Haiti to Manhattan's West Village.

Even capital is not immune to the novel challenges of the "borderless economy": the BCCI scandal was, in part, a reflection of what can happen when a charming stranger arrives at the door and we do not know what to make of him. The Bank of America, remember, acquired a 25 percent share of BCCI in 1972, and the Bank of England gave BCCI a license. Both, in their way, were simply unprepared to deal with an entity whose codes they could not read.

Technology has, to be sure, eliminated some of our old divisions and corruptions; but it has also given us new ways of refining and compounding them. Even as many countries are now proudly marching down the Information Highway, many others (think of North Korea, Iraq, Myanmar) are better able than ever to bind their people to the Disinformation Highway. And while Salman Rushdie, the apostle of a new internationalism, sings the possibilities of a fresh, cross-pollinating world, he is stalked by an old ancestral order that embodies an almost medieval sense of self-enclosedness—and that prosecutes its *fatwa* in Tokyo and Istanbul and Bradford, England. We may say that the age-old pattern of migration from countryside to city is now global—that the bright student from rural India can now set his sights not on Bombay but on Cambridge, Massachusetts. But we must also add that the divisions that haunt many a big city are now global, so that much of the world resembles one big city, with South-Central on one side and Bel-Air on the other.

Deeper than the problems of sudden connectedness, however, are the fundamental disconnections that the new globalism obscures. As Edward Said has pointed out, the exile's predicament is made more agonized these days by the fact that he can see what he has left behind.

He is surrounded by reminders of his home and reinforcements of his seeming closeness to it. The Cambodian in California can see Phnom Penh on his TV, and see the streets where he courted his wife, and watch his old neighbors setting up their shops again, and the ones who murdered his father saying "cheese" before the cameras; he can even— and this is the ultimate tease—get on a plane and be back there tomorrow. But if he makes the trip, he will likely find that Phnom Penh is no closer to Long Beach than it ever was, and that he is as much a foreigner there as in the new home he has gained.

That is one of the great shadows of the illusory smallness our new world offers. We are often told—and it *is* heartening—that on the West Bank, Palestinians and Israelis both watch *L.A. Law* on Sunday nights, on screens that have subtitles in both Arabic and Hebrew. We read that the Khmer Rouge are tuning in to *Santa Barbara,* and we feel that this establishes their humanity, or at least a common link between us. But what they are learning about us from *Santa Barbara* is doubtless as limited as what we learn about them from the (already Western-filtered) movie *The Killing Fields.* And when a Cambodian comes to America eager to deal with Robin Wright, he will be as lost as one of us who goes to Phnom Penh with images of Dith Pran in our heads. Vietnam was famously the "living-room war." But now every war is in our living room, and in half the living rooms of the world. Rodney King is being beaten up in Johannesburg, and Bosnia is in Miami every night. But the knowledge we get from this is no deeper than the image, and the fact that we believe we have seen the "real Cambodia" on our screens may well put us behind our grandfathers, who could scarcely countenance such illusions.

Thus a man in Louisiana says "Freeze!" and a Japanese boy, looking for a Halloween party, doesn't get it—and a life is lost, and trust undermined. The problem is not one of complete misunderstanding but rather—and more dangerously—of a partial understanding, or the illusion of understanding. People may play contract bridge across several countries on the Internet, but they cannot communicate bluffs or poker faces on their computer screens; faxes transmit words instantaneously, but they are not so good with nuances or pauses.

Homogeneity, in fact, is not the fear: every culture sings Madonna with a different accent. It is disguised heterogeneity that is the threat, a world of differences that is veiled by surface similarities. And a world of differences made more difficult when everyone's living down the block. It is not just that the Afghan down the street has different customs from ours; even when he watches *Rambo III,* he is getting something very different from the screen than we are—is seeing it as a political piece and not an entertainment. For him McDonald's may be a status symbol, as surely as that quaint Central Asian restaurant is for us. And the very diversity of costumes and colors that seems so beguiling in the Opening Ceremonies of the Olympic Games becomes more charged when it's to be found in the divisions and rivalries within Timmy's classroom.

None of this, of course, is an argument for hardening our differ- 11
ences, or for living alone, or for denying the richness and opportunities
that polyculturalism makes available. A little knowledge may be a dangerous thing, but ignorance is ten times worse, and suspicion can fulfill
its prophecies as easily as trust. But the mingling of cultures that is our
new inheritance makes imaginative and moral demands on us much
harder than just the business of trying to "get along" or to "see the
world through others' eyes," and forces us to carry our assumptions
more lightly than we have ever done before.

In Michael Ondaatje's beautiful novel *The English Patient,* he presents 12
a lyrical, often radiant vision of a world beyond nationalities, in which
people are simply individuals, of indistinguishable origins, with a hundred different cultures singing inside them. That is a lovely and a liberating notion, and it is one echoed by those executives who tell us that
soon there will be "no Japan, only Japanese." But it underestimates, perhaps, a need, a basic human need, for affiliation with something larger
and a sense of belonging to a higher order. For Ondaatje, the desert is the
model of a place where all distinctions are dissolved and people live as
people; but as the fourteenth-century Arab writer Ibn Khaldun wrote,
"Only tribes held together by group feeling can live in a desert."

If there is a real virtue to all the blessings of the global village, it 13
inheres mostly in our recognition of how much our sense of obligation
must be expanded and diversified, and how much our family responsibilities, if you will, must be extended more than they have ever been
before. Insofar as we aspire to be our brothers' keepers, we have to
acknowledge that we have five—soon eight—billion brothers, and that
they are in Borneo and Bolivia and Benin. Insofar as we try to love our
neighbors as ourselves, we have to admit that our neighbors are people
with whom we share no common language, or past, or value. And the
smaller the distance between people, Freud reminded us, the greater,
often, the dispute.

COMPREHENSION

1. What is the meaning of the title of this piece?
2. From where and from whom does the term "global village" come? What
   does it mean?
3. The author suggests that popular-culture icons like Michael Jackson,
   Madonna, and American television are universal. Does the author believe
   that their universal appreciation brings the citizens of the world closer
   together? Explain.

RHETORIC

1. The introductory paragraph in this piece includes some stock phrases about
   brotherhood, or sisterhood. What is the function of providing these various
   examples at the start of the essay?

2. In paragraph 4, the author provides a number of examples of the dangers of mobility. How does the diversity of these examples serve to strengthen the author's argument? How does the content of this paragraph mirror the very topic about which he is writing?

3. How does the author use the technique of comparison and contrast in paragraphs 8 through 10 to show the contradictions of the new world order?

4. The essay is divided into three parts. Study each part, and explain the main topic of each and the relationship of each to the others.

5. This essay is replete with examples of the new information age and its effects on culture. For example, the author refers to eleven different cultures, nationalities, or countries in paragraph 6. What can you infer about the intended audience of this essay given the range of specific references to world culture?

6. The final sentence of the essay dramatically concludes and summarizes the substance of the essay. Why does the author include the ideas of the famous psychoanalyst Sigmund Freud, who died long before the concept of the global village?

7. The dash is a punctuation mark little used in student writing. The author, however, exploits its function often in this essay. Select five examples of his use of this device, and explain its purpose and effect in each of the examples. Also, consider the use of the dash as a writing device that fits in with modern modes of communication. Why might its popularity be on the rise?

WRITING

1. Argue for or against the proposition that the term *diversity* is meaningless given the fact that most people have the same basic material needs and desires for luxuries.

2. Write a personal essay wherein you describe the effect mass media or access to speedy transportation has had on your life.

3. Describe an incident you witnessed or participated in that involved "intercultural miscommunication"—in other words, an event that was interpreted differently by members of two distinct cultures.

RUTH PRAWER JHABVALA   Ruth Prawer Jhabvala (b. 1927) has long been associated with the Merchant-Ivory team of filmmakers, who specialize in translating literary works onto the screen. Jhabvala, born in Germany, also lived in India for many years before coming to the United States in 1975. Along with screenplays for *A Room with a View* (1985), for which she won an Academy Award, and *Howard's End* (1992), she has written a novel, *Heat and Dust* (1975), and *Out of India: Selected Stories* (1986). In this narrative essay from the latter, Jhabvala tells of her struggles to accept the spiritually demanding conditions of life in India.

RUTH PRAWER JHABVALA

Myself in India

I have lived in India for most of my adult life. My husband is Indian   1
and so are my children. I am not, and less so every year.

India reacts very strongly on people. Some loathe it, some love it,   2
most do both. There is a special problem of adjustment for the sort of
people who come today, who tend to be liberal in outlook and have
been educated to be sensitive and receptive to other cultures. But it is
not always easy to be sensitive and receptive to India: There comes a
point where you have to close up in order to protect yourself. The place
is very strong and often proves too strong for European nerves. There
is a cycle that Europeans—by Europeans I mean all Westerners, including Americans—tend to pass through. It goes like this: first stage,
tremendous enthusiasm—everything Indian is marvelous; second stage,
everything Indian not so marvelous; third stage, everything Indian
abominable. For some people it ends there, for others the cycle renews
itself and goes on. I have been through it so many times that now I
think of myself as strapped to a wheel that goes round and round and
sometimes I'm up and sometimes I'm down. When I meet other Europeans, I can usually tell after a few moments' conversation at what stage
of the cycle they happen to be. Everyone likes to talk about India,
whether they happen to be loving or loathing it. It is a topic on which
a lot of things can be said, and on a variety of aspects—social, economic, political, philosophical: It makes fascinating viewing from every
side.

However, I must admit that I am no longer interested in India. What   3
I am interested in now is myself in India—which sometimes, in
moments of despondency, I tend to think of as my survival in India. I
had better say straightaway that the reason I live in India is that my
strongest human ties are here. If I hadn't married an Indian, I don't
think I would ever have come here for I am not attracted—or used not
to be attracted—to the things that usually bring people to India. I know
I am the wrong type of person to live here. To stay and endure, one
should have a mission and a cause, to be patient, cheerful, unselfish,
strong. I am a central European with an English education and a
deplorable tendency to constant self-analysis. I am irritable and have
weak nerves.

The most salient fact about India is that it is very poor and very   4
backward. There are so many other things to be said about it but this
must remain the basis of all of them. We may praise Indian democracy,
go into raptures over Indian music, admire Indian intellectuals—but

whatever we say, not for one moment should we lose sight of the fact that a very great number of Indians never get enough to eat. Literally that: From birth to death they never for one day cease to suffer from hunger. *Can* one lose sight of that fact? God knows, I've tried. But after seeing what one has to see here every day, it is not really possible to go on living one's life the way one is used to. People dying of starvation in the streets, children kidnapped and maimed to be sent out as beggars— but there is no point in making a catalog of the horrors with which one lives, *on* which one lives, as on the back of an animal. Obviously, there has to be some adjustment.

There are several ways. The first and best is to be a strong person who plunges in and does what he can as a doctor or social worker. I often think that perhaps this is the only condition under which Europeans have any right to be here. I know several people like that. They are usually attached to some mission. They work very hard and stay very cheerful. Every few years they are sent on home leave. Once I met such a person—a woman doctor—who had just returned from her first home leave after being out here for twelve years. I asked her: But what does it feel like to go back after such a long time? How do you manage to adapt yourself? She didn't understand. This question, which was of such tremendous import to me—how to adapt oneself to the differences between Europe and India—didn't mean a thing to her. It simply didn't matter. And she was right, for in view of the things she sees and does every day, the delicate nuances of one's own sensibilities are best forgotten.

Another approach to India's basic conditions is to accept them. This seems to be the approach favored by most Indians. Perhaps it has something to do with their belief in reincarnation. If things are not to your liking in this life, there is always the chance that in your next life everything will be different. It appears to be a consoling thought for both rich and poor. The rich man stuffing himself on pilau can do so with an easy conscience because he knows he has earned this privilege by his good conduct in previous lives; and the poor man can watch him with some degree of equanimity, for he knows that next time around it may well be *he* who will be digging into that pilau while the other will be crouching outside the door with an empty stomach. However, this path of acceptance is not open to you if you don't have a belief in reincarnation ingrained within you. And if you don't accept, then what can you do? Sometimes one wants just to run away and go to a place where everyone has enough to eat and clothes to wear and a home fit to live in. But even when you get there, can you ever forget? Having once seen the sights in India, and the way it has been ordained that people must live out their lives, nowhere in the world can ever be all that good to be in again.

None of this is what I wanted to say. I wanted to concentrate only on myself in India. But I could not do so before indicating the basis on which everyone who comes here has to live. I have a nice house, I do my best to live in an agreeable way. I shut all my windows, I let down the blinds, I turn on the air-conditioner; I read a lot of books, with a special preference for the great masters of the novel. All the time I know myself to be on the back of this great animal of poverty and backwardness. It is not possible to pretend otherwise. Or rather, one does pretend, but retribution follows. Even if one never rolls up the blinds and never turns off the air-conditioner, something is bound to go wrong. People are not meant to shut themselves up in rooms and pretend there is nothing outside.

Now I think I am drawing nearer to what I want to be my subject. 8 Yes, something is wrong: I am not happy this way. I feel lonely, shut in, shut off. It is my own fault. I should go out more and meet people and learn what is going on. All right, so I am not a doctor nor a social worker nor a saint nor at all a good person; then the only thing to do is to try to push that aspect of India out of sight and turn to others. There are many others. I live in the capital, where so much is going on. The winter is one round of parties, art exhibitions, plays, music and dance recitals, visiting European artists: There need never be a dull moment. Yet all my moments are dull. Why? It is my own fault, I know. I can't quite explain it to myself but somehow I have no heart for these things here. Is it because all the time underneath I feel the animal moving? But I have decided to ignore the animal. I wish to concentrate only on modern, Westernized India, and on modern, well-off, cultured Westernized Indians.

Let me try and describe a Westernized Indian woman with whom I 9 ought to have a lot in common and whose company I ought to enjoy. She has been to Oxford or Cambridge or some smart American college. She speaks flawless, easy, colloquial English with a charming lilt of an accent. She has a degree in economics or political science or English literature. She comes from a good family. Her father may have been an I. C. S. officer or some other high-ranking government official; he too was at Oxford or Cambridge, and he and her mother traveled in Europe in prewar days. They have always lived a Western-style life, with Western food and an admiration for Western culture. The daughter now tends rather to frown on this. She feels one should be more deeply Indian, and with this end in view, she wears handloom saris and traditional jewelry and has painted an abnormally large vermilion mark on her forehead. She is interested in Indian classical music and dance. If she is rich enough—she may have married into one of the big Indian business houses—she will become a patroness of the arts and hold delicious parties on her lawn on summer nights. All her friends are there— and she has so many, both Indian and European, all interesting people—and trays of iced drinks are carried around by servants in uniform and there is intelligent conversation and then there is a superbly arranged buffet supper and more intelligent conversation, and then the crown of the evening: a famous Indian maestro performing on the sitar. The guests recline on carpets and cushions on the lawn. The sky sparkles with stars and the languid summer air is fragrant with jasmine. There are many pretty girls reclining against bolsters; their faces are melancholy, for the music is stirring their hearts, and sometimes they sigh with yearning and happiness and look down at their pretty toes (adorned with a tiny silver toe ring) peeping out from under the sari. Here is Indian life and culture at its highest and best. Yet, with all that, it need not be thought that our hostess has forgotten her Western education. Not at all. In her one may see the best of East and West combined. She is interested in a great variety of topics and can hold her own in any discussion. She loves to exercise her emancipated mind, and whatever the subject of conversation—economics, or politics, or literature, or film—she has a well-formulated opinion on it and knows how to express herself. How lucky for me if I could have such a person for a friend! What enjoyable, lively times we two could have together!

In fact, my teeth are set on edge if I have to listen to her for more than five minutes—yes, even though everything she says is so true and in line with the most advanced opinions of today. But when she says it, somehow, even though I know the words to be true, they ring completely false. It is merely lips moving and sounds coming out: It doesn't mean anything, nothing of what she says (though she says it with such conviction, skill, and charm) is of the least importance to her. She is only making conversation in the way she knows educated women have to make conversation. And so it is with all of them. Everything they say, all that lively conversation around the buffet table, is not prompted by anything they really feel strongly about but by what they think they ought to feel strongly about. This applies not only to subjects that are naturally alien to them—for instance, when they talk oh so solemnly! and with such profound intelligence! of Godard and Becket and ecology—but when they talk about themselves too. They know modern India to be an important subject and they have a lot to say about it: But though they themselves *are* modern India, they don't look at themselves, they are not conditioned to look at themselves except with the eyes of foreign experts whom they have been taught to respect. And while they are fully aware of India's problems and are up on all the statistics and all the arguments for and against nationalization and a socialistic pattern of society, all the time it is as if they were talking about some *other* place—as if it were a subject for debate—an abstract subject—and not a live animal actually moving under their feet.

But if I have no taste for the company of these Westernized Indians, then what else is there? Other Indians don't really have a social life, not in our terms; the whole conception of such a life is imported. It is true that Indians are gregarious insofar as they hate to be alone and always like to sit together in groups; but these groups are clan-units—it is the family, or clan members, who gather together and enjoy each other's company. And again, their conception of enjoying each other's company is different from ours. For them it is enough just to *be* together; there are long stretches of silence in which everyone stares into space. From time to time there is a little spurt of conversation, usually on some commonplace everyday subject as rising prices, a forthcoming marriage, or a troublesome neighbor. There is no attempt at exercising the mind or testing one's wits against those of others: The pleasure lies only in having other familiar people around and enjoying the air together and looking forward to the next meal. There is actually something very restful about this mode of social intercourse, and certainly holds more pleasure than the synthetic social life led by Westernized Indians. It is also more adapted to the Indian climate, which invites one to be absolutely relaxed in mind and body, to do nothing, to think nothing, just to feel, to *be*. I have in fact enjoyed sitting around like that for hours on end. But there is something in me that after some time revolts against such lassitude. I can't just *be!* Suddenly I jump up and rush away out of that contented circle. I want to do something terribly difficult like climbing a mountain or reading the *Critique of Pure Reason*. I feel tempted to bang my head against the wall as if to wake myself up. Anything to prevent myself from being sucked down into the bog of passive, intuitive being. I feel I cannot, I must not allow myself to live this way.

Of course there are other Europeans more or less in the same situation as myself. For instance, other women married to Indians. But I hesitate to seek them out. People suffering from the same disease do not usually make good company for one another. Who is to listen to whose complaints? On the other hand, with what enthusiasm I welcome visitors from abroad. Their physical presence alone is a pleasure to me. I love to see their fresh complexions, their red cheeks that speak of wind and rain; and I like to see their clothes and their shoes, to admire the texture of these solid European materials and the industrial skills that have gone into making them. I also like to hear the way in which these people speak. In some strange way their accents, their intonations are redolent to me of the places from which they have come, so that as voices rise and fall I hear in them the wind stirring in English trees or a mild brook murmuring through a summer wood. And apart from these sensuous pleasures, there is also the pleasure of hearing what they have to say. I listen avidly to what is said about people I know or have heard of and about new plays and restaurants and changes and fashions. However, neither the subject nor my interest in it is inexhaustible; and after that, it is my turn. What about India? Now they want to hear, but I don't want to say. I feel myself growing sullen. I don't want to talk about India. There is nothing I can tell them. There is nothing they would understand. However, I do begin to talk, and after a time even to talk with passion. But everything I say is wrong. I listen to myself with horror; they too listen with horror. I want to stop and reverse, but I can't. I want to cry out, this is not what I mean! You are listening to me in entirely the wrong context! But there is no way of explaining the context. It would take too long, and anyway what is the point? It's such a small, personal thing. I fall silent. I have nothing more to say. I turn my face and want them to go away.

12

So I am back again alone in my room with the blinds drawn and the air-conditioner on. Sometimes, when I think of my life, it seems to have contracted to this one point and to be concentrated in this one room, and it is always a very hot, very long afternoon when the air-conditioner has failed. I cannot describe the *oppression* of such afternoons. It is a physical oppression—heat pressing down on me and pressing in the walls and the ceiling and congealing together with time that has stood still and will never move again. And it is not only those two—heat and time—that are laying their weight on me but behind them, or held within them, there is something more, which I can only describe as the whole of India. This is hyperbole, but I need hyperbole to express my feelings about those countless afternoons spent over what now seem to me countless years in a country for which I was not born. India swallows me up and now it seems to me that I am no longer in my room but in the white-hot city streets under a white-hot sky; people cannot live in such heat, so everything is deserted—no, not quite, for here comes a smiling leper in a cart being pushed by another leper; there is also the carcass of a dog and vultures have swooped down on it. The river has dried up and stretches in miles of flat cracked earth; it is not possible to make out where the river ceases and the land begins, for this too is as flat, as cracked, as dry as the riverbed and stretches on forever. Until we come to a jungle in which wild beasts live, and then there are ravines and here live outlaws with the hearts of wild beasts. Sometimes they make raids into the villages and they rob and burn and mutilate and kill for sport. More mountains and these are very, very high, and now it is no longer hot but terribly cold, we are in snow and ice and here is Mount Kailash on which sits Siva the Destroyer wearing a necklace of human skulls. Down in the plains they are worshiping him. I can see them from here—they are doing something strange—what is it? I draw nearer. Now I can see. They are killing a boy. They hack him to pieces and now they bury the pieces into the foundations dug for a new bridge. There is a priest with them who is quite naked except for ash smeared all over him; he is reciting some holy verses over the foundations, to bless and propitiate.

I am using these exaggerated images in order to give some idea of how intolerable India—the idea, the sensation of it—can become. A point is reached where one must escape, and if one can't do so physically, then some other way must be found. And I think it is not only Europeans but Indians too who feel themselves compelled to seek refuge from their often unbearable environment. Here perhaps less than anywhere else is it possible to believe that this world, this life, is all there is for us, and the temptation to write it off and substitute something more satisfying becomes overwhelming. This brings up the question whether religion is such a potent force in India because life is so terrible, or is it the other way around—is life so terrible because, with the eyes of the spirit turned elsewhere, there is no incentive to improve its quality? Whichever it is, the fact remains that the eyes of the spirit *are* turned elsewhere, and it really is true that God seems more present in India than in other places. Every morning I wake up at 3 A.M. to the sound of someone pouring out his spirit in devotional song; and then at dawn the temple bells ring, and again at dusk, and conch shells are blown, and there is the smell of incense and of the slightly overblown flowers that are placed at the feet of smiling, pink-cheeked idols. I read in the papers that the Lord Krishna has been reborn as the son of a weaver woman in a village somewhere in Madhya Pradesh. On the banks of the river there are figures in meditation and one of them may turn out to be the teller in your bank who cashed your check just a few days ago; now he is in the lotus pose and his eyes are turned up and he is in ecstasy. There are ashrams full of little old half-starved widows who skip and dance about, they giggle and play hide-and-seek because they are Krishna's milkmaids. And over all this there is a sky of enormous proportions—so much larger than the earth on which you live, and often so incredibly beautiful, an unflawed unearthly blue by day, all shining with stars at night, that it is difficult to believe that something grand and wonderful beyond the bounds of human comprehension does not emanate from there.

I love listening to Indian devotional songs. They seem pure like water drawn from a well; and the emotions they express are both beautiful and easy to understand because the imagery employed is so human. The soul crying out for God is always shown as the beloved yearning for the lover in an easily recognizable way ("I wait for Him. Do you hear His step? He has come."). I feel soothed when I hear such songs and all my discontentment falls away. I see that everything I have been fretting about is of no importance at all because all that matters is this promise of eternal bliss in the Lover's arms. I become patient and good and feel that everything is good. Unfortunately this tranquil state does not last for long, and after a time it again seems to me that nothing is good and neither am I. Once somebody said to me: "Just see, how sweet is the Indian soul that can see God in a cow!" But when I try to assume this sweetness, it turns sour: For, however much I may try to fool myself, whatever veils I may try, for the sake of peace of mind, to draw over my eyes, it is soon enough clear to me that the cow *is* a cow, and a very scrawny, underfed, diseased one at that. And then I feel that I want to keep this knowledge, however painful it is, and not exchange it for some other that may be true for an Indian but can never quite become that for me. 15

And here, it seems to me, I come to the heart of my problem. To live in India and be at peace, one must to a very considerable extent become Indian and adopt Indian attitudes, habits, beliefs, assume if possible an Indian personality. But how is this possible? And even if it were possible—without cheating oneself—would it be desirable? Should one want to try to become something other than what one is? I don't always say no to this question. Sometimes it seems to me how pleasant it would be to say yes and give in and wear a sari and be meek and accepting and see God in a cow. Other times it seems worthwhile to be defiant and European and—all right, be crushed by one's envi- 16 ronment, but all the same have made some attempt to remain standing. Of course, this can't go on indefinitely and in the end I'm bound to lose—if only at the point where my ashes are immersed in the Ganges to the accompaniment of Vedic hymns, and then who will say that I have not truly merged with India?

I do sometimes go back to Europe. But after a time I get bored there and want to come back here. I also find it hard now to stand the European climate. I have got used to intense heat and seem to need it.

17

COMPREHENSION

1. Does Jhabvala truly hate India? What evidence suggests the opposite?
2. What is it about India that makes it "too strong for European nerves"? What does this suggest about European sensibilities?
3. How does Jhabvala describe the Indian character?

RHETORIC

1. Comment on Jhabvala's animal metaphor. Is it a suitable one for India? Cite other uses of figurative language in the essay. How does the language evoke a sense of place? Why is this important to the writer's purposes?
2. How would you describe Jhabvala's writing style and approach to her topic? Is this a successful stylistic treatment of her subject?
3. How do the topic sentences of paragraphs 7 and 8 reveal the writer's state of mind? Why does she use this device? What response is she trying to elicit?
4. Jhabvala employs numerous rhetorical strategies to develop her essay. Identify key passages that reflect these strategies.
5. How does Jhabvala's juxtaposition of opposites reflect her attitude in paragraph 10? How does this technique lend force to the thesis of the essay?
6. Is Jhabvala's conclusion satisfying? Why, or why not? How does it relate to the content of the essay and the author's thesis?

WRITING

1. In paragraph 7 of her essay, Jhabvala states: "People are not meant to shut themselves up in rooms and pretend there is nothing outside." Write an essay in which you agree or disagree with this opinion. Consider the problems outside your door, both national and global. Can you ignore them? How? On the other hand, is it your duty to try to remedy these problems? Is it ever necessary to escape?
2. Jhabvala attributes the Indian character to the belief in reincarnation. What is reincarnation? In a research paper, examine the teachings of this belief. Use the information you gather to comment on the validity of Jhabvala's remarks.
3. Write a personal narrative similar to Jhabvala's in which you examine and analyze your feelings about the country in which you were born or raised.

What ambivalent feelings do you have about the place, if any? How does it feel to be a product of a particular culture? What effect has it had on your identity or your sense of the world?

ISHMAEL REED Ishmael Reed (b. 1938), an American novelist and poet, is the founder and editor (along with Al Young) of *Quilt* magazine, begun in 1981. In his writing, Reed uses a combination of standard English, black dialect, and slang to satirize American society. He believes that African Americans must move away from identification with Europe in order to rediscover their African qualities. Reed's books include *Flight to Canada* (1976), *The Terrible Twos* (1982), and *The Terrible Threes* (1989). In addition, he has written volumes of verse, including *Secretary to the Spirits* (1975), and a play, *Hell Hath No Fury* (1960). In the following essay from *Writin' Is Fightin'*, Reed seeks to debunk the myth of the European ideal and argues for a universal definition of *culture*.

ISHMAEL REED

America: The Multinational Society

At the annual Lower East Side Jewish Festival yesterday, a Chinese woman ate a pizza slice in front of Ty Thuan Duc's Vietnamese grocery store. Beside her a Spanish-speaking family patronized a cart with two signs: "Italian Ices" and "Kosher by Rabbi Alper." And after the pastrami ran out, everybody ate knishes. —*The New York Times*, June 23, 1983

On the day before Memorial Day, 1983, a poet called me to describe 1 a city he had just visited. He said that one section included mosques, built by the Islamic people who dwelled there. Attending his reading, he said, were large numbers of Hispanic people, forty thousand of whom lived in the same city. He was not talking about a fabled city located in some mysterious region of the world. The city he'd visited was Detroit.

A few months before, as I was leaving Houston, Texas, I heard it 2 announced on the radio that Texas's largest minority was Mexican American, and though a foundation recently issued a report critical of bilingual education, the taped voice used to guide the passengers on the air trams connecting terminals in Dallas Airport is in both Spanish and English. If the trend continues, a day will come when it will be difficult to travel through some sections of the country without hearing commands in both English and Spanish; after all, for some western states, Spanish was the first written language and the Spanish style lives on in the western way of life.

Shortly after my Texas trip, I sat in an auditorium located on the
campus of the University of Wisconsin at Milwaukee as a Yale professor—whose original work on the influence of African cultures upon
those of the Americas has led to his ostracism from some monocultural
intellectual circles—walked up and down the aisle, like an old-time
southern evangelist, dancing and drumming the top of the lectern, illus-
trating his points before some serious Afro-American intellectuals and
artists who cheered and applauded his performance and his mastery of
information. The professor was "white." After his lecture, he joined a
group of Milwaukeeans in a conversation. All of the participants spoke
Yoruban, though only the professor had ever traveled to Africa.

One of the artists told me that his paintings, which included African
and Afro-American mythological symbols and imagery, were hanging
in the local McDonald's restaurant. The next day I went to McDonald's
and snapped pictures of smiling youngsters eating hamburgers below
paintings that could grace the walls of any of the country's leading
museums. The manager of the local McDonald's said, "I don't know
what you boys are doing, but I like it," as he commissioned the local
painters to exhibit in his restaurant.

Such blurring of cultural styles occurs in everyday life in the United
States to a greater extent than anyone can imagine and is probably
more prevalent than the sensational conflict between people of different backgrounds that is played up and often encouraged by the media.
The result is what the Yale professor, Robert Thompson, referred to as
a cultural bouillabaisse, yet members of the nation's present educational
and cultural Elect still cling to the notion that the United States belongs
to some vaguely defined entity they refer to as "Western civilization,"
by which they mean, presumably, a civilization created by the people of
Europe, as if Europe can be viewed in monolithic terms. Is Beethoven's
Ninth Symphony, which includes Turkish marches, a part of Western
civilization, or the late nineteenth- and twentieth-century French paintings, whose creators were influenced by Japanese art? And what of the
cubists, through whom the influence of African art changed modern
painting, or the surrealists, who were so impressed with the art of the
Pacific Northwest Indians that, in their map of North America, Alaska
dwarfs the lower forty-eight in size?

Are the Russians, who are often criticized for their adoption of
"Western" ways by Tsarist dissidents in exile, members of Western civ-
ilization? And what of the millions of Europeans who have black
African and Asian ancestry, black Africans having occupied several
countries for hundreds of years? Are these "Europeans" members of
Western civilization, or the Hungarians, who originated across the
Urals in a place called Greater Hungary, or the Irish, who came from
the Iberian Peninsula?

Even the notion that North America is part of Western civilization
because our "system of government" is derived from Europe is being
challenged by Native American historians who say that the founding
fathers, Benjamin Franklin especially, were actually influenced by the

643

system of government that had been adopted by the Iroquois hundreds of years prior to the arrival of large numbers of Europeans.

Western civilization, then, becomes another confusing category like 8 Third World, or Judeo-Christian culture, as man attempts to impose his small-screen view of political and cultural reality upon a complex world. Our most publicized novelist recently said that Western civilization was the greatest achievement of mankind, an attitude that flourishes on the street level as scribbles in public restrooms: "White Power," "Niggers and Spics Suck," or "Hitler was a prophet," the latter being the most telling, for wasn't Adolph Hitler the archetypal monoculturalist who, in his pigheaded arrogance, believed that one way and one blood was so pure that it had to be protected from alien strains at all costs? Where did such an attitude, which has caused so much misery and depression in our national life, which has tainted even our noblest achievements, begin? An attitude that caused the incarceration of Japanese-American citizens during World War II, the persecution of Chicanos and Chinese Americans, the near-extermination of the Indians, and the murder and lynchings of thousands of Afro-Americans.

Virtuous, hardworking, pious, even though they occasionally would 9 wander off after some fancy clothes, or rendezvous in the woods with the town prostitute, the Puritans are idealized in our schoolbooks as "a hardy band" of no-nonsense patriarchs whose discipline razed the forest and brought order to the New World (a term that annoys Native American historians). Industrious, responsible, it was their "Yankee ingenuity" and practicality that created the work ethic. They were simple folk who produced a number of good poets, and they set the tone for the American writing style, of lean and spare lines, long before Hemingway. They worshiped in churches whose colors blended in with the New England snow, churches with simple structures and ornate lecterns.

The Puritans were a daring lot, but they had a mean streak. They 10 hated the theater and banned Christmas. They punished people in a cruel and inhuman manner. They killed children who disobeyed their parents. When they came in contact with those whom they considered heathens or aliens, they behaved in such a bizarre and irrational manner that this chapter in the American history comes down to us as a late-movie horror film. They exterminated the Indians, who taught them how to survive in a world unknown to them, and their encounter with the calypso culture of Barbados resulted in what the tourist guide in Salem's Witches' House refers to as the Witchcraft Hysteria.

The Puritan legacy of hard work and meticulous accounting led to 11 the establishment of a great industrial society; it is no wonder that the American industrial revolution began in Lowell, Massachusetts, but there was the other side, the strange and paranoid attitudes toward those different from the Elect.

The cultural attitudes of that early Elect continue to be voiced in 12 everyday life in the United States: the president of a distinguished university, writing a letter to the *Times,* belittling the study of African civilizations; the television network that promoted its show on the Vatican art with the boast that this art represented "the finest achievements of the human spirit." A modern up-tempo state of complex rhythms that depends upon contacts with an international community can no longer behave as if it dwelled in a "Zion Wilderness" surrounded by beasts and pagans.

When I heard a schoolteacher warn the other night about the invasion of the American educational system by foreign curriculums, I wanted to yell at the television set, "Lady, they're already here." It has already begun because the world is here. The world has been arriving at these shores for at least ten thousand years from Europe, Africa, and Asia. In the late nineteenth and early twentieth centuries, large numbers of Europeans arrived, adding their cultures to those of the European, African, and Asian settlers who were already here, and recently millions have been entering the country from South America and the Caribbean, making Yale Professor Bob Thompson's bouillabaisse richer and thicker.

One of our most visionary politicians said that he envisioned a time when the United States could become the brain of the world, by which he meant the repository of all of the latest advanced information systems. I thought of that remark when an enterprising poet friend of mine called to say that he had just sold a poem to a computer magazine and that the editors were delighted to get it because they didn't carry fiction or poetry. Is that the kind of world we desire? A humdrum homogeneous world of all brains but no heart, no fiction, no poetry; a world of robots with human attendants bereft of imagination, of culture? Or does North America deserve a more exciting destiny? To become a place where the cultures of the world crisscross. This is possible because the United States is unique in the world: The world is here.

COMPREHENSION

1. Why does Reed believe that the notion of Western or European civilization is fallacious?
2. According to Reed, what are the origins of our monoculturalist view?
3. What are the dangers of such a narrow view? What historical examples does Reed allude to?

RHETORIC

1. How do paragraphs 1 to 4 help set the stage for Reed's discourse? Does this section contain Reed's thesis?
2. Does the computer analogy in Reed's conclusion work? Do his rhetorical questions underscore the thesis?
3. Comment on the author's extensive use of details and examples. How do they serve to support his point? Which examples are especially illuminating? Why?

4. What kind of humor does Reed use in his essay? Does its use contribute to the force of his essay? Why, or why not?
5. Is Reed's reasoning inductive or deductive? Justify your answer.
6. How does Reed employ definitions to structure his essay?

WRITING

1. Write an essay arguing that a multinational society is often riddled with complex problems. What are some of the drawbacks or disadvantages of such a society? What causes these conflicts? Explore these issues in your writing.
2. How does America's insistence that it is a European country affect its dealings with other nations? How does it influence the way it treats its own citizens? Explore these questions in a causal-analysis essay, using support from Reed.
3. Write an essay in which you consider how a multinational United States affects you on a day-to-day basis. How does it enrich your life or the life of the country? Use specific examples and details to support your opinion.

LANCE MORROW   Lance Morrow, who was born in Lewisburg, Pennsylvania, in 1939, is a graduate of Harvard University. Morrow began working at *Time* magazine in 1965 and has been with that publication ever since. His book about the relationship between himself and his father, entitled *The Chief: A Memoir of Fathers and Sons* (1984), was widely praised upon publication for its honesty and integrity. He is a National Magazine Award winner for his *Time* essays.

LANCE MORROW

The Evil at the Dragon's Feet

Beneath Carpaccio's dragon lies a kind of Bosnian litter: half-devoured   1
bodies . . . skulls . . . busy, slithering snakes. The painting *St. George and the Dragon* is a vision of evil perfectly at home in the late 20th century, even though the artist imagined it almost 500 years ago. It gleams like a premonition in the garage-dim Scuola di San Giorgio degli Schiavoni in Venice. What is missing from the picture in 1995, of course, is the St. George part—the rescue: Evil impaled, Good's shining blond revenge.

It made some sense that Elie Wiesel chose Venice as the place to   2
bring together 30 interesting adolescents ("Tomorrow's Leaders") from various battlefields around the world (Bosnia, several African

countries, Northern Ireland, the Middle East, some of the more violent neighborhoods of American cities) to talk about their lives. Venice, with its gorgeous, impastoed melancholy, exhausted the possibilities of human glory and depravity centuries ago. Wiesel's young, all vulnerability and fire, assembled at the other end of history altogether. Furious at what the blackhearted past has done to them, they made friends across their inherited fault lines (Israeli with Palestinian, Irish Protestant with Irish Catholic, for example) and inspected the future with a kind of fervent wariness, a provisional hope.

In the meantime, of course, the dragon proceeded with his projects. Beside the Venice lagoon, you could practically hear the noise from Bosnia, an hour's hop across the Adriatic. (Some sporting Italians, it is said, fly over for the weekend, hoping to see some shooting and maybe even to do some violence themselves.) Nineteen-year-old Tarja Krehic from Bosnia told the others about the mysterious onset of evil in her neighborhood: "Hate came, I don't know from where." A 19-year-old from Kenya, Kim Muhota, reported that in the streets of Nairobi, children are known to wield discarded hypodermic needles (carrying God knows what viruses of doom) and threaten to jab passersby unless given money—the needles becoming grotesquely miniaturized moral inversions of the St. George lance.

Wiesel meant, in part, to audition the future while it is still in its teens. He told the young, "Some of us have access to the leaders of the world. But all the meetings we have had have been disappointments. So we wanted to start before you become leaders."

Some of the kids' short, traumatized biographies supported an underlying premise—a motif that the older speakers elaborated upon a bit too automatically. Bernard Kouchner, the French doctor who co-founded Médecins Sans Frontières and Médecins du Monde, stated the theme when he spoke about Bosnia: Today there are 37 wars going on in the world. The adults have failed, he said. Youth must succeed.

Is it true that the adults of the world have so hideously failed? The multilingual hordes of early June tourists surging around the Piazza San Marco suggested the freedom, democracy, prosperity and astonishing mobility achieved in portions of the post–World War II and post–cold war planet. The adults defeated Hitler and dismantled communism. The world remains filled with persistent, ragged atavisms that kill en masse—Rwanda and the Sudan, for example. But there is a fecklessness in the spectacle of adults demonizing their own generation (as, when young, they demonized their elders by saying "Don't trust anyone over 30") and declaring that it is now up to the children to save the world. Nonsense. It is up to the adults to face their responsibilities and protect the children. That is what adults are for. We should not prematurely "empower" children. Tomorrow's leaders will take care of tomorrow.

The suffering of any child shames a decent conscience. The simplest definition of evil begins with whatever makes a child suffer. The most terrible failure of adults has been their inability, or unwillingness, to shoulder the responsibilities of adults and protect children not only from war but also from other, newer, nonmartial forms of destruction.

The theme of parentlessness has become pervasive in the world, not 8 merely in Kouchner's 37 wars but also in the supposedly peaceful cultures of success. Hell is answered prayers: greed has an omnivorous life of its own. During the 1960s, American fathers failed in their responsibilities to the young whom they involved in the Vietnam War. Now the moral abdications of adults in the economically successful world have brought down upon their own young inundations of drugs, guns, and a slithering, id-ridden chaos of cultural violence—all the highly profitable artifacts, legal and illegal, of a spiritual devolution as destructive as war.

Adults, whom nature has given the task of protecting children, have 9 made it their business instead to corrupt them. In a degraded culture, the unprotected minds of children come to resemble the litter at the feet of Carpaccio's dragon—filled with an evil imagery.

While presiding over the Venice conference, Elie Wiesel passed the 10 51st anniversary of his arrival, as an adolescent, at Auschwitz. Wiesel spent time in the heart of evil. Having thus been brought to a knowledge of darkness, he tries to lift the future—meaning the young—into a brighter orbit. That is the work of a moral grownup.

COMPREHENSION

1. What is the analogy between the ancient images in the painting *St. George and the Dragon* and the victims of war and neglect of today?

2. The final sentence of paragraph 8 is rather complex in form and ideas. Explain the meaning of this sentence in your own words.

3. Morrow speaks of two types of violence. What are they?

RHETORIC

1. Why has the author chosen to introduce his essay with a reference from art history? What does it imply about the author's assumptions about his audience?

2. Although the author reflects on the current high level of violence in the world, his tone is not an angry one. How would you describe his tone? Explain.

3. The author shifts between despair and hope in his essay. Which paragraphs denote hopefulness; which denote despair? How does he weave the two together?

4. Why has the author chosen to focus on Elie Wiesel in the final paragraph? In what way does the experience of Wiesel synthesize the aspects of good and evil discussed in the essay?

5. The dragon is a central metaphor. Identify the way in which the author exploits it in the essay. Explain how it lends coherence to the writing.

6. Examine the topic sentences of each paragraph. How do they serve to introduce the subject matter of the paragraph they lead? Are any faulty in this
regard? Explain your view.
7. Examine the four uses of parentheses in the essay. Why has the author chosen to use them? What is their purpose? Compare them to your use of
parentheses. How does the author's use differ from your own?

WRITING

1. Argue for or against the proposition that violence has always been a part of
human existence and that today's world is no exception.
2. As a creative writing exercise, assume the persona of someone lecturing to
a group of young people who have suffered from violence. Persuade them
that there is good reason to maintain optimism.
3. Study Picasso's painting *Guernica,* and research its historical and cultural
context. Write an essay exploring your response to the painting.

V. S. NAIPAUL   V. S. Naipaul (b. 1932), whose given name is Vidiadhari
Surajprasad, is a West-Indian novelist and essayist who has lived in England
since 1950. His parents were Hindus, but Naipaul was educated in Trinidad
and at Oxford. Naipaul's work reflects his inner conflicts about his dual heritage and offers an ironic view of life. His novels, including *A House for Mr.
Biswas* (1961) and *Guerillas* (1975), demonstrate his elegant prose, while
Among the Believers: An Islamic Journey (1981) and *India: A Million Mutinies
Now* (1990) offer penetrating nonfictional analyses. In the following essay
from *The New York Times,* Naipaul explores the efforts to achieve an international community and confronts issues of ethnic identity.

V. S. NAIPAUL

Our Universal Civilization

I never formulated the idea of the universal civilization until 11 years ₁
ago, when I traveled for many months in a number of non-Arab Muslim countries—Iran, Indonesia, Malaysia and Pakistan—to try to
understand what had driven them to their rage. That Muslim rage was
just beginning to be apparent.

I thought I would be traveling among people who would be like the ₂
people of my own community, the Trinidad Indian community. A large
portion of Indians were Muslims; we both had a similar 19th century
imperial or colonial history. But it wasn't like that.

Despite the history we had in common, I had traveled a different ₃
way. Starting with the Hindu background of the instinctive, ritualized

life; growing up in the unpromising conditions of colonial Trinidad; I had gone through many stages of knowledge and self-knowledge. I had been granted the ideas of inquiry and the tools of scholarship. I could carry four or five or six different cultural ideas in my head. Now, traveling among non-Arab Muslims, I found myself among a colonized people who had been stripped by their faith of all that expanding cultural and historical knowledge of the world that I had been growing into on the other side of the world.

Before I began my journey—while the Shah still ruled—there had 4 appeared in the United States a small novel, *Foreigner,* by Nahid Rachlin, a young Iranian woman, that in its subdued, unpolitical way foreshadowed the hysteria that was to come. The central figure is a young Iranian woman who does research work in Boston as a biologist. She is married to an American, and she might seem well adapted.

But when she goes back on a holiday to Teheran, she begins to feel 5 lost. She reflects on her time in the United States. It is not a time of clarity; she sees it now to be a time of emptiness. She has never been in control. We can see that she was not prepared for the movement out of the shut-in Iranian world—where the faith was the complete way, filled everything, left no spare corner of the mind or will or soul—to the other world where it was necessary to be an individual and responsible; where people developed vocations and were stirred by ambition and achievement, and believed in perfectibility.

In her distress, she falls ill. She goes to a hospital. The doctor under- 6 stands her unhappiness. He tells the young woman that her pain comes from an old ulcer. "What you have," he says in his melancholy, seductive way, "is a Western disease." And the research biologist arrives at a decision. She will give up that Boston-imposed life of the intellect and meaningless work; she will stay in Iran and put on the veil.

Immensely satisfying, that renunciation. But it is intellectually 7 flawed: it assumes that there will continue to be people striving out there, in the stressed world, making drugs and medical equipment, to keep the Iranian doctor's hospital going.

Again and again, on my Islamic journey in 1979, I found a similar 8 unconscious contradiction in people's attitudes. I remember especially a newspaper editor in Teheran. His paper had been at the heart of the revolution. In the middle of 1979 it was busy, in a state of glory. Seven months later, when I went back to Teheran, it had lost its heart; the once busy main room was empty; all but two of the staff had disappeared. The American Embassy had been seized; a financial crisis had followed; many foreign firms had closed down; advertising had dried up; the newspaper editor could hardly see his way ahead; every issue of the paper lost money; the editor, it might be said, had become as much a hostage as the diplomats.

He also, as I now learned, had two sons of university age. One was 9 studying in the United States; the other had applied for a visa, but then the hostage crisis had occurred. This was news to me—that the United States should have been so important to the sons of one of the spokesmen of the Islamic revolution. I told the editor I was surprised. He said, speaking especially of the son waiting for the visa, "It's his future."

Emotional satisfaction on one hand; thought for the future on the other. The editor was as divided as nearly everyone else.

One of Joseph Conrad's earliest stories of the East Indies, from the 1890's, was about a local raja or chieftain, a murderous man, a Muslim (though it is never explicitly said), who, in a crisis, having lost his magical counselor, swims out one night to one of the English merchant ships in the harbor to ask the sailors, representatives of the immense power that had come from the other end of the world, for an amulet, a magical charm. The sailors are at a loss; but then someone among them gives the raja a British coin, a sixpence commemorating Queen Victoria's Jubilee; and the raja is well pleased. Conrad didn't treat the story as a joke; he loaded it with philosophical implications for both sides, and I feel now that he saw truly.

In the 100 years since that story, the wealth of the world has grown, power has grown, education has spread; the disturbance, the "philosophical shriek" of men at the margin (to use Conrad's words), has been amplified. The division in the revolutionary editor's spirit, and the renunciation of the fictional biologist, both contain a tribute—unacknowledged, but all the more profound—to the universal civilization. Simple charms alone cannot be acquired from it; other, difficult things come with it as well: ambition, endeavor, individuality.

The universal civilization has been a long time in the making. It wasn't always universal; it wasn't always as attractive as it is today. The expansion of Europe gave it for at least three centuries a racial taint, which still causes pain.

In Trinidad I grew up in the last days of that kind of racialism. And that, perhaps, has given me a greater appreciation of the immense changes that have taken place since the end of the war, the extraordinary attempt to accommodate the rest of the world, and all the currents of that world's thought.

Because my movement within this civilization has been from Trinidad to England, from the periphery to the center, I may have felt certain of its guiding principles more freshly than people to whom these things were everyday. One such realization—I suppose I have sensed it most of my life, but I have understood it philosophically only during the preparation of this talk—has been the beauty of the idea of the pursuit of happiness. Familiar words, easy to take for granted; easy to misconstrue.

This idea of the pursuit of happiness is at the heart of the attractiveness of the civilization to so many outside it or on its periphery. I find it marvelous to contemplate to what an extent, after two centuries, and after the terrible history of the earlier part of this century, the idea has come to a kind of fruition. It is an elastic idea; it fits all men. It implies a certain kind of society, a certain kind of awakened spirit. I don't imagine my father's Hindu parents would have been able to understand the idea. So much is contained in it: the idea of the indi-

vidual, responsibility, choice, the life of the intellect, the idea of vocation and perfectibility and achievement. It is an immense human idea.
It cannot be reduced to a fixed system. It cannot generate fanaticism.
But it is known to exist, and because of that, other more rigid systems
in the end blow away.

COMPREHENSION

1. What does Naipaul mean by "universal civilization"?
2. What are the differences between Naipaul's Muslims and the ones he
   encounters in his travels? What factors does the author cite to explain those
   differences?
3. What conflicts do the non-Arab Muslims face in a universal civilization?

RHETORIC

1. What is Naipaul's thesis? Where does it appear?
2. In paragraph 8, how does the author structure his example? Comment on
   his choice of punctuation and his ordering of events.
3. How does Naipaul use other literary sources to structure the essay? How do
   they serve to amplify his points?
4. How does Naipaul employ comparative analysis and definition? Is his overall approach deductive or inductive? Explain your views.
5. Cite uses of parallel structure in Naipaul's essay. How is it used?
6. The author introduces and expands on the theme of "the pursuit of happiness" in his conclusion. Is there any hint to the reader that it's an important
   issue for Naipaul before it's mentioned? What is the purpose of placing it in
   the final paragraphs?

WRITING

1. In an essay, develop Naipaul's remark: "I could carry four or five or six cultural ideas around in my head." What does the writer mean by this? How
   can such an attitude enhance a person's perception of the world? Can most
   people make the same claim? Do you feel that your own perspective is
   broad or narrow?
2. Write an essay exploring the meaning of "the pursuit of happiness." Is it a
   concept that most Americans and other Westerners take for granted? What
   does it mean? Can it be abused?
3. In a brief essay using Naipaul's observations as support, explore the role of
   religion in defining a country's philosophy and customs. How can religion
   narrow a country's global vision?

JAMES BALDWIN   James Baldwin (1924–1988), a major American essayist,
novelist, short-story writer, and playwright, was born and grew up in Harlem.
He won a Eugene Saxon Fellowship and lived in Europe from 1948 to 1956.

Always an activist in civil-rights causes, Baldwin focused in his essays and fiction on the black search for identity in modern America and on the myth of white superiority. Among his principal works are *Go Tell It on the Mountain* (1953), *Notes of a Native Son* (1955), *Giovanni's Room* (1956), *Nobody Knows My Name* (1961), *Another Country* (1962), and *If Beale Street Could Talk* (1974). One of the finest contemporary essayists, Baldwin had a rare talent for portraying the deepest concerns about civilization in an intensely personal style, as the following essay indicates.

JAMES BALDWIN

Stranger in the Village

From all available evidence no black man had ever set foot in this tiny Swiss village before I came. I was told before arriving that I would probably be a "sight" for the village; I took this to mean that people of my complexion were rarely seen in Switzerland, and also that city people are always something of a "sight" outside of the city. It did not occur to me—possibly because I am an American—that there could be people anywhere who had never seen a Negro.

It is a fact that cannot be explained on the basis of the inaccessibility of the village. The village is very high, but it is only four hours from Milan and three hours from Lausanne. It is true that it is virtually unknown. Few people making plans for a holiday would elect to come here. On the other hand, the villagers are able, presumably, to come and go as they please—which they do: to another town at the foot of the mountain, with a population of approximately five thousand, the nearest place to see a movie or go to the bank. In the village there is no movie house, no bank, no library, no theater; very few radios, one jeep, one station wagon; and, at the moment, one typewriter, mine, an invention which the woman next door to me here had never seen. There are about six hundred people living here, all Catholic—I conclude this from the fact that the Catholic church is open all year round, whereas the Protestant chapel, set off on a hill a little removed from the village, is open only in the summertime when the tourists arrive. There are four or five hotels, all closed now, and four or five *bistros*, of which, however, only two do any business during the winter. These two do not do a great deal, for life in the village seems to end around nine or ten o'clock. There are a few stores, butcher, baker, *épicerie*, a hardware store, and a money-changer—who cannot change travelers' checks, but must send them down to the bank, an operation which takes two or three days. There is something called the *Ballet Haus*, closed in the winter and used for God knows what, certainly not ballet, during the summer. There seems to be only one schoolhouse in the village, and this for the quite young children; I suppose this to mean that their older brothers and sisters at some point descend from these mountains in order to complete their education—possibly, again, to the town just below. The landscape is absolutely forbidding, mountains towering on all four sides, ice and snow as far as the eye can reach. In this white wilderness, men and women and children move all day, carrying washing, wood, buckets of milk or water, sometimes skiing on Sunday afternoons. All week long boys and young men are to be seen shoveling snow off the rooftops, or dragging wood down from the forest in sleds.

The village's only real attraction, which explains the tourist season, is the hot spring water. A disquietingly high proportion of these tourists are cripples, or semi-cripples, who come year after year—from other parts of Switzerland, usually—to take the waters. This lends the village, at the height of the season, a rather terrifying air of sanctity, as though it were a lesser Lourdes. There is often something beautiful, there is always something awful, in the spectacle of a person who has lost one of his faculties, a faculty he never questioned until it was gone, and who struggles to recover it. Yet people remain people, on crutches or indeed on deathbeds; and wherever I passed, the first summer I was here, among the native villagers or among the lame, a wind passed with me— of astonishment, curiosity, amusement, and outrage. The first summer I stayed two weeks and never intended to return. But I did return in the winter, to work; the village offers, obviously, no distractions whatever and has the further advantage of being extremely cheap. Now it is winter again, a year later, and I am here again. Everyone in the village knows my name, though they scarcely ever use it, knows that I come from America—though this, apparently, they will never really believe: black men come from Africa—and everyone knows that I am the friend of the son of a woman who was born here, and that I am staying in their chalet. But I remain as much a stranger today as I was the first day I arrived, and the children shout *Neger! Neger!* as I walk along the streets.

It must be admitted that in the beginning I was far too shocked to have any real reaction. In so far as I reacted at all, I reacted by trying to be pleasant—it being a great part of the American Negro's education (long before he goes to school) that he must make people "like" him. This smile-and-the-world-smiles-with-you routine worked about as well in this situation as it had in the situation for which it was designed, which is to say that it did not work at all. No one, after all, can be liked whose human weight and complexity cannot be, or has not been, admitted. My smile was simply another unheard-of phenomenon which allowed them to see my teeth—they did not, really, see my smile and I began to think that, should I take to snarling, no one would notice any difference. All of the physical characteristics of the Negro which had caused me, in America, a very different and almost forgotten pain were nothing less than miraculous—or infernal—in the eyes of the village people. Some thought my hair was the color of tar, that it had the texture of wire, or the texture of cotton. It was jocularly suggested that

I might let it all grow long and make myself a winter coat. If I sat in the sun for more than five minutes some daring creature was certain to come along and gingerly put his fingers on my hair, as though he were afraid of an electric shock, or put his hand on my hand, astonished that the color did not rub off. In all of this, in which it must be conceded there was the charm of genuine wonder and in which there was certainly no element of intentional unkindness, there was yet no suggestion that I was human: I was simply a living wonder.

I knew that they did not mean to be unkind, and I know it now; it is necessary, nevertheless, for me to repeat this to myself each time I walk out of the chalet. The children who shout *Neger!* have no way of knowing the echoes this sound raises in me. They are brimming with good humor and the more daring swell with pride when I stop to speak with them. Just the same, there are days when I cannot pause and smile, when I have no heart to play with them; when, indeed, I mutter sourly to myself, exactly as I muttered on the streets of a city these children have never seen, when I was no bigger than these children are now: *Your* mother *was a nigger.* Joyce is right about history being a nightmare—but it may be the nightmare from which no one *can* awaken. People are trapped in history and history is trapped in them.

There is a custom in the village—I am told it is repeated in many villages—of "buying" African natives for the purpose of converting them to Christianity. There stands in the church all year round a small box with a slot for money, decorated with a black figurine, and into this box the villagers drop their francs. During the *carnaval* which precedes Lent, two village children have their faces blackened—out of which bloodless darkness their blue eyes shine like ice—and fantastic horsehair wigs are placed on their blond heads; thus disguised, they solicit among the villagers for money for the missionaries in Africa. Between the box in the church and the blackened children, the village "bought" last year six or eight African natives. This was reported to me with pride by the wife of one of the *bistro* owners and I was careful to express astonishment and pleasure at the solicitude shown by the village for the souls of black folk. The *bistro* owner's wife beamed with a pleasure far more genuine than my own and seemed to feel that I might now breathe more easily concerning the souls of at least six of my kinsmen.

I tried not to think of these so lately baptized kinsmen, of the price paid for them, or the peculiar price they themselves would pay, and said nothing about my father, who having taken his own conversion too literally never, at bottom, forgave the white world (which he described as heathen) for having saddled him with a Christ in whom, to judge at least from their treatment of him, they themselves no longer believed. I thought of white men arriving for the first time in an African village, strangers there, as I am a stranger here, and tried to imagine the astounded populace touching their hair and marveling at the color of their skin. But there is a great difference between being the first white man to be seen by Africans and being the first black man to be seen by

655

whites. The white man takes the astonishment as tribute, for he arrives to conquer and to convert the natives, whose inferiority in relation to himself is not even to be questioned; whereas I, without a thought of conquest, find myself among a people whose culture controls me, has even, in a sense, created me, people who have cost me more in anguish and rage than they will ever know, who yet do not even know of my existence. The astonishment with which I might have greeted them, should they have stumbled into my African village a few hundred years ago, might have rejoiced their hearts. But the astonishment with which they greet me today can only poison mine.

And this is so despite everything I may do to feel differently, despite ⁸ my friendly conversations with the *bistro* owner's wife, despite their three-year-old son who has at last become my friend, despite the *saluts* and *bonsoirs* which I exchange with people as I walk, despite the fact that I know that no individual can be taken to task for what history is doing, or has done. I say that the culture of these people controls me— but they can scarcely be held responsible for European culture. America comes out of Europe, but these people have never seen America nor have most of them seen more of Europe than the hamlet at the foot of their mountain. Yet they move with an authority which I shall never have; and they regard me, quite rightly, not only as a stranger in their village but as a suspect latecomer, bearing no credentials, to everything they have—however unconsciously—inherited.

For this village, even were it incomparably more remote and incred- ⁹ ibly more primitive, is the West, the West onto which I have been so strangely grafted. These people cannot be, from the point of view of power, strangers anywhere in the world; they have made the modern world, in effect, even if they do not know it. The most illiterate among them is related, in a way that I am not, to Dante, Shakespeare, Michelangelo, Aeschylus, Da Vinci, Rembrandt, and Racine; the cathedral at Chartres says something to them which it cannot say to me, as indeed would New York's Empire State Building, should anyone here ever see it. Out of their hymns and dances come Beethoven and Bach. Go back a few centuries and they are in their full glory—but I am in Africa, watching the conquerors arrive.

The rage of the disesteemed is personally fruitless, but it is also ¹⁰ absolutely inevitable; this rage, so generally discounted, so little understood even among the people whose daily bread it is, is one of the things that makes history. Rage can only with difficulty, and never entirely, be brought under the domination of the intelligence and is therefore not susceptible to any arguments whatever. This is a fact which ordinary representatives of the *Herrenvolk*, having never felt this rage and being unable to imagine it, quite fail to understand. Also, rage cannot be hidden, it can only be dissembled. This dissembling deludes the thoughtless, and strengthens rage and adds, to rage, contempt. There are, no doubt, as many ways of coping with the resulting complex of tensions as there are black men in the world, but no black man can hope ever to be entirely liberated from this internal warfare—rage, dissembling, and contempt having inevitably accompanied his first realization of the power of white men. What is crucial here is that, since white men represent in the black man's world so heavy a weight, white men have for black men a reality which is far from being reciprocal; and hence all black men have toward all white men an attitude which is designed, really, either to rob the white man of the jewel of his naïveté, or else to make it cost him dear.

The black man insists, by whatever means he finds at his disposal, that the white man cease to regard him as an exotic rarity and recognize him as a human being. This is a very charged and difficult moment, for there is a great deal of will power involved in the white man's naïveté. Most people are not naturally reflective any more than they are naturally malicious, and the white man prefers to keep the black man at a certain human remove because it is easier for him thus to preserve his simplicity and avoid being called to account for crimes committed by his forefathers, or his neighbors. He is inescapably aware, nevertheless, that he is in a better position in the world than black men are, nor can he quite put to death the suspicion that he is hated by black men therefore. He does not wish to be hated, neither does he wish to change places, and at this point in his uneasiness he can scarcely avoid having recourse to those legends which white men have created about black men, the most usual effect of which is that the white man finds himself enmeshed, so to speak, in his own language which describes hell, as well as the attributes which lead one to hell, as being as black as night.

Every legend, moreover, contains its residuum of truth, and the root function of language is to control the universe by describing it. It is of quite considerable significance that black men remain, in the imagination, and in overwhelming numbers in fact, beyond the disciplines of salvation; and this despite the fact the West has been "buying" African natives for centuries. There is, I should hazard, an instantaneous necessity to be divorced from this so visibly unsaved stranger, in whose heart, moreover, one cannot guess what dreams of vengeance are being nourished; and, at the same time, there are few things on earth more attractive than the idea of the unspeakable liberty which is allowed the unredeemed. When, beneath the black mask, a human being begins to make himself felt one cannot escape a certain awful wonder as to what kind of human being it is. What one's imagination makes of other people is dictated, of course, by the laws of one's own personality and it is one of the ironies of black-white relations that, by means of what the white man imagines the black man to be, the black man is enabled to know who the white man is.

I have said, for example, that I am as much a stranger in this village today as I was the first summer I arrived, but this is not quite true. The villagers wonder less about the texture of my hair than they did then, and wonder rather more about me. And the fact that their wonder now exists on another level is reflected in their attitudes and in their eyes. There are the children who make those delightful, hilarious, sometimes astonishingly grave overtures of friendship in the unpredictable fashion of children; other children, having been taught that the devil is a black man, scream in genuine anguish as I approach. Some of the older women never pass without a friendly greeting, never pass, indeed, if it seems that they will be able to engage me in conversation; other women look down or look away or rather contemptuously smirk. Some of the men drink with me and suggest that I learn how to ski—partly, I gather, because they cannot imagine what I would look like on skis—and want to know if I am married, and ask questions about my *métier.* But some of the men have accused *le sale négre*—behind my back—of stealing wood and there is already in the eyes of some of them that peculiar, intent, paranoiac malevolence which one sometimes surprises in the eyes of American white men when, out walking with their Sunday girl, they see a Negro male approach.

There is a dreadful abyss between the streets of this village and the streets of the city in which I was born, between the children who shout *Neger!* today and those who shouted *Nigger!* yesterday—the abyss is experience, the American experience. The syllable hurled behind me today expresses, above all, wonder: I am a stranger here. But I am not a stranger in America and the same syllable riding on the American air expresses the war my presence has occasioned in the American soul. 14

For this village brings home to me this fact: that there was a day, and not really a very distant day, when Americans were scarcely Americans at all but discontented Europeans, facing a great unconquered continent and strolling, say, into a marketplace and seeing black men for the first time. The shock this spectacle afforded is suggested, surely, by the promptness with which they decided that these black men were not really men but cattle. It is true that the necessity on the part of the settlers of the New World of reconciling their moral assumptions with the fact—and the necessity—of slavery enhanced immensely the charm of this idea, and it is also true that this idea expresses, with a truly American bluntness, the attitude which to varying extents all masters have had toward all slaves. 15

But between all former slaves and slave-owners and the drama which begins for Americans over three hundred years ago at Jamestown, there are at least two differences to be observed. The American Negro slave could not suppose, for one thing, as slaves in past epochs had supposed and often done, that he would ever be able to wrest the power from his master's hands. This was a supposition which the modern era, which was to bring about such vast changes in the aims and dimensions of power, put to death; it only begins, in unprecedented fashion, and with dreadful implications, to be resurrected today. But even had this supposition persisted with undiminished force, the American Negro slave could not have used it to lend his condition dignity, for the reason that this supposition rests on another: that the slave in exile yet remains related to his past, has some means—if only in memory—of revering and sustaining the forms of his former life, is able, in short, to maintain his identity. 16

This was not the case with the American Negro slave. He is unique among the black men of the world in that his past was taken from him, almost literally, at one blow. One wonders what on earth the first slave found to say to the first dark child he bore. I am told that there are Haitians able to trace their ancestry back to African kings, but any American Negro wishing to go back so far will find his journey through time abruptly arrested by the signature on the bill of sale which served as the entrance paper for his ancestor. At the time—to say nothing of the circumstances—of the enslavement of the captive black man who was to become the American Negro, there was not the remotest possibility that he would ever take power from his master's hands. There was no reason to suppose that his situation would ever change, nor was there, shortly, anything to indicate that his situation had ever been different. It was his necessity, in the words of E. Franklin Frazier, to find a "motive for living under American culture or die." The identity of the American Negro comes out of this extreme situation, and the evolution of this identity was a source of the most intolerable anxiety in the minds and the lives of his masters.

For the history of the American Negro is unique also in this: that the question of his humanity, and of his rights therefore as a human being, became a burning one for several generations of Americans, so burning a question that it ultimately became one of those used to divide the nation. It is out of this argument that the venom of the epithet *Nigger!* is derived. It is an argument which Europe has never had, and hence Europe quite sincerely fails to understand how or why the argument arose in the first place, why its effects are so frequently disastrous and always so unpredictable, why it refuses until today to be entirely settled. Europe's black possessions remained—and do remain—in Europe's colonies, at which remove they represented no threat whatever to European identity. If they posed any problem at all for the European conscience, it was a problem which remained comfortingly abstract: in effect, the black man, *as a man*, did not exist for Europe. But in America, even as a slave, he was an inescapable part of the general social fabric and no American could escape having an attitude toward him. Americans attempt until today to make an abstraction of the Negro, but the very nature of these abstractions reveals the tremendous effects the presence of the Negro has had on the American character.

When one considers the history of the Negro in America it is of the greatest importance to recognize that the moral beliefs of a person, or a people, are never really as tenuous as life—which is not moral—very often causes them to appear; these create for them a frame of reference and a necessary hope, the hope being that when life has done its worst they will be enabled to rise above themselves and to triumph over life. Life would scarcely be bearable if this hope did not exist. Again, even when the worst has been said, to betray a belief is not by any means to have put oneself beyond its power; the betrayal of a belief is not the same thing as ceasing to believe. If this were not so there would be no

659

moral standards in the world at all. Yet one must also recognize that morality is based on ideas and that all ideas are dangerous—dangerous because ideas can only lead to action and where the action leads no man can say. And dangerous in this respect: that confronted with the impossibility of becoming free of them, one can be driven to the most inhuman excesses. The ideas on which American beliefs are based are not, though Americans often seem to think so, ideas which originated in America. They came out of Europe. And the establishment of democracy on the American continent was scarcely as radical a break with the past as was the necessity, which Americans faced, of broadening this concept to include black men.

This was, literally, a hard necessity. It was impossible, for one thing, for Americans to abandon their beliefs, not only because these beliefs alone seemed able to justify the sacrifices they had endured and the blood that they had spilled, but also because these beliefs afforded them their only bulwark against a moral chaos as absolute as the physical chaos of the continent it was their destiny to conquer. But in the situation in which Americans found themselves, these beliefs threatened an idea which, whether or not one likes to think so, is the very warp and woof of the heritage of the West, the idea of white supremacy.   20

Americans have made themselves notorious by the shrillness and the brutality with which they have insisted on this idea, but they did not invent it; and it has escaped the world's notice that those very excesses of which Americans have been guilty imply a certain, unprecedented uneasiness over the idea's life and power, if not, indeed, the idea's validity. The idea of white supremacy rests simply on the fact that white men are the creators of civilization (the present civilization, which is the only one that matters; all previous civilizations are simply "contributions" to our own) and are therefore civilization's guardians and defenders. Thus it was impossible for Americans to accept the black man as one of themselves, for to do so was to jeopardize their status as white men. But not so to accept him was to deny his human reality, his human weight and complexity, and the strain of denying the overwhelmingly undeniable forced Americans into rationalizations so fantastic that they approached the pathological.   21

At the root of the American Negro problem is the necessity of the American white man to find a way of living with the Negro in order to be able to live with himself. And the history of this problem can be reduced to the means used by Americans—lynch law and law, segregation and legal acceptance, terrorization and concession—either to come to terms with this necessity, or to find a way around it, or (most usually) to find a way of doing both these things at once. The resulting spectacle, at once foolish and dreadful, led someone to make the quite accurate observation that "the Negro-in-America is a form of insanity which overtakes white men."   22

In this long battle, a battle by no means finished, the unforeseeable effects of which will be felt by many future generations, the white man's motive was the protection of his identity; the black man was motivated   23 by the need to establish an identity. And despite the terrorization which the Negro in America endured and endures sporadically until today, despite the cruel and totally inescapable ambivalence of his status in his country, the battle for his identity has long ago been won. He is not a visitor to the West, but a citizen there, an American; as American as the Americans who despise him, the Americans who fear him, the Americans who love him—the Americans who became less than themselves, or rose to be greater than themselves by virtue of the fact that the challenge he represented was inescapable. He is perhaps the only black man in the world whose relationship to white men is more terrible, more subtle, and more meaningful than the relationship of bitter possessed to uncertain possessor. His survival depended, and his development depends, on his ability to turn his peculiar status in the Western world to his own advantage and, it may be, to the very great advantage of that world. It remains for him to fashion out of his experience that which will give him sustenance, and a voice.

The cathedral at Chartres, I have said, says something to the people 24 of this village which it cannot say to me; but it is important to understand that this cathedral says something to me which it cannot say to them. Perhaps they are struck by the power of the spires, the glory of the windows; but they have known God, after all, longer than I have known him, and in a different way, and I am terrified by the slippery bottomless well to be found in the crypt, down which heretics were hurled to death, and by the obscene, inescapable gargoyles jutting out of the stone and seeming to say that God and the devil can never be divorced. I doubt that the villagers think of the devil when they face a cathedral because they have never been identified with the devil. But I must accept the status which myth, if nothing else, gives me in the West before I can hope to change the myth.

Yet, if the American Negro has arrived at his identity by virtue of 25 the absoluteness of his estrangement from his past, American white men still nourish the illusion that there is some means of recovering the European innocence, of returning to a state in which black men do not exist. This is one of the greatest errors Americans can make. The identity they fought so hard to protect has, by virtue of that battle, undergone a change: Americans are as unlike any other white people in the world as it is possible to be. I do not think, for example, that it is too much to suggest that the American vision of the world—which allows so little reality, generally speaking, for any of the darker forces in human life, which tends until today to paint moral issues in glaring black and white—owes a great deal to the battle waged by Americans to maintain between themselves and black men a human separation which could not be bridged. It is only now beginning to be borne in on us— very faintly, it must be admitted, very slowly, and very much against our will—that this vision of the world is dangerously inaccurate, and perfectly useless. For it protects our moral high-mindedness at the terrible expense of weakening our grasp of reality. People who shut their eyes to reality simply invite their own destruction, and anyone who insists on remaining in a state of innocence long after that innocence is dead turns himself into a monster.

The time has come to realize that the interracial drama acted out on 26 the American continent has not only created a new black man, it has created a new white man, too. No road whatever will lead Americans back to the simplicity of this European village where white men still have the luxury of looking on me as a stranger. I am not, really, a stranger any longer for any American alive. One of the things that distinguishes Americans from other people is that no other people has ever been so deeply involved in the lives of black men, and vice versa. This fact faced, with all its implications, it can be seen that the history of the American Negro problem is not merely shameful, it is also something of an achievement. For even when the worst has been said, it must also be added that the perpetual challenge posed by this problem was always, somehow, perpetually met. It is precisely this black-white experience which may prove of indispensable value to us in the world we face today. This world is white no longer, and it will never be white again.

COMPREHENSION

1. According to Baldwin, what distinguishes Americans from other people? What is his purpose in highlighting these differences?

2. What connections between Europe, Africa, and America emerge from this essay? What is the relevance of the Swiss village to this frame of reference?

3. In the context of the essay, explain what Baldwin means by his statement, "People are trapped in history and history is trapped in them" (paragraph 5).

RHETORIC

1. Analyze the effect of Baldwin's repetition of "there is" and "there are" constructions in paragraph 2. What does the parallelism at the start of paragraph 8 accomplish? Locate other examples of parallelism in the essay.

2. Analyze the image of winter in paragraph 3 and its relation to the rest of the essay.

3. Where in the essay is Baldwin's complex thesis condensed for the reader? What does this placement of thesis reveal about the logical method of development in the essay?

4. How does Baldwin create his introduction? What is the focus? What key motifs does the author present that will inform the rest of the essay? What is the relationship of paragraph 5 to paragraph 6?

5. What paragraphs constitute the second section of the essay? What example serves to unify this section? What major shift in emphasis occurs in the third part of the essay? Explain the cathedral of Chartres as a controlling motif between these two sections.

6. What comparisons and contrasts help to structure and unify the essay?

1. Examine the paradox implicit in Baldwin's statement in the last paragraph that the history of the American Negro problem is "something of an achievement."
2. Write an essay on civilization based on the last sentence in Baldwin's essay: "This world is white no longer, and it will never be white again."
3. Describe a time when you felt yourself a "stranger" in a certain culture.

MARTIN LUTHER KING, JR. Martin Luther King, Jr. (1929–1968) was born in Atlanta, Georgia, and earned degrees from Moorehouse College, Crozer Theological Seminary, Boston University, and Chicago Theological Seminary. As a Baptist clergyman, civil-rights leader, founder and president of the Southern Christian Leadership Council, and, in 1964, Nobel Peace Prize winner, King was a celebrated advocate of nonviolent resistance to achieve equality and racial integration in the world. King was a gifted orator and a highly persuasive writer. His books include *Letter from Birmingham City Jail* (1963), *Why We Can't Wait* (1964), *Stride toward Freedom* (1958), *Strength to Love* (1963), and *Where Do We Go from Here: Chaos or Community?* (1967), a book published shortly before he was assassinated on April 4, 1968, in Memphis, Tennessee. In "The World House," a section from his last book, King uses analogy to promote his long-standing vision of a peaceful and united world civilization.

MARTIN LUTHER KING, JR.

The World House

Some years ago a famous novelist died. Among his papers was found a list of suggested plots for future stories, the most prominently underscored being this one: "A widely separated family inherits a house in which they have to live together." This is the great new problem of mankind. We have inherited a large house, a great "world house" in which we have to live together—black and white, Easterner and Westerner, Gentile and Jew, Catholic and Protestant, Moslem and Hindu— a family unduly separated in ideas, culture and interest, who, because we can never again live apart, must learn somehow to live with each other in peace.

However deeply American Negroes are caught in the struggle to be at last at home in our homeland of the United States, we cannot ignore the larger world house in which we are also dwellers. Equality with whites will not solve the problem of either whites or Negroes if it means equality in a world society stricken by poverty and in a universe doomed to extinction by war.

All inhabitants of the globe are now neighbors. This world-wide ₃ neighborhood has been brought into being largely as a result of the modern scientific and technological revolutions. The world of today is vastly different from the world of just one hundred years ago. A century ago Thomas Edison had not yet invented the incandescent lamp to bring light to many dark places of the earth. The Wright brothers had not yet invented that fascinating mechanical bird that would spread its gigantic wings across the skies and soon dwarf distance and place time in the service of man. Einstein had not yet challenged an axiom and the theory of relativity had not yet been posited.

Human beings, searching a century ago as now for better under- ₄ standing, had no television, no radios, no telephones and no motion pictures through which to communicate. Medical science had not yet discovered the wonder drugs to end many dread plagues and diseases. One hundred years ago military men had not yet developed the terrifying weapons of warfare that we know today—not the bomber, an airborne fortress raining down death; nor napalm, that burner of all things and flesh in its path. A century ago there were no skyscraping buildings to kiss the stars and no gargantuan bridges to span the waters. Science had not yet peered into the unfathomable ranges of interstellar space, nor had it penetrated oceanic depths. All these new inventions, these new ideas, these sometimes fascinating and sometimes frightening developments came later. Most of them have come within the past sixty years, sometimes with agonizing slowness, more characteristically with bewildering speed, but always with enormous significance for our future.

The years ahead will see a continuation of the same dramatic devel- ₅ opments. Physical science will carve new highways through the stratosphere. In a few years astronauts and cosmonauts will probably walk comfortably across the uncertain pathways of the moon. In two or three years it will be possible, because of the new supersonic jets, to fly from New York to London in two and one-half hours. In the years ahead medical science will greatly prolong the lives of men by finding a cure for cancer and deadly heart ailments. Automation and cybernation will make it possible for working people to have undreamed-of amounts of leisure time. All this is a dazzling picture of the furniture, the workshop, the spacious rooms, the new decorations and the architectural pattern of the large world house in which we are living.

Along with the scientific and technological revolution, we have also ₆ witnessed a world-wide freedom revolution over the last few decades. The present upsurge of the Negro people of the United States grows out of a deep and passionate determination to make freedom and equality a reality "here" and "now." In one sense the civil rights movement in the United States is a special American phenomenon which must be understood in the light of American history and dealt with in terms of the American situation. But on another and more important level, what is happening in the United States today is a significant part of a world development.

We live in a day, said the philosopher Alfred North Whitehead, 7 "when civilization is shifting its basic outlook; a major turning point in history where the pre-suppositions on which society is structured are being analyzed, sharply challenged, and profoundly changed." What we are seeing now is a freedom explosion, the realization of "an idea whose time has come," to use Victor Hugo's phrase. The deep rumbling of discontent that we hear today is the thunder of disinherited masses, rising from dungeons of oppression to the bright hills of freedom. In one majestic chorus the rising masses are singing, in the words of our freedom song, "Ain't gonna let nobody turn us around." All over the world like a fever, freedom is spreading in the widest liberation movement in history. The great masses of people are determined to end the exploitation of their races and lands. They are awake and moving toward their goal like a tidal wave. You can hear them rumbling in every village street, on the docks, in the houses, among the students, in the churches and at political meetings. For several centuries the direction of history flowed from the nations and societies of Western Europe out into the rest of the world in "conquests" of various sorts. That period, the era of colonialism, is at an end. East is moving West. The earth is being redistributed. Yes, we are "shifting our basic outlooks."

These developments should not surprise any student of history. 8 Oppressed people cannot remain oppressed forever. The yearning for freedom eventually manifests itself. The Bible tells the thrilling story of how Moses stood in Pharaoh's court centuries ago and cried, "Let my people go." This was an opening chapter in a continuing story. The present struggle in the United States is a later chapter in the same story. Something within has reminded the Negro of his birthright of freedom, and something without has reminded him that it can be gained. Consciously or unconsciously, he has been caught up by the spirit of the times, and with his black brothers of Africa and his brown and yellow brothers in Asia, South America and the Caribbean, the United States Negro is moving with a sense of great urgency toward the promised land of racial justice.

Nothing could be more tragic than for men to live in these revo- 9 lutionary times and fail to achieve the new attitudes and the new mental outlooks that the new situation demands. In Washington Irving's familiar story of Rip Van Winkle, the one thing that we usually remember is that Rip slept twenty years. There is another important point, however, that is almost always overlooked. It was the sign on the inn in the little town on the Hudson from which Rip departed and scaled the mountain for his long sleep. When he went up, the sign had a picture of King George III of England. When he came down, twenty years later, the sign had a picture of George Washington. As he looked at the picture of the first President of the United States, Rip was confused, flustered and lost. He knew not who Washington was. The most striking thing about this story is not that Rip slept twenty years, but that he slept through a revolution that would alter the course of human history.

*Chapter
Thirteen
Civilization*

One of the great liabilities of history is that all too many people fail to remain awake through great periods of social change. Every society has its protectors of the status quo and its fraternities of the indifferent who are notorious for sleeping through revolutions. But today our very survival depends on our ability to stay awake, to adjust to new ideas, to remain vigilant and to face the challenge of change. The large house in which we live demands that we transform this world-wide neighborhood into a world-wide brotherhood. Together we must learn to live as brothers or together we will be forced to perish as fools.

We must work passionately and indefatigably to bridge the gulf between our scientific progress and our moral progress. One of the great problems of mankind is that we suffer from a poverty of the spirit which stands in glaring contrast to our scientific and technological abundance. The richer we have become materially, the poorer we have become morally and spiritually.

Every man lives in two realms, the internal and the external. The internal is that realm of spiritual ends expressed in art, literature, morals and religion. The external is that complex of devices, techniques, mechanisms and instrumentalities by means of which we live. Our problem today is that we have allowed the internal to become lost in the external. We have allowed the means by which we live to outdistance the ends for which we live. So much of modern life can be summarized in that suggestive phrase of Thoreau: "Improved means to an unimproved end." This is the serious predicament, the deep and haunting problem, confronting modern man. Enlarged material powers spell enlarged peril if there is not proportionate growth of the soul. When the external of man's nature subjugates the internal, dark storm clouds begin to form.

Western civilization is particularly vulnerable at this moment, for our material abundance has brought us neither peace of mind nor serenity of spirit. An Asian writer has portrayed our dilemma in candid terms:

> You call your thousand material devices "labor-saving machinery," yet you are forever "busy." With the multiplying of your machinery you grow increasingly fatigued, anxious, nervous, dissatisfied. Whatever you have, you want more; and wherever you are you want to go somewhere else . . . your devices are neither time-saving nor soul-saving machinery. They are so many sharp spurs which urge you on to invent more machinery and to do more business.[1]

This tells us something about our civilization that cannot be cast aside as a prejudiced charge by an Eastern thinker who is jealous of Western prosperity. We cannot escape the indictment.

This does not mean that we must turn back the clock of scientific progress. No one can overlook the wonders that science has wrought

---

[1] Abraham Mitrie Rihbany, *Wise Men from the East and from the West,* Houghton, Mifflin, 1922.

for our lives. The automobile will not abdicate in favor of the horse and buggy, or the train in favor of the stagecoach, or the tractor in favor of the hand plow, or the scientific method in favor of ignorance and superstition. But our moral and spiritual "lag" must be redeemed. When scientific power outruns moral power, we end up with guided missiles and misguided men. When we foolishly minimize the internal of our lives and maximize the external, we sign the warrant for our own day of doom.

Our hope for creative living in this world house that we have inher- 15 ited lies in our ability to re-establish the moral ends of our lives in personal character and social justice. Without this spiritual and moral reawakening we shall destroy ourselves in the misuse of our own instruments.

COMPREHENSION

1. What does the author mean by the concept of a "world house"? How is the modern era drawing the peoples of the world together? How does King explain the dangers confronting the world house? What is his proposal for "creative living"?
2. According to King, what are the two "realms" that we live in? How are these realms reflected in the content of this selection?
3. Explain the connection that King draws between oppression, freedom, and revolution.

RHETORIC

1. King, a compelling preacher and speaker (see his "I Have a Dream" speech in Chapter 6, a contemporary classic delivered in 1963 at the end of the March on Washington), often delivered his prose in biblical and oratorical rhythms. Find three examples of rhythmical, carefully balanced cadences in this essay, and explain their effect. Compare these rhythms with those in "I Have a Dream."
2. A second characteristic of King's oratorical and literary style is his fondness for figurative language. Locate and identify five examples of figurative language.
3. What is King's thesis? How does the key rhetorical strategy of analogy help to advance it? What minor analogies exist in the essay?
4. Describe King's relationship with his reading audience. Identify words and phrases that clarify this relationship. Why, for example, does the author use the prounoun *we?*
5. How do the first and last paragraphs serve as a frame for this selection? How effective are they? Why?
6. What argumentative and persuasive techniques do you detect in this essay? How does King use illustration, comparison, and contrast to advance his proposition?

1. Comment on the relevance of King's analogy to the 1990s.
2. Write a paper on "the world house," using contemporary events, quotations from authorities, and your own ideas about today's conflicts to frame the analogy.
3. Using Whitehead's quotation (paragraph 7) as a guide, develop an argumentative essay on whether we are at a turning point in civilization.

MARGARET ATWOOD   Margaret Atwood (b. 1939) is a Canadian-born poet, novelist, short-story writer, and critic whose work explores the role of personal consciousness in a troubled world. While her second collection of poems, *The Circle Game* (1966), brought her recognition, she is also well known for her novels, which include *Surfacing* (1973), *Life before Man* (1979), *The Handmaid's Tale* (1986), and *Cat's Eye* (1988). Atwood is interested in the complexities of language, and her subjects range from the personal to the global. In the following piece from *Mother Jones* magazine, Atwood draws a provocative parallel between male behavior and the American influence in Canada.

MARGARET ATWOOD

Canadians: What Do They Want?

Last month, during a poetry reading, I tried out a short prose poem   1
called "How to Like Men." It began by suggesting that one start with the feet. Unfortunately, the question of jackboots soon arose, and things went on from there. After the reading I had a conversation with a young man who thought I had been unfair to men. He wanted men to be liked totally, not just from the heels to the knees, and not just as individuals but as a group; and he thought it negative and inegalitarian of me to have alluded to war and rape. I pointed out that as far as any of us knew these were two activities not widely engaged in by women, but he was still upset. "We're both in this together," he protested. I admitted that this was so; but could he, maybe, see that our relative positions might be a little different.

This is the conversation one has with Americans, even, uh, *good*   2
Americans, when the dinner-table conversation veers round to Canadian-American relations. "We're in this together," they like to say, especially when it comes to continental energy reserves. How do you *explain* to them, as delicately as possible, why they are not categorically beloved? It gets like the old Lifebuoy ads: even their best friends won't tell them. And Canadians are supposed to be their best friends, right? Members of the family?

Well, sort of. Across the river from Michigan, so near and yet so far, there I was at the age of eight, reading *their* Donald Duck comic books (originated however by one of *ours;* yes, Walt Disney's parents were Canadian) and coming at the end to Popsicle Pete, who promised me the earth if only I would save wrappers, but took it all away from me again with a single asterisk: Offer Good Only in the United States. Some cynical members of the world community may be forgiven for thinking that the same asterisk is there, in invisible ink, on the Constitution and the Bill of Rights.

But quibbles like that aside, and good will assumed, how does one go about liking Americans? Where does one begin? Or, to put it another way, why did the Canadian women lock themselves in the john during a '70s, "international" feminist conference being held in Toronto? Because the American sisters were being "imperialist," that's why.

But then, it's always a little naive of Canadians to expect that Americans, of whatever political stamp, should stop being imperious. How can they? The fact is that the United States is an empire and Canada is to it as Gaul was to Rome.

It's hard to explain to Americans what it feels like to be a Canadian. Pessimists among us would say that one has to translate the experience into their own terms and that this is necessary because Americans are incapable of thinking in any other terms—and this in itself is part of the problem. (Witness all those draft dodgers who went into culture shock when they discovered to their horror that Toronto was not Syracuse.)

Here is a translation: Picture a Mexico with a population ten times larger than that of the United States. That would put it at about two billion. Now suppose that the official American language is Spanish, that 75 percent of the books Americans buy and 90 percent of the movies they see are Mexican, and that the profits flow across the border to Mexico. If an American does scrape it together to make a movie, the Mexicans won't let him show it in the States, because they own the distribution outlets. If anyone tries to change this ratio, not only the Mexicans but many fellow Americans cry "National chauvinism," or, even more effectively, "National socialism." After all, the American public prefers the Mexican product. It's what they're used to.

Retranslate and you have the current American-Canadian picture. It's changed a little recently, not only on the cultural front. For instance, Canada, some think a trifle late, is attempting to regain control of its own petroleum industry. Americans are predictably angry. They think of Canadian oil as *theirs.*

"What's mine is yours," they have said for years, meaning exports: "What's yours is mine" means ownership and profits. Canadians are supposed to do retail buying, not controlling, or what's an empire for? One could always refer Americans to history, particularly that of their own revolution. They objected to the colonial situation when they themselves were a colony; but then, revolution is considered one of a

669

very few homegrown American products that definitely are not for export.

Objectively, one cannot become too self-righteous about this state 10 of affairs. Canadians owned lots of things, including their souls, before World War II. After that they sold, some say because they had put too much into financing the war, which created a capital vacuum (a position they would not have been forced into if the Americans hadn't kept out of the fighting for so long, say the sore losers). But for whatever reason, capital flowed across the border in the '50s, and Canadians, traditionally sock-under-the-mattress hoarders, were reluctant to invest in their own country. Americans did it for them and ended up with a large part of it, which they retain to this day. In every sellout there's a seller as well as a buyer, and the Canadians did a thorough job of trading their birthright for a mess.

That's on the capitalist end, but when you turn to the trade union 11 side of things you find much the same story, except that the sellout happened in the '30s under the banner of the United Front. Now Canadian workers are finding that in any empire the colonial branch plants are the first to close, and what could be a truly progressive labor movement has been weakened by compromised bargains made in international union headquarters south of the border.

Canadians are sometimes snippy to Americans at cocktail parties. 12 They don't like to feel owned and they don't like having been sold. But what really bothers them—and it's at this point that the United States and Rome part company—is the wide-eyed innocence with which their snippiness is greeted.

Innocence becomes ignorance when seen in the light of interna- 13 tional affairs, and though ignorance is one of the spoils of conquest— the Gauls always knew more about the Romans than the Romans knew about them—the world can no longer afford America's ignorance. Its ignorance of Canada, though it makes Canadians bristle, is a minor and relatively harmless example. More dangerous is the fact that individual Americans seem not to know that the United States is an imperial power and is behaving like one. They don't want to admit that empires dominate, invade and subjugate—and live on the proceeds—or, if they do admit it, they believe in their divine right to do so. The export of divine right is much more harmful than the export of Coca-Cola, though they may turn out to be much the same thing in the end.

Other empires have behaved similarly (the British somewhat better, 14 Genghis Khan decidedly worse); but they have not expected to be *liked* for it. It's the final Americanism, this passion for being liked. Alas, many Americans are indeed likable; they are often more generous, more welcoming, more enthusiastic, less picky and sardonic than Canadians, and it's not enough to say it's only because they can afford it. Some of that revolutionary spirit still remains: the optimism, the eighteenth-century belief in the fixability of almost anything, the conviction of the possibility of change. However, at cocktail parties and elsewhere one must be able to tell the difference between an individual and a foreign policy. Canadians can no longer afford to think of Americans as only a spectator sport. If Reagan blows up the world, we will unfortunately be doing more than watching it on television. "No annihilation without representation" sounds good as a slogan, but if we run it up the flagpole, who's going to salute?

We *are* all in this together. For Canadians, the question is how to 15 survive it. For Americans there is no question, because there does not have to be. Canada is just that vague, cold place where their uncle used to go fishing, before the lakes went dead from acid rain.

How do you like Americans? Individually, it's easier. Your average 16 American is no more responsible for the state of affairs than your average man is for war and rape. Any Canadian who is so narrow-minded as to dislike Americans merely on principle is missing out on one of the good things in life. The same might be said, to women, of men. As a group, as a foreign policy, it's harder. But if you like men, you can like Americans. Cautiously. Selectively. Beginning with the feet. One at a time.

COMPREHENSION

1. Atwood makes a connection between men and an imperialistic America. How does the title help expand this link? Is this thread woven into the total essay?
2. How has Canada's sometimes reluctant connection to the United States imperiled its sense of identity? How does America's attitude continue to worsen the problem?
3. How does Atwood define the American character?

RHETORIC

1. Who is Atwood's intended audience? Does she expect a sympathetic reader? An antagonist? What in her language and approach suggest the answer to these questions?
2. Describe Atwood's tone in the essay. Provide evidence from her writing.
3. How does the comparative method serve to unify this essay? What points of comparison does Atwood draw?
4. What historical analogy recurs in Atwood's essay? How does it strengthen Atwood's contention? Why does she choose not to recount the event?
5. Comment on the writer's use of generalization in her essay. Cite an example of this, and critique Atwood's support of it.
6. How does Atwood bring the reader back to her original point? What effect do the final phrases in her conclusion have on the reader?

1. Write a rebuttal essay defending America's forays into other countries. List the ways in which America has benefited Canada and other countries it has formed bonds with. How has American "imperialism" raised these countries' economy and standard of living? Use Atwood's article as it applies. Some research may be necessary.

2. Write an essay entitled "What's Wrong with Nationalism?" You may treat the topic in a tongue-in-cheek fashion, or you may approach it seriously.

3. Is America's influence on Canada's national identity and culture an example of Reed's "multinational society"? Explore this question in a brief essay. Use support from both essays.

CLASSIC AND CONTEMPORARY

OLIVER GOLDSMITH Oliver Goldsmith (1730–1774), the son of an Anglican curate, was an Anglo-Irish essayist, poet, novelist, dramatist, and journalist. His reputation as an enduring figure in English literature is based on his novel, *The Vicar of Wakefield* (1766); his play, *She Stoops to Conquer* (1773); his major poem, *The Deserted Village* (1770); and the essays and satiric letters collected in *The Bee* (1759) and *The Citizen of the World* (1762). In this essay from the latter, Goldsmith argues quietly for a new type of citizen, one who can transcend the xenophobia governing national behavior.

OLIVER GOLDSMITH

National Prejudices

As I am one of that sauntering tribe of mortals, who spend the greatest part of their time in taverns, coffee houses, and other places of public resort, I have thereby an opportunity of observing an infinite variety of characters, which, to a person of a contemplative turn, is a much higher entertainment than a view of all the curiosities of art or nature. In one of these, my late rambles, I accidentally fell into the company of half a dozen gentlemen, who were engaged in a warm dispute about some political affair; the decision of which, as they were equally divided in their sentiments, they thought proper to refer to me, which naturally drew me in for a share of the conversation.

Amongst a multiplicity of other topics, we took occasion to talk of the different characters of the several nations of Europe; when one of the gentlemen, cocking his hat, and assuming such an air of importance as if he had possessed all the merit of the English nation in his own person, declared that the Dutch were a parcel of avaricious wretches; the French a set of flattering sycophants; that the Germans were drunken sots, and beastly gluttons; and the Spaniards proud, haughty, and surly tyrants; but that in bravery, generosity, clemency, and in every other virtue, the English excelled all the rest of the world.

This very learned and judicious remark was received with a general smile of approbation by all the company—all, I mean, but your humble servant; who, endeavoring to keep my gravity as well as I could, and reclining my head upon my arm, continued for some time in a posture of affected thoughtfulness, as if I had been musing on something else, and did not seem to attend to the subject of conversation; hoping by these means to avoid the disagreeable necessity of explaining myself, and thereby depriving the gentleman of his imaginary happiness.

But my pseudo-patriot had no mind to let me escape so easily. Not satisfied that his opinion should pass without contradiction, he was determined to have it ratified by the suffrage of every one in the company; for which purpose addressing himself to me with an air of inexpressible confidence, he asked me if I was not of the same way of thinking. As I am never forward in giving my opinion, especially when I have reason to believe that it will not be agreeable; so, when I am obliged to give it, I always hold it for a maxim to speak my real sentiments. I therefore told him that, for my own part, I should not have ventured to talk in such a peremptory strain, unless I had made the tour of Europe, and examined the manners of these several nations with great care and accuracy: that, perhaps, a more impartial judge would not scruple to affirm that the Dutch were more frugal and industrious, the French more temperate and polite, the Germans more hardy and patient of labour and fatigue, and the Spaniards more staid and sedate, than the English; who, though undoubtedly brave and generous, were at the same time rash, headstrong, and impetuous; too apt to be elated with prosperity, and to despond in adversity.

I could easily perceive that all the company began to regard me with a jealous eye before I had finished my answer, which I had no sooner done, than the patriotic gentleman observed, with a contemptuous sneer, that he was greatly surprised how some people could have the conscience to live in a country which they did not love, and to enjoy the protection of a government, to which in their hearts they were inveterate enemies. Finding that by this modest declaration of my sentiments I had forfeited the good opinion of my companions, and given them occasion to call my political principles in question, and well knowing that it was in vain to argue with men who were so very full of themselves, I threw down my reckoning and retired to my own lodgings, reflecting on the absurd and ridiculous nature of national prejudice and prepossession.

Among all the famous sayings of antiquity, there is none that does greater honour to the author, or affords greater pleasure to the reader (at least if he be a person of a generous and benevolent heart), than that of the philosopher, who, being asked what "countryman he was,"

673

replied, that he was, "a citizen of the world."—How few are there to be found in modern times who can say the same, or whose conduct is consistent with such a profession!—We are now become so much Englishmen, Frenchmen, Dutchmen, Spaniards, or Germans, that we are no longer citizens of the world; so much the natives of one particular spot, or members of one petty society, that we no longer consider ourselves as the general inhabitants of the globe, or members of that grand society which comprehends the whole human kind.

Did these prejudices prevail only among the meanest and lowest 7 of the people, perhaps they might be excused, as they have few, if any, opportunities of correcting them by reading, travelling, or conversing with foreigners; but the misfortune is, that they infect the minds, and influence the conduct, even of our gentlemen; of those, I mean, who have every title to this appellation but an exemption from prejudice, which however, in my opinion, ought to be regarded as the characteristical mark of a gentleman; for let a man's birth be ever so high, his station ever so exalted, or his fortune ever so large, yet if he is not free from national and other prejudices, I should make bold to tell him, that he had a low and vulgar mind, and had no just claim to the character of a gentleman. And in fact, you will always find that those are most apt to boast of national merit, who have little or no merit of their own to depend on; than which, to be sure, nothing is more natural: the slender vine twists around the sturdy oak, for no other reason in the world but because it has not strength sufficient to support itself.

Should it be alleged in defense of national prejudice, that it is the 8 natural and necessary growth of love to our country, and that therefore the former cannot be destroyed without hurting the latter, I answer, that this is a gross fallacy and delusion. That it is the growth of love to our country, I will allow; but that it is the natural and necessary growth of it, I absolutely deny. Superstition and enthusiasm too are the growth of religion; but who ever took it in his head to affirm that they are the necessary growth of this noble principle? They are, if you will, the bastard sprouts of this heavenly plant, but not its natural and genuine branches, and may safely enough be lopped off, without doing any harm to the parent stock; nay, perhaps, till once they are lopped off, this goodly tree can never flourish in perfect health and vigour.

It is not very possible that I may love my own country, without hat- 9 ing the natives of other countries? that I may exert the most heroic bravery, the most undaunted resolution, in defending its laws and liberty, without despising all the rest of the world as cowards and poltroons? Most certainly it is; and if it were not—But why need I suppose what is absolutely impossible?—But if it were not, I must own, I should prefer the title of the ancient philosopher, viz. a citizen of the world, to that of an Englishman, a Frenchman, a European, or to any other appellation whatever.

COMPREHENSION

1. Why does Goldsmith maintain that he is "a citizen of the world"? According to the author, could such an individual also be a patriot? Explain.
2. What connection does Goldsmith make between national prejudices and the conduct of gentlemen? Why does he allude to the manners of gentlemen?
3. Compare and contrast Goldsmith's observations with those of Priestley in "Wrong Ism" (Chapter 6).

RHETORIC

1. Locate in the essay examples of the familiar style in writing. What is the relationship between this style and the tone and substance of the essay?
2. Explain the metaphors at the end of paragraphs 7 and 8.
3. What is the relevance of the introductory narrative, with its description of characters, to the author's declaration of thesis? Where does the author state his proposition concerning national prejudices?
4. Analyze the function of classification and contrast in paragraphs 2 to 5. How does the entire essay serve as a pattern of definition?
5. Examine the pattern of reasoning involved in the author's presentation of his argument in the essay, notably in paragraphs 6 to 8. What appeals to emotion and to reason does he make?
6. Assess the rhetorical effectiveness of Goldsmith's concluding paragraph.

WRITING

1. Why has it been difficult to eliminate the problem that Goldsmith posed in 1762? Are we better able today to function as citizens of the world? In what ways? What role does the United Nations play in this issue? What factors contribute to a new world citizenry? Explore these questions in an essay.
2. Write an argumentative essay on the desirability of world government or on the need to be a citizen of the world.
3. Write a paper on contemporary *national* prejudices—from the viewpoint of an *ingenious* foreigner.

ARTHUR M. SCHLESINGER, Jr.   Arthur Meien Schlesinger, Jr., was born in Columbus, Ohio, in 1917 and received his A.B. degree from Harvard University in 1938. Schlesinger has combined careers as a writer, college professor, political activist, and President Kennedy's special assistant for Latin American affairs. Schlesinger is perhaps most responsible for the intellectual position of what is today generally known as *liberalism.* He has written more than a dozen books on history and politics, among the most famous being *The Age of Jackson,* for which he won the 1946 Pulitzer Prize for history; *Robert Kennedy and His Times* (1978); and *A Thousand Days,* for which he won the 1966 Pulitzer Prize for biography. He has also edited many books on the American political process. While never earning an advanced degree as a student, he has been awarded numerous honorary degrees from universities in the United States and England. Critic Alan Brinkley wrote of Schlesinger in the *New Republic,* "He is a reminder to professional historians of the possibilities of reaching beyond their own ranks to the larger world in which they live."

ARTHUR M. SCHLESINGER, JR.

The Cult of Ethnicity

The history of the world has been in great part the history of the mix- 1 ing of peoples. Modern communication and transport accelerate mass migrations from one continent to another. Ethnic and racial diversity is more than ever a salient fact of the age.

But what happens when people of different origins, speaking differ- 2 ent languages and professing different religions, inhabit the same local-ity and live under the same political sovereignty? Ethnic and racial con-flict—far more than ideological conflict—is the explosive problem of our times.

On every side today ethnicity is breaking up nations. The Soviet 3 Union, India, Yugoslavia, Ethiopia, are all in crisis. Ethnic tensions dis-turb and divide Sri Lanka, Burma, Indonesia, Iraq, Cyprus, Nigeria, Angola, Lebanon, Guyana, Trinidad—you name it. Even nations as sta-ble and civilized as Britain and France, Belgium and Spain, face grow-ing ethnic troubles. Is there any large multiethnic state that can be made to work?

The answer to that question has been, until recently, the United 4 States. "No other nation," Margaret Thatcher has said, "has so suc-cessfully combined people of different races and nations within a single culture." How have Americans succeeded in pulling off this almost unprecedented trick?

We have always been a multiethnic country. Hector St. John de 5 Crevecoeur, who came from France in the 18th century, marveled at the astonishing diversity of the settlers—"a mixture of English, Scotch, Irish, French, Dutch, Germans and Swedes . . . this promiscuous breed." He propounded a famous question: "What then is the Ameri-can, this new man?" And he gave a famous answer: "Here individuals of all nations are melted into a new race of men." *E pluribus unum.*

The U.S. escaped the divisiveness of a multiethnic society by a bril- 6 liant solution: the creation of a brand-new national identity. The point of America was not to preserve old cultures but to forge a new, Amer-ican culture. "By an intermixture with our people," President George Washington told Vice President John Adams, immigrants will "get assimilated to our customs, measures and laws: in a word, soon become one people." This was the ideal that a century later Israel Zangwill crys-tallized in the title of his popular 1908 play *The Melting Pot.* And no institution was more potent in molding Crevecoeur's "promiscuous breed" into Washington's "one people" than the American public school.

The new American nationality was inescapably English in language, ideas and institutions. The pot did not melt everybody, not even all the white immigrants; deeply bred racism put black Americans, yellow Americans, red Americans and brown Americans well outside the pale. Still, the infusion of other stocks, even of nonwhite stocks, and the experience of the New World reconfigured the British legacy and made the U.S., as we all know, a very different country from Britain.

In the 20th century, new immigration laws altered the composition of the American people, and a cult of ethnicity erupted both among non-Anglo whites and among nonwhite minorities. This had many healthy consequences. The American culture at last began to give shamefully overdue recognition to the achievements of groups subordinated and spurned during the high noon of Anglo dominance, and it began to acknowledge the great swirling world beyond Europe. Americans acquired a more complex and invigorating sense of their world—and of themselves.

But, pressed too far, the cult of ethnicity has unhealthy consequences. It gives rise, for example, to the conception of the U.S. as a nation composed not of individuals making their own choices but of inviolable ethnic and racial groups. It rejects the historic American goals of assimilation and integration.

And, in an excess of zeal, well-intentioned people seek to transform our system of education from a means of creating "one people" into a means of promoting, celebrating and perpetuating separate ethnic origins and identities. The balance is shifting from *unum* to *pluribus*.

That is the issue that lies behind the hullabaloo over "multiculturalism" and "political correctness," the attack on the "Eurocentric" curriculum and the rise of the notion that history and literature should be taught not as disciplines but as therapies whose function is to raise minority self-esteem. Group separatism crystallizes the differences, magnifies tensions, intensifies hostilities. Europe—the unique source of the liberating ideas of democracy, civil liberties and human rights—is portrayed as the root of all evil, and non-European cultures, their own many crimes deleted, are presented as the means of redemption.

I don't want to sound apocalyptic about these developments. Education is always in ferment, and a good thing too. The situation in our universities, I am confident, will soon right itself. But the impact of separatist pressures on our public schools is more troubling. If a Kleagle of the Ku Klux Klan wanted to use the schools to disable and handicap black Americans, he could hardly come up with anything more effective than the "Afrocentric" curriculum. And if separatist tendencies go unchecked, the result can only be the fragmentation, resegregation and tribalization of American life.

I remain optimistic. My impression is that the historic forces driving toward "one people" have not lost their power. The eruption of ethnicity is, I believe, a rather superficial enthusiasm stirred by romantic ideologues on the one hand and by unscrupulous con men on the other: self-appointed spokesmen whose claim to represent their minority groups is carelessly accepted by the media. Most American-born members of minority groups, white or nonwhite, see themselves primarily as Americans rather than primarily as members of one or another ethnic group. A notable indicator today is the rate of intermarriage across ethnic lines, across religious lines, even (increasingly) across racial lines. "We Americans," said Theodore Roosevelt, "are children of the crucible."

The growing diversity of the American population makes the quest 14 for unifying ideals and a common culture all the more urgent. In a world savagely rent by ethnic and racial antagonisms, the U.S. must continue as an example of how a highly differentiated society holds itself together.

COMPREHENSION

1. What is a *cult?* What is the significance of the word in Schlesinger's title?
2. According to Schlesinger, what social institution has been the most significant in forgoing a commonality among Americans?
3. Why does Schlesinger claim that an "Afrocentric curriculum" would disable and handicap black Americans?

RHETORIC

1. This essay might be considered a problem/solution essay. What evidence is there in its structure to support this view?
2. In paragraph 3, the author cites many countries where internal ethnic conflict has or is occurring. Why are they merely listed without being explained on a case-by-case basis? What does this imply about the author's expectations of his audience?
3. Nearly all of the appeals to authority used by the author are historical figures. Why has he chosen to refer to thinkers hundreds of years old rather than contemporary ones?
4. The author places terms such as "one people," "multiculturalism," "political correctness," and "Eurocentric" in quotation marks. Why?
5. The introductory material to the essay is in the form of two paragraphs, separated by the conjunction *but.* Why didn't the author simply join these paragraphs into one?
6. Examine the rather lengthy sentence that begins paragraph 11. What formal device does the author use in order to keep the sentence coherent?

WRITING

1. Argue for or against the proposition that personal identification with a specific ethnic or cultural group results in alienation from society as a whole.

2. For a research project, define and describe the idea of a *cult,* and argue for or against the proposition that the author is using the term in an appropriate way regarding ethnicity.
3. Argue for or against the view that the United States should adopt English as its official language.

CLASSIC AND CONTEMPORARY

1. How do the respective tones of Goldsmith's and Schlesinger's essays differ? What clues are contained in the text that make this difference evident? Use examples from both.
2. In his essay, Goldsmith argues against nationalism and professes to be a "citizen of the world." Compare Schlesinger's argument that someone deciding to live as an American should consider himself or herself an American first. Are these opposing arguments, are they similar arguments, or do they contain both opposing *and* similar arguments?
3. Discuss both Schlesinger's and Goldsmith's essays in terms of formality of voice. Does one author speak with more authority than the other? If so, what elements of language contribute toward this formality. Use examples from both essays.

1. How does a country maintain a strong sense of self and still remain open to outside influences? Is a national identity crucial to a country's survival? Use the opinions of Atwood, Reed, Naipaul, or Jhabvala to address the question.

2. In his essay, Naipaul expresses his belief that Muslims have been "stripped by their faith." How do his views of religion as an impediment to a "universal civilization" clash with Martin Luther King's overtly religious approach to the issue? Use support from both writers to compare and contrast their points of view.

3. Compare America's involvement in Canada's cultural and economic life to that of Europe's in India's. What are the advantages and disadvantages of such an involvement?

4. How does Baldwin's contention that there is no longer a home to which the American white man can return illustrate Reed's rejection of the concept of a Western civilization?

5. Is there such a thing as a "national character," something that distinguishes an Indian from a European, an American from a Canadian? What factors contribute to this identification with country? Use the works of Jhabvala, Naipaul, Iyer, and Atwood to explore this issue.

6. Although Lance Morrow takes an apocalyptic approach to global problems, what concerns does he share with the other writers in this section?

7. Use the essays of Goldsmith, Naipaul, and King to explore the dangers of nationalism to a country's relation to its own people and the larger world. What are the consequences of a "monoculturalist" outlook?

8. Compare Baldwin's belief that the African American has only one home with King's dreams of a "world house." Have we yet achieved an "American House"? Where do the two writers come together on issues? Where do they differ?

9. Based on your reading of the essays in this chapter and throughout the anthology, write an extended definition of the term *civilization.*

10. Argue for or against the proposition that we are becoming a one-world civilization. Refer to the essays in this chapter to support your position.

Glossary of Terms

Abstract/concrete: patterns of language reflect an author's word choice. Abstract words (for example, *wisdom, power, beauty*) refer to general ideas, qualities, or conditions. Concrete words name material objects and items associated with the five senses—words like *rock, pizza,* and *basketball.* Both abstract and concrete language are useful in communicating ideas. Generally you should not be too abstract in writing. It is best to employ concrete words, naming things that can be seen, touched, smelled, heard, or tasted in order to support generalizations, topic sentences, or more abstract ideas.

Acronym: is a word formed from the first or first few letters of several words, as in OPEC (Organization of Petroleum Exporting Countries).

Action: in narrative writing is the sequence of happenings or events. This movement of events may occupy just a few minutes or extend over a period of years or centuries.

Alliteration: is the repetition of initial consonant sounds in words placed closely next to each other, as in "what a *t*ale of *t*error now their *t*urbulency *t*ells." Prose that is highly rhythmical or "poetic" often makes use of this method.

Allusion: is a literary, biographical, or historical reference, whether real or imaginary. It is a "figure of speech" (a fresh, useful comparison) employed to illuminate an idea. A writer's prose style can be made richer through this economical method of evoking an idea or emotion, as in E. M. Forster's biblical allusion in this sentence: "Property produces men of weight, and it was a man of weight who failed to get into the Kingdom of Heaven."

Analogy: is a form of comparison that uses a clear illustration to explain a difficult idea or function. It is unlike a formal comparison in that its subjects of comparison are from different categories or areas. For example, an analogy likening "division of labor" to the activity of bees in a hive makes the first concept more concrete by showing it to the reader through the figurative comparison with the bees. Analogy in exposition can involve a few sentences, a paragraph or set of paragraphs, or an entire essay. Analogies can also be used in argumentation to heighten an appeal to emotion, but they cannot actually *prove* anything.

Analysis: is a method of exposition in which a subject is broken up into its parts so as to explain their nature, function, proportion, or relationship. Analysis thus explores connections and processes within the context of a given subject. (See *Causal analysis* and *Process analysis*.)

Anecdote: is a brief, engaging account of some happening, often historical, biographical, or personal. As a technique in writing, anecdote is especially effective in creating interesting essay introductions and also in illuminating abstract concepts in the body of the essay.

Antecedent: in grammar refers to the word, phrase, or clause to which a pronoun refers. In writing, antecedent also refers to any happening or thing that is prior to another, or to anything that logically precedes a subject.

Antithesis: is the balancing of one idea or term against another for emphasis.

Antonym: is a word whose meaning is opposite to that of another word.

Aphorism: is a short, pointed statement expressing a general truism or an idea in an original or imaginative way. Marshall McLuhan's statement that "the medium is the message" is a well-known contemporary aphorism.

Archaic: language is vocabulary or usage that belongs to an early period and is old-fashioned today. A word like *thee* for *you* would be an archaism still in use in certain situations.

Archetypes: are special images or symbols that, according to Carl Jung, appeal to the total racial or cultural understanding of a people. Such images or symbols as the mother archetype, the cowboy in American film, a sacred mountain, or spring as a time of renewal tend to trigger the "collective unconscious" of the human race.

Argumentation: is a formal variety of writing that offers reasons for or against something. Its goal is to persuade or convince the reader through logical reasoning and carefully controlled emotional appeal. Argumentation as a formal mode of writing contains many properties that distinguish it from exposition. (See *Assumption, Deduction, Evidence, Induction, Logic, Persuasion, Proposition,* and *Refutation.*)

Assonance: defined generally is likeness or rough similarity of sound. Its specific definition is a partial rhyme in which the stressed vowel sounds are alike but the consonant sounds are unlike, as in *late* and *make*. Although more common to poetry, assonance can also be detected in highly rhythmic prose.

Assumption: in argumentation is anything taken for granted or presumed to be accepted by the audience and therefore unstated. Assumptions in argumentative writing can be dangerous because the audience might not always accept the idea implicit in them. (See *Begging the question*.)

Audience: is that readership toward which an author directs his or her essay. In composing essays, writers must acknowledge the nature of their expected readers—whether specialized or general, minimally educated or highly educated, sympathetic or unsympathetic toward the writer's opinions, and so forth. Failure to focus on the writer's true audience can lead to confusions in language and usage, presentation of inappropriate content, and failure to appeal to the expected reader.

Balance: in sentence structure refers to the assignment of equal treatment in the arrangement of coordinate ideas. It is often used to heighten a contrast of ideas.

Begging the question: is an error or a fallacy in reasoning and argumentation in which the writer assumes as a truth something for which evidence or proof is actually needed.

Causal analysis: is a form of writing that examines causes and effects of events or conditions as they relate to a specific subject. Writers can investigate the causes of a particular effect or the effects of a particular cause or combine both methods. Basically, however, causal analysis looks for connections between things and reasons behind them.

Characterization: especially in narrative or descriptive writing is the creation of people involved in the action. Authors use techniques of dialogue, description, reportage, and observation in attempting to present vivid and distinctive characters.

Chronology or **Chronological order:** is the arrangement of events in the order in which they happened. Chronological order can be used in such diverse narrative situations as history, biography, scientific process, and personal account. Essays that are ordered by chronology move from one step or point to the next in time.

Cinematic technique: in narration, description, and occasionally exposition is the conscious application of film art to the development of the contemporary essay. Modern writers often are aware of such film techniques as montage (the process of cutting and arranging film so that short scenes are presented in rapid succession), zoom (intense enlargement of subject), and various forms of juxtaposition using these methods to enhance the quality of their essays.

Classification is a form of exposition in which the writer divides a subject into categories and then groups elements in each of those cate-

683

gories according to their relationships with one another. Thus a writer using classification takes a topic, divides it into several major groups, and then often subdivides these groups, moving always from larger categories to smaller ones.

Cliché: is an expression that once was fresh and original but has lost much of its vitality through overuse. Because terms like "as quick as a wink" and "blew her stack" are trite or common today, they should be avoided in writing.

Climactic ordering: is the arrangement of a paragraph or essay so that the most important items are saved for last. The effect is to build slowly through a sequence of events or ideas to the most critical part of the composition.

Coherence: is a quality in effective writing that results from the careful ordering of each sentence in a paragraph and each paragraph in the essay. If an essay is coherent, each part will grow naturally and logically from those parts that come before it. Following careful chronological, logical, spatial, or sequential order is the most natural way to achieve coherence in writing. The main devices used in achieving coherence are transitions, which help to connect one thought with another.

Colloquial language: is conversational language used in certain types of informal and narrative writing but rarely in essays, business writing, or research writing. Expressions like "cool," "pal," or "I can dig it" often have a place in conversational settings. However, they should be used sparingly in essay writing for special effects.

Comparison/contrast: as an essay pattern treats similarities and differences between two subjects. Any useful comparison involves two items from the same class. Moreover, there must be a clear reason for the comparison or contrast. Finally, there must be a balanced treatment of the various comparative or contrasting points between the two subjects.

Conclusions: are the endings of essays. Without a conclusion, an essay would be incomplete, leaving the reader with the feeling that something important has been left out. There are numerous strategies for conclusions available to writers: summarizing main points in the essay, restating the main idea, using an effective quotation to bring the essay to an end, offering the reader the climax to a series of events, returning to the beginning and echoing it, offering a solution to a problem, emphasizing the topic's significance, or setting a new frame of reference by generalizing from the main thesis. A conclusion should end the essay in a clear, convincing, or emphatic way.

Concrete: (See *Abstract/concrete.*)

Conflict: in narrative writing is the clash or opposition of events, characters, or ideas that makes the resolution of action necessary.

Connotation/denotation: are terms specifying the way a word has meaning. Connotation refers to the "shades of meaning" that a word might have because of various emotional associations it calls up for writers and readers alike. Words like *patriotism, pig,* and *rose* have strong connotative overtones to them. Denotation refers to the "dictionary" definition of a word—its exact meaning. Good writers understand the connotative and denotative value of words and must control the shades of meaning that many words possess.

Context: is the situation surrounding a word, group of words, or sentence. Often the elements coming before or after a certain confusing or difficult construction will provide insight into the meaning or importance of that item.

Coordination: in sentence structure refers to the grammatical arrangement of parts of the same order or equality in rank.

Declarative sentences: make a statement or assertion.

Deduction: is a form of logic that begins with a generally stated truth or principle and then offers details, examples, and reasoning to support the generalization. In other words, deduction is based on reasoning from a known principle to an unknown principle, from the general to the specific, or from a premise to a logical conclusion. (See *Syllogism.*)

Definition: in exposition is the extension of a word's meaning through a paragraph or an entire essay. As an extended method of explaining a word, this type of definition relies on other rhetorical methods, including detail, illustration, comparison and contrast, and anecdote.

Denotation: (See *Connotation/denotation.*)

Description: in the prose essay is a variety of writing that uses details of sight, sound, color, smell, taste, and touch to create a word picture and to explain or illustrate an idea.

Development: refers to the way a paragraph or an essay elaborates or builds upon a topic or theme. Typical development proceeds either from general illustrations to specific ones or from one generalization to another. (See *Horizontal/vertical.*)

Dialogue: is the reproduction of speech or conversation between two or more persons in writing. Dialogue can add concreteness and vividness to an essay and can also help to reveal character. A writer who reproduces dialogue in an essay must use it for a purpose and not simply as a decorative device.

Diction: is the manner of expression in words, choice of words, or wording. Writers must choose vocabulary carefully and precisely to communicate a message and also to address an intended audience effectively; this is good diction.

Digression: is a temporary departure from the main subject in writing. Any digression in the essay must serve a purpose or be intended for a specific effect.

Glossary of Terms

Discourse (forms of): relates conventionally to the main categories of writing—narration, description, exposition, and argumentation. In practice, these forms of discourse often blend or overlap. Essayists seek the ideal fusion of forms of discourse in the treatment of their subject.

Division: is that aspect of classification in which the writer divides some large subject into categories. Division helps writers to split large and potentially complicated subjects into parts for orderly presentation and discussion.

Dominant impression: in description is the main impression or effect that writers attempt to create for their subject. It arises from an author's focus on a single subject and from the feelings the writer brings to that subject.

Editorialize: is to express personal opinions about the subject of the essay. An editorial tone can have a useful effect in writing, but at other times an author might want to reduce editorializing in favor of a better balanced or more objective tone.

Effect: is a term used in causal analysis to describe the outcome or expected result of a chain of happenings.

Emphasis: indicates the placement of the most important ideas in key positions in the essay. As a major principle, emphasis relates to phrases, sentences, paragraphs—the construction of the entire essay. Emphasis can be achieved by repetition, subordination, careful positioning of thesis and topic sentences, climactic ordering, comparison and contrast, and a variety of other methods.

Episodic: relates to that variety of narrative writing that develops through a series of incidents or events.

Essay: is the name given to a short prose work on a limited topic. Essays take many forms, ranging from personal narratives to critical or argumentative treatments of a subject. Normally an essay will convey the writer's personal ideas about the subject.

Etymology: is the origin and development of a word—tracing a word back as far as possible.

Evidence: is material offered to support an argument or a proposition. Typical forms of evidence are facts, details, and expert testimony.

Example: is a method of exposition in which the writer offers illustrations in order to explain a generalization or a whole thesis. (See *Illustration.*)

Exclamatory sentences: in writing express surprise or strong emotion.

Expert testimony: as employed in argumentative essays and in expository essays is the use of statements by authorities to support a writer's position or idea. This method often requires careful quotation and acknowledgment of sources.

Exposition: is a major form of discourse that informs or explains. Exposition is the form of expression required in much college writing, for it provides facts and information, clarifies ideas, and establishes meaning. The primary methods of exposition are illustration, comparison and contrast, analogy, definition, classification, causal analysis, and process analysis (see entries).

Extended metaphor: is a figurative comparison that is used to structure a significant part of the composition or the whole essay. (See *Figurative language* and *Metaphor*.)

Fable: is a form of narrative containing a moral that normally appears clearly at the end.

Fallacy: in argumentation is an error in logic or the reasoning process. Fallacies occur because of vague development of ideas, lack of awareness on the part of writers of the requirements of logical reasoning, or faulty assumptions about the proposition.

Figurative language: as opposed to literal language is a special approach to writing that departs from what is typically a concrete, straightforward style. It is the use of vivid, imaginative statements to illuminate or illustrate an idea. Figurative language adds freshness, meaning, and originality to a writer's style. Major figures of speech include allusion, hyperbole, metaphor, personification, and simile (see entries).

Flashback: is a narrative technique in which the writer begins at some point in the action and then moves into the past in order to provide crucial information about characters and events.

Foreshadowing: is a technique that indicates beforehand what is to occur at a later point in the essay.

Frame: in narration and description is the use of a key object or pattern—typically at the start and end of the essay—that serves as a border or structure to contain the substance of the composition.

General/specific words: are the basis of writing, although it is wise in college composition to keep vocabulary as specific as possible. General words refer to broad categories and groups, whereas specific words capture with force and clarity the nature of a term. General words refer to large classes, concepts, groups, and emotions; specific words are more particular in providing meanings. The distinction between general and specific language is always a matter of degree.

Generalization: is a broad idea or statement. All generalizations require particulars and illustrations to support them.

Genre: is a type or form of literature—for example, short fiction, novel, poetry, drama.

Grammatical structure: is a systematic description of language as it relates to the grammatical nature of a sentence.

Horizontal/vertical: paragraph and essay development refers to the basic way a writer moves either from one generalization to another in a carefully related series of generalizations (horizontal) or from a generalization to a series of specific supporting examples (vertical).

Hortatory style: is a variety of writing designed to encourage, give advice, or urge to good deeds.

Hyperbole: is a form of figurative language that uses exaggeration to overstate a position.

Hypothesis: is an unproven theory or proposition that is tentatively accepted to explain certain facts. A working hypothesis provides the basis for further investigation or argumentation.

Hypothetical examples: are illustrations in the form of assumptions that are based on the hypothesis. As such, they are conditional rather than absolute or certain facts.

Identification: as a method of exposition refers to focusing on the main subject of the essay. It involves the clear location of the subject within the context or situation of the composition.

Idiomatic language: is the language or dialect of a people, region, or class—the individual nature of a language.

Ignoring the question: in argumentation is a fallacy that involves the avoidance of the main issue by developing an entirely different one.

Illustration: is the use of one or more examples to support an idea. Illustration permits the writer to support a generalization through particulars or specifics.

Imagery: is clear, vivid description that appeals to our sense of sight, smell, touch, sound, or taste. Much imagery exists for its own sake, adding descriptive flavor to an essay. However, imagery (especially when it involves a larger pattern) can also add meaning to an essay.

Induction: is a method of logic consisting of the presentation of a series of facts, pieces of information, or instances in order to formulate or build a likely generalization. The key is to provide prior examples before reaching a logical conclusion. Consequently, as a pattern of organization in essay writing, the inductive method requires the careful presentation of relevant data and information before the conclusion is reached at the end of the paper.

Inference: involves arriving at a decision or opinion by reasoning from known facts or evidence.

Interrogative sentences: are sentences that ask or pose a question.

Introduction: is the beginning or opening of an essay. The introduction should alert the reader to the subject by identifying it, set the limits of the essay, and indicate what the thesis (or main idea) will be. Moreover, it should arouse the reader's interest in the subject.

Glossary of Terms

Among the devices available in the creation of good introductions are making a simple statement of thesis; giving a clear, vivid description of an important setting; posing a question or series of questions; referring to a relevant historical event; telling an anecdote; using comparison and contrast to frame the subject; using several examples to reinforce the statement of the subject; and presenting a personal attitude about a controversial issue.

Irony: is the use of language to suggest the opposite of what is stated. Writers use irony to reveal unpleasant or troublesome realities that exist in life or to poke fun at human weaknesses and foolish attitudes. In an essay there may be verbal irony, in which the author says one thing but means another, or situational irony, in which the result of a sequence of ideas or events is the opposite of what normally would be expected. A key to the identification of irony in an essay is our ability to detect where the author is stating the opposite of what he or she actually believes.

Issue: is the main question upon which an entire argument rests. It is the idea that the writer attempts to prove.

Jargon: is the use of special words associated with a specific area of knowledge or a particular profession. Writers who employ jargon either assume that readers know specialized terms or take care to define terms for the benefit of the audience.

Juxtaposition: as a technique in writing or essay organization is the placing of elements—either similar or contrasting—close together, positioning them side by side in order to illuminate the subject.

Levels of language: refer to the kinds of language used in speaking and writing. Basically there are three main levels of language—formal, informal, and colloquial. Formal English, used in writing or speech, is the type of English employed to address special groups and professional people. Informal English is the sort of writing found in newspapers, magazines, books, and essays. It is popular English for an educated audience but still more formal than conversational English. Finally, colloquial English is spoken (and occasionally written) English used in conversations with friends, employees, and peer group members; it is characterized by the use of slang, idioms, ordinary language, and loose sentence structure.

Linear order: in paragraph development means the clear line of movement from one point to another.

Listing: is a simple technique of illustration in which facts or examples are used in order to support a topic or generalization.

Logic: as applied to essay writing is correct reasoning based on induction or deduction. The logical basis of an essay must offer reasonable criteria or principles of thought, present these principles in an orderly manner, avoid faults in reasoning, and result in a complete and satisfactory outcome in the reasoning process.

689

Metaphor: is a type of figurative language in which an item from one category is compared briefly and imaginatively with an item from another area. Writers use such implied comparisons to assign meaning in a fresh, vivid, and concrete way.

Metonymy: is a figure of language in which a thing is not designated by its own name but by another associated with or suggested by it, as in "The Supreme Court has decided" (meaning that the judges of the Supreme Court have decided).

Mood: is the creation of atmosphere in descriptive writing.

Motif: in an essay is any series of components that can be detected as a pattern. For example, a particular detail, idea, or image can be elaborated upon or designed so as to form a pattern or motif in the essay.

Myth: in literature is a traditional story or series of events explaining some basic phenomenon of nature; the origin of humanity; or the customs, institutions, and religious rites of a people. Myth often relates to the exploits of gods, goddesses, and heroes.

Narration: as a form of essay writing is the presentation of a story in order to illustrate an idea.

Non sequitur: in argumentation is a conclusion or inference that does not follow from the premises or evidence on which it is based. The non sequitur thus is a type of logical fallacy.

Objective/subjective: writing refers to the attitude that writers take toward their subject. When writers are objective, they try not to report their personal feelings about the subject; they attempt to be detached, impersonal, and unbiased. Conversely, subjective writing reveals an author's personal attitudes and emotions. For many varieties of college writing, such as business or laboratory reports, term papers, and literary analyses, it is best to be as objective as possible. But for many personal essays in composition courses, the subjective touch is fine. In the hands of skilled writers, the objective and subjective tones often blend.

Onomatopoeia: is the formation of a word by imitating the natural sound associated with the object or action, as in *buzz* or *click*.

Order: is the arrangement of information or materials in an essay. The most common ordering techniques are *Chronological order* (time in sequence); *Spatial order* (the arrangement of descriptive details); *process order* (a step-by-step approach to an activity); *deductive order* (a thesis followed by information to support it); and *inductive order* (evidence and examples first, followed by the thesis in the form of a conclusion). Some rhetorical patterns such as comparison and contrast, classification, and argumentation require other ordering methods. Writers should select those ordering principles that permit them to present materials clearly.

Overstatement: is an extravagant or exaggerated claim or statement.

690